THE DOCUMENTS OF VATICAN II

ALL SIXTEEN OFFICIAL TEXTS PROMULGATED

BY THE ECUMENICAL COUNCIL

1963-1965

TRANSLATED FROM THE LATIN

THE DOCUMENTS OF VATICAN II

*In a New and Definitive Translation
With Commentaries and Notes
By Catholic, Protestant and Orthodox
Authorities*

WALTER M. ABBOTT, S.J.
General Editor

Introduction by Lawrence Cardinal Shehan

Translations Directed by Joseph Gallagher

A Herder and Herder Book
CROSSROAD • NEW YORK

1989

The Crossroad Publishing Company
370 Lexington Avenue, New York, N.Y. 10017

Copyright ©1966 by The America Press

Printed in the United States of America

Library of Congress Cataloging-in-Publication Data

Vatican Council (2nd : 1962-1965)
    The documents of Vatican II : in a new and definitive translation,
with commentaries and notes by Catholic, Protestant, and Orthodox
authorities / Walter M. Abbott, general editor ; introduction by
Lawrence Cardinal Shehan ; translations directed by Joseph
Gallagher.
        p.   cm.
    Issued in a set with: Commentary on the documents of Vatican II.
    ISBN 0-8245-0980-3   —ISBN 0-8245-0979-X (set)
    1. Vatican Council (2nd : 1962-1965)   2. Catholic Church—
Doctrines.   I. Abbott, Walter M.   II. Title.
BX830 1962.A3G3   1989
262'.52—dc20   89-38818
                                                                         CIP

CONTENTS

Preface to the Translation ix

Abbreviations xiii

Introduction, *Lawrence Cardinal Shehan* xv

An Adventure in Ecumenical Cooperation,
  Bishop Reuben H. Mueller xx

Prayer of the Council Fathers xxii

OPENING MESSAGE 1

THE CHURCH

Introduction, *Rev. Avery Dulles, S.J.* 9

DOGMATIC CONSTITUTION ON THE CHURCH
  (LUMEN GENTIUM) 14

A Response, *Dr. Albert C. Outler* 102

REVELATION

Introduction,
  Very Rev. R. A. F. MacKenzie, S.J. 107

DOGMATIC CONSTITUTION ON DIVINE REVELATION
  (DEI VERBUM) 111

A Response, *Prof. Frederick C. Grant* 129

LITURGY

Introduction, *Rev. C. J. McNaspy, S.J.* 133

CONSTITUTION ON THE SACRED LITURGY
  (SACROSANCTUM CONCILIUM) 137

A Response, *Prof. Jaroslav J. Pelikan* 179

THE CHURCH TODAY

Introduction, *Rev. Donald R. Campion, S.J.*   183

PASTORAL CONSTITUTION ON THE CHURCH

     IN THE MODERN WORLD (GAUDIUM ET SPES)   199

A Response, *Dr. Robert McAfee Brown*   309

COMMUNICATIONS

Introduction, *Rev. Thomas J. M. Burke, S.J.*   317

DECREE ON THE INSTRUMENTS OF SOCIAL

     COMMUNICATION (INTER MIRIFICA)   319

A Response, *Dr. Stanley I. Stuber*   332

ECUMENISM

Introduction, *Rev. Walter M. Abbott, S.J.*   336

DECREE ON ECUMENISM (UNITATIS REDINTEGRATIO)   341

A Response, *Dr. Samuel McCrea Cavert*   367

EASTERN CHURCHES

Introduction, *Rev. Paul Mailleux, S.J.*   371

DECREE ON EASTERN CATHOLIC CHURCHES

     (ORIENTALIUM ECCLESIARUM)   373

A Response, *Very Rev. Alexander Schmemann*   387

BISHOPS

Introduction, *Most Rev. Paul J. Hallinan*   389

DECREE ON THE BISHOPS' PASTORAL

     OFFICE IN THE CHURCH (CHRISTUS DOMINUS)   396

A Response, *Bishop Fred Pierce Corson*   430

PRIESTLY FORMATION

Introduction, *Most Rev. Alexander Carter*   434

DECREE ON PRIESTLY FORMATION (OPTATAM TOTIUS)   437

A Response, *Prof. Warren A. Quanbeck*   458

RELIGIOUS LIFE

Introduction, *Most Rev. John J. McEleney, S.J.*   462

DECREE ON THE APPROPRIATE RENEWAL OF THE
RELIGIOUS LIFE (PERFECTAE CARITATIS)   466

A Response, *Rev. William A. Norgren*   483

LAITY

Introduction, *Mr. Martin Work*   486

DECREE ON THE APOSTOLATE OF THE LAITY
(APOSTOLICAM ACTUOSITATEM)   489

A Response, *Mrs. Theodore O. Wedel*   522

PRIESTS

Introduction, *Most Rev. Guilford C. Young*   526

DECREE ON THE MINISTRY AND LIFE OF PRIESTS
(PRESBYTERORUM ORDINIS)   532

A Response, *Dr. John Oliver Nelson*   577

MISSIONS

Introduction, *Rev. Calvert Alexander, S.J.*   580

DECREE ON THE CHURCH'S MISSIONARY ACTIVITY
(AD GENTES)   584

A Response, *Dr. Eugene L. Smith*   631

EDUCATION

Introduction, *Most Rev. G. Emmett Carter*   634

DECLARATION ON CHRISTIAN EDUCATION
(GRAVISSIMUM EDUCATIONIS)   637

A Response, *Dr. John C. Bennett*   652

NON-CHRISTIANS

Introduction, *Rev. Robert A. Graham, S.J.*   656

DECLARATION ON THE RELATIONSHIP OF THE CHURCH
TO NON-CHRISTIAN RELIGIONS (NOSTRA AETATE)   660
A Response, *Dr. Claude Nelson*   669

RELIGIOUS FREEDOM
Introduction, *Rev. John Courtney Murray, S.J.*   672
DECLARATION ON RELIGIOUS FREEDOM
(DIGNITATIS HUMANAE)   675
A Response, *Dr. Franklin H. Littell*   697

APPENDIX   701
Pope John Convokes the Council   703
Pope John's Opening Speech to the Council   710
Synod of Bishops Established   720
Catholic-Orthodox Declaration   725
Closing Messages of the Council   728
Papal Brief Declaring the Council Completed   738
The Ecumenical Councils   740
Important Dates of Vatican II   741
Contributors   743

INDEX   749
Prayer of Pope John XXIII to the Holy Spirit
for the Success of the Ecumenical Council   793

PREFACE TO THE TRANSLATION

What the Second Vatican Council said is what it said in its official Latin texts. Exclusive of 992 footnotes of varying length, the sixteen promulgated texts run to approximately 103,014 words.*

There are three main sources of these Latin texts: 1) the final versions distributed at the Council usually just before the last vote on a text and the actual promulgation of it by the Holy Father; 2) the Vatican newspaper, *L'Osservatore Romano*, which printed the full Latin texts, one at a time, shortly after each one was promulgated; 3) the official Vatican periodical, *Acta Apostolicae Sedis*. So far only the first five Council documents have appeared in the *Acta*.

The translations in this volume are based on the Latin texts. In the case of the documents promulgated at the final Council session, slight differences exist between available Latin texts. Future editions of this volume will take advantage of whatever light is thrown on these discrepancies by the eventual appearance of the texts in the *Acta*. Where these differences have been caught they are noted in the present volume.

There are as yet no "official" English translations of these Council documents. A few translations, however, have been produced by highly knowledgeable and reliable persons. For the most part, there has not been sufficient time for production of truly authenticated translations, which would require, among other things, officially authorized translators with an intimate knowledge of the meetings held by the commissions

---

*1. Dogmatic Constitution on the Church: 16,200 words;
2. Dogmatic Constitution on Divine Revelation: 2,996 words;
3. Constitution on the Sacred Liturgy: 7,806 words;
4. Pastoral Constitution on the Church in the Modern World: 23,335 words;
5. Decree on the Instruments of Social Communication: 2,225 words;
6. Decree on Ecumenism: 4,790 words;
7. Decree on Eastern Catholic Churches: 1,806 words;
8. Decree on the Bishops' Pastoral Office in the Church: 5,982 words;
9. Decree on Priestly Formation: 2,987 words;
10. Decree on the Appropriate Renewal of the Religious Life: 3,189 words;
11. Decree on the Apostolate of the Laity: 7,016 words;
12. Decree on the Ministry and Life of Priests: 7,896 words;
13. Decree on the Church's Missionary Activity: 9,870 words;
14. Declaration on Christian Education: 2,604 words;
15. Declaration on the Relationship of the
    Church to Non-Christian Religions: 1,117 words;
16. Declaration on Religious Freedom: 3,195 words;

that helped to produce each document. The notes of these meetings remain unpublished.

A translation could be technically accurate and yet fail to be intelligible and readable from the point of view of the general public. Such would surely be the case if the very long, involved sentences and paragraphs of the original were not broken into digestible portions. For example, one sentence in the text on the priestly ministry runs to 68 words; a paragraph in the document on the Church contains 276 words. At the same time, some Council paragraphs are only a few words long. As a general rule, the translations in this volume start a new paragraph wherever the original does, but they often start one where the original does not.

Every word in these translations was chosen in the light of their purpose: to provide the average American reader with as clear, accurate, and readable a rendering of the original documents as the subject matter, the available time, and resources of information would permit.

At times the original Latin deliberately treats a subject in an incomplete, indirect, or highly technical manner. In such cases the translator chose to adhere closely to the original, even at some cost to style.

Style was also a problem in view of the tendency of the Council Latin to be less specific and concrete than current American idiom would suggest. In its use of adjectives, the Council Latin often resorts to superlatives when less exuberant English style would use the positive degree. Again, the Council Latin uses words such as "holy" or "most holy" to an extent which may grate on some ears more attuned to Anglo-Saxon simplicity and understatement, especially in religious matters.

That the translations might reflect as nearly as possible exactly what the Council said—and there are times when such exactness can be crucial—a literal rendering was chosen over a literary one whenever the choice seemed necessary.

Another problem is Latin's lack of a word for "a" and "the." Hence there were times when the translator was not sure whether the Council was calling something "a most important duty" or "the most important duty." He has tried to choose the sense which seemed better suited to the context.

When it cited the Bible, Vatican II most often quoted from a particular version of the Latin translation produced by St. Jerome in the late 4th or early 5th century (the Vulgate). Hence in this volume it was deemed advisable to use an English version of the Bible based on the Vulgate. Unless otherwise noted, then, the New Testament excerpts are from the 1941 American Catholic translation sponsored by the Confraternity of Christian Doctrine; Old Testament quotations are from the Douay-Challoner version.

Although these translations are to a major extent my own, there is one exception, and there are several qualifications. The translation of the Declaration on Religious Freedom was chiefly prepared by one of the architects of the Latin original, Father John Courtney Murray, S.J. For this volume, he slightly emended the translation that he had prepared for the National Catholic Welfare Conference. A small number of other changes were made editorially, in favor of consistency of style throughout the book.

The translations of the Decree on Ecumenism and the Declaration on the Relationship of the Church to Non-Christian Religions rely to a notable extent on the informed version produced by members of the Vatican Secretariat for Promoting Christian Unity.

All the translations prepared for, and by, the National Catholic Welfare Conference were carefully consulted. The one on the sacred liturgy proved especially adaptable to the aims of this volume. I myself prepared for the N.C.W.C. the major part of the translation of the Pastoral Constitution on the Church in the Modern World—whose 23,335 words make it the Council's longest text. The translation has been completely reviewed for this book.

The N.C.W.C. translations were generally done under great pressure and served the immediate purpose of providing newsmen with a basic translation at the time the documents were promulgated. What this pressure could mean in practice can be illustrated by the history of the so-called Schema 13 (on the Church in the Modern World). Five days before it was promulgated, the final version became available to translators. It contained 743 lines which had been thoroughly or partially changed since the previous version. Also, sentences and paragraphs had been rearranged and various items had been omitted, often without notice.

While the translation editor accepts final responsibility for the translations, he gladly acknowledges the "collegiality" of contributions which helped bring about the final product. Special thanks are due to my own Archbishop, Lawrence Cardinal Shehan, who permitted me to devote myself to this work almost exclusively over a period of several months; to

Thurston N. Davis, S.J., editor-in-chief of *America,* who first invited me to provide translations for this book; to Walter M. Abbott, S.J., general editor of the book, who worked closely with me every step along the way.

For various other kinds of help I must also thank the staff of the *Baltimore Catholic Review;* the staff and fellow guests at Rome's celebrated *pensione, Istituto Villanova;* my secretary, Miss Audrey McCarthy; and the Sisters at the Motherhouse of the Mission Helpers of the Sacred Heart, Towson, Maryland.

Special translation help was provided by Rev. Raymond Brown, S.S., Rev. John F. Cronin, S.S., Very Rev. F. Joseph Gossman, Rev. John A. Gray, Rt. Rev. George G. Higgins, Rev. John King, O.M.I., Rev. James A. Laubacher, S.S., Rev. William Leahy, Rev. John McGraw, Rev. Charles K. Riepe, Rev. James R. Schaefer, Rev. J. Francis Stafford, Rev. Robert Trisco, Rev. Eugene A. Walsh, S.S., Rt. Rev. Porter J. White, Very Rev. Vincent A. Yzermans, and students at the North American College and the Graduate House of Studies in Rome. Also, in several instances, scholars who serve as commentators in this book made valuable suggestions about the translation. Comments, criticisms, and recommendations pertaining to these translations are most welcome and will be taken into account when future editions are prepared.

VERY REV. MSGR. JOSEPH GALLAGHER

January 15, 1966

ABBREVIATIONS OF THE BOOKS OF THE BIBLE

Acts The Acts of the Apostles
Am. Amos
Apoc. Apocalypse (Revelation)
Bar. Baruch
Cant. Canticle of Canticles
    (S. of S.)
1 Chr. 1 Chronicles (Paralip.)
2 Chr. 2 Chronicles (Paralip.)
Col. Colossians
1 Cor. 1 Corinthians
2 Cor. 2 Corinthians
Dan. Daniel
Dt. Deuteronomy
Ec. Ecclesiastes
Eccl. Ecclesiasticus (Sirach)
Eph. Ephesians
1 Esd. 1 Esdras
2 Esd. 2 Esdras
Est. Esther
Ex. Exodus
Ezek. Ezekiel
Ezra Ezra
Gal. Galatians
Gen. Genesis
Hab. Habakkuk
Hag. Haggai (Aggeus)
Heb. Hebrews
Hos. Hosea (Osee)
Is. Isaiah
Jas. James
Jdt. Judith
Jer. Jeremiah
Jg. Judges
Jl. Joel
Jn. John (Gospel)
1 Jn. 1 John (Epistle)
2 Jn. 2 John
3 Jn. 3 John
Job Job
Jon. Jonah
Jos. Joshua
Jude Jude
1 Kg. 1 Kings

2 Kg. 2 Kings
Lam. Lamentations
Lev. Leviticus
Lk. Luke
1 Macc. 1 Maccabees
2 Macc. 2 Maccabees
Mal. Malachi
Mic. Micah
Mk. Mark
Mt. Matthew
Nah. Nahum
Neh. Nehemiah
Num. Numbers
Ob. Obadiah (Abdias)
Os. Osee (Hosea)
1 Paralip. 1 Paralipomenon
    (1 Chronicles)
2 Paralip. 2 Paralipomenon
    (2 Chronicles)
1 Pet. 1 Peter
2 Pet. 2 Peter
Phil. Philippians
Philem. Philemon
Pr. Proverbs
Ps. Psalms
Rev. Revelation (Apocalypse)
Rom. Romans
Ru. Ruth
1 Sam. 1 Samuel
2 Sam. 2 Samuel
Sir. Sirach (Ecclesiasticus)
S. of S. Song of Solomon
    (Canticle of Canticles)
Soph. Sophoniah (Zephaniah)
1 Th. 1 Thessalonians
2 Th. 2 Thessalonians
1 Tim. 1 Timothy
2 Tim. 2 Timothy
Tit. Titus
Tob. Tobit (Tobias)
Wis. Wisdom of Solomon
Zech. Zechariah
Zeph. Zephaniah (Sophoniah)

OTHER ABBREVIATIONS

AAS *Acta Apostolicae Sedis* ("Acts of the Apostolic See"), with subtitle *Commentarium Officiale* ("Official Commentary"). This periodical, published at Vatican City, is the official record of papal statements, appointments, etc.

CCD Confraternity of Christian Doctrine translation of the Bible, by members of the Catholic Biblical Association of America.

CIC *Codex Iuris Canonici* (Code of Canon Law).

CSEL *Corpus Scriptorum Ecclesiasticorum Latinorum* ("Collected Works of Latin Church Writers"), published at Vienna, from 1866.

Denz. *Enchiridion Symbolorum, Definitionum et Declarationum de Rebus Fidei et Morum* ("Manual of Creeds, Definitions and Declarations on Matters of Faith and Morals"), compiled by H. Denzinger (1854), continued by C. Bannwart and others to the present.

PG *Patrologia Graeca* (Writings of the Greek Church Fathers), ed. by J. B. Migne (Paris).

PL *Patrologia Latina* (Writings of the Latin Church Fathers), ed. by J. B. Migne (Paris).

RSV Revised Standard Version of the Bible (National Council of the Churches of Christ in the U.S.A.)

Vg. Vulgate (St. Jerome's Latin translation of the Bible).

For the convenience of students who may wish to consult the sources, and for the sake of brevity, references to Migne's collection are, for the most part, left in the traditional abbreviated form as used in the official footnotes of the Council documents.

Official notes accompanying the Council documents are printed in italic type; notes in Roman type are the work of the commentator (whose name is at the end of the essay introducing the document).

Most biblical references in the official notes have been brought up into the text (in parentheses).

INTRODUCTION

It was a sense of continuity which inspired the saying, "The king is dead; long live the king." A similar sense would justify the statement, "The Council is over; the Council has just begun."

The Council is indeed over. John XXIII had been Pope for merely ninety days when, on January 25, 1959, he made the first and completely unexpected announcement of his plan to convoke the Church's Twenty-First Ecumenical Council, the first since Vatican I of 1869-70. On October 11, 1962, after nearly four years of exhaustive preparation, the Council finally opened.

In a positive and optimistic speech, the eighty-year-old Pope John gently chided the prophets of doom within the Church and spoke of the world's need for the medicine of mercy. Thus, less than nine months before his death, he set the pastoral tone which was to dominate the Council deliberations. The first period of these deliberations ended on December 8, 1962.

On September 29 of the following year, Pope Paul opened the second session by stressing the various areas of dialogue in which the Council and the Church must today engage. Upon his election the previous June 21, Pope Paul VI had taken as a main program of his pontificate the completion and implementation of the Council which his revered predecessor had summoned.

By the end of this second session, on December 4, 1963, the first two Council documents were ready for promulgation: the Constitution on the Sacred Liturgy and the Decree on the Instruments of Social Communication. On this same day, Peter's successor revealed his plan to pay history's first papal visit to the homeland of our Lord and His vicar, St. Peter. There, on January 5, 1964, Paul, the Patriarch of the West, embraced Athenagoras, the chief Orthodox Patriarch of the East. A thousand years of unhappy estrangement were beginning to be reversed.

The Council's third session began on September 14, 1964, and lasted until November 21. This session produced the Council's master and pivotal document on the nature of the Church. It presents a panoramic and richly biblical view of the Church as the People of God. Concluding the main unfinished business of Vatican I, it formulated with solemn conciliar authority the traditional doctrine of collegiality.

According to this doctrine, the whole college of bishops, as successors to the college of the apostles, shares in responsibility for the shepherding of the entire Church of Christ. This the bishops do in union with and under the ultimate authority of the Bishop of Rome, the successor of Peter, who was the divinely appointed head of the Apostolic College. Now that world conditions both allow and require greater contact between the Bishop of Rome and his brother bishops, this formulation of the concept of collegiality is full of practical implications both within the Church herself and in her efforts to foster Christian unity.

This third session also produced the Decree on Ecumenism and the Decree on Eastern Catholic Churches. These two documents, especially the former, have an immediate and promising bearing on this cherished dream of Pope John, the reunion of all Christians.

Yet the Church's concern for the non-Christian world was not being overlooked. In the Constitution on the Church, the Council had quoted an ancient statement to the effect that the See of Peter looks upon the people of even distant India as its concern. Eleven days after this Constitution was promulgated, Peter, in the person of Pope Paul, paid his first visit to India. Thus did this pilgrim Pope, this "apostle on the move," who bears the name of the great missionary Apostle to the Gentiles, end a year which he had begun by visiting Jordan and Israel.

The final session began on September 14, 1965, and concluded ceremonially with a Mass in St. Peter's Square on December 8. This most productive of sessions saw the completion of eleven documents. Five were promulgated on October 28, the seventh anniversary of Pope John's election: 1) the Decree on the Bishops' Pastoral Office in the Church; 2) the Decree on Priestly Formation; 3) the Decree on the Appropriate Renewal of the Religious Life; 4) the Declaration on the Relationship of the Church to Non-Christian Religions; and 5) the Declaration on Christian Education.

On November 18, two more texts were promulgated: the Dogmatic Constitution on Divine Revelation and the Decree on the Apostolate of the Laity.

Finally, during the last Council event held within St. Peter's, four more texts were promulgated: 1) the Pastoral Constitution on the Church in the Modern World; 2) the Decree on the Ministry and Life of Priests; 3) the Decree on the Church's Missionary Activity; and 4) the Declaration on Religious Freedom.

The very variety of Council topics and the diversity of interest in them would probably keep any two persons from agreeing on the relative importance of each of the sixteen documents produced. For my own part, I would certainly rank the Constitutions on the Church, on Divine Revelation, and on the Sacred Liturgy, and the Decree on Ecumenism as among the most significant. As an American, I would also consider the Council's Declarations on Religious Freedom and the Church's Relationship with Non-Christian Religions, including the statement against anti-Semitism, as among its most satisfying achievements.

Taken as a whole, the documents are especially noteworthy for their concern with the poor, for their insistence on the unity of the human family and therefore on the wrongness of discrimination, for their repeated emphasis on the Christian's duty to help build a just and peaceful world, a duty which he must carry out in brotherly cooperation with all men of good will.

Among other notable features of Vatican II must surely be listed the influential presence of non-Catholic observers and guests, the introduction of Catholic men and women auditors, the lively interest of the general press, and the growing availability of Council information. An abundant measure of gratitude is due to those many members of the communications media who brought to the Council coverage their professional skill and dedication.

For their part, members of the English-speaking press have already expressed their appreciation for the contribution made to their work by Father Edward Heston, C.S.C., in his duties on behalf of the Council Press Office, and to the members and guests of the press panel established by the U.S. Catholic bishops. His loss to this panel was one of the manifold grounds on which the mid-Council death of Father Gustave Weigel, S.J., was so widely and deeply lamented.

A word of special appreciation is likewise due to the press department of the National Catholic Welfare Conference, and to its small but highly dedicated Rome bureau. In proportion to its size the N.C.W.C. Bureau of Information also rendered most valuable service in the work of making the Council better known and understood. The Religious News Service, too, though having a broader scope of concern than the N.C.W.C. press department, gave most generous and sympathetic attention to the Council.

Although they were not, strictly speaking, conciliar events, two occurrences toward the very end of Vatican II were undoubtedly of immense significance for one of its long-range goals, namely, the realization of our Lord's prayer that all His followers be united in one mind and one heart. These events were the prayer service involving Pope Paul, the Council Fathers, and the non-Catholic observers, which was held on December 4 of last year. The choice of the Basilica of St. Paul's Outside-the-Walls was certainly appropriate, since it was there that Pope John first announced the Council almost seven years earlier.

The second event, in which I was privileged to play a role, was the joint declaration pronounced at Istanbul and Vatican City on December 7 of last year. Through this declaration of regret for past mistakes, of esteem and charity for the present, and of hope for future reconciliation, the Church of Constantinople and the See of Peter took a beautiful and promising step toward each other. On that historic day, the joint declaration signed by Pope Paul VI and Patriarch Athenagoras I was read in St. Peter's in the presence of the Pope and the Council Fathers, and in the Church of St. George in the presence of the Patriarch, his Synod, his clergy, and his people. Before the Metropolitan Meliton, who headed the Patriarch's delegation, left Rome, he placed nine white roses at the tomb of Pope John as a symbol of the nine centuries of division which were now beginning to be undone.

"Beginning" is the key word, for much remains to be done. That is why it can be said, "The Council has ended; the Council has just begun." As Pope Paul noted during the final session, "From now on *aggiornamento* will signify for us a wisely undertaken quest for a deeper understanding of the spirit of the Council and the faithful application of the norms it has happily and prayerfully provided."

In this work of understanding, the Council texts themselves must play a central role. For most people, access to the Council's work must come through translations into their own language. In this case the quality of the translation, which exactly renders the thought of the text in an idiom worthy of the original, bears witness to the unique competence of the translator and to the meticulous care he has given his work. Hence the importance of this book, made available with remarkable speed and at a remarkably low cost.

The value of this book is heightened by the explanations provided by especially competent and knowledgeable experts from within the Church. The book's value is even further enhanced by the courteous but frank evaluations given to each Council document by an impressive group of Protestant and Orthodox commentators, some of whom have followed the work of the Council even with their personal presence.

Pope John and Pope Paul as well as the Council documents themselves call for Catholics to engage in that sincere dialogue which knows how to listen humbly as well as how to speak candidly. Hence it is most appropriate that as this book presents and explains the work of Vatican II it should likewise provide an example of the spirit of the Council.

Since it is obviously the aim of these non-Catholic essays neither to teach Catholic doctrine nor to attack it polemically, the customary authentication given to this kind of book should be taken as applying only to the translations and the commentaries by Catholics. No kind of *imprimatur* or official Catholic review was either sought or required for the non-Catholic contributions. As their authors surely wish, these essays are presented in the spirit of ecumenism as the considered personal opinion of the individuals as such.

May this volume find a readership worthy of its contents and its contributors. If the purpose of the Council is to be achieved, a book such as this is an indispensable tool. With respect to Vatican II, sermons, lectures, articles, study and discussion clubs, ecumenical dialogues, religion classes, private reading and meditation stand to gain immensely from a thoughtful pondering of these pages. Though the Council has ended, for many people it will begin with the acquisition of this book. That is praise enough for it.

✛ LAWRENCE CARDINAL SHEHAN
Archbishop of Baltimore,
January 25, 1966

AN ADVENTURE IN
ECUMENICAL COOPERATION

It is my great privilege to introduce a new adventure in ecumenical cooperation among the followers of our Lord Jesus Christ.

The preparation and publication of this volume, *The Documents of Vatican II,* is a significant demonstration of the new spirit of Christian brotherhood and fellowship that is flowering from the Second Vatican Council, called by Pope John XXIII, and continued by Pope Paul VI. The deeply significant drama which began in the Basilica of St. Peter's in Rome in the fall of 1962, and recently came to formal adjournment, is now being moved to all parts of the world.

A great religious community in process of renewal and change, the Roman Catholic Church has, through this Council, won the respectful attention of all who have carefully and prayerfully watched its developments. As the results of the work of the Second Vatican Council now move into dioceses and parishes in response to the admonishment of His Holiness, the world outside will continue to watch with interest and hope. We who are numbered among those whom good Pope John XXIII called "separated brethren" will add our sincere prayers as the evidence of our hopes.

The purpose of the book is to help to carry the impact of the Council into all American communities. It is because of this purpose that a new and meaningful procedure has been followed in writing and publishing this book. Roman Catholic, Protestant, and Orthodox Christians have been involved in planning the volume. A significant aspect of the plan is that, in addition to Roman Catholic contributors who provide the commentaries on the sixteen official documents, Protestant and Orthodox contributors were invited to provide a response or reaction to each of these documents. By this method it is hoped that the actions of Vatican II will move out from St. Peter's into the world at large for dialogue and ecumenical support.

Publishing these essays under one cover is a striking symbol of our new ecumenical fellowship. Surely, we have entered an era when Christians, long separated from each other, will cooperate increasingly in a wide range of Christian ventures under God. As this happens, we will be enriching each other and benefiting the world as a whole.

The charters for renewal and change in the Roman Catholic Church lie within the pages of this book. Anyone who hopes to follow the actual developments as we move onward will need to study and discuss and understand the basic documents, as well as Catholic and non-Catholic commentaries on them.

Pope Paul VI has called for the prompt application of the teachings of the Council in the life of the Church. Men and women of good will everywhere can applaud his determination and can pray that the gifts of the Holy Spirit will continue to be poured upon the Church which He leads.

More than that, it is my personal hope and prayer (and I believe that I can venture to speak for most of those Christians who constitute our Protestant and Orthodox constituencies) that the new movement for renewal in the Roman Catholic Church, as expressed through the Second Vatican Council, may assist us in our sectors of the Christian movement to enter into a wonderful new era of renewal through the living Christ until, together, we enter fully into the transformed Church of Christ.

BISHOP REUBEN H. MUELLER, President
The National Council of the Churches
of Christ in the U.S.A.

Prayer of the Council Fathers[1]

We are here before You, O Holy Spirit, conscious of our innumerable sins, but united in a special way in Your Holy Name. Come and abide with us. Deign to penetrate our hearts.

Be the guide of our actions, indicate the path we should take, and show us what we must do so that, with Your help, our work may be in all things pleasing to You.

May You be our only inspiration and the overseer of our intentions, for You alone possess a glorious name together with the Father and the Son.

May You, who are infinite justice, never permit that we be disturbers of justice. Let not our ignorance induce us to evil, nor flattery sway us, nor moral and material interest corrupt us. But unite our hearts to You alone, and do it strongly, so that, with the gift of Your grace, we may be one in You and may in nothing depart from the truth.

Thus, united in Your name, may we in our every action follow the dictates of Your mercy and justice, so that today and always our judgments may not be alien to You and in eternity we may obtain the unending reward of our actions. Amen.

1. It is believed that this prayer was composed by St. Isidore of Seville, to be used during the Second Provincial Council of Seville, Spain, in 619. It was also used during the Fourth Provincial Council of Toledo, Spain, in 633. With this prayer the sessions of the First Vatican Council began, in 1869, and it was used before every meeting (in Latin) of preparatory commissions and conciliar commissions of Vatican II.

OPENING MESSAGE

WHEN THE SECOND VATICAN COUNCIL formally opened on October 11, 1962, many wondered how long it would take the Council Fathers to begin producing the documents that had been planned by the preparatory commissions. It would be more than a year before the first of them could be promulgated: the Constitution on the Sacred Liturgy and the Decree on the Instruments of Social Communication (both promulgated on December 4, 1963).

Nine days after the opening of the Council, however, an unscheduled document was presented to the world by the Council Fathers. Pope John himself had sent it to the Council hall with the request that the Fathers discuss it, and amend it if they felt it necessary to do so. He desired that it should be the first official act of the Council.

A number of bishops had earlier requested that the Council present a message to the world before going to work on the planned documents. Two French theologians had drafted a message and sent it around to some of the cardinals. It was a good text, based on principles of natural morality. The cardinals urged, however, that an Ecumenical Council should focus on Christ and His message. Another text drawn up by four French bishops was more to their liking, and Pope John's liking. It was essentially this text that the Council Fathers considered throughout the morning of October 20, 1962, in St. Peter's Basilica.

Various amendments were proposed. Some Fathers wanted to include a condemnation of communism; others were against having any opening message. It was finally decided to add only one amendment (a reference to the Blessed Virgin), and the document was approved for publication.

The message, a noble beginning for the Council, is one of the most beautiful and significant products of the Council. It presents the kernel of the Christian faith, in terms resonant with biblical strength. It presents what will emerge as key themes of the future Council documents: Christ, the Light of the world; hope in the power of the Holy Spirit; the bishops as shepherds devoted to service of the people. The message gave promise that the Council would, indeed, strive to recapture the youthful bloom of the Church, as Pope John had put it.

These opening words of the Council look to renewal of the Catholic Church, to compassionate dialogue with modern men, to peace, to social justice, to whatever concerns the dignity of man and the unity of mankind. The message shows awareness of the world's problems and a keen desire to help. It emphasizes the quest for a community of peoples, the motivation that comes from Christ's love, the need for co-operation with all men of good will. It is remarkable how this first document contains the seeds of the great Constitution on the Church; how it foreshadows the great texts that will come on ecumenism, religious freedom, relations with non-Christians; how it outlines so much of what will be in the Council's concluding document, the Pastoral Constitution on the Church in the Modern World.

The document was released to—literally—the world. That very fact made it a remarkable first in the history of the Ecumenical Councils. It was like Pope John to have arranged it so, and in its contents the message is faithful to the desires of Pope John's heart. It was all to come to fruition in the subsequent Constitutions, Decrees, and Declarations of Vatican II. The message was thus proved to have been faithful to urgings of the Holy Spirit.

WALTER M. ABBOTT, S.J.

Message to Humanity

ISSUED AT THE BEGINNING OF THE SECOND VATICAN COUNCIL[1] BY ITS FATHERS, WITH THE ENDORSEMENT OF THE SUPREME PONTIFF

THE FATHERS OF THE COUNCIL TO ALL MEN[2]

We take great pleasure in sending to all men and nations a message concerning that well-being,[3] love, and peace which were brought into the world by Christ Jesus, the Son of the living God, and entrusted to the Church.

For this is the reason why, at the direction of the most blessed Pope John XXIII, we successors of the apostles have gathered here, joined in singlehearted prayer with Mary the Mother of Jesus,[4] and forming one apostolic body headed by the successor of Peter.

MAY THE FACE OF CHRIST JESUS SHINE OUT[5]

In this assembly, under the guidance of the Holy Spirit, we wish to inquire[6] how we ought to renew ourselves, so that

1. This message was approved and released by the Council on Saturday, Oct. 20, 1962, nine days after the Council opened (and two days before the crisis over Soviet missiles in Cuba became public).
2. For the first time in the history of Ecumenical Councils, a Council addresses itself to all men, not just members of the Catholic Church. In the following year, Pope John XXIII added, for the first time, the salutation "and to all men of good will" as the opening of a papal encyclical (*Pacem in Terris*, Apr. 11, 1963).
3. *Salutis*, often translated "salvation."
4. There is a strong biblical flavor in this first message from the Council. This sentence, for example, is reminiscent of Acts 1:14: "All these with one mind continued steadfastly in prayer with the women and Mary, the mother of Jesus, and with his brethren." All of the document's explicit references are biblical, except for the two references to Pope John.
5. The theme of light, as Pope John himself pointed out, is the key theme of the Second Vatican Council, and its motto, as he suggested, was *Lumen Christi, Lumen Gentium* ("Light of Christ, Light of the Nations"). *Lumen Gentium* was to become the opening phrase of the Council's greatest work, the Dogmatic Constitution on the Church (Nov. 21, 1964).
6. The Council Fathers state the purpose of the Council as they understand it.

we may be found increasingly faithful to the gospel of Christ. We shall take pains so to present to the men of this age God's truth in its integrity and purity that they may understand it and gladly assent to it.

Since we are shepherds, we desire that all those may have their longing satisfied who seek God[7] "if perhaps they might find Him as they grope after Him; though indeed He is not far from each of us."[8]

Hence, obeying the will of Christ, who delivered Himself to death "that He might present to Himself the Church, not having spot or wrinkle . . . but that she might be holy and without blemish,"[9] we as pastors devote all our energies and thoughts to the renewal of ourselves and the flocks committed to us, so that there may radiate before all men the lovable features of Jesus Christ, who shines in our hearts "that God's splendor may be revealed."[10]

GOD SO LOVED THE WORLD . . .

We believe that the Father so loved the world that He gave His own Son to save it. Indeed, through this same Son of His He freed us from bondage to sin, reconciling all things unto Himself through Him, "making peace through the blood of his cross,"[11] so that "we might be called sons of God, and truly be such."

The Spirit too has been bestowed on us by the Father, that living the life of God, we might love God and the brethren, who are all of us one in Christ.

It is far from true that because we cling to Christ we are diverted from earthly duties and toils.[12] On the contrary, faith, hope, and the love of Christ impel us to serve our brothers, thereby patterning ourselves after the example of

---

7. Pope Paul VI, in his Christmas message for 1965, would write: "The dominant mood of the Council was inspired by the gospel image of the shepherd setting out in pursuit of the lost sheep, allowing himself no peace until he has found it. The awareness that mankind, represented with touching simplicity by the straying sheep, belongs to the Church was the guiding principle of the Council. For mankind, by a universally valid decree, does belong to the Church . . . mankind belongs to her by right of love, since the Church, no matter how distant or uncooperative or hostile mankind may be, can never be excused from loving the human race for which Christ shed His blood."
8. *Acts 17:27.*
9. *Cf. Eph. 5:27.*
10. *Cf. 2 Cor. 4:6.*
11. *Cf. Col. 1:20.*
12. The Fathers of the Council reject the notion that they may be out of contact with reality.

the Divine Teacher, who "came not to be served but to serve."[13] Hence, the Church too was not born to dominate but to serve.[14] He laid down His life for us, and we too ought to lay down our lives for our brothers.[15]

Accordingly, while we hope that the light of faith will shine more clearly and more vigorously as a result of this Council's efforts, we look forward to a spiritual renewal from which will also flow a happy impulse on behalf of human values such as scientific discoveries, technological advances, and a wider diffusion of knowledge.

THE LOVE OF CHRIST IMPELS US

Coming together in unity from every nation under the sun, we carry in our hearts the hardships, the bodily and mental distress, the sorrows, longings, and hopes of all the peoples entrusted to us.[16] We urgently turn our thoughts to all the anxieties by which modern man is afflicted. Hence, let our concern swiftly focus first of all on those who are especially lowly, poor, and weak. Like Christ, we would have pity on the multitude weighed down with hunger, misery, and lack of knowledge. We want to fix a steady gaze on those who still lack the opportune help to achieve a way of life worthy of human beings.[17]

As we undertake our work, therefore, we would emphasize whatever concerns the dignity of man, whatever contributes to a genuine community of peoples. "Christ's love impels us,"[18] for "he who sees his brother in need and closes his heart against him, how does the love of God abide in him?"[19]

TWO ISSUES OF SPECIAL URGENCY CONFRONT US

The Supreme Pontiff, John XXIII, in a radio address delivered on September 11, 1962, stressed two points especially.

The first dealt with peace between peoples. There is no one who does not hate war, no one who does not strive for peace

---

13. *Mt. 20:28.*
14. The strong stress on service will run throughout the Council's documents.
15. *Cf. 1 Jn. 3:16.*
16. Before the Council was over, some bishops would also have to bear the burdens of worry resulting from war (e.g., between India and Pakistan, in Vietnam).
17. A reference to underdeveloped countries, depressed areas in developed countries, etc.
18. *2 Cor. 5:14.*
19. *1 Jn. 3:17.*

with burning desire. But the Church desires it most of all, because she is the Mother of all. Through the voice of the Roman Pontiffs, she never ceases to make an open declaration of her love for peace, her desire for peace. She is always ready to lend aid with her whole heart to any sincere effort on behalf of peace.[20] She strives with all her might to bring peoples together and to develop among them a mutual respect for interests and feelings. This very conciliar congress of ours,[21] so impressive in the diversity of the races, nations, and languages it represents, does it not bear witness to a community of brotherly love, and shine as a visible sign of it? We are giving witness that all men are brothers, whatever their race or nation.[22]

The Supreme Pontiff also pleads for social justice. The teaching expounded in his encyclical *Mater et Magistra* clearly shows that the Church is supremely necessary for the modern world if injustices and unworthy inequalities are to be denounced, and if the true order of affairs and of values is to be restored, so that man's life can become more human according to the standards of the gospel.

THE POWER OF THE HOLY SPIRIT

To be sure, we are lacking in human resources and earthly power.[23] Yet we lodge our trust in the power of God's Spirit, who was promised to the Church by the Lord Jesus Christ. Hence we humbly and ardently call for all men to work along with us in building up a more just and brotherly city in this world. We call not only upon our brothers whom we serve as shepherds, but also upon all our brother Christians, and

20. On Oct. 4, 1965, Pope Paul brought to the General Assembly of the United Nations his personal greetings "and those of the Second Vatican Ecumenical Council now meeting in Rome and represented here by the eminent cardinals who accompany us for this purpose." The Pope's "ratification, a solemn moral ratification of this lofty institution" which "represents the obligatory path of modern civilization and of world peace" was an evident effort to act in the spirit of this sentence in the Council's opening message to the world.
21. *Conventus noster Conciliaris.* Throughout the first two years of the Council, some bishops complained about newspaper references to the Council as a "congress" or "parliament" with "conservative" and "progressive" (or "liberal") parties. They wished it to be understood that the Council was quite unlike political bodies. The word "congress" here is used in the general sense of "meeting," "assembly," etc.
22. In their first message the Council Fathers include a reference to racial justice. Later, in the Declaration on Relationship of the Church to Non-Christian Religions (Art. 5) they will make a very strong statement about racial discrimination.
23. At the beginning of his historic address to the United Nations General Assembly, Oct. 4, 1965, Pope Paul touched upon this same idea.

the rest of men of good will, whom God "wills that they be saved and come to the knowledge of the truth."[24] For this is the divine plan, that through love God's kingdom may already shine out on earth in some fashion as a preview of God's eternal kingdom.

The world is still far from the desired peace because of threats arising from the very progress of science, marvelous though it be, but not always responsive to the higher law of morality. Our prayer is that in the midst of this world there may radiate the light of our great hope in Jesus Christ, our only Savior.

24. *Cf. 1 Tim. 2:4.*

THE CHURCH

THE TWENTIETH CENTURY has often been called the century of the Church. The official work of Church bodies, both within and outside of Roman Catholicism, reflects a mounting interest in this theme. For the past fifty years Protestant, Anglican, and Orthodox Christians in world organizations such as the Faith and Order Movement and the World Council of Churches have been intensely studying the nature and structure of the Church. The same topics have been coming into ever-increasing prominence in the pronouncements of the Catholic Church since the First Vatican Council (1869-70).

A preparatory commission of Vatican I drew up a lengthy draft declaration on the Church, but the deliberations of the Council were cut short by the Franco-Prussian War and the invasion of the Papal States by the Piedmontese armies. Instead of the planned Constitution on the Church of Christ consisting of fifteen chapters, the Council succeeded in enacting only four chapters on the papacy. The definitions regarding the primacy and infallibility of the Pope, unaccompanied by any treatment of the other bishops and members of the Church, gave a somewhat unbalanced picture. Many critics of the Council charged that it had converted the Catholic Church into an absolute monarchy in which the other bishops would be mere lackeys of the Pope.

Other facets of the Catholic doctrine concerning the Church were set forth by Leo XIII in his encyclical on the unity of the Church *(Satis Cognitum,* 1896) and especially by Pius XII in his great encyclical on the Mystical Body *(Mystici Corporis,* 1943), which dwelt on the mysterious vital relationship of the Church to Christ and to the Holy Spirit. But other questions regarding the nature and organization of the Church still clamored for attention. Thus in 1959, when John XXIII announced his intention of convening an Ecumenical Council, it was generally surmised that the coming Council would deal with the Church as its major theme. Paul VI made this clear in his first encyclical, "The Paths of the Church" *(Ecclesiam Suam,* 1964), in which he stated (Art. 33) that the Church was "the principal object of attention of the Second Vatican Ecumenical Council."

The present document—known as "Light of All Nations" from the first two words of the Latin text *(Lumen Gentium)* —is one of the two Dogmatic Constitutions issued by Vatican II, the other being that on Revelation. It is the second longest of the conciliar statements, next in length after the Pastoral Constitution on the Church in the Modern World. With something like unanimity it has been hailed as the most momentous achievement of the Council, both because of its important contents and because of its central place among the Council documents. The other constitutions, decrees, and declarations, for the most part, deal either with particular sections or elements in the Church (Eastern Churches, bishops, religious, seminarians, laity), or with particular activities of the Church (such as liturgy, communications, education, and the missions), or with the relations of the Church to outside groups (ecumenism, the non-Christian religions, the modern world). The Constitution on Divine Revelation deals with the sources of the Church's doctrine, and the Declaration on Religious Freedom with the relations between the Church and civil society. Thus in one way or another the entire work of the Council is centered about the theme of the Church.

Among all the documents of Vatican II, probably none underwent more drastic revision between the first schema and the finally approved text. The successive drafts of the Constitution, compared with one another, strikingly reveal the tremendous development of the Church's self-understanding which resulted from the dialogue within the Council. The original schema, prepared by the Theological Commission before the first session in 1962, resembled the standard treatise on the Church as found, for example, in most of the theological manuals published between the two world wars. Influenced by centuries of anti-Protestant polemics, the writers of this period placed heavy emphasis on the hierarchical and juridical aspects of the Church, including the supremacy of the Pope.

When the Council Fathers came together, they immediately saw the need of setting forth a radically different vision of the Church, more biblical, more historical, more vital and dynamic. An entirely new document was therefore drafted during the interval between the first and second sessions. This schema was itself subjected to thorough revision in the light of the debates at the second session (1963). The debate was completed at the third session, at the close of which the final vote on the text, as amended, was taken. On November 21, 1964, it was accepted by a majority of 2,151 Fathers in favor and 5 opposed, and was immediately promulgated by Pope Paul VI. Thus the mighty document, hammered into shape on the anvil of vigorous controversy, at length won almost unanimous approval.

Although called a Dogmatic Constitution, the most solemn form of conciliar utterance, *Lumen Gentium* does not actually define any new dogmas. It sets forth, with conciliar authority, the Church's present understanding of her own nature. In accordance with Pope John's directive that the Council should be predominantly pastoral in character, Vatican II wished to propose its teaching without anathemas and condemnations. It exhibits the Church, as Pope John expressed it in his opening allocution at the first session, as the "loving mother of all," spreading everywhere the fullness of Christian charity.

Avoiding rigid definitions and scholastic or juridical subtleties, the Council shows a marked preference for vivid and biblical language. It envisages the Church as continuing the work of the Good Shepherd, who came to serve and not to be served, and who did not hesitate to lay down His life for the sheep. But the Church is represented very realistically as a "little flock" made up of frail and sinful men. Weak and humble, it stands in constant need of purification and renewal. At the same time, however, it feels confident of God's loving help which guides its steps.

Throughout this Constitution, the mystery of the Church is viewed in terms of the paradoxical union between the human and the divine. Because the Church is human, it exists in time, and is subject to the forces of history. But because of its divine element, it presses forward, full of optimism, toward a goal beyond history. In all its prayer and labors it is sustained by the glorious vision of the final kingdom in which God will be all in all (1 Cor. 15:28).

The orientations of *Lumen Gentium* are therefore pastoral, Christocentric, biblical, historical, and eschatological. The tone of the document is, moreover, strongly ecumenical.

Every effort is made to speak in language which will be readily understood by other Christians and by all men of good will, and to explain Catholic teaching in a way that avoids giving unnecessary offense to persons accustomed to other modes of thought and speech.

Instead of beginning with a discussion of the structures and government of the Church—as was the tendency at Vatican I—the Constitution starts with the notion of the Church as a people to whom God communicates Himself in love. This provides an excellent foundation for a new and creative approach to the role of the laity in the Church. Not only in the chapter expressly devoted to the laity (Chapter 4) but in other sections (especially Chapter 2 and Chapter 5) the dignity and responsibilities of lay Christians are presented in an inspiring manner.

In other chapters attention is given to the clergy and religious, but always within the general picture of the Church's total mission. Authority is therefore viewed in terms of service rather than domination. In many respects the Constitution strikes a "democratic" note.

The most important doctrinal achievements of *Lumen Gentium* are contained in the third and longest chapter, dealing with the hierarchy. This chapter deals primarily with the episcopate, a theme which Vatican I would perhaps have taken up, had its deliberations not been interrupted. The teaching of Vatican II puts the accent clearly on the priestly role of the bishop and on his sacramental consecration rather than on the powers conferred by his appointment to a particular diocese. The bishops collectively are seen to constitute a stable body or "college," which is collectively responsible for the tasks of the entire Church. To avoid all danger of misunderstanding, the so-called principle of collegiality is explained in more precise and technical language in the "Prefatory Note" to Chapter III, composed by the Theological Commission (cf. infra. pp. 98-101).

In its teaching regarding the Church as a whole, the hierarchy, and the laity, the Council frequently divides its considerations under three headings, corresponding to what traditional theology has recognized as the threefold office of Christ. Christ, according to this conception, may be viewed as prophet, priest, and king. Those who have authority in the Church must carry on his work by the three functions of teaching, sanctifying, and governing the People of God. And the Church as a whole, including the laity, has a total task which may suitably be summarized under the three captions of witness, ministry, and fellowship. These last three terms are strongly biblical; they appear in the Greek New Testament as *martyrion, diakonia,* and *koinōnia.* From an ecumenical point of view, it is significant that these were the three terms about which the Third General Assembly of the World Council of Churches, meeting at New Delhi in 1961, centered its discussions.

The inclusion of a final chapter on the Blessed Virgin in this Constitution on the Church calls for some explanation. Actually, a separate document on the Blessed Virgin was contemplated, and was presented in draft form by the Theological Commission at the first session in 1962. But the Fathers saw a danger in treating Mariology too much in isolation; they preferred to link her role more closely with the main theme of the Council, the Church. The chapter on the Blessed Virgin, as finally adopted, goes considerably beyond the mere discussion of her relation to the Church, but this theme is sufficiently central to justify the inclusion of the chapter in this Constitution.

Lumen Gentium is not and does not purport to be a definitive document. As Père Dejaifve has said, "The greatest merit of the Constitution is that, far from canonizing the past, or even consecrating the present, it prepares for the future."[1] And Dom Christopher Butler, in a similar vein, declares: "I have no hesitation in saying that the Constitution is a great document, even though, being the fruit of the Holy Spirit working in imperfect human beings, it is a stepping-stone and not a final accomplishment."[2] Some later Council documents, such as that on the Church and the world, show a further advance of thinking in some respects surpassing *Lumen Gentium.* But this Constitution, because of its central importance and its wealth of doctrine, probably deserves to be called the most imposing achievement of Vatican II.

AVERY DULLES, S.J.

---

1. G. Dejaifve, S.J., "La 'Magna Charta' de Vatican II," *Nouvelle revue théologique* 87 (Jan. 1965), p. 21.
2. Foreword to the Paulist Press edition of *The Constitution on the Church* (New York: Deus Books, 1965), pp. 8-9.

Dogmatic Constitution on the Church

PAUL, BISHOP

SERVANT OF THE SERVANTS OF GOD

TOGETHER WITH THE FATHERS OF THE SACRED COUNCIL

FOR EVERLASTING MEMORY

CHAPTER I

THE MYSTERY[1] OF THE CHURCH

1. Christ is the light of all nations.[2] Hence this most sacred
Synod, which has been gathered in the Holy Spirit, eagerly

1. The term "mystery" indicates that the Church, as a divine reality inserted
into history, cannot be fully captured by human thought or language. As
Paul VI said in his opening allocution at the second session (Sept. 29, 1963):
"The Church is a mystery. It is a reality imbued with the hidden presence
of God. It lies, therefore, within the very nature of the Church to be always
open to new and greater exploration."
2. Although the document has a title in its official heading, Dogmatic Constitution on the Church, it may also be called *Lumen Gentium* ("Light of
All Nations") because these are the opening words of the Latin text. This
designation of Christ is biblical (cf. Lk. 2:32, Jn. 8:12, etc.) and therefore
serves to set a biblical and Christological tone for the entire document. It
likewise suggests the optimism and universal concern which is manifest
throughout the following pages. Prompted by similar considerations, the
Third General Assembly of the World Council of Churches, meeting at New
Delhi in 1961, had selected for its general theme, "Jesus Christ, the Light
of the World." [The document is also frequently called "De Ecclesia," from
the Latin of the title *Constitutio Dogmatica de Ecclesia.*—Ed.]

desires to shed on all men that radiance of His which brightens the countenance of the Church. This it will do by proclaiming the gospel to every creature (cf. Mk. 16:15).

By her relationship with Christ, the Church is a kind of sacrament[3] or sign of intimate union with God, and of the unity of all mankind. She is also an instrument for the achievement of such union and unity. For this reason, following in the path laid out by its predecessors, this Council wishes to set forth more precisely to the faithful and to the entire world the nature and encompassing mission of the Church. The conditions of this age lend special urgency to the Church's task of bringing all men to full union with Christ, since mankind today is joined together more closely than ever before by social, technical, and cultural bonds.

2. By an utterly free and mysterious decree of His own wisdom and goodness, the eternal Father,[4] created the whole world. His plan was to dignify men with a participation in His own divine life. He did not abandon men after they had fallen in Adam, but ceaselessly offered them helps to salvation, in anticipation of Christ the Redeemer, "who is the image of the invisible God, the firstborn of every creature" (Col. 1:15). All the elect, before time began, the Father "foreknew and predestined to become conformed to the image of his Son, that he should be the firstborn among many brethren" (Rom. 8:29).

He planned to assemble in the holy Church all those who would believe in Christ. Already from the beginning of the world the foreshadowing of the Church took place. She was prepared for in a remarkable way throughout the history of the people of Israel and by means of the Old Covenant.[5] Established in the present era of time, the Church was made manifest by the outpouring of the Spirit. At the end of time she will achieve her glorious fulfillment. Then, as may be

---

3. The term "sacrament" is here applied to the Church by analogy with the seven sacraments properly so called, which are particular actions of Christ in and through the Church. The Church itself is a sort of "general sacrament," since, as the Constitution here explains, it is a "sign and instrument" of the grace which unites men supernaturally to God and to one another.

4. Art. 2-4 show how the Church in its successive phases can be attributed to each of the divine Persons, Father, Son, and Holy Spirit. The preparation of the Church in the Old Testament is particularly attributed to God the Father, who began to put into effect His plan for the redemption of mankind immediately after the fall of our first parents.

5. Cf. St. Cyprian, "Epist.," 64, 4: PL 3, 1017 (CSEL [Hartel], III B, p. 720); St. Hilary of Poitiers, "In Matth.," 23, 6: PL 9, 1047; St. Augustine, passim; and St. Cyril of Alexandria, "Glaph. in Gen.," 2, 10: PG 69, 110 A.

read in the holy Fathers, all just men from the time of Adam, "from Abel, the just one, to the last of the elect,"[6] will be gathered together with the Father in the universal Church.

3. The Son, therefore, came on mission from His Father.[7] It was in Him, before the foundation of the world, that the Father chose us and predestined us to become adopted sons, for in Him it has pleased the Father to re-establish all things (cf. Eph. 1:4-5 and 10). To carry out the will of the Father, Christ inaugurated the kingdom of heaven on earth and revealed to us the mystery of the Father. By His obedience He brought about redemption. The Church, or, in other words, the kingdom of Christ now present in mystery, grows visibly in the world through the power of God.

This inauguration and this growth are both symbolized by the blood and water which flowed from the open side of the crucified Jesus (cf. Jn. 19:34), and are foretold in the Lord's words concerning His death on the cross: "And I, if I be lifted up from the earth, will draw all men to myself" (Jn. 12:32, Greek text). As often as the sacrifice of the cross in which "Christ, our passover, has been sacrificed" (1 Cor. 5:7) is celebrated on an altar, the work of our redemption is carried on. At the same time, in the sacrament of the Eucharistic bread the unity of all believers who form one body in Christ (cf. 1 Cor. 10:17) is both expressed and brought about. All men are called to this union with Christ, who is the light of the world, from whom we go forth, through whom we live, and toward whom our journey leads us.

4. When the work which the Father had given the Son to do on earth (cf. Jn. 17:4) was accomplished, the Holy Spirit was sent on the day of Pentecost in order that He might forever sanctify the Church,[8] and thus all believers would have

6. *Cf. St. Gregory the Great, "Hom. in Evang.," 19, 1: PL 76, 1154 B; St. Augustine, "Serm.," 341, 9, 11: PL 39, 1499 f.; St. John of Damascus, "Adv. iconocl.," 11: PG 96, 1357.*
7. Turning now to Christ, the Second Person of the Blessed Trinity, the Council explains that He is related to the Church as having founded it, thereby making His kingdom already present in a mysterious way. Christ continues to carry on His redemptive work in the Church, especially through the Eucharist in which, as the Council here notes with a quotation from the Prayer over the Gifts for the 9th Sunday after Pentecost, "the work of our redemption is carried on."
8. The role of the Holy Spirit in the Church is set forth in the numerous quotations from the New Testament in this paragraph. The Council especially mentions the Spirit's work in renewing and rejuvenating the Church. Pope John XXIII had prayed that Vatican II might be a "new Pentecost."

access to the Father through Christ in the one Spirit (cf. Eph. 2:18). He is the Spirit of life, a fountain of water springing up to life eternal (cf. Jn. 4:14; 7:38-39). Through Him the Father gives life to men who are dead from sin, till at last He revives in Christ even their mortal bodies (cf. Rom. 8:10-11).

The Spirit dwells in the Church and in the hearts of the faithful as in a temple (cf. 1 Cor. 3:16; 6:19). In them He prays and bears witness to the fact that they are adopted sons (cf. Gal. 4:6; Rom. 8:15-16 and 26). The Spirit guides the Church into the fullness of truth (cf. Jn. 16:13) and gives her a unity of fellowship and service. He furnishes and directs her with various gifts, both hierarchical and charismatic, and adorns her with the fruits of His grace (cf. Eph. 4:11-12; 1 Cor. 12:4; Gal. 5:22). By the power of the gospel He makes the Church grow, perpetually renews her, and leads her to perfect union with her Spouse.[9] The Spirit and the Bride both say to the Lord Jesus, "Come!" (cf. Apoc. 22:17).

Thus, the Church shines forth as "a people made one with the unity of the Father, the Son, and the Holy Spirit."[10]

5. The mystery of the holy Church is manifest in her very foundation, for the Lord Jesus inaugurated her by preaching the good news, that is, the coming of God's Kingdom,[11] which, for centuries, had been promised in the Scriptures: "The time is fulfilled, and the kingdom of God is at hand" (Mk. 1:15; cf. Mt. 4:17). In Christ's word, in His works, and in His presence this kingdom reveals itself to men. The word of the Lord is like a seed sown in a field (Mk. 4:14). Those who hear the word with faith and become part of the little flock of Christ (Lk. 12:32) have received the kingdom itself. Then, by its own power the seed sprouts and ripens until harvest time (cf. Mk. 4:26-29).

The miracles of Jesus also confirm that the kingdom has already arrived on earth: "If I cast out devils by the finger

---

9. Cf. St. Irenaeus, "Adv. haer.," III, 24, 1: PG 7, 966 B (Harvey, 2, 131; ed. Sagnard, "Sources Chr.," p. 398).
10. St. Cyprian, "De orat. Dom.," 23: PL 4, 553 (Hartel, III A, p. 285); St. Augustine, "Serm.," 71, 20, 33: PL 38, 463 f.; and St. John of Damascus, "Adv. iconocl.," 12: PG 96, 1358 D.
11. The kingdom of God, which Jesus inaugurated in His public life by His own preaching and by His very person, is not fully identical with the Church. But since Pentecost the Church has had the task of announcing and extending the kingdom here on earth, and in this way initiating in itself the final kingdom, which will be realized in glory at the end of time.

of God, then the kingdom of God has come upon you" (Lk.
11:20; cf. Mt. 12:28).

Before all things, however, the kingdom is clearly visible
in the very person of Christ, Son of God and Son of Man,
who came "to serve, and to give his life as a ransom for
many" (Mk. 10:45).

When Jesus rose up again after suffering death on the cross
for mankind, He manifested that He had been appointed
Lord, Messiah, and Priest forever (cf. Acts 2:36; Heb. 5:6;
7:17-21), and He poured out on His disciples the Spirit
promised by the Father (cf. Acts 2:33). The Church, consequently, equipped with the gifts of her Founder and faithfully guarding His precepts of charity, humility, and self-
sacrifice, receives the mission to proclaim and to establish
among all peoples the kingdom of Christ and of God. She
becomes on earth the initial budding forth of that kingdom.
While she slowly grows, the Church strains toward the consummation of the kingdom and, with all her strength, hopes
and desires to be united in glory with her King.

6. In the Old Testament the revelation of the kingdom had
often been conveyed by figures of speech. In the same way
the inner nature of the Church was now to be made known
to us through various images.[12] Drawn from pastoral life,
agriculture, building construction, and even from family and
married life, these images served a preparatory role in the
writings of the prophets.

Thus, the Church is a sheepfold whose one and necessary
door is Christ (Jn. 10:1-10). She is a flock of which God
Himself foretold that He would be the Shepherd (cf. Is.
40:11; Ez. 34:11 ff.). Although guided by human shepherds,
her sheep are nevertheless ceaselessly led and nourished by
Christ Himself, the Good Shepherd and the Prince of Shepherds (cf. Jn. 10:11; 1 Pet. 5:4), who gave His life for the
sheep (cf. Jn. 10:11-15).

The Church is a tract of land to be cultivated, the field
of God (1 Cor. 3:9). On that land grows the ancient olive
tree whose holy roots were the patriarchs and in which the

12. Since the Church is a mystery, it cannot be exhaustively defined, but its
nature is best communicated by studying the various biblical metaphors. The
following four paragraphs of this article call attention to four groups of
images: the Church is the Flock of Christ, the Vineyard of God, the Temple
of the Holy Spirit, and the Spouse of the Immaculate Lamb. These images,
taken from different spheres of human life (pastoral life, agriculture, building, and matrimony), magnificently supplement one another and indicate in
different ways Christ's tender love for, and intimate union with, the Church.

reconciliation of Jew and Gentile has been brought about and will be brought about (Rom. 11:13-26). The Church has been cultivated by the heavenly Vinedresser as His choice vineyard (Mt. 21:33-43 par.; cf. Is. 5:1 ff.). The true Vine is Christ who gives life and fruitfulness to the branches, that is, to us. Through the Church, we abide in Christ, without whom we can do nothing (Jn. 15:1-5).

The Church has more often been called the edifice of God (1 Cor. 3:9). Even the Lord likened Himself to the stone which the builders rejected, but which became the corner-stone (Mt. 21:42 par.; cf. Acts 4:11; 1 Pet. 2:7; Ps. 117:22). On this foundation the Church is built by the apostles (cf. 1 Cor. 3:11), and from it the Church receives durability and solidity. This edifice is adorned by various names: the house of God (1 Tim. 3:15) in which dwells His family; the household of God in the Spirit (Eph. 2:19-22); the dwelling place of God among men (Apoc. 21:3); and, especially, the holy temple. This temple, symbolized by places of worship built out of stone, is praised by the holy Fathers and, not without reason, is compared in the liturgy to the Holy City, the New Jerusalem.[13] As living stones we here on earth are being built up along with this City (1 Pet. 2:5). John contemplates this Holy City, coming down out of heaven from God when the world is made anew, and prepared like a bride adorned for her husband (Apoc. 21:1 f.).

The Church, "that Jerusalem which is above," is also called "our Mother" (Gal. 4:26; cf. Apoc. 12:17). She is described as the spotless spouse of the spotless Lamb (Apoc. 19:7; 21:2 and 9; 22:17). She it was whom Christ "loved and delivered himself up for her that he might sanctify her" (Eph. 5:26), whom He unites to Himself by an unbreakable covenant, and whom He unceasingly "nourishes and cherishes" (Eph. 5:29). Once she had been purified, He willed her to be joined unto Himself and to be subject to Him in love and fidelity (cf. Eph. 5:24). Finally, He filled her with heavenly gifts for all eternity, in order that we might know the love of God and of Christ for us, a love which surpasses all knowledge (cf. Eph. 3:19). The Church on earth, while

13. *Cf. Origen, "In Matth.," 16, 21: PG 13, 1443 C; and Tertullian, "Adv. Marc.," 3, 7: PL 2, 357 C (CSEL, 47, 3, p. 386). For liturgical documents, see "Sacramentarium Gregorianum": PL 78, 160 B or C. Mohlberg, "Liber Sacramentorum Romanae Ecclesiae" (Rome, 1960), p. III, XC: "Deus, qui ex omni coaptatione sanctorum aeternum tibi condis habitaculum . . ." ["O God, who by the formation of all your saints are preparing for Yourself an eternal habitation . . ."]; and the hymns "Urbs Ierusalem beata" in the Monastic Breviary and "Coelestis urbs Ierusalem" in the Roman Breviary.*

journeying in a foreign land away from her Lord (cf. 2 Cor. 5:6), regards herself as an exile. Hence she seeks and experiences those things which are above, where Christ is seated at the right hand of God, where the life of the Church is hidden with Christ in God until she appears in glory with her Spouse (cf. Col. 3:1-4).

7. In the human nature which He united to Himself, the Son of God redeemed man and transformed him into a new creation (cf. Gal. 6:15; 2 Cor. 5:17) by overcoming death through His own death and resurrection. By communicating His Spirit to His brothers, called together from all peoples, Christ made them mystically into His own body.[14]

In that body, the life of Christ is poured into the believers, who, through the sacraments, are united in a hidden and real way to Christ who suffered and was glorified.[15] Through baptism we are formed in the likeness of Christ: "For in one Spirit we were all baptized into one body" (1 Cor. 12:13). In this sacred rite, a union with Christ's death and resurrection is both symbolized and brought about: "For we were buried with him by means of Baptism into death." And if "we have been united with him in the likeness of his death, we shall be so in the likeness of his resurrection also" (Rom. 6:4-5).

Truly partaking of the body of the Lord in the breaking of the Eucharistic bread, we are taken up into communion with Him and with one another. "Because the bread is one, we though many, are one body, all of us who partake of the one bread" (1 Cor. 10:17). In this way all of us are made members of His body (cf. 1 Cor. 12:27), "but severally members one of another" (Rom. 12:5).

As all the members of the human body, though they are many, form one body, so also are the faithful in Christ (cf. 1 Cor. 12:12). Also, in the building up of Christ's body there is a flourishing variety of members and functions. There is

---

14. This relatively long article takes up and develops the Pauline doctrine of the Church as the Body of Christ, which had already formed the subject of Pius XII's important encyclical on the Church, *Mystici Corporis* (1943). But rather than beginning from the modern technical term, "Mystical Body," the Constitution prefers to show from Scripture that Christ brings men together in such wise that they constitute "in a mystical manner" his own Body. (The term "Mystical Body" is used below in Art. 8.) The analogy of the Body, considered from various points of view, strikingly illustrates the relations of men in the Church to one another, to Christ as Head, and to the Holy Spirit as Soul.

15. *Cf. St. Thomas, "Summa Theol.," 3, q. 62, a. 5, ad 1.*

only one Spirit who, according to His own richness and the needs of the ministries, distributes His different gifts for the welfare of the Church (cf. 1 Cor. 12:1-11). Among these gifts stands out the grace given to the apostles. To their authority, the Spirit Himself subjected even those who were endowed with charisms (cf. 1 Cor. 14). Giving the body unity through Himself and through His power and through the internal cohesion of its members, this same Spirit produces and urges love among the believers. Consequently, if one member suffers anything, all the members suffer it too, and if one member is honored, all the members rejoice together (cf. 1 Cor. 12:26).

The Head of this body is Christ. He is the image of the invisible God and in Him all things came into being. He has priority over everyone and in Him all things hold together. He is the Head of that body which is the Church. He is the beginning, the firstborn from the dead, so that in all things He might have the first place (cf. Col. 1:15-18). By the greatness of His power He rules the things of heaven and the things of earth, and with His all-surpassing perfection and activity He fills the whole body with the riches of His glory (cf. Eph. 1:18-23).[16]

All the members ought to be molded into Christ's image until He is formed in them (cf. Gal. 4:19). For this reason we who have been made like unto Him, who have died with Him and been raised up with Him, are taken up into the mysteries of His life, until we reign together with Him (cf. Phil. 3:21; 2 Tim. 2:11; Eph. 2:6; Col. 2:12; etc.). Still in pilgrimage upon the earth, we trace in trial and under oppression the paths He trod. Made one with His sufferings as the body is one with the head, we endure with Him, that with Him we may be glorified (cf. Rom. 8:17).

From Him, "the whole body, supplied and built up by joints and ligaments, attains a growth that is of God" (Col. 2:19). He continually distributes in His body, that is, in the Church, gifts of ministries through which, by His own power, we serve each other unto salvation so that, carrying out the truth in love, we may through all things grow up into Him who is our head (cf. Eph. 4:11-16, Greek text).

In order that we may be unceasingly renewed in Him (cf. Eph. 4:23), He has shared with us His Spirit who, existing as one and the same being in the head and in the members,

---

16. *Cf. Pius XII, encyclical "Mystici Corporis," June 29, 1943: AAS 35 (1943), p. 208.*

vivifies, unifies, and moves the whole body. This He does in such a way that His work could be compared by the holy Fathers with the function which the soul fulfills in the human body, whose principle of life the soul is.[17]

Having become the model of a man loving his wife as his own body, Christ loves the Church as His bride (cf. Eph. 5:25-28). For her part, the Church is subject to her Head (cf. Eph. 5:22-23). "For in him dwells all the fullness of the Godhead bodily" (Col. 2:9). He fills the Church, which is His Body and His fullness, with His divine gifts (cf. Eph. 1:22-23) so that she may grow and reach all the fullness of God (cf. Eph. 3:19).

8. Christ, the one Mediator, established and ceaselessly sustains here on earth His holy Church, the community of faith, hope, and charity, as a visible structure.[18] Through her He communicates truth and grace to all. But the society furnished with hierarchical agencies and the Mystical Body of Christ are not to be considered as two realities, nor are the visible assembly and the spiritual community, nor the earthly Church and the Church enriched with heavenly things. Rather they form one interlocked reality which is comprised of a divine and a human element.[19] For this reason, by an excellent analogy, this reality is compared to the mystery of the incarnate Word.[20] Just as the assumed nature inseparably united to the divine Word serves Him as a living instrument of salvation, so, in a similar way, does the communal structure of the Church serve Christ's Spirit, who vivifies it by way of building up the body (cf. Eph. 4:16).[21]

This is the unique Church of Christ which in the Creed

17. *Cf. Leo XIII, encyclical "Divinum Illud," May 9, 1897: AAS 29 (1896-7), p. 650; Pius XII, encyclical "Mystici Corporis": AAS 35 (1943), pp. 219-20 (Denz. 2288 [3808]); St. Augustine, "Serm.," 268, 2: PL 38, 1232, and in other works; St. John Chrysostom, "In Eph. Hom.," 9, 3: PG 62, 72; Didymus of Alexandria, "Trin.," 2, 1: PG 39, 449 f.; and St. Thomas, "In Col.," 1, 18, lect. 5 (ed. Marietti, II, no. 46): "Sicut constituitur unum corpus ex unitate animae, ita Ecclesia ex unitate Spiritus . . ." [As one body is constituted by the unity of the soul, so the Church by the unity of the Spirit . . ."].*
18. *Leo XIII, encyclical "Sapientiae Christianae," Jan. 10, 1890: AAS 22 (1889-90), p. 392; the same Pontiff's encyclical "Satis Cognitum," June 29, 1896: AAS 28 (1895-6), pp. 710 and 724 ff.; Pius XII, encyclical "Mystici Corporis": AAS 35 (1943), pp. 199-200.*
19. *Cf. Pius XII, encyclical "Mystici Corporis": AAS 35 (1943), pp. 221 ff.; Pius XII, encyclical "Humani Generis," Aug. 12, 1950: AAS 42 (1950), p. 571.*
20. The Church as a mystery (or divine reality appearing in visible form) is in some way comparable to Christ Himself, whose visible presence on earth both manifested and cloaked His divinity.
21. *Leo XIII, encyclical "Satis Cognitum": AAS 28 (1895-6), p. 713.*

we avow as one, holy, catholic, and apostolic.[22] After His Resurrection our Savior handed her over to Peter to be shepherded (Jn. 21:17), commissioning him and the other apostles to propagate and govern her (cf. Mt. 28:18 ff.). Her He erected for all ages as "the pillar and mainstay of the truth" (1 Tim. 3:15).[23] This Church, constituted and organized in the world as a society, subsists in the Catholic Church, which is governed by the successor of Peter and by the bishops in union with that successor,[24] although many elements of sanctification and of truth can be found outside of her visible structure. These elements, however, as gifts properly belonging to the Church of Christ, possess an inner dynamism toward Catholic unity.

Just as Christ carried out the work of redemption in poverty and under oppression, so the Church is called to follow the same path in communicating to men the fruits of salvation.[25] Christ Jesus, "though He was by nature God . . . emptied himself, taking the nature of a slave" (Phil. 2:6), and "being rich, he became poor" (2 Cor. 8:9) for our sakes. Thus, although the Church needs human resources to carry out her mission, she is not set up to seek earthly glory, but to proclaim humility and self-sacrifice, even by her own example.

22. Cf. Apostles' Creed: Denz. 6-9 (10-13); the Niceno-Constantinopolitan Creed: Denz. 86 (150); and the Tridentine Profession of Faith: Denz. 994 and 999 (1862 and 1868).

23. The Constitution here takes up the very delicate point of the relationship of the Catholic Church as it presently exists (governed by the Roman Pontiff and by the bishops in communion with him) to the Church of Christ. According to the Constitution, the Church of Christ survives in the world today in its institutional fullness in the Catholic Church, although elements of the Church are present in other Churches and ecclesial communities—a point which will be more fully developed in the Decree on Ecumenism. These "ecclesial elements" in other Churches, far from shattering the unity of the Mystical Body, are dynamic realities which tend to bring about an ever greater measure of unity among all who believe in Christ and are baptized in Him.

24. It is called "Sancta (catholica, apostolica) Romana Ecclesia" ["the holy (catholic, apostolic) Church"] in the Tridentine Profession of Faith (as cited in the preceding footnote) and in Vatican Council I, Session 3, the dogmatic constitution "De fide cath.": Denz. 1782 (3001).

25. The comparison between the Church and Christ is a reminder that the Church, like its Master, should not seek to be served but to serve. But of course there is no complete parallelism. Unlike Christ, the Church is not a divine Person; in its concrete historical existence, it is capable of being tarnished by sin. The theme of the Church's continuous need for purification is no innovation, but is found in various ancient liturgical prayers such as the Collects for the First Sunday of Lent and the 15th Sunday after Pentecost. The Decree on Ecumenism, building on this idea of inner renewal and reform in the Church, shows its great ecumenical importance, especially for facilitating better understanding with the Protestants.

Christ was sent by the Father "to bring good news to the poor, to heal the contrite of heart"* (Lk. 4:18), "to seek and to save what was lost" (Lk. 19:10). Similarly, the Church encompasses with love all those who are afflicted with human weakness. Indeed, she recognizes in the poor and the suffering the likeness of her poor and suffering Founder. She does all she can to relieve their need and in them she strives to serve Christ. While Christ, "holy, innocent, undefiled" (Heb. 7:26) knew nothing of sin (2 Cor. 5:21), but came to expiate only the sins of the people (cf. Heb. 2:17), the Church, embracing sinners in her bosom, is at the same time holy and always in need of being purified, and incessantly pursues the path of penance and renewal.

The Church, "like a pilgrim in a foreign land, presses forward amid the persecutions of the world and the consolations of God,"[26] announcing the cross and death of the Lord until He comes (cf. 1 Cor. 11:26). By the power of the risen Lord, she is given strength to overcome patiently and lovingly the afflictions and hardships which assail her from within and without, and to show forth in the world the mystery of the Lord in a faithful though shadowed way, until at the last it will be revealed in total splendor.

CHAPTER II

THE PEOPLE OF GOD[27]

9. At all times and among every people, God has given welcome to whosoever fears Him and does what is right (cf.

---

*Like many other versions, the 1941 Confraternity translation omits the last six words.—Ed.

26. *St. Augustine, "Civ. Dei," XVIII, 51, 2: PL 41, 614.*

27. Completing the study of the biblical images and designations in the second half of Chap. I, the Constitution devotes an entire chapter to the description of the Church as the "new People of God." This title, solidly founded in Scripture, met a profound desire of the Council to put greater emphasis on the human and communal side of the Church, rather than on the institutional and hierarchical aspects which have sometimes been overstressed in the past for polemical reasons. While everything said about the

Acts 10:35). It has pleased God, however, to make men holy and save them not merely as individuals without any mutual bonds, but by making them into a single people, a people which acknowledges Him in truth and serves Him in holiness. He therefore chose the race of Israel as a people unto Himself. With it He set up a covenant. Step by step He taught this people by manifesting in its history both Himself and the decree of His will, and by making it holy unto Himself. All these things, however, were done by way of preparation and as a figure of that new and perfect covenant which was to be ratified in Christ, and of that more luminous revelation which was to be given through God's very Word made flesh.

"Behold the days shall come, saith the Lord, and I will make a new covenant with the house of Israel, and with the house of Judah. . . . I will give my law in their bowels, and I will write it in their heart: and I will be their God, and they shall be my people. . . . For all shall know me, from the least of them even to the greatest, saith the Lord" (Jer. 31:31-34). Christ instituted this new covenant, that is to say, the new testament, in His blood (cf. 1 Cor. 11:25), by calling together a people made up of Jew and Gentile, making them one, not according to the flesh but in the Spirit.

This was to be the new People of God. For, those who believe in Christ, who are reborn not from a perishable but from an imperishable seed through the Word of the living God (cf. 1 Pet. 1:23), not from the flesh but from water and the Holy Spirit (cf. Jn. 3:5-6), are finally established as "a chosen race, a royal priesthood, a holy nation, a purchased people. . . . You who in times past were not a people, but are now the people of God" (1 Pet. 2:9-10).

That messianic people has for its head Christ, "who was delivered up for our sins, and rose again for our justification" (Rom. 4:25), and who now, having won a name which is above all names, reigns in glory in heaven.[28] The heritage of this people are the dignity and freedom of the sons of God, in whose hearts the Holy Spirit dwells as in His temple. Its law is the new commandment to love as Christ loved us

People of God as a whole is applicable to the laity, it should not be forgotten that the term "People of God" refers to the total community of the Church, including the pastors as well as the other faithful.

28. This paragraph, one of the most beautiful in the entire Constitution, touches on a number of characteristic themes of Vatican II: the universal expansiveness of the Church, its role as a sacrament of unity, its weakness and dependence upon God's help during its earthly pilgrimage, and its ardent hope for the final fulfillment of God's kingdom.

(cf. Jn. 13:34). Its goal is the kingdom of God, which has been begun by God Himself on earth, and which is to be further extended until it is brought to perfection by Him at the end of time. Then Christ our life (cf. Col. 3:4), will appear, and "creation itself also will be delivered from its slavery to corruption into the freedom of the glory of the sons of God" (Rom. 8:21).

So it is that this messianic people, although it does not actually include all men, and may more than once look like a small flock, is nonetheless a lasting and sure seed of unity, hope, and salvation for the whole human race. Established by Christ as a fellowship of life, charity, and truth, it is also used by Him as an instrument for the redemption of all, and is sent forth into the whole world as the light of the world and the salt of the earth (cf. Mt. 5:13-16).

Israel according to the flesh, which wandered as an exile in the desert, was already called the Church of God (2 Esd. 13:1; cf. Num. 20:4; Dt. 23:1 ff). Likewise the new Israel which, while going forward in this present world, goes in search of a future and abiding city (cf. Heb. 13:14) is also called the Church of Christ (cf. Mt. 16:18). For He has bought it for Himself with His blood (cf. Acts 20:28), has filled it with His Spirit, and provided it with those means which befit it as a visible and social unity. God has gathered together as one all those who in faith look upon Jesus as the author of salvation and the source of unity and peace, and has established them as the Church, that for each and all she may be the visible sacrament of this saving unity.[29]

While she transcends all limits of time and of race, the Church is destined to extend to all regions of the earth and so to enter into the history of mankind. Moving forward through trial and tribulation, the Church is strengthened by the power of God's grace promised to her by the Lord, so that in the weakness of the flesh she may not waver from perfect fidelity, but remain a bride worthy of her Lord; that moved by the Holy Spirit she may never cease to renew herself, until through the cross she arrives at the light which knows no setting.

10. Christ the Lord, High Priest taken from among men (cf. Heb. 5:1-5), "made a kingdom and priests to God his Fa-

---

29. *Cf. St. Cyprian. "Epist.," 69, 6: PL 3, 1142 B (Hartel, III B, p. 754): "inseparabile unitatis sacramentum" ["the unbreakable sacrament of unity"].*

ther" (Apoc. 1:6; cf. 5:9-10) out of this new people.[30] The baptized, by regeneration and the anointing of the Holy Spirit, are consecrated into a spiritual house and a holy priesthood. Thus through all those works befitting Christian men they can offer spiritual sacrifices and proclaim the power of Him who has called them out of darkness into His marvelous light (cf. 1 Pet. 2:4-10). Therefore all the disciples of Christ, persevering in prayer and praising God (cf. Acts 2:42-47), should present themselves as living sacrifice, holy and pleasing to God (cf. Rom. 12:1). Everywhere on earth they must bear witness to Christ and give an answer to those who seek an account of that hope of eternal life which is in them (cf. 1 Pet. 3:15).

Though they differ from one another in essence and not only in degree, the common priesthood of the faithful and the ministerial or hierarchical priesthood are nonetheless interrelated. Each of them in its own special way is a participation in the one priesthood of Christ.[31] The ministerial priest, by the sacred power he enjoys, molds and rules the priestly people. Acting in the person of Christ, he brings about the Eucharistic Sacrifice, and offers it to God in the name of all the people. For their part, the faithful join in the offering of the Eucharist by virtue of their royal priesthood.[32] They likewise exercise that priesthood by receiving the sacraments, by prayer and thanksgiving, by the witness of a holy life, and by self-denial and active charity.

11. It is through the sacraments[33] and the exercise of the virtues that the sacred nature and organic structure of the

30. Art. 10-13 form a unit in which the Church is considered as reflecting in itself the triple office of Christ as priest, prophet, and king. This the Church does by its threefold function of worship (ministry), witness, and communal life. The present paragraph deals particularly with the priestly office. The common priesthood of all the baptized provides the basis for, and requires for its completion, the ministerial priesthood of the ordained clergy.

31. Cf. Pius XII, allocution "Magnificate Dominum," Nov. 2, 1954: AAS 46 (1954), p. 669; Pius XII, encyclical "Mediator Dei," Nov. 20, 1947: AAS 39 (1947), p. 555.

32. Cf. Pius XI, encyclical "Miserentissimus Redemptor," May 8, 1928: AAS 20 (1928), pp. 171 f.; Pius XII, allocution "Vous nous avez," Sept. 22, 1956: AAS 48 (1956) p. 714.

33. Amplifying Art. 10, the Council goes on to show that the priestly function of the Church is exercised in various ways in the administration and reception of the sacraments. Three of these (baptism, confirmation, and holy orders) make their recipients sharers in various degrees in the priestly office of Christ, thus qualifying them to receive or administer the other sacraments. The sacraments are here envisaged not as the actions of individuals but in their relation to the entire Church, whose life they articulate.

priestly community is brought into operation. Incorporated into the Church through baptism, the faithful are consecrated by the baptismal character to the exercise of the cult of the Christian religion. Reborn as sons of God, they must confess before men the faith which they have received from God through the Church.[34] Bound more intimately to the Church by the sacrament of confirmation, they are endowed by the Holy Spirit with special strength. Hence they are more strictly obliged to spread and defend the faith both by word and by deed as true witnesses of Christ.[35]

Taking part in the Eucharistic Sacrifice, which is the fount and apex of the whole Christian life, they offer the divine Victim to God, and offer themselves along with It.[36] Thus, both by the act of oblation and through holy Communion, all perform their proper part in this liturgical service, not, indeed, all in the same way but each in that way which is appropriate to himself. Strengthened anew at the holy table by the Body of Christ, they manifest in a practical way that unity of God's People which is suitably signified and wondrously brought about by this most awesome sacrament.

Those who approach the sacrament of penance obtain pardon from the mercy of God for offenses committed against Him. They are at the same time reconciled with the Church, which they have wounded by their sins, and which by charity, example, and prayer seeks their conversion. By the sacred anointing of the sick and the prayer of her priests, the whole Church commends those who are ill to the suffering and glorified Lord, asking that He may lighten their suffering and save them (cf. Jas. 5:14-16). She exhorts them, moreover, to contribute to the welfare of the whole People of God by associating themselves freely with the passion and death of Christ (cf. Rom. 8:17; Col. 1:24; 2 Tim. 2:11-12; 1 Pet. 4:13). Those of the faithful who are consecrated by holy orders are appointed to feed the Church in Christ's name with the Word and the grace of God.

Finally, Christian spouses, in virtue of the sacrament of matrimony, signify and partake of the mystery of that unity

They constitute public, communal worship, and the grace which flows from them serves to build up the life of the whole Church.

34. Cf. St. Thomas, "Summa Theol.," 3, q. 63, a. 2.
35. Cf. St. Cyril of Jerusalem, "Catech.," 17, De Spiritu Sancto, II, 35-7: PG 33, 1009-12; Nic. Cabasilas, "De vita in Christo," bk. III, De utilate chrismatis: PG 150, 569-80; and St. Thomas, "Summa Theol.," 3, q. 65, a. 3 and q. 72, a. 1 and 5.
36. Cf. Pius XII, encyclical "Mediator Dei," Nov. 20, 1947: AAS 39 (1947), especially pp. 552 f.

and fruitful love which exists between Christ and His Church (cf. Eph. 5:32). The spouses thereby help each other to attain to holiness in their married life and by the rearing and education of their children. And so, in their state and way of life, they have their own special gift among the People of God (cf. 1 Cor. 7:7).[37]

For from the wedlock of Christians there comes the family, in which new citizens of human society are born. By the grace of the Holy Spirit received in baptism these are made children of God, thus perpetuating the People of God through the centuries. The family is, so to speak, the domestic Church. In it parents should, by their word and example, be the first preachers of the faith to their children. They should encourage them in the vocation which is proper to each of them, fostering with special care any religious vocation.

Fortified by so many and such powerful means of salvation, all the faithful, whatever their condition or state, are called by the Lord, each in his own way, to that perfect holiness whereby the Father Himself is perfect.

12. The holy People of God shares also in Christ's prophetic office.[38] It spreads abroad a living witness to Him, especially by means of a life of faith and charity and by offering to God a sacrifice of praise, the tribute of lips which give honor to His name (cf. Heb. 13:15). The body of the faithful as a whole, anointed as they are by the Holy One (cf. Jn. 2:20, 27), cannot err in matters of belief. Thanks to a supernatural sense of the faith which characterizes the People as a whole, it manifests this unerring quality when, "from the bishops down to the last member of the laity,"[39] it shows universal agreement in matters of faith and morals.[40]

For, by this sense of faith which is aroused and sustained by the Spirit of truth, God's People accepts not the word of

---

37. *1 Cor 7:7: "Everyone has his own particular gift* ["*idion charisma*"] *from God, some one thing and some another." Cf. St. Augustine, "De dono persev.," 14, 37: PL 45, 1015 f.: "It is not just continence that is a gift of God —so also is the chastity of the married."*
38. The entire People of God, just as it shares in Christ's priestly office, shares in his role as prophet, bearing witness to the gospel.
39. *Cf. St. Augustine, "De praed. sanct.," 14, 27: PL 44, 980.*
40. The idea that the "sense of the faithful," imprinted on their hearts by the Holy Spirit, cannot err, was a favorite theme of Cardinal Newman, who foresaw its importance for the theology of the laity, which was in its infancy in his day. The fact that the faithful as a whole bear witness to the gospel does not make superfluous the teaching of the hierarchy. To them it falls to shepherd the whole flock by clear, authoritative doctrine.

men but the very Word of God (cf. 1 Th. 2:13). It clings without fail to the faith once delivered to the saints (cf. Jude 3), penetrates it more deeply by accurate insights, and applies it more thoroughly to life. All this it does under the lead of a sacred teaching authority to which it loyally defers.

It is not only through the sacraments and Church ministries that the same Holy Spirit sanctifies and leads the People of God and enriches it with virtues. Allotting His gifts "to everyone according as he will" (1 Cor. 12:11), He distributes special graces among the faithful of every rank. By these gifts He makes them fit and ready to undertake the various tasks or offices advantageous for the renewal and upbuilding of the Church, according to the words of the Apostle: "The manifestation of the Spirit is given to everyone for profit" (1 Cor. 12:7). These charismatic gifts, whether they be the most outstanding or the more simple and widely diffused, are to be received with thanksgiving and consolation, for they are exceedingly suitable and useful for the needs of the Church.[41]

Still, extraordinary gifts are not to be rashly sought after, nor are the fruits of apostolic labor to be presumptuously expected from them. In any case, judgment as to their genuineness and proper use belongs to those who preside over the Church, and to whose special competence it belongs, not indeed to extinguish the Spirit, but to test all things and hold fast to that which is good (cf. 1 Th. 5:12, 19-21).

13. All men are called to belong to the new People of God.[42] Wherefore this People, while remaining one and unique, is to be spread throughout the whole world and must exist in all ages, so that the purpose of God's will may be fulfilled. In the beginning God made human nature one. After His children were scattered, He decreed that they should at length be unified again (cf. Jn. 11:52). It was for this

---

41. To guard against a common misunderstanding, the Constitution makes it clear that charisms should not necessarily be identified with extraordinary and spectacular phenomena, which are by their very nature rare. The whole question of charisms is well treated by Karl Rahner in his book *The Dynamic Element in the Church* (New York: Herder and Herder, 1964).

42. Thirdly, the People of God is considered in its relationship to Christ as King. In this regard it is a fellowship of life. Reflecting the universal Lordship of Christ, the Church spontaneously tends to spread everywhere, thereby bringing men of every nation into intimate spiritual union with one another. Since the Church's unity is vital and organic, it does not impose rigid uniformity, but rather thrives on a variety of gifts and functions.

reason that God sent His Son, whom He appointed heir of all things (cf. Heb. 1:2), that He might be Teacher, King, and Priest of all, the Head of the new and universal people of the sons of God. For this God finally sent His Son's Spirit as Lord and Lifegiver. He it is who, on behalf of the whole Church and each and every one of those who believe, is the principle of their coming together and remaining together in the teaching of the apostles and in fellowship, in the breaking of bread and in prayers (cf. Acts 2:42, Greek text).

It follows that among all the nations of earth there is but one People of God, which takes its citizens from every race, making them citizens of a kingdom which is of a heavenly and not an earthly nature. For all the faithful scattered throughout the world are in communion with each other in the Holy Spirit, so that "he who occupies the See of Rome knows the people of India are his members."[43] Since the kingdom of Christ is not of this world (cf. Jn. 18:36), the Church or People of God takes nothing away from the temporal welfare of any people by establishing that kingdom. Rather does she foster and take to herself, insofar as they are good, the ability, resources, and customs of each people. Taking them to herself she purifies, strengthens, and ennobles them. The Church in this is mindful that she must harvest with that King to whom the nations were given for an inheritance (cf. Ps. 2:8) and into whose city they bring gifts and presents (cf. Ps. 71[72]:10; Is. 60:4-7; Apoc. 21:24). This characteristic of universality which adorns the People of God is a gift from the Lord Himself. By reason of it, the Catholic Church strives energetically and constantly to bring all humanity with all its riches back to Christ its Head in the unity of His Spirit.[44]

In virtue of this catholicity each individual part of the Church contributes through its special gifts to the good of the other parts and of the whole Church. Thus through the common sharing of gifts and through the common effort to attain fullness in unity, the whole and each of the parts receive increase. Not only, then, is the People of God made up of different peoples but even in its inner structure it is composed of various ranks. This diversity among its members arises either by reason of their duties, as is the case with those who

---

43. Cf. St. John Chrysostom, "In Io.," Hom. 65, 1: PG 59, 361.
44. Cf. St. Irenaeus, "Adv. haer.," III, 16, 6; III, 22, 1-3: PG 7, 925 C-926 A and 955 C-958 A (Harvey, 2, 87 f. and 120-3; Sagnard, pp. 290-2 and 372 ff.).

exercise the sacred ministry for the good of their brethren, or by reason of their situation and way of life, as is the case with those many who enter the religious state and, tending toward holiness by a narrower path, stimulate their brethren by their example.

Moreover, within the Church particular Churches hold a rightful place. These Churches retain their own traditions without in any way lessening the primacy of the Chair of Peter. This Chair presides over the whole assembly of charity[45] and protects legitimate differences, while at the same time it sees that such differences do not hinder unity but rather contribute toward it. Finally, between all the parts of the Church there remains a bond of close communion with respect to spiritual riches, apostolic workers, and temporal resources. For the members of the People of God are called to share these goods, and to each of the Churches the words of the Apostle apply: "According to the gift that each has received, administer it to one another as good stewards of the manifold grace of God" (1 Pet. 4:10).

All men are called to be part of this catholic unity of the People of God, a unity which is harbinger of the universal peace it promotes. And there belong to it or are related to it in various ways, the Catholic faithful as well as all who believe in Christ, and indeed the whole of mankind. For all men are called to salvation by the grace of God.[46]

14. This sacred Synod turns its attention first to the Catholic faithful. Basing itself upon sacred Scripture and tradition, it teaches that the Church, now sojourning on earth as an exile, is necessary for salvation.[47] For Christ, made present to us in His Body, which is the Church, is the one Mediator and the unique Way of salvation. In explicit terms He Himself affirmed the necessity of faith and baptism (cf. Mk. 16:16; Jn. 3:5) and thereby affirmed also the necessity of the Church, for through baptism as through a door men enter the Church. Whosoever, therefore, knowing that the Catholic

---

45. Cf. St. Ignatius of Antioch, "Ad Rom.," Praef.: ed. Funk, I, p. 252.
46. The Constitution now passes on to consider in the last section of this Chapter the various ways in which men can be united or linked with the people of God.
47. To indicate the importance of union with the Church, the Council first reiterates the traditional Catholic teaching on the necessity of the Church for salvation. This necessity is a double one arising both from the positive precept of Christ that men should enter the Church and from the efficacy of the Church's means of grace (especially her proclamation of the faith and her administration of the sacrament of baptism) for imparting and sustaining an authentically Christian life.

Church was made necessary by God through Jesus Christ, would refuse to enter her or to remain in her could not be saved.

They are fully incorporated into the society of the Church who, possessing the Spirit of Christ, accept her entire system and all the means of salvation given to her, and through union with her visible structure are joined to Christ, who rules her through the Supreme Pontiff and the bishops.[48] This joining is effected by the bonds of professed faith, of the sacraments, of ecclesiastical government, and of communion. He is not saved, however, who, though he is part of the body of the Church, does not persevere in charity. He remains indeed in the bosom of the Church, but, as it were, only in a "bodily" manner and not "in his heart."[49] All the sons of the Church should remember that their exalted status is to be attributed not to their own merits but to the special grace of Christ. If they fail moreover to respond to that grace in thought, word, and deed, not only will they not be saved but they will be the more severely judged.[50]

Catechumens who, moved by the Holy Spirit, seek with explicit intention to be incorporated into the Church are by that very intention joined to her. With love and solicitude Mother Church already embraces them as her own.

15. The Church recognizes[51] that in many ways she is linked with those who, being baptized, are honored with the name of Christian, though they do not profess the faith in its entirety or do not preserve unity of communion with the suc-

48. The Council here makes it clear that only Catholic Christians are fully incorporated in the Church. But for full incorporation it is not sufficient to be externally a Catholic; one must also be animated by the Spirit of Christ. Where charity is absent, a bond of union essential to salvation is lacking.

49. *Cf St. Augustine, "Bapt. c. Donat.," V, 28, 39: PL 43, 197: "It is certainly clear that when we speak of 'within' and 'without' with regard to the Church, our consideration must be directed to what is in the heart, not to what is in the body." See also in the same work, III, 19, 26: PL 43, 152; V, 18, 24: PL 43, 189; and the same author's "In Jo.," tr. 61, 2: PL 35, 1800, as well as many texts in other of his works.*

50. *Cf. Lk. 12:48: "Much will be expected from the one who has been given much." Also, Mt. 5:19-20; 7:21-2; 25:41-6; Jas. 2:14.*

51. This paragraph gives a concise summary of the ways in which those Christians who do not have full visible union with the Catholic Church may nevertheless be linked to the Church by salutary bonds. The Decree on Ecumenism treats this point more fully, especially in Art. 3, which details the various elements of the Church that can subsist outside the visible boundaries of Catholicism. By treating the relationship of the other Christians to the Catholic Church under the heading of the "People of God" rather than that of the "Mystical Body" (treated in Chap. I), the Constitution is able to avoid various subtle and controverted questions concerning "degrees of membership" which have been much discussed since the time of *Mystici Corporis.*

cessor of Peter.[52] For there are many who honor sacred Scripture, taking it as a norm of belief and of action, and who show a true religious zeal. They lovingly believe in God the Father Almighty and in Christ, Son of God and Savior.[53] They are consecrated by baptism, through which they are united with Christ. They also recognize and receive other sacraments within their own Churches or ecclesial communities. Many of them rejoice in the episcopate, celebrate the Holy Eucharist, and cultivate devotion toward the Virgin Mother of God.[54] They also share with us in prayer and other spiritual benefits.

Likewise, we can say that in some real way they are joined with us in the Holy Spirit, for to them also He gives His gifts and graces, and is thereby operative among them with His sanctifying power. Some indeed He has strengthened to the extent of the shedding of their blood. In all of Christ's disciples the Spirit arouses the desire to be peacefully united, in the manner determined by Christ, as one flock under one shepherd, and He prompts them to pursue this goal.[55] Mother Church never ceases to pray, hope, and work that they may gain this blessing. She exhorts her sons to purify and renew themselves so that the sign of Christ may shine more brightly over the face of the Church.

16. Finally, those who have not yet received the gospel[56] are related in various ways to the People of God.[57] In the first place there is the people to whom the covenants and the promises were given and from whom Christ was born according to the flesh (cf. Rom. 9:4-5). On account of their fathers, this people remains most dear to God, for God does not repent of the gifts He makes nor of the calls He issues (cf. Rom. 11:28-29).

---

52. Cf. Leo XIII, apostolic epistle "Praeclara gratulationis," June 20, 1894: Acta Sanctae Sedis, 26 (1893-4), p. 707.

53. Cf. Leo XIII, encyclical "Satis Cognitum," June 29, 1896: Acta Sanctae Sedis, 28 (1895-6), p. 738; Leo XIII, encyclical "Caritatis studium," July 25, 1898; Acta Sanctae Sedis, 31 (1898-9), p. 11; and the radio message of Pius XII, "Nell'abla," Dec. 24, 1941: AAS 34 (1942), p. 21.

54. Cf. Pius XI, encyclical "Rerum Orientalium," Sept. 8, 1928: AAS 20 (1928), p. 287; Pius XII, encyclical "Orientalis Ecclesiae," Apr. 9, 1944: AAS 36 (1944), p. 137.

55. Cf. instruction of the Holy Office, Dec. 20, 1949: AAS 42 (1950), p. 142.

56. Extending the range of its view beyond the Christian fold, the Council now touches on the relationship of non-Christian communities to the Church, thus preparing the way for the Declaration on the Relationship of the Church to Non-Christian Religions. Special mention is here made of the Jews and Mohammedans because of the biblical basis of their respective faiths.

57. Cf. St. Thomas, "Summa Theol.," 3, q. 8, a. 3, ad 1.

But the plan of salvation also includes those who acknowledge the Creator. In the first place among these there are the Moslems, who, professing to hold the faith of Abraham, along with us adore the one and merciful God, who on the last day will judge mankind. Nor is God Himself far distant from those who in shadows and images seek the unknown God, for it is He who gives to all men life and breath and every other gift (cf. Acts 17:25-28), and who as Savior wills that all men be saved (cf. 1 Tim. 2:4).

Those also can attain to everlasting salvation who through no fault of their own do not know the gospel of Christ or His Church, yet sincerely seek God and, moved by grace, strive by their deeds to do His will as it is known to them[58] through the dictates of conscience.[59] Nor does divine Providence deny the help necessary for salvation to those who, without blame on their part, have not yet arrived at an explicit knowledge of God, but who strive to live a good life, thanks to His grace. Whatever goodness or truth is found for the gospel.[60] She regards such qualities as given by Him among them is looked upon by the Church as a preparation who enlightens all men so that they may finally have life.

But rather often men, deceived by the Evil One, have become caught up in futile reasoning and have exchanged the truth of God for a lie, serving the creature rather than the Creator (cf. Rom. 1:21,25). Or some there are who, living and dying in a world without God, are subject to utter hopelessness. Consequently, to promote the glory of God and procure the salvation of all such men, and mindful of the command of the Lord, "Preach the gospel to every creature" (Mk. 16:16), the Church painstakingly fosters her missionary work.

17. Just as the Son was sent by the Father, so He too sent the apostles (cf. Jn. 20:21), saying: "Go, therefore, and make disciples of all nations, baptizing them in the name of the Father and of the Son and of the Holy Spirit, teaching them to observe all that I have commanded you; and behold,

58. The Council is careful to add that men unacquainted with the biblical revelation, and even those who have not arrived at explicit faith in God, may by the grace of Christ attain salvation if they sincerely follow the lights God gives them. In a footnote, the Council makes reference to the important 1949 letter of the Holy Office to Archbishop (now Cardinal) Cushing of Boston, which lucidly explained how according to Catholic doctrine it can be possible for non-Catholics to attain salvation through the grace of God.
59. *Cf. letter of the Holy Office to the Archbishop of Boston: Denz. 3869-72.*
60. *Cf. Eusebius of Caesarea, "Praeparatio evangelica," 1, 1: PG 21, 28 AB.*

I am with you all days even unto the consummation of the world" (Mt. 28:18-20).

The Church has received from the apostles as a task to be discharged even to the ends of the earth this solemn mandate of Christ to proclaim the saving truth (cf. Acts 1:8).[61] Hence she makes the words of the Apostle her own: "Woe to me, if I do not preach the gospel" (1 Cor. 9:16), and continues unceasingly to send heralds of the gospel until such time as the infant churches are fully established and can themselves carry on the work of evangelizing. For the Church is compelled by the Holy Spirit to do her part towards the full realization of the will of God, who has established Christ as the source of salvation for the whole world.[62] By the proclamation of the gospel, she prepares her hearers to receive and profess the faith, disposes them for baptism, snatches them from the slavery of error, and incorporates them into Christ so that through charity they may grow up into full maturity in Christ.

Through her work, whatever good is in the minds and hearts of men, whatever good lies latent in the religious practices and cultures of diverse peoples, is not only saved from destruction but is also healed, ennobled, and perfected unto the glory of God, the confusion of the devil, and the happiness of man. The obligation of spreading the faith is imposed on every disciple of Christ, according to his ability.[63] Though all the faithful can baptize, the priest alone can complete the building up of the Body in the Eucharistic Sacrifice. Thus are fulfilled the Words of God, spoken through His prophet: "From the rising of the sun even to the going down, my name is great among the Gentiles, and in every place there is sacrifice, and there is offered to my name a clean oblation" (Mal. 1:11).[64] In this way the Church simultaneously prays and labors in order that the entire world

---

61. The concluding lines of the preceding paragraph lead naturally to a consideration of the missionary mandate of the Church, which brings this important chapter to a dynamic conclusion.

62. As in the Gospels, so here the missionary mandate of the Church is closely related to the doctrine of the Trinity, the heart of the Church's faith. The respective roles of hierarchy and laity in the missions, here briefly intimated, will be more fully spelled out in the Decree on the Church's Missionary Activity.

63. Cf. Benedict XV, apostolic epistle "Maximum illud": AAS 11 (1919), p. 440 and especially pp. 451˙ff.; Pius XI, encyclical "Rerum Ecclesiae": AAS 18 (1926), pp. 68-70; Pius XII, encyclical "Fidei donum," Apr. 21, 1957: AAS 49 (1957), pp. 236-7.

64. Cf. the "Didache," 14: ed. Funk, I, p. 32; St. Justin, "Dial.," 41: PG 6, 564; St. Irenaeus, "Adv. haer.," IV, 17, 5: PG 7, 1023 (Harvey, 2, pp. 199f.); and the Council of Trent, Session 22, Chap. 1: Denz. 939 (1742).

may become the People of God, the Body of the Lord, and the Temple of the Holy Spirit, and that in Christ, the Head of all, there may be rendered to the Creator and Father of the Universe all honor and glory.

CHAPTER III

THE HIERARCHICAL STRUCTURE OF THE CHURCH, WITH SPECIAL REFERENCE TO THE EPISCOPATE [65]

18. For the nurturing and constant growth of the People of God, Christ the Lord instituted in His Church a variety of ministries, which work for the good of the whole body. For those ministers who are endowed with sacred power are servants of their brethren, so that all who are of the People of God, and therefore enjoy a true Christian dignity, can work toward a common goal freely and in an orderly way, and arrive at salvation.[66]

This most sacred Synod, following in the footsteps of the First Vatican Council, teaches and declares with that Council that Jesus Christ, the eternal Shepherd, established His holy Church by sending forth the apostles as He Himself had been sent by the Father (cf. Jn. 20:21). He willed that their successors, namely the bishops, should be shepherds in His Church even to the consummation of the world.[67]

65. This lengthy chapter deals with the ordained ministers in the Church, especially the bishops, and contains the most important doctrinal affirmations in the Constitution, namely, the sacramentality of episcopal consecration and the collegiality of the bishops. Vatican I, after defining the primacy and infallibility of the Roman Pontiff, had intended to consider the episcopal office, but the labors of the Council were interrupted by political upheavals. Thus Vatican II on this point resumes where Vatican I left off, but makes great advances which would scarcely have been possible a century ago.
66. The authority of the hierarchy, here as elsewhere in the Constitution, is explained in terms of service, not of dominion.
67. The Council begins with a consideration of what Jesus instituted during his life on earth. It repeats the doctrine of Vatican I concerning the primacy

In order that the episcopate itself might be one and undivided, He placed blessed Peter over the other apostles, and instituted in him a permanent and visible source and foundation of unity of faith and fellowship.[68] And all this teaching about the institution, the perpetuity, the force and reason for the sacred primacy of the Roman Pontiff and of his infallible teaching authority, this sacred Synod again proposes to be firmly believed by all the faithful.

Continuing in the same task of clarification begun by Vatican I, this Council has decided to declare and proclaim before all men its teaching concerning bishops, the successors of the apostles, who together with the successor of Peter, the Vicar of Christ[69] and the visible Head of the whole Church, govern the house of the living God.[70]

19. The Lord Jesus, after praying to the Father and calling to Himself those whom He desired, appointed twelve men who would stay in His company, and whom He would send to preach the kingdom of God (cf. Mk. 3:13-19; Mt. 10:1-42). These apostles (cf. Lk. 6:13) He formed after the manner of a college or a fixed group, over which He placed Peter, chosen from among them (cf. Jn. 21:15-17).[71] He sent them first to the children of Israel and then to all nations (cf. Rom. 1:16), so that as sharers in His power they might make all peoples His disciples, sanctifying and governing them (cf. Mt. 28:16-20; Mk. 16:15; Lk. 24:45-48; Jn. 20: 21-23). Thus they would spread His Church, and by ministering to it under the guidance of the Lord, would shepherd it all days even to the consummation of the world (cf. Mt. 28:20).

They were fully confirmed in this mission on the day of Pentecost (cf. Acts 2:1-26) in accordance with the Lord's promise: "You shall receive power when the Holy Spirit comes upon you, and you shall be witnesses for me in Jerusalem and in all Judea and in Samaria and even to the very

of Peter among the apostles, and reaffirms the primacy and infallibility of the Pope as Peter's successor.
68. Cf. Vatican Council I, Session 4, the dogmatic constitution "Pastor aeternus": Denz. 1821 (3050 f.).
69. Cf. the Council of Florence, "Decretum pro Graecis": Denz. 694 (1307); and Vatican Council I as cited in the preceding footnote: Denz. 1826 (3059).
70. In applying to the Pope the traditional title, "Vicar of Christ," the Council does not intend to deny that all bishops are in some sense Christ's vicars or ambassadors; cf. Art. 27 below.
71. Christ formed the apostles and commissioned them as a "collegial" group in the sense that he gave them certain collective powers and responsibilities for the dissemination of the gospel.

ends of the earth" (Acts 1:8). By everywhere preaching the
gospel (cf. Mk. 16:20), which was accepted by their hearers
under the influence of the Holy Spirit, the apostles gathered
together the universal Church, which the Lord established on
the apostles and built upon blessed Peter, their chief, Christ
Jesus Himself remaining the supreme cornerstone (cf. Apoc.
21:14; Mt. 16:18; Eph. 2:20).[72]

20. That divine mission, entrusted by Christ to the apostles,
will last until the end of the world (Mt. 28:20), since the
gospel which was to be handed down by them is for all time
the source of all life for the Church. For this reason the
apostles took care to appoint successors in this hierarchically
structured society.[73]

For they not only had helpers in their ministry,[74] but also,
in order that the mission assigned to them might continue
after their death, they passed on to their immediate cooperators, as a kind of testament, the duty of perfecting and consolidating the work begun by themselves,[75] charging them to
attend to the whole flock in which the Holy Spirit placed
them to shepherd the Church of God (cf. Acts 20:28). They
therefore appointed such men, and authorized the arrangement that, when these men should have died, other approved
men would take up their ministry.[76]

Among those various ministries which, as tradition witnesses, were exercised in the Church from the earliest times,
the chief place belongs to the office of those who, appointed
to the episcopate in a sequence running back to the beginning,[77] are the ones who pass on the apostolic seed.[78] Thus,

72. *Cf. St. Gregory, "Liber sacramentorum," Praef. in natali S. Matthiae et
S. Thomae: PL 78, 51 and 152—compare Cod. Vat. lat. 3548, f. 18; St.
Hilary, "In Ps.," 67, 10: PL 9, 450 (CSEL, 22, p. 286); St. Jerome, "Adv.
Iovin.," 1, 26: PL 23, 247 A; St. Augustine, "In Ps.," 86, 4: PL 37, 1103; St.
Gregory the Great, "Mor. in Iob," XXVIII, V: PL 76, 455-6; Primasius,
"Comm. in Apoc.," V: PL 68, 924 BC; and Paschasius Radbertus, "In
Matth.," Bk. VIII, c. 16: PL 120, 561 C. Also, Leo XIII, epistle "Et sane,"
Dec. 17, 1888: Acta Sanctae Sedis 21 (1888), 321.*
73. After considering the apostles, the Council now goes on to the status of
the bishops, first repeating, with numerous citations from the Church Fathers,
the doctrine of Vatican I that the bishops are "successors" of the apostles;
that is to say, they have supreme authority in the Church as the apostles
did in the first generation.
74. *Cf. Acts 6:2-6; 11:30; 13:1; 14:23; 20:17; 1 Th. 5:12; Phil. 1:1;
Col. 4:11 and passim.*
75. *Cf. Acts 20:25-7; 2 Tim. 4:6 f., taken together with 1 Tim. 5:22; 2 Tim.
2:2; Tit. 1:5; and St. Clement of Rome, "Ad Cor.," 44, 3: ed. Funk, I, p. 156.*
76. *St. Clement of Rome, "Ad Cor.," 44, 2: ed. Funk, I, pp. 154 f.*
77. *Tertullian, "Praescr. haer.," 32: PL 2, 52 f.; and St. Ignatius of Antioch,
passim.*
78. *Cf. Tertullian, "Praescr. haer.," 32: PL 2, 53.*

as St. Irenaeus testifies, through those who were appointed bishops by the apostles, and through their successors down to our own time, the apostolic tradition is manifested[79] and preserved[80] throughout the world.

With their helpers, the priests and deacons, bishops have therefore taken up the service of the community,[81] presiding in place of God over the flock[82] whose shepherds they are, as teachers of doctrine, priests of sacred worship, and officers of good order.[83] Just as the role that the Lord gave individually to Peter, the first among the apostles, is permanent and was meant to be transmitted to his successors, so also the apostles' office of nurturing the Church is permanent, and was meant to be exercised without interruption by the sacred order of bishops.[84] Therefore, this sacred Synod teaches that by divine institution bishops have succeeded to the place of the apostles[85] as shepherds of the Church, and that he who hears them, hears Christ, while he who rejects them, rejects Christ and Him who sent Christ (cf. Lk. 10:16).[86]

21. In the bishops, therefore, for whom priests are assistants, our Lord Jesus Christ, the supreme High Priest, is present in the midst of those who believe.[87] For sitting at the right hand of God the Father, He is not absent from the gathering of His high priests,[88] but above all through their excellent service He is preaching the Word of God to all nations, and

---

79. *Cf. St. Irenaeus, "Adv. haer.," III, 3, 1: PG 7, 848 A (Harvey, 2, 8; Sagnard, pp. 100 f.): "manifestatam" ["having been made manifest"].*
80. *Cf. Irenaeus, "Adv. haer.," III, 2, 2: PG 7, 847 (Harvey, 2, 7; Sagnard, p. 100): "custoditur" ["is guarded"]. And see also St. Irenaeus, "Adv. haer.," IV, 26, 2: PG 7, 1053 (Harvey, 2, 236); IV, 33, 8: PG 7, 1077 (Harvey, 2, 262).*
81. *St. Ignatius of Antioch, "Ad Philad.," Praef.: ed. Funk, I, p. 264.*
82. *St. Ignatius of Antioch, "Ad Philad.," 1, 1; "Ad Magn.," 6, 1: ed. Funk, I, pp. 264 and 234.*
83. *St. Clement of Rome, "Ad Cor.," 42, 3-4; 57, 1-2: ed. Funk, I, 152, 156, 171 f.; St. Ignatius of Antioch, "Ad Philad.," 2; "Ad Smyrn.," 8; "Ad Magn.," 3; "Ad Trall.," 7: ed. Funk, I, pp. 265 f., 282, 232, 246 f. etc.; St. Justin, "Apol.," 1, 65: PG 6, 428; and St. Cyprian, "Epist.," passim.*
84. *Cf. Leo XIII, encyclical "Satis Cognitum," June 29, 1896: Acta Sanctae Sedis 28 (1895-6), p. 732.*
85. *Cf. the Council of Trent, Session 23, the decree "De sacr. Ordinis," c. 4: Denz. 960 (1768); Vatican Council I, Session 4, the first dogmatic constitution "De Ecclesia Christi," c. 3: Denz. 1828 (3061); Pius XII, encyclical "Mystici Corporis," June 29, 1943: AAS 35 (1943), pp. 209 and 212; and the Code of Canon Law, c. 329, 1.*
86. *Cf. Leo XIII, epistle "Et sane," Dec. 17, 1888: Acta Sanctae Sedis 21 (1888), pp. 321 f.*
87. Having completed its discussion of the relationship between bishops and the apostles, the Constitution turns to the nature of the episcopacy.
88. *St. Leo the Great, "Serm.," 5, 3: PL 54, 154.*

constantly administering the sacraments of faith to those who believe. By their paternal role (cf. 1 Cor. 4:15), He incorporates new members into His body by a heavenly regeneration, and finally by their wisdom and prudence He directs and guides the people of the New Testament in its pilgrimage toward eternal happiness.

These pastors, selected to shepherd the Lord's flock, are servants of Christ and stewards of the mysteries of God (cf. 1 Cor. 4:1). To them has been assigned the bearing of witness to the gospel of God's grace (cf. Rom. 15:16; Acts 20:24), and to the ministration of the Spirit and of God's glorious power to make men just (cf. 2 Cor. 3:8-9).

For the discharging of such great duties, the apostles were enriched by Christ with a special outpouring of the Holy Spirit, who came upon them (cf. Acts 1:8; 2:4; Jn. 20:22-23). This spiritual gift they passed on to their helpers by the imposition of hands (cf. 1 Tim. 4:14; 2 Tim. 1:6-7), and it has been transmitted down to us in episcopal consecration.[89] This sacred Synod teaches that by episcopal consecration is conferred the fullness of the sacrament of orders,[90] that fullness which in the Church's liturgical practice and in the language of the holy Fathers of the Church is undoubtedly called the high priesthood, the apex of the sacred ministry.[91]

But episcopal consecration, together with the office of sanctifying, also confers the offices of teaching and of governing. (These, however, of their very nature, can be exercised only in hierarchical communion with the head and the members of the college.)[92] For from tradition, which is expressed especially in liturgical rites and in the practice of the

---

89. *The Council of Trent, Session 23, c. 3, cites the words of 2 Tim. 1:6-7 to show that order is a true sacrament: Denz., 959 (1766).*

90. Ending what little controversy still remained on the point, the Council teaches that the bishop is not just a priest with greater powers of jurisdiction, but that he receives through sacramental consecration the fullness of the power of orders. This is a permanent and inalienable gift, involving powers to sanctify, teach, and govern.

91. *In the "Apostolic Tradition," 3, ed. Botte, "Sources Chr.," pp. 27-30, there is attributed to the bishop "primatus sacerdotii" ["primacy of priesthood"]. See the "Sacramentarium Leonianum," ed. C. Mohlberg, "Sacramentarium Vernonense" (Rome, 1955), p. 119: ". . . ad summi sacerdotii ministerium. . . . Comple in sacerdotibus tuis mysterii tui summam . . ."* [". . . to the ministry of the high priest. . . . Fill up in Your priests the highest point of Your mystery . . ."]; *and the same editor's "Liber Sacramentorum Romanae Ecclesiae" (Rome, 1960), pp. 121-2: "Tribuas eis, Domine, cathedram episcopalem ad regendam Ecclesiam tuam et plebem universam"* ["Give them, Lord, the episcopal see to rule Your Church and Your entire people"]. *See PL 78, 224.*

92. The teaching and ruling functions cannot be exercised except by those

Church both of the East and of the West, it is clear that, by
means of the imposition of hands and the words of consecration, the grace of the Holy Spirit is so conferred,[93] and
the sacred character so impressed,[94] that bishops in an eminent and visible way undertake Christ's own role as Teacher,
Shepherd, and High Priest, and that they act in His person.[95]
Therefore it devolves on the bishops to admit newly elected
members into the episcopal body by means of the sacrament
of orders.

22. Just as, by the Lord's will, St. Peter and the other apostles constituted one apostolic college, so in a similar way the
Roman Pontiff as the successor of Peter, and the bishops as
the successors of the apostles are joined together.[96] The collegial nature and meaning of the episcopal order found expression in the very ancient practice by which bishops
appointed the world over were linked with one another and
with the Bishop of Rome by the bonds of unity, charity, and
peace;[97] also, in the conciliar assemblies[98] which made com-

bishops in "hierarchical communion" with the Pope and the bishops in
union with him. The term "hierarchical communion" is not here precisely
defined, but its meaning is further clarified by the "Prefatory Note" (par. 2
and the "N.B." at the end) (see below pp. 98-101).

93. "Apostolic Tradition," 2: ed. Botte, p. 27.

94. The Council of Trent, Session 23, c. 4, teaches that the sacrament of
order imprints an indelible character: Denz. 960 (1767). See the allocution of
John XXIII, "Jubilate Deo," May 8, 1960: AAS 52 (1960), p. 466; and the
homily of Paul VI in St. Peter's Basilica, Oct. 20, 1963: AAS 55 (1963), p.
1014.

95. St. Cyprian, "Epist.," 63, 14: PL 4, 386 (Hartel, IIIB, p. 713): "Sacerdos
vice Christi vere fungitur" ["The priest truly acts in the place of Christ"];
St. John Chrysostom, "In 2 Tim.," Hom. 2, 4: PG 62, 612: The priest is
the "symbolon" of Christ; St. Ambrose, "In Ps.," 38, 25-6: PL 14, 1051-2
(CSEL, 64, 203-4); Ambrosiaster, "In 1 Tim.," 5, 19: PL 17, 479 C and
"In Eph.," 4, 11-2: PL 17, 387C; Theodore of Mopsuestia, "Hom. Catech.,"
XV, 21 and 24: ed. Tonneau, pp. 497 and 503; and Hesychius of Jerusalem,
"In Lev.," 2, 9, 23: PG 93, 894 B.

96. The chief doctrinal point of the chapter is set forth in Art. 22. All
bishops who are united to the Pope and to their fellow bishops by the
hierarchical communion just referred to, constitute a collegial body enjoying supreme power in governing the Church. Such supreme power is exercised not only when the college is united in an Ecumenical Council but also
through other forms of "appropriate collegiate action" not yet specified. In
the coming years we shall doubtless see many practical applications of this
doctrine of collegiality. One important step which has already been taken
is the establishment of a world-wide Episcopal Synod, announced by Paul
VI in his motu proprio of Sept. 15, 1965.

97. Cf. Eusebius of Caesarea, "Hist. Eccl.," V, 24, 10: GCS II, 1, p. 495 (ed.
Bardy, "Sources chr.," II, p. 69); and Dionysius as given in Eusebius of
Caesarea, "Hist. Eccl.," VII, 5, 2: GCS II, pp. 638 f. (ed. Bardy, II, pp.
168 f.).

98. For the ancient Councils, cf. Eusebius of Caesarea, "Hist. Eccl.," V,

mon judgments about more profound matters[99] in decisions reflecting the views of many.[100] The ecumenical councils held through the centuries clearly attest this collegial aspect. And it is suggested also in the practice, introduced in ancient times, of summoning several bishops to take part in the elevation of someone newly elected to the ministry of the high priesthood. Hence, one is constituted a member of the episcopal body by virtue of sacramental consecration and by hierarchical communion with the head and members of the body.

But the college or body of bishops has no authority unless it is simultaneously conceived of in terms of its head, the Roman Pontiff, Peter's successor, and without any lessening of his power of primacy over all, pastors as well as the general faithful.[101] For in virtue of his office, that is, as Vicar of Christ and pastor of the whole Church, the Roman Pontiff has full, supreme, and universal power over the Church. And he can always exercise this power freely.

The order of bishops is the successor to the college of the apostles in teaching authority and pastoral rule; or, rather, in the episcopal order the apostolic body continues without a break. Together with its head, the Roman Pontiff, and never without this head, the episcopal order is the subject of supreme and full power over the universal Church.[102] But this power can be exercised only with the consent of the Roman Pontiff. For our Lord made Simon Peter alone the rock and keybearer of the Church (cf. Mt. 16:18-19), and appointed him shepherd of the whole flock (cf. Jn. 21:15 ff.).

It is definite, however, that the power of binding and loosing, which was given to Peter (Mt. 16:19), was granted also to the college of apostles, joined with their head (Mt. 18:18; 28:16-20).[103] This college, insofar as it is composed of many, expresses the variety and universality of the People of

23-4: GCS II, 1, pp. 488 ff. (ed. Bardy, II, p. 66 ff.) and passim, Council of Nicaea, can. 5: "Conc. Oec. Decr.," p. 7.
99. *Tertullian, "De ieiunio," 13: PL 2, 972 B (CSEL, 20, p. 292, lines 13-6).*
100. *St. Cyprian, "Epist.," 56, 3: Hartel, III B, p. 650 (ed. Bayard, p. 154).*
101. The Council is careful to explain that the doctrine of collegiality in no way impugns the primacy of the Pope, as defined by Vatican I. The relation between the Pope and the rest of the episcopal college is explained more precisely in the "Prefatory Note" (infra. pp. 98-101).
102. *Cf. official "Relatio" of Zinelli during Vatican Council I: Mansi, 52, 1109 C.*
103. *Cf. Vatican Council I, schema for the second dogmatic constitution "De Ecclesia Christi," c. 4: Mansi, 53, 310. See also the "Relatio" of Kleutgen on the revised schema: Mansi, 53, 321 B-322 B; and the statement by Zinelli: Mansi, 52, 1110 A. And see, too, St. Leo the Great, "Serm.," 4, 3: PL 54, 151 A.*

God, but insofar as it is assembled under one head, it expresses the unity of the flock of Christ. In it, the bishops, faithfully recognizing the primacy and pre-eminence of their head, exercise their own authority for the good of their own faithful, and indeed of the whole Church, with the Holy Spirit constantly strengthening its organic structure and inner harmony.

The supreme authority with which this college is empowered over the whole Church is exercised in a solemn way through an ecumenical council. A council is never ecumenical unless it is confirmed or at least accepted as such by the successor of Peter. It is the prerogative of the Roman Pontiff to convoke these councils, to preside over them, and to confirm them.[104] The same collegiate power can be exercised in union with the Pope by the bishops living in all parts of the world, provided that the head of the college calls them to collegiate action, or at least so approves or freely accepts the united action of the dispersed bishops, that it is made a true collegiate act.

23. This collegial union is apparent also in the mutual relations of the individual bishops with particular churches and with the universal Church. The Roman Pontiff, as the successor of Peter, is the perpetual and visible source and foundation of the unity of the bishops and of the multitude of the faithful.[105] The individual bishop, however, is the visible principle and foundation of unity in his particular church,[106] fashioned after the model of the universal Church. In and from such individual churches there comes into being the one and only Catholic Church.[107] For this reason each individual bishop represents his own church, but all of them together in union with the Pope represent the entire Church joined in the bond of peace, love, and unity.

The individual bishops, who are placed in charge of particular churches, exercise their pastoral government over the portion of the People of God committed to their care, and

104. *Cf. Code of Canon Law, c. 227.*
105. *Cf. Vatican Council I, the dogmatic constitution "Pastor aeternus": Denz. 1821 (3050 f.).*
106. *Cf. St. Cyprian, "Epist.," 66, 8: Hartel, III B, p. 733: "Episcopus in Ecclesia et Ecclesia in episcopo"* ["The bishop is in the Church and the Church in the bishop"].
107. *Cf. St. Cyprian, "Epist.," 55:24: Hartel, III B, p. 642, line 13: "Una Ecclesia per totum mundum in multa membra divisa"* ["The one Church divided throughout the entire world into many members"]; *and "Epist.," 36, 4: Hartel, III B, p. 575, lines 20-1.*

not over other churches nor over the universal Church.[108] But each of them, as a member of the episcopal college and a legitimate successor of the apostles, is obliged by Christ's decree and command[109] to be solicitous for the whole Church.

This solicitude, though it is not exercised by an act of jurisdiction, contributes immensely to the welfare of the universal Church. For it is the duty of all bishops to promote and to safeguard the unity of faith and the discipline common to the whole Church, to instruct the faithful in love for the whole Mystical Body of Christ, especially for its poor and sorrowing members and for those who are suffering persecution for justice' sake (cf. Mt. 5:10), and, finally, to foster every activity which is common to the whole Church, especially efforts to spread the faith and make the light of full truth dawn on all men.[110] For the rest, it is a sacred reality that by governing well their own church as a portion of the universal Church, they themselves are effectively contributing to the welfare of the whole Mystical Body, which is also the body of the churches.[111]

The task of proclaiming the gospel everywhere on earth devolves on the body of pastors, to all of whom in common Christ gave His command, thereby imposing upon them a common duty, as Pope Celestine in his time reminded the Fathers of the Council of Ephesus.[112] From this it follows that the individual bishops, insofar as the discharge of their duty permits, are obliged to enter into a community of effort among themselves and with the successor of Peter, upon whom was imposed in a special way the great duty of spreading the Christian name.[113] With all their energy, therefore,

108. While residential bishops other than the Pope exercise pastoral government only over a particular portion of the Church, their pastoral solicitude, as members of the episcopal college, must extend to the whole Church.
109. Cf. Pius XII, encyclical "Fidei donum," Apr. 21, 1957: AAS 49 (1957), p. 237.
110. An important consequence of this universal pastoral solicitude is that all the bishops must have a concern for the missions, a point repeated in the Decree on the Church's Missionary Activity, Art. 6. Bishops are also obliged, in cases of need, to give spiritual and material assistance to each other's Churches.
111. Cf. St. Hilary of Poitiers, "In Ps.," 14, 3: PL 9, 206 (CSEL 22, p. 86); St. Gregory the Great, "Moral," IV, 7, 12: PL 75, 643; and pseudo-Basil, "In Is.," 15, 296: PG 30, 637 C.
112. St. Celestine, "Epist.," 18, 1-2 to the Council of Ephesus: PL 50, 505 AB (Schwartz, "Acta Conc. Oec.," I, 1, 1, p. 22). Cf. Benedict XV, apostolic epistle "Maximum illud": AAS 11 (1919), p. 440; Pius IX, encyclical "Rerum Ecclesiae," Feb. 28, 1926: AAS 18 (1926), p. 69; Pius XII, encyclical "Fidei Donum," April 21, 1957: AAS 49 (1957), p. 237.
113. Cf. Leo XIII, encyclical "Grande Munus," Sept. 30, 1880: AAS 13 (1880), p. 145. Cf. Code of Canon Law, c. 1327; c. 1350, §2.

they must supply to the missions both workers for the harvest and also spiritual and material aid, both directly and on their own account, as well as by arousing the ardent cooperation of the faithful. And finally, in a universal fellowship of charity, bishops should gladly extend their fraternal aid to other churches, especially to neighboring and more needy dioceses, in accordance with the venerable example of antiquity.

By divine Providence it has come about that various churches established in diverse places by the apostles and their successors have in the course of time coalesced into several groups, organically united, which, preserving the unity of faith and the unique divine constitution of the universal Church, enjoy their own discipline, their own liturgical usage, and their own theological and spiritual heritage. Some of these churches, notably the ancient patriarchal churches, as parent-stocks of the faith, so to speak, have begotten others as daughter churches. With these they are connected down to our own time by a close bond of charity in their sacramental life and in their mutual respect for rights and duties.[114]

This variety of local churches with one common aspiration is particularly splendid evidence of the catholicity of the undivided Church. In like manner the episcopal bodies of today are in a position to render a manifold and fruitful assistance, so that this collegiate sense may be put into practical application.[115]

24. To the Lord was given all power in heaven and on earth. As successors of the apostles, bishops receive from Him the mission to teach all nations and to preach the gospel to every creature, so that all men may attain to salvation by faith, baptism, and the fulfillment of the commandments (cf. Mt.

---

114. *On the rights of patriarchal sees, see the Council of Nicaea, canon 6 on Alexandria and Antioch, canon 7 on Jerusalem:* "Conc. Oec. Decr.," p. 8; *Lateran Council IV in the year 1215, Constitution V:* "De dignitate Patriarcharum": "Conc. Oec. Decr.," p. 212; *and the Council of Ferrara-Florence:* "Conc. Oec. Decr.," p. 504.

115. The Council here gives official recognition to the territorial Episcopal Conferences, such as that of the hierarchy of the United States. These groups are comparable in some ways to the ancient Patriarchates—e.g., those of Constantinople, Alexandria, Antioch, and Jerusalem—which retain certain important privileges in our day. Further specifications regarding the composition of the Episcopal Conferences and the binding force of their decisions may be found in the Decree on the Bishops' Pastoral Office in the Church, Art. 37-8.

28:18; Mk. 16:15-16; Acts 26:17 f.). To fulfill this mission, Christ the Lord promised the Holy Spirit to the apostles, and on Pentecost day sent the Spirit from heaven. By His power they were to be witnesses to Christ before the nations and peoples and kings, even to the ends of the earth (cf. Acts 1:8; 2:1 ff.; 9:15). Now, that duty, which the Lord committed to the shepherds of His people, is a true service, and in sacred literature is significantly called "diakonia" or ministry (cf. Acts 1:17, 25; 21:19; Rom. 11:13; 1 Tim. 1:12).

The canonical mission of bishops[116] can come about by legitimate customs which have not been revoked by the supreme and universal authority of the Church, or by laws made or recognized by that same authority, or directly through the successor of Peter himself. If the latter refuses or denies apostolic communion, a bishop cannot assume office.[117]

25. Among the principal duties of bishops, the preaching of the gospel occupies an eminent place.[118] For bishops are preachers of the faith who lead new disciples to Christ. They are authentic teachers,[119] that is, teachers endowed with the authority of Christ, who preach to the people committed to them the faith they must believe and put into practice. By the light of the Holy Spirit, they make that faith clear, bringing forth from the treasury of revelation new things and old (cf. Mt. 13:52), making faith bear fruit and vigilantly warding off any errors which threaten their flock (cf. 2 Tim. 4:1-4).

Bishops, teaching in communion with the Roman Pontiff,

116. The Council here makes it clear that the "canonical mission" by which a bishop is assigned to a particular task or diocese need not in every case come by the positive activity of the Pope, although in the Latin Church this is today the normal procedure. On the authority of the Patriarchs in the Eastern Churches, see the Decree on the Eastern Catholic Churches, Art. 9.
117. Cf. Code of Law for Eastern Churches cc. 216-314: on Patriarchs; cc. 324-39: on major archbishops; cc. 362-91: on other dignitaries; and in particular, cc. 238, §3; 216; 240; 251; 255: on the naming of bishops by a Patriarch.
118. Cf. Council of Trent, Decree on reform, Session 5, c. 2, n. 9; and Session 24, c. 4: "Conc. Oec. Decr.," pp. 645 and 739.
119. Having completed its discussion of collegiality, the Council goes on in the next three articles to consider the role of the individual bishop under the three headings of prophetic (Art. 25), priestly (Art. 26), and kingly (Art. 27). In treating of the prophetic or teaching office, the Council compares the "religious assent" due to the non-infallible teaching of the Pope or of the individual bishop teaching his own flock with the total submission of faith which is due to the infallible teaching of the whole college of bishops or to the Pope when he speaks ex cathedra, formally defining the contents of the Christian revelation.

are to be respected by all as witnesses to divine and Catholic truth. In matters of faith and morals, the bishops speak in the name of Christ and the faithful are to accept their teaching and adhere to it with a religious assent of soul. This religious submission of will and of mind must be shown in a special way to the authentic teaching authority of the Roman Pontiff, even when he is not speaking ex cathedra. That is, it must be shown in such a way that his supreme magisterium is acknowledged with reverence, the judgments made by him are sincerely adhered to, according to his manifest mind and will. His mind and will in the matter may be known chiefly either from the character of the documents, from his frequent repetition of the same doctrine, or from his manner of speaking.

Although the individual bishops do not enoy the prerogative of infallibility, they can nevertheless proclaim Christ's doctrine infallibly. This is so, even when they are dispersed around the world, provided that while maintaining the bond of unity among themselves and with Peter's successor, and while teaching authentically on a matter of faith or morals, they concur in a single viewpoint as the one which must be held conclusively.[120] This authority is even more clearly verified when, gathered together in an ecumenical council, they are teachers and judges of faith and morals for the universal Church. Their definitions must then be adhered to with the submission of faith.[121]

This infallibility with which the divine Redeemer willed His Church to be endowed in defining a doctrine of faith and morals extends as far as extends the deposit of divine revelation, which must be religiously guarded and faithfully expounded.[122] This is the infallibility which the Roman Pontiff, the head of the college of bishops, enjoys in virtue of his office, when, as the supreme shepherd and teacher of all the faithful, who confirms his brethren in their faith (cf.

---

120. *Cf. Vatican Council I, the dogmatic constitution "Dei Filius," 3: Denz. 1712 (3011). Cf. note (taken from St. Robert Bellarmine) adjoined to Schema I "De Ecclesia": Mansi, 51, 579 C; as well as the revised Schema for the second constitution "De Ecclesia Christi" with the commentary of Kleutgen: Mansi, 53, 313 AB. Cf. Pius IX, epistle, "Tuas libenter": Denz. 1683 (2879).*
121. *Cf. Code of Canon Law, cc. 1322-3.*
122. In this connection the Council declares that the infallibility of the Church—and consequently that of a Council or Pope making a doctrinal definition—extends "as far as the deposit of revelation extends." For a fuller explanation of the notion of the "sacred deposit," see the Constitution on Divine Revelation, especially Art. 10.

Lk. 22:32), he proclaims by a definitive act some doctrine of faith or morals.[123] Therefore his definitions, of themselves, and not from the consent of the Church, are justly styled irreformable, for they are pronounced with the assistance of the Holy Spirit, an assistance promised to him in blessed Peter. Therefore they need no approval of others, nor do they allow an appeal to any other judgment. For then the Roman Pontiff is not pronouncing judgment as a private person. Rather, as the supreme teacher of the universal Church, as one in whom the charism of the infallibility of the Church herself is individually present, he is expounding or defending a doctrine of Catholic faith.[124]

The infallibility promised to the Church resides also in the body of bishops when that body exercises supreme teaching authority with the successor of Peter. To the resultant definitions the assent of the Church can never be wanting,[125] on account of the activity of that same Holy Spirit, whereby the whole flock of Christ is preserved and progresses in unity of faith.[126]

But when either the Roman Pontiff or the body of bishops together with him defines a judgment, they pronounce it in accord with revelation itself. All are obliged to maintain and be ruled by this revelation, which, as written or preserved by tradition, is transmitted in its entirety through the legitimate succession of bishops and especially through the care of the Roman Pontiff himself.

Under the guiding light of the Spirit of truth, revelation is thus religiously preserved and faithfully expounded in the Church.[127] The Roman Pontiff and the bishops, in view of their office and of the importance of the matter, strive painstakingly and by appropriate means to inquire properly into that revelation and to give apt expression to its con-

---

123. *Cf. Vatican Council I, the dogmatic constitution "Pastor aeternus":* Denz. 1839 (3074).
124. *Cf. explanation of Gasser at Vatican Council I: Mansi, 52, 1213 AC.*
125. To the difficulty sometimes raised, "What if the Pope were to define something to which the rest of the episcopal college or the faithful did not agree?" the Constitution replies that the case is a purely imaginary one, since one and the same Holy Spirit directs the Pope, the college of bishops, and the whole body of the faithful. In practice, the Pope always consults the other bishops and the faithful before making a doctrinal decision, but the validity of his action does not legally depend upon any kind of ratification by them.
126. *Gasser, Vatican Council I: Mansi, 52, 1214 A.*
127. *Gasser, Vatican Council I: Mansi, 52, 1215 CD, 1216-7 A.*

tents.[128] But they do not allow that there could be any new public revelation pertaining to the divine deposit of faith.[129]

26. A bishop, marked with the fullness of the sacrament of orders,[130] is "the steward of the grace of the supreme priesthood,"[131] especially in the Eucharist, which he offers or causes to be offered,[132] and by which the Church constantly lives and grows. This Church of Christ is truly present in all legitimate local congregations of the faithful which, united with their pastors, are themselves called churches in the New Testament.[133] For in their own locality these are the new people called by God, in the Holy Spirit and in much fullness (cf. 1 Th. 1:5). In them the faithful are gathered together by the preaching of the gospel of Christ, and the mystery of the Lord's Supper is celebrated, "that by the flesh and blood of the Lord's body the whole brotherhood may be joined together."[134]

In any community existing around an altar, under the sacred ministry of the bishop,[135] there is manifested a symbol of that charity and "unity of the Mystical Body, without which there can be no salvation."[136] In these communities, though frequently small and poor, or living far from any other, Christ is present. By virtue of Him the one, holy, catholic, and apostolic Church gathers together.[137] For "the partaking of the Body and Blood of Christ does nothing other than transform us into that which we consume."[138]

Every legitimate celebration of the Eucharist is regulated by the bishop, to whom is committed the office of offering the worship of Christian religion to the divine Majesty and of administering it in accordance with the Lord's command-

---

128. *Gasser, Vatican Council I, Mansi, 52, 1213.*
129. *Vatican Council I, the dogmatic constitution "Pastor aeternus," 4: Denz. 1836 (3070).*
130. The article has to do with the "priestly" functions of the bishop, which stem from his reception of the fullness of the sacrament of orders. The bishop either celebrates or regulates the celebration of the Eucharist, which, more than any other sacrament, signifies and effects the unity of the Church. In the local church, actualized in the Eucharistic celebration, the mystery of the whole Church is present representatively.
131. *Prayer of episcopal consecration in the Byzantine rite: "Euchologion to mega" (Rome, 1873), p. 139.*
132. *Cf. St. Ignatius of Antioch, "Ad Smyrn.," 8, 1: ed. Funk, I, p. 282.*
133. *Cf. Acts 8:1; 14:22-3; 20:17; and passim.*
134. *Mozarabic prayer: PL 96, 759 B.*
135. *Cf. St. Ignatius of Antioch, "Ad Smyrn.," 8, 1: ed. Funk, I, p. 282.*
136. *Cf. St. Thomas, "Summa Theol.," 3, q. 73, a. 3.*
137. *Cf. St. Augustine, "C. Faustum," 12, 20: PL 42, 265; "Serm.," 57, 7: PL 38, 389; and elsewhere.*
138. *St. Leo the Great, "Serm.," 63, 7: PL 54, 357 C.*

ments and with the Church's laws, as further defined by his particular judgment for his diocese.

By thus praying and laboring for the people, bishops channel the fullness of Christ's holiness in many ways and abundantly. By the ministry of the word they communicate God's power to those who believe unto salvation (cf. Rom. 1:16). Through the sacraments, the regular and fruitful distribution of which they direct by their authority,[139] they sanctify the faithful. They govern the conferring of baptism, by which a sharing in the kingly priesthood of Christ is granted. They are the original ministers of confirmation, dispensers of sacred orders, and the moderators of penitential discipline. They earnestly exhort and instruct their people to carry out with faith and reverence their part in the liturgy and especially in the holy Sacrifice of the Mass. Finally, by the example of their manner of life they must be an influence for good on those over whom they preside, by refraining from all evil and, as far as they are able with God's help, turning evil to good. Thus, together with the flock committed to their care, they can arrive at eternal life.[140]

27. Bishops govern[141] the particular churches entrusted to them as the vicars and ambassadors of Christ.[142] This they do by their counsel, exhortations, and example, as well, indeed, as by their authority and sacred power. This power they use only for the edification of their flock in truth and holiness, remembering that he who is greater should become as the lesser and he who is the more distinguished, as the servant (cf. Lk. 22:26-27). This power, which they personally exercise in Christ's name, is proper, ordinary, and immediate, although its exercise is ultimately regulated by the supreme authority of the Church, and can be circumscribed by certain limits, for the advantage of the Church or of the faith-

139. *The "Apostolic Tradition" of Hippolytus*, 2-3: ed. Botte, pp. 26-30.
140. Cf. text of the "Examen" at the beginning of the consecration of a bishop and the Prayer at the end of the Mass of the same consecration after the Te Deum.
141. Finally, the power of the bishops to govern the dioceses entrusted to them (a participation in Christ's "kingly" office) is discussed. Following the teaching of Vatican I, this Council makes it clear that bishops govern by their proper authority as bishops, and not simply as delegates of the Pope.
142. *Benedict XIV*, brief, "Romana Ecclesia," Oct. 5, 1752, §1: "Bullarium Benedicti XIV," t. IV ·(Rome, 1758), 21: "Episcopus Christi typum gerit, Eiusque munere fungitur" ["The bishop is an image of Christ and performs His work"]; and Pius XII, encyclical "Mystici Corporis," June 29, 1943: AAS 35 (1943), p. 211: "Assignatos sibi greges singuli singulos Christi nomine pascunt et regunt" ["In the name of Christ each one takes care of and rules the individual flock assigned to him"].

ful. In virtue of this power, bishops have the sacred right and the duty before the Lord to make laws for their subjects, to pass judgment on them, and to moderate everything pertaining to the ordering of worship and the apostolate.

The pastoral office or the habitual and daily care of their sheep is entrusted to them completely. Nor are they to be regarded as vicars of the Roman Pontiff, for they exercise an authority which is proper to them, and are quite correctly called "prelates," heads of the people whom they govern.[143] Their power, therefore, is not destroyed by the supreme and universal power. On the contrary it is affirmed, strengthened, and vindicated thereby,[144] since the Holy Spirit unfailingly preserves the form of government established by Christ the Lord in His Church.

Since he is sent by the Father to govern His family, a bishop must keep before his eyes the example of the Good Shepherd, who came not to be ministered unto but to minister (cf. Mt. 20:28; Mk. 10:45), and to lay down His life for His sheep (cf. Jn. 10:11). Taken from among men, and himself beset with weakness, he is able to have compassion on the ignorant and erring (cf. Heb. 5:1-2). Let him not refuse to listen to his subjects, whom he cherishes as his true sons and exhorts to cooperate readily with him. As having one day to render to God an account for their souls (cf. Heb. 13:17), he takes care of them by his prayer, preaching, and all the works of charity, and not only of them, but also of those who are not yet of the one flock. For these also are commended to him in the Lord.

Since, like Paul the Apostle, he is debtor to all men, let him be ready to preach the gospel to all (cf. Rom. 1:14-15), and to urge his faithful to apostolic and missionary activity. For their part, the faithful must cling to their bishop, as the Church does to Christ, and Jesus Christ to the Father, so that everything may harmonize in unity,[145] and abound to the glory of God (cf. 2 Cor. 4:15).

28. Christ, whom the Father sanctified and sent into the world (Jn. 10:36) has, through His apostles, made their suc-

---

143. *Leo XII, encyclical "Satis cognitum," June 29, 1896: Acta Sanctae Sedis 28 (1895-6), p. 732; the same Pontiff's epistle "Officio sanctissimo," Dec. 22, 1887: Acta Sanctae Sedis 20 (1887), p. 264; Pius IX, apostolic letter to the bishops of Germany, Mar. 12, 1875, and his consistorial allocution of Mar. 15, 1875: Denz. 3112-7 (only in the new edition).*
144. *Vatican Council I, the dogmatic constitution "Pastor aeternus," 3: Denz. 1828 (3061). Cf. "Relatio" of Zinelli: Mansi, 52, 1114D.*
145. *Cf. St. Ignatius of Antioch, "Ad Ephes.," 5, 1: ed. Funk, 1, p. 216.*

cessors, the bishops, partakers of His consecration and His mission.[146] These in their turn have legitimately handed on to different individuals in the Church various degrees of participation in this ministry.[147] Thus the divinely established ecclesiastical ministry is exercised on different levels by those who from antiquity have been called bishops, priests, and deacons.[148] Although priests do not possess the highest degree of the priesthood, and although they are dependent on the bishops in the exercise of their power, they are nevertheless united with the bishops in sacerdotal dignity.[149] By the power of the sacrament of orders,[150] and in the image of Christ the eternal High Priest (Heb. 5:1-10; 7:24; 9:11-28), they are consecrated to preach the gospel, shepherd the faithful, and celebrate divine worship as true priests of the New Testament.[151] Partakers of the function of Christ the sole Mediator (1 Tim. 2:5) on their level of ministry, they announce the divine word to all. They exercise this sacred function of Christ most of all in the Eucharistic liturgy or synaxis. There, acting in the person of Christ,[152] and proclaiming His mystery, they join the offering of the faithful to the sacrifice of their Head. Until the coming of the Lord (cf. 1 Cor. 11:26), they re-present and apply in the Sacrifice of the Mass the one sacrifice of the New Testament, namely the sacrifice of Christ offering Himself once and for all to His Father as a spotless victim (cf. Heb. 9:11-28).[153]

For the penitent or ailing among the faithful, priests exercise fully the ministry of reconciliation and alleviation, and

146. *Cf. St. Ignatius of Antioch, "Ad Ephes.," 6, 1: ed. Funk, I, p. 218.*
147. Rounding out this chapter on the hierarchy, the Council adds two articles dealing with simple priests (presbyters) and deacons, who hold hierarchical ranks beneath that of bishop. The brief remarks on the priesthood in this Constitution are supplemented by what is said in the Decree on the Ministry and Life of Priests.
148. *Cf. Council of Trent, Session 23, "De sacr. Ordinis," c. 2: Denz. 958 (1765); and c. 6: Denz. 966 (1776).*
149. *Cf. Innocent I, "Epist. ad Decentium": PL 20, 554 A (Mansi, 3, 1029; Denz. 98 [215]: "Presbyteri, licet secundi sint sacerdotes, pontificatus tamen apicem non habent" ["The presbyters, though they are priests of the second grade, do not possess the crown of being pontiffs"]); and St. Cyprian, "Epist.," 61, 3: ed. Hartel, III B, p. 696.*
150. *Cf. Council of Trent as cited in footnote 148, Denz. 956a-968 (1763-78) and in particular c. 7: Denz. 967 (1777); and the apostolic constitution of Pius XII, "Sacramentum Ordinis": Denz. 2301 (3857-61).*
151. *Cf. Innocent I as cited in footnote 149; St. Gregory Nazianzen, "Apol.," II, 22: PG 35, 432 B; and pseudo-Dionysius, "Eccl. Hier.," 1, 2: PG 3 372D.*
152. *Cf. Council of Trent, Session 22: Denz. 940 (1743); and Pius XII, encyclical "Mediator Dei," Nov. 20, 1947: AAS 39 (1947), p. 553 (Denz. 2300 [3850]).*
153. *Cf. Council of Trent, Session 22: Denz. 938 (1739-40); and Vatican Council II, "Constitution on the Sacred Liturgy," Art. 7 and 47.*

they present the needs and the prayers of the faithful to God
the Father (cf. Heb. 5:1-4). Exercising within the limits of
their authority the function of Christ as Shepherd and
Head,[154] they gather together God's family as a brotherhood all of one mind[155] and lead them in the Spirit, through
Christ, to God the Father. In the midst of the flock they
adore Him in spirit and in truth (cf. Jn. 4:24). Finally, they
labor in word and doctrine (cf. 1 Tim. 5:17), believing what
they have read and meditated upon in the law of the Lord,
teaching what they believe, and practicing what they
teach.[156]

Priests, prudent cooperators with the episcopal order[157]
as well as its aids and instruments, are called to serve the
People of God. They constitute one priesthood[158] with their
bishop, although that priesthood is comprised of different
functions. Associated with their bishop in a spirit of trust and
generosity, priests make him present in a certain sense in the
individual local congregations of the faithful, and take upon
themselves, as far as they are able, his duties and concerns,
discharging them with daily care. As they sanctify and govern under the bishop's authority that part of the Lord's flock
entrusted to them, they make the universal Church visible
in their own locality and lend powerful assistance to the upbuilding of the whole body of Christ (cf. Eph. 4:12). Intent
always upon the welfare of God's children, they must strive
to lend their effort to the pastoral work of the whole diocese,
and even of the entire Church.

On account of this sharing in his priesthood and mission,
let priests sincerely look upon the bishop as their father, and
reverently obey him. And let the bishop regard his priests,
who are his co-workers, as sons and friends, just as Christ
called His disciples no longer servants but friends (cf. Jn.
15:15). All priests, both diocesan and religious, by reason
of orders and ministry, are associated with this body of bishops, and serve the good of the whole Church according to
their vocation and the grace given to them.

In virtue of their common sacred ordination and mission,
all priests are bound together in an intimate brotherhood,
which should naturally and freely manifest itself in mutual

154. *Cf. Pius XII, encyclical "Mediator Dei," as cited in footnote 152.*
155. *Cf. St. Cyprian, "Epist.," 11, 3: PL 4, 242 B (Hartel, III B, p. 497).*
156. *Ceremony of priestly ordination, at the imposition of the vestments.*
157. *Ceremony of priestly ordination, the Preface.*
158. *Cf. St. Ignatius of Antioch, "Ad Philad.," 4: ed. Funk, I, p. 266; and
St. Cornelius I as given in St. Cyprian, "Epist.," 48, 2: Hartel, III B, p. 610.*

aid, spiritual as well as material, pastoral as well as personal, in meetings and in a community of life, of labor, of charity.

Let them, as fathers in Christ, take care of the faithful whom they have spiritually begotten by baptism and by their teaching (cf. 1 Cor. 4:15; 1 Pet. 1:23). Having become from the heart a pattern to the flock (1 Pet. 5:3), let them so lead and serve their local community that it may worthily be called by that name by which the one and entire People of God is distinguished, namely, the Church of God (cf. 1 Cor. 1:2; 2 Cor. 1:1 and passim). They should remember that by their daily life and interests they are showing the face of a truly priestly and pastoral ministry to the faithful and the unbeliever, to Catholics and non-Catholics, and that to all men they should bear witness about truth and life, and, as good shepherds, go after those also (cf. Lk. 15:4-7) who, though baptized in the Catholic Church, have fallen away from the sacraments, or even from the faith.

Because the human race today is joining more and more into a civic, economic, and social unity, it is that much more necessary that priests, united in concern and effort, under the leadership of the bishops and the Supreme Pontiff, wipe out every kind of division, so that the whole human race may be brought into the unity of the family of God.

29. At a lower level of the hierarchy are deacons,[159] upon whom hands are imposed "not unto the priesthood, but unto a ministry of service."[160] For strengthened by sacramental grace, in communion with the bishop and his group of priests, they serve the People of God in the ministry of the liturgy, of the word, and of charity. It is the duty of the deacon, to the extent that he has been authorized by competent authority, to administer baptism solemnly, to be custodian and dispenser of the Eucharist, to assist at and bless marriages in the name of the Church, to bring Viaticum to the dying, to read the sacred Scripture to the faithful, to instruct and exhort the people, to preside at the worship and prayer of the faithful, to administer sacramentals, and to officiate at funeral and burial services. Dedicated to duties of charity and

159. The final article on the deacons is of great practical moment. It makes provision for the future restoration of the diaconate as a permanent grade in the Churches of the Latin rite and even, eventually, for the ordaining of married deacons of mature years. The implementing of these two provisions is made subject to the decision of the competent territorial bodies of bishops, with the approval or consent of the Pope.

160. "Constitutiones Ecclesiae aegyptiacae," III, 2: ed. Funk, "Didascalia," II, p. 103; and "Statuta Ecclesiae antiquae," 37-41: Mansi, 3, 954.

of administration, let deacons be mindful of the admonition of Blessed Polycarp: "Be merciful, diligent, walking according to the truth of the Lord, who became the servant of all."[161]

These duties, so very necessary for the life of the Church, can in many areas be fulfilled only with difficulty according to the prevailing discipline of the Latin Church. For this reason, the diaconate can in the future be restored as a proper and permanent rank of the hierarchy. It pertains to the competent territorial bodies of bishops, of one kind or another, to decide, with the approval of the Supreme Pontiff, whether and where it is opportune for such deacons to be appointed for the care of souls. With the consent of the Roman Pontiff, this diaconate will be able to be conferred upon men of more mature age, even upon those living in the married state. It may also be conferred upon suitable young men. For them, however, the law of celibacy must remain intact.

CHAPTER IV

THE LAITY

30. Having set forth the functions of the hierarchy, this holy Synod gladly turns its attention to the status of those faithful called the laity.[162] Everything which has been said so far concerning the People of God applies equally to the laity, religious, and clergy. But there are certain things which pertain in a particular way to the laity, both men and women, by reason of their situation and mission. Because of the spe-

---

161. *St. Polycarp, "Ad Phil.," 5, 2: ed. Funk, I, p. 300: Christ is said "to have become the deacon of all." See "Didache," 15, 1: ed. Funk, I, p. 32; St. Ignatius of Antioch, "Ad Trall.," 2, 3: ed. Funk, I, p. 242; and "Constitutiones Apostolorum," 8, 28, 4: ed. Funk, "Didascalia," I, p. 530.*
1   .   .. ..g dealt with the hierarchical ministries of the Church, the Constitution quite naturally goes on to speak of the remaining members, the laity. This brief but inspiring chapter should be read in close connection with Chap. II on the People of God, the general teaching of which is here applied to the special condition of lay people.

cial circumstances of our time the foundations of these particularities must be examined more thoroughly.

For their sacred pastors know how much the laity contribute to the welfare of the entire Church. Pastors also know that they themselves were not meant by Christ to shoulder alone the entire saving mission of the Church toward the world. On the contrary, they understand that it is their noble duty so to shepherd the faithful and recognize their services and charismatic gifts that all according to their proper roles may cooperate in this common undertaking with one heart. For we must all "practice the truth in love, and so grow up in all things in him who is head, Christ. For from him the whole body (being closely joined and knit together through every joint of the system according to the functioning in due measure of each single part) derives its increase to the building up of itself in love" (Eph. 4:15-16).

31. The term laity[163] is here understood to mean all the faithful except those in holy orders and those in a religious state sanctioned by the Church. These faithful are by baptism made one body with Christ and are established among the People of God. They are in their own way made sharers in the priestly, prophetic, and kingly functions of Christ. They carry out their own part in the mission of the whole Christian people with respect to the Church and the world.

A secular quality is proper and special to laymen.[164] It is true that those in holy orders can at times engage in secular activities, and even have a secular profession. But by reason of their particular vocation they are chiefly and professedly ordained to the sacred ministry. Similarly, by their state in life, religious give splendid and striking testimony that the world cannot be transfigured and offered to God without the spirit of the beatitudes.

But the laity, by their very vocation, seek the kingdom of God by engaging in temporal affairs and by ordering them according to the plan of God. They live in the world, that is, in each and in all of the secular professions and occupations. They live in the ordinary circumstances of family and social

163. The laity are here defined not only negatively (as those not ordained and not in the religious state) but positively, in terms of their baptism and their active role in the People of God.
164. The emphasis on the "secular" mission of the laity links this chapter closely with the Decree on the Church in the Modern World. Note that while non-ordained religious are technically or canonically lay persons they are not considered in this chapter on the laity since they are the subject of Chap. VI below.

life, from which the very web of their existence is woven.

They are called there by God so that by exercising their proper function and being led by the spirit of the gospel they can work for the sanctification of the world from within, in the manner of leaven. In this way they can make Christ known to others, especially by the testimony of a life resplendent in faith, hope, and charity. The layman is closely involved in temporal affairs of every sort. It is therefore his special task to illumine and organize these affairs in such a way that they may always start out, develop, and persist according to Christ's mind, to the praise of the Creator and the Redeemer.

32. By divine institution Holy Church is structured and governed with a wonderful diversity.[165] "For just as in one body we have many members, yet all the members have not the same function, so we, the many, are one body in Christ, but severally members one of another" (Rom. 12:4-5).

Therefore, the chosen People of God is one: "one Lord, one faith, one baptism" (Eph. 4:5). As members, they share a common dignity from their rebirth in Christ. They have the same filial grace and the same vocation to perfection. They possess in common one salvation, one hope, and one undivided charity. Hence, there is in Christ and in the Church no inequality on the basis of race or nationality, social condition or sex, because "there is neither Jew nor Greek; there is neither slave nor freeman; there is neither male nor female. For you are all 'one' in Christ Jesus" (Gal. 3:28, Greek text; cf. Col. 3:11).

If therefore everyone in the Church does not proceed by the same path, nevertheless all are called to sanctity and have received an equal privilege of faith through the justice of God (cf. 2 Pet. 1:1). And if by the will of Christ some are made teachers, dispensers of mysteries, and shepherds on behalf of others, yet all share a true equality with regard to the dignity and to the activity common to all the faithful for the building up of the Body of Christ.

For the distinction which the Lord made between sacred ministers and the rest of the People of God entails a unifying purpose, since pastors and the other faithful are bound to each other by a mutual need. Pastors of the Church, follow-

---

165. Here and throughout the chapter, pains are taken to dispel the common misconception that the laity are in all respects subject to, and dependent upon, their pastors. On the contrary, the Constitution teaches that there is a mutual relationship of support and dependence between laity and clergy.

ing the example of the Lord, should minister to one another and to the other faithful. The faithful in their turn should enthusiastically lend their cooperative assistance to their pastors and teachers. Thus in their diversity all bear witness to the admirable unity of the Body of Christ. This very diversity of graces, ministries, and works gathers the children of God into one, because "all these things are the work of one and the same Spirit" (1 Cor. 12:11).

Therefore, by divine condescension the laity have Christ for their brother who, though He is the Lord of all, came not to be served but to serve (cf. Mt. 20:28). They also have for their brothers those in the sacred ministry who by teaching, by sanctifying, and by ruling with the authority of Christ so feed the family of God that the new commandment of charity may be fulfilled by all. St. Augustine puts this very beautifully when he says: "What I am for you terrifies me; what I am with you consoles me. For you I am a bishop; but with you I am a Christian. The former is a title of duty; the latter, one of grace. The former is a danger; the latter, salvation."[166]

33. The laity are gathered together in the People of God and make up the Body of Christ under one Head. Whoever they are, they are called upon, as living members, to expend all their energy for the growth of the Church and its continuous sanctification. For this very energy is a gift of the Creator and a blessing of the Redeemer.

The lay apostolate, however, is a participation in the saving mission of the Church itself.[167] Through their baptism and confirmation, all are commissioned to that apostolate by the Lord Himself. Moreover, through the sacraments, especially the Holy Eucharist, there is communicated and nourished that charity toward God and man which is the soul of the entire apostolate. Now, the laity are called in a special way to make the Church present and operative in those places and circumstances where only through them can she become the salt of the earth.[168] Thus every layman, by vir-

---

166. *St. Augustine, "Serm.," 340, 1: PL 38, 1483.*
167. The lay apostolate according to some earlier conceptions had been limited to the cooperation of the laity in the apostolic tasks proper to the hierarchy. The present document, as well as the Decree on the Apostolate of the Laity, make it clear that while laymen may laudably assist in the hierarchical apostolate as collaborators, the term "lay apostolate" refers primarily to apostolic tasks pertaining to the laity as such.
168. *Cf. Pius XI, encyclical "Quadragesimo anno," May 15, 1931: AAS 23 (1931), pp. 221 f.; and the allocution of Pius XII, "De quelle consolation," Oct. 14, 1951: AAS 43 (1951), pp. 790 f.*

tue of the very gifts bestowed upon him, is at the same time
a witness and a living instrument of the mission of the
Church herself, "according to the measure of Christ's be-
stowal" (Eph. 4:7).

Besides this apostolate, which pertains to absolutely every
Christian, the laity can also be called in various ways to a
more direct form of cooperation in the apostolate of the
hierarchy.[169] This was the case with certain men and women
who assisted Paul the Apostle in the gospel, laboring much
in the Lord (cf. Phil. 4:3; Rom. 16:3 ff.). Further, laymen
have the capacity to be deputed by the hierarchy to exercise
certain church functions for a spiritual purpose.

Upon all the laity, therefore, rests the noble duty of working to extend the divine plan of salvation ever increasingly
to all men of each epoch and in every land. Consequently,
let every opportunity be given them so that, according to
their abilities and the needs of the times, they may zealously
participate in the saving work of the Church.

34. Since the supreme and eternal Priest, Christ Jesus, wills
to continue His witness and serve through the laity too, He
vivifies them in His Spirit and unceasingly urges them on to
every good and perfect work.[170]

For besides intimately associating them with His life and
His mission, Christ also gives them a share in His priestly
function of offering spiritual worship for the glory of God
and the salvation of men. For this reason the laity, dedicated
to Christ and anointed by the Holy Spirit, are marvelously
called and equipped to produce in themselves ever more
abundant fruits of the Spirit. For all their works, prayers,
and apostolic endeavors, their ordinary married and family
life, their daily labor, their mental and physical relaxation, if
carried out in the Spirit, and even the hardships of life, if
patiently borne—all of these become spiritual sacrifices acceptable to God through Jesus Christ (cf. 1 Pet. 2:5). During the celebration of the Eucharist, these sacrifices are most
lovingly offered to the Father along with the Lord's body.
Thus, as worshipers whose every deed is holy, the laity con-
secrate the world itself to God.

169. *Cf. Pius XII, allocution "Six ans se sont écoulés," Oct. 5, 1957: AAS
49 (1957), p. 927.*
170. The duties and powers of the laity, like those of the hierarchy in
Chap. III, are discussed in relation to the triple office of Christ. This paragraph explains their priestly ministry, which, without interfering with the
proper autonomy of worldly affairs, brings about a certain "consecration"
of the world to God its Creator.

35. Christ, the great Prophet, who proclaimed the kingdom of His Father by the testimony of His life and the power of His words, continually fulfills His prophetic office until His full glory is revealed.[171] He does this not only through the hierarchy who teach in His name and with His authority, but also through the laity. For that very purpose He made them His witnesses and gave them understanding of the faith and the grace of speech (cf. Acts 2:17-18; Apoc. 19:10), so that the power of the gospel might shine forth in their daily social and family life.

They show themselves to be children of the promise, if, strong in faith and in hope, they make the most of the present time (cf. Eph. 5:16; Col. 4:5), and with patience await the glory that is to come (cf. Rom. 8:25). Let them not, then, hide this hope in the depths of their hearts, but even in the framework of secular life let them express it by a continual turning toward God and by wrestling "against the world-rulers of this darkness, against the spiritual forces of wickedness" (Eph. 6:12).

The sacraments of the New Law, by which the life and the apostolate of the faithful are nourished, prefigure a new heaven and a new earth (cf. Apoc. 21:1). So too the laity go forth as powerful heralds of a faith in things to be hoped for (cf. Heb. 11:1) provided they steadfastly join to their profession of faith a life springing from faith. This evangelization, that is, this announcing of Christ by a living testimony as well as by the spoken word, takes on a specific quality and a special force in that it is carried out in the ordinary surroundings of the world.

In connection with this function, that state of life which is sanctified by a special sacrament is obviously of great value, namely, married and family life. For where Christianity pervades a whole way of life and ever increasingly transforms it, there will exist both the practice and an excellent school of the lay apostolate. In such a home, husband and wife find their proper vocation in being witnesses to one another and to their children of faith in Christ and love for Him. The Christian family loudly proclaims both the present virtues of the kingdom of God and the hope of a blessed life to come.

---

171. The present explanation of the prophetic role of the laity supplements Chap. II. where it was indicated that their function as witnesses stems from the sacraments of baptism and confirmation (Art. 11) and from the charisms freely bestowed by the Holy Spirit (Art 12). This theological foundation and the particular forms of witness proper to the laity are further explained in the Decree on the Apostolate of the Laity.

Thus by its example and its witness it accuses the world of sin and enlightens those who seek the truth.

Consequently, even when preoccupied with temporal cares, the laity can and must perform eminently valuable work on behalf of bringing the gospel to the world. Some of them do all they can to provide sacred services when sacred ministers are lacking or are blocked by a persecuting regime. Many devote themselves entirely to apostolic work. But all ought to cooperate in the spreading and intensifying of the kingdom of Christ in the world. Therefore, let the laity strive skillfully to acquire a more profound grasp of revealed truth, and insistently beg of God the gift of wisdom.

36. Christ obeyed even at the cost of death, and was therefore raised up by the Father (cf. Phil. 2:8-9). Thus He entered into the glory of His kingdom.[172] To Him all things are made subject until He subjects Himself and all created things to the Father, that God may be all in all (cf. 1 Cor. 15:27-28). Now, Christ has communicated this power of subjection to His disciples that they might be established in royal freedom and that by self-denial and a holy life they might conquer the reign of sin in themselves (cf. Rom. 6:12). Further, He has shared this power so that by serving Him in their fellow men they might through humility and patience lead their brother men to that King whom to serve is to reign.

For the Lord wishes to spread His kingdom by means of the laity also, a kingdom of truth and life, a kingdom of holiness and grace, a kingdom of justice, love, and peace.[173] In this kingdom, creation itself will be delivered out of its slavery to corruption and into the freedom of the glory of the sons of God (cf. Rom. 8:21). Clearly then a great promise and a great mandate are committed to the disciples: "For all are yours, and you are Christ's, and Christ is God's" (1 Cor. 3:23).

The faithful, therefore, must learn the deepest meaning and the value of all creation, and how to relate it to the praise of God. They must assist one another to live holier lives even in their daily occupations. In this way the world is per-

---

172. This article on the participation of the laity in the royal office of Christ shows a marked advance beyond anything contained in previous official documents of the Church. Note that the laity discharge this function not only by contributing to the moral improvement of mankind but also by assisting the advance of culture and civilization.
173. *From the Preface of the Feast of Christ the King.*

meated by the spirit of Christ and more effectively achieves its purpose in justice, charity, and peace. The laity have the principal role in the universal fulfillment of this purpose.

Therefore, by their competence in secular fields and by their personal activity, elevated from within by the grace of Christ, let them labor vigorously so that by human labor, technical skill, and civic culture created goods may be perfected for the benefit of every last man, according to the design of the Creator and the light of His Word. Let them work to see that created goods are more fittingly distributed among men, and that such goods in their own way lead to general progress in human and Christian liberty. In this manner, through the members of the Church, Christ will progressively illumine the whole of human society with His saving light.

Moreover, let the laity also by their combined efforts remedy any institutions and conditions of the world which are customarily an inducement to sin, so that all such things may be conformed to the norms of justice and may favor the practice of virtue rather than hinder it. By so doing, laymen will imbue culture and human activity with moral values. They will better prepare the field of the world for the seed of the Word of God. At the same time they will open wider the Church's doors, through which the message of peace can enter the world.

Because the very plan of salvation requires it, the faithful should learn how to distinguish carefully between those rights and duties which are theirs as members of the Church, and those which they have as members of human society.[174] Let them strive to harmonize the two, remembering that in every temporal affair they must be guided by a Christian conscience. For even in secular affairs there is no human activity which can be withdrawn from God's dominion. In our own time, however, it is most urgent that this distinction and also this harmony should shine forth as radiantly as possible in the practice of the faithful, so that the mission of the Church may correspond more adequately to the special conditions of the world today. For while it must be recognized that the temporal sphere is governed by its own principles, since it is properly concerned with the interests of this world, that ominous doctrine must rightly be rejected which attempts to build a society with no regard whatever for reli-

174. For a more complete statement on the rights of Christian conscience in temporal affairs, see the Declaration on Religious Freedom.

gion, and which attacks and destroys the religious liberty of its citizens.[175]

37. The laity have the right,[176] as do all Christians, to receive in abundance from their sacred pastors the spiritual goods of the Church, especially the assistance of the Word of God and the sacraments.[177] Every layman should openly reveal to them his needs and desires with that freedom and confidence which befits a son of God and a brother in Christ. An individual layman, by reason of the knowledge, competence, or outstanding ability which he may enjoy, is permitted and sometimes even obliged to express his opinion on things which concern the good of the Church.[178] When occasions arise, let this be done through the agencies set up by the Church for this purpose. Let it always be done in truth, in courage, and in prudence, with reverence and charity toward those who by reason of their sacred office represent the person of Christ.

With ready Christian obedience, laymen as well as all disciples of Christ should accept whatever their sacred pastors, as representatives of Christ, decree in their role as teachers and rulers in the Church. Let laymen follow the example of Christ, who, by His obedience even at the cost of death, opened to all men the blessed way to the liberty of the children of God. Nor should they omit to pray to God for those placed over them, who keep watch as having to render an account of their souls, so that they may render this account with joy and not with grief (cf. Heb. 13:17).

Let sacred pastors recognize and promote the dignity as well as the responsibility of the layman in the Church. Let them willingly make use of his prudent advice. Let them con-

175. *Cf. Leo XIII, encyclical "Immortale Dei," Nov. 1, 1885: Acta Sanctae Sedis 18 (1885), pp. 166 ff.; the same Pontiff's encyclical "Sapientiae Christianae," Jan. 10, 1890: Acta Sanctae Sedis 22 (1889-90), pp. 397 ff.; and the allocution of Pius XII, "Alla vostra filiale," March 23, 1958: AAS 50 (1958), p. 220: "la legittima sana laicità dello Stato"* ["the legitimate and healthy laicity of the State"].
176. This paragraph is liberal in stressing the rights and the active role of the laity in the Church. It suggests, at least indirectly, that there should be institutions such as diocesan councils in which "familiar dialogue" can be carried on between the laity and their pastors. Here again the reciprocal assistance and dependence of pastors and laity is acknowledged.
177. *Code of Canon Law, c. 682.*
178. *Cf. Pius XII, allocution "De quelle consolation": AAS 43 (1951), p. 789: "Dans les batailles décisives, c'est parfois du front que partent les plus heureuses initiatives . . ."* ("In the case of decisive battles, it happens at times that the best initiatives come from the frontline"); *and the same Pontiff's allocution "L'importance de la presse catholique," Feb. 17, 1950: AAS 42 (1950), p. 256.*

fidently assign duties to him in the service of the Church, allowing him freedom and room for action. Further, let them encourage the layman so that he may undertake tasks on his own initiative. Attentively in Christ, let them consider with fatherly love the projects, suggestions, and desires proposed by the laity.[179] Furthermore, let pastors respectfully acknowledge that just freedom which belongs to everyone in this earthly city.

A great many benefits are to be hoped for from this familiar dialogue between the laity and their pastors: in the laity, a strengthened sense of personal responsibility, a renewed enthusiasm, a more ready application of their talents to the projects of their pastors. The latter, for their part, aided by the experience of the laity, can more clearly and more suitably come to decisions regarding spiritual and temporal matters. In this way, the whole Church, strengthened by each one of its members, can more effectively fulfill its mission for the life of the world.

38. Each individual layman must stand before the world as a witness to the resurrection and life of the Lord Jesus and as a sign that God lives. As a body and individually, the laity must do their part to nourish the world with spiritual fruits (cf. Gal. 5:22), and to spread abroad in it that spirit by which are animated those poor, meek, and peacemaking men whom the Lord in the gospel calls blessed (cf. Mt. 5:3-9). In a word, "what the soul is to the body, let Christians be to the world."[180]

CHAPTER V

THE CALL OF THE
WHOLE CHURCH TO HOLINESS [181]

39. Faith teaches that the Church, whose mystery is being set forth by this sacred Synod, is holy in a way which can

---

179. *Cf. 1 Th. 5:19 and 1 Jn. 4:1.*
180. *"Epist. ad Diognetum," 6: ed. Funk, I, p. 400. Cf. St. John Chrysostom, "In Matth.," Hom. 46 (47), 2: PG 58, 478, on the leaven in the dough.*
181. Having considered the various classes of members in the Church (the

never fail. For Christ, the Son of God, who with the Father and the Spirit is praised as being "alone holy,"[182] loved the Church as His Bride, delivering Himself up for her. This He did that He might sanctify her (cf. Eph. 5:25-26). He united her to Himself as His own body and crowned her with the gift of the Holy Spirit, for God's glory. Therefore in the Church, everyone belonging to the hierarchy, or being cared for by it, is called to holiness, according to the saying of the Apostle: "For this is the will of God, your sanctification" (1 Th. 4:3; cf. Eph. 1:4).

Now, this holiness of the Church is unceasingly manifested, as it ought to be, through those fruits of grace that the Spirit produces in the faithful. It is expressed in multiple ways by those individuals who, in their walk of life, strive for the perfection of charity, and thereby help others to grow. In a particularly appropriate way this holiness shines out in the practice of the counsels customarily called "evangelical."[183] Under the influence of the Holy Spirit, the practice of these counsels is undertaken by many Christians, either privately or in some Church-approved situation or state, and produces in the world, as produce it should, a shining witness and model of holiness.

40. The Lord Jesus, the divine Teacher and Model of all perfection, preached holiness of life to each and every one of His disciples, regardless of their situation:[184] "You therefore are to be perfect, even as your heavenly Father is perfect" (Mt. 5:48).[185] He Himself stands as the Author and Finisher of this holiness of life. For He sent the Holy Spirit upon all men that He might inspire them from within to love God with their whole heart and their whole soul, with all their

hierarchy in its several degrees and the laity), the Constitution goes on to deal with the activity of the Church. A special chapter is devoted to holiness, or sanctity, which essentially consists in separation from sin and union with God, and which may be called the very goal of the Church both in this life and in the next.

182. *Roman Missal, the Gloria in Excelsis. Cf. LK. 1:35; Mk. 1:24; Lk. 4:34; Jn. 6:69 (ho hagios tou theou [the holy one of God]); Acts 3:14; 4:27 and 30; Heb. 7:26; 1 Jn. 2:20; Apoc. 3:7.*

183. The "evangelical counsels"—traditionally enumerated as poverty, chastity, and obedience—are discussed more fully in Art. 42 below.

184. The New Testament texts cited in this article make it evident that not only those who live according to the evangelical counsels but all Christians are called to "the fullness of Christian life and to the perfection of charity." It would be an error to think of holiness as the special preserve of some one class of Christians, e.g., the religious.

185. *Cf. Origen, "Comm. in Rom.," 7, 7: PG 14, 1122 B; pseudo-Macarius, "De oratione," 11: PG 34, 861 AB; and St. Thomas, "Summa Theol.," 2-2, q. 184, a. 3.*

mind and all their strength (cf. Mk. 12:30) and that they might love one another as Christ loved them (cf. Jn. 13:34; 15:12).

The followers of Christ are called by God, not according to their accomplishments, but according to His own purpose and grace. They are justified in the Lord Jesus, and through baptism sought in faith they truly become sons of God and sharers in the divine nature. In this way they are really made holy. Then, too, by God's gifts they must hold on to and complete in their lives this holiness which they have received. They are warned by the Apostle to live "as becomes saints" (Eph. 5:3), and to put on "as God's chosen ones, holy and beloved, a heart of mercy, kindness, humility, meekness, patience" (Col. 3:12), and to possess the fruits of the Spirit unto holiness (cf. Gal. 5:22; Rom. 6:22). Since we all truly offend in many things (cf. Jas. 3:2), we all need God's mercy continuously and must daily pray: "Forgive us our debts" (Mt. 6:12).[186]

Thus it is evident to everyone that all the faithful of Christ of whatever rank or status are called to the fullness of the Christian life and to the perfection of charity.[187] By this holiness a more human way of life is promoted even in this earthly society. In order that the faithful may reach this perfection, they must use their strength according as they have received it, as a gift from Christ. In this way they can follow in His footsteps and mold themselves in His image, seeking the will of the Father in all things, devoting themselves with all their being to the glory of God and the service of their neighbor. In this way too, the holiness of the People of God will grow into an abundant harvest of good, as is brilliantly proved by the lives of so many saints in Church history.

41. In the various types and duties of life,[188] one and the same holiness is cultivated by all who are moved by the Spirit of God, and who obey the voice of the Father, worshiping God the Father in spirit and in truth. These souls follow the

---

186. *Cf. St. Augustine, "Retract.," II, 18: PL 32, 637 f.; and the encyclical of Pius XII, "Mystici Corporis," June 29, 1943: AAS 35 (1943), p. 225.*
187. *Cf. Pius XI, encyclical "Rerum omnium," Jan. 26, 1923: AAS 15 (1923), pp. 50 and 59-60; Pius XI, encyclical "Casti connubii," Dec. 31, 1930: AAS 22 (1930), p. 548; the apostolic constitution of Pius XII, "Provida Mater," Feb. 2, 1947: AAS 39 (1947), p. 177; the same Pontiff's allocution "Annus sacer," Dec. 8, 1950: AAS 43 (1951), pp. 27-8; and his allocution, "Nel darvi," July 2, 1956: AAS 48 (1956), pp. 574 f.*
188. This article shows the great variety of ways in which different classes of persons within the Church are called to pursue holiness.

poor Christ, the humble and cross-bearing Christ, in order to be made worthy of being partakers in His glory. Every person should walk unhesitatingly according to his own personal gifts and duties in the path of a living faith which arouses hopes and works through charity.

In the first place, the shepherds of Christ's flock[189] ought to carry out their ministry with holiness, eagerness, humility, and courage, in imitation of the eternal High Priest, the Shepherd and Guardian of our souls. They will thereby make this ministry the principal means of their own sanctification. Those chosen for the fullness of the priesthood are gifted with sacramental grace enabling them to exercise a perfect role of pastoral charity through prayer, sacrifice, and preaching, as through every form of a bishop's care and service.[190] They are enabled to lay down their life for their sheep fearlessly, and, made a model for their flock (cf. 1 Pet. 5:3), can lead the Church to ever-increasing holiness through their own example.

Thanks to Christ, the eternal and sole Mediator, priests share in the grace of the bishop's rank and form his spiritual crown.[191] Like bishops, priests should grow in love for God and neighbor through the daily exercise of their duty. They should preserve the bond of priestly fraternity, abound in every spiritual good, and give living evidence of God to all men.[192] Let their heroes be those priests who have lived during the course of the centuries, often in lowly and hidden service, and have left behind them a bright pattern of holiness. Their praise lives on in the Church.

A priest's task is to pray and offer sacrifice for his own people and indeed the entire People of God, realizing what he does and reproducing in himself the holiness of the things he handles.[193] Let him not be undone by his apostolic cares, dangers, and toils, but rather led by them to higher sanctity. His activities should be fed and fostered by a wealth of meditation, to the delight of the whole Church of God. All priests,

189. The first class considered are the bishops, whose high calling demands close imitation of the Good Shepherd.
190. Cf. St. Thomas, "Summa Theol.," 2-2, q. 184, aa. 5 and 6; the same author's "De perf. vitae spir.," c. 18; and Origen, "In Is.," Hom. 6, 1: PG 13, 239.
191. Cf. St. Ignatius of Antioch, "Ad Magn.," 13, 1: ed. Funk, I, p. 241.
192. Cf. St. Pius X, exhortation "Haerent animo," Aug. 4, 1908: Acta Sanctae Sedis 41 (1908), pp. 560 f.; Code of Canon Law, c. 124; and Pius XI, encyclical "Ad catholici sacerdotii," Dec. 20, 1935: AAS 28 (1936), pp. 22 f.
193. Ceremony of priestly ordination, the initial exhortation.

especially those who are called diocesan[194] in view of the particular title of their ordination, should bear in mind how much their sanctity profits from loyal attachment to the bishop and generous collaboration with him.

In their own special way, ministers of lesser rank also share in the mission and grace of the supreme priest. First among these are deacons. Since they are servants of the mysteries of Christ and the Church,[195] they should keep themselves free from every fault, be pleasing to God, and be a source of all goodness in the sight of men (cf. 1 Tim. 3:8-10, 12-13).

Called by the Lord and set aside as His portion, other clerics prepare themselves for various ministerial offices under the watchful eye of pastors. They are bound to bring their hearts and minds into accord with the splendid calling which is theirs, and will do so by constancy in prayer, burning love, and attention to whatever is true, just, and of good repute, all for the glory and honor of God. In addition, there are laymen chosen by God and called by the bishop to devote themselves exclusively to apostolic labors, working with great fruitfulness in the Lord's field.[196]

Married couples and Christian parents should follow their own proper path to holiness by faithful love, sustaining one another in grace throughout the entire length of their lives. They should imbue their offspring, lovingly welcomed from God, with Christian truths and evangelical virtues. For thus they can offer all men an example of unwearying and generous love, build up the brotherhood of charity, and stand as witnesses to and cooperators in the fruitfulness of Holy Mother Church. By such lives, they signify and share in that very love with which Christ loved His Bride and because of which He delivered Himself up on her behalf.[197] A like example, but one given in a different way, is that offered by widows and single people, who are able to make great contributions toward holiness and apostolic endeavor in the Church.

Finally, laborers, whose work is often toilsome, should by

194. Special mention is made of diocesan priests because some have erroneously imagined that only religious priests were called to the path of perfection.
195. *Cf. St. Ignatius of Antioch, "Ad Trall.," 2, 3: ed. Funk, 1, p. 244.*
196. *Cf. Pius XII, allocution "Sous la maternelle protection," Dec. 9, 1957: AAS 50 (1958), p. 36.*
197. *Pius XI, encyclical "Casti connubii," Dec. 31, 1930: AAS 22 (130), pp. 548 f. Cf. St. John Chrysostom, "In Ephes.," Hom. 20, 2: PG 62, 136 ff.*

their human exertions try to perfect themselves, aid their fellow citizens, and raise all of society, and even creation itself, to a better mode of existence.[198] By their lively charity, joyous hope, and sharing of one another's burdens, let them also truly imitate Christ, who roughened His hands with carpenter's tools, and who in union with His Father is always at work for the salvation of all men. By their daily work itself laborers can achieve greater apostolic sanctity.

Those who are oppressed by poverty, infirmity, sickness, or various other hardships, as well as those who suffer persecution for justice' sake—may they all know that in a special way they are united with the suffering Christ for the salvation of the world.[199] The Lord called them blessed in His gospel. They are those whom "the God of all grace, who has called us unto his eternal glory in Christ Jesus, will himself, after we have suffered a little while, perfect, strengthen, and establish" (1 Pet. 5:10).

All of Christ's faithful, therefore, whatever be the conditions, duties, and circumstances of their lives, will grow in holiness day by day through these very situations, if they accept all of them with faith from the hand of their heavenly Father, and if they cooperate with the divine will by showing every man through their earthly activities the love with which God has loved the world.

42. "God is love, and he who abides in love abides in God, and God in him" (1 Jn. 4:16).[200] God pours out His love into our hearts through the Holy Spirit, who has been given to us (cf. Rom. 5:5). Thus the first and most necessary gift is that charity by which we love God above all things and our neighbor because of God. If that love, as good seed, is to grow and bring forth fruit in the soul, each one of the faithful must willingly hear the Word of God and with the help of His grace act to fulfill His will.

Each must share frequently in the sacraments, the Eucharist especially, and in liturgical rites. Each must apply himself

198. The Christian value of labor, already touched on in Chap. IV, is a theme which has emerged with increasing clarity in the present century, as men have become conscious of their immense power to contribute by their efforts to the perfection of the material universe, thus bringing creation itself, so to speak, to completion, to the greater glory of the Creator.
199. The Christian, in faith, should esteem the passive purification which can result from a patient acceptance of hardship and suffering.
200. To free us from a legalistic view of holiness, which would overemphasize external good works and conformity to law, the Constitution reminds us that the true measure of holiness is a sincere and efficacious love of God and neighbor.

constantly to prayer, self-denial, active brotherly service, and the exercise of all the virtues. For charity, as the bond of perfection and the fulfillment of the law (cf. Col. 3:14; Rom. 13:10), rules over all the means of attaining holiness, gives life to them, and makes them work.[201] Hence it is the love of God and of neighbor which points out the true disciple of Christ.

Since Jesus, the Son of God, manifested His charity by laying down His life for us, no one has greater love than he who lays down his life for Christ and his brothers (cf. 1 Jn. 3:16; Jn. 15:13). From the earliest times, then, some Christians have been called upon—and some will always be called upon—to give this supreme testimony of love to all men, but especially to persecutors. The Church, therefore, considers martyrdom as an exceptional gift and as the highest proof of love.

By martyrdom a disciple is transformed into an image of his Master, who freely accepted death on behalf of the world's salvation; he perfects that image even to the shedding of blood. Though few are presented with such an opportunity, nevertheless all must be prepared to confess Christ before men, and to follow Him along the way of the cross through the persecutions which the Church will never fail to suffer.

The holiness of the Church is also fostered in a special way by the observance of the manifold counsels[202] proposed in the gospel by our Lord to His disciples.[203] Outstanding among them is that precious gift of divine grace which the Father gives to some men (cf. Mt. 19:11; 1 Cor. 7:7) so that by virginity, or celibacy, they can more easily devote their entire selves to God alone with undivided heart (cf. 1 Cor. 7:32-34).[204] This total continence embraced on behalf of the kingdom of heaven has always been held in par-

---

201. *Cf. St. Augustine, "Enchir.," 121, 32: PL 40, 288; St. Thomas, "Summa Theol.," 2-2, q. 184, a. 1; and the apostolic exhortation of Pius XII, "Menti nostrae," Sept. 23, 1950: AAS 42 (1950), p. 660.*
202. This and the following paragraph single out for praise those who, even without embracing the religious state, practice one or more of the evangelical counsels of poverty, chastity, and obedience in accordance with the special grace given to them by God.
203. *On the counsels in general, see Origen, "Comm. in Rom.," X, 14: PG 14, 1275 B; St. Augustine, "De s. virginitate," 15, 15: PL 40, 403; and St. Thomas, "Summa Theol.," 1-2, q. 100, a. 2 c at the end and 2-2, q. 44, a. 4, ad 3.*
204. *On the excellence of holy virginity, see Tertullian, "Exhort. cast.," 10: PL 2, 925 C; St. Cyprian, "Hab. virg.," 3 and 22: PL 4, 443 B and 461 A f.; St. Athanasius (?), "De virg.,": PG 28, 252 ff.; and St. John Chrysostom, "De virg.," PG 48, 533 ff.*

ticular honor by the Church as being a sign of charity and stimulus towards it, as well as a unique fountain of spiritual fertility in the world.

The Church also keeps in mind the advice of the Apostle, who summoned the faithful to charity by exhorting them to share the mind of Christ Jesus—He who "emptied himself, taking the nature of a slave . . . becoming obedient to death" (Phil. 2:7-8), and, because of us, "being rich, he became poor" (2 Cor. 8:9).

Since the disciples must always imitate and give witness to this charity and humility of Christ, Mother Church rejoices at finding within her bosom men and women who more closely follow and more clearly demonstrate the Savior's self-giving by embracing poverty with the free choice of God's sons, and by renouncing their own wills. They subject the latter to another person on God's behalf, in pursuit of an excellence surpassing what is commanded. Thus they liken themselves more thoroughly to Christ in His obedience.[205]

All of Christ's followers, therefore, are invited and bound to pursue holiness and the perfect fulfillment of their proper state. Hence, let them all see that they guide their affections rightly. Otherwise, they will be thwarted in the search for perfect charity by the way they use earthly possessions and by a fondness for riches which goes against the gospel spirit of poverty. The Apostle has sounded the warning: let those who make use of this world not get bogged down in it, for the structure of this world is passing away (cf. 1 Cor. 7:31, Greek text).[206]

---

205. *On spiritual poverty, Cf. Mt. 5:3 and 19-21; Mk. 10:21; Lk. 18:22; with regard to obedience, the example of Christ is given: Jn. 4:34; 6:38; Phil. 2:8-10; Heb. 10:5-7. The Fathers and the founders of orders have much to say about these matters.*
206. *On the effective practice of the counsels which is not imposed on all, see St. John Chrysostom, "In Matth.," Hom. 7, 7: PG 57, 81 f.; and St. Ambrose, "De viduis," 4, 23: PL 16, 241 f.*

CHAPTER VI

RELIGIOUS[207]

43. The evangelical counsels of chastity dedicated to God, poverty, and obedience are based upon the words and example of the Lord.[208] They were further commended by the apostles and the Fathers, and other teachers and shepherds of the Church. The counsels are a divine gift, which the Church has received from her Lord and which she ever preserves with the help of His grace. Church authority has the duty, under the inspiration of the Holy Spirit, of interpreting these evangelical counsels, of regulating their practice, and finally of establishing stable forms of living according to them.

Thus it has come about that various forms of solitary and community life, as well as different religious families have grown up. Advancing the progress of their members and the welfare of the whole body of Christ,[209] these groups have been like branches sprouting out wondrously and abundantly from a tree growing in the field of the Lord from a seed divinely planted.

These religious families give their members the support of

207. This chapter may be regarded as an extension of Chap. V, especially the last paragraphs. It deals with a special manner of following the universal call to holiness. The religious are not a third state in addition to the clergy and laity, but they are clerics or lay people who have dedicated themselves to a life according to the evangelical counsels, and thus differ from those pursuing the secular form of life discussed in Chap. IV. In order to indicate its special esteem for the religious life, the Council wished to devote to it a special chapter of the Constitution on the Church. Some aspects of the religious state are discussed more fully in the Decree on the Appropriate Renewal of the Religious Life.

208. In this compact paragraph, the Constitution explains in what sense the three counsels of poverty, chastity, and obedience deserve to be called "evangelical." The religious life, considered as a stable form of existence, was not directly established by Christ Himself, but it has become a permanent feature of the Church by a legitimate and necessary development. In connection with the variety of forms which the religious life has taken in the course of history, the Council distinguishes between the solitary life and life in community, pointing out some advantages of the latter.

209. *Cf. H. Rosweyde, "Vitae patrum" (Antwerp, 1628); "Apophthegmata patrum": PG 65; Palladius, "Historia lausiaca": PG 34, 995 ff. (ed. C. Butler, Cambridge, 1898 [1904]); the apostolic constitution of Pius XI, "Umbratilem," July 8, 1924: AAS 16 (1924), pp. 386-7; and Pius XII, allocution "Nous sommes heureux," Apr. 11, 1958: AAS 50 (1958), p. 283.*

greater stability in their way of life, a proven method of acquiring perfection, fraternal association in the militia of Christ, and liberty strengthened by obedience. Thus these religious can securely fulfill and faithfully observe their religious profession, and rejoicing in spirit make progress on the road of charity.[210]

From the point of view of the divine and hierarchical structure of the Church, the religious state of life is not an intermediate one between the clerical and lay states. Rather, the faithful of Christ are called by God from both these latter states of life so that they may enjoy this particular gift in the life of the Church and thus each in his own way can forward the saving mission of the Church.[211]

44. The faithful of Christ can bind themselves to the three previously mentioned counsels either by vows, or by other sacred bonds which are like vows in their purpose.[212] Through such a bond a person is totally dedicated to God by an act of supreme love, and is committed to the honor and service of God under a new and special title.

It is true that through baptism he has died to sin and has been consecrated to God. However, in order to derive more abundant fruit from this baptismal grace, he intends, by the profession of the evangelical counsels in the Church, to free himself from those obstacles which might draw him away from the fervor of charity and the perfection of divine worship. Thus he is more intimately consecrated to divine service.[213] This consecration gains in perfection since by virtue of firmer and steadier bonds it serves as a better symbol of the unbreakable link between Christ and His Spouse, the Church.

By the charity to which they lead,[214] the evangelical counsels join their followers to the Church and her mystery

---

210. *Paul VI, allocution "Magno Gaudio," May 23, 1964: AAS 56 (1964), p. 566.*

211. *Cf. Code of Canon Law, cc. 487 and 488, 4; Pius XII, allocution "Annus sacer," Dec. 8, 1950: AAS 43 (1951), pp. 27 f.; and Pius XII, apostolic constitution "Provida Mater," Feb. 2, 1947: AAS 39 (1947), pp. 120 ff.*

212. To constitute a person a "religious" in the wide sense here used, it is sufficient that he embrace an approved form of life in which he is permanently bound to live according to the three "evangelical counsels," whether the bond takes the form of vows or some other sacred commitment (such as a promise or oath). See the various categories enumerated in the Decree on the Appropriate Renewal of the Religious Life.

213. *Paul VI, as cited in footnote 210, p. 567.*

214. *Cf. St. Thomas, "Summa Theol.," 2-2, q. 184, a. 3 and q. 188, a. 2;*

in a special way.[215] Since this is so, the spiritual life of these followers should be devoted to the welfare of the whole Church. Thence arises their duty of working to implant and strengthen the kingdom of Christ in souls and to extend that kingdom to every land. This duty is to be discharged to the extent of their capacities and in keeping with the form of their proper vocation. The chosen means may be prayer or active undertakings. It is for this reason that the Church preserves and fosters the special character of her various religious communities.

The profession of the evangelical counsels, then, appears as a sign which can and ought to attract all the members of the Church to an effective and prompt fulfillment of the duties of their Christian vocation. The People of God has no lasting city here below, but looks forward to one which is to come. This being so, the religious state by giving its members greater freedom from earthly cares more adequately manifests to all believers the presence of heavenly goods already possessed here below.

Furthermore, it not only witnesses to the fact of a new and eternal life acquired by the redemption of Christ. It foretells the resurrected state and the glory of the heavenly kingdom. Christ also proposed to His disciples that form of life which He, as the Son of God, accepted in entering this world to do the will of the Father. In the Church this same state of life is imitated with particular accuracy and perpetually exemplified. The religious state reveals in a unique way that the kingdom of God and its overmastering necessities are superior to all earthly considerations. Finally, to all men it shows wonderfully at work within the Church the surpassing greatness of the force of Christ the King and the boundless power of the Holy Spirit.

Thus, although the religious state constituted by the profession of the evangelical counsels does not belong to the hierarchical structure of the Church, nevertheless it belongs inseparably to her life and holiness.

45. Since it is the duty of the hierarchy of the Church to

and St. Bonaventure, Opusc. XI, "Apologia pauperum," c. 3, 3: ed. Opera, Quaracchi, t. 8, 1898, p. 245 a.

215. This document, because its subject matter is the Church, takes occasion to stress the way in which the religious profession unites a person to the Church, thus offsetting an excessively individualistic theology of the religious life, which has sometimes prevailed in the past. The way in which the religious life contributes to the life of the Church by giving testimony to the kingdom of heaven was already mentioned earlier in Art. 31.

nourish the People of God and lead them to the choicest pastures (cf. Ezek. 34:14), it devolves on the same hierarchy to govern with wise legislation[216] the practice of the evangelical counsels. For by that practice is uniquely fostered the perfection of love for God and neighbor.

Submissively following the promptings of the Holy Spirit, the hierarchy also endorses rules formulated by eminent men and women, and authentically approves later modifications. Moreover, by its watchful and shielding authority, the hierarchy keeps close to communities established far and wide for the upbuilding of Christ's body, so that they can grow and flourish in accord with the spirit of their founders.

Any institute of perfection and its individual members can be removed from the jurisdiction of the local Ordinaries by the Supreme Pontiff and subjected to himself alone.[217] This is possible by virtue of his primacy over the entire Church. He does so in order to provide more adequately for the necessities of the entire flock of the Lord and in consideration of the common good.[218] In like manner, these communities can be left or committed to the charge of their proper patriarchical authorities. In fulfilling their duty toward the Church in accord with the special form of their life, the members of these communities should show toward bishops the reverence and obedience required by canonical laws. For bishops possess pastoral authority over individual churches, and apostolic labor demands unity and harmony.[219]

By her approval the Church not only raises the religious profession to the dignity of a canonical state. By the liturgical setting of that profession she also manifests that it is a state consecrated to God. The Church herself, by the au-

---

216. Cf. Vatican Council I, Schema "De Ecclesia Christi," c. XV and Annotation 48: Mansi, 51, 549 f. and 619 f.; Leo XIII, epistle "Au milieu des consolations," Dec. 23, 1900: Acta Sanctae Sedis 33 (1900-1), p. 361; and Pius XII, apostolic constitution "Provida Mater," as cited in footnote 211, pp. 114 f.

217. To correct the impression that papal exemption withdraws the members of an exempt order from obedience to the hierarchy, the Constitution stresses that they are directly subject to the Pope himself; in addition they are, in certain respects further specified in the Decree on the Bishops' Pastoral Office in the Church, subject to the local Ordinary. Exemption is a privilege granted for the sake of more effective service in the interests of the universal Church.

218. Cf. Leo XIII, constitution "Romanos Pontifices," May 8, 1881: Acta Sanctae Sedis 13 (1880-1), p. 483; and Pius XII, allocution "Annus Sacer," Dec. 8, 1950: AAS 43 (1951), pp. 28 f.

219. Pius XII, allocution "Annus Sacer," as cited in the preceding footnote, p. 28; the same Pontiff's apostolic constitution "Sedes Sapientiae," May 31, 1956: AAS 48 (1956), p. 355; and the allocution of Paul VI, as cited in footnote 210, pp. 570-1.

thority given to her by God, accepts the vows of those professing them. By her public prayer she begs aid and grace from God for them. She commends them to God, imparts a spiritual blessing to them, and accompanies their self-offering with the Eucharistic sacrifice.

46. Religious should carefully consider that through them, to believers and non-believers alike, the Church truly wishes to give an increasingly clearer revelation of Christ.[220] Through them Christ should be shown contemplating on the mountain, announcing God's kingdom to the multitude, healing the sick and the maimed, turning sinners to wholesome fruit, blessing children, doing good to all, and always obeying the will of the Father who sent Him.[221]

Finally, everyone should realize that the profession of the evangelical counsels, though entailing the renunciation of certain values which undoubtedly merit high esteem, does not detract from a genuine development of the human person.[222] Rather by its very nature it is most beneficial to that development. For the counsels, voluntarily undertaken according to each one's personal vocation, contribute greatly to purification of heart and spiritual liberty. They continually kindle the fervor of charity. As the example of so many saintly founders shows, the counsels are especially able to pattern the Christian man after that manner of virginal and humble life which Christ the Lord elected for Himself, and which His Virgin Mother also chose.

Let no one think that by their consecration religious have become strangers to their fellow men or useless citizens of this earthly city. For even though in some instances religious do not directly mingle with their contemporaries, yet in a more profound sense these same religious are united with them in the heart of Christ and cooperate with them spiritually. In this way the work of building up the earthly city can always have its foundation in the Lord and can tend toward Him. Otherwise, those who build this city will perhaps have labored in vain.[223]

220. The true meaning of the religious life cannot be grasped except in relation to Christ, whose ministries the religious seek to mirror and to perpetuate.
221. Cf. Pius XII, encyclical "Mystici Corporis," June 29, 1943: AAS 35 (1943), pp. 214 f.
222. The Council here replies to two charges commonly directed against the religious life—that it impedes the full development of personality and that it cuts one off from effectively helping his fellow man.
223. Cf. Pius XII, allocution "Annus Sacer," as cited in footnote 218, p. 30;

In summary, therefore, this sacred Synod encourages and praises the men and women, brothers and sisters, who in monasteries, or in schools and hospitals, or on the missions, adorn the Bride of Christ. They do so by their unswerving and humble loyalty to their chosen consecration, while rendering to all men generous services of every variety.

47. Let all who have been called to the profession of the vows take painstaking care to persevere and excel increasingly in the vocation to which God has summoned them. Let their purpose be a more vigorous flowering of the Church's holiness and the greater glory of the one and undivided Trinity, which in Christ and through Christ is the fountain and the wellspring of all holiness.

CHAPTER VII

THE ESCHATOLOGICAL NATURE OF THE PILGRIM CHURCH AND HER UNION WITH THE HEAVENLY CHURCH[224]

48. The Church, to which we are all called in Christ Jesus, and in which we acquire sanctity through the grace of God, will attain her full perfection only in the glory of heaven. Then will come the time of the restoration of all things (Acts 3:21).[225] Then the human race as well as the entire world,

---

and the same Pontiff's allocution "Sous la maternelle protection," Dec. 9, 1957: AAS 50 (1958), pp. 39 f.

224. This chapter, one of the most original and inspiring in the entire Constitution, sets the Church in perspective by relating it to the "future and abiding city" already referred to in Art. 9 above. Pope John XXIII insisted on the inclusion of a chapter on this subject. The term "eschatological" in the title means "pertaining to the last times" when history will draw to a close and God's final kingdom will be inaugurated.

225. This article, richly studded with quotations from the New Testament, shows that the eschatological consummation is not simply a gift for which we wait but, in some manner, a present reality. Christ, who has already entered into His Father's glory, sustains the Church by His Holy Spirit, whose workings in the Church are signs and pledges of eternal life.

which is intimately related to man and achieves its purpose through him, will be perfectly re-established in Christ (cf. Eph. 1:10; Col. 1:20; 2 Pet. 3:10-13).

Christ, having been lifted up from the earth, is drawing all men to Himself (Jn. 12:32, Greek text). Rising from the dead (cf. Rom. 6:9), He sent His life-giving Spirit upon His disciples and through this Spirit has established His body, the Church, as the universal sacrament of salvation. Sitting at the right hand of the Father, He is continually active in the world, leading men to the Church, and through her joining them more closely to Himself and making them partakers of His glorious life by nourishing them with His own body and blood.

Therefore, the promised restoration which we are awaiting has already begun in Christ, is carried forward in the mission of the Holy Spirit, and through Him continues in the Church. There we learn through faith the meaning, too, of our temporal life, as we perform, with hope of good things to come, the task committed to us in this world by the Father, and work out our salvation (cf. Phil. 2:12).

The final age of the world has already come upon us (cf. 1 Cor. 10:11). The renovation of the world has been irrevocably decreed and in this age is already anticipated in some real way. For even now on this earth the Church is marked with a genuine though imperfect holiness. However, until there is a new heaven and a new earth where justice dwells (cf. 2 Pet. 3:13), the pilgrim Church in her sacraments and institutions, which pertain to this present time, takes on the appearance of this passing world. She herself dwells among creatures who groan and travail in pain until now and await the revelation of the sons of God (cf. Rom. 8:19-22).

Joined with Christ in the Church and signed with the Holy Spirit "who is the pledge of our inheritance" (Eph. 1:14), we are truly called sons of God and such we are (cf. 1 Jn. 3:1). But we have not yet appeared with Christ in the state of glory (cf. Col. 3:4), in which we shall be like to God, since we shall see Him as He is (cf. 1 Jn. 3:2). Therefore "while we are in the body, we are exiled from the Lord" (2 Cor. 5:6), and having the first fruits of the Spirit we groan within ourselves (cf. Rom. 8:23) and desire to be with Christ (cf. Phil. 1:23). A common love urges us to live more for Him, who died for us and rose again (cf. 2 Cor. 5:15). We strive therefore to please the Lord in all things (cf. 2 Cor.

5:9). We put on the armor of God that we may be able to stand against the wiles of the devil and resist on the evil day (cf. Eph. 6:11-13).

Since we know not the day nor the hour, on our Lord's advice we must constantly stand guard. Thus when we have finished the one and only course of our earthly life (cf. Heb. 9:27) we may merit to enter into the marriage feast with Him and to be numbered among the blessed (cf. Mt. 25:31-46). Thus we may not be commanded to go into eternal fire (cf. Mt. 25:41) like the wicked and slothful servant (cf. Mt. 25:26), into the exterior darkness where "there will be the weeping and the gnashing of teeth" (Mt. 22:13; 25:30). For before we reign with the glorious Christ, all of us will be made manifest "before the tribunal of Christ, so that each one may receive what he has won through the body, according to his works, whether good or evil" (2 Cor. 5:10). At the end of the world, "they who have done good shall come forth unto resurrection of life; but who have done evil unto resurrection of judgment" (Jn. 5:29; cf. Mt. 25:46).

We reckon therefore that "the sufferings of the present time are not worthy to be compared with the glory to come that will be revealed in us" (Rom. 8:18; cf. 2 Tim. 2:11-12). Strong in faith we look for "the blessed hope and glorious coming of our great God and Savior, Jesus Christ" (Tit. 2:13) "who will refashion the body of our lowliness, conforming it to the body of his glory" (Phil. 3:21) and who will come "to be glorified in his saints, and to be marveled at in all those who have believed" (2 Th. 1:10).

49. When the Lord comes in His majesty, and all the angels with Him (cf. Mt. 25:31), death will be destroyed and all things will be subject to Him (cf. 1 Cor. 15:26-27). Meanwhile some of His disciples are exiles on earth.[226] Some have finished with this life and are being purified. Others are in glory, beholding "clearly God Himself triune and one, as He is."[227]

But in various ways and degrees we all partake in the same love for God and neighbor, and all sing the same hymn of

---

226. According to a venerable theological tradition, the Church exists in three conditions: the pilgrim Church on earth, the suffering Church in purgatory, and the triumphant Church in heaven. In faith the Christian should recognize his solidarity with those who, as the Canon of the Roman Mass expresses it, "have gone before us with the sign of faith and sleep in the sleep of peace."

227. *Council of Florence, "Decretum pro Graecis": Denz. 693 (1305).*

glory to our God. For all who belong to Christ, having His Spirit, form one Church and cleave together in Him (cf. Eph. 4:16). Therefore the union of the wayfarers with the brethren who have gone to sleep in the peace of Christ is not in the least interrupted. On the contrary, according to the perennial faith of the Church, it is strengthened through the exchanging of spiritual goods.[228]

For by reason of the fact that those in heaven are more closely united with Christ, they establish the whole Church more firmly in holiness, lend nobility to the worship which the Church offers on earth to God, and in many ways contribute to its greater upbuilding (cf. 1 Cor. 12:12-27).[229] For after they have been received into their heavenly home and are present to the Lord (cf. 2 Cor. 5:8), through Him and with Him and in Him, they do not cease to intercede[230] with the Father for us. Rather, they show forth the merits which they won on earth through the one Mediator between God and man, Christ Jesus (cf. 1 Tim. 2:5). There they served God in all things and filled up in their flesh whatever was lacking of the sufferings of Christ on behalf of His body which is the Church (cf. Col. 1:24).[231] Thus by their brotherly interest our weakness is very greatly strengthened.

50. Very much aware of the bonds linking the whole Mystical Body of Jesus Christ, the pilgrim Church from the very first ages of the Christian religion has cultivated with great piety the memory of the dead.[232] Because it is "a holy and wholesome thought to pray for the dead that they may be loosed from sins" (2 Mach. 12:46), she has also offered prayers for them.[233]

The Church has always believed that the apostles, and Christ's martyrs who had given the supreme witness of faith

228. *Besides the older documents against any evoking of the spirits, from the time of Alexander IV (Sept. 27, 1258), see the encyclical of the Holy Office, "De magnetismi abusu," Aug. 4, 1856: Acta Sanctae Sedis 1 (1865), pp. 177-8, (Denz. 1653-4 2823-5); and the response of the Holy Office, Apr. 24, 1917: AAS 9 (1917), p. 268 (Denz. 2182 [3642]).*
229. *For a synthetic presentation of this Pauline doctrine, see the encyclical of Pius XII, "Mystici Corporis": AAS 35 (1943), p. 200 and passim.*
230. *Cf., among others, St. Augustine, "Enarr. in Ps.," 85, 24: PL 37, 1099; St. Jerome, "Liber contra Vigilantium," 6: PL 23, 344; St. Thomas, "In 4 Sent.," d. 45, q. 3, a. 2; and St. Bonaventure, "In 4 Sent.," d. 45, a. 3, q. 2; etc.*
231. *Cf. Pius XII, encyclical "Mystici Corporis": AAS 35 (1943), p. 245.*
232. *Cf. many inscriptions in the Roman catacombs.*
233. *Prayers for the dead and the veneration of the saints take on an added meaning when viewed not simply individualistically but, as here, in an ecclesial context.*

and charity by the shedding of their blood, are quite closely joined with us in Christ. She has always venerated them with special devotion, together with the Blessed Virgin Mary and the holy angels.[234] The Church too has devoutly implored the aid of their intercession. To these were soon added those who had imitated Christ's virginity and poverty more exactly,[235] and finally others whom the outstanding practice of the Christian virtues[236] and the divine charisms recommended to the pious devotion and imitation of the faithful.[237]

For when we look at the lives of those who have faithfully followed Christ, we are inspired with a new reason for seeking the city which is to come (Heb. 13:14; 11:10). At the same time we are shown a most safe path by which, among the vicissitudes of this world and in keeping with the state in life and condition proper to each of us, we will be able to arrive at perfect union with Christ, that is, holiness.[238] In the lives of those who shared in our humanity and yet were transformed into especially successful images of Christ (cf. 2 Cor. 3:18), God vividly manifests to men His presence and His face.[239] He speaks to us in them, and gives us a sign of His kingdom,[240] to which we are powerfully drawn, surrounded as we are by so many witnesses (cf. Heb. 12:1), and having such an argument for the truth of the gospel.

Now, it is not only by the title of example that we cherish the memory of those in heaven. We do so still more in order that the union of the whole Church may be strengthened in the Spirit by the practice of fraternal charity (cf. Eph. 4:1-6). For just as Christian communion among wayfarers brings us closer to Christ, so our companionship with the saints joins

234. Cf. Gelasius I, the decretal "De libris recipiendis," 3: PL 59, 160 (Denz. 165 [353]).
235. Cf. St. Methodius, "Symposium," VII, 3: GCS (Bonwetsch), p. 74.
236. Benedict XV, "Decretum approbationis virtutum in causa beatificationis et canonizationis Servi Dei Ioannis Nepomuceni Neumann": AAS 14 (1922), p. 23; a number of the allocutions of Pius XI on the saints as collected in "Inviti all'eroismo, Discorsi . . . ," 1-3, Rome, 1941-2, passim; and Pius XII, "Discorsi e radiomessaggi," 10 (1949), pp. 37-43.
237. Cf. Pius XII, encyclical "Mediator Dei": AAS 39 (1947), p. 581.
238. Cf. Heb. 13:7; Sir. 44-50; Heb. 11:3-40. Cf. Pius XII, encyclical "Mediator Dei": AAS 39 (1947), pp. 582-3.
239. The manner in which God continues to give signs of His power and grace through the example of the saints in every generation makes it possible to say that, without prejudice to the fullness of revelation which has been given once and for all in Christ, God continues to reveal Himself and to speak of men through the Church.
240. Cf. Vatican Council I, the constitution "De fide catholics," c. 3: Denz. 1794 (3013).

us to Christ, from whom as from their fountain and head issue every grace and the life of God's People itself.[241]

It is supremely fitting, therefore, that we love those friends and fellow heirs of Jesus Christ, who are also our brothers and extraordinary benefactors, that we render due thanks to God for them[242] and "suppliantly invoke them and have recourse to their prayers, their power and help in obtaining benefits from God through His Son, Jesus Christ, our Lord, who is our sole Redeemer and Savior." [243] For by its very nature every genuine testimony of love which we show to those in heaven tends toward and terminates in Christ,[244] who is the "crown of all saints." [245] Through Him it tends toward and terminates in God, who is wonderful in His saints and is magnified in them.[246]

Our union with the Church in heaven is put into effect in its noblest manner when with common rejoicing we celebrate together the praise of the divine Majesty.[247] Then all those from every tribe and tongue and people and nation (cf. Apoc. 5:9) who have been redeemed by the blood of Christ and gathered together into one Church, with one song of praise magnify the one and triune God. Such is especially the case in the sacred liturgy, where the power of the Holy Spirit acts upon us through sacramental signs. Celebrating the Eucharistic sacrifice, therefore, we are most closely united to the worshiping Church in heaven as we join with and venerate the memory first of all of the glorious ever-Virgin Mary, of Blessed Joseph and the blessed apostles and martyrs, and of all the saints.[248]

51. This most sacred Synod accepts with great devotion the venerable faith of our ancestors regarding this vital fellowship with our brethren who are in heavenly glory or who are

241. *Cf. Pius XII, encyclical "Mystici Corporis": AAS 35 (1943), p. 216.*

242. *With regard to the giving of thanks to saints, see E. Diehl, "Inscriptiones latinae christianae veteres," I (Berlin, 1925), nn. 2008, 2382, and passim.*

243. *Council of Trent, Session 25, "De invocatione . . . sanctorum": Denz. 984 (1821).*

244. Because some have imagined that the veneration and invocation of the saints, as practiced by Catholics, necessarily interferes with the relationship which the Christian should have to Christ, the Council here points out that a properly ordered devotion to the saints should cement more closely the believer's relationship to Christ. This point is reaffirmed with reference to the entire Trinity in Art. 51 below.

245. *Roman Breviary, Invitatory Antiphon of the Feast of All Saints.*

246. *Cf. 2 Th. 1:10.*

247. *Vatican Council II, "Constitution on the Sacred Liturgy," Chap. 5, Art. 104.*

248. *Canon of the Roman Mass.*

still being purified after death. It proposes again[249] the decrees of the Second Council of Nicea,[250] the Council of Florence,[251] and the Council of Trent.[252] And at the same time, as part of its own pastoral solicitude, this Synod urges all concerned to work hard to prevent or correct any abuses, excesses, or defects which may have crept in here and there, and to restore all things to a more ample praise of Christ and of God.

Let the faithful be taught, therefore, that the authentic cult of the saints consists not so much in the multiplying of external acts, but rather in the intensity of our active love. By such love, for our own greater good and that of the Church, we seek from the saints "example in their way of life, fellowship in their communion, and aid by their intercession."[253] At the same time, let the people be instructed that our communion with those in heaven, provided that it is understood in the more adequate light of faith, in no way weakens, but conversely, more thoroughly enriches the supreme worship we give to God the Father, through Christ, in the Spirit.[254]

For as long as all of us, who are sons of God and comprise one family in Christ (cf. Heb. 3:6), remain in communion with one another in mutual charity and in one praise of the most Holy Trinity, we are responding to the deepest vocation of the Church and partaking in a foretaste of the liturgy of consummate glory.[255] For when Christ shall appear and the glorious resurrection of the dead takes place, the splendor of God will brighten the heavenly city and the Lamb will be the lamp thereof (cf. Apoc. 21:24). Then in the supreme happiness of charity the whole Church of the

---

249. The Councils of Nicaea II (787) and Florence (1439) are ecumenically important because they express points of agreement between the Greek and Latin Churches regarding the invocation of saints, the veneration of sacred images, and suffrages for the souls in Purgatory. The Council of Trent (1549-63) treated these questions once more in the context of the Protestant Reformation.
250. *Council of Nicaea II, Act. VII:* Denz. 302 (600).
251. *Council of Florence, "Decretum pro Graecis":* Denz. 693 (1304).
252. *Council of Trent, Session 25, "De invocatione, veneratione, et reliquiis sanctorum et sacris imaginibus":* Denz. 984-8 (1821-4); *Session 25, "Decretum de Purgatorio":* Denz. 983 (1820); *and Session 6, "Decretum de iustificatione,"* c. 30: Denz. 840 (1580).
253. *From the Preface granted for use in various dioceses.*
254. *Cf. St. Peter Canisius, "Catechismus maior seu Summa doctrinae christianae,"* c. III (ed. crit. F. Streicher), par. I, pp. 15-6, n. 44 and pp. 100-1, n. 49.
255. *Cf. Vatican Council II, "Constitution on the Sacred Liturgy,"* Chap. 1, Art. 8.

saints will adore God and "the Lamb who was slain" (Apoc. 5:12), proclaiming with one voice: "To him who sits upon the throne, and to the Lamb, blessing and honor and glory and dominion, forever and ever" (Apoc. 5:13-14).

CHAPTER VIII

THE ROLE OF THE BLESSED VIRGIN MARY, MOTHER OF GOD, IN THE MYSTERY OF CHRIST AND THE CHURCH[256]

I. Preface[257]

52. Wishing in His supreme goodness and wisdom to effect the redemption of the world, "when the fullness of time came, God sent his Son, born of a woman, . . . that we might receive the adoption of sons" (Gal. 4:4-5). "He for us men, and for our salvation, came down from heaven, and was incarnate by the Holy Spirit from the Virgin Mary."[258] This divine mystery of salvation is revealed to us and continued in the Church, which the Lord established as His own body. In this Church, adhering to Christ the Head and having

256. This eighth chapter was appended to the Constitution on the Church as a result of a vote in the Council on Oct. 29, 1963, in which the Fathers, by a small majority, decided not to issue a separate document on the Blessed Virgin, as had originally been planned. The present chapter, while it treats of Mary's relationship to the Church, speaks also of her relation to Christ, as indicated in the title of the chapter. The entire text represents a skillful and prudent compromise between two tendencies in modern Catholic theology, one of which would emphasize Mary's unique connection with Christ the Redeemer; the other, her close connection with the Church and all the redeemed.

257. This is the only chapter with official headings; and the headings clearly indicate the structure.

258. *The Creed in the Roman Mass: the Constantinopolitan creed: Mansi, 3, 566. Cf. Council of Ephesus: Mansi, 4, 1130 (as well as Mansi, 2, 665, and 4, 1071); the Council of Chalcedon: Mansi, 7, III-6; and the Council of Constantinople II: Mansi, 9, 375-96.*

communion with all His saints, the faithful must also venerate the memory "above all of the glorious and perpetual Virgin Mary, Mother of our God and Lord Jesus Christ."[259]

53. At the message of the angel, the Virgin Mary received the Word of God in her heart and in her body, and gave Life to the world. Hence she is acknowledged and honored as being truly the Mother of God and Mother of the Redeemer. Redeemed in an especially sublime manner by reason of the merits of her Son, and united to Him by a close and indissoluble tie, she is endowed with the supreme office and dignity of being the Mother of the Son of God.[260] As a result she is also the favorite daughter of the Father and the temple of the Holy Spirit. Because of this gift of sublime grace she far surpasses all other creatures, both in heaven and on earth.

At the same time, however, because she belongs to the offspring of Adam she is one with all human beings in their need for salvation. Indeed she is "clearly the mother of the members of Christ . . . since she cooperated out of love so that there might be born in the Church the faithful, who are members of Christ their Head."[261] Therefore she is also hailed as a pre-eminent and altogether singular member of the Church, and as the Church's model and excellent exemplar in faith and charity. Taught by the Holy Spirit, the Catholic Church honors her with filial affection and piety as a most beloved mother.[262]

54. Therefore, as it clarifies Catholic teaching concerning the Church, in which the divine Redeemer works salvation, this sacred Synod intends to describe with diligence the role of the Blessed Virgin in the mystery of the Incarnate Word and the Mystical Body. It also wishes to describe the duties of redeemed mankind toward the Mother of God, who is mother of Christ and mother of men, particularly of the faithful.[263]

The Synod does not, however, have it in mind to give a

259. *Canon of the Roman Mass.*
260. The foundation of all Mary's other privileges is her dignity as Mother of the Son of God.
261. *St. Augustine, "De s. virginitate," 6: PL 40, 399.*
262. The Council comes very close here to calling Mary "Mother of the Church." This title, while not bestowed by the Council itself, was actually conferred by Paul VI in his closing allocution at the end of the third session, Nov. 21, 1964.
263. This paragraph succinctly states the purposes of the whole chapter.

complete doctrine on Mary, nor does it wish to decide those questions which have not yet been fully illuminated by the work of theologians. Those opinions therefore may be lawfully retained which are freely propounded by schools of Catholic thought concerning her who occupies a place in the Church which is the highest after Christ and yet very close to us.[264]

II. The Role of the Blessed Virgin in the Economy of Salvation

55. The sacred Scriptures of both the Old and the New Testament, as well as ancient tradition, show the role of the Mother of the Savior in the economy of salvation in an ever clearer light and propose it as something to be probed into.[265] The books of the Old Testament recount the period of salvation history during which the coming of Christ into the world was slowly prepared for. These earliest documents, as they are read in the Church and are understood in the light of a further and full revelation, bring the figure of the woman, Mother of the Redeemer, into a gradually sharper focus.

When looked at in this way, she is already prophetically foreshadowed in that victory over the serpent which was promised to our first parents after their fall into sin (cf. Gen. 3:15). Likewise she is the Virgin who is to conceive and bear a son, whose name will be called Emmanuel (cf. Is. 7:14; Mic. 5:2-3; Mt. 1:22-23). She stands out among the poor and humble of the Lord, who confidently await and receive salvation from Him. With her, the exalted Daughter of Sion, and after a long expectation of the promise, the times were at length fulfilled and the new dispensation established. All this occurred when the Son of God took a human nature from her, that He might in the mysteries of His flesh free man from sin.

56. The Father of mercies willed that the consent of the predestined mother should precede the Incarnation, so that

---

264. *Cf. Paul VI, allocution, the Council, Dec. 4, 1963: AAS 56 (1964), p. 37.*
265. The first sentence gives the topic of the next five articles (55-59), which summarize, in language generally close to that of the Bible itself, Mary's role in the economy of salvation. Throughout this section her proximity to Christ is strongly emphasized.

just as a woman contributed to death, so also a woman should contribute to life. This contrast was verified in outstanding fashion by the Mother of Jesus. She gave to the world that very Life which renews all things, and she was enriched by God with gifts befitting such a role.

It is no wonder, then, that the usage prevailed among the holy Fathers whereby they called the mother of God entirely holy and free from all stain of sin, fashioned by the Holy Spirit into a kind of new substance and new creature.[266] Adorned from the first instant of her conception with the splendors of an entirely unique holiness, the Virgin of Nazareth is, on God's command, greeted by an angel messenger as "full of grace" (cf. Lk. 1:28). To the heavenly messenger she replies: "Behold the handmaid of the Lord; be it done to me according to thy word" (Lk. 1:38).

By thus consenting to the divine utterance, Mary, a daughter of Adam, became the mother of Jesus. Embracing God's saving will with a full heart and impeded by no sin, she devoted herself totally as a handmaid of the Lord to the person and work of her Son. In subordination to Him and along with Him, by the grace of almighty God she served the mystery of redemption.

Rightly therefore the holy Fathers see her as used by God not merely in a passive way, but as cooperating in the work of human salvation through free faith and obedience. For, as St. Irenaeus says, she, "being obedient, became the cause of salvation for herself and for the whole human race."[267] Hence in their preaching not a few of the early Fathers gladly assert with him: "The knot of Eve's disobedience was untied by Mary's obedience. What the virgin Eve bound through her unbelief, Mary loosened by her faith."[268] Comparing Mary with Eve, they call her "the mother of the living,"[269] and still more often they say: "death through Eve, life through Mary."[270]

266. *Cf. St. Germanus of Constantinople, "Hom. in Annunt. Deiparae": PG 98, 328 A and his "Hom. in Dorm.," 2: PG 98, 357; St. Anastasius of Antioch, "Serm. 2 de Annunt.," 2 PG 89, 1377 AB and his "Serm. 3 de Annunt.," 2 PG 89, 1388 C; St. Andrew of Crete, "Can. in B.V. Nat.," 4: PG 97, 1321 B and his "In B.V. Nat.," 1: PG 97, 812 A, as well as his "Hom. in dorm.," 1: PG 97, 1068 C; and St. Sophronius, "Or. 2 in Annunt.," 18: PG 87 (3), 3237 BD.*
267. *St. Irenaeus, "Adv. haer.," III, 22, 4: PG 7, 959, A (Harvey, 2, 123).*
268. *St. Irenaeus, as cited in the preceding footnote (Harvey, 2, 124).*
269. *St. Epiphanius, "Haer.," 78, 18: PG 42, 728 CD-729 AB.*
270. *St. Jerome, "Epist.," 22, 21: PL 22, 408. Cf. St. Augustine, "Serm.," 51, 2, 3: PL 38, 335 and his "Serm." 232, 2: PL 38, 1108; St. Cyril of Jerusalem, "Catech.," 12, 15: PG 33, 741 AB; St. John Chrysostom, "In*

57. This union of the Mother with the Son in the work of salvation was manifested from the time of Christ's virginal conception up to His death. It is shown first of all when Mary, arising in haste to go to visit Elizabeth, was greeted by her as blessed because of her belief in the promise of salvation, while the precursor leaped with joy in the womb of his mother (cf. Lk. 1:41-45). This association was shown also at the birth of our Lord, who did not diminish His mother's virginal integrity but sanctified it,[271] when the Mother of God joyfully showed her first-born Son to the shepherds and Magi.

When she presented Him to the Lord in the temple, making the offering of the poor, she heard Simeon foretelling at the same time that her Son would be a sign of contradiction and that a sword would pierce the mother's soul, that out of many hearts thoughts might be revealed (cf. Lk. 2:34-35). When the Child Jesus was lost and they had sought Him sorrowing, His parents found Him in the temple, taken up with the things which were His Father's business. They did not understand the reply of the Son. But His Mother, to be sure, kept all these things to be pondered over in her heart (cf. Lk. 2:41-51).

58. In the public life of Jesus, Mary made significant appearances. This was so even at the very beginning, when she was moved by pity at the marriage feast of Cana, and her intercession brought about the beginning of miracles by Jesus the Messiah (cf. Jn. 2: 1-11). In the course of her Son's preaching she received His praise when, in extolling a kingdom beyond the calculations and bonds of flesh and blood, He declared blessed (cf. Mk. 3:35 par.; Lk. 11:27-28) those who heard and kept the Word of God, as she was faithfully doing (cf. Lk. 2:19, 51).

Thus the Blessed Virgin advanced in her pilgrimage of faith, and loyally persevered in her union with her Son unto the cross. There she stood, in keeping with the divine plan (cf. Jn. 19:25), suffering grievously with her only-begotten Son. There she united herself with a maternal heart to His sacrifice, and lovingly consented to the immolation of this

Ps.," 44, 7: PG 55, 193; and St. John of Damascus, "Hom. 2 in dorm. B.M.V.," 3: PG 96, 728.
271. Cf. Lateran Council of the year 649, can. 3: Mansi, 10, 1151; St. Leo the Great, "Epist. ad Flav.": PL 54, 759; Council of Chalcedon: Mansi, 7, 462; and St. Ambrose, "De inst. virg.": PL 16, 320.

Victim which she herself had brought forth. Finally, the same Christ Jesus dying on the cross gave her as a mother to His disciple. This He did when He said: "Woman, behold thy son" (Jn. 19:26-27).[272]

59. But since it pleased God not to manifest solemnly the mystery of the salvation of the human race until He poured forth the Spirit promised by Christ, we see the apostles before the day of Pentecost "continuing with one mind in prayer with the women and Mary, the Mother of Jesus, and with his brethren" (Acts 1:14). We see Mary prayerfully imploring the gift of the Spirit, who had already overshadowed her in the Annunciation.

Finally, preserved free from all guilt of original sin,[273] the Immaculate Virgin was taken up body and soul into heavenly glory upon the completion of her earthly sojourn.[274] She was exalted by the Lord as Queen of all, in order that she might be the more thoroughly conformed to her Son, the Lord of lords (cf. Apoc. 19:16) and the conqueror of sin and death.[275]

III. The Blessed Virgin and the Church

60. We have but one Mediator, as we know from the words of the Apostle: "For there is one God, and one Mediator between God and men, himself man, Christ Jesus, who gave himself a ransom for all" (1 Tim. 2:5-6).[276] The maternal duty of Mary toward men in no way obscures or diminishes this unique mediation of Christ, but rather shows its power. For all the saving influences of the Blessed Virgin on men originate, not from some inner necessity, but from the divine

272. *Cf. Pius XII, encyclical "Mystici Corporis," June 29, 1943: AAS 35 (1943), pp. 247-8.*
273. *Cf. Pius IX, bull "Ineffabilis," Dec. 8, 1854: "Acta Pii IX," 1, I, p. 616; Denz. 1641 (2803).*
274. *Cf. Pius XII, apostolic constitution "Munificentissimus," Nov. 1, 1950: AAS 42 (1950), p. 770 (Denz. 2333 [3903]). Cf. St. John of Damascus, "Enc. in dorm. Dei genitricis," Hom. 1 and 3: PG 96, 721-61 especially 728 B; St. Germanus of Constantinople, "In S. Dei gen. dorm.," Serm. 1: PG 98 (6), 340-8 as well as his Serm. 3: PG 98 (6), 361; and St. Modestus of Jerusalem, "In dorm. SS. Deiparae": PG 86 (2), 3277-3312.*
275. *Cf. Pius XII, encyclical "Ad Caeli Reginam," Oct. 11, 1954: AAS 46 (1954), pp. 633-6 (Denz. 3913 ff.). Cf. St. Andrew of Crete, "Hom. 3 in dorm. SS. Deiparae": PG 97, 1089-1109; and St. John of Damascus, "De fide orth.," IV, 14: PG 94, 1153-61.*
276. The following six articles (60-65) stress the second facet of Mary's role, her solidarity with the redeemed.

pleasure. They flow forth from the superabundance of the merits of Christ, rest on His mediation, depend entirely on it, and draw all their power from it. In no way do they impede the immediate union of the faithful with Christ. Rather, they foster this union.

61. The Blessed Virgin was eternally predestined, in conjunction with the incarnation of the divine Word, to be the Mother of God. By decree of divine Providence, she served on earth as the loving mother of the divine Redeemer, an associate of unique nobility, and the Lord's humble handmaid. She conceived, brought forth, and nourished Christ. She presented Him to the Father in the temple, and was united with Him in suffering as He died on the cross. In an utterly singular way she cooperated by her obedience, faith, hope, and burning charity in the Savior's work of restoring supernatural life to souls. For this reason she is a mother to us in the order of grace.

62. This maternity of Mary in the order of grace began with the consent which she gave in faith at the Annunciation and which she sustained without wavering beneath the cross. This maternity will last without interruption until the eternal fulfillment of all the elect. For, taken up to heaven, she did not lay aside this saving role, but by her manifold acts of intercession continues to win for us gifts of eternal salvation.[277]

By her maternal charity, Mary cares for the brethren of her Son who still journey on earth surrounded by dangers and difficulties, until they are led to their happy fatherland. Therefore the Blessed Virgin is invoked by the Church under the titles of Advocate, Auxiliatrix, Adjutrix, and Mediatrix.[278] These, however, are to be so understood[279] that

---

277. Cf. Kleutgen, the revised text of "De mysterio Verbi incarnati," c. IV: Mansi, 53, 290. Cf. St. Andrew of Crete, "In nat. Mariae," Sermo 4: PG 97, 865 A; St. Germanus of Constantinople, "In annunt. Deiparae": PG 98, 321 BC and his "In dorm. Deiparae," III: PG 98, 361 D; and St. John of Damascus, "In dorm. B.V. Mariae," Hom. 1, 8: PG 96, 712 BC-712A.

278. Cf. Leo XIII, encyclical "Adiutricem populi," Sept. 5, 1895: Acta Sanctae Sedis 15 (1895-6), p. 303; St. Pius X, encyclical "Ad diem illum," Feb. 2, 1904: "Pii X Pontificis Maximi Acta," I, p. 154 (Denz. 1978 a [3370]), Pius XI, encyclical "Miserentissimus," May 8, 1928: AAS 20 (1928), p. 178; Pius XII, radio message, May 13, 1946: AAS 38 (1946), p. 266.

279. The Council applies to the Blessed Virgin the title of Mediatrix, but carefully explains this so as to remove any impression that it could detract from the uniqueness and sufficiency of Christ's position as Mediator (cf. 1 Tim. 2:5), already referred to in Chap. I (Art. 8).

they neither take away from nor add anything to the dignity and efficacy of Christ the one Mediator.[280]

For no creature could ever be classed with the Incarnate Word and Redeemer. But, just as the priesthood of Christ is shared in various ways both by sacred ministers and by the faithful, and as the one goodness of God is in reality communicated diversely to His creatures, so also the unique mediation of the Redeemer does not exclude but rather gives rise among creatures to a manifold cooperation which is but a sharing in this unique source.

The Church does not hesitate to profess this subordinate role of Mary. She experiences it continuously and commends it to the hearts of the faithful, so that encouraged by this maternal help they may more closely adhere to the Mediator and Redeemer.

63. Through the gift and role of divine maternity, Mary is united with her Son, the Redeemer, and with His singular graces and offices. By these, the Blessed Virgin is also intimately united with the Church. As St. Ambrose taught, the Mother of God is a model of the Church[281] in the matter of faith, charity, and perfect union with Christ.[282] For in the mystery of the Church, herself rightly called mother and virgin, the Blessed Virgin stands out in eminent and singular fashion as exemplar of both virginity and motherhood.[283]

For, believing and obeying, Mary brought forth on earth the Father's Son. This she did, knowing not man but overshadowed by the Holy Spirit. She was the new Eve, who put her absolute trust not in the ancient serpent but in God's messenger. The Son whom she brought forth is He whom God placed as the first-born among many brethren (cf. Rom. 8:29), namely, the faithful. In their birth and development she cooperates with a maternal love.

64. The Church, moreover, contemplating Mary's mysterious sanctity, imitating her charity, and faithfully fulfilling the Fa-

280. St. Ambrose, "Epist.," 63: PL 16, 1218.
281. The theme of Mary as type of the Church, developed in this and the following two articles, is central to the chapter and partly accounts for the decision of the Council to treat Mariology in the Constitution on the Church.
282. St. Ambrose, "Expos. Lc.," II, 7: PL 15, 1555.
283. Cf. pseudo-Peter Damian, "Serm.," 63: PL 144, 861 AB; Godfrey of St. Victor, "In nat. B.M.," Ms. Paris, Mazarine, 1002, fol. 109r; Gerhoh of Reichersberg, "De gloria et honore Filii hominis," 10: PL 194, 1105 AB.

ther's will, becomes herself a mother by accepting God's word in faith. For by her preaching and by baptism she brings forth to a new and immortal life children who are conceived of the Holy Spirit and born of God. The Church herself is a virgin, who keeps whole and pure the fidelity she has pledged to her Spouse. Imitating the Mother of her Lord, and by the power of the Holy Spirit, she preserves with virginal purity an integral faith, a firm hope, and a sincere charity.[284]

65. In the most holy Virgin the Church has already reached that perfection whereby she exists without spot or wrinkle (cf. Eph. 5:27). Yet the followers of Christ still strive to increase in holiness by conquering sin. And so they raise their eyes to Mary who shines forth to the whole community of the elect as a model of the virtues. Devotedly meditating on her and contemplating her in the light of the Word made man, the Church with reverence enters more intimately into the supreme mystery of the Incarnation and becomes ever increasingly like her Spouse.

For Mary figured profoundly in the history of salvation and in a certain way unites and mirrors within herself the central truths of the faith. Hence when she is being preached and venerated, she summons the faithful to her Son and His sacrifice, and to love for the Father. Seeking after the glory of Christ, the Church becomes more like her exalted model, and continually progresses in faith, hope, and charity, searching out and doing the will of God in all things. Hence the Church in her apostolic work also rightly looks to her who brought forth Christ, conceived by the Holy Spirit and born of the Virgin, so that through the Church Christ may be born and grow in the hearts of the faithful also. The Virgin Mary in her own life lived an example of that maternal love by which all should be fittingly animated who cooperate in the apostolic mission of the Church on behalf of the rebirth of men.

---

284. *St. Ambrose as cited in footnote 282, as well as his "Expos. Lc.," X, 24-5: PL 15, 1810; St. Augustine, "In Io.," tr. 13, 12: PL 35, 1499, and see also his "Serm.," 191, 2, 3: PL 38, 1010 as well as other of his texts. Cf. Venerable Bede, "In Lc. expos.," I, c. 2: PL 92, 330; and Isaac of Stella, "Serm.," 51: PL 194, 1863 A.*

IV. Devotion to the Blessed
Virgin in the Church

66. Mary was involved in the mysteries of Christ. As the most holy Mother of God she was, after her Son, exalted by divine grace above all angels and men. Hence the Church appropriately honors her with special reverence.[285] Indeed, from most ancient times the Blessed Virgin has been venerated under the title of "God-bearer." In all perils and needs, the faithful have fled prayerfully to her protection.[286] Especially after the Council of Ephesus the cult of the People of God toward Mary wonderfully increased in veneration and love, in invocation and imitation, according to her own prophetic words: "All generations shall call me blessed; because He who is mighty has done great things for me" (Lk. 1:48).

As it has always existed in the Church, this cult is altogether special. Still, it differs essentially from the cult of adoration which is offered to the Incarnate Word, as well as to the Father and Holy Spirit. Yet devotion to Mary is most favorable to this supreme cult. The Church has endorsed many forms of piety toward the Mother of God, provided that they were within the limits of sound and orthodox doctrine. These forms have varied according to the circumstances of time and place and have reflected the diversity of native characteristics and temperament among the faithful. While honoring Christ's Mother, these devotions cause her Son to be rightly known, loved, and glorified, and all His commands observed. Through Him all things have their being (cf. Col. 1:15-16) and in Him "it has pleased [the eternal Father] that . . . all his fullness should dwell" (Col. 1:19).

67. This most holy Synod deliberately teaches this Catholic doctrine. At the same time, it admonishes all the sons of the Church that the cult, especially the liturgical cult, of the Blessed Virgin, be generously fostered. It charges that prac-

285. The last major division of the chapter deals with the way in which the Church venerates Mary. The Council commends a generous devotion to her which is at the same time Christ-centered and free from all exaggeration. Here as elsewhere, the Council in its choice of language and emphasis tries to avoid anything which might unnecessarily offend the sensibilities of the separated brethren.
286. *"We fly to thy patronage."*

tices and exercises of devotion toward her be treasured as
recommended by the teaching authority of the Church in the
course of centuries, and that those decrees issued in earlier
times regarding the veneration of images of Christ, the
Blessed Virgin, and the saints, be religiously observed.[287]

But this Synod earnestly exhorts theologians and preachers
of the divine word that in treating of the unique dignity of
the Mother of God, they carefully and equally avoid the
falsity of exaggeration on the one hand, and the excess of
narrow-mindedness on the other.[288] Pursuing the study of
sacred Scripture, the holy Fathers, the doctors, and liturgies
of the Church, and under the guidance of the Church's teaching authority, let them rightly explain the offices and privileges of the Blessed Virgin which are always related to
Christ, the Source of all truth, sanctity, and piety.

Let them painstakingly guard against any word or deed
which could lead separated brethren or anyone else into error regarding the true doctrine of the Church. Let the faithful remember moreover that true devotion consists neither
in fruitless and passing emotion, nor in a certain vain credu-
lity. Rather, it proceeds from true faith, by which we are led
to know the excellence of the Mother of God, and are moved
to a filial love toward our mother and to the imitation of
her virtues.

V. Mary, a Sign of Sure Hope and of Solace for God's People in Pilgrimage

68. In the bodily and spiritual glory which she possesses in
heaven, the Mother of Jesus continues in this present world
as the image and first flowering of the Church as she is to
be perfected in the world to come. Likewise, Mary shines
forth on earth, until the day of the Lord shall come (cf. 2
Pet. 3:10), as a sign of sure hope and solace for the pilgrim
People of God.

69. It gives great joy and comfort to this most holy Synod
that among the separated brethren, too, there are those who

---

287. *Council of Nicaea II in the year 787: Mansi, 13, 378-9 (Denz. 302
[600-1]); Council of Trent, Session 25: Mansi, 33, 171-2.*
288. *Cf. Pius XII, radio message, Oct. 24, 1954: AAS 46 (1954), p. 679;
and the same Pontiff's encyclical "Ad Caeli Reginam," Oct. 11, 1954: AAS
46 (1954), p. 637.*

give due honor to the Mother of our Lord and Savior. This is especially so among the Easterners, who with ardent emotion and devout mind concur in reverencing the Mother of God, ever virgin.[289]

Let the entire body of the faithful pour forth persevering prayer to the Mother of God and Mother of men. Let them implore that she who aided the beginnings of the Church by her prayers may now, exalted as she is in heaven above all the saints and angels, intercede with her Son in the fellowship of all the saints. May she do so until all the peoples of the human family, whether they are honored with the name of Christian or whether they still do not know their Savior, are happily gathered together in peace and harmony into the one People of God, for the glory of the Most Holy and Undivided Trinity.[290]

Each and every one of the things set forth in this Dogmatic Constitution has won the consent of the Fathers of this most sacred Council. We, too, by the apostolic authority conferred on us by Christ, join with the Venerable Fathers in approving, decreeing and establishing these things in the Holy Spirit, and we direct that what has thus been enacted in synod be published to God's glory.

Rome, at St. Peter's, November 21, 1964

I, Paul, Bishop of the Catholic Church

There follow the signatures of the Fathers.

---

289. *Cf. Pius XI, encyclical "Ecclesiam Dei," Nov. 12, 1923: AAS 15 (1923), p. 581; and Pius XII, encyclical, "Fulgens Corona," Sept. 8, 1953: AAS 45 (1953), pp. 590-1.*
290. The last sentence, returning to the theme of the People of God, eloquently sums up the goal for which the Church unceasingly prays and labors.

FROM THE ACTS OF THE MOST HOLY SECOND ECUMENICAL COUNCIL OF THE VATICAN[1]

Announcements Made by the Most Excellent Secretary General of the Most Holy Council at the 123rd General Congregation, November 16, 1964

The question has been raised, what ought to be the *theological qualification*[2] of the doctrine which is set forth in the schema *De Ecclesia* and is being voted on.

The Theological Commission gave the answer to this ques-

---

1. This excerpt from the Acts of the Council is not an integral part of the Constitution on the Church but an appendix to the text of the Constitution as found in the *Acta Apostolicae Sedis*. It consists of two announcements by the Secretary General of the Council made on the eve of the final vote. These announcements quote two statements made by the Theological Commission (the committee of bishops charged with the drafting of the Constitution on the Church), both of great importance for the correct interpretation of the Constitution itself, especially Chapter III.

2. The "theological qualification" of a proposition has reference to the degree and kind of assent which it calls for on the part of the faithful. With regard to the Constitution on the Church, the question had been raised whether it defined any new dogmas, e.g., that episcopal consecration is a sacrament or that the bishops are divinely constituted as a corporate body (college). The Theological Commission replied that, especially in view of the predominantly pastoral aims of Vatican II, the teachings of the Constitution were not to be regarded as infallible definitions unless clearly and specifically proposed as such.

The doctrinal pronouncements of this and other documents of Vatican II, since they come from the highest magisterial organ in the Church, should of course be accepted and believed by Catholics with that "religious assent" which is due to the official teaching authority (cf. what is said about this religious assent to the teaching of the individual bishops in Art. 25). But nothing in the language of the Constitution on the Church indicates that the Council wished to propose its teaching in this document with the irrevocable binding force proper to infallible definitions. On this question see Gregory Baum, "Teaching Authority of Vatican II," *The Ecumenist* 3, (1965), 89-93.

tion when it evaluated the *modi* pertaining to Chapter III of
De Ecclesia in these words:

"As is self-evident, a conciliar text must always be interpreted according to the general rules known by all."

On that occasion the Theological Commission referred to
its own *Declaration* of March 6, 1964. We repeat that text
here:

"In view of conciliar practice and the pastoral purpose of
the present Council, this sacred Synod defines matters of
faith or morals as binding on the Church only when the
Synod itself openly declares so.

"Other matters which the sacred Synod proposes as the
doctrine of the supreme teaching authority of the Church,
each and every member of the faithful is obliged to accept
and embrace according to the mind of the sacred Synod itself, which becomes known either from the subject matter or
from the language employed, according to the norms of
theological interpretation."

                              *   *   *   *

From a higher authority[3] there is communicated to the
Fathers an explanatory and prefatory note on the *modi* concerning Chapter III of the schema *De Ecclesia*. The doctrine
set forth in this same Chapter III ought to be interpreted
and understood according to the mind and opinion of this
note.

PREFATORY NOTE OF EXPLANATION

The Commission decrees that the following general observations should precede the evaluation of the *modi:*

1) *College* is not understood in a *strictly juridical* sense,
namely, of a group of equals who entrust their power to

---

3. The original purpose of this Prefatory Note by the Theological Commission was to explain to the Council Fathers the reasons why certain proposed
amendments *(modi)* to Chap. III were handled as they were. But since the
Note throws valuable light on the proper understanding of the text itself,
"higher authority" (presumably Pope Paul himself) directed that it should
be published as an authentic norm of interpretation. All commentators agree
that this Note does not weaken or modify the teaching of Chap. III. Rather,
it sets forth in more technical and juridical language how certain points in
the text are to be understood. In particular it clarifies the meaning of the
term "college," the manner by which one is made a member, the significance
of "hierarchical communion," and the relationship between the collegial
authority of the bishops and the primacy of the Pope. The precision with
which these thorny points are here handled went far to remove the
lingering doubts of some Council Fathers and thus to pave the way for
the almost unanimous acceptance which the Constitution on the Church
finally received.

their president, but of a stable group whose structure and authority is to be deduced from revelation. Hence in reply to Modus 12 it is explicitly asserted of the Twelve that the Lord established them "in the manner of a college or *a stable group*." Cf. also Modus 53, C.

For the same reason the words *Order* or *Body* are also used here and there of the College of Bishops. The parallel between Peter and the other apostles on the one hand, and the Supreme Pontiff and the bishops on the other, does not imply any transmission of the extraordinary power of the apostles to their successors, nor, as is clear, any *equality* between the head and the members of the College, but only a *proportionality* between the first relationship (Peter/apostles) and the second (Pope/bishops). Hence the Commission decided to write, in #22, not "by the *same* reason," but "by a *like* reason." Cf. Modus 57.

2) A person becomes a *member of the College* by virtue of episcopal consecration and hierarchical communion with the head of the College and its members. Cf. Article 22, §1, at the end.

In *consecration* is given an ontological participation in *sacred* functions, as is clear beyond doubt from tradition, even liturgical. The word *functions* is deliberately employed, rather than *powers,* since this latter word could be understood as *ready to go into action.* But for such ready power to be had, it needs *canonical* or *juridical determination* by hierarchical authority. This determination of power can consist in the granting of a particular office, or in an assigning of subjects; and it is given according to *norms* approved by the highest authority. Such an ulterior norm is demanded *by the nature of the case,* since there is question of functions which must be exercised by several subjects working together by Christ's will in a hierarchical manner. It is clear that this "communion" has been *in the life* of the Church according to circumstances of the times, before it was, so to speak, codified *in law*.

Therefore, it is significantly stated that *hierarchical* communion is required with the head of the Church and its members. *Communion* is an idea which was held in high honor by the ancient Church (as it is even today, especially in the East). It is understood, however, not of a certain vague feeling, but of an *organic reality* which demands a juridical form, and is simultaneously animated by charity. Hence the Commission by practically unanimous consent decreed that it must be written: "in *hierarchical* communion." Cf. Modus 40, and also what is said of *canonical mission* under Article 24.

The documents of the more recent Popes dealing with the jurisdiction of bishops must be interpreted in the light of this necessary determination of powers.

3) Of the College, which cannot exist without its head, it is said that "it is *the subject also of supreme and full power* over the whole Church." This must be allowed of necessity if the fullness of power of the Roman Pontiff is not to be jeopardized. For necessarily and always the College carries with it the idea of its head, *who preserves intact in the College his role of Vicar of Christ and shepherd of the universal Church.* In other words there is no distinction between the Roman Pontiff and the bishops taken collectively, but between the Roman Pontiff by himself and the Roman Pontiff together with the bishops. Since the Supreme Pontiff is the *head* of the College, he alone can perform certain acts which in no wise belong to the bishops, for example, convoking and directing the College, approving the norms of action, etc. Cf. Modus 81.

The care of the whole flock of Christ has been entrusted to the Supreme Pontiff. It belongs to him, according to the changing needs of the Church during the passage of time, to determine the way in which it is fitting for this care to be exercised, whether personally or collegially. The Roman Pontiff proceeds according to his own discretion and in view of the welfare of the Church in structuring, promoting, and endorsing any exercise of collegiality.

4) As supreme pastor of the Church, the Sovereign Pontiff can always exercise his authority as he chooses, as is demanded by his office itself. While the College always exists, it does not for that reason permanently operate through *strictly* collegial action, as the tradition of the Church shows. In other words, it is not always "in full act"; indeed, it operates through collegial actions only at intervals and only *with the consent of its head.* The phrase is *"with the consent of its head";* for there should be no thought of a *dependence* on some *outside* person. The word "consent," on the contrary, recalls the *communion* existing between head and members, and implies the necessity of the *act* which properly belongs to the head. This idea is explicitly asserted in Article 22, §2, and is explained at the end of the same location. The negative word *"only"* takes in every case. Thus it is evident that

the *norms* approved by the supreme authority must always be observed. Cf. Modus 84.

In every instance it is clear that *the union* of the bishops *with their head* is contemplated, and never any action of the bishops taken *independently* of the Pope. For in the latter case the head would be inoperative, and the bishops could not function as a college, as is evident from the very concept of a "college." This hierarchical communion of all the bishops with the Supreme Pontiff is undoubtedly a recurring feature of tradition.

N.B. Without hierarchical communion, the sacramental-ontological office, as distinct from its canonical-juridical aspect, *cannot* be exercised. The Commission has decided not to go into questions of *liceity* and *validity*, which are left to the debate of theologians, especially with regard to the power which is *de facto* exercised among the separated Easterners and which is explained in various ways.

PERICLE FELICI, Titular Archbishop of Samosata
Secretary General of the Most Holy Second
Ecumenical Council of the Vatican

A RESPONSE

There are at least two decisive reasons why the Dogmatic Constitution on the Church may rightly be regarded as *the* masterpiece of Vatican II. In the first place—and strange as it may seem—this is the first full-orbed *conciliar* exposition of the doctrine of the Church in Christian history. Earlier Councils took the Church for granted and focused their energies on one or another challenge to her teaching or unity. Vatican II, however, was an unprecedented venture in ecclesiological self-examination and self-understanding. Its working premise was the conviction that any significant renovation of the Church-in-action would have to begin with a valid doctrinal statement concerning her basic nature.

Thus, the Constitution on the Church is important both in its own right and also as the *fundamentum* of the other fifteen documents of the Second Vatican Council. The Roman Catholic Church at worship (On the Sacred Liturgy), her norm of authority (On Divine Revelation), her relations with other Christians (On Ecumenism), with the devotees of other religions (On the Relationship of the Church to Non-Christian Religions) and with the rest of the human community (The Church in the Modern World), etc.—all of these rest back on the Constitution on the Church as their ground, and each of them, in one degree or another, provides significant development for one or another of its major motifs. This emphasis on the Church and her renewal for mission in the world is what gave Vatican II its most distinctive character as a Council.

The second reason for On the Church's cardinal importance lies in its truly pastoral tone and ecumenical spirit. Here, in welcome contrast to the polemical tempers of Trent and Vatican I, we have a vision of the Church that enlivens the prospects of effective ecumenical dialogue: the Church aware of her mission under God and therefore capable of self-criticism; the Church in dialogue with the world and therefore capable of historical development; the Church in which all are called to holiness and therefore to Christian witness and service.

The atmosphere of On the Church is neither partisan nor immobilist. Indeed, it calls to mind the spirit of those great Catholic reformers of the sixteenth century (Contarini, Sadoleto, Gropper, Morone) whose efforts on behalf of unity were thwarted then by both the "Papalists" and the "Protestants." There is a very real sense in which *De Ecclesia* has reopened the way to serious and fruitful discussion of Christian unity after four centuries of cloture.

That it should have turned out this way was very far from certain—or even hopeful—at the beginning of the Council. The first text submitted to the bishops in the summer of 1962 was an ominous sample of what has been called "the siege mentality of pre-conciliar Rome." Even in its second and third revised versions, it still reflected the formalistic tendency that spoke blandly of "the Church as a mystery" and then proceeded to *define* the *mystery!* The most crucial conflict of the Council centered on the doctrine of "collegiality"; its resolution (October 30, 1963) marked the turning point in the Council's history. The decision to include the chapter on the Blessed Virgin Mary in *this* Constitution (instead of in a separate schema) was the closest of all the votes taken in St. Peter's.

Thus it was that, in the course of their protracted, and painful, efforts to perfect On the Church, the Council Fathers succeeded in clarifying their basic understanding and judgment, not only in the area of ecclesiology but also on the other issues before them. The result is a remarkable demonstration of the efficacy of the conciliar process as it worked in Vatican II.

To begin with the notion of the Church as "mystery" (Chapter I) is at once to lift the discussion above the level of institutional organization and management, and to establish as the first premise of sound ecclesiology the reality of the Church's divine origin, maintenance, and destiny. The Church in history is "human, all-too human," but her true dynamic—what accounts for her continuity through history and her effective witness in the world—lies beyond human manipulation or merit. To speak of the Church as mystery is to confess God's constant sovereignty and to remind all Christians that we "belong to the Church"—the Church does not belong to us! It also implies that the whole Church is mysteriously present in each local congregation but that no congregation (or "denomination" for that matter) exhausts the fullness of the Church catholic.

The kernel of Chapter II recalls the biblical theme of the *People of God* and points to the literal marvel of the Church's survival through the vicissitudes of her historical existence. There are at least two significant ecumenical implications here. The first (cf. Article 15) is that "the People of God" includes the entire Christian community and, therefore, that the problem of the recomposition of Christian unity has to be tackled within the bond of Christian brotherhood —separated brethren, yes, but separated *Christian brethren.* Another implication is that, being richly human and infinitely diverse, the People of God have not been immune from the faults and failings of human affairs—and are, therefore, subject to self-criticism and self-correction. No *status quo* will serve the pilgrim Church for long; she marches with the march of time. This was, one thinks, the point to John XXIII's now famous slogan, *aggiornamento.*

The notion of the hierarchy as collegial (Chapter III) opens a new era in Roman Catholic conceptions of Church order. Now once again, as in the patristic Church, it is to be understood that the entire episcopacy, under the presidency of the Bishop of Rome, shares in the leadership of the entire Catholic Church. This is a striking advance beyond the sterile extremes of traditional "ultramontanism," on the one hand, and traditional "conciliarism" on the other. No one has any longer to choose between the primacy of the Petrine Office and the authority of the episcopal "college." This ought also to mean important developments in the responsibility and effectiveness of Episcopal Conferences and of local Ordinaries, without any corresponding loss of unity among the bishops or in their communion with the Head of the College.

The notion of the laity as *the presence of the Church in the world* (Chapter IV) restores yet another biblical emphasis upon the general priesthood of all believers (as constituted by their baptism and confirmation) and lays out the theory for their apostolate in and for the world. Thus, the Constitution on the Church serves as the doctrinal foundation for the more practical concerns of the Decree on the Apostolate of the Laity.

The universal call to holiness (in Chapter V) erases the false distinction between higher and lower levels of Christian faithfulness, since holiness (defined here as the utterly earnest love of God and neighbor) is affirmed as both a possibility and an imperative for all Christians. The restatement of the distinctive contribution of "the religious" (in Chapter VI) in and for "the People of God" has the makings of a new pattern of Christian monasticism—one which could be as relevant and useful in this age of ours as its earlier forms in other ages. The emphasis upon the living link between the Church militant and the Church triumphant (in Chapter VII) gives fresh meaning to the old phrase "communion of the saints"—and rescues eschatology from its conventional preoccupations with the sweet bye-and-bye. Finally, the identification of the Blessed Virgin (in Chapter VIII) as the foremost of all those who have shared in, and who still enrich, the communion of saints may well have the effect, among other things, of recalling Protestants to an important aspect of Christian faith that they have tended to underestimate in their reaction to what was deemed the excesses of conventional Mariology.

Given the new ecumenical climate which has been generated by Vatican II and the guidelines for the ecumenical enterprise provided by On Ecumenism and On Religious Liberty, it is obvious that all who dream of the healing of "the sixth wound of Christ" (disunity) will have the Dogmatic Constitution on the Church as a basic text for study, analysis, and negotiation. There is much here to ponder, much to recognize as integral in our common history as Christians, much to appropriate in the various parts of divided Christendom. The Orthodox, who would have rejected out of hand a restatement of the ecclesiology of Florence and Vatican I, may find here a valid basis for new and fruitful colloquy with Rome. Protestants (and Anglicans) who would have braced themselves defiantly before new *anathemata* (in the vein of Trent) will find little here that offends and much that edifies. The faithful of other religions, and the secularists who encompass the Christian remnant in the world today, can find in On the Church (if they can somehow be persuaded to take it seriously) a vision of a community of faith, hope, and love that answers to their deep and unsatisfied hungers for a truly human, truly meaningful existence. Lastly, but certainly not least, Roman Catholics will find in this constitution a *Magna Carta* that will reshape many of their conventional notions about the Church in her nature and mission and that will furnish both inspiration and direction for their further experimentation and developments in the postconciliar period that now begins.

There is, of course, the tragic possibility that even so magnificent a document as this may suffer the fate of many of its antecedents (one thinks, for example, of the celebrated *Consilium de Emendanda Ecclesia* [1537]): that it should promptly be interred in the vast mausoleum of ecumenical literature—rated as a classic by the *cognoscenti* but not wide-ly read or actually implemented in the ongoing life of the Church. There is the equally tragic danger that it may be interpreted and implemented *piecemeal:* that the progressives will stress only its progressive ideas, even as the immobilists attend only to its traditional residues; that the bishops may be more preoccupied with the implications of collegiality at the level of their dioceses than at the level of parish life and work; that the laity mistake On the Church as a warrant for self-assertion without fully assuming their commission to an apostolate of Christian witness in the world; that members of religious orders may become too intent upon their life apart; that the studied ambiguities of Chapter VIII may be over-simplified in one direction or another.

All of this is to say that the real meaning of On the Church has still to be deciphered—and translated into action in the polity and program of the Roman Catholic Church. This now becomes the paramount task in the years ahead. It is certain that the Council intended this Constitution to be the major resource in the renovation and reform of the Catholic Church—and in the further progress of the ecumenical dia-logue. It is equally certain that history's verdict on Vatican II will turn largely on how far this intention is realized.

ALBERT C. OUTLER

REVELATION

IMPORTANT AS THE Constitution on the Church is generally agreed to be, it is equaled in stature by the Constitution on Divine Revelation; the two are the most fundamental documents produced by the Second Vatican Council. To the casual reader, the latter may not appear to be either novel or dramatic, but to the theologian it is of basic importance. Other constitutions and decrees will have more obvious practical effects for people within the Church (e.g., the Constitution on the Liturgy), or for those still separated from her (e.g., the Decree on Ecumenism), but all the documents depend on the faith in God's word to men, which the Council has spelled out in this Constitution.

Drama was not lacking in the document's history. Before the Council assembled, the Theological Commission had prepared a preliminary draft. When this was presented for discussion in the first session (November, 1962), it met with severe criticism. After a few days, a vote was taken to decide whether the draft should be returned to the commission to be rewritten. The result was affirmative by about 60%; but, according to the regulations set up beforehand, a two-thirds majority was required for this somewhat drastic step. It was at this point that Pope John XXIII made his famous intervention: he overrode the regulation, confirmed the majority preference, and constituted a new joint commission to recast the text.

The schema therefore was largely rewritten. The original first chapter, "Two Sources of Revelation" (namely, Scripture and tradition), was replaced by two chapters, on revelation itself and on its transmission, in which Scripture and tradition were not explicitly distinguished as separate "sources." The treatment in general became less philosophical, more biblical and historical. More stress was laid on modern methods of interpretation of Scripture, in accordance with the forward-looking doctrine of the encyclical *Divino Afflante Spiritu* of 1943.

Although this text was ready for the second session, in 1963, it was not presented then. Instead, it underwent further revision the following year in the commission, and was brought up for discussion, and voted on, in the third session, 1964. Many *modi* (amendments) were presented by the Council Fathers, and further alterations were made by the commission in consideration of these. In the fourth session, additional last-minute corrections were made, some at the request of Pope Paul VI. Finally, the definitive text was approved by an almost unanimous vote, and was promulgated on November 18, 1965.

This is in fact, if not in name, the Second Vatican Council's pronouncement on the Bible. Four of its six chapters (3 to 6) expressly deal with sacred Scripture. Chapters 1 and 2 set the Bible in the context of the whole Christian doctrine of salvation, and in this light explain its origin and its function.

It is basic to Christian belief (as to the tenets of Judaism) that God is a personal God who has spoken to men. He has initiated a dialogue with them, in which they are invited to listen to his words, and to respond. His words are revelation, and man's response is faith.

Faith is briefly touched on in Article 5 of the Constitution (it is more fully treated in the Constitution on the Church). The important point is here made that biblical faith is far more than an intellectual assent to propositions. It is a loyal adherence to a personal God.

The document's main subject is revelation. This is a manifestation by God—primarily, of Himself; secondarily, of His will and intentions—granted to particular men at particular times. Every single such communication from God is part of a larger pattern, is destined ultimately for the good of all men. Revelation by its nature is public (possible private "revelations" are another thing, not touched on here). Therefore it has to be made known to others by the testimony of its recipient. Passed on orally, it becomes tradition; recorded in writing, it becomes Scripture.

More precisely, Scripture *contains* revelation, namely, in the form of a written record; but not all of Scripture *is* revelation. Much of it is the record of revelation's effects, of the human reactions to it, of men's faith or lack of it. All of Scripture is inspired, but not all is revealed. Similarly, tradition comes to include much that is only of human origin, however venerable and valuable. At the time of the Council of Trent, great difficulty was experienced in drawing a line between traditions which merely witnessed to ancient usages in the Church, and those which represented the revelation of Christ. Considerable progress has been made since then by theologians and Church historians in clarifying the point, but not all such questions are yet solved.

Hence, the written record in the New Testament is vitally important—the permanent and unchanging testimony of the apostolic generation. The New Testament writings do not claim to be—in fact they obviously are not—a complete and balanced inventory of the early Church's beliefs. Nevertheless, they lay down what cannot be changed: the rule of faith as it was recorded, to which the Church is always bound, and which she can develop and expand but never falsify.

On the other hand, a written record is a dead letter, needing constant interpretation and commentary in succeeding ages. It cannot of itself answer new questions, or explain what was once clear and has now become obscure. But the writings transmitted in a living community, from one generation to another, are accompanied by a continuous tradition of understanding and explanation, which preserves and re-expresses their meaning, and which applies them, from time to time, to the solving of new problems. If this tradition were only human, it would be liable to grave error. But such a consequence is avoided by the Church's magisterium, which, however much exposed to human vagaries and mistakes in secondary matters, is preserved from going wrong in essentials by the indwelling presence of Christ's Spirit.

The Constitution especially emphasizes (in Article 10) the coordination and interplay of Scripture, tradition, and the magisterium. In whatever way the question of the separate values of the first two may be answered in theory, in practice all three function together, and all are necessary for the Church's life.

The generous encouragement of Bible reading on the part of all the faithful (Articles 22, 25) is coupled with reminders of tradition and the magisterium. No Christian comes, or should come, to the reading of Scripture in utter ignorance of what is to be found there. He comes to it with his faith in Christ, who is the last and definitive utterance of God's word; with his faith in the Church, which is the depository and custodian of that word; with his faith in Scripture itself, which is the expression in human language of the message delivered by God. All of that prepares him to understand it rightly, and to make his reading, and his prayerful reaction to what he reads, an act of loving and hopeful faith in Christ, who has revealed the Father to men.

R. A. F. MacKenzie, S.J.

Dogmatic Constitution on Divine Revelation

PAUL, BISHOP

SERVANT OF THE SERVANTS OF GOD

TOGETHER WITH THE FATHERS OF THE SACRED COUNCIL

FOR EVERLASTING MEMORY

PREFACE

1. Hearing the word of God with reverence and proclaiming it confidently, this most sacred Synod takes its direction from these words of St. John: "We announce to you the eternal life which was with the Father, and has appeared to us. What we have seen and have heard we announce to you, in order that you also may have fellowship with us, and that our fellowship may be with the Father, and with his son Jesus Christ" (1 Jn. 1:2-3). Therefore, following in the footsteps of the Councils of Trent and of First Vatican, this present Council wishes to set forth authentic teaching about divine revelation and about how it is handed on, so that by hearing the message of salvation the whole world may believe;[1] by believing, it may hope; and by hoping, it may love.[2]

1. This Constitution is not intended merely as a theological document, but as a proclamation to the world. It is a fresh announcement of the gospel, of the "kerygma" preached by the apostles.
2. Cf. St. Augustine, "De Catechizandis Rudibus," C. IV, 8:PL 40,316.

CHAPTER I

REVELATION ITSELF

2. In His goodness and wisdom, God chose to reveal Himself and to make known to us the hidden purpose of His will (cf. Eph. 1:9) by which through Christ, the Word made flesh, man has access to the Father in the Holy Spirit and comes to share in the divine nature (cf. Eph. 2:18; 2 Pet. 1:4). Through this revelation, therefore, the invisible God (cf. Col. 1:15; 1 Tim. 1:17) out of the abundance of His love speaks to men as friends (cf. Ex. 33:11; Jn. 15:14-15) and lives among them (cf. Bar. 3:38), so that He may invite and take them into fellowship with Himself. This plan of revelation is realized by deeds and words having an inner unity: the deeds wrought by God in the history of salvation manifest and confirm the teaching and realities signified by the words, while the words proclaim the deeds and clarify the mystery contained in them. By this revelation then, the deepest truth about God and the salvation of man is made clear to us in Christ, who is the Mediator and at the same time the fullness of all revelation.[3]

3. God, who through the Word creates all things (cf. Jn. 1:3) and keeps them in existence, gives men an enduring witness to Himself in created realities (cf. Rom. 1:19-20).[4] Planning to make known the way of heavenly salvation, He went further and from the start manifested Himself to our first parents. Then after their fall His promise of redemption aroused in them the hope of being saved (cf. Gen. 3:15), and from that time on He ceaselessly kept the human race in His care, in order to give eternal life to those who perseveringly do good in search of salvation (cf. Rom. 2:6-7). Then, at the

3. Cf. Mt. 11:27; Jn. 1:14 and 17; 14:6; 17:1-3; 2 Cor. 3:16 and 4:6; Eph. 1:3-14.

4. The first sentence of Art. 3 refers to so-called "natural" revelation: the indications of God's nature and activity to be gathered from the existence of created things. (See also Art. 6.) But what follows deals with supernatural revelation, which is not dumb "evidence," hard to interpret, but a series of personal acts and utterances. The last and definitive one is the Incarnation (Art. 4).

time He had appointed, He called Abraham in order to make of him a great nation (cf. Gen. 12:2). Through the patriarchs, and after them through Moses and the prophets, He taught this nation to acknowledge Himself as the one living and true God, provident Father and just Judge, and to wait for the Savior promised by Him. In this manner He prepared the way for the gospel down through the centuries.

4. Then, after speaking in many places and varied ways through the prophets, God "last of all in these days has spoken to us by his* son" (Heb. 1:1-2). For he sent His Son, the eternal Word, who enlightens all men, so that He might dwell among men and tell them the innermost realities about God (cf. Jn. 1:1-18). Jesus Christ, therefore, the Word made flesh, sent as "a man to men,"[5] "speaks the words of God" (Jn. 3:34), and completes the work of salvation which His Father gave Him to do (cf. Jn. 5:36, 17:4). To see Jesus is to see His Father (Jn. 14:9). For this reason Jesus perfected revelation by fulfilling it through His whole work of making Himself present and manifesting Himself: through His words and deeds, His signs and wonders, but especially through His death and glorious resurrection from the dead and final sending of the Spirit of truth. Moreover, He confirmed with divine testimony what revelation proclaimed: that God is with us to free us from the darkness of sin and death, and to raise us up to life eternal.

The Christian dispensation, therefore, as the new and definitive covenant, will never pass away, and we now await no further new public revelation before the glorious manifestation of our Lord Jesus Christ (cf. 1 Tim. 6:14 and Tit. 2:13).

5. "The obedience of faith" (Rom. 16:26; cf. 1:5; 2 Cor. 10:5-6) must be given to God who reveals, an obedience by which man entrusts his whole self freely to God, offering "the full submission of intellect and will to God who reveals,"[6] and freely assenting to the truth revealed by Him.[7]

---

*Like the original Greek, the Latin has no "his."—Ed.
5. *Epistle to Diognetus, C. VII, 4: Funk, Apostolic Fathers, I, p. 403.*
6. *First Vatican Council, Dogmatic Constitution on the Catholic Faith, Chap. 3, "On Faith": Denz. 1789 (3008).*
7. Art. 5 describes the response to be made by men to God's loving invitation. Note the general description of faith, "by which a man commits his whole self": the Council desired to get away from a too intellectualist conception. Christian faith is not merely assent to a set of statements; it is a personal engagement, a continuing act of loyalty and self-commitment, offered by man to God.

If this faith is to be shown, the grace of God and the interior help of the Holy Spirit must precede and assist, moving the heart and turning it to God, opening the eyes of the mind, and giving "joy and ease to everyone in assenting to the truth and believing it."[8] To bring about an ever deeper understanding of revelation, the same Holy Spirit constantly brings faith to completion by His gifts.[9]

6. Through divine revelation, God chose to show forth and communicate Himself and the eternal decisions of His will regarding the salvation of men. That is to say, He chose "to share those divine treasures which totally transcend the understanding of the human mind."[10]

This sacred Synod affirms, "God, the beginning and end of all things, can be known with certainty from created reality by the light of human reason" (cf. Rom. 1:20); but the Synod teaches that it is through His revelation "that those religious truths which are by their nature accessible to human reason can be known by all men with ease, with solid certitude, and with no trace of error, even in the present state of the human race."[11]

CHAPTER II

THE TRANSMISSION
OF DIVINE REVELATION

7. In His gracious goodness, God has seen to it that what He had revealed for the salvation of all nations would abide perpetually in its full integrity and be handed on to all genera-

---

8. *Second Council of Orange, Canon 7: Denz. 180 (377); First Vatican Council, loc. cit.: Denz. 1791 (3010).*
9. Since this faith is supernatural, God must and does act on men interiorly, to enable them to realize it. Without His effective interior help, which we call grace, we could do nothing "profitable for salvation."
10. *First Vatican Council, Dogmatic Constitution on the Catholic Faith, Chap. 2, "On Revelation": Denz. 1786 (3005).*
11. *Ibid.: Denz. 1785 and 1786 (3004 and 3005).*

tions. Therefore Christ the Lord, in whom the full revelation of the supreme God is brought to completion (cf. 2 Cor. 1: 20; 3:16; 4:6), commissioned the apostles to preach to all men that gospel which is the source of all saving truth and moral teaching,[12] and thus to impart to them divine gifts. This gospel had been promised in former times through the prophets, and Christ Himself fulfilled it and promulgated it with His own lips. This commission was faithfully fulfilled by the apostles who, by their oral preaching, by example, and by ordinances, handed on what they had received from the lips of Christ, from living with Him, and from what He did, or what they had learned through the prompting of the Holy Spirit. The commission was fulfilled, too, by those apostles and apostolic men who under the inspiration of the same Holy Spirit committed the message of salvation to writing.[13]

But in order to keep the gospel forever whole and alive within the Church, the apostles left bishops as their successors, "handing over their own teaching role" to them.[14] This sacred tradition, therefore, and sacred Scripture of both the Old and the New Testament[15] are like a mirror in which the pilgrim Church on earth looks at God, from whom she has received everything, until she is brought finally to see Him as He is, face to face (cf. 1 Jn. 3:2).

8. And so the apostolic preaching, which is expressed in a special way in the inspired books, was to be preserved by a continuous succession of preachers until the end of time. Therefore the apostles, handing on what they themselves had

12. Cf. Mt. 28:19-20, and Mk. 16:15; Council of Trent, session IV, Decree on Scriptural Canons: Denz. 783 (1501).
13. Cf. Council of Trent, loc. cit.; First Vatican Council, session III, Dogmatic Constitution on the Catholic Faith, Chap. 2, "On Revelation": Denz. 1787 (3006).
14. St. Ireneus, "Against Heretics" III, 3, 1: PG 7, 848; Harvey, 2, p. 9.
15. Here arises the question of the "two sources" of divine revelation. Scripture is clearly something different from a living oral tradition; but as sources from which we may learn what God has in the past revealed, can Scripture and tradition be treated separately, or must they always be taken together?

The prevailing view since the Council of Trent has been that they may be treated separately, and statements of revealed truth (dogmas) may be gathered from tradition alone, though they are in no way contained in Scripture.

The other opinion, recently revived, which claims to be the pre-Tridentine teaching, maintains that all Christian revelation is contained in Scripture, not necessarily in explicit terms sufficient to "prove" it, but at least by implication, which can be made explicit in the light of tradition.

The question was much debated in the Council, and the majority of the Fathers preferred not to decide it one way or the other. The final text in Art. 8 explains the nature of each of the two forms of transmission, and in Art. 9 insists on their functional unity.

received,[16] warn the faithful to hold fast to the traditions which they have learned either by word of mouth or by letter (cf. 2 Th. 2:15), and to fight in defense of the faith handed on once and for all (cf. Jude 3).[17] Now what was handed on by the apostles includes everything which contributes to the holiness of life, and the increase in faith of the People of God; and so the Church, in her teaching, life, and worship, perpetuates and hands on to all generations all that she herself is, all that she believes.

This tradition which comes from the apostles develops in the Church with the help of the Holy Spirit.[18] For there is a growth in the understanding of the realities and the words which have been handed down. This happens through the contemplation and study made by believers, who treasure these things in their hearts (cf. Lk. 2:19, 51), through the intimate understanding of spiritual things they experience, and through the preaching of those who have received through episcopal succession the sure gift of truth.[19] For, as the centuries succeed one another, the Church constantly moves forward toward the fullness of divine truth until the words of God reach their complete fulfillment in her.

The words of the holy Fathers[20] witness to the living presence of this tradition, whose wealth is poured into the practice and life of the believing and praying Church. Through the same tradition the Church's full canon of the sacred books is known, and the sacred writings themselves are more profoundly understood and unceasingly made active in her; and thus God, who spoke of old, uninterruptedly converses with the Bride of His beloved Son; and the Holy Spirit, through

---

16. This the apostles did, in the first place, by word of mouth. That oral transmission has never ceased in the Church. Preaching, instruction of converts, catechetics, are still oral, person-to-person communication. The message must normally be passed on by personal contact. Christianity can never become a mere book-religion.

At the same time, in the New Testament the exact form of the apostolic message, with all its characteristics of time and place, is permanently preserved.

17. Cf. Second Council of Nicea: Denz. 303 (602); Fourth Council of Constance, session X, Canon 1: Denz. 336 (650-652).

18. Cf. First Vatican Council, Dogmatic Constitution on the Catholic Faith, Chap. 4, "On Faith and Reason": Denz. 1800 (3020).

19. A description of the "development of dogma." Note that the first medium of this development is the consideration and contemplation of revealed truth by the faithful, who are implicity compared with Mary, treasuring "these things" in her heart.

20. I.e., the ancient Fathers of the Church, early orthodox Christian writers up to and including St. Gregory I (the Great) in the West and St. John of Damascus in the East.—Ed.

whom the living voice of the gospel resounds in the Church,
and through her, in the world, leads unto all truth those who
believe and makes the word of Christ dwell abundantly in
them (cf. Col. 3:16).

9. Hence there exist a close connection and communication
between sacred tradition and sacred Scripture. For both of
them, flowing from the same divine wellspring, in a certain
way merge into a unity and tend toward the same end. For
sacred Scripture is the word of God inasmuch as it is consigned to writing under the inspiration of the divine Spirit.
To the successors of the apostles, sacred tradition hands on in
its full purity God's word, which was entrusted to the apostles
by Christ the Lord and the Holy Spirit. Thus, led by the light
of the Spirit of truth, these successors can in their preaching
preserve this word of God faithfully, explain it, and make it
more widely known. Consequently, it is not from sacred Scripture alone that the Church draws her certainty about everything which has been revealed.[21] Therefore both sacred tradition and sacred scripture are to be accepted and venerated
with the same sense of devotion and reverence.[22]

10. Sacred tradition and sacred Scripture form one sacred
deposit of the word of God, which is committed to the
Church. Holding fast to this deposit, the entire holy people
united with their shepherds remain always steadfast in the
teaching of the apostles, in the common life, in the breaking
of the bread, and in prayers (cf. Acts 2, 42, Greek text), so
that in holding to, practicing, and professing the heritage of
the faith, there results on the part of the bishops and faithful
a remarkable common effort.[23]
    The task of authentically interpreting the word of God,
whether written or handed on,[24] has been entrusted exclusively

21. This careful formula was one of the last additions to the text, made at
the Pope's request. It does not exclude the opinion that all revelation is in
some way, though perhaps obscurely, contained in Scripture. But this may
not suffice for certitude, and in fact the Church always understands and interprets Scripture in the light of her continuous tradition. See the end of
Art. 12.
22. Cf. *Council of Trent, session IV, loc. cit.*: Denz. 783 (1501).
23. Cf. *Pius XII, apostolic constitution "Munificentissimus Deus," Nov. 1,
1950: AAS 42 (1950), p. 756; Collected Writings of St. Cyprian, Letter 66,
8: Hartel, III, B, p. 733:* "The Church [is] people united with the priest and
the pastor together with his flock."
24. Cf. *First Vatican Council, Dogmatic Constitution on the Catholic Faith,
Chap. 3 "On Faith"*: Denz. 1792 (3011).

to the living teaching office of the Church,[25] whose authority is exercised in the name of Jesus Christ.[26] This teaching office is not above the word of God, but serves it, teaching only what has been handed on, listening to it devoutly, guarding it scrupulously, and explaining it faithfully by divine commission and with the help of the Holy Spirit; it draws from this one deposit of faith everything which it presents for belief as divinely revealed.

It is clear, therefore, that sacred tradition, sacred Scripture, and the teaching authority of the Church, in accord with God's most wise design, are so linked and joined together that one cannot stand without the others, and that all together and each in its own way under the action of the one Holy Spirit contribute effectively to the salvation of souls.

CHAPTER III

THE DIVINE INSPIRATION AND THE INTERPRETATION OF SACRED SCRIPTURE

11. Those divinely revealed realities which are contained and presented in sacred Scripture have been committed to writing under the inspiration of the Holy Spirit. Holy Mother Church, relying on the belief of the apostles, holds that the books of both the Old and New Testament in their entirety, with all their parts, are sacred and canonical because, having been written under the inspiration of the Holy Spirit (cf. Jn. 20:31; 2 Tim. 3:16; 2 Pet. 1:19-21; 3:15-16) they have God as their author and have been handed on as such to the Church

---

25. Cf. Pius XII, encyclical "Humani Generis," Aug. 12, 1950: AAS 42 (1950), pp. 568-69: Denz. 2314 (3886).
26. The Latin term for the teaching office is magisterium, including in its broadest sense all who proclaim the word with authority in the Church. It generally refers to the Pope and the bishops collectively. Their duty is to serve the word of God.

herself.[27] In composing the sacred books, God chose men and while employed by Him they made use of their powers and abilities,[28] so that with Him acting in them and through them,[29] they, as true authors, consigned to writing everything and only those things which He wanted.[30]

Therefore, since everything asserted by the inspired authors or sacred writers must be held to be asserted by the Holy Spirit, it follows that the books of Scripture must be acknowledged as teaching firmly, faithfully, and without error that truth[31] which God wanted put into the sacred writings for the sake of our salvation.[32] Therefore "all Scripture is inspired by God and useful for teaching, for reproving, for correcting, for instruction in justice; that the man of God may be perfect, equipped for every good work" (2 Tim. 3:16-17, Greek text).

27. *Cf. First Vatican Council, Dogmatic Constitution on the Catholic Faith, Chap. 2 "On Revelation": Denz. 1787 (3006); Biblical Commission, Decree of June 18, 1915: Denz. 2180 (3629): EB 420; Holy Office, letter of Dec. 22, 1923: EB 499.*
28. *Cf. Pius XII, encyclical "Divino Afflante Spiritu," Sept. 30, 1943: AAS 35 (1943), p. 314; EB 556.*
29. *"In" and "through" man: cf. Heb. 1, and 4:7 ("in"): 2 Sam. 23:2; Mt. 1, 22 and various places ("through"): First Vatican Council, Schema on Catholic Doctrine, note 9: Coll. Lac. VII, 522.*
30. *Leo XIII, encyclical "Providentissimus Deus," Nov. 18, 1893: Denz. 1952 (3293); EB 125.*
31. An earlier draft of the Constitution had joined the adjective *salutaris* ("tending to salvation") to the word "truth." Another last-minute change substituted the phrase "for the sake of our salvation," to avoid seeming to limit the truth itself. The point remains the same, and can be shown by quoting a text from the following official footnote. St. Thomas Aquinas says: "Any knowledge which is profitable to salvation may be the object of prophetic inspiration. But things which cannot affect our salvation do not belong to inspiration." Hence, Augustine says that although the sacred writers may have known astronomy, nevertheless the Holy Spirit did not intend to utter through them any truth apart from that which is profitable to salvation. He adds that this may concern either teachings to be believed or morals to be practiced.

The Bible was not written in order to teach the natural sciences, nor to give information on merely political history. It treats of these (and all other subjects) only insofar as they are involved in matters concerning salvation. It is only in this respect that the veracity of God and the inerrancy of the inspired writers are engaged. This is not a quantitative distinction, as though some sections treated of salvation (and were inerrant), while others gave merely natural knowledge (and were fallible). It is formal, and applies to the whole text. The latter is authoritative and inerrant in what it affirms about the revelation of God and the history of salvation. According to the intentions of its authors, divine and human, it makes no other affirmations.
32. *Cf. St. Augustine, "Gen. ad Litt." 2, 9, 20: PL 34, 270-271; Epistle 82, 3: PL 33,277: CSEL 34, 2, p. 354; St. Thomas, "On Truth," Q. 12, A. 2, C.; Council of Trent, session IV, Scriptural Canons: Denz. 783 (1501); Leo XIII, encyclical "Providentissimus Deus": EB 121, 124, 126-127; Pius XII, encyclical "Divino Afflante Spiritu": EB 539.*

12. However, since God speaks in sacred Scripture through men in human fashion,[33] the interpreter of sacred Scripture, in order to see clearly what God wanted to communicate to us, should carefully investigate what meaning the sacred writers really intended, and what God wanted to manifest by means of their words.[34]

Those who search out the intention of the sacred writers must, among other things, have regard for "literary forms." For truth is proposed and expressed in a variety of ways, depending on whether a text is history of one kind or another, or whether its form is that of prophecy, poetry, or some other type of speech. The interpreter must investigate what meaning the sacred writer intended to express and actually expressed in particular circumstances as he used contemporary literary forms in accordance with the situation of his own time and culture.[35] For the correct understanding of what the sacred author wanted to assert, due attention must be paid to the customary and characteristic styles of perceiving, speaking, and narrating which prevailed at the time of the sacred writer, and to the customs men normally followed at that period in their everyday dealings with one another.[36]

But, since holy Scripture must be read and interpreted according to the same Spirit by whom it was written,[37] no less serious attention must be given to the content and unity of the whole of Scripture, if the meaning of the sacred texts is to be correctly brought to light. The living tradition of the whole Church must be taken into account along with the harmony which exists between elements of the faith. It is the task of exegetes to work according to these rules toward a better understanding and explanation of the meaning of sacred Scripture, so that through preparatory study the judgment of the

33. St. Augustine, "City of God," XVII, 6, 2: PL 41,537: CSEL XL, 2,228.
34. Art. 12 insists on two of the main points made in Pius XII's encyclical "Divino Afflante Spiritu." The first is the importance of the intention of the human author of a scriptural book or passage. We must understand what he was aiming at, in order to interpret his words aright. The second is the distinction of "literary forms." In ancient Israelite literature (as in any other), there were many distinct types of literary composition, each with its recognized and conventional style, idioms, and usages. There were different conventional ways of representing the past, i.e., of writing history, with varying proportions of literalness or symbolism. The comparitive study of these conventions has greatly clarified for us some difficult parts of the Old Testament.
35. St. Augustine, "On Christian Doctrine" III, 18, 26: PL 34, 75-76.
36. Pius XII, loc. cit.: Denz. 2294 (3829-3830); EB 557-562.
37. Cf. Benedict XV, encyclical "Spiritus Paraclitus," Sept. 15, 1920: EB 469; St. Jerome, "On Galatians," 5, 19-20: PL 26, 417 A.

Church may mature.[38] For all of what has been said about the way of interpreting Scripture is subject finally to the judgment of the Church, which carries out the divine commission and ministry of guarding and interpreting the word of God.[39]

13. In sacred Scripture, therefore, while the truth and holiness of God always remain intact, the marvelous "condescension" of eternal wisdom is clearly shown, "that we may learn the gentle kindness of God, which words cannot express, and how far He has gone in adapting His language with thoughtful concern for our weak human nature."[40] For the words of God, expressed in human language, have been made like human discourse, just as of old the Word of the eternal Father, when he took to Himself the weak flesh of humanity, became like other men.

CHAPTER IV

THE OLD TESTAMENT

14. In carefully planning and preparing the salvation of the whole human race, the God of supreme love, by a special dispensation, chose for Himself a people to whom He might entrust His promises. First He entered into a covenant with Abraham (cf. Gen. 15:18) and, through Moses, with the people of Israel (cf. Ex. 24:8). To this people which He had acquired for Himself, He so manifested Himself through words and deeds as the one true and living God that Israel came to know by experience the ways of God with men, and with God Himself speaking to them through the mouth of the

---

38. Scripture is its own best commentary. It must be treated as a whole, and understood according to the analogy of the faith. Note that one function of Scripture scholars is to help the Church's understanding of Scripture to "mature."

39. *Cf. First Vatican Council, Dogmatic Constitution on the Catholic Faith, Chap. 2, "On Revelation": Denz. 1788 (3007).*

40. *St. John Chrysostom, "On Genesis" 3, 8 (Homily 17, 1): PG 53,134; "Attemperatio" in Greek "synkatabasis."*

prophets, Israel daily gained a deeper and clearer understanding of His ways and made them more widely known among the nations (cf. Ps. 21:28-29; 95:1-3; Is. 2:1-4; Jer. 3: 17). The plan of salvation, foretold by the sacred authors, recounted and explained by them, is found as the true word of God in the books of the Old Testament: these books, therefore, written under divine inspiration, remain permanently valuable. "For whatever things have been written have been written for our instruction, that through the patience and the consolation afforded by the Scriptures we may have hope" (Rom. 15:4).

15. The principal purpose to which the plan of the Old Covenant was directed was to prepare for the coming both of Christ, the universal Redeemer, and of the messianic kingdom, to announce this coming by prophecy (cf. Lk. 24:44; Jn. 5:39; 1 Pet. 1:10), and to indicate its meaning through various types (cf. 1 Cor. 10:11). Now the books of the Old Testament, in accordance with the state of mankind before the time of salvation established by Christ, reveal to all men the knowledge of God and of man and the ways in which God, just and merciful, deals with men. These books, though they also contain some things which are incomplete and temporary, nevertheless show us true divine pedagogy.[41] These same books, then, give expression to a lively sense of God, contain a store of sublime teachings about God, sound wisdom about human life, and a wonderful treasury of prayers, and in them the mystery of our salvation is present in a hidden way. Christians should receive them with reverence.

16. God, the inspirer and author of both testaments, wisely arranged that the New Testament be hidden in the Old and the Old be made manifest in the New.[42] For, though Christ established the New Covenant in His blood (cf. Lk. 22: 20; 1 Cor. 11:25), still the books of the Old Testament with all their parts, caught up into the proclamation of the gospel,[43] acquire and show forth their full meaning in the New Testament (cf. Mt. 5:17; Lk. 24:27; Rom. 16:25-26; 2 Cor. 3:14-16) and in turn shed light on it and explain it.

41. *Pius XI, encyclical "Mit Brennender Sorge," Mar. 14, 1937: AAS 29 (1937), p. 51.*
42. *St. Augustine, "Quest. in Hept." 2, 73: PL 34,623.*
43. *St. Irenaeus, "Against Heretics" III, 21, 3: PG 7,950; (Same as 25, 1: Harvey 2, p. 115). St. Cyril of Jerusalem, "Catech." 4, 35: PG 33,497. Theodore of Mopsuestia, "In Soph." 1, 4-6: PG 66,452D-453A.*

CHAPTER V

THE NEW TESTAMENT

17. The word of God, which is the power of God for the
salvation of all who believe (cf. Rom. 1:16), is set forth and
shows its power in a most excellent way in the writings of
the New Testament. For when the fullness of time arrived
(cf. Gal. 4:4), the Word was made flesh and dwelt among
us in the fullness of grace and truth (cf. Jn. 1:14). Christ
established the Kingdom of God on earth, manifested His
Father and Himself by deeds and words, and completed His
work by His death, resurrection, and glorious ascension and
by the sending of the Holy Spirit. Having been lifted up from
the earth, He draws all men to Himself (cf. Jn. 12:32, Greek
text), He who alone has the words of eternal life (cf. Jn. 6:
68). This mystery had not been manifested to other generations as it was now revealed to His holy apostles and prophets
in the Holy Spirit (cf. Eph. 3:4-6, Greek text), so that they
might preach the gospel, stir up faith in Jesus, Christ and
Lord, and gather the Church together. To these realities, the
writings of the New Testament stand as a perpetual and divine
witness.

18. It is common knowledge that among all the Scriptures,
even those of the New Testament, the Gospels have a special
pre-eminence, and rightly so, for they are the principal witness
of the life and teaching of the incarnate Word, our Savior.

The Church has always and everywhere held and continues
to hold that the four Gospels are of apostolic origin. For
what the apostles preached in fulfillment of the commission of
Christ, afterwards they themselves and apostolic men,[44] under
the inspiration of the divine Spirit, handed on to us in writing:
the foundation of faith, namely, the fourfold Gospel, according to Matthew, Mark, Luke, and John.[45]

44. "Apostolic men" refers to the generation partly contemporary with the
apostles, but younger than they; e.g., Mark and Luke.
45. Cf. St. Irenaeus, "Against Heretics" III, 11, 8: PG 7,885; Sagnard
Edition, p. 194.

19. Holy Mother Church has firmly and with absolute constancy held, and continues to hold, that the four Gospels just named, whose historical character the Church unhesitatingly asserts, faithfully hand on what Jesus Christ, while living among men, really did and taught for their eternal salvation until the day He was taken up into heaven (see Acts 1:1-2). Indeed, after the ascension of the Lord the apostles handed on to their hearers what He had said and done. This they did with that clearer understanding which they enjoyed[46] after they had been instructed by the events of Christ's risen life* and taught by the light of the Spirit of truth.[47] The sacred authors wrote the four Gospels, selecting some things from the many which had been handed on by word of mouth or in writing, reducing some of them to a synthesis, explicating† some things in view of the situation of their churches, and preserving the form of proclamation[48] but always in such fashion that they told us the honest truth about Jesus.[49] For their intention in writing was that either from their own memory and recollections, or from the witness of those who themselves "from the beginning were eyewitnesses and ministers of the word" we might know "the truth" concerning those matters about which we have been instructed (cf. Lk. 1:2-4).

20. Besides the four Gospels, the canon of the New Testament also contains the Epistles of St. Paul and other apostolic writings, composed under the inspiration of the Holy Spirit. In these writings, by the wise plan of God, those matters which concern Christ the Lord are confirmed, His true teaching is more and more fully stated, the saving power of the divine work of Christ is preached, the story is told of the beginnings of the Church and her marvelous growth, and her glorious fulfillment is foretold.

46. *Jn.* 2:22; 12:16; *Cf.* 14:26; 16:12-13; 7:39.
*Literally, "the glorious events of Christ" (*eventibus gloriosis Christi*).—Ed.
47. *Cf. Jn.* 14:26; 16:13.
48. This Article summarizes much of the Instruction of the Pontifical Biblical Commission cited in the following footnote. On the one hand, the four Gospels are complex literary compositions, each put together, according to a definite plan, from a variety of materials; on the other, they are guaranteed reliable and truthful presentations of the Person, the work, and the teaching of Jesus.
49. *Cf. instruction "Holy Mother Church" edited by Pontifical Commission for Promotion of Bible Studies: AAS 56 (1964), p. 715.*
† The Latin word is *explanantes,* and it is taken from the document mentioned in note 49. For the importance of this word, cf. Joseph A. Fitzmyer, S.J., in *Theological Studies,* Vol. 25, 1964, esp. p. 400.—Ed.

For the Lord Jesus was with His apostles as He had promised (cf. Mt. 28:20) and sent to them as Paraclete the Spirit who would lead them into the fullness of truth (cf. Jn. 16: 13).

CHAPTER VI

SACRED SCRIPTURE IN THE LIFE OF THE CHURCH

21. The Church has always venerated the divine Scriptures just as she venerates the body of the Lord, since from the table of both the word of God and of the body of Christ she unceasingly receives and offers to the faithful the bread of life, especially in the sacred liturgy. She has always regarded the Scriptures together with sacred tradition as the supreme rule of faith, and will ever do so. For, inspired by God and committed once and for all to writing, they impart the word of God Himself without change, and make the voice of the Holy Spirit resound in the words of the prophets and apostles. Therefore, like the Christian religion itself, all the preaching of the Church must be nourished and ruled by sacred Scripture. For in the sacred books, the Father who is in heaven meets His children with great love and speaks with them; and the force and power in the word of God is so great that it remains the support and energy of the Church, the strength of faith for her sons, the food of the soul, the pure and perennial source of spiritual life. Consequently, these words are perfectly applicable to sacred Scripture: "For the word of God is living and efficient" (Heb. 4:12) and is "able to build up and give the inheritance among all the sanctified" (Acts 20: 32; cf. 1 Th. 2:13).

22. Easy access to sacred Scripture should be provided for all the Christian faithful.[50] That is why the Church from the very

50. This is perhaps the most novel section of the Constitution. Not since

beginning accepted as her own that very ancient Greek translation of the Old Testament which is named after seventy men;[51] and she has always given a place of honor to other translations, Eastern and Latin, especially the one known as the Vulgate. But since the word of God should be available at all times, the Church with maternal concern sees to it that suitable and correct translations are made into different languages, especially from the original texts of the sacred books.[52] And if, given the opportunity and the approval of Church authority, these translations are produced in cooperation with the separated brethren as well, all Christians will be able to use them.

23. The Bride of the incarnate Word, and the Pupil of the Holy Spirit, the Church is concerned to move ahead daily toward a deeper understanding of the sacred Scriptures so that she may unceasingly feed her sons with the divine words. Therefore, she also rightly encourages the study of the holy Fathers of both East and West and of sacred liturgies. Catholic exegetes then and other students of sacred theology, working diligently together and using appropriate means, should devote their energies, under the watchful care of the sacred teaching office of the Church, to an exploration and exposition of the divine writings. This task should be done in such a way that as many ministers of the divine word as possible will be able effectively to provide the nourishment of the Scriptures for the people of God, thereby enlightening their minds, strengthening their wills, and setting men's hearts on fire with the love of God.[53] This sacred Synod encourages the sons of the Church who are biblical scholars to continue energetically with the work they have so well begun, with a constant renewal of vigor and with loyalty to the mind of the Church.[54]

the early centuries of the Church has an official document urged the availability of the Scriptures for all. See also Art. 25.

51. I.e., the Septuagint.

52. This draws the practical consequence from the affirmation of "Divino Afflante Spiritu": "The original text has more authority and more weight than any translation, old or new." Modern-language versions therefore should by preference be made from that text, not from a pre-existing translation.

53. Cf. Pius XII, encyclical "Divino Afflante Spiritu": EB 551, 553, 567. Pontifical Biblical Commission, Instruction on Proper Teaching of Sacred Scripture in Seminaries and Religious Colleges, May 13, 1950: AAS 42 (1950), pp. 495-505.

54. Cf. Pius XII, ibid.: EB 569.

24. Sacred theology rests on the written word of God, together with sacred tradition, as its primary and perpetual foundation. By scrutinizing in the light of faith all truth stored up in the mystery of Christ, theology is most powerfully strengthened and constantly rejuvenated by that word. For the sacred Scriptures contain the word of God and, since they are inspired, really are the word of God; and so the study of the sacred page is, as it were, the soul of sacred theology.[55] By the same word of Scripture the ministry of the word also takes wholesome nourishment and yields fruits of holiness. This ministry includes pastoral preaching, catechetics, and all other Christian instruction, among which the liturgical homily should have an exceptional place.

25. Therefore, all the clergy must hold fast to the sacred Scriptures through diligent sacred reading and careful study, especially the priests of Christ and others, such as deacons and catechists, who are legitimately active in the ministry of the word. This cultivation of Scripture is required lest any of them become "an empty preacher of the word of God outwardly, who is not a listener to it inwardly"[56] since they must share the abundant wealth of the divine word with the faithful committed to them, especially in the sacred liturgy. This sacred Synod earnestly and specifically urges all the Christian faithful, too, especially religious, to learn by frequent reading of the divine Scriptures the "excelling knowledge of Jesus Christ" (Phil. 3:8). "For ignorance of the Scriptures is ignorance of Christ."[57] Therefore, they should gladly put themselves in touch with the sacred text itself, whether it be through the liturgy, rich in the divine word, or through devotional reading, or through instructions suitable for the purpose and other aids which, in our time, are commendably available everywhere, thanks to the approval and active support of the shepherds of the Church. And let them remember that prayer should accompany the reading of sacred Scripture, so that God and man may talk together; for "we speak to Him when we pray; we hear Him when we read the divine sayings."[58]

55. *Cf. Leo XIII, encyclical "Providentissimus Deus": EB 114; Benedict XV, encyclical "Spiritus Paraclitus": EB 483.*
56. *St. Augustine, Sermons, 179, 1: PL 38,966.*
57. *St. Jerome, Commentary on Isaiah, Prol.: PL 24, 17.*
    Cf. Benedict XV, encyclical "Spiritus Paraclitus": EB 475-480; Pius XII, encyclical "Divino Afflante Spiritu": EB 544.
58. *St. Ambrose, On the Duties of Ministers I, 20, 88: PL 16, 50.*

It devolves on sacred bishops, "who have the apostolic teaching,"[59] to give the faithful entrusted to them suitable instruction in the right use of the divine books, especially the New Testament and above all the Gospels, through translations of the sacred texts. Such versions are to be provided with necessary and fully adequate explanations so that the sons of the Church can safely and profitably grow familiar with the sacred Scriptures and be penetrated with their spirit.

Furthermore, editions of the sacred Scriptures, provided with suitable comments, should be prepared also for the use of non-Christians and adapted to their situation. Both pastors of souls and Christians generally should see to the wise distribution of these in one way or another.[60]

26. In this way, therefore, through the reading and study of the sacred books, let "the word of the Lord* run and be glorified" (2 Th. 3:1) and let the treasure of revelation entrusted to the Church increasingly fill the hearts of men.[61] Just as the life of the Church grows through persistent participation in the Eucharistic mystery, so we may hope for a new surge of spiritual vitality from intensified veneration for God's word, which "lasts forever" (Is. 40:8; cf. 1 Pet. 1:23-25).

Each and every one of the things set forth in this Constitution has won the consent of the Fathers of this most sacred Council. We too, by the apostolic authority conferred on us by Christ, join with the Venerable Fathers in approving, decreeing, and establishing these things in the Holy Spirit, and we direct that what has thus been enacted in synod be published to God's glory.

Rome, at St. Peter's, November 18, 1965

I, Paul, Bishop of the Catholic Church

There follow the signatures of the Fathers.

---

59. *St. Irenaeus, "Against Heretics" IV, 32, 1: PG 7, 1071; (same as 49, 2) Harvey, 2, p. 255.*
60. This is another novel departure; it envisages and encourages the establishment of Catholic Bible Societies.
*The Latin has "God" for "the Lord."—Ed.
61. The last Article returns from the apostolic aspect of Scripture reading, to the internal ecclesial aspect. The Council hopes that familiarity with the Word of God will make us all better followers, and stronger members, of Christ.

A RESPONSE

The final form of the schema on *Divine Revelation* is a great improvement on the original draft submitted to the Council in 1962. It goes a long way to meet the problems of today, though it could have gone farther.

The theological basis is certainly sound: there are not two sources of Revelation, but only one, namely God, who reveals Himself and His purposes. This has always been the Church's teaching, beginning with the New Testament, and is not an echo of modern biblical theology with its emphasis on the covenant-idea or upon *Heilsgeschichte*—as if they were new and recent discoveries. Rather, the discovery is the other way about. In this respect, Neo-Orthodoxy is really *Vetusta Orthodoxia*.

Moreover, it seems that the theory of two sources is an unsuspected, uncondemned modernism. Both Trent and Vatican I used the language of *one* source with two modes of transmission, written and oral. The quotations from Vatican I form a very fine summary of the first chapter in this Constitution. The Article rules out the erroneous idea that God is the Great Unknown, not only to all men in general but even to Christians, for it safeguards the sound principle that God has revealed Himself to all men, in nature, in history, and may be known by the light of human reason. This has always been one of the most stable and dependable principles in Catholic theology, and its modern repudiation in some areas of Protestantism has been a major tragedy, whose full consequences are now becoming apparent among those who speak lightly of the "death of God" and of "religionless Christianity." The Christian faith, as many of us believe, reflects the climax of a divine revelation which began long before human history and has been available to all men everywhere (Jn. 1:9; Acts 14:17). This revelation was available not only to the descendants of Abraham but to all men—Greeks, Romans, Arabs, Scythians, Persians, Indians, Chinese, and to nations on the far outskirts of the habitable earth.

Chapter II continues the statement of principles underlying revelation and its transmission. God Himself devised the way in which His revelation should be transmitted or handed on, and preserved, the Old Testament among the Jews, the

Old and the New alike by the Church. Fundamentally, the preaching of the gospel is oral, and from the apostles' days has been promulgated thus by apostles, bishops, priests, missionaries and teachers, and translators, all working under the guidance of God the Holy Spirit. The *tradition* enshrined, and was enshrined by, the luminous splendor of the *written* Word. This is the continuing miracle of the revelation, as it reaches out to all men everywhere, in every age. But, I believe, it might be well to lay more emphasis on the fact that not everything contained in holy Scripture is on one common high level of inspiration—the Old Testament genealogies, for example, or the secular poetry of *Canticles*. As Pope Pius XII pointed out in his great encyclical *Divino Afflante Spiritu* (1943), there are statements in the Bible that are purely figurative, illustrative, and must be understood as "tropes," figures of speech. As St. Augustine said long ago, the Christian teacher must begin his preparation by studying "tropes." For example, the parables of our Lord are not necessarily taken from actual events—though in many cases it is quite probable that they were. What the Council states in Chap. III, Art. 12, about "literary forms" is precisely in point, if we are to "search out the intention of the sacred writers."

Many a phrase in this Constitution echoes the Bible itself, especially the New Testament, and the early Church fathers, and also the Councils, especially Trent and Vatican I. Most Christians everywhere, East and West, North and South, will agree with its statements, including those about the relation of theology to Scripture and the duty of the clergy as "ministers of the Word." It will do much to encourage the revival of Bible reading in all Churches, since the good example of Rome is far-reaching. I only wish that more had been said about two or three things:

(1) The rich and rewarding consequences of constant Bible reading, not only by the clergy but also by the laity. Time was when many people supposed the Catholic Church "kept the Bible from the people." There was ample evidence of it in some areas, and also ample excuse for the effort. The barely literate tailors of London with their five-hour street-corner sermons on one text, in the days of Cromwell, and the vagaries of sects, in all ages, who cherish a half-dozen texts as if they were the whole Bible, and who went off in all directions, repudiating the traditional teaching and practice of the Church—but those days are now past! Why not

tell people what joyful discoveries lie before them in the Scriptures, what feasts of learning, what inspiration and encouragement, what sound teaching, what help in facing the problems and frustrations of life? As the prophet shouted,

> Ho, every one who thirsts,
>   come to the waters;
> and he who has no money,
>   come, buy and eat!
> Come, buy wine and milk
>   without money and without price. (Is. 55:1)

But we get the impression that from being forbidden, the reading of the Bible is now commanded. Why not simply invited, and encouraged?

(2) Why is not more said about the importance of Bible study in the training of the clergy, and in their whole way of life? By that I mean more than the selections used in the liturgy and the Offices, and much more than patristic or mediaeval allegorism in interpretation, or purely homiletical expositions, whatever the date. I mean the solid linguistic, historical, critical study of holy Scripture in the "sacred languages," Hebrew and Greek as well as Latin, and with all the most up-to-date texts and reference books—such, for example, as the magnificent *Dictionary of the Bible* by Father John McKenzie, S.J. (Bruce, 1965). This is the kind of scholarship all clergy should aspire to, and should constantly use—and also all laymen and women seriously concerned with the study of holy Scripture. And teachers—of course! Many of the outstanding works of Catholic biblical scholarship, especially those produced on the Continent but also some in Great Britain (and therefore in the English language), are almost unknown over here.

(3) Finally, how can such study continue without freedom for research? The Appendix to Cardinal Bea's *The Study of the Synoptic Gospels* (Harper, 1965) warns Ordinaries (bishops and superiors) to "keep watch with great care over popular writings . . . on biblical subjects." This is clearly censorship, and suffocating. The Constitution does not go that far, but it could—and should, I think—have said something about the *scholar's* liberty of conscience, and his duty to follow truth wherever it leads, for "Truth is mighty, and prevails" (1 Esd. 4:38), as all modern efforts at suppression and dictation of religious convictions and of scientific research are making dreadfully clear! For the sake of safeguarding the ancient

common faith of all Christians, the Church's scholars must be free and unfettered in pursuing their tasks. Of course they must be responsible. But to whom? To God, not merely the ecclesiastical authorities with their traditional interpretations.

(4) One word more. If only the Constitution had said something about the claims made for such doctrines as the Assumption of the Blessed Virgin, as based upon sound tradition, it would have clarified the minds of many inquirers. And it might have started a "dialogue" destined to open the whole question of the criteria of true tradition, and the tests by which extra-biblical teaching should be re-evaluated, and if possible reinstated in the category of "pious opinion" where it belongs (many of us think), not in the category of dogma. As Cardinal Léger of Montreal said, speaking of the effects of the Council, "The minds of Catholics are bound to be shaken up." Protestants think this not a dangerous consequence of the tremendous work of the Council, but in fact a very good thing, wherever and whenever needed. Whatever compels men to take their religion seriously and *think* about it is surely a good thing, provided they have the material for serious thinking, and can reach out toward balanced judgments.

Though I have listed a few items on which I wish the Council had been more explicit or more up to date, I would not wish to leave the impression that I am disappointed. A beginning has been made, a wonderful reawakening has taken place, which will reach out to the utmost bounds of earth and human history. As another eminent and very influential Cardinal, Archbishop Cushing of Boston, has said, "The work of the Council has not ended. It has just begun." It may take several generations to see the full working out of the consequences of Pope John's "up-dating" of the Church. What I really wish is that we could all go back to the days of Erasmus and work together in harmony, especially in biblical studies, and forget all about the intervening four centuries of confusion, distrust, and antagonism. But history is irreversible. We must go on from where we are. Thank God, a brighter path is now opening before us than any our fathers were compelled to tread!

FREDERICK C. GRANT

LITURGY

IT WAS NO accident that the first completed work of Vatican Council II proved to be the Constitution on the Sacred Liturgy. For, as Pope Paul said, "the liturgy was the first subject to be examined and the first too, in a sense, in intrinsic worth and in importance for the life of the Church." These two reasons bear some study.

It could be said, no doubt, that all the topics taken up by the Council had already been "examined"; ecumenical councils never take place in a vacuum but work on problems that are related to the Church's present needs and development. Yet the liturgy was in a privileged position when the Council began. For decades a vigorous liturgical movement had been going on, notably in such northern European countries as Belgium, Holland, Germany, and France. In 1956, however, the movement had become so international as to lead to the momentous Assisi Congress, which took place right in the Pope's back yard and with his enthusiastic blessing.

In America, too, the movement had grown from a timid trickle into a mighty tide. Back in the twenties and thirties, we witnessed the pioneer work of men like Fathers Virgil Michel, O.S.B., Gerald Ellard, S.J., H. A. Reinhold, Martin Hellriegel, and others. The astonishing growth of the Liturgical Conference, in twenty-five years, from a courageous nucleus to countless thousands of members, manifested the fact that liturgical awareness was no mere European phenomenon.

Meantime, serious scholarly work buttressed the pastoral instincts of liturgical pioneers. The vast research of Father Joseph Jungmann, S.J., for example, and scores of other probing historians, made it possible for a series of reforms to be undertaken in line with the Church's deepest traditions. Thus, when the Council addressed itself to the liturgy, all the basic spadework had been done. The magnificent text proposed to the Council Fathers was, accordingly, no haphazard or improvised sketch, but the fruit of serious preliminary work.

The preconciliar commission, headed by Cardinal Gaetano Cicognani, seemed at first disinclined to include French and German bishops and the directors of the national liturgical centers at Trier and Paris. Soon it became clear that their help was needed, and five of them were accordingly co-opted into the commission. These included such scholars as Fathers A.–M. Roguet, O.P., A. G. Martimort, and J. Wagner—all of them among the world's most esteemed liturgical experts. Father A. Bugnini, who had been secretary to the commission set up by Pope Pius XII, was happily made secretary of the commission.

Sub-committees were thereupon set up to devote four months of intensive work on each of the Constitution's proposed chapters. The entire text was worked over three times by the commission in its entirety; no point was left unexamined. Its tone was altogether biblical, stressing salvation history, though at times it uses the very phrasing of Pius XII's great encyclical *Mediator Dei*. From October 22 to November 13, 1962, the proposed text was debated at length in the Council. In fact, there were 328 oral interventions during this time.

On November 14, 2,162 Council fathers voted in favor of the schema, with only forty-six negative votes. It was thus accepted in principle. Amendments were then studied, and as much as possible incorporated into the final text, which was voted on and passed overwhelmingly just about a year later. Pope Paul, who had voted in favor of it back on October 22, 1962, when he was Archbishop Montini, now promulgated it as head of the Church. (Cf. article by Pierre Marie Gy, O.P., in *The Liturgy Constitution* [Deus Books, Paulist Press] for a good summary of the document's history.)

Pope Paul's other point—the liturgy's "intrinsic worth and importance for the life of the Church"—is almost too evident to demand comment. For, while many of the issues discussed in the Council have only an indirect bearing on the everyday life of the faithful, the liturgy touches everyone immediately and vitally. Nothing is more evidently at the core of the Christian life than our public worship—which, in fact, is precisely what liturgy means. Further, the explanation of the Church as the People of God, given in the Constitution, anticipated the fuller development to be given in the great Constitution on the Church.

Several points of emphasis in the Constitution are useful for our understanding of the whole work of the Council. Article 50, for example, stresses the need of revising the rite of the Mass "in such a way that the intrinsic nature and purpose of its several parts, as also the connection between them, can be more clearly manifested." Thus, the meaning of the Mass and its various sections should be made more intelligible, and that precisely for the sake of "devout and active participation by the faithful." In the course of centuries, much of this had been lost, and, while reverence for the awesome mystery had always remained strong among the faithful, much of its sacramental usefulness had been diminished by obscurity.

The Constitution goes on to make this explicit: "Elements which, with the passage of time, came to be duplicated, or were added with but little advantage, are now to be discarded." Here the principle of change is accepted, not with a view to change for change's sake, or returning to the past for the past's sake, but all for the pastoral benefit of the faithful. This practical, pastoral note may be found everywhere in the Council's work.

The liturgical Constitution had another advantage in coming first. In a very short time after its promulgation, Catholics began to participate in a more meaningful, more communal celebration of the Holy Sacrifice. This had the added effect of dramatizing in a concrete way (a sacramental way, one might say) the reality of Church renewal, or *aggiornamento*. The Council quickly ceased to be something remote, occupying the bishops gathered in Rome and the newspaper columnists who tried to give it vivid treatment. The Constitution made a difference right in the parishes. By sharing actively in worship, even the ordinary Catholic began to take part in the great work launched by Pope John and continued by Pope Paul.

The Council's Commission on the Liturgy lost no time translating the Constitution into action. Under the leadership of venerable Cardinal Lercaro, the new Commission gave a series of specific, concrete directives. True, some opposition was only to be expected; but the overwhelming majority of the faithful found the "new liturgy" intelligible and authentically helpful. The Holy Father himself, by celebrating Mass according to the new patterns, helped to show how effective they were. After witnessing the historic Mass celebrated by Pope Paul in Yankee Stadium, only the most recalcitrant could question that the new way was better than the old.

At the same time, the present reforms are by no means

final or fixed. As I have tried to show in *Our Changing Liturgy* (Hawthorn), they mark only a beginning and are part of a dynamic, ongoing process of renewal inspired by God and directed by our spiritual shepherds.

C. J. McNaspy, S.J.

Constitution on the Sacred Liturgy [1]

PAUL, BISHOP

SERVANT OF THE SERVANTS OF GOD

TOGETHER WITH THE FATHERS OF THE SACRED COUNCIL

FOR EVERLASTING MEMORY

1. It is the goal of this most sacred Council to intensify the daily growth of Catholics in Christian living; to make more responsive to the requirements of our times those Church observances which are open to adaptation; to nurture whatever can contribute to the unity of all who believe in Christ; and to strengthen those aspects of the Church which can help summon all of mankind into her embrace. Hence the Council has special reasons for judging it a duty to provide for the renewal and fostering of the liturgy.

2. For it is through the liturgy, especially the divine Eucharistic Sacrifice, that "the work of our redemption is exercised." [2] The liturgy is thus the outstanding means by which the faithful can express in their lives, and manifest to others, the mystery of Christ and the real nature of the true Church. [3] It is of the essence of the Church that she be both human and divine, visible and yet invisibly endowed, eager to act and yet devoted to contemplation, present in this world and yet not at home in it. She is all these things in such a way that in

1. This document, promulgated on Dec. 4, 1963, was the first Constitution published by Vatican Council II. It came at the end of the Council's second session.
2. *Secret* (prayer in the Mass now called Prayer over the Offerings) *for the ninth Sunday after Pentecost.*
3. Liturgy is seen as something profound rather than merely external. In many ways this Constitution is the germ of the Constitution on the Church, promulgated on Nov. 21, 1964.

her the human is directed and subordinated to the divine,
the visible likewise to the invisible, action to contemplation,
and this present world to that city yet to come, which we
seek (cf. Heb. 13:14). Day by day the liturgy builds up those
within the Church into the Lord's holy temple, into a spiritual
dwelling for God (cf. Eph. 2:21-22)—an enterprise which
will continue until Christ's full stature is achieved (cf. Eph.
4:13). At the same time the liturgy marvelously fortifies the
faithful in their capacity to preach Christ. To outsiders the
liturgy thereby reveals the Church as a sign raised above the
nations (cf. Is. 11:12). Under this sign the scattered sons of
God are being gathered into one (cf. Jn. 11:52) until there
is one fold and one shepherd (cf. Jn. 10:16).

3. Therefore this most sacred Council judges that the following principles concerning the promotion and reform of the
liturgy should be called to mind, and that practical norms
should be established.

Among these principles and norms there are some which
can and should be applied both to the Roman rite and also
to all the other rites. The practical norms which follow, however, should be taken as pertaining only to the Roman rite,
except for those which, in the very nature of things, affect
other rites as well.[4]

4. Finally, in faithful obedience to tradition, this most sacred
Council declares that holy Mother Church holds all lawfully
acknowledged rites to be of equal authority and dignity; that
she wishes to preserve them in the future and to foster them
in every way. The Council also desires that, where necessary,
the rites be carefully and thoroughly revised in the light of
sound tradition, and that they be given new vigor to meet the
circumstances and needs of modern times.

4. The rites of the Eastern Church, which are in no way inferior to the
Roman rite, are envisioned here only in the broadest principles; for details,
they follow their own venerable traditions.

CHAPTER I

GENERAL PRINCIPLES FOR THE RESTORATION AND PROMOTION OF THE SACRED LITURGY

I. The Nature of the Sacred Liturgy and Its Importance in the Church's Life

5. God, who "wishes all men to be saved and come to the knowledge of the truth" (1 Tim. 2:4), "in many and various ways . . . spoke of old to our fathers by the prophets"* (Heb. 1:1). When the fullness of time had come He sent His Son, the Word made flesh, anointed by the Holy Spirit, to preach the gospel to the poor, to heal the contrite of heart (cf. Is. 61:1; Lk. 4:18), to be a "bodily and spiritual medicine,"[5] the Mediator between God and man (cf. 1 Tim. 2:5).[6] For His humanity, united with the person of the Word, was the instrument of our salvation. Thus in Christ "there came forth the perfect satisfaction needed for our reconcilation, and we received the means for giving worthy worship to God."[7]

The wonders wrought by God among the people of the Old Testament were but a prelude to the work of Christ the Lord in redeeming mankind and giving perfect glory to God. He achieved His task principally by the paschal mystery of His blessed passion, resurrection from the dead, and glorious ascension, whereby "dying, he destroyed our death and, rising,

---

*Revised Standard Version (Confraternity: "at sundry times and in divers manners").—Ed.
5. *St. Ignatius of Antioch, "To the Ephesians," 7, 2; ed. F. X. Funk, Patres Apostolici I, Tübingen, 1901, p. 218.*
6. The central position of Christ as our Mediator is the theme of Pius XII's important encyclical, *Mediator Dei*, which was the Magna Carta of the liturgical renewal (1947). The present Constitution, however, goes far beyond its development.
7. *Sacramentarium Veronense (Leonianum); ed. C. Mohlberg, Rome, 1956 n. 1265.*

he restored our life."[8] For it was from the side of Christ as He slept the sleep of death upon the cross that there came forth the wondrous sacrament which is the whole Church.[9]

6. Just as Christ was sent by the Father, so also He sent the apostles, filled with the Holy Spirit. This He did so that, by preaching the gospel to every creature (cf. Mk. 16:15), they might proclaim that the Son of God, by His death and resurrection, had freed us from the power of Satan (cf. Acts 26: 18) and from death, and brought us into the kingdom of His Father. His purpose was also that they might exercise the work of salvation which they were proclaiming, by means of sacrifice and sacraments, around which the entire liturgical life revolves. Thus, by baptism, men are plunged into the paschal mystery of Christ: they die with Him, are buried with Him, and rise with Him (cf. Rom. 6:4; Eph. 2:6; Col. 3:1; 2 Tim. 2:11); they receive the spirit of adoption as sons "by virtue of which we cry: Abba, Father" (Rom. 8:15), and thus become those true adorers whom the Father seeks (cf. Jn. 4:23). In like manner, as often as they eat the supper of the Lord they proclaim the death of the Lord until He comes (cf. 1 Cor. 11:26). For that reason, on the very day of Pentecost, when the Church appeared before the world, "those who received the word" of Peter "were baptized." And "they continued steadfastly in the teaching of the apostles and in the communion of the breaking of the bread and in the prayers ... praising God and being in favor with all the people" (Acts 2:41-47). From that time onward the Church has never failed to come together to celebrate the paschal mystery: reading "in all the scriptures the things referring to himself" (Lk. 24:27), celebrating the Eucharist in which "the victory and triumph of his death are again made present,[10] and at the same time giving thanks "to God for his unspeakable gift" (2 Cor. 9:15) in Christ Jesus, "to the praise of his glory" (Eph. 1:12), through the power of the Holy Spirit.

7. To accomplish so great a work, Christ is always present in

8. *Easter Preface in the Roman Missal.*
9. *Cf. St. Augustine, "Enarr. in Ps. 138" 2, Corpus Christianorum XL, Tournai, 1956, p. 1991, and prayer after the second lesson for Holy Saturday, as it was in the Roman Missal before the restoration of Holy Week.*
10. *Council of Trent, Session 13, Oct. 11, 1551, Decree on the Holy Eucharist, c. 5: Concilium Tridentinum, Diariorum, Actorum, Epistolarum, Tractatuum nova collectio, ed. Soc. Goerresiana, VII, Actorum pars IV, Freiburg im Breisgau, 1961, p. 202.*

His Church, especially in her liturgical celebrations. He is present in the sacrifice of the Mass, not only in the person of His minister, "the same one now offering, through the ministry of priests, who formerly offered himself on the cross,"[11] but especially under the Eucharistic species. By His power He is present in the sacraments, so that when a man baptizes it is really Christ Himself who baptizes.[12] He is present in His word, since it is He Himself who speaks when the holy Scriptures are read in the church. He is present, finally, when the Church prays and sings, for He promised: "Where two or three are gathered together for my sake, there am I in the midst of them" (Mt. 18:20).

Christ indeed always associates the Church with Himself in the truly great work of giving perfect praise to God and making men holy. The Church is His dearly beloved Bride who calls to her Lord, and through Him offers worship to the Eternal Father.

Rightly, then, the liturgy is considered as an exercise of the priestly office of Jesus Christ. In the liturgy the sanctification of man is manifested by signs perceptible to the senses, and is effected in a way which is proper to each of these signs; in the liturgy full public worship is performed by the Mystical Body of Jesus Christ, that is, by the Head and His members.[13]

From this it follows that every liturgical celebration, because it is an action of Christ the priest and of His Body the Church, is a sacred action surpassing all others. No other action of the Church can match its claim to efficacy, nor equal the degree of it.

8. In the earthly liturgy, by way of foretaste, we share in that heavenly liturgy which is celebrated in the holy city of Jerusalem toward which we journey as pilgrims, and in which Christ is sitting at the right hand of God, a minister of the sanctuary and of the true tabernacle (cf. Apoc. 21:2; Col. 3:1; Heb. 8:2); we sing a hymn to the Lord's glory with all the warriors of the heavenly army; venerating the memory of the saints, we hope for some part and fellowship with them;

11. *Council of Trent, Session 22, Sept. 17, 1562, Doctrine on the Holy Sacrifice of the Mass, c. 2: Concilium Tridentinum, ed. cit., VIII, Actorum pars V, Freiburg im Breisgau, 1919, p. 960.*
12. *Cf. St. Augustine, "In Ioannis Evangelium tractatus VI," c. 1, n. 7; PL 35, 1428.*
13. Another important encyclical of Pius XII, *Mystici Corporis* (1943), stressed the fact of the Church as Christ's Mystical Body. This has been incorporated (and in some ways greatly surpassed) by the present Constitution and the Constitution on the Church.

we eagerly await the Savior, our Lord Jesus Christ, until He, our life, shall appear and we too will appear with Him in glory (cf. Phil. 3:20; Col. 3:4).

9. The sacred liturgy does not exhaust the entire activity of the Church. Before men can come to the liturgy they must be called to faith and to conversion: "How then are they to call upon him in whom they have not believed? But how are they to believe him whom they have not heard? And how are they to hear, if no one preaches? And how are men to preach unless they be sent?" (Rom. 10:14-15).

Therefore the Church announces the good tidings of salvation to those who do not believe, so that all men may know the true God and Jesus Christ whom He has sent, and may repent and mend their ways (cf. Jn. 17:3; Lk. 24:27; Acts 2:38). To believers also the Church must ever preach faith and repentance. She must prepare them for the sacraments, teach them to observe all that Christ has commanded (cf. Mt. 28:20), and win them to all the works of charity, piety, and the apostolate. For all these activities make it clear that Christ's faithful, though not of this world, are the light of the world and give glory to the Father in the sight of men.

10. Nevertheless the liturgy is the summit toward which the activity of the Church is directed; at the same time it is the fountain from which all her power flows.[14] For the goal of apostolic works is that all who are made sons of God by faith and baptism should come together to praise God in the midst of His Church, to take part in her sacrifice, and to eat the Lord's supper.

The liturgy in its turn inspires the faithful to become "of one heart in love"[15] when they have tasted to their full of the paschal mysteries; it prays that "they may grasp by deed what they hold by creed."[16] The renewal in the Eucharist of the covenant between the Lord and man draws the faithful into the compelling love of Christ and sets them afire. From the liturgy, therefore, and especially from the Eucharist, as from a fountain, grace is channeled into us; and the sanctification of men in Christ and the glorification of God, to

14. This solemn paragraph represents the core of the Church's official teaching on the liturgy. It is thus something central, by no means secondary or peripheral.
15. *Postcommunion in the Easter Vigil Mass and the Mass of Easter Sunday.*
16. *Collect* (prayer) *of the Mass for Tuesday of Easter Week.*

which all other activities of the Church are directed as toward
their goal, are most powerfully achieved.

11. But in order that the sacred liturgy may produce its
full effect, it is necessary that the faithful come to it with
proper dispositions, that their thoughts match their words, and
that they cooperate with divine grace lest they receive it in
vain (cf. 2 Cor. 6:1). Pastors of souls must therefore realize
that, when the liturgy is celebrated, more is required than the
mere observance of the laws governing valid and licit celebration. It is their duty also to ensure that the faithful take part
knowingly, actively, and fruitfully.[17]

12. The spiritual life, however, is not confined to participation
in the liturgy. The Christian is assuredly called to pray with
his brethren, but he must also enter into his chamber to pray
to the Father in secret (cf. Mt. 6:6); indeed, according to
the teaching of the Apostle Paul, he should pray without ceasing (cf. 1 Th. 5:17). We learn from the same Apostle that
we must always carry about in our body the dying of Jesus, so
that the life of Jesus too may be made manifest in our bodily
frame (cf. 2 Cor. 4:10-11). This is why we ask the Lord in
the sacrifice of the Mass that, "receiving the offering of the
spiritual victim," He may fashion us for Himself "as an
eternal gift."[18]

13. Popular devotions of the Christian people are warmly
commended, provided they accord with the laws and norms of
the Church. Such is especially the case with devotions called
for by the Apostolic See.

Devotions proper to individual churches also have a special
dignity if they are conducted by mandate of the bishops in
accord with customs or books lawfully approved.

Nevertheless these devotions should be so drawn up that
they harmonize with the liturgical seasons, accord with the
sacred liturgy, are in some fashion derived from it, and lead
the people to it, since the liturgy by its very nature far surpasses any of them.[19]

17. This theme of awareness and active participation by the faithful is
another basic theme of the Constitution. It reinforces recent papal teaching
on the meaning of liturgy.
18. *Secret* (prayer of the Mass) *for Monday of Pentecost Week.*
19. While liturgy is not the whole of the Christian life and does not supplant personal prayer, all devotions must harmonize with its spirit.

II. The Promotion of Liturgical Instruction and Active Participation

14. Mother Church earnestly desires that all the faithful be led to that full, conscious, and active participation in liturgical celebrations which is demanded by the very nature of the liturgy. Such participation by the Christian people as "a chosen race, a royal priesthood, a holy nation, a purchased people" (1 Pet. 2:9; cf. 2:4-5), is their right and duty by reason of their baptism.

In the restoration and promotion of the sacred liturgy, this full and active participation by all the people is the aim to be considered before all else; for it is the primary and indispensable source from which the faithful are to derive the true Christian spirit. Therefore, through the needed program of instruction, pastors of souls must zealously strive to achieve it in all their pastoral work.[20]

Yet it would be futile to entertain any hopes of realizing this goal unless the pastors themselves, to begin with, become thoroughly penetrated with the spirit and power of the liturgy, and become masters of it. It is vitally necessary, therefore, that attention be directed, above all, to the liturgical instruction of the clergy.[21] Therefore this most sacred Council has decided to enact as follows:

15. Professors who are appointed to teach liturgy in seminaries, religious houses of study, and theological faculties must be properly trained for their work in institutes which specialize in this subject.

16. The study of sacred liturgy is to be ranked among the compulsory and major courses in seminaries and religious houses of studies; in theological faculties it is to rank among the principal subjects. It is to be taught under its theological, historical, spiritual, pastoral, and juridical aspects. Moreover,

20. Again the emphasis on active and conscious participation by the whole Church. Liturgy is thus not a clerical preserve. Rather, the whole people of God has a priestly function which must not be treated as unimportant.
21. The Council anticipates the danger that some priests, used to different patterns of thought and behavior, may not grasp the central position of worship. Accordingly, priests and future priests are required to become deeply imbued with the liturgical spirit. This section of the Constitution may, in the practical order, prove the most momentous of all.

other professors, while striving to expound the mystery of Christ and the history of salvation from the angle proper to each of their own subjects, must nevertheless do so in a way which will clearly bring out the connection between their subjects and the liturgy, as also the unity which underlies all priestly training. This consideration is especially important for professors of dogmatic, spiritual, and pastoral theology and holy Scripture.

17. In seminaries and houses of religious, clerics are to be given a liturgical formation in their spiritual life. For this they will need proper direction, so that they can understand the sacred rites and take part in them wholeheartedly; and they will also need to celebrate the sacred mysteries personally, as well as popular devotions which are animated with the spirit of the liturgy. In addition they must learn how to observe liturgical laws. Thus life in seminaries and houses of religion will be thoroughly influenced by the spirit of the liturgy.

18. Secular and religious priests already at work in the Lord's vineyard are to be helped by every suitable means to understand ever more deeply what it is that they do when they perform sacred rites; they are to be aided to live the liturgical life and to share it with the faithful entrusted to their care.

19. With zeal and patience,[22] pastors of souls must promote the liturgical instruction of the faithful, and also their active participation in the liturgy both internally and externally. The age and condition of their people, their way of life, and degree of religious culture should be taken into account. By so doing, pastors will be fulfilling one of the chief duties of a faithful dispenser of the mysteries of God; and in this matter they must lead their flock not only in word but also by example.

20. The broadcasting and televising of sacred rites must be done with discretion and dignity, under the guidance and guarantee of a suitable person appointed for this office by the bishops. This is especially important when the service in question is a Mass.

22. The two-pronged insistence on "zeal and patience" recognizes the fact that some priests will tend to move faster than the faithful, while others (perhaps the majority) will be inclined to stress patience at the expense of zeal.

III. The Reform of the Sacred Liturgy

21. In order that the Christian people may more securely derive an abundance of graces from the sacred liturgy, holy Mother Church desires to undertake with great care a general restoration of the liturgy itself. For the liturgy is made up of unchangeable elements divinely instituted, and elements subject to change. The latter not only may but ought to be changed with the passing of time if features have by chance crept in which are less harmonious with the intimate nature of the liturgy, or if existing elements have grown less functional.[23]

In this restoration, both texts and rites should be drawn up so that they express more clearly the holy things which they signify. Christian people, as far as possible, should be able to understand them with ease and to take part in them fully, actively, and as befits a community.

Therefore this most sacred Council establishes the following general norms:

(A) GENERAL NORMS

22. §1. Regulation of the sacred liturgy depends solely on the authority of the Church, that is, on the Apostolic See and, as laws may determine, on the bishop.

§2. In virtue of power conceded by the law, the regulation of the liturgy within certain defined limits belongs also to various kinds of competent territorial bodies of bishops legitimately established.

§3. Therefore, absolutely no other person, not even a priest, may add, remove, or change anything in the liturgy on his own authority.

23. That sound tradition may be retained, and yet the way be open for legitimate progress, a careful investigation is always to be made into each part of the liturgy which is to be revised. This investigation should be theological, historical, and pastoral.[24] Also, the general laws governing the structure

---

23. The Catholic inclination to accept all religious practices as unchangeable is here given a sharp and much needed corrective. There are, indeed, unchangeable elements in the liturgy; but others "may and ought to be changed." For a futher development of this point, see the editor's volume, *Our Changing Liturgy* (Hawthorn, 1965).
24. Liturgical changes involve not primarily a return to the past but due adaptation to present needs. However, historical and theological study is

and meaning of the liturgy must be studied in conjunction with the experience derived from recent liturgical reforms and from the indults conceded to various places. Finally, there must be no innovations unless the good of the Church genuinely and certainly requires them; and care must be taken that any new forms adopted should in some way grow organically from forms already existing.

As far as possible, notable differences between the rites used in adjacent regions are to be carefully avoided.

24. Sacred Scripture is of paramount importance in the celebration of the liturgy. For it is from Scripture that lessons are read and explained in the homily, and psalms are sung; the prayers, collects, and liturgical songs are scriptural in their inspiration, and it is from Scripture that actions and signs derive their meaning. Thus if the restoration, progress, and adaptation of the sacred liturgy are to be achieved, it is necessary to promote that warm and living love for Scripture to which the venerable tradition of both Eastern and Western rites gives testimony.[25]

25. The liturgical books are to be revised as soon as possible; from various parts of the world, experts are to be employed and bishops are to be consulted.

(B) Norms Drawn from the Hierarchic and Communal Nature of the Liturgy

26. Liturgical services are not private functions, but are celebrations of the Church, which is the "sacrament of unity," namely, a holy people united and organized under their bishops.[26]

Therefore liturgical services pertain to the whole body of the Church; they manifest it and have effects upon it; but they concern individual members of the Church in different ways, according to the diversity of holy orders, functions, and degrees of participation.[27]

required for a full understanding of the rites in question. Otherwise, the changes may prove ineffectual, if not counterproductive.
25. The paramount role of sacred Scripture, God's Word, in the liturgy needs stress. The biblical movement and deeper grasp of salvation history are two of the central currents of Catholic thought today.
26. *St. Cyprian, "On the Unity of the Catholic Church," 7; ed. G. Hartel, in CSEL, III, 1, Vienna, 1868, pp. 215-16. Cf. Ep. 66, n. 8:3; ed. cit., III, 2, Vienna, 1871, pp. 732-33.*
27. While every Christian is involved in public worship, each has a special

27. It is to be stressed that whenever rites, according to their specific nature, make provision for communal celebration involving the presence and active participation of the faithful, this way of celebrating them is to be preferred, as far as possible, to a celebration that is individual and quasi-private.

This rule applies with special force to the celebration of Mass and the administration of the sacraments, even though every Mass has of itself a public and social nature.

28. In liturgical celebrations, whether as a minister or as one of the faithful, each person should perform his role by doing solely and totally what the nature of things and liturgical norms require of him.

29. Servers, lectors, commentators, and members of the choir also exercise a genuine liturgical ministry. They ought, therefore, to discharge their office with the sincere piety and decorum demanded by so exalted a ministry and rightly expected of them by God's people.

Consequently they must all be deeply penetrated with the spirit of the liturgy, each in his own measure, and they must be trained to perform their functions in a correct and orderly manner.

30. By way of promoting active participation, the people should be encouraged to take part by means of acclamations, responses, psalmody, antiphons, and songs, as well as by actions, gestures, and bodily attitudes. And at the proper times all should observe a reverent silence.[28]

31. In the revision of liturgical books, it should be carefully provided that the rubrics take the role of the people into account.

32. The liturgy makes distinctions between persons according to their liturgical function and sacred Orders, and there are liturgical laws providing for due honors to be given to civil authorities. Apart from these instances, no special honors are to be paid in the liturgy to any private persons or classes of persons, whether in the ceremonies or by external display.

role which he alone must perform. This is developed in Art. 28. The social consciousness implied in the liturgical renewal is another great spiritual development of contemporary Catholicism.

28. The people's role, while always active, will take different forms (including a "social silence") in various parts of liturgical worship. Passivity or exaggerated isolation is foreign to the authentic Christian spirit, as seen everywhere in the teachings of the Council.

(C) Norms Based upon the Educative
and Pastoral Nature of the Liturgy

33. Although the sacred liturgy is above all things the worship
of the divine Majesty, it likewise contains abundant instruction for the faithful.[29] For in the liturgy God speaks to His
people and Christ is still proclaiming His gospel. And the
people reply to God both by song and by prayer.[30]

Moreover, the prayers addressed to God by the priest who
presides over the assembly in the person of Christ are said in
the name of the entire holy people as well as of all present.
And the visible signs used by the liturgy to signify invisible
divine things have been chosen by Christ or the Church.
Thus, not only when things are read "which have been written
for our instruction" (Rom. 15:4), but also when the Church
prays or sings or acts, the faith of those taking part is nourished and their minds are raised to God, so that they may
offer Him the worship which reason requires and more copiously receive His grace.

Therefore, in the revision of the liturgy, the following general norms should be observed:

34. The rites should be distinguished by a noble simplicity;
they should be short, clear, and unencumbered by useless
repetitions; they should be within the people's powers of com-
prehension, and normally should not require much explanation.[31]

35. That the intimate connection between words and rites
may be apparent in the liturgy:

(1) In sacred celebrations there is to be more reading from
holy Scripture, and it is to be more varied and suitable.

(2) Since the sermon is part of the liturgical service, the
preferred place for it is to be indicated even in the rubrics, as
far as the nature of the rite will allow; and the ministry of
preaching is to be fulfilled with exactitude and fidelity. The
sermon, moreover, should draw its content mainly from scriptural and liturgical sources. Its character should be that

29. *Cf. Council of Trent, Session 22, Sept. 17, 1562, Doctrine on the Holy
Sacrifice of the Mass, c. 8: Concilium Tridentinum, ed. cit., VIII, p. 961.*
30. While worship is directed to God, it is a consequence of the Incarnation,
recognizing the need of going "through the visible to the invisible" (Preface
for the Mass of Christmas). Worship, thus, is in great part instructional.
31. The "noble simplicity" and clarity called for here are consequences of
liturgy itself and the whole sacramental system. They are particularly relevant
to our age, with its stress on the values of sincerity and authenticity.

of a proclamation of God's wonderful works in the history of salvation, that is, the mystery of Christ, which is ever made present and active within us, especially in the celebration of the liturgy.[32]

(3) Instruction which is more explicitly liturgical should also be imparted in a variety of ways; if necessary, should directives to be spoken by the priest or proper minister should be provided within the rites themselves. But they should occur only at the more suitable moments, and be in prescribed words or their equivalent.

(4) Bible services should be encouraged, especially on the vigils of the more solemn feasts, on some weekdays in Advent and Lent, and on Sundays and feast days. They are particularly to be commended in places where no priest is available; when this is so, a deacon or some other person authorized by the bishop should preside over the celebration.[33]

36. §1. Particular law remaining in force, the use of the Latin language is to be preserved in the Latin rites.

§2. But since the use of the mother tongue, whether in the Mass, the administration of the sacraments, or other parts of the liturgy, may frequently be of great advantage to the people, the limits of its employment may be extended. This extension will apply in the first place to the readings and directives, and to some of the prayers and chants, according to the regulations on this matter to be laid down separately in subsequent chapters.

§3. It is for the competent territorial ecclesiastical authority mentioned in Article 22, §2, to decide whether, and to what extent, the vernacular language is to be used according to these norms; their decrees are to be approved, that is, confirmed, by the Apostolic See. And, whenever the procedure seems to be called for, this authority is to consult with bishops of neighboring regions employing the same language.[34]

32. The homily is not meant to be a sort of autonomous service, but the normal outflowing of holy Scripture as applied to the spiritual needs of God's people here and now.
33. Bible services represent both a return to ancient Christian practice and a fuller use of God's Word. A large measure of variety here becomes possible, which will relieve the tedium of repetitious familiar devotions. In line with the scriptural movement, Catholics now have a chance to enrich their spiritual lives by exploring the full treasury of revelation, instead of only a few truths.
34. While Latin is officially retained as the language of the Roman rite, a wide opening is made for the use of local tongues (the "vernacular"). In great part the amount of vernacular is left to the discretion of bishops. Preliminary "experiments" in the use of the vernacular have received

§4. Translations from the Latin text into the mother tongue which are intended for use in the liturgy must be approved by the competent territorial ecclesiastical authority mentioned above.

(D) NORMS FOR ADAPTING THE LITURGY TO THE GENIUS AND TRADITIONS OF PEOPLES

37. Even in the liturgy, the Church has no wish to impose a rigid uniformity in matters which do not involve the faith or the good of the whole community. Rather she respects and fosters the spiritual adornments and gifts of the various races and peoples. Anything in their way of life that is not indissolubly bound up with superstition and error she studies with sympathy and, if possible, preserves intact. Sometimes in fact she admits such things into the liturgy itself, as long as they harmonize with its true and authentic spirit.[35]

38. Provided that the substantial unity of the Roman rite is maintained, the revision of liturgical books should allow for legitimate variations and adaptations to different groups, regions, and peoples, especially in mission lands. Where opportune, the same rule applies to the structuring of rites and the devising of rubrics.

39. Within the limits set by the typical editions of the liturgical books, it shall be for the competent territorial ecclesiastical authority mentioned in Article 22, §2, to specify adaptations, especially in the case of the administration of the sacraments, the sacramentals, processions, liturgical language, sacred music, and the arts, but according to the fundamental norms laid down in this Constitution.

40. In some places and circumstances, however, an even more radical adaptation of the liturgy is needed and entails greater difficulties.
Therefore:
(1) The competent territorial ecclesiastical authority mentioned in Article 22, §2, must, in this matter, carefully and

generally enthusiastic acceptance by the faithful, despite the less-than-perfect texts used at present.
35. The unity of the Church does not demand uniformity, as we learn from the experience of Eastern Catholics. However, the principle of diversity is now widened in its application to the faithful of the Roman rite. This is one of the most revolutionary Articles of the Constitution and is likely to have important effects both in missionary countries and at home.

prudently consider which elements from the traditions and genius of individual peoples might appropriately be admitted into divine worship. Adaptations which are judged to be useful or necessary should then be submitted to the Apostolic See, by whose consent they may be introduced.

(2) To ensure that adaptations are made with all necessary circumspection, the Apostolic See will grant power to this same territorial ecclesiastical authority to permit and to direct, as the case requires, the necessary preliminary experiments over a determined period of time among certain groups suited for the purpose.

(3) Because liturgical laws often involve special difficulties with respect to adaptation, particularly in mission lands, men who are experts in these matters must be employed to formulate them.

IV. Promotion of Liturgical Life in Diocese and Parish

41. The bishop is to be considered the high priest of his flock. In a certain sense it is from him that the faithful who are under his care derive and maintain their life in Christ.[36]

Therefore all should hold in very high esteem the liturgical life of the diocese which centers around the bishop, especially in his cathedral church. Let them be persuaded that the Church reveals herself most clearly when a full complement of God's holy people, united in prayer and in a common liturgical service (especially the Eucharist), exercise a thorough and active participation at the very altar where the bishop presides in the company of his priests and other assistants.[37]

42. But because it is impossible for the bishop always and everywhere to preside over the whole flock in his Church, he cannot do other than establish lesser groupings of the faithful. Among these, parishes set up locally under a pastor who takes the place of the bishop are the most important: for in a certain way they represent the visible Church as it is established throughout the world.

36. The primary role of the bishop is that of priest. Parishes are seen as local expressions of the diocese and the entire Church. Chapter 3 of the Constitution on the Church develops the theology of the bishop's roles.
37. Cf. St. Ignatius of Antioch, "To the Magnesians," 7; "To the Philadelphians," 4; "To the Smyrnans," 8; ed. F. X. Funk, op. cit., I, pp. 236, 266, 281.

Therefore the liturgical life of the parish and its relationship to the bishop must be fostered in the thinking and practice of both laity and clergy; efforts also must be made to encourage a sense of community within the parish, above all in the common celebration of the Sunday Mass.

V. The Promotion of Pastoral-Liturgical Action

43. Zeal for the promotion and restoration of the liturgy is rightly held to be a sign of the providential dispositions of God in our time, as a movement of the Holy Spirit in His Church. It is today a distinguishing mark of the Church's life, indeed of the whole tenor of contemporary religious thought and action.

So that this pastoral-liturgical action may become even more vigorous in the Church, this most sacred Council decrees:

44. It is desirable that the competent territorial ecclesiastical authority mentioned in Article 22, §2, set up a liturgical commission, to be assisted by experts in liturgical science, sacred music, art, and pastoral practice. As far as possible, the commission should be aided by some kind of Institute for Pastoral Liturgy, consisting of persons who are eminent in these matters, and including laymen, as circumstances suggest. Under the direction of the aforementioned territorial ecclesiastical authority the commission is to regulate pastoral-liturgical action throughout the territory, and to promote studies and necessary experiments whenever there is question of adaptations to be proposed to the Apostolic See.[38]

45. Likewise, by way of advancing the liturgical apostolate, every diocese is to have a commission on the sacred liturgy under the direction of the bishop.

Sometimes it may be expedient for several dioceses to form between them one single commission which will be able to promote the liturgy by common consultation.

46. Besides the commission on the sacred liturgy, every diocese, as far as possible, should have commissions for sacred music and sacred art.

38. The bishops are to set up various commissions of liturgical experts and other professionals to assist in the work of adaptation, which is the explicit aim of this Constitution. It is recognized that no single person can be fully competent in an area which touches on all Christian life.

These three commissions must harmonize their activities. Indeed it will frequently be advisable to fuse the three of them into a single commission.

CHAPTER II

THE MOST SACRED MYSTERY OF THE EUCHARIST

47. At the Last Supper, on the night when He was betrayed, our Savior instituted the Eucharistic Sacrifice of His Body and Blood. He did this in order to perpetuate the sacrifice of the Cross throughout the centuries until He should come again, and so to entrust to His beloved spouse, the Church, a memorial of His death and resurrection: a sacrament of love, a sign of unity, a bond of charity,[39] a paschal banquet in which Christ is consumed, the mind is filled with grace, and a pledge of future glory is given to us.[40]

48. The Church, therefore, earnestly desires that Christ's faithful, when present at this mystery of faith, should not be there as strangers or silent spectators. On the contrary, through a proper appreciation of the rites and prayers they should participate knowingly, devoutly, and actively. They should be instructed by God's word and be refreshed at the table of the Lord's body; they should give thanks to God; by offering the Immaculate Victim, not only through the hands of the priest, but also with him, they should learn to offer themselves too. Through Christ the Mediator,[41] they should be drawn day by day into ever closer union with God and with each other, so that finally God may be all in all.[42]

39. Cf. St. Augustine, "In Ioannis Evangelium tractatus 26," c. 6, n. 13: PL 35, 1613.
40. Roman Breviary, Feast of Corpus Christi, Second Vespers, antiphon to the Magnificat.
41. Cf. St. Cyril of Alexandria, "Commentary on the Gospel of John," Book 11, c. 11-12: PG 74, 557-564.
42. The Eucharist, our daily sacrament, is the center of the Christian life.

49. Consequently, this sacred Council, having in mind those Masses which are celebrated with the assistance of the faithful, especially on Sundays and feasts of obligation, issues the following decrees so that the sacrifice of the Mass, even in the ritual forms of its celebration, can achieve its pastoral effects to the fullest.

50. The rite of the Mass is to be revised in such a way that the intrinsic nature and purpose of its several parts, as also the connection between them, can be more clearly manifested, and that devout and active participation by the faithful can be more easily accomplished.

For this purpose the rites are to be simplified, while due care is taken to preserve their substance. Elements which, with the passage of time, came to be duplicated, or were added with but little advantage, are now to be discarded. Where opportunity allows or necessity demands, other elements which have suffered injury through accidents of history are now to be restored to the earlier norm of the holy Fathers.[43]

51. The treasures of the Bible are to be opened up more lavishly, so that richer fare may be provided for the faithful at the table of God's Word. In this way a more representative portion of the holy Scriptures will be read to the people over a set cycle of years.

52. By means of the homily the mysteries of the faith and the guiding principles of the Christian life are expounded from the sacred text during the course of the liturgical year. The homily, therefore, is to be highly esteemed as part of the liturgy itself; in fact, at those Masses which are celebrated with the assistance of the people on Sundays and feasts of obligation, it should not be omitted except for a serious reason.

53. Especially on Sundays and feasts of obligation, there is to be restored, after the Gospel and the homily, "the common prayer" or "the prayer of the faithful." By this prayer,

---

The encyclical *Mediator Dei* (84) had previously insisted that it is our "duty and highest privilege to take part in the Eucharistic Sacrifice." It is there, especially, that we are nourished by God's Word and the Lord's Body; it is there that we offer Christ our Mediator and ourselves in Him and through Him to the Father.

43. The ceremonies of the Mass are to be clarified and simplified for the sake of deeper participation. The fact that certain features of our present liturgical rites are less than perfect is honestly admitted.

in which the people are to take part, intercession will be made for holy Church, for the civil authorities, for those oppressed by various needs, for all mankind, and for the salvation of the entire world (cf. 1 Tim. 2:1-2).[44]

54. In Masses which are celebrated with the people, a suitable place may be allotted to their mother tongue. This provision is to apply in the first place to the readings and "the common prayer," but also, as local conditions may warrant, to those parts which pertain to the people, according to the norm laid down in Article 36 of this Constitution.

Nevertheless steps should be taken so that the faithful may also be able to say or to sing together in Latin those parts of the Ordinary of the Mass which pertain to them.

And wherever a more extended use of the mother tongue within the Mass appears desirable, the regulation laid down in Article 40 of this Constitution is to be observed.

55. Hearty endorsement is given to that closer form of participation in the Mass whereby the faithful, after the priest's communion, receive the Lord's body under elements consecrated at that very sacrifice.

The dogmatic principles which were laid down by the Council of Trent remaining intact,[45] communion under both kinds may be granted when the bishops think fit, not only to clerics and religious, but also to the laity, in cases to be determined by the Apostolic See, as, for instance, to the newly ordained in the Mass of their sacred ordination, to the newly professed in the Mass of their religious profession, and to the newly baptized in a Mass following their baptism.[46]

56. The two parts which, in a certain sense, go to make up the Mass, namely, the liturgy of the word and the Eucharistic

44. The ancient "Bidding Prayers" are to be restored, offering an element of variety and flexibility to the structure of the Mass. They will replace the incidental "Five Our Fathers" and other prayers often inserted into parish announcements, and are accepted as an official part of the Mass. They offer another chance for the faithful to participate actively in their response.

45. *Session 21, July 16, 1562, Doctrine on Communion under Both Species, c. 1-3: Concilium Tridentinum, ed. cit., VIII, pp. 698-699.*

46. Communion "under both kinds" (or "under both species") is recognized. While the reason is not specified, it is plainly because Communion in this form is a fuller expression of the Eucharistic symbolism (Christ did order the apostles both to eat and drink). For reasons of convenience, however, this ancient practice is now permitted only during events of special solemnity. At all Masses, however, it is urged that the faithful receive a Host consecrated at that Mass. This had previously been urged in *Mediator Dei* and in the Liturgical Instruction of 1958, but was seldom put into practice.

liturgy, are so closely connected with each other that they
form but one single act of worship. Accordingly this sacred
Synod strongly urges pastors of souls that, when instructing
the faithful, they insistently teach them to take their part in
the entire Mass, especially on Sundays and feasts of obligation.

57. §1. Concelebration, by which the unity of the priesthood
is appropriately manifested, has remained in use to this day
in the Church both in the East and in the West.[47] For this
reason it has seemed good to the Council to extend permission
for concelebration to the following cases:
    1. (a) on the Thursday of the Lord's Supper, not only
          at the Mass of the Chrism, but also at the evening
          Mass;
     (b) at Masses during councils, bishops' conferences,
          and synods;
     (c) at the Mass for the blessing of an abbot.
    2. Also, with permission of the ordinary, to whom it be-
      longs to decide whether concelebration is opportune:
     (a) at conventual Mass, and at the principal Mass
          in churches when the needs of the faithful do
          not require that all the priests available should
          celebrate individually;
     (b) at Masses celebrated at any kind of priests'
          meetings, whether the priests be secular clergy
          or religious.
§2.   1. Rules concerning concelebration within a diocese
        are under the control of the bishop.
      2. Nevertheless, each priest shall always retain his
        right to celebrate Mass individually, though not at
        the same time in the same church as a concele-
        brated Mass, nor on Thursday of the Lord's Sup-
        per.

58. A new rite for concelebration is to be drawn up and
incorporated into the Pontifical and into the Roman Missal.

---

47. Concelebration is another ancient liturgical custom revived by the Constitution. It is desirable because it stresses the social nature of the Holy
Sacrifice, especially by symbolizing the unity of the priesthood. Since the
Constitution was promulgated, concelebration has been rather widely permitted, and participants have found it a great aid to themselves and to the
faithful. It is particularly appropriate where large numbers of priests are
together and "private" Masses are not needed.

CHAPTER III

THE OTHER SACRAMENTS
AND THE SACRAMENTALS

59. The purpose of the sacraments is to sanctify men, to build up the body of Christ, and finally, to give worship to God. Because they are signs they also instruct. They not only presuppose faith, but by words and objects they also nourish, strengthen, and express it; that is why they are called "sacraments of faith." They do indeed impart grace, but, in addition, the very act of celebrating them disposes the faithful most effectively to receive this grace in a fruitful manner, to worship God duly, and to practice charity.

It is therefore of capital importance that the faithful easily understand the sacramental signs, and with great eagerness have frequent recourse to those sacraments which were instituted to nourish the Christian life.[48]

60. Holy Mother Church has, moreover, instituted sacramentals. These are sacred signs which bear a resemblance to the sacraments: they signify effects, particularly of a spiritual kind, which are obtained through the Church's intercession. By them men are disposed to receive the chief effect of the sacraments, and various occasions in life are rendered holy.

61. Thus, for well-disposed members of the faithful, the liturgy of the sacraments and sacramentals sanctifies almost every event in their lives; they are given access to the stream of divine grace which flows from the paschal mystery of the passion, death, and resurrection of Christ, the fountain from which all sacraments and sacramentals draw their power. There is hardly any proper use of material things which cannot thus be directed toward the sanctification of men and the praise of God.

48. Again the reiterated emphasis on intelligibility. Since the sacraments are there to "nourish, strengthen, and express" faith and to give grace, they must be made as effective and fruitful as possible.

62. With the passage of time, however, there have crept into the rites of the sacraments and sacramentals certain features which have rendered their nature and purpose less clear to the people of today; and hence to that extent the need arises to adjust certain aspects of these rites to the requirements of our times. For this reason the sacred Council decrees as follows concerning their revision.[49]

63. Because the use of the mother tongue in the administration of the sacraments and sacramentals can often be of considerable help to the people, this use is to be extended according to the following norms:

(a) The vernacular language may be used in administering the sacraments and sacramentals, according to the norm of Article 36.

(b) Following the pattern of the new edition of the Roman Ritual, particular rituals are to be prepared as soon as possible by the competent territorial ecclesiastical authority mentioned in Article 22, §2, of this Constitution. These rituals, adapted to the linguistic and other needs of the different regions, are to be reviewed by the Apostolic See and then introduced into the regions for which they have been prepared. But in drawing up these rituals or particular collections of rites, the instructions prefixed to the individual rites in the Roman Ritual, whether they be pastoral and rubrical or whether they have special social import, are not to be omitted.

64. The catechumenate for adults, comprising several distinct steps, is to be restored and to be put into use at the discretion of the local ordinary. By this means the period of the catechumenate, which is intended as a time of suitable instruction, may be sanctified by sacred rites to be celebrated at successive intervals.

65. In mission lands initiation rites are found in use among individual peoples. Elements from these, when capable of being adapted to Christian ritual, may be admitted along with those already found in Christian tradition, according to the norm laid down in Articles 37-40 of this Constitution.

66. Both of the rites for the baptism of adults are to be

49. Again the recognition that certain features of the liturgy are no longer functional. Thus, the changeable elements that call for changing will be revised.

revised: not only the simpler rite, but also the more solemn
one, which must take into account the restored catechumenate. A special Mass "for the conferring of baptism" is to be
inserted into the Roman Missal.

67. The rite for the baptism of infants is to be revised, and
should be adapted to the circumstance that those to be baptized are, in fact, infants. The roles of parents and godparents, and also their duties, should be brought out more sharply in the rite itself.

68. The baptismal rite should contain adaptations, to be used
at the discretion of the local ordinary, for occasions when a
very large number are to be baptized together. Moreover, a
shorter rite is to be drawn up, especially for mission lands,
for use by catechists, but also by the faithful in general when
there is danger of death, and neither priest nor deacon is
available.

69. In place of the rite called the "Order of Supplying What
Was Omitted in the Baptism of an Infant," a new rite is to
be drawn up which manifests more fittingly and clearly that
the infant, baptized by the short rite, has already been received into the Church.

   A new rite is also to be drawn up for converts who have
already been validly baptized; it should indicate that they are
now admitted to communion with the Church.[50]

70. Except during Eastertide, baptismal water may be blessed
within the rite of baptism itself by an approved shorter formula.

71. The rite of confirmation is to be revised and the intimate
connection which this sacrament has with the whole of Christian initiation is to be more lucidly set forth; for this reason
it will be fitting for candidates to renew their baptismal promises just before they are confirmed.

   Confirmation may be given within the Mass when convenient; when it is given outside the Mass, the rite that is
used should be introduced by a formula to be drawn up for
this purpose.

50. It is obvious from the Decree on Ecumenism (Art. 3, par. 1, and Art.
22), that what is referred to here is admission into the fullest communion
with the Church.

72. The rite and formulas for the sacrament of penance are to be revised so that they give more luminous expression to both the nature and effect of the sacrament.

73. "Extreme unction," which may also and more fittingly be called "anointing of the sick," is not a sacrament for those only who are at the point of death.[51] Hence, as soon as any one of the faithful begins to be in danger of death from sickness or old age, the appropriate time for him to receive this sacrament has certainly already arrived.

74. In addition to the separate rites for anointing of the sick and for Viaticum, a continuous rite shall be prepared according to which the sick man is anointed after he has made his confession and before he receives Viaticum.

75. The number of the anointings is to be adapted to the occasion, and the prayers accompanying the rite of anointing are to be revised so as to correspond with the varying conditions of the sick who receive the sacrament.

76. Both the ceremonies and texts of the ordination rites are to be revised. The address given by the bishop at the beginning of each ordination or consecration may be in the mother tongue.

When a bishop is consecrated, the imposition of hands may be done by all the bishops present.

77. The marriage rite now found in the Roman Ritual is to be revised and enriched in a way which more clearly expresses the grace of the sacrament and the duties of the spouses.

"If certain locales traditionally use other praiseworthy customs and ceremonies when celebrating the sacrament of matrimony, this sacred Synod earnestly desires that these by all means be retained."[52]

Moreover, the competent territorial ecclesiastical authority mentioned in Article 22, §2, of this Constitution is free to draw up its own rite suited to the usages of place and people,

---

51. "Anointing of the sick" is a much happier term than "Extreme Unction," since it does not suggest imminent death. This comforting sacrament should be given, not at the moment of death, but as soon as there is some danger of death from sickness or old age.

52. *Council of Trent, Session 24, Nov. 11, 1563, On Reform, c. 1: Concilium Tridentinum, ed. cit., IX, Actorum pars VI, Freiburg im Breisgau, 1924, p. 969. Cf. Roman Ritual, title 8, c. 2, n. 6.*

according to the provision of Article 63. But the rite is always to honor the requirement that the priest assisting at the marriage must ask for and obtain the consent of the contracting parties.

78. Matrimony is normally to be celebrated within the Mass, after the reading of the Gospel and the homily, and before "the prayer of the faithful." The prayer for the bride, duly amended to remind both spouses of their equal obligation to remain faithful to each other, may be said in the mother tongue.

But if the sacrament of matrimony is celebrated apart from Mass, the Epistle and Gospel from the nuptial Mass are to be read at the beginning of the rite, and a blessing should always be given to the spouses.

79. The sacramentals are to undergo a revision based on the primary principle of enabling the faithful to participate intelligently, actively, and easily; the requirements of our own times should also be weighed. When rituals are revised, as laid down in Article 63, new sacramentals may also be added as the need for these becomes apparent.

Reserved blessings shall be very few and only in favor of bishops or ordinaries.

Let provision be made that some sacramentals, at least in special circumstances and at the discretion of the ordinary, may be administered by qualified lay persons.

80. The rite for the consecration of virgins which is currently found in the Roman Pontifical is to be revised.

Moreover, a rite of religious profession and renewal of vows shall be drawn up, in order to achieve greater unity, sobriety, and dignity. Apart from exceptions in particular law, this rite should be adopted by those who make their profession or renewal of vows within the Mass.

It would be praiseworthy for religious professions to be made during Mass.

81. The rite for the burial of the dead should evidence more clearly the paschal character of Christian death, and should correspond more closely to the circumstances and traditions found in various regions. This latter provision holds good also for the liturgical color to be used.[53]

53. The traditional rites for Christian burial have been too often expressive

82. The rite for the burial of infants is to be revised, and a special Mass for the occasion provided.

CHAPTER IV

THE DIVINE OFFICE

83. Christ Jesus, high priest of the new and eternal covenant, taking human nature, introduced into this earthly exile that hymn which is sung throughout all ages in the halls of heaven. He joins the entire community of mankind to Himself, associating it with His own singing of this canticle of divine praise.

For He continues His priestly work through the agency of His Church, which is ceaselessly engaged in praising the Lord and interceding for the salvation of the whole world. This she does not only by celebrating the Eucharist, but also in other ways, especially by praying the divine Office.[54]

84. By tradition going back to early Christian times, the divine Office is arranged so that the whole course of the day and night is made holy by the praises of God. Therefore, when this wonderful song of praise is worthily rendered by priests and others who are deputed for this purpose by Church ordinance, or by the faithful praying together with the priest in an approved form, then it is truly the voice of the bride addressing her bridegroom; it is the very prayer which Christ Himself, together with His body, addresses to the Father.

85. Hence all who perform this service are not only fulfilling a duty of the Church, but also are sharing in the greatest hon-

---

of gloom rather than of the paschal mystery. Christ's resurrection and our own entrance into His Life and resurrection should be the themes of Christian death and its ritual expression.

54. The priestly work of the Church is not restricted to the sacraments; the Church must praise God ceaselessly and pray for the whole world. However, the divine Office has become badly adjusted to certain needs of priests and faithful and needs revision. Some provisional changes are given here, while a more thorough revision is being prepared by experts.

or accorded to Christ's spouse, for by offering these praises to God they are standing before God's throne in the name of the Church their Mother.

86. Priests engaged in the sacred pastoral ministry will offer the praises of the hours with fervor to the extent that they vividly realize that they must heed St. Paul's exhortation: "Pray without ceasing" (1 Th. 5:17). For only the Lord can give fruitfulness and increase to the works in which they are engaged. "Without me," He said, "you can do nothing" (Jn. 15:5). That is why the apostles, appointing deacons, said: "We will devote ourselves to prayer and to the ministry of the word" (Acts 6:4).

87. In order that the divine Office may be better and more worthily prayed in existing circumstances, whether by priests or by other members of the Church, this sacred Council, carrying forward the restoration already so happily begun by the Apostolic See, has seen fit to decree as follows concerning the Office of the Roman rite.

88. Because the purpose of the Office is to sanctify the day, the traditional sequence of the hours is to be restored so that as far as possible they may once again be genuinely related to the time of the day at which they are prayed. Moreover, it will be necessary to take into account the modern conditions in which daily life has to be lived, especially by those who are called to labor in apostolic works.

89. Therefore, when the Office is revised, these norms are to be observed:
(a) By the venerable tradition of the universal Church, Lauds as morning prayer and Vespers as evening prayer are the two hinges on which the daily Office turns; hence they are to be considered as the chief hours and are to be celebrated as such.
(b) Compline is to be drawn up so that it will be a suitable prayer for the end of the day.
(c) The hour known as Matins, although it should retain the character of nocturnal praise when celebrated in choir, should be adapted so that it may be recited at any hour of the day; it is to be made up of fewer psalms and longer readings.
(d) The hour of Prime is to be suppressed.

(e) In choir the minor hours of Terce, Sext, and None are to be maintained. But outside choir it will be lawful to select any one of these three, according to the respective time of the day.

90. Because it is the public prayer of the Church, the divine Office is a source of piety and nourishment for personal prayer. Therefore priests and all others who take part in the divine Office are earnestly exhorted in the Lord to attune their minds to their voices when praying it. The better to achieve this ideal, let them take steps to improve their understanding of the liturgy and of the Bible, especially the psalms.

In the revision of the Roman Office, its ancient and venerable treasures are to be so adapted that all those to whom they are bequeathed may more extensively and easily draw riches from them.

91. So that it may really be possible in practice to observe the course of the hours proposed in Article 89, the psalms are no longer to be distributed throughout one week, but through some longer period of time.

The work of revising the psalter, already happily begun, is to be finished as soon as possible, and is to take into account the style of Christian Latin, the liturgical use of psalms, also when sung, and the entire tradition of the Latin Church.

92. As regards the readings, the following shall be observed:

(a) Readings from sacred Scripture are to be arranged so that the riches of God's word may be easily accessible in more abundant measure.

(b) Readings excerpted from the works of the Fathers, doctors, and other ecclesiastical writers ought to be better selected.

(c) The accounts of martyrdom or the lives of the saints are to accord with the facts of history.

93. To whatever extent seems desirable, the hymns are to be restored to their original form, and whatever smacks of mythology or ill accords with Christian piety is to be removed or changed. Also, as occasion arises, let other selections from the treasury of hymns be incorporated.

94. That the day may be truly sanctified, and that the hours themselves may be recited with spiritual advantage, it is best

that each of them be prayed at a time which most closely corresponds with its true canonical time.

95. Communities obliged to choral Office are bound to celebrate the Office in choir every day in addition to the conventual Mass. In particular:

(a) Orders of canons, of monks, and of nuns, and of other regulars bound by law or constitutions to choral Office must celebrate the entire Office.

(b) Cathedral or collegiate chapters are bound to recite those parts of the Office imposed on them by general or particular law.

(c) All members of the aforementioned communities who are in major orders or who are solemnly professed, except for lay brothers, are bound to recite individually those canonical hours which they do not pray in choir.

96. Clerics not bound to Office in choir, if they are in major orders, are bound to pray the entire Office every day, either in common or individually, as laid down in Article 89.

97. Appropriate instances are to be defined by the rubrics in which a liturgical service may be substituted for the divine Office.

In particular cases, and for a just reason, ordinaries can dispense their subjects wholly or in part from the obligation of reciting the divine Office, or may commute the obligation.

98. Members of any institute dedicated to acquiring perfection who, according to their constitutions, are obliged to recite any parts of the divine Office are thereby performing the public prayer of the Church.

They too perform the public prayer of the Church who, in virtue of their constitutions, recite any short Office, provided this is drawn up after the pattern of the divine Office and is duly approved.

99. Since the divine Office is the voice of the Church, that is, of the whole mystical body publicly praising God, those clerics who are not obliged to Office in choir, especially priests who live together or who assemble for any purpose, are urged to pray at least some part of the divine Office in common.

All who pray the divine Office, whether in choir or in common, should fulfill the task entrusted to them as perfectly as possible: this admonition refers not only to the internal devotion of their minds but also to their external manner of celebration.

It is, moreover, fitting that the Office, both in choir and in common, be sung when this is possible.

100. Pastors of souls should see to it that the chief hours, especially Vespers, are celebrated in common in church on Sundays and the more solemn feasts. And the laity, too, are encouraged to recite the divine Office, either with the priests, or among themselves, or even individually.

101. §1. In accordance with the centuries-old tradition of the Latin rite, the Latin language is to be retained by clerics in reciting the divine Office. But in individual cases the ordinary has the power of granting the use of a vernacular translation to those clerics for whom the use of Latin constitutes a grave obstacle to their praying the Office properly. The vernacular version, however, must be one that is drawn up according to the provision of Article 36.

§2. The competent superior has the power to grant the use of the vernacular in the celebration of the divine Office, even in choir, to nuns and to members of institutes dedicated to acquiring perfection, both men who are not clerics and women. The version, however, must be an approved one.

§3. Any cleric bound to the divine Office fulfills his obligation if he prays the Office in the vernacular together with a group of the faithful or with those mentioned in §2 above, provided that the text of the translation is approved.

CHAPTER V

THE LITURGICAL YEAR

102. Holy Mother Church is conscious that she must celebrate the saving work of her divine Spouse by devoutly recalling it on certain days throughout the course of the year.

Every week, on the day which she has called the Lord's day, she keeps the memory of His resurrection. In the supreme solemnity of Easter she also makes an annual commemoration of the resurrection, along with the Lord's blessed passion.

Within the cycle of a year, moreover, she unfolds the whole mystery of Christ, not only from His incarnation and birth until His ascension, but also as reflected in the day of Pentecost, and the expectation of a blessed, hoped-for return of the Lord.

Recalling thus the mysteries of redemption, the Church opens to the faithful the riches of her Lord's powers and merits, so that these are in some way made present at all times, and the faithful are enabled to lay hold of them and become filled with saving grace.[55]

103. In celebrating this annual cycle of Christ's mysteries, holy Church honors with special love the Blessed Mary, Mother of God, who is joined by an inseparable bond to the saving work of her Son. In her the Church holds up and admires the most excellent fruit of the redemption, and joyfully contemplates, as in a faultless model, that which she herself wholly desires and hopes to be.[56]

104. The Church has also included in the annual cycle days devoted to the memory of the martyrs and the other saints. Raised up to perfection by the manifold grace of God, and already in possession of eternal salvation, they sing God's perfect praise in heaven and offer prayers for us. By celebrating the passage of these saints from earth to heaven the Church proclaims the paschal mystery as achieved in the saints who have suffered and been glorified with Christ; she proposes them to the faithful as examples who draw all to the Father through Christ, and through their merits she pleads for God's favors.

105. Finally, in the various seasons of the year and according

55. The Church year, too, has become somewhat obscured through the multiplication of feasts. It is to be restored, with due emphasis on the central paschal (Easter) mystery. Every Sunday is the memory of Christ's resurrection.
56. The Council, both here and in Chapter 8 of the Constitution on the Church, focuses attention on a true understanding of the role of Mary and proper devotion to her and to the saints. While Christ is our one Mediator (1 Tim. 2:5), Mary has a true maternal role. Further, she is the "most perfect fruit of the redemption." The saints are honored, too, as manifestations of God's grace. At the same time, Art. 108 insists on the primary emphasis to be given to the feasts of Christ in His mysteries of salvation.

to her traditional discipline, the Church completes the formation of the faithful by means of pious practices for soul and body, by instruction, prayer, and works of penance and of mercy.

Accordingly, this most sacred Council has seen fit to decree as follows:

106. By an apostolic tradition which took its origin from the very day of Christ's resurrection, the Church celebrates the paschal mystery every eighth day; with good reason this, then, bears the name of the Lord's day or the day of the Lord. For on this day Christ's faithful should come together into one place so that, by hearing the word of God and taking part in the Eucharist, they may call to mind the passion, the resurrection, and the glorification of the Lord Jesus, and may thank God who "has begotten us again, through the resurrection of Jesus Christ from the dead, unto a living hope" (1 Pet. 1:3). Hence the Lord's day is the original feast day, and it should be proposed to the piety of the faithful and taught to them in such a way that it may become in fact a day of joy and of freedom from work. Other celebrations, unless they be truly of overriding importance, must not have precedence over this day, which is the foundation and nucleus of the whole liturgical year.

107. The liturgical year is to be revised so that the traditional customs and discipline of the sacred seasons can be preserved or restored to meet the conditions of modern times; their specific character is to be retained, so that they duly nourish the piety of the faithful who celebrate the mysteries of Christian redemption, and above all the paschal mystery. If certain adaptations are considered necessary on account of local conditions, they are to be made in accordance with the provisions of Articles 39 and 40.

108. The minds of the faithful must be directed primarily toward the feasts of the Lord in which the mysteries of salvation are celebrated in the course of the year. Therefore, the Proper of the Time,[57] shall be given the preference which is its due over the feasts of the saints, so that the entire cycle of the mysteries of salvation can be suitably recalled.

109. The Lenten season has a twofold character: 1) it recalls

---

57. I.e., the sequence of feasts pertaining directly to Christ in the whole sequence of the mystery of salvation.

baptism or prepares for it; 2) it stresses a penitential spirit. By these means especially, Lent readies the faithful for celebrating the paschal mystery after a period of closer attention to the Word of God, and more ardent prayer. In the liturgy itself and in liturgy-centered instructions, these baptismal and penitential themes should be more pronounced. Hence:

(a) Wider use is to be made of the baptismal features proper to the Lenten liturgy; some elements which belonged to a now-lapsed tradition may be opportunely restored.

(b) The same approach holds for the penitential elements. As regards instruction, it is important to impress on the minds of the faithful not only the social consequences of sin but also the fact that the real essence of the virtue of penance is hatred for sin as an offence against God; the role of the Church in penitential practices is not to be passed over, and the people must be exhorted to pray for sinners.

110. During Lent, penance should not be only internal and individual but also external and social. The practice of penance should be fostered according to the possibilities of the present day and of a given area, as well as of individual circumstances. Such practice should be encouraged by the authorities mentioned in Article 22.

In any event, let the paschal fast be kept sacred. It should be observed everywhere on Good Friday and, where possible, prolonged throughout Holy Saturday, so that the joys of the Sunday of the resurrection may be visited on uplifted and responsive spirits.

111. The saints have been traditionally honored in the Church and their authentic relics and images held in veneration. For the feasts of the saints proclaim the wonderful works of Christ in His servants, and display to the faithful fitting examples for their imitation.

Lest the feasts of the saints, however, take precedence over the feasts which commemorate the very mysteries of salvation, many of them should be left to be celebrated by a particular Church or nation or religious community; only those should be extended to the universal Church which commemorate saints who are truly of universal significance.

CHAPTER VI

SACRED MUSIC

112. The musical tradition of the universal Church is a treasure of immeasurable value, greater even than that of any other art. The main reason for this pre-eminence is that, as sacred melody united to words, it forms a necessary or integral part of the solemn liturgy.

Holy Scripture, indeed, has bestowed praise upon sacred song (cf. Eph. 5:19; Col. 3:16), and the same may be said of the Fathers of the Church and of the Roman pontiffs who in recent times, led by St. Pius X, have explained more precisely the ministerial function rendered by sacred music in the service of the Lord.

Therefore sacred music increases in holiness to the degree that it is intimately linked with liturgical action, winningly expresses prayerfulness, promotes solidarity, and enriches sacred rites with heightened solemnity. The Church indeed approves of all forms of true art, and admits them into divine worship when they show appropriate qualities.

Accordingly, this sacred Council, keeping to the norms and precepts of ecclesiastical tradition and discipline, and having regard for the purpose of sacred music, which is the glory of God and the sanctification of the faithful, decrees as follows:

113. Liturgical action is given a more noble form when sacred rites are solemnized in song, with the assistance of sacred ministers and the active participation of the people.

As regards the language to be used, the provisions of Article 36 are to be observed; for the Mass, Article 54; for the sacraments, Article 63; for the divine Office, Article 101.

114. The treasure of sacred music is to be preserved and fostered with very great care. Choirs must be diligently promoted, especially in cathedral churches; but bishops and other pastors of souls must be at pains to ensure that, whenever the sacred action is to be celebrated with song, the whole body of the

faithful may be able to contribute that active participation
which is rightly theirs, as laid down in Articles 28 and 30.[58]

115. Great importance is to be attached to the teaching and
practice of music in seminaries, in the novitiates and houses
of study of religious of both sexes, and also in other Catholic
institutions and schools. To impart this instruction, teachers
are to be carefully trained and put in charge of the teaching of sacred music.

It is desirable also to found higher institutes of sacred music
whenever this can be done.

Composers and singers, especially boys, must also be given
a genuine liturgical training.

116. The Church acknowledges Gregorian chant as proper
to the Roman liturgy: therefore, other things being equal, it
should be given pride of place in liturgical services.

But other kinds of sacred music, especially polyphony, are
by no means excluded from liturgical celebrations, so long as
they accord with the spirit of the liturgical action, as laid
down in Article 30.

117. The typical edition of the books of Gregorian chant is
to be completed; and a more critical edition is to be prepared
of those books already published since the restoration by St.
Pius X.

It is desirable also that an edition be prepared containing
simpler melodies, for use in small churches.

118. Religious singing by the people is to be skillfully fostered, so that in devotions and sacred exercises, as also during liturgical services, the voices of the faithful may ring out
according to the norms and requirements of the rubrics.[59]

119. In certain parts of the world, especially mission lands,
there are peoples who have their own musical traditions, and
these play a great part in their religious and social life. For

58. This balanced Article (114) insists on the active participation of the
faithful in sacred music, but insists no less that choirs be diligently promoted. To abolish choirs, as experience has taught, is to deprive the liturgy
of important support to the congregation, as well as to strip it of due
solemnity and "delight in prayer" (Art. 112).
59. People are urged to sing both in devotions and in official liturgical services,
and some adaptation to local traditions and needs must be made. While
Art. 119 seems to refer explicitly to missionary countries, some adaptation
seems called for everywhere.

this reason due importance is to be attached to their music, and a suitable place is to be given to it, not only by way of forming their attitude toward religion, but also when there is question of adapting worship to their native genius, as indicated in Articles 39 and 40.

Therefore, when missionaries are being given training in music, every effort should be made to see that they become competent in promoting the traditional music of these peoples, both in schools and in sacred services, as far as may be practicable.

120. In the Latin Church the pipe organ is to be held in high esteem, for it is the traditional musical instrument, and one that adds a wonderful splendor to the Church's ceremonies and powerfully lifts up man's mind to God and to heavenly things.

But other instruments also may be admitted for use in divine worship, with the knowledge and consent of the competent territorial authority, as laid down in Articles 22, §2; 37; and 40. This may be done, however, only on condition that the instruments are suitable for sacred use, or can be made so, that they accord with the dignity of the temple, and truly contribute to the edification of the faithful.

121. Composers, filled with the Christian spirit, should feel that their vocation is to cultivate sacred music and increase its store of treasures.

Let them produce compositions which have the qualities proper to genuine sacred music, not confining themselves to works which can be sung only by large choirs, but providing also for the needs of small choirs and for the active participation of the entire assembly of the faithful.

The texts intended to be sung must always be in conformity with Catholic doctrine; indeed they should be drawn chiefly from holy Scripture and from liturgical sources.[60]

---

60. There is need for new music, both for Mass and for devotions; new hymns should be liturgically and scripturally inspired, and not in the sentimental "devotional" manner that has proved the bane of much Catholic hymnody.

CHAPTER VII

SACRED ART AND SACRED FURNISHINGS

122. Very rightly the fine arts are considered to rank among the noblest expressions of human genius. This judgment applies especially to religious art and to its highest achievement, which is sacred art. By their very nature both of the latter are related to God's boundless beauty, for this is the reality which these human efforts are trying to express in some way. To the extent that these works aim exclusively at turning men's thoughts to God persuasively and devoutly, they are dedicated to God and to the cause of His greater honor and glory.

Holy Mother Church has therefore always been the friend of the fine arts and has continuously sought their noble ministry, with the special aim that all things set apart for use in divine worship should be truly worthy, becoming, and beautiful, signs and symbols of heavenly realities.[61] For this purpose, too, she has trained artists. In fact, the Church has, with good reason, always reserved to herself the right to pass judgment upon the arts, deciding which of the works of artists are in accordance with faith, piety, and cherished traditional laws, and thereby suited to sacred purposes.

The Church has been particularly careful to see that sacred furnishings should worthily and beautifully serve the dignity of worship, and has welcomed those changes in materials, style, or ornamentation which the progress of the technical arts has brought with the passage of time.

Therefore it has pleased the Fathers to issue the following decrees on these matters:

61. This optimistic paragraph expresses the Church's official acceptance of the fine arts in her worship. Pope Paul, on Ascension Day, 1964, referred to this chapter as "the new alliance" between the Church and artists, and pleaded for it to be taken as "a pact of reconciliation and of rebirth of religious art." For it cannot be denied that sacred art, for some centuries, has been less than effective or relevant to contemporary man. A true renewal must take place.

123. The Church has not adopted any particular style of art as her very own; she has admitted fashions from every period according to the natural talents and circumstances of peoples, and the needs of the various rites. Thus, in the course of the centuries, she has brought into being a treasury of art which must be very carefully preserved. The art of our own days, coming from every race and region, shall also be given free scope in the Church, provided that it adorns the sacred buildings and holy rites with due honor and reverence. It will thereby be enabled to contribute its own voice to that wonderful chorus of praise in honor of the Catholic faith sung by great men in times gone by.[62]

124. Ordinaries, by the encouragement and favor they show to art which is truly sacred, should strive after noble beauty rather than mere extravagance. This principle is to apply also in the matter of sacred vestments and ornaments.

Let bishops carefully exclude from the house of God and from other sacred places those works of artists which are repugnant to faith, morals, and Christian piety, and which offend true religious sense either by their distortion of forms or by lack of artistic worth, by mediocrity or by pretense.

When churches are to be built, let great care be taken that they be suitable for the celebration of liturgical services and for the active participation of the faithful.

125. The practice of placing sacred images in churches so that they may be venerated by the faithful is to be firmly maintained. Nevertheless, their number should be moderate and their relative location should reflect right order. Otherwise they may create confusion among the Christian people and promote a faulty sense of devotion.

126. When passing judgment on works of art, local ordinaries shall give a hearing to the diocesan commission on sacred art and, if needed, also to others who are truly experts, and to the commissions referred to in Articles 44, 45, and 46.

Ordinaries must be very careful to see that sacred furnishings and works of value are not disposed of or allowed to deteriorate; for they are the ornaments of the house of God.

---

62. This marks a strong welcome to the art of our day, which is the art that should participate in our worship. The stress on "noble beauty rather than sumptuous display" is particularly urgent, since too often recent churches have striven for the monumental and pretentious, rather than an honest, functional style that fits the needs of God's people at worship.

127. Bishops should take pains to instill artists with the spirit of sacred art and of the sacred liturgy. This they may do in person or through suitable priests who are gifted with a knowledge and love of art.

For the training of artists it is also recommended that schools or academies of sacred art be founded in those parts of the world where they would be useful.

All artists who, in view of their talents, desire to serve God's glory in holy Church should ever bear in mind that they are engaged in a kind of sacred imitation of God the Creator, and are concerned with works destined for use in Catholic worship and for the edification, devotion, and religious instruction of the faithful.

128. Along with the revision of the liturgical books, as laid down in Article 25, there is to be an early revision of the canons and ecclesiastical statutes which govern the disposition of material things involved in sacred worship. These laws refer especially to the worthy and well-planned construction of sacred buildings, the shape and construction of altars, the nobility, location, and security of the Eucharistic tabernacle, the suitability and dignity of the baptistery, the proper use of sacred images, embellishments, and vestments. Laws which seem less suited to the reformed liturgy are to be brought into harmony with it, or else abolished; and any which are helpful are to be retained if already in use, and introduced where they are lacking.

According to the norm of Article 22 of the Constitution, the territorial bodies of bishops are empowered to adapt matters to the needs and customs of their different regions; this applies especially to the materials and form of sacred furnishings and vestments.

129. During their philosophical and theological studies, clerics are to be taught about the history and development of sacred art, and about the sound principles underlying the production of its works. As a result, they will be able to appreciate and preserve the Church's venerable monuments, and be in a position to aid, by good advice, artists who are engaged in producing works of art.[63]

63. This regulation (and the one contained in Art. 115) will make all the difference. If it is observed, and priests receive the required training, our churches and other sacred art and music can be expected to be relevant to our time. Otherwise, Chapters 6 and 7 will become a dead letter. For the Church possesses no divine guarantee of infallibility in matters of art.

130. It is fitting that the use of pontificals be reserved to those ecclesiastical persons who have episcopal rank or some particular jurisdiction.

APPENDIX[64]

DECLARATION OF THE MOST SACRED SECOND ECUMENICAL COUNCIL OF THE VATICAN ON REVISION OF THE CALENDAR

The most sacred Second Ecumenical Council of the Vatican recognizes the importance of the wishes expressed by many concerning the assignment of the feast of Easter to a fixed Sunday and concerning an unchanging calendar. Having carefully considered the effects which could result from the introduction of a new calendar, the most sacred Council declares as follows:

1. It would not object if the feast of Easter were assigned to a particular Sunday of the Gregorian Calendar, provided that those whom it may concern give their consent, especially the brethren who are not in communion with the Apostolic See.

2. The most sacred Council likewise declares that it does not oppose efforts designed to introduce a perpetual calendar into civil society.

But among the various systems which are being devised for establishing a perpetual calendar and introducing it into civil life, the Church has no objection only in the case of those systems which would retain and safeguard a seven-day week including Sunday, without the introduction of any days outside the week. In other words, the sequence of seven-day weeks should remain unbroken. Only the weightiest of rea-

---

64. In addition to this Appendix there has also appeared the *Instruction,* Sept. 26, 1964 (cf. appendix of documents at end of this volume; the Instruction can also be found in *Our Changing Liturgy* and in *Church Architecture: The Shape of Reform* [Liturgical Conference, 1965]).

sons, acknowledged as such by the Apostolic See, would make the contrary acceptable.

Each and every one of the things set forth in this Constitution has won the consent of the Fathers of this most sacred Council. We too, by the apostolic authority conferred on us by Christ, join with the Venerable Fathers in approving, decreeing and establishing these things in the Holy Spirit, and we direct that what has thus been enacted in synod be published to God's glory.

Rome, at St. Peter's, December 4, 1963

I, Paul, Bishop of the Catholic Church

There follow the signatures of the Fathers.

A RESPONSE

Worship is the metabolism of the Christian life. In the liturgy, through the Word of God and the sacraments, the Church receives the grace of God by which she lives; in the liturgy, through prayer and sacrificial action, she offers herself. to God for His service in the world. This Constitution on the Sacred Liturgy, therefore, does not merely tinker with the formalities of liturgical worship, but seeks to form and to reform the very life of the Church. Since that was also the aim of the Reformers of the 16th century, it will perhaps be appropriate for me, as a Reformation scholar, to summarize my reactions to the Constitution under three of the rubrics I have employed in my book *Obedient Rebels* (Harper, 1964) for an interpretation of the liturgical thought of Martin Luther.

Liturgy as Accommodation. The Constitution contains many remarkable expressions of the insight that liturgy must adjust itself to the state of spirituality and of culture among a particular people. There is the explicit recognition (21) that while the fundamental elements of the liturgy cannot be changed, everything else is changeable. From this there follows the demand (50) that the liturgy of the Mass be trimmed of useless accretions and be restored to a "noble simplicity" (34), as well as the prescription (62) that other sacramental practices be reformed, "to adjust certain aspects of these rites to the requirements of our times."

Not only the distinctiveness of modern times, but the uniqueness of each culture must be respected. In its acknowledgement of that uniqueness, the Constitution goes very far (37-40). It "has no wish to impose a rigid uniformity" (37), even though that is precisely what missionaries have often done. Pagan rituals of initiation may be adapted to Christian usage (65), since, after all, both circumcision and baptism had been in use before being instituted. Although Gregorian chant has "pride of place" (116), other forms of music, expressive of "the native genius" of a culture, may and should be adopted (119). Above all, there should be a more generous use of the vernacular in the liturgy (36).

But liturgy represents an accommodation in another sense as well, for it must be related also to popular devotion. One of the prime needs in liturgical reform is to supplant certain popular devotions with authentically liturgical piety. The Constitution urges that the use of images in the church, while legitimate, be controlled (125) and that feasts of the saints not be allowed to "take precedence over the feasts which commemorate the very mysteries of salvation" (111). Yet it does seem unfortunate that the Fathers do not speak out more strongly against the abuses connected with these observances and against "individual and quasi-private" (27) celebrations of the Mass. Therefore simultaneously—and perhaps inconsistently—they commend popular devotions and warn that they must conform to liturgical devotion, "since the liturgy . . . surpasses any of them" (13).

The Centrality of Scripture. One of the most striking features of the Constitution is its emphasis on Scripture, which is said to be "of paramount importance in the celebration of the liturgy" (24). It would have to be conceded that this paramount importance has not always been as obvious in the Roman Catholic liturgy as that axiomatic statement suggests. It is heartening, therefore, that the Constitution becomes quite specific, prescribing that "there is to be more reading from holy Scripture, and it is to be more varied and suitable" (35), with the result that "a more representative portion of the holy Scriptures will be read to the people over a set cycle of years" (51).

Of particular moment for the recovery of the centrality of Scripture in worship is the restoration of preaching. The theological basis for that restoration is the doctrine that Christ is present not only in the sacraments, but also "in His word. since it is He Himself who speaks when the holy Scriptures are read in the church" (7). This real presence of Christ in the word must not be set into opposition with the real presence in the Eucharist, as it has been by some Protestants. Nor dare it be overlooked, as it has sometimes been in Roman Catholicism; for when it is, the sermon becomes mere exhortation or a moral harangue, rather than "a proclamation of God's wonderful works in the history of salvation" (35).

Such statements are bound to evoke the enthusiastic approval of anyone who believes that the Reformation was the work of the Holy Spirit, but this reaction is turned to disappointment at one crucial point. In view of the explicit commandment of Christ and the evident practice of the early Church, what is the justification for still denying the chalice to the laity except at a few very special occasions "in cases to be determined by the Apostolic See" (55)? At the very least, the restoration of the form of communion prescribed by our Lord must be a primary task for the reform of the liturgy in the future.

The Church Year. The reform of the liturgy does not make very much sense without some reform of the ecclesiastical calendar. Like the liturgy, the Church year has grown in a manner that has often been haphazard, retaining holidays long after their reason for being had disappeared, and heaping up additional feasts and special days until it takes an expert to decide which of the observances falling on a particular day takes precedence.

Into this chaos the Council has stepped with the command that "the liturgical year be revised" (107). This implies that the feasts of the saints must yield to the sequence of the feasts describing the history of salvation in the life and work of Christ (108). There is no need for each parish or diocese to observe all the feasts of all the saints, for these could overshadow the liturgical order devoted to that history (111). Even the feasts of Mary are subject to this rule and take their proper place as part of "this annual cycle of Christ's mysteries" (103).

It is consistent with this emphasis when the Constitution decrees that "the accounts of martyrdom or the lives of the saints [in the divine Office] are to accord with the facts of history" (92); but if past experience is any indication, the devotion to legends and the sentimental pictures and ditties will continue to resist liturgical reformation, especially when some of them carry official endorsement.

The reform of the calendar is the issue on which the Constitution strikes its most explicitly ecumenical note; the proviso of its appendix that the adoption of a fixed Sunday for Easter have the consent of "the brethren who are not in communion with the Apostolic See."

As these brief comments suggest, there is much in the Constitution on the Sacred Liturgy for which Christians who stand in the heritage of the Reformation ought to be grateful. In fact, several of its fundamental principles represent the acceptance, however belated, of the liturgical program set forth by the Reformers: the priesthood of all believers (14); the requirement "that the faithful take part knowingly, actively, and fruitfully" (11); "the intimate connection between words and rites" (35). These principles also represent the best in the Roman Catholic tradition. If the Constitution can be translated into action creatively and imaginatively—and that still remains to be seen—it will indeed, as the Council Fathers hope, "contribute to the unity of all who believe in Christ" (1).

JAROSLAV PELIKAN

THE CHURCH
TODAY

VATICAN II's Pastoral Constitution on the Church in the Modern World, entitled *Gaudium et Spes* from the initial words of its Latin text, enjoys the interesting distinction of being the only major document to have originated directly from a suggestion made on the floor of the conciliar Aula itself. For this reason, but much more of course for the universal interest attaching to the basic human problems dealt with in the text, this Constitution must rank as perhaps the most characteristic achievement of an essentially "pastoral" Council.

To be sure, as the Constitution states, most of what it sets forth is "teaching already accepted in the Church" (91) as befits a conciliar pronouncement. Though there are significant new emphases and occasional advances in thought or attitude revealed in the lengthy document (which we shall endeavor to highlight in this commentary), it remains primarily a synthesis of Catholic thinking as laid down in many sources but particularly in the vast corpus of papal statements on social issues from Leo XIII to Paul VI.

What is noteworthy, perhaps, is that despite the existence of such a body of authoritative pronouncements in the Church, the several commissions charged with drafting tentative texts for consideration by the Council had not felt it necessary or desirable to prepare a document dealing with the theme of the Church in the modern world. One could speculate endlessly on the circumstances that might account for what seems in hindsight to have been an amazing omission. When one takes into consideration the rigid traditionalism that dominated so much of the preparatory work lead-

ing up to the first session in October of 1962, however, it
might well have been more amazing still had one of the
preparatory commissions actually planned for a document
without precedent in previous Ecumenical Councils.

The immediate impetus for drafting what was to become
the Pastoral Constitution finally promulgated on December
7, 1965, came from a challenging intervention at the close
of the first session. The speaker was Cardinal Léon-Joseph
Suenens, and the date was December 4, 1962. The Belgian
primate began by voicing sentiments of concern over the future course of the Council. In this he spoke the mind of
many of the Council Fathers. On successive days, December
5 and 6, his remarks would be echoed by two other leaders
of the progressive majority, Cardinals Giovanni Battista
Montini and Giacomo Lercaro.

The accomplishments of the first session insofar as they
involved breaking out of tradition-caked attitudes made it
possible to embark on genuine *aggiornamento*. Those accomplishments were essential for the ultimate success of a
reform Council. However, it was necessary to go beyond
them. Cardinal Suenens remarked that this could only be
done if the Council found an architectonic theme or central
vision. He urged that such a vision might focus on the answer to a question put by the world: Church of Christ, what
do you say of yourself? This question asked for more, however, than a statement of the Church's own sense of identity
or consciousness of its inner nature. The Council must speak
also of the Church *ad extra,* of how it conceived its relation
to the world of today. This latter reply is what Vatican II
finally attempted to furnish in the pages of *Gaudium et Spes.*

Before entering on a sketch of the Constitution's highlights,
it may help to say a word about the formal intent or purpose
of the Council Fathers in issuing it. We are told at the outset
that the Council has addressed this message "to the whole of
humanity" and that it contains a statement of "how it conceives of the presence and activity of the Church in the
world today" (2). Theologians will quickly remark, also, that
the text has been deliberately designated as a *pastoral* constitution. (The Constitution on the Church, *Lumen Gentium,*
would be known as a dogmatic constitution.) This matter of
a title for the document received close attention within the
special commission created to draft the text. While it is obviously the Council's intention to indicate that the text is a
major conciliar document, one ranking with the other prime

texts on the sacred liturgy, on the Church, and on divine revelation, it is also clearly one whose unique character derives from its strictly pastoral import.

Gaudium et Spes is an unusually lengthy conciliar text, one that inevitably repeats itself as it explores basic doctrinal issues in the four chapters of its first part, and then undertakes a series of pastoral applications to urgent contemporary issues in the chapters of the second half.

What further distinguishes the Constitution is the tone or mood pervading its pages. Though there are many qualifications and cautions attached to the major discussions aired in its two parts, one quickly observes a tendency to accentuate the positive in a realistic appraisal of trends and movements at work today in the City of Man. Time and again, even the most casual reader must be struck by the document's evident openness to fundamental elements in the intellectual climate of 20th-century civilization, to the dimensions of human culture opened up by advances in the historical, social, and psychological sciences. Again, though it is true that much of what the Constitution has to say on modern man's economic and political life merely echoes teachings of Leo XIII or Pius XI and Pius XII, the very restatement of well-known passages sometimes uncovers a nuance of personalism that owes much to later Catholic thought in France and elsewhere.

Perhaps the most telling immediate influence on much of the document is that of John XXIII and his two historic encyclicals, *Mater et Magistra* and *Pacem in Terris*. Indeed, there are some who will judge that the final version of *Gaudium et Spes* could have been improved by even more forthright repetition of classic passages from the Johannine encyclicals. Certainly this is true, in the judgment of many, with respect to the Constitution's treatment of specific questions on war and peace. By contrast, however, many would also hold that the Constitution's discussion of responsible parenthood and birth control marks a clear advance over the late Pope John's statements on population problems and birth control in *Mater et Magistra*.

The most distinctive note sounded in the text, many already agree, is that of the Church putting itself consciously at the service of the family of man. It may well be that in generations to come men will read this as a highly significant step toward a rethinking of conventional ecclesiological images, e.g., that of the Church viewed as a "perfect society" standing over against the perfect society of the *Civitas*. Thus, in the life of the Church itself this document makes a precious contribution to the work of doctrinal development carried forward in *Lumen Gentium*, Vatican II's Constitution on the Church. This has come about precisely as it seeks "to speak to all men in order to shed light on the mystery of man and to cooperate in finding the solution to the outstanding problems of our time" (10).

The Constitution is divided into two main parts: one deals with "the Church and man's calling" (11-45); the other, with "some problems of special urgency" (46-90). Articles 1 to 10 form an introduction to the whole text; Articles 91 to 93 are a general conclusion. The first part is chiefly doctrinal in nature and treats in separate chapters of "the dignity of the human person" (11-22); "the community of mankind" (23-32); "man's activity throughout the world" (33-39); and the "role of the Church in the modern world" (40-45). The second part, dealing with "the dignity of marriage and the family" (46-52), "the proper development of culture" (53-62), "economic and social life" (63-72), "the life of the political community" (73-76), and "the fostering of peace and the promotion of a community of nations" (77-90), contains many important doctrinal points, but is primarily pastoral in tone, as the headings suggest.

"The root reason for human dignity lies in man's call to communion with God" (19). This affirmation contains the essence of the Council's teaching on the dignity of the human person (11-22). Its approach to the question of human worth is strongly positive and, on balance, quite optimistic. While vividly aware of dark conflict in the history of the human situation, the Council Fathers stress the Christian understanding of man's dignity in consequence of his creation "in the image of God."

This creature made in God's image is endowed with conscience, "the most secret core and sanctuary of a man" (16). But conscience implies responsibility and the responsible actor must have true freedom, not merely immunity from coercion, but guaranteed opportunity to share in some of life's meaningful decisions. Anyone familiar with the basic line of argumentation employed in Vatican II's Declaration on Religious Freedom will readily recognize its consistency with the line of reasoning followed here.

It is also easy to grasp the necessity of the Council's facing up to the question and the fact of atheism, one of the "most serious problems of the day." For the Christian believer confronting atheism, there can only be opposition to "doctrines and actions which contradict reason and the common experience of humanity, and dethrone man from his native excellence" (21). In the spirit of Vatican II, however, the Constitution does not take on itself the task of issuing a mere declaration of hostility or condemnatory fulminations. It teaches, rather, that the Christian must be "conscious of how weighty are the questions which atheism raises." Then, following the lead of John XXIII in *Pacem in Terris* and in his wholly remarkable address opening the Council on October 11, 1962, as well as of Paul VI in *Ecclesiam Suam,* the whole assembly of bishops declares that the Church stands ready to enter on sincere dialogue with unbelievers. From the atheist is asked only evidence of an open mind and respect for the basic rights of believers.

Borrowing yet another theme from John XXIII's *Mater et Magistra,* the Constitution next calls attention to "socialization," a characteristic phenomenon of our age. The growth of a community of mankind (23-32) must parallel the emergence of socialization or the growing interdependence of men. "The beginning, the subject, and the goal of all social institutions is and must be the human person, which for its part and by its very nature stands completely in need of social life" (25). This means a serious concern over the danger of men becoming mere automata caught up in the workings of a highly complex structure, as the late Pope had warned in *Mater et Magistra.*

Neither the Pope nor the Council remain content with cautions, however. Socialization, they insist, can result in a truly human world community, and it can greatly enhance the possibility of responsible action on the part of individual human persons.

Throughout the Constitution, finally, there is a strongly personalist note and a concurrent optimism about the future of the human family if all communities can come to emphasize the importance not only of truth, justice, and love but also of freedom, for a sound society of men.

With respect to man's activity throughout the world (33-39), the Council takes pains to dispel false conceptions of the Christian attitude toward temporal involvement. "It is clear that men are not deterred by the Christian message from building up the world or impelled to neglect the welfare of their fellows, but that they are rather the more stringently bound to do these very things" (34).

What, then, is the meaning of human endeavor and what are its valid goals? The Council views man's activity, when entered on responsibly, as being a means of personal fulfillment and as having importance insofar as it contributes to human progress and social advance. For its part, the Church has something to contribute in the realm of temporal affairs, but it freely admits the limited nature of this contribution. "The Church guards the heritage of God's Word and draws moral and religious principles without always having at hand the solution to particular problems" (33). Though there may still be some who yield to the temptation to claim omnicompetence for ecclesiastical commentators on the human scene and its contingent social, economic, and political complexities, they cannot appeal to this Constitution for support of such a pretension. On the contrary, the text tells us something significant about the Church's true understanding of its own nature and function, as well as about the modesty and humility with which it regards its relation to the world.

How, then, does the Council speak of the Church's conception of its role in the modern world (40-45)? "Through her individual members and her whole community, the Church believes she can contribute greatly toward making the family of man and its history more human" (40). One objective in spelling out this view is to provide "basis for dialogue between the Church and the world" (40).

Here it is necessary to note that the aim is true dialogue, not a one-sided laying down of dictates on the part of the Church. "Though the same God is Savior and Creator, Lord of human history as well as of salvation history, in the divine arrangement itself, the rightful autonomy of the creature, and particularly of man, is not withdrawn, but is rather reestablished in its own dignity and strengthened" (41). The Church stands ready to serve mankind and human institutions, humbly conscious of what it can learn from history and from the social context.

Here is a work in which both clergy and laity can and must collaborate for a ministry of service. Concerning the unique role of the Christian layman in the temporal city, we have the pertinent conciliar teaching of the fourth chapter in the Constitution on the Church, as well as the practical norms of the Decree on the Apostolate of the Laity. At all times, we are here reminded, "while helping the world and receiving many benefits from it, the Church has a single intention: that God's kingdom may come, and that the salvation of the whole human race may come to pass" (44).

In the second, predominantly pastoral part of the Constitution, the Council Fathers turn to some "subjects arousing universal concern today" (46). They propose to take up in succession the topics of marriage, family life, human culture, life in its economic, social, and political dimensions, and finally the most vexing issues of modern war and the formation of a true family of nations.

In their discussion on fostering the dignity of marriage and the family (47-52), the Council Fathers state their desire to aid those who "are trying to preserve the holiness and to foster the natural dignity of the married state and its superlative value" (47). To this end they set forth a Christian understanding of marriage that emphasizes the centrality of conjugal love and of the concept of a covenant relationship between two persons. Christian marriage is seen, moreover, as a reflection of "the loving covenant uniting Christ with the Church" (49). This stress on conjugal love and the strongly personalist tone of the entire section on marriage carries us far beyond legalisms and philosophical abstractions indeed. They shape the very context, it is important to note, for the sharply debated and carefully framed passages that deal with family morality and the extremely urgent issues of responsible parenthood and the regulation of births.

The Constitution insists that "marriage and conjugal love are by their nature ordained toward the begetting and educating of children." Thus it is, too, that the Council, "while not making the other purposes of marriage of less account," holds that "the true practice of conjugal love, and the whole meaning of the family life which results from it, have this aim: that the couple be ready with stout hearts to cooperate with the love of the Creator and Savior, who through them will enlarge and enrich His own family day by day" (50). At the same time, however, the Council Fathers explicitly remind parents of their personal responsibility to verify the existence of conditions which make procreation at a given time the responsible act of mature Christians. This means that the decision to undertake parenthood in a given instance must be made with full regard for the parents' duty to themselves and their mutual love, to children already born and that might be anticipated in years ahead, to the common welfare of their family or other communities to which they are bound.

With respect to the debate over the moral acceptability of various methods of regulating births, the text reminds all believers that "sons of the Church may not undertake methods of birth control which are found blameworthy by the teaching authority of the Church in its unfolding of the divine law" (51). Against the current background of energetic debate on the "pill" and related issues of family morality and birth control, it seems clear that the most significant aspect of this section of the conciliar text is what it does not state. Evidently the Council Fathers had no intention of settling any concrete issues in the debate over birth control as it has evolved within Catholic theological circles in recent years. It is likewise clear that nothing they state in the Constitution presently forecloses any new lines of development in Catholic understanding on the matter.

Many readers of *Gaudium et Spes* will judge that the section treating of the proper development of culture (53-62) represents the Constitution's most novel venture in theological exploration. The arduous nature of its task here can be understood if one studies the several attempts made in the opening paragraphs of this chapter to come up with a satisfactory definition of culture itself. Whatever the problems inherent in arriving at a definition, it is possible to speak of a new age in human history characterized by profound changes in the ways contemporary man "strives by his knowledge and by his labor to bring the world itself under his control" (53). What the Constitution accepts as its point of departure is the emergence of valid new intellectual disciplines, chiefly those of the psychological, social, and historical sciences, as well as the unfolding of world-wide trends such as urbanization and industrialization with their inevitable impact on man and his works (54).

Coupled to these developments is a heightened sense of modern man's ability to shape a more truly human culture and to see to it that all men share in this culture on a meaningful level. Grave obstacles stand in the way of such accomplishments, however, and the task of altering significantly the situation of great segments of the world population now deprived of literacy is formidable (60).

The Constitution also takes into account the danger of dehumanization of a culture when technological or political considerations take over as the principal determinants of appropriate cultural development. Culture, the text insists, "because it flows immediately from the spiritual and social character of man, has constant need of a just liberty in order to develop; it needs also the legitimate possibility of exercising its autonomy according to its own principles" (59). As contemporary human culture unfolds, the Christian—and especially the theologian—must maintain close contact with all its aspects, particularly those emerging from the research of secular sciences (62).

Within the theological or ecclesiastical sciences, of course, there must be respect for the freedom of the scholar. In a sense, the closing lines of this section of *Gaudium et Spes* represent a most welcome and significant charter for Catholic intellectual pursuit: "In order that they may fulfill their function, let it be recognized that all the faithful, whether clerics or laity, possess a lawful freedom of inquiry, freedom of thought and of expressing their mind with humility and fortitude in those matters on which they enjoy competence" (62).

What the Constitution has to say concerning economic and social life (63-72) will not surprise anyone familiar with the main lines of papal social pronouncements over the past seventy-five years and the specific formulations made by Pope John XXIII in his two major social encyclicals. Once again, the *leitmotif* of this section is the dignity of the human person, "for man is the source, the center, and the purpose of all economic and social life" (63).

Taking up the theme of inequalities among men and nations sounded so strongly in Pope John's *Mater et Magistra,* the Constitution calls attention to the import of widespread sensitivity to such inequalities: "Our contemporaries are coming to feel these inequalities with an ever sharper awareness, since they are thoroughly convinced that the ampler technical and economic possibilities which the world of today enjoys can and should correct this unhappy state of affairs" (63). Thus Vatican II confronts that "revolution of rising expectations" that is so powerful a force on the world scene today. It follows that "today more than ever before attention is rightly given to the increase of the production of . . . goods and . . . services" (64) and that where reforms of the economic or social structure are needed, "doctrines which obstruct the necessary reforms under the guise of a false liberty, and those which subordinate the basic rights of individual persons and groups to the collective organization of production, must be shown to be erroneous" (65).

Human labor itself must always be seen in its true dignity, and workers must never be treated as mere automata in the organization of a complex productive process (67). The principle of maximizing responsible participation by all members of a group in the planning of common efforts and the securing of common interests is here repeated from *Mater et Magistra.* "Without doing harm to the necessary unity of management, the active sharing of all in the administration and profits of these enterprises . . . is to be promoted." Moreover, "since more often . . . decisions concerning economic and social conditions . . . are made not within the business itself but by the institutions on a higher level, the workers themselves should have a share also in determining these conditions—in person or through freely elected delegates" (68).

Private property is upheld as a right that often is an essential safeguard of man's freedom, but this point is made, significantly, only after the text has stressed the common destiny of earthly goods as such. "God intended the earth with everything in it for the use of all human beings and peoples." Thus, "whatever the forms of property may be . . . attention must always be paid to this universal destination of earthly goods" (69). The immediately relevant significance of this deliberate choice to reaffirm the earliest Christian tradition concerning property appears from a patristic citation made at this very point in the Constitution: " 'Feed the man dying of hunger, because if you have not fed him, you have killed him' " (69).

There is, in addition, written into the final version of the text an explicit openness to such communitarian patterns of ownership as one might encounter in some parts of Africa or Asia. Here is one of the clearest examples of successful efforts to rid the document of the overly Europeanized outlook and tone that characterized initial drafts of the document on the Church in the modern world and that drew sharp complaint in the Council hall. The same may be said of the document's careful handling of the pressing matter of land reform (71).

Profound changes in the life of the political community (73-76) of men make it fitting for the Council to offer some comments on the function of political society. "The present keener sense of human dignity has given rise in many parts

of the world to attempts to bring about a politico-juridical
order which will give better protection to the rights of the
person in public life" (73). Among these rights, the Constitution stresses once more that of participation in responsible decision-making within the civic order. "Along with cultural, economic and social development, there is a growing
desire among many people to play a greater part in organizing the life of the political community" (73).

Of special interest in this section is the positive reference
to the fact of social and political pluralism: "The people
who come together in the political community are many and
diverse, and they have every right to prefer divergent solutions" (74). Within the community, therefore, there must be
an organ of political authority charged with promoting the
common good. A characteristically modern note sounded in
the text is the statement that "political authority . . . must
always be . . . directed toward the common good—with a
dynamic concept of that good" (74). Immediately after this
embrace of a concept of authority that must be concerned
with doing more than to preserve an existing order of things
or status quo, we find a cautious nod in the direction of the
"right of revolution" when the Constitution states that "where
citizens are oppressed by a public authority . . . it is legitimate for them to defend their own rights and the rights of
their fellow citizens against the abuse of this authority" (74).

The state itself, the text notes, must shoulder many new
responsibilities, since "the complex circumstances of our day
make it necessary for public authority to intervene more
often in social, economic, and cultural matters" (75). Perhaps the Council Fathers felt relatively little concern over
expanding state intervention because they look to the creation of a built-in mechanism of control on arbitrary use of
power. This seems to be the intent of their recommendation
that "there must be a statute of positive law providing for a
suitable division of the functions and bodies of authority and
an efficient and independent system for the protection of
rights" (75).

As for its own status in the world, the Church declares
that "it is very important, especially where a pluralistic society prevails, that there be a correct notion of the relationship between the political community and the Church." While
the Church, "by reason of her role and competence, is not
identified in any way with the political community nor bound
to any political system," it does seek by "ways and means

proper to the gospel" to demonstrate that it "respects and fosters the political freedom and responsibility of citizens" (76). The emphasis, therefore, is once more on service to the modern world and mankind, with the assurance further that the Church "does not place her trust in the privileges offered by civil authority" and that she stands ready to renounce even legitimate rights where their use might "cast doubt on the sincerity of her witness" (76). It seems fair to say that the language here chosen deliberately disavows any lingering sentiment favoring a ghettoized Church or any attempts to implement some medieval vision of a Christian theocracy.

The last chapter of the "pastoral" part of *Gaudium et Spes* is divided into two sections. Both deal with relations among nations today. Few, surely, will disagree with the introductory statement that "the whole human family faces an hour of supreme crisis in its advance toward maturity." Hence most will anticipate the reason for making a conciliar declaration on fostering peace (77-82). True to the gospel, "the Council wishes passionately to summon Christians to co-operate . . . with all men in securing among themselves a peace based on justice and love and in setting up the instruments of peace" (77).

Peace, the Constitution remarks, "is not merely the absence of war; nor can it be reduced solely to the maintenance of a balance of power between enemies; nor is it brought about by dictatorship" (78). The Council Fathers testify that they "cannot fail to praise those who renounce the use of violence in the vindication of their rights and who resort to methods of defense which are otherwise available to weaker parties too" (78). But the task of banishing war today is complicated by the present state of international misunderstanding and tension and by the very ingenuity of modern science. The text notes, for instance, that "the complexity of the modern world and the intricacy of international relations allow guerrilla warfare to be drawn out by new methods of deceit and subversion" and that "in many cases the use of terrorism is regarded as a new way to wage war" (79). As a result, though the Constitution speaks out for the conscientious objector in declaring that "it seems right that laws make humane provision for the case of those who for reasons of conscience refuse to bear arms," it concedes that "as long as the danger of war remains and there is no competent and sufficiently powerful authority at the international level, governments cannot be denied the right to legitimate defense once every means of peaceful settlement has been exhausted" (79).

Since "the horror and perversity of war is immensely magnified by the addition of scientific weapons," it becomes necessary, exactly in the spirit of Pope John's *Pacem in Terris,* "to undertake an evaluation of war with an entirely new attitude" (80). Identifying itself with Pius XII and John XXIII, the Council makes an "unequivocal and unhesitating condemnation" of war "aimed indiscriminately at the destruction of cities or extensive areas along with their population." It seeks, moreover, to persuade men and rulers that "the arms race is an utterly treacherous trap for humanity, and one which ensnares the poor to an intolerable degree" (81).

Divine Providence calls for a supreme effort to free mankind from the "age-old slavery of war." Therefore, the Constitution argues, "it is our clear duty . . . to strain every muscle in working for the time when all war can be completely outlawed by international consent." Realistically, the text adds that "this goal undoubtedly requires the establishment of some universal public authority acknowledged as such by all and endowed with the power to safeguard on the behalf of all, security, regard for justice, and respect for rights" (82). The duty of striving for this goal does not rest on public officials alone, however, and thus "there is above all a pressing need for a renewed education of attitudes and for new inspiration in public opinion." Educators and others in a position to mold public opinion must accept this heavy responsibility (82).

Clearly, the crisis confronting a world threatened by universal and lethal war points up the importance of the second section of the Constitution's last chapter, one dealing with the task of setting up an international community (83-90). Present dangers to world peace and justice make it "absolutely necessary for countries to cooperate more advantageously and more closely together" and that they organize "as international bodies." (83). These organizations "must make provision for men's different needs . . . such as food supplies, health, education, labor," and for special problem cases such as those posed by the needs of developing nations, refugees, or migrants (84).

There is special need for "greater international cooperation in the economic field" and the effort here must be vast. The Constitution argues, for instance, that "developing nations

will not be able to procure material assistance unless radical
changes are made in the established procedures of modern
world commerce" (85). In any form of international economic exchange, there must be an end to "profiteering, to
national ambitions, to the appetite for political supremacy,
to militaristic calculations, and to machinations for the sake
of spreading and imposing ideologies" (85). In a positive
vein, the document continues, economic cooperation must
follow these norms: "Developing nations should . . . seek
. . . to express and secure the total human fulfillment of
their citizens. . . . It is a very important duty of the advanced nations to help the developing nations. . . . It is the
role of the international community to coordinate and promote development . . . with complete equity. . . . In many
cases there is an urgent need to revamp economic and social
structures" (86).

International cooperation is also needed particularly to aid
peoples with problems aggravated by a rapid increase in
population. Here the Council Fathers agree that "governments undoubtedly have rights and duties, within the limits
of their proper competency, regarding the population problem in their respective countries" (87). In view of the drastic solutions to population problems proposed in some quarters, however, "the Council urges everyone to guard against
solutions, whether publicly or privately supported, or at times
even imposed, which are contrary to the moral law" (87).
The Church's concern here is with man's inalienable rights
and the necessity of guaranteeing human responsibility and
hence human freedom.

Gaudium et Spes does not rest content with warning
against immoral efforts to combat the population problem,
or with urging more or less realistic programs for increased
food production or better land distribution in order to meet
the needs of rapidly growing populations. Here we see a new
emphasis added to the teaching of a document like John
XXIII's *Mater et Magistra*. The Council Fathers now recommend that "men should discreetly be informed, furthermore,
of scientific advances in exploring methods whereby spouses
can be helped in regulating the number of their children and
whose safeness has been well proven and whose harmony
with the moral order has been ascertained" (87).

Vatican II affirms that in the quest for international justice and world community "those Christians are to be praised
and supported, therefore, who volunteer their services to

help other men and nations" (88). In the spirit of the conciliar Decree on Ecumenism, this Constitution recommends
that "wherever it seems convenient, this activity of Catholics should be carried on in unison with other Christian
brothers" (88). Indeed, "to encourage and stimulate cooperation among men, the Church must be clearly present in the
midst of the community of nations," seeking a collaboration
motivated solely by the desire to be of service to all" (89).
Recognizing the need for organization and coordination of
efforts for effective international aid and development, the
Constitution finally speaks on behalf of regional and world-
wide secretariats. It lends support specifically to a "most opportune" proposal for setting up an organism of the universal Church "to stimulate the Catholic community to promote
progress in needy regions and international social justice"
(90).

The concluding paragraphs (91-93) of the Pastoral Constitution on the Church in the Modern World briefly recapit-
ulate certain basic themes of the document as a whole. It is
stated that "the proposals of this sacred Synod look to the
assistance of every man of our time" (91). Conceding that
the document as it stands "is but a general one in several of
its parts," and that in most places "it presents teaching already accepted in the Church," or else that it speaks only
tentatively since "it sometimes deals with matters in a constant state of development," the Council Fathers insist that
throughout they have relied on "the Word of God and the
spirit of the gospel" (91).

Following in the footsteps of the late Pope John and even
more immediately of Pope Paul VI in his encyclical *Ecclesiam Suam,* the Constitution speaks of the Church's awareness of its mission to stand forth "as a sign of that brotherhood which allows honest dialogue and gives it vigor" (92).
Within its own ranks, then, "such a mission requires in the
first place that we foster . . . mutual esteem, reverence, and
harmony, through the full recognition of lawful diversity."
Repeating a citation employed more than once by Pope John,
the Council Fathers urge: "Let there be unity in what is
necessary, freedom in what is unsettled, and charity in any
case" (92). But the dialogue as Vatican II would conceive
of it must extend also to "those brothers and communities
not yet living with us in full communion" and, indeed, "for
our part, the desire for such dialogue . . . excludes no one"
(92).

What the Council Fathers have had at heart throughout their labors in the Second Vatican Council is that the Church of Christ be ever more true to its own divinely instituted nature. Hence, they can boldly conclude this historic document by declaring that "mindful of the Lord's saying . . . Christians cannot yearn for anything more ardently than to serve the men of the modern world with mounting generosity and effectiveness" (93). For in a sense, by thus giving witness to the truth that Christ exists in all men, their brothers, the Christian faithful, "will share with others the mystery of the heavenly Father's love" (93).

DONALD R. CAMPION, S.J.

Pastoral Constitution on the Church in the Modern World

PAUL, BISHOP

SERVANT OF THE SERVANTS OF GOD

TOGETHER WITH THE FATHERS OF THE SACRED COUNCIL

FOR EVERLASTING MEMORY

PREFACE

THE INTIMATE BOND BETWEEN THE CHURCH AND MANKIND

1. The joys and the hopes, the griefs and the anxieties of the men of this age, especially those who are poor or in any way

---

1. An explanatory note was appended to the title of the text in order to satisfy the misgivings of some Fathers of the Council concerning the application of the term "constitution" to a document that of its nature does not define or decree immutable dogma. Though a special vote revealed that a majority of the Council Fathers approved use of the term "pastoral constitution," several hundred voted variously to substitute the terms "declaration," "letter," "exposition," or similar designations.

2. *The pastoral constitution "De Ecclesia in Mundo Huius Temporis" is made up of two parts; yet it constitutes an organic unity.*

By way of explanation: the constitution is called "pastoral" because, while resting on doctrinal principles, it seeks to express the relation of the Church to the world and modern mankind. The result is that, on the one hand, a pastoral slant is present in the first part, and, on the other hand, a doctrinal slant is present in the second part.

In the first part, the Church develops her teaching on man, on the world which is the enveloping context of man's existence, and on man's relations to his fellow men. In part two, the Church gives closer consideration to various aspects of modern life and human society; special consideration is given to those questions and problems which, in this general area, seem to have a greater urgency in our day. As a result, in part two the subject matter which is viewed in the light of doctrinal principles is made up of diverse elements. Some elements have a permanent value; others, only a transitory one.

Consequently, the Constitution must be interpreted according to the general norms of theological interpretation. Interpreters must bear in mind—especially in part two—the changeable circumstances which the subject matter, by its very nature, involves.

afflicted, these too are the joys and hopes, the griefs and anxieties of the followers of Christ. Indeed, nothing genuinely human fails to raise an echo in their hearts. For theirs is a community composed of men. United in Christ, they are led by the Holy Spirit in their journey to the kingdom of their Father and they have welcomed the news of salvation which is meant for every man. That is why this community realizes that it is truly and intimately linked with mankind and its history.

FOR WHOM THIS MESSAGE IS INTENDED

2. Hence this Second Vatican Council, having probed more profoundly into the mystery of the Church, now addresses itself without hesitation, not only to the sons of the Church and to all who invoke the name of Christ, but to the whole of humanity.[3] For the Council yearns to explain to everyone how it conceives of the presence and activity of the Church in the world of today.

Therefore, the Council focuses its attention on the world of men, the whole human family along with the sum of those realities in the midst of which that family lives. It gazes upon that world which is the theater of man's history, and carries the marks of his energies, his tragedies, and his triumphs; that world which the Christian sees as created and sustained by its Maker's love, fallen indeed into the bondage of sin, yet emancipated now by Christ. He was crucified and rose again to break the stranglehold of personified Evil,[4] so that this world might be fashioned anew according to God's design and reach its fulfillment.

THE SERVICE TO BE OFFERED TO HUMANITY

3. Though mankind today is struck with wonder at its own discoveries and its power, it often raises anxious questions about the current trend of the world, about the place and role of man in the universe, about the meaning of his individual and collective strivings, and about the ultimate destiny of reality and of humanity. Hence, giving witness and

3. It should be recalled that John XXIII set a widely hailed precedent in addressing his encyclical on peace, "Pacem in Terris," to "all men of good will." Paul VI adopted the same formula when he issued his inaugural encyclical "Ecclesiam Suam" on Aug. 6, 1964.
4. The Latin text at this point speaks of the power of "Malignus," a biblical usage. The editors of the text indicate the special sense of the term here by capitalizing the initial letter.

voice to the faith of the whole People of God[5] gathered together by Christ, this Council can provide no more eloquent proof of its solidarity with the entire human family with which it is bound up, as well as its respect and love for that family, than by engaging with it in conversation about these various problems.

The Council brings to mankind light kindled from the gospel, and puts at its disposal those saving resources which the Church herself, under the guidance of the Holy Spirit, receives from her Founder. For the human person deserves to be preserved; human society deserves to be renewed. Hence the pivotal point of our total presentation will be man himself, whole and entire, body and soul, heart and conscience, mind and will.

Therefore, this sacred Synod proclaims the highest destiny of man and champions the godlike seed which has been sown in him. It offers to mankind the honest assistance of the Church in fostering that brotherhood of all men which corresponds to this destiny of theirs. Inspired by no earthly ambition,[6] the Church seeks but a solitary goal: to carry forward the work of Christ Himself under the lead of the befriending Spirit. And Christ entered this world to give witness to the truth, to rescue and not to sit in judgment, to serve and not to be served.[7]

INTRODUCTORY STATEMENT

The Situation of Men in the Modern World

HOPE AND ANGUISH

4. To carry out such a task, the Church has always had the duty of scrutinizing the signs of the times[8] and of interpret-

5. Reference here to the "People of God" recalls the new emphasis given that image of the Church in the second chapter of "Lumen Gentium," Vatican II's historic Constitution on the Church.
6. This formal declaration of the Council had been anticipated in Paul VI's address to the United Nations General Assembly in New York City on Oct. 4, 1965.
7. *Cf. Jn. 18:37; Mt. 20:28; Mk. 10:45.*
8. "Signs of the times" was a phrase frequently used by John XXIII. It won

ing them in the light of the gospel. Thus, in language intelligible to each generation, she can respond to the perennial questions which men ask about this present life and the life to come, and about the relationship of the one to the other. We must therefore recognize and understand the world in which we live, its expectations, its longings, and its often dramatic characteristics. Some of the main features of the modern world can be sketched as follows:

Today, the human race is passing through a new stage of its history. Profound and rapid changes are spreading by degrees around the whole world. Triggered by the intelligence and creative energies of man, these changes recoil upon him, upon his decisions and desires, both individual and collective, and upon his manner of thinking and acting with respect to things and to people. Hence we can already speak of a true social and cultural transformation, one which has repercussions on man's religious life as well.

As happens in any crisis of growth,[9] this transformation has brought serious difficulties in its wake. Thus while man extends his power in every direction, he does not always succeed in subjecting it to his own welfare. Striving to penetrate farther into the deeper recesses of his own mind, he frequently appears more unsure of himself. Gradually and more precisely he lays bare the laws of society, only to be paralyzed by uncertainty about the direction to give it.

Never has the human race enjoyed such an abundance of wealth, resources, and economic power. Yet a huge proportion of the world's citizens is still tormented by hunger and poverty,[10] while countless numbers suffer from total illiteracy. Never before today has man been so keenly aware of freedom, yet at the same time, new forms of social and psychological slavery make their appearance.

Although the world of today has a very vivid sense of its unity and of how one man depends on another in needful

special attention when employed as the heading for several notable passages in his "Pacem in Terris." Though some professed to find the usage disturbingly unfamiliar or misleading, it is now obviously a part of the Christian vocabulary as a result of this usage by the Council. Indeed, its source is ultimately biblical.

9. It should be remarked that the Council Fathers do not necessarily attribute existing difficulties in society to the cultural and social changes that have occurred, but see them rather as possibly normal concomitants of any "crisis of growth."

10. This theme has been sounded with telling effect by experts like Barbara Ward in her essays and lectures on inequalities between rich and poor nations. Michael Harrington's "The Other America" (Macmillan, 1963) brought home to a great many citizens of the United States the fact that similar inequalities can exist between "haves" and "have nots" even in the richest nation on earth.

solidarity, it is most grievously torn into opposing camps by conflicting forces. For political, social, economic, racial, and ideological disputes still continue bitterly, and with them the peril of a war which would reduce everything to ashes. True, there is a growing exchange of ideas, but the very words by which key concepts are expressed take on quite different meanings in diverse ideological systems. Finally, man painstakingly searches for a better world, without working with equal zeal for the betterment of his own spirit.

Caught up in such numerous complications, very many of our contemporaries are kept from accurately identifying permanent values and adjusting them properly to fresh discoveries. As a result, buffeted between hope and anxiety and pressing one another with questions about the present course of events, they are burdened down with uneasiness. This same course of events leads men to look for answers. Indeed, it forces them to do so.

PROFOUNDLY CHANGED CONDITIONS

5. Today's spiritual agitation and the changing conditions of life are part of a broader and deeper revolution. As a result of the latter, intellectual formation is ever increasingly based on the mathematical and natural sciences and on those dealing with man himself, while in the practical order the technology which stems from these sciences takes on mounting importance.

This scientific spirit exerts a new kind of impact on the cultural sphere and on modes of thought. Technology is now transforming the face of the earth, and is already trying to master outer space. To a certain extent, the human intellect is also broadening its dominion over time: over the past by means of historical knowledge; over the future by the art of projecting and by planning.

Advances in biology, psychology, and the social sciences not only bring men hope of improved self-knowledge. In conjunction with technical methods, they are also helping men to exert direct influence on the life of social groups. At the same time, the human race is giving ever-increasing thought to forecasting and regulating its own population growth.

History itself speeds along on so rapid a course that an individual person can scarcely keep abreast of it. The destiny of the human community has become all of a piece, where once the various groups of men had a kind of private history of their own. Thus, the human race has passed from a rather static concept of reality to a more dynamic, evolutionary one.[11] In consequence, there has arisen a new series of problems, a series as important as can be, calling for new efforts of analysis and synthesis.

CHANGES IN THE SOCIAL ORDER

6. By this very circumstance, the traditional local communities such as father-centered families, clans, tribes, villages, various groups and associations stemming from social contacts experience more thorough changes every day.

The industrial type of society is gradually being spread, leading some nations to economic affluence, and radically transforming ideas and social conditions established for centuries. Likewise, the practice and pursuit of city living has grown, either because of a multiplication of cities and their inhabitants, or by a transplantation of city life to rural settings.

New and more efficient media of social communication are contributing to the knowledge of events. By setting off chain reactions, they are giving the swiftest and widest possible circulation to styles of thought and feeling.

It is also noteworthy how many men are being induced to migrate on various counts, and are thereby changing their manner of life. Thus a man's ties with his fellows are constantly being multiplied. At the same time "socialization"[12] brings further ties, without, however, always promoting appropriate personal development and truly personal relationships ("personalization").

This kind of evolution can be seen more clearly in those nations which already enjoy the conveniences of economic and technological progress, though it is also astir among peoples still striving for such progress and eager to secure for themselves the advantages of an industrialized and urbanized society. These peoples, especially those among them who are

---

11. A later section of the Constitution (Art. 74) will speak of the duty governments have to take a "dynamic" concept of the common good as their norm and goal. The reference to dynamic evolutionary forces here is perhaps one reason why some critics early objected to the influence of the thought of Pierre Teilhard de Chardin on the document.

12. "Socialization" appeared in John XXIII's encyclical "Mater et Magistra" (59-67). It quickly drew fire from those who neglected to analyze the late Pope's definition of the term. For further discussion of the phenomenon in the present document, cf. Arts. 63 and 74.

attached to older traditions, are simultaneously undergoing a movement toward more mature and personal exercise of liberty.

PSYCHOLOGICAL, MORAL, AND RELIGIOUS CHANGES

7. A change in attitudes and in human structures frequently calls accepted values into question. This is especially true of young people, who have grown impatient on more than one occasion, and indeed become rebels in their distress. Aware of their own influence in the life of society, they want to assume a role in it sooner. As a result, parents and educators frequently experience greater difficulties day by day in discharging their tasks.

The institutions, laws, and modes of thinking and feeling as handed down from previous generations do not always seem to be well adapted to the contemporary state of affairs. Hence arises an upheaval in the manner and even the norms of behavior.

Finally, these new conditions have their impact on religion. On the one hand a more critical ability to distinguish religion from a magical view of the world and from the superstitions which still circulate purifies religion and exacts day by day a more personal and explicit adherence to faith. As a result many persons are achieving a more vivid sense of God.

On the other hand, growing numbers of people are abandoning religion in practice. Unlike former days, the denial of God or of religion, or the abandonment of them, are no longer unusual and individual occurrences.[13] For today it is not rare for such decisions to be presented as requirements of scientific progress or of a certain new humanism. In numerous places these views are voiced not only in the teachings of philosophers, but on every side they influence literature, the arts, the interpretation of the humanities and of history, and civil laws themselves. As a consequence, many people are shaken.

IMBALANCES IN THE MODERN WORLD

8. Because they are coming so rapidly, and often in a disorderly fashion, all these changes beget contradictions and

13. For a formal treatment at length of atheism, cf. Arts. 19-21 of this Constitution.

imbalances, or intensify them. Indeed the very fact that men are more conscious than ever of the inequalities in the world has the same effect.

Within the individual person there too often develops an imbalance between an intellect which is modern in practical matters, and a theoretical system of thought which can neither master the sum total of its ideas, nor arrange them adequately into a synthesis. Likewise, an imbalance arises between a concern for practicality and efficiency, and the demands of moral conscience; also, very often, between the conditions of collective existence and the requisites of personal thought, and even of contemplation.[14] Specialization in any human activity can at length deprive a man of a comprehensive view of reality.

As for the family, discord results from demographic, economic, and social pressures, or from difficulties which arise between succeeding generations, or from new social relationships between men and women.

Significant differences crop up too between races and between various kinds of social orders; between wealthy nations and those which are less influential or are needy; finally, between international institutions born of the popular desire for peace, and the ambition to propagate one's own ideology, as well as collective greed existing in nations or other groups.

What results is mutual distrust, enmities, conflicts, and hardships. Of such is man at once the cause and the victim.

THE BROADER DESIRES OF MANKIND

9. Meanwhile, the conviction grows not only that humanity can and should increasingly consolidate its control over creation, but even more, that it devolves on humanity to establish a political, social, and economic order which will to an ever better extent serve man and help individuals as well as groups to affirm and develop the dignity proper to them.

As a result very many persons are quite aggressively demanding those benefits of which with vivid awareness they judge themselves to be deprived either through injustice or unequal distribution. Nations on the road to progress, like

---

14. The Council ought not here to be understood as intending to enter into a peripheral debate on the proper relation between "contemplative prayer" and the communitarian aspects of that active liturgy fostered by the Vatican Council's Constitution on the Sacred Liturgy. What this passage offers is simply a reminder of the value perennially placed by the Christian community on contemplation.

those recently made independent, desire to participate in the goods of modern civilization, not only in the political field but also economically, and to play their part freely on the world scene. Still they continually fall behind while very often their dependence on wealthier nations deepens more rapidly, even in the economic sphere.

People hounded by hunger call upon those better off. Where they have not yet won it, women claim for themselves an equity with men before the law and in fact. Laborers and farmers seek not only to provide for the necessities of life but to develop the gifts of their personality by their labors, and indeed to take part in regulating economic, social, political, and cultural life. Now, for the first time in human history, all people are convinced that the benefits of culture ought to be and actually can be extended to everyone.[15]

Still, beneath all these demands lies a deeper and more widespread longing. Persons and societies thirst for a full and free life worthy of man—one in which they can subject to their own welfare all that the modern world can offer them so abundantly. In addition, nations try harder every day to bring about a kind of universal community.

Since all these things are so, the modern world shows itself at once powerful and weak, capable of the noblest deeds or the foulest. Before it lies the path to freedom or to slavery, to progress or retreat, to brotherhood or hatred. Moreover, man is becoming aware that it is his responsibility to guide aright the forces which he has unleashed and which can enslave him or minister to him. That is why he is putting questions to himself.[16]

MAN'S DEEPER QUESTIONINGS

10. The truth is that the imbalances under which the modern world labors are linked with that more basic imbalance rooted in the heart of man. For in man himself many elements wrestle with one another. Thus, on the one hand, as a creature he experiences his limitations in a multitude of ways. On the other, he feels himself to be boundless in his desires and summoned to a higher life.

15. Even if, in the past, one individual or group had entertained such ambitions, the Council would be correct here in speaking of a new "universal" conviction, one that is a "first" in human history.
16. This description of the "human condition" can be accepted by any man who is willing to consider the data of day-to-day experience. The specific impact of sin in the world, a realization derived in part at least from the data of revelation, is treated in Arts. 10 and 13 of the Constitution.

Pulled by manifold attractions, he is constantly forced to choose among them and to renounce some. Indeed, as a weak and sinful being, he often does what he would not, and fails to do what he would.[17] Hence he suffers from internal divisions, and from these flow so many and such great discords in society.

No doubt very many whose lives are infected with a practical materialism are blinded against any sharp insight into this kind of dramatic situation. Or else, weighed down by wretchedness, they are prevented from giving the matter any thought.

Thinking that they have found serenity in an interpretation of reality everywhere proposed these days, many look forward to a genuine and total emancipation of humanity wrought solely by human effort. They are convinced that the future rule of man over the earth will satisfy every desire of his heart.

Nor are there lacking men who despair of any meaning to life and praise the boldness of those who think that human existence is devoid of any inherent significance and who strive to confer a total meaning on it by their own ingenuity alone.

Nevertheless, in the face of the modern development of the world, an ever-increasing number of people are raising the most basic questions or recognizing them with a new sharpness: what is man? What is this sense of sorrow, of evil, of death, which continues to exist despite so much progress? What is the purpose of these victories, purchased at so high a cost? What can man offer to society, what can he expect from it? What follows this earthly life?

The Church believes that Christ, who died and was raised up for all,[18] can through His Spirit offer man the light and the strength to measure up to his supreme destiny. Nor has any other name under heaven been given to man by which it is fitting for him to be saved.[19] She likewise holds that in her most benign Lord and Master can be found the key, the focal point, and the goal of all human history.

The Church also maintains that beneath all changes there are many realities which do not change and which have their ultimate foundation in Christ, who is the same yesterday and

17. Cf. Rom. 7:14 ff.
18. Cf. 2 Cor. 5:15.
19. Cf. Acts 4:12.

today, yes and forever.[20] Hence in the light of Christ, the image of the unseen God, the firstborn of every creature,[21] the Council wishes to speak to all men in order to illuminate the mystery of man and to cooperate in finding the solution to the outstanding problems of our time.

PART I

THE CHURCH AND MAN'S CALLING

THE IMPULSES OF THE SPIRIT
DEMAND A RESPONSE

11. The People of God believes that it is led by the Spirit of the Lord, who fills the earth. Motivated by this faith, it labors to decipher authentic signs of God's presence and purpose in the happenings, needs, and desires[22] in which this People has a part along with other men of our age. For faith throws a new light on everything, manifests God's design for man's total vocation, and thus directs the mind to solutions which are fully human.

This Council, first of all, wishes to assess in this light those values which are most highly prized today, and to relate them to their divine source. For insofar as they stem from endowments conferred by God on man, these values are exceedingly good. Yet they are often wrenched from their rightful function by the taint in man's heart, and hence stand in need of purification.

What does the Church think of man? What recommendations seem needful for the upbuilding of contemporary society? What is the ultimate significance of human activity

20. Cf. Heb. 13:8.
21. Cf. Col. 1:15.
22. A further elaboration of the sense in which the Council chooses to speak of the "signs of the times." It should be clear that not all events necessarily manifest God's true purpose. Hence the Council notes that the People of God must labor to discern the working of God's will from that of the Evil One.

throughout the world? People are waiting for an answer to these questions. From the answers it will be increasingly clear that the People of God and the human race in whose midst it lives render service to each other. Thus the mission of the Church will show its religious, and by that very fact, its supremely human character.

CHAPTER I

THE DIGNITY OF THE HUMAN PERSON

MAN AS MADE IN GOD'S IMAGE

12. According to the almost unanimous opinion of believers and unbelievers alike, all things on earth should be related to man as their center and crown.

But what is man? About himself he has expressed, and continues to express, many divergent and even contradictory opinions. In these he often exalts himself as the absolute measure of all things or debases himself to the point of despair. The result is doubt and anxiety.

The Church understands these problems. Endowed with light from God, she can offer solutions to them so that man's true situation can be portrayed and his defects explained, while at the same time his dignity and destiny are justly acknowledged.

For sacred Scripture teaches that man was created "to the image of God," is capable of knowing and loving his Creator, and was appointed by Him as master of all earthly creatures[23] that he might subdue them and use them to God's glory.[24] "What is man that thou art mindful of him or the son of man that thou visitest him? Thou hast made him a little less than the angels, thou hast crowned him with glory and honor: thou hast set him over the works of thy hands,

23. Cf. Gen. 1:26; Wis. 2:23.
24. Cf. Eccl. (Sir.) 17:3-10.

thou hast subjected all things under his feet" (Ps. 8:5-6).

But God did not create man as a solitary. For from the beginning "male and female he created them" (Gen. 1:27). Their companionship produces the primary form of interpersonal communion.[25] For by his innermost nature man is a social being, and unless he relates himself to others he can neither live nor develop his potential.

Therefore, as we read elsewhere in holy Scripture, God saw "all the things that he had made, and they were very good" (Gen. 1:31).

SIN

13. Although he was made by God in a state of holiness, from the very dawn of history man abused his liberty, at the urging of personified Evil. Man set himself against God and sought to find fulfillment apart from God. Although he knew God, he did not glorify Him as God, but his senseless mind was darkened and he served the creature rather than the Creator.[26]

What divine revelation makes known to us agrees with experience. Examining his heart, man finds that he has inclinations toward evil too, and is engulfed by manifold ills which cannot come from his good Creator. Often refusing to acknowledge God as his beginning, man has disrupted also his proper relationship to his own ultimate goal. At the same time he became out of harmony with himself, with others, and with all created things.[27]

Therefore man is split within himself. As a result, all of human life, whether individual or collective, shows itself to be a dramatic struggle between good and evil, between light and darkness. Indeed, man finds that by himself he is incapable of battling the assaults of evil successfully, so that everyone feels as though he is bound by chains.

But the Lord Himself came to free and strengthen man, renewing him inwardly and casting out that prince of this world (cf. Jn. 12:31) who held him in the bondage of sin.[28] For sin has diminished man, blocking his path to fulfillment.

---

25. This concept of marriage as fundamentally an interpersonal communion is at the heart of the subsequent conciliar teaching (Art. 48) on the dignity of married life.
26. Cf. Rom. 1:21-25.
27. One ought to understand that the Council wishes to take note of the "cosmic" dimension of sin by its reference to disorder in relation to all created things.
28. Cf. Jn. 8:34.

The call to grandeur and the depths of misery are both a part of human experience. They find their ultimate and simultaneous explanation in the light of God's revelation.

THE MAKE-UP OF MAN

14. Though made of body and soul, man is one. Through his bodily composition he gathers to himself the elements of the material world. Thus they reach their crown through him, and through him raise their voice in free praise of the Creator.[29]

For this reason man is not allowed to despise his bodily life. Rather, he is obliged to regard his body as good and honorable since God has created it and will raise it up on the last day. Nevertheless, wounded by sin, man experiences rebellious stirrings in his body. But the very dignity of man postulates that man glorify God in his body[30] and forbid it to serve the evil inclinations of his heart.

Now, man is not wrong when he regards himself as superior to bodily concerns, and as more than a speck of nature or a nameless constituent of the city of man. For by his interior qualities[31] he outstrips the whole sum of mere things. He finds re-enforcement in this profound insight* whenever he enters into his own heart. God, who probes the heart,[32] awaits him there. There he discerns his proper destiny beneath the eyes of God. Thus, when man recognizes in himself a spiritual and immortal soul, he is not being mocked by a deceptive fantasy springing from mere physical or social influences. On the contrary he is getting to the depths of the very truth of the matter.

THE DIGNITY OF THE MIND; TRUTH; WISDOM

15. Man judges rightly that by his intellect he surpasses the material universe, for he shares in the light of the divine mind. By relentlessly employing his talents through the ages, he has indeed made progress in the practical sciences, tech-

29. *Cf. Dan. 3:57-90.*
30. *Cf. 1 Cor. 6:13-20.*
31. The Latin text here uses the word "interioritas." This usage rightly reflects the impact of modern insights into the significance of this distinctively human capacity.
* The sources vary here. The Latin text published by *L'Osservatore Romano* (Dec. 19, 1965) reads: *ad hanc profundam agnitionem redit.* The Latin text distributed in St. Peter's just before promulgation read: *ad haec profunda redit.*—Ed.
32. *Cf. 1 Kg. 16:7; Jer. 17:10.*

nology, and the liberal arts.[33] In our times he has won superlative victories, especially in his probing of the material world and in subjecting it to himself.

Still he has always searched for more penetrating truths, and finds them. For his intelligence is not confined to observable data alone. It can with genuine certitude attain to reality itself as knowable, though in consequence of sin that certitude is partly obscured and weakened.

The intellectual nature of the human person is perfected by wisdom and needs to be. For wisdom gently attracts the mind of man to a quest and a love for what is true and good. Steeped in wisdom, man passes through visible realities to those which are unseen.

Our era needs such wisdom more than bygone ages if the discoveries made by man are to be further humanized. For the future of the world stands in peril unless wiser men are forthcoming. It should also be pointed out that many nations, poorer in economic goods, are quite rich in wisdom and can offer noteworthy advantages to others.[34]

It is, finally, through the gift of the Holy Spirit that man comes by faith to the contemplation and appreciation of the divine plan.[35]

THE DIGNITY OF THE MORAL CONSCIENCE

16. In the depths of his conscience, man detects a law which he does not impose upon himself, but which holds him to obedience. Always summoning him to love good and avoid evil, the voice of conscience can when necessary speak to his heart more specifically: do this, shun that. For man has in his heart a law written by God. To obey it is the very dignity of man; according to it he will be judged.[36]

Conscience is the most secret core and sanctuary of a man. There he is alone with God, whose voice echoes in his depths.[37] In a wonderful manner conscience reveals that law

---

33. Though the reference to the "liberal arts" comes last in this particular enumeration, the fact need not be taken as proof of the Council's wish to tip the balance in the controversy over what C. P. Snow has called the "two cultures."
34. This comment in the text should be read as a reference to nations outside the West. It points up the openness of the Council, under pressure from spokesmen for some of the "new" Churches, to viewpoints other than those familiar to lands that have long known the gospel.
35. *Cf. Eccl. (Sir.) 17:7-8.*
36. *Cf. Rom. 2:15-16.*
37. *Cf. Pius XII, radio address on the correct formation of a Christian conscience in the young, Mar. 23, 1952: AAS (1952), p. 271.*

which is fulfilled by love of God and neighbor.[38] In fidelity
to conscience, Christians are joined with the rest of men in
the search for truth, and for the genuine solution to the
numerous problems which arise in the life of individuals and
from social relationships. Hence the more that a correct conscience holds sway, the more persons and groups turn aside
from blind choice and strive to be guided by objective norms
of morality.

Conscience frequently errs from invincible ignorance without losing its dignity. The same cannot be said of a man who
cares but little for truth and goodness, or of a conscience
which by degrees grows practically sightless as a result of
habitual sin.

THE EXCELLENCE OF LIBERTY

17. Only in freedom can man direct himself toward goodness. Our contemporaries make much of this freedom and
pursue it eagerly; and rightly so, to be sure. Often, however,
they foster it perversely as a license for doing whatever
pleases them, even if it is evil.

For its part, authentic freedom is an exceptional sign of
the divine image within man. For God has willed that man
be left "in the hand of his own counsel"[39] so that he can
seek his Creator spontaneously, and come freely to utter and
blissful perfection through loyalty to Him. Hence man's dignity demands that he act according to a knowing and free
choice. Such a choice is personally motivated and prompted
from within. It does not result from blind internal impulse
nor from mere external pressure.[40]

Man achieves such dignity when, emancipating himself
from all captivity to passion, he pursues his goal in a spontaneous choice of what is good, and procures for himself,
through effective and skillful action, apt means to that end.
Since man's freedom has been damaged by sin, only by the
help of God's grace can he bring such a relationship with
God into full flower. Before the judgment seat of God each

38. *Cf. Mt. 22:37-40; Gal. 5:14.*
39. *Cf. Eccl. (Sir.) 15:14.*
40. The reasoning here is clearly pertinent to any discussion on a basis for true
religious freedom. One finds it repeated in the Council's declaration on that subject. It should be remarked that at one point in the life cycle of Vatican II it was
strongly advocated by some that the subject of religious freedom be dealt with
in the proposed text on the Church in the modern world.

man must render an account of his own life, whether he has done good or evil.[41]

THE MYSTERY OF DEATH

18. It is in the face of death that the riddle of human existence becomes most acute. Not only is man tormented by pain and by the advancing deterioration of his body, but even more so by a dread of perpetual extinction. He rightly follows the intuition of his heart when he abhors and repudiates the absolute ruin and total disappearance of his own person.

Man rebels against death because he bears in himself an eternal seed which cannot be reduced to sheer matter. All the endeavors of technology, though useful in the extreme, cannot calm his anxiety. For a prolongation of biological life is unable to satisfy that desire for a higher life which is inescapably lodged in his breast.

Although the mystery of death utterly beggars the imagination, the Church has been taught by divine revelation, and herself firmly teaches, that man has been created by God for a blissful purpose beyond the reach of earthly misery. In addition, that bodily death from which man would have been immune had he not sinned[42] will be vanquished, according to the Christian faith, when man who was ruined by his own doing is restored to wholeness by an almighty and merciful Savior.

For God has called man and still calls him so that with his entire being he might be joined to Him in an endless sharing of a divine life beyond all corruption. Christ won this victory when He rose to life, since by His death He freed man from death.[43] Hence to every thoughtful man a solidly established faith provides the answer to his anxiety about what the future holds for him. At the same time faith gives him the power to be united in Christ with his loved ones who have already been snatched away by death. Faith arouses the hope that they have found true life with God.

THE FORMS AND ROOTS OF ATHEISM

19. An outstanding cause of human dignity lies in man's call to communion with God. From the very circumstance of his

41. *Cf. 2 Cor. 5:10.*
42. *Cf. Wis. 1:13; 2:23-24; Rom. 5:21; 6:23; Jas. 1:15.*
43. *Cf. 1 Cor. 15:56-57.*

origin, man is already invited to converse with God. For man would not exist were he not created by God's love and constantly preserved by it. And he cannot live fully according to truth unless he freely acknowledges that love and devotes himself to his Creator.

Still, many of our contemporaries have never recognized this intimate and vital link with God, or have explicitly rejected it. Thus atheism must be accounted among the most serious problems of this age, and is deserving of closer examination.

The word atheism is applied to phenomena which are quite distinct from one another.[44] For while God is expressly denied by some, others believe that man can assert absolutely nothing about Him. Still others use such a method so to scrutinize the question of God as to make it seem devoid of meaning. Many, unduly transgressing the limits of the positive sciences, contend that everything can be explained by this kind of scientific reasoning alone, or, by contrast, they altogether disallow that there is any absolute truth.

Some laud man so extravagantly that their faith in God lapses into a kind of anemia, though they seem more inclined to affirm man than to deny God. Again some form for themselves such a fallacious idea of God that when they repudiate this figment they are by no means rejecting the God of the gospel. Some never get to the point of raising questions about God, since they seem to experience no religious stirrings nor do they see why they should trouble themselves about religion.

Moreover, atheism results not rarely from a violent protest against the evil in this world, or from the absolute character with which certain human values are unduly invested, and which thereby already accords them the stature of God. Modern civilization itself often complicates the approach to God, not for any essential reason, but because it is excessively engrossed in earthly affairs.

Undeniably, those who willfully shut out God from their hearts and try to dodge religious questions are not following

44. Historians of the Second Vatican Council may some day recount in full the extensive efforts made to commit the Council to a direct and explicit condemnation of atheistic materialism. In general, the mood of the Council was to remain true to its providential nature as defined by Pope John, and thus to avoid negative measures or harsh condemnations. The analysis of atheism set forth in the text is an attempt to uncover some of the complexities behind the phenomenon of atheism and agnosticism in their many contemporary guises.

the dictates of their consciences. Hence they are not free of blame.

Yet believers themselves frequently bear some responsibility for this situation. For, taken as a whole, atheism is not a spontaneous development but stems from a variety of causes, including a critical reaction against religious beliefs, and in some places against the Christian religion in particular. Hence believers can have more than a little to do with the birth of atheism. To the extent that they neglect their own training in the faith, or teach erroneous doctrine, or are deficient in their religious, moral, or social life,[45] they must be said to conceal rather than reveal the authentic face of God and religion.

SYSTEMATIC ATHEISM

20. Modern atheism[46] often takes on a systematic expression, which, in addition to other arguments against God, stretches the desire for human independence to such a point that it finds difficulties with any kind of dependence on God. Those who profess atheism of this sort maintain that it gives man freedom to be an end unto himself, the sole artisan and creator of his own history. They claim that this freedom cannot be reconciled with the affirmation of a Lord who is author and purpose of all things, or at least that this freedom makes such an affirmation altogether superfluous. The sense of power which modern technical progress generates in man can give color to such a doctrine.

Not to be overlooked among the forms of modern atheism

45. The Council here proposes an examination of conscience for believers. Have they contributed by their shortcomings to the disaffection of those who cannot or will not believe? The text specifically mentions defects of social conscience among Christians. One is reminded of John XXIII's forthright declaration in "Mater et Magistra" (222): "We reaffirm strongly that Christian social doctrine is an integral part of the Christian conception of life."

46. Lest there be confusion the drafters of the Constitution wished to make it plain that this paragraph treats directly of "systematic" atheism as a "contemporary" phenomenon and not merely of its manifestations in past ages. Despite all efforts, the drafting of this passage occasioned considerable tension in some circles during the Council's closing days. Through unintentional oversight members of the drafting commission had not seen copies of identical suggestions by 334 Fathers of which 297 had been filed with the Council's secretariat in due time, urging an "explicit" condemnation of Marxist atheistic communism. The commission felt it had reviewed the substantial issue, however, and gave it a second consideration when 220 Fathers again submitted the same suggestion in the form of "modi" (emendations) on the next-to-last revision of the text. Economic, social, and philosophical aspects of communism were dealt with positively in other sections of the Constitution. The commission judged that its references to atheism satisfied the wishes of the Council as a whole.

is that which anticipates the liberation of man especially through his economic and social emancipation. This form argues that by its nature religion thwarts such liberation by arousing man's hope for a deceptive future life, thereby diverting him from the constructing of the earthly city. Consequently, when the proponents of this doctrine gain governmental power they vigorously fight against religion. They promote atheism by using those means of pressure which public power has at its disposal. Such is especially the case in the work of educating the young.

THE CHURCH'S ATTITUDE TOWARD ATHEISM

21. In her loyal devotion to God and men, the Church has already repudiated[47] and cannot cease repudiating, sorrowfully but as firmly as possible, those poisonous doctrines and actions which contradict reason and the common experience of humanity, and dethrone man from his native excellence.

Still, she strives to detect in the atheistic mind the hidden causes for the denial of God. Conscious of how weighty are the questions which atheism raises, and motivated by love for all men, she believes these questions ought to be examined seriously and more profoundly.

The Church holds that the recognition of God is in no way hostile to man's dignity, since this dignity is rooted and perfected in God. For man was made an intelligent and free member of society by the God who created him. Even more importantly, man is called as a son to commune with God and to share in His happiness. She further teaches that a hope related to the end of time does not diminish the importance of intervening duties, but rather undergirds the acquittal of them with fresh incentives. By contrast, when a divine substructure and the hope of life eternal are wanting, man's dignity is most grievously lacerated, as current events often attest. The riddles of life and death, of guilt and of grief go unsolved, with the frequent result that men succumb to despair.

Meanwhile, every man remains to himself an unsolved puzzle, however obscurely he may perceive it. For on cer-

47. *Cf. Pius XI, encyclical letter "Divini Redemptoris," March 19, 1937: AAS 29 (1937), pp. 65-106; Pius XII, encyclical letter "Ad Apostolorum Principis," June 29, 1958: AAS 50 (1958), pp. 601-614; John XXIII, encyclical letter "Mater et Magistra," May 15, 1961: AAS 35 (1961), pp. 451-453; Paul VI, encyclical letter "Ecclesiam Suam," Aug. 6, 1964: AAS 56 (1964), pp. 651-653.*

tain occasions no one can entirely escape the kind of self-questioning mentioned earlier, especially when life's major events take place. To this questioning only God fully and most certainly provides an answer as He summons man to higher knowledge and humbler probing.

The remedy which must be applied to atheism, however, is to be sought in a proper presentation of the Church's teaching as well as in the integral life of the Church and her members. For it is the function of the Church, led by the Holy Spirit who renews and purifies[48] her ceaselessly,[49] to make God the Father and His Incarnate Son present and in a sense visible.

This result is achieved chiefly by the witness of a living and mature faith, namely, one trained to see difficulties clearly and to master them. Very many martyrs have given luminous witness to this faith and continue to do so. This faith needs to prove its fruitfulness by penetrating the believer's entire life, including its worldly dimensions, and by activating him toward justice and love, especially regarding the needy. What does the most to reveal God's presence, however, is the brotherly charity of the faithful who are united in spirit as they work together for the faith of the gospel[50] and who prove themselves a sign of unity.[51]

While rejecting atheism, root and branch, the Church sincerely professes that all men, believers and unbelievers alike, ought to work for the rightful betterment of this world in which all alike live. Such an ideal cannot be realized, however, apart from sincere and prudent dialogue.[52] Hence the

48. There are some who may express wonder at this description of the Church itself undergoing purification since it is to be recognized as holy. The text carries a reference, therefore, to the teaching of "Lumen Gentium." Speaking of the pilgrim Church, that Constitution confesses that "the Church, embracing sinners in her bosom, at the same time holy and always in need of being purified, follows the way of penance and renewal."

49. Cf. Second Vatican Council, dogmatic constitution "Lumen Gentium," Chap. I, Art. 8: AAS 57 (1965), p. 12.

50. Cf. Phil. 1:27.

51. In a moving paragraph of his encyclical "Ecclesiam Suam" (108), Pope Paul VI held out the importance of Christians manifesting such a sign of unity: "Sometimes, too, the atheist is spurred on by noble sentiments and by impatience with the mediocrity and self-seeking of so many contemporary social settings. He knows well how to borrow from our gospel modes and expressions of solidarity and human compassion. Shall we not be able to lead him back one day to the Christian source of such manifestations of moral worth?"

52. To understand the presuppositions necessary for a dialogue of Christians with professed atheists, it is important to recall the famous distinction laid down by John XXIII in his "Pacem in Terris" (158-159): "One must never confuse error and the person who errs, not even when there is question of error, or inadequate knowledge of truth, in the moral or religious field.... It must be borne in mind,

Church protests against the distinction which some state authorities unjustly make between believers and unbelievers, thereby ignoring fundamental rights of the human person. The Church calls for the active liberty of believers to build up in this world God's temple too. She courteously invites atheists to examine the gospel of Christ with an open mind.

Above all the Church knows that her message is in harmony with the most secret desires of the human heart when she champions the dignity of the human vocation, restoring hope to those who have already despaired of anything higher than their present lot. Far from diminishing man, her message brings to his development light, life, and freedom. Apart from this message nothing will avail to fill up the heart of man: "Thou hast made us for Thyself," O Lord, "and our hearts are restless till they rest in Thee."[53]

CHRIST AS THE NEW MAN

22. The truth is that only in the mystery of the incarnate Word does the mystery of man take on light. For Adam, the first man, was a figure of Him who was to come,[54] namely, Christ the Lord. Christ, the final Adam, by the revelation of the mystery of the Father and His love, fully reveals man to man himself and makes his supreme calling clear. It is not surprising, then, that in Him all the aforementioned truths find their root and attain their crown.

He who is "the image of the invisible God" (Col. 1:15),[55] is Himself the perfect man. To the sons of Adam He restores the divine likeness which had been disfigured from the first sin onward. Since human nature as He assumed it was not annulled,[56] by that very fact it has been raised up to a divine dignity in our respect too. For by His incarnation the

furthermore, that neither can false philosophical teachings regarding the nature, origin, and destiny of the universe and of man be identified with historical movements that have economic, social, cultural or political ends, not even when these movements have originated from those teachings...."

53. *St. Augustine, Confessions I, 1: PL 32, 661.*

54. *Cf. Rom. 5:14. Cf. Tertullian, "De carnis resurrectione" 6: "The shape that the slime of the earth was given was intended with a view to Christ, the future man.": p. 2, 282; CSEL 47, p. 33, 1. 12-13.*

55. *Cf. 2 Cor. 4:4.*

56. *Cf. Second Council of Constantinople, can. 7: "The divine Word was not changed into a human nature, nor was a human nature absorbed by the Word." Denz. 219 (428). Cf. also Third Council of Constantinople: "For just as His most holy and immaculate human nature, though deified, was not destroyed (theotheisa ouk anerethe), but rather remained in its proper state and mode of being": Denz. 291 (556). Cf. Council of Chalcedon: "to be acknowledged in two natures, without confusion, change, division, or separation." Denz. 148 (302).*

Son of God has united Himself in some fashion with every man. He worked with human hands, He thought with a human mind, acted by human choice,[57] and loved with a human heart. Born of the Virgin Mary, He has truly been made one of us, like us in all things except sin.[58]

As an innocent lamb He merited life for us by the free shedding of His own blood. In Him God reconciled us[59] to Himself and among ourselves. From bondage to the devil and sin, He delivered us, so that each one of us can say with the Apostle: The Son of God "loved me and gave himself up for me" (Gal. 2:20). By suffering for us He not only provided us with an example for our imitation.[60] He blazed a trail, and if we follow it, life and death are made holy and take on a new meaning.

The Christian man, conformed to the likeness of that Son who is the firstborn of many brothers,[61] receives "the first-fruits of the Spirit" (Rom. 8:23) by which he becomes capable of discharging the new law of love.[62] Through this Spirit, who is "the pledge of our inheritance" (Eph. 1:14), the whole man is renewed from within, even to the achievement of "the redemption of the body" (Rom. 8:23): "If the Spirit of him who raised Jesus from the death dwells in you, then he who raised Jesus Christ from the dead will also bring to life your mortal bodies because of his Spirit who dwells in you" (Rom. 8:11).[63]

Pressing upon the Christian, to be sure, are the need and the duty to battle against evil through manifold tribulations and even to suffer death. But, linked with the paschal mystery and patterned on the dying Christ, he will hasten forward to resurrection in the strength which comes from hope.[64]

All this holds true not only for Christians, but for all men of good will in whose hearts grace works in an unseen way.[65] For, since Christ died for all men,[66] and since the

57. Cf. Third Council of Constantinople: "and so His human will, though deified, is not destroyed": Denz. 291 (556).
58. Cf. Heb. 4:15.
59. Cf. 2 Cor. 5:18-19; Col. 1:20-22.
60. Cf. 1 Pet. 2:21; Mt. 16:24; Lk. 14:27.
61. Cf. Rom. 8:29; Col. 3:10-14.
62. Cf. Rom. 8:1-11.
63. Cf. 2 Cor. 4:14.
64. Cf. Phil. 3:19; Rom. 8:17.
65. Cf. Second Vatican Council, dogmatic constitution "Lumen Gentium," Chap. II, Art. 16: AAS 57 (1965), p. 20.
66. Cf. Rom. 8:32.

ultimate vocation of man is in fact one, and divine, we ought to believe that the Holy Spirit in a manner known only to God offers to every man[67] the possibility of being associated with this paschal mystery.

Such is the mystery of man, and it is a great one, as seen by believers in the light of Christian revelation. Through Christ and in Christ, the riddles of sorrow and death grow meaningful. Apart from His gospel, they overwhelm us. Christ has risen, destroying death by His death. He has lavished life upon us[68] so that, as sons in the Son, we can cry out in the Spirit: Abba, Father![69]

CHAPTER II

THE COMMUNITY OF MANKIND

THE COUNCIL'S INTENTION

23. One of the salient features of the modern world is the growing interdependence of men one on the other, a development very largely promoted by modern technical advances. Nevertheless, brotherly dialogue among men does not reach its perfection on the level of technical progress, but on the deeper level of interpersonal relationships. These demand a mutual respect for the full spiritual dignity of the person. Christian revelation contributes greatly to the promotion of this communion between persons, and at the same time leads us to a deeper understanding of the laws of social life which the Creator has written into man's spiritual and moral nature.

---

67. This statement ratifies traditional interpretations of the well-known dictum: "Extra Ecclesiam nulla salus" ("outside the Church there is no salvation"). It stands in harmony with Vatican II's own teaching in the Declaration on the Relationship of the Church to non-Christian Religions.
68. Cf. the Byzantine Easter Liturgy.
69. Cf. Rom. 8:15 and Gal. 4:6; cf. also Jn. 1:22 and Jn. 3:1-2.

Since rather recent documents of the Church's teaching authority have dealt at considerable length with Christian doctrine about human society,[70] this Council is merely going to call to mind some of the more basic truths, treating their foundations under the light of revelation. Then it will dwell more at length on certain of their implications having special significance for our day.

GOD'S PLAN GIVES MAN'S VOCATION A COMMUNITARIAN NATURE

24. God, who has fatherly concern for everyone, has willed that all men should constitute one family and treat one another in a spirit of brotherhood. For having been created in the image of God, who "from one man has created the whole human race and made them live all over the face of the earth" (Acts 17:26), all men are called to one and the same goal, namely, God Himself.

For this reason, love for God and neighbor is the first and greatest commandment. Sacred Scripture, however, teaches us that the love of God cannot be separated from love of neighbor: "If there is any other commandment, it is summed up in this saying, Thou shalt love thy neighbor as thyself. . . . Love therefore is the fulfillment of the Law" (Rom. 13:9-10; cf. 1 Jn. 4:20). To men growing daily more dependent on one another, and to a world becoming more unified every day, this truth proves to be of paramount importance.

Indeed, the Lord Jesus, when He prayed to the Father, "that all may be one . . . as we are one" (Jn. 17:21-22) opened up vistas closed to human reason.[71] For He implied a certain likeness between the union of the divine Persons, and in the union of God's sons in truth and charity. This likeness reveals that man, who is the only creature on earth which God willed for itself, cannot fully find himself except through a sincere gift of himself.[72]

---

70. Cf. John XXIII, encyclical letter, "Mater et Magistra," May 15, 1961: AAS 53 (1961), pp. 401-464, and encyclical letter "Pacem in Terris," Apr. 11, 1963: AAS 55 (1963), pp. 257-304; Paul VI, encyclical letter "Ecclesiam Suam," Aug. 6, 1964: AAS 54 (1964), pp. 609-659.
71. For the Christian this Constitution probably contains no bolder invitation to theological reflection than this brief allusion to the light divine revelation sheds on the meaning of man's vocation to find human and personal fulfillment in and through society.
72. Cf. Lk. 17:33.

THE INTERDEPENDENCE OF PERSON AND SOCIETY

25. Man's social nature makes it evident that the progress of the human person and the advance of society itself hinge on each other. For the beginning, the subject and the goal of all social institutions is and must be the human person, which for its part and by its very nature stands completely in need of social life.[73] This social life is not something added on to man. Hence, through his dealings with others, through reciprocal duties, and through fraternal dialogue he develops all his gifts and is able to rise to his destiny.

Among those social ties which man needs for his development some, like the family and political community, relate with greater immediacy to his innermost nature. Others originate rather from his free decision. In our era, for various reasons, reciprocal ties and mutual dependencies increase day by day and give rise to a variety of associations and organizations, both public and private. This development, which is called socialization,[74] while certainly not without its dangers, brings with it many advantages with respect to consolidating and increasing the qualities of the human person, and safeguarding his rights.[75]

But if by this social life the human person is greatly aided in responding to his destiny, even in its religious dimensions, it cannot be denied that men are often diverted from doing good and spurred toward evil by the social circumstances in which they live and are immersed from their birth. To be sure the disturbances which so frequently occur in the social order result in part from the natural tensions of economic, political, and social forms. But at a deeper level they flow from man's pride and selfishness, which contaminate even the social sphere. When the structure of affairs is flawed by the consequences of sin, man, already born with a bent toward evil, finds there new inducements to sin, which cannot be

73. Cf. St. Thomas, 1 Ethica Lect. 1.
74. The use of "socialization" upset some commentators when John XXIII first employed the term in his "Mater et Magistra," even though it had previously appeared in letters from the Vatican Secretariat of State. It is true that the Latin text of that encyclical resorted to involved paraphrases of a term that appeared in the several modern-language versions from the Vatican. Here, however, the Council uses the Latin "socializatio" and indicates by paraphrase that it means exactly what John XXIII had in mind back in 1961.
75. Cf. John XXIII, encyclical letter "Mater et Magistra": AAS 53 (1961), p. 418. Cf. also Pius XI, encyclical letter "Quadragesimo Anno": AAS 23 (1931), p. 222 ff.

overcome without strenuous efforts and the assistance of grace.

PROMOTING THE COMMON GOOD

26. Every day human interdependence grows more tightly drawn and spreads by degrees over the whole world. As a result the common good, that is, the sum of those conditions of social life which allow social groups and their individual members relatively thorough and ready access to their own fulfillment, today takes on an increasingly universal complexion and consequently involves rights and duties with respect to the whole human race. Every social group must take account of the needs and legitimate aspirations of other groups, and even of the general welfare of the entire human family.[76]

At the same time, however, there is a growing awareness of the exalted dignity proper to the human person, since he stands above all things, and his rights and duties are universal and inviolable. Therefore, there must be made available to all men everything necessary for leading a life truly human, such as food, clothing, and shelter; the right to choose a state of life freely and to found a family, the right to education, to employment, to a good reputation, to respect, to appropriate information, to activity in accord with the upright norm of one's own conscience, to protection of privacy and to rightful freedom in matters religious too.

Hence, the social order and its development must unceasingly work to the benefit of the human person if the disposition of affairs is to be subordinate to the personal realm and not contrariwise, as the Lord indicated when He said that the Sabbath was made for man, and not man for the Sabbath.[77]

This social order requires constant improvement. It must be founded on truth, built on justice, and animated by love; in freedom it should grow every day toward a more humane balance.[78] An improvement in attitudes and widespread changes in society[79] will have to take place if these objectives are to be gained.

---

76. *Cf. John XXIII, encyclical letter "Mater et Magistra": AAS 53 (1961).*
77. *Cf. Mk. 2:27.*
78. *Cf. John XXIII, encyclical letter "Pacem in Terris": AAS 55 (1963), p. 266.*
79. It is known that a number of Council Fathers expressed concern over the wording of this sentence. Many felt that it stood as an encouragement to social

God's Spirit, who with a marvelous providence directs the unfolding of time and renews the face of the earth, is not absent from this development. The ferment of the gospel, too, has aroused and continues to arouse in man's heart the irresistible requirements of his dignity.

REVERENCE FOR THE HUMAN PERSON

27. Coming down to practical and particularly urgent consequences, this Council lays stress on reverence for man; everyone must consider his every neighbor without exception as another self, taking into account first of all his life and the means necessary to living it with dignity,[80] so as not to imitate the rich man who had no concern for the poor man Lazarus.[81]

In our times a special obligation binds us to make ourselves the neighbor of absolutely every person, and of actively helping him when he comes across our path, whether he be an old person abandoned by all, a foreign laborer unjustly looked down upon, a refugee, a child born of an unlawful union and wrongly suffering for a sin he did not commit, or a hungry person who disturbs our conscience by recalling the voice of the Lord: "As long as you did it for one of these, the least of my brethren, you did it for me" (Mt. 25:40).

Furthermore, whatever is opposed to life itself, such as any type of murder, genocide, abortion, euthanasia, or willful self-destruction, whatever violates the integrity of the human person, such as mutilation, torments inflicted on body or mind, attempts to coerce the will itself; whatever insults human dignity, such as subhuman living conditions, arbitrary imprisonment, deportation, slavery, prostitution, the selling of women and children; as well as disgraceful working conditions, where men are treated as mere tools for profit, rather than as free and responsible persons; all these things and others of their like are infamies indeed.[82] They poison hu-

revolution and thus should be revised. It is clear from the context, however, that any such revolution—urged by the Council—would be a Christian one, "founded on truth, built on justice, and animated by love." For this reason, the Constitution can go on to assert that "God's spirit is not absent from this development ('evolutioni')."
80. Cf. Jas. 2:15-16.
81. Cf. Lk. 16:18-31.
82. It is clear that the list of abuses against human life, integrity, or dignity could be extended. It will be recalled that on several occasions Council Fathers from the United States had urged explicit condemnations of segregation and racial discrimination. The evil of discrimination is taken up specifically in 29.

man society, but they do more harm to those who practice them than those who suffer from the injury. Moreover, they are a supreme dishonor to the Creator.

REVERENCE AND LOVE FOR ENEMIES

28. Respect and love ought to be extended also to those who think or act differently than we do in social, political, and religious matters, too. In fact, the more deeply we come to understand their ways of thinking through such courtesy and love, the more easily will we be able to enter into dialogue with them.

This love and good will, to be sure, must in no way render us indifferent to truth and goodness. Indeed love itself impels the disciples of Christ to speak the saving truth to all men. But it is necessary to distinguish between error, which always merits repudiation, and the person in error, who never loses the dignity of being a person, even when he is flawed by false or inadequate religious notions.[83] God alone is the judge and searcher of hearts; for that reason He forbids us to make judgments about the internal guilt of anyone.[84]

The teaching of Christ even requires that we forgive injuries,[85] and extends the law of love to include every enemy, according to the command of the New Law: "You have heard that it was said, 'Thou shalt love thy neighbor, and shalt hate thy enemy.' But I say to you, love your enemies, do good to those who hate you, and pray for those who persecute and calumniate you" (Mt. 5:43-44).

THE ESSENTIAL EQUALITY OF MEN; AND SOCIAL JUSTICE

29. Since all men possess a rational soul and are created in God's likeness, since they have the same nature and origin, have been redeemed by Christ, and enjoy the same divine calling and destiny, the basic equality of all must receive increasingly greater recognition.

True, all men are not alike from the point of view of varying physical power and the diversity of intellectual and moral resources. Nevertheless, with respect to the fundamental rights of the person, every type of discrimination, whether

---

83. Cf. John XXIII, encyclical letter "Pacem in Terris": AAS 55 (1963), pp. 299 and 300.
84. Cf. Lk. 6:37-38; Mt. 7:1-2; Rom. 2:1-11; 14:10; 14:10-12.
85. Cf. Mt. 5:43-47.

social or cultural, whether based on sex, race, color, social condition, language, or religion, is to be overcome and eradicated as contrary to God's intent. For in truth it must still be regretted that fundamental personal rights are not yet being universally honored. Such is the case of a woman who is denied the right and freedom to choose a husband, to embrace a state of life, or to acquire an education or cultural benefits equal to those recognized for men.

Moreover, although rightful differences exist between men, the equal dignity of persons demands that a more humane and just condition of life be brought about. For excessive economic and social differences between the members of the one human family or population groups cause scandal, and militate against social justice, equity, the dignity of the human person, as well as social and international peace.

Human institutions, both private and public, must labor to minister to the dignity and purpose of man. At the same time let them put up a stubborn fight against any kind of slavery, whether social or political, and safeguard the basic rights of man under every political system. Indeed human institutions themselves must be accommodated by degrees to the highest of all realities, spiritual ones, even though meanwhile, a long enough time will be required before they arrive at the desired goal.

MORE THAN AN INDIVIDUALISTIC ETHIC IS REQUIRED

30. Profound and rapid changes make it particularly urgent that no one, ignoring the trend of events or drugged by laziness, content himself with a merely individualistic morality. It grows increasingly true that the obligations of justice and love are fulfilled only if each person, contributing to the common good, according to his own abilities and the needs of others, also promotes and assists the public and private institutions dedicated to bettering the conditions of human life.

Yet there are those who, while professing grand and rather noble sentiments, nevertheless in reality live always as if they cared nothing for the needs of society. Many in various places even make light of social laws and precepts, and do not hesitate to resort to various frauds and deceptions in avoiding just taxes or other debts due to society. Others think little of certain norms of social life, for example those designed for the protection of health, or laws establishing speed limits. They do not even avert to the fact that by such in-difference they imperil their own life and that of others.

Let everyone consider it his sacred obligation to count so-cial necessities among the primary duties of modern man, and to pay heed to them.[86] For the more unified the world becomes, the more plainly do the offices of men extend be-yond particular groups and spread by degrees to the whole world. But this challenge cannot be met unless individual men and their associations cultivate in themselves the moral and social virtues, and promote them in society. Thus, with the needed help of divine grace, men who are truly new and artisans of a new humanity can be forthcoming.

RESPONSIBILITY AND PARTICIPATION

31. In order for individual men to discharge with greater ex-actness the obligations of their conscience toward themselves and the various groups to which they belong, they must be carefully educated to a higher degree of culture through the use of the immense resources available today to the human race. Above all the education of youth from every social background has to be undertaken, so that there can be pro-duced not only men and women of refined talents, but those great-souled persons who are so desperately required by our times.

Now a man can scarcely arrive at the needed sense of responsibility unless his living conditions allow him to be-come conscious of his dignity, and to rise to his destiny by spending himself for God and for others. But human freedom is often crippled when a man falls into extreme poverty, just as it withers when he indulges in too many of life's comforts and imprisons himself in a kind of splendid isolation. Free-dom acquires new strength, by contrast, when a man con-sents to the unavoidable requirements of social life, takes on the manifold demands of human partnership, and commits himself to the service of the human community.

Hence, the will to play one's role in common endeavors should be everywhere encouraged. Praise is due to those na-tional procedures which allow the largest possible number of citizens to participate in public affairs with genuine freedom. Account must be taken, to be sure, of the actual conditions

86. Many will see in this and the preceding sentences of this paragraph a healthy reaction against an excessively casuistic approach to "merely" penal law, and a welcome stress in this conciliar pronouncement on the Christian's proper response to demands of the common welfare.

of each people and the vigor required by public authority.

If every citizen is to feel inclined to take part in the activities of the various groups which make up the social body, these must offer advantages which will attract members and dispose them to serve others. We can justly consider that the future of humanity lies in the hands of those who are strong enough to provide coming generations with reasons for living and hoping.

THE INCARNATE WORD AND HUMAN SOLIDARITY

32. God did not create man for life in isolation, but for the formation of social unity. So also "it has pleased God to make men holy and save them not merely as individuals, without any mutual bonds, but by making them into a single people, a people which acknowledges Him in truth and serves Him in holiness."[87] So from the beginning of salvation history He has chosen men not just as individuals but as members of a certain community. Revealing His mind to them, God called these chosen ones "His people" (Ex. 3:7-12), and, furthermore, made a covenant with them on Sinai.[88]

This communitarian character is developed and consummated in the work of Jesus Christ. For the very Word made flesh willed to share in the human fellowship. He was present at the wedding of Cana, visited the house of Zacchaeus, ate with publicans and sinners. He revealed the love of the Father and the sublime vocation of man in terms of the most common of social realities and by making use of the speech and the imagery of plain everyday life. Willingly obeying the laws of his country, He sanctified those human ties, especially family ones, from which social relationships arise. He chose to lead the life proper to an artisan of His time and place.

In His preaching He clearly taught the sons of God to treat one another as brothers. In His prayers He pleaded that all His disciples might be "one." Indeed, as the Redeemer of all, He offered Himself for all even to point of death. "Greater love than this no one has, that one lay down his life for his friends" (Jn. 15:13). He commanded His apostles to preach to all peoples the gospel message so that the human race might become the Family of God, in which the fullness of the Law would be love.

87. Cf. dogmatic constitution "Lumen Gentium," Chap. II, Art. 9: AAS 57 (1965), pp. 12-13.
88. Cf. Ex. 24:1-8.

As the first-born of many brethren and through the gift of His Spirit, He founded after His death and resurrection a new brotherly community composed of all those who receive Him in faith and in love. This He did through His Body, which is the Church. There everyone, as members one of the other, would render mutual service according to the different gifts bestowed on each.

This solidarity must be constantly increased until that day on which it will be brought to perfection. Then, saved by grace, men will offer flawless glory to God as a family beloved of God and of Christ their Brother.

CHAPTER III

MAN'S ACTIVITY THROUGHOUT THE WORLD

THE PROBLEM DEFINED

33. Through his labors and his native endowments man has ceaselessly striven to better his life. Today, however, especially with the help of science and technology, he has extended his mastery over nearly the whole of nature and continues to do so. Thanks primarily to increased opportunities for many kinds of interchange among nations, the human family is gradually recognizing that it comprises a single world community and is making itself so.[89] Hence many benefits once looked for, especially from heavenly powers, man has now enterprisingly procured for himself.

In the face of these immense efforts which already preoccupy the whole human race, men raise numerous questions among themselves. What is the meaning and value of this feverish activity? How should all these things be used? To the

89. The Constitution does not suggest that the basic unity of the human family is something new, but it does wish to call attention to mankind's growing awareness of common bonds forming a world community, one that is heightened particularly by vastly improved means of communication.

achievement of what goal are the strivings of individuals and societies heading?

The Church guards the heritage of God's Word and draws from it religious and moral principles, without always having at hand the solution to particular problems.[90] She desires thereby to add the light of revealed truth to mankind's store of experience, so that the path which humanity has taken in recent times will not be a dark one.

THE VALUE OF HUMAN ACTIVITY

34. Throughout the course of the centuries, men have labored to better the circumstances of their lives through a monumental amount of individual and collective effort. To believers, this point is settled: considered in itself, such human activity accords with God's will. For man, created to God's image, received a mandate to subject to himself the earth and all that it contains, and to govern the world with justice and holiness;[91] a mandate to relate himself and the totality of things to Him who was to be acknowledged as the Lord and Creator of all. Thus, by the subjection of all things to man, the name of God would be wonderful in all the earth.[92]

This mandate concerns even the most ordinary everyday activities. For while providing the substance of life for themselves and their families, men and women are performing their activities in a way which appropriately benefits society. They can justly consider that by their labor they are unfolding the Creator's work, consulting the advantages of their brother men, and contributing by their personal industry to the realization in history of the divine plan.[93]

Thus, far from thinking that works produced by man's own talent and energy are in opposition to God's power, and that the rational creature exists as a kind of rival to the Creator, Christians are convinced that the triumphs of the human race are a sign of God's greatness and the flowering of His own mysterious design. For the greater man's power becomes, the farther his individual and community responsi-

90. It is known that many Fathers wished to see to it that the Council resist any temptation to claim that the Church has all the answers in so-called mixed areas where there is need for application of general principles to specific instances. There is a conscious effort here to avoid anything that suggests triumphalism.
91. Cf. Gen. 1:26-27; 9:3; Wis. 9:3.
92. Cf. Ps. 8:7 and 10.
93. Cf. John XXIII, encyclical letter "Pacem in Terris": AAS 55 (1963), p. 297.

bility extends. Hence it is clear that men are not deterred by the Christian message from building up the world, or impelled to neglect the welfare of their fellows. They are, rather, more stringently bound to do these very things.[94]

THE REGULATION OF HUMAN ACTIVITY

35. Just as human activity proceeds from man, so it is ordered toward man. For when a man works he not only alters things and society, he develops himself as well. He learns much, he cultivates his resources, he goes outside of himself and beyond himself.

Rightly understood, this kind of growth is of greater value than any external riches which can be garnered. A man is more precious for what he is than for what he has.[95] Similarly, all that men do to obtain greater justice, wider brotherhood, and a more humane ordering of social relationships has greater worth than technical advances. For these advances can supply the material for human progress, but of themselves alone they can never actually bring it about.

Hence, the norm of human activity is this: that in accord with the divine plan and will, it should harmonize with the genuine good of the human race, and allow men as individuals and as members of society to pursue their total vocation and fulfill it.[96]

THE RIGHTFUL INDEPENDENCE
OF EARTHLY AFFAIRS

36. Now, many of our contemporaries seem to fear that a closer bond between human activity and religion will work against the independence of men, of societies, or of the sciences.

If by the autonomy of earthly affairs we mean that created things and societies themselves enjoy their own laws and values which must be gradually deciphered, put to use, and regulated by men, then it is entirely right to demand that autonomy. Such is not merely required by modern man, but harmonizes also with the will of the Creator. For by the very

94. Cf. "Message to All Mankind" sent by the Fathers at the beginning of the Second Vatican Council, Oct. 20, 1962: AAS 54 (1962), p. 823.
95. Cf. Paul VI, address to the diplomatic corps, Jan. 7, 1965: AAS 57 (1965), p. 232.
96. These paragraphs have formulated the basis of a true Christian humanism. There is here a clear hierarchy of human values, but no room for hostility toward, or suspicion of, the truly humane.

circumstance of their having been created, all things are endowed with their own stability, truth, goodness, proper laws, and order.[97] Man must respect these as he isolates them by the appropriate methods of the individual sciences or arts.

Therefore, if methodical investigation within every branch of learning is carried out in a genuinely scientific manner and in accord with moral norms, it never truly conflicts with faith. For earthly matters and the concerns of faith derive from the same God.[98] Indeed, whoever labors to penetrate the secrets of reality with a humble and steady mind, is, even unawares, being led by the hand of God, who holds all things in existence, and gives them their identity.

Consequently, we cannot but deplore certain habits of mind, sometimes found too among Christians,[99] which do not sufficiently attend to the rightful independence of science. The arguments and controversies which they spark lead many minds to conclude that faith and science are mutually opposed.[100]

But if the expression, the independence of temporal affairs, is taken to mean that created things do not depend on God, and that man can use them without any reference to their Creator, anyone who acknowledges God will see how false such a meaning is. For without the Creator the creature would disappear. For their part, however, all believers of whatever religion have always heard His revealing voice in the discourse of creatures. But when God is forgotten the creature itself grows unintelligible.

HUMAN ACTIVITY AS INFECTED BY SIN

37. Sacred Scripture teaches the human family what the experience of the ages confirms: that while human progress is

97. The confidence implicit in these lines makes it possible for the Christian scholar to approach all questions with scientific boldness. The Council shuns any fundamentalism in dealing with the findings of science, whether ecclesiastical or natural.

98. Cf. First Vatican Council, Dogmatic Constitution on the Catholic Faith, Chap. III: Denz. 1785-1786 (3004-3005).

99. The official annotation at the close of this sentence is to a recently published study on Galileo. It seems fair to say that the conciliar text intends here to warn against another Galileo affair. Several speakers in the Council had called for some such warning and Bishop Arthur Elchinger had asked for an official rehabilitation and act of amend. It is interesting to note that publication of the two-volume study by Msgr. Pio Paschini had been delayed a number of years and was only finally undertaken at papal urging.

100. Cf. Msgr. Pio Paschini, "Vita e opere di Galileo Galilei," 2 volumes, Vatican Press (1964).

a great advantage to man, it brings with it a strong temptation. For when the order of values is jumbled, and bad is mixed with the good, individuals and groups pay heed solely to their own interests, and not to those of others. Thus it happens that the world ceases to be a place of true brotherhood. In our own day, the magnified power of humanity threatens to destroy the race itself.

For a monumental struggle against the powers of darkness pervades the whole history of man. The battle was joined from the very origins of the world and will continue until the last day, as the Lord has attested.[101] Caught in this conflict, man is obliged to wrestle constantly if he is to cling to what is good. Nor can he achieve his own integrity without valiant efforts and the help of God's grace.

That is why Christ's Church, trusting in the design of the Creator, acknowledges that human progress can serve man's true happiness. Yet she cannot help echoing the Apostle's warning: "Be not conformed to this world" (Rom. 12:2). By the world is here meant that spirit of vanity and malice which transforms into an instrument of sin those human energies intended for the service of God and man.[102]

Hence if anyone wants to know how this unhappy situation can be overcome, Christians will tell him that all human activity, constantly imperiled by man's pride and deranged self-love, must be purified and perfected by the power of Christ's cross and resurrection. For, redeemed by Christ and made a new creature in the Holy Spirit, man is able to love the things themselves created by God, and ought to do so. He can receive them from God, and respect and reverence them as flowing constantly from the hand of God.

Grateful to his Benefactor for these creatures, using and enjoying them in detachment and liberty of spirit, man is led forward into a true possession of the world, as having nothing, yet possessing all things.[103] "All are yours, and you are Christ's, and Christ is God's" (1 Cor. 3:22-23).

HUMAN ACTIVITY FINDS PERFECTION IN THE PASCHAL MYSTERY

38. For God's Word, through whom all things were made,

---

101. *Cf. Mt. 24:13; 13:24-30 and 36-43.*
102. Having stoutly affirmed the positive value of human endeavor and progress, the Constitution must allow for the consequences of human vanity, malice, and disordered self-love. Here is a sense in which the Christian can and must practice "contempt of the world."
103. *Cf. 2 Cor. 6:10.*

was Himself made flesh and dwelt on the earth of men.[104] Thus He entered the world's history as a perfect man, taking that history up into Himself and summarizing it.[105] He Himself revealed to us that "God is love" (1 Jn. 4:8). At the same time He taught us that the new command of love was the basic law of human perfection and hence of the world's transformation.

To those, therefore, who believe in divine love, He gives assurance that the way of love lies open to all men and that the effort to establish a universal brotherhood is not a hopeless one. He cautions them at the same time that this love is not something to be reserved for important matters, but must be pursued chiefly in the ordinary circumstances of life.

Undergoing death itself for all of us sinners,[106] He taught us by example that we too must shoulder that cross which the world and the flesh inflict upon those who search after peace and justice. Appointed Lord by His resurrection and given plenary power in heaven and on earth,[107] * Christ is now at work in the hearts of men through the energy of His Spirit. He arouses not only a desire for the age to come, but, by that very fact, He animates, purifies, and strengthens those noble longings too by which the human family strives to make its life more human and to render the whole earth submissive to this goal.

Now, the gifts of the Spirit are diverse. He calls some to give clear witness to the desire for a heavenly home and to keep that desire green among the human family. He summons others to dedicate themselves to the earthly service of men and to make ready the material of the celestial realm by this ministry of theirs. Yet He frees all of them so that by putting aside love of self and bringing all earthly resources into the service of human life they can devote themselves to that future when humanity itself will become an offering accepted by God.[108]

The Lord left behind a pledge of this hope and strength for life's journey in that sacrament of faith where natural elements refined by man are changed into His glorified Body

---

104. *Cf. Jn. 1:3 and 14.*
105. *Cf. Eph. 1:10.*
106. *Cf. Jn. 3:16; Rom. 5:8.*
107. *Cf. Acts 2:36; Mt. 28:18.*
*This is a literal translation of the Vulgate (Latin) quoted here by the Council Fathers.—Ed.
108. *Cf. Rom. 15:16.*

and Blood, providing a meal of brotherly solidarity and a foretaste of the heavenly banquet.

A NEW EARTH AND A NEW HEAVEN

39. We do not know the time for the consummation of the earth and of humanity.[109] Nor do we know how all things will be transformed. As deformed by sin, the shape of this world will pass away.[110] But we are taught that God is preparing a new dwelling place and a new earth where justice will abide,[111] and whose blessedness will answer and surpass all the longings for peace which spring up in the human heart.[112]

Then, with death overcome, the sons of God will be raised up in Christ. What was sown in weakness and corruption will be clothed with incorruptibility.[113] While charity and its fruits endure,[114] all that creation[115] which God made on man's account will be unchained from the bondage of vanity.

Therefore, while we are warned that it profits a man nothing if he gain the whole world and lose himself,[116] the expectation of a new earth must not weaken but rather stimulate our concern for cultivating this one. For here grows the body of a new human family, a body which even now is able to give some kind of foreshadowing of the new age.

Earthly progress must be carefully distinguished from the growth of Christ's kingdom. Nevertheless, to the extent that the former can contribute to the better ordering of human society, it is of vital concern to the kingdom of God.[117]

For after we have obeyed the Lord, and in His Spirit nurtured on earth the values of human dignity, brotherhood and freedom, and indeed all the good fruits of our nature and enterprise, we will find them again, but freed of stain, burnished and transfigured. This will be so when Christ hands over to the Father a kingdom eternal and universal: "a kingdom of truth and life, of holiness and grace, of justice, love, and peace."[118] On this earth that kingdom is already pres-

---

109. Cf. Acts 1:7.
110. Cf. 1 Cor. 7:31; St. Irenaeus, "Adversus haereses," V, 36, PG, VIII, 1221.
111. Cf. 2 Cor. 5:2; 2 Pet. 3:13.
112. Cf. 1 Cor. 2:9; Apoc. 21:4-5.
113. Cf. 1 Cor. 15:42 and 53.
114. Cf. 1 Cor. 13:8; 3:14.
115. Cf. Rom. 8:19-21.
116. Cf. Lk. 9:25.
117. Cf. Pius XI, encyclical letter "Quadragesimo Anno": AAS 23 (1931), p. 207.
118. Preface of the Feast of Christ the King.

ent in mystery. When the Lord returns, it will be brought into full flower.

CHAPTER IV

THE ROLE OF THE CHURCH IN THE MODERN WORLD

THE CHURCH AND THE WORLD AS MUTUALLY RELATED

40. Everything we have said about the dignity of the human person, and about the human community and the profound meaning of human activity, lays the foundation for the relationship between the Church and the world, and provides the basis for dialogue between them.[119] In this chapter, presupposing everything which has already been said by this Council concerning the mystery of the Church, we must now consider this same Church inasmuch as she exists in the world, living and acting with it.[120]

Coming forth from the eternal Father's love,[121] founded in time by Christ the Redeemer, and made one in the Holy Spirit,[122] the Church has a saving and an eschatological purpose which can be fully attained only in the future world. But she is already present in this world, and is composed of men, that is, of members of the earthly city who have a call to form the family of God's children during the present history of the human race, and to keep increasing it until the Lord returns.

119. *Cf. Paul VI, encyclical letter "Ecclesiam Suam," III: AAS 56 (1964), pp. 637-659.*
120. The Constitution is here linked explicitly with "Lumen Gentium," the Constitution on the Church. Having looked within itself, the Church now looks—as Cardinal Suenens had urged in his address of Dec. 4, 1962—"ad extra": to its relations with the world.
121. *Cf. Tit. 3:4: "love of mankind."*
122. *Cf. Eph. 1:3; 5:6, 13-14, 23.*

United on behalf of heavenly values and enriched by them, this family has been "constituted and organized in the world as a society"[123] by Christ, and is equipped with "those means which befit it as a visible and social unity."[124] Thus the Church, at once a visible assembly and a spiritual community,[125] goes forward together with humanity and experiences the same earthly lot which the world does. She serves as a leaven and as a kind of soul for human society[126] as it is to be renewed in Christ and transformed into God's family.

That the earthly and the heavenly city penetrate each other is a fact accessible to faith alone. It remains a mystery of human history, which sin will keep in great disarray until the splendor of God's sons is fully revealed. Pursuing the saving purpose which is proper to her, the Church not only communicates divine life to men, but in some way casts the reflected light of that life over the entire earth.

This she does most of all by her healing and elevating impact on the dignity of the person, by the way in which she strengthens the seams of human society and imbues the everyday activity of men with a deeper meaning and importance.[127] Thus, through her individual members and her whole community, the Church believes she can contribute greatly toward making the family of man and its history more human.

In addition, the Catholic Church gladly holds in high esteem the things which other Christian Churches or ecclesial communities have done or are doing cooperatively by way of achieving the same goal. At the same time, she is firmly convinced that she can be abundantly and variously helped by the world in the matter of preparing the ground for the gospel. This help she gains from the talents and industry of individuals and from human society as a whole. The Council now sets forth certain general principles for the proper fostering of this mutual exchange and assistance in concerns which are in some way common to the Church and the world.

123. *Second Vatican Council, dogmatic constitution "Lumen Gentium," Chap. I, Art. 8: AAS 57 (1965), p. 12.*
124. *Ibid., Chap. II, Art. 9: AAS 57 (1965), p. 14; cf. Art. 8: AAS loc. cit., p. 11.*
125. *Ibid., Chap. I, Art. 8: AAS 57 (1965), p. 11.*
126. *Cf. ibid., Chap. IV, Art. 38: AAS 57 (1965), p. 43, with Art. 120.*
127. The Church's ministry of healing or reconciliation is clearly one that it is called on to exercise in many areas of modern life where divisions exist among men and between groups.

THE HELP WHICH THE CHURCH STRIVES
TO BRING TO INDIVIDUALS

41. Modern man is on the road to a more thorough development of his own personality, and to a growing discovery and vindication of his own rights. Since it has been entrusted to the Church to reveal the mystery of God, who is the ultimate goal of man, she opens up to man at the same time the meaning of his own existence, that is, the innermost truth about himself. The Church truly knows that only God, whom she serves, meets the deepest longings of the human heart, which is never fully satisfied by what this world has to offer.

She also knows that man is constantly worked upon by God's Spirit, and hence can never be altogether indifferent to the problems of religion. The experience of past ages proves this, as do numerous indications in our own times. For man will always yearn to know, at least in an obscure way, what is the meaning of his life, of his activity, of his death. The very presence of the Church recalls these problems to his mind.

But only God, who created man to His own image and ransomed him from sin, provides a fully adequate answer to these questions. This He does through what He has revealed in Christ His Son, who became man. Whoever follows after Christ, the perfect man, becomes himself more of a man.

Thanks to this belief, the Church can anchor the dignity of human nature against all tides of opinion, for example, those which undervalue the human body or idolize it. By no human law can the personal dignity and liberty of man be so aptly safeguarded as by the gospel of Christ which has been entrusted to the Church.

For this gospel announces and proclaims the freedom of the sons of God, and repudiates all the bondage which ultimately results from sin.[128] The gospel has a sacred reverence for the dignity of conscience and its freedom of choice, constantly advises that all human talents be employed in God's service and men's, and, finally, commends all to the charity of all.[129]

All this corresponds with the basic law of the Christian dispensation. For though the same God is Savior and Creator, Lord of human history as well as of salvation history, in

128. *Cf. Rom. 8:14-17.*
129. *Cf. Mt. 22:39.*

the divine arrangement itself the rightful autonomy of the creature, and particularly of man, is not withdrawn. Rather it is re-established in its own dignity and strengthened in it.

Therefore, by virtue of the gospel committed to her, the Church proclaims the rights of man. She acknowledges and greatly esteems the dynamic movements of today by which these rights are everywhere fostered.[130] Yet these movements must be penetrated by the spirit of the gospel and protected against any kind of false autonomy. For we are tempted to think that our personal rights are fully ensured only when we are exempt from every requirement of divine law. But this way lies not the maintenance of the dignity of the human person, but its annihilation.

THE HELP WHICH THE CHURCH STRIVES TO GIVE TO SOCIETY

42. The union of the human family is greatly fortified and fulfilled by the unity, founded on Christ,[131] of the family of God's sons.

Christ, to be sure, gave His Church no proper mission in the political, economic, or social order. The purpose which He set before her is a religious one.[132] But out of this religious mission itself come a function, a light, and an energy which can serve to structure and consolidate the human community according to the divine law. As a matter of fact, when circumstances of time and place create the need, she can and indeed should initiate activities on behalf of all men. This is particularly true of activities designed for the needy, such as the works of mercy and similar undertakings.

The Church further recognizes that worthy elements are found in today's social movements, especially an evolution

---

130. Whatever the regrettable misunderstandings that turned the "rights of man" into a rallying cry of the Church's bitter foes in the 18th and 19th centuries and entrenched the Church in a role of intransigent resistance to movements for social revolution in many parts of the world, the Council now makes it unequivocally plain that the Church intends to play its true historic role as a champion of human rights and to align itself with those who fight for these rights.

131. *Dogmatic constitution "Lumen Gentium," Chap. II, Art. 9: AAS 57 (1956), pp. 12-14.*

132. *Cf. Pius XII, Address to the International Union of Institutes of Archeology, History and History of Art, Mar. 9, 1956: AAS 48 (1965), p. 212: "Its divine Founder, Jesus Christ, has not given it any mandate or fixed any end of the cultural order. The goal which Christ assigns to it is strictly religious....The Church must lead men to God, in order that they may be given over to him without reserve....The Church can never lose sight of the strictly religious, supernatural goal. The meaning of all its activities, down to the last canon of its code, can only cooperate directly or indirectly in this goal."*

toward unity, a process of wholesome socialization and of association in civic and economic realms. For the promotion of unity belongs to the innermost nature of the Church, since she is, "by her relationship with Christ, both a sacramental sign and an instrument of intimate union with God, and of the unity of all mankind."[133]

Thus she shows the world that an authentic union, social and external, results from a union of minds and hearts, namely, from that faith and charity by which her own unity is unbreakably rooted in the Holy Spirit. For the force which the Church can inject into the modern society of man consists in that faith and charity put into vital practice, not in any external dominion exercised by merely human means.

Moreover, in virtue of her mission and nature, she is bound to no particular form of human culture, nor to any political, economic, or social system. Hence the Church by her very universality can be a very close bond between diverse human communities and nations, provided these trust her and truly acknowledge her right to true freedom in fulfilling her mission. For this reason, the Church admonishes her own sons, but also humanity as a whole, to overcome all strife between nations and races in this family spirit of God's children, and in the same way, to give internal strength to human associations which are just.

This Council, therefore, looks with great respect upon all the true, good, and just elements found in the very wide variety of institutions which the human race has established for itself and constantly continues to establish. The Council affirms, moreover, that the Church is willing to assist and promote all these institutions to the extent that such a service depends on her and can be associated with her mission. She has no fiercer desire than that, in pursuit of the welfare of all, she may be able to develop herself freely under any kind of government which grants recognition to the basic rights of person and family and to the demands of the common good.[134]

THE HELP WHICH THE CHURCH STRIVES TO GIVE TO HUMAN ACTIVITY THROUGH CHRISTIANS

43. This Council exhorts Christians, as citizens of two cities,

133. *Dogmatic constitution "Lumen Gentium," Chap. I, Art. 1: AAS 57 (1965), p. 5.*
134. The foregoing rights represent, in the Council's view, the necessary conditions for "peaceful coexistence."

to strive to discharge their earthly duties conscientiously and in response to the gospel spirit. They are mistaken who, knowing that we have here no abiding city but seek one which is to come,[135] think that they may therefore shirk their earthly responsibilities. For they are forgetting that by the faith itself they are more than ever obliged to measure up to these duties, each according to his proper vocation.[136]

Nor, on the contrary, are they any less wide of the mark who think that religion consists in acts of worship alone and in the discharge of certain moral obligations, and who imagine they can plunge themselves into earthly affairs in such a way as to imply that these are altogether divorced from the religious life. This split between the faith which many profess and their daily lives deserves to be counted among the more serious errors of our age. Long since, the prophets of the Old Testament fought vehemently against this scandal[137] and even more so did Jesus Christ Himself in the New Testament threaten it with grave punishments.[138]

Therefore, let there be no false opposition between professional and social activities on the one part, and religious life on the other. The Christian who neglects his temporal duties neglects his duties toward his neighbor and even God, and jeopardizes his eternal salvation. Christians should rather rejoice that they can follow the example of Christ, who worked as an artisan. In the exercise of all their earthly activities, they can thereby gather their humane, domestic, professional, social, and technical enterprises into one vital synthesis with religious values, under whose supreme direction all things are harmonized unto God's glory.[139]

Secular duties and activities belong properly although not exclusively to laymen. Therefore acting as citizens of the world, whether individually or socially, they will observe the laws proper to each discipline, and labor to equip themselves with a genuine expertise in their various fields. They will gladly work with men seeking the same goals. Acknowledging the demands of faith and endowed with its force, they

135. *Cf. Heb. 13:14.*
136. *Cf. 2 Th. 3:6-13; Eph. 4:28.*
137. *Cf. Is. 58:1-12.*
138. *Cf. Mt. 23:3-23; Mk. 7:10-13.*
139. Pope John XXIII had made the same point in his "Mater et Magistra" (255): "We should not foolishly dream up an artificial opposition—where none really exists—between one's own spiritual perfection and one's active contact with the everyday world, as if a man could not perfect himself as a Christian except by putting aside all temporal activity."

will unhesitatingly devise new enterprises, where they are appropriate, and put them into action.

Laymen should also know that it is generally the function of their well-formed Christian conscience to see that the divine law is inscribed in the life of the earthly city. From priests they may look for spiritual light and nourishment. Let the layman not imagine that his pastors are always such experts, that to every problem which arises, however complicated, they can readily give him a concrete solution, or even that such is their mission. Rather, enlightened by Christian wisdom and giving close attention to the teaching authority of the Church,[140] let the layman take on his own distinctive role.

Often enough the Christian view of things will itself suggest some specific solution in certain circumstances. Yet it happens rather frequently, and legitimately so, that with equal sincerity some of the faithful will disagree with others on a given matter. Even against the intentions of their proponents, however, solutions proposed on one side or another may be easily confused by many people with the gospel message. Hence it is necessary for people to remember that no one is allowed in the aforementioned situations to appropriate the Church's authority for his opinion. They should always try to enlighten one another through honest discussion, preserving mutual charity and caring above all for the common good.

Since they have an active role to play in the whole life of the Church, laymen are not only bound to penetrate the world with a Christian spirit. They are also called to be witnesses to Christ in all things in the midst of human society.

Bishops, to whom is assigned the task of ruling the Church of God, should, together with their priests, so preach the message of Christ that all the earthly activities of the faithful will be bathed in the light of the gospel. All pastors should remember too that by their daily conduct and concern[141] they are revealing the face of the Church to the world. Men will judge the power and truth of the Christian message thereby. By their lives and speech, in union with religious and their faithful, may pastors demonstrate that even now the Church, by her presence alone and by all the gifts which she

140. *Cf. John XXIII, encyclical letter "Mater et Magistra," IV: AAS 53 (1961), pp. 456-457; cf. I: AAS loc. cit., pp. 407, 410-411.*
141. *Cf. dogmatic constitution "Lumen Gentium," Chapter III, Art. 28: AAS 57 (1965), p. 35.*

possesses, is an unspent fountain of those virtues which the modern world most needs.

By unremitting study they should fit themselves to do their part in establishing dialogue with the world and with men of all shades of opinion. Above all let them take to heart the words which this Council has spoken: "Because the human race today is joining more and more in civic, economic, and social unity, it is that much more necessary that priests, united in concern and effort under the leadership of the bishops and the Supreme Pontiff, wipe out every ground of division, so that the whole human race may be brought into the unity of the family of God."[142]

Although by the power of the Holy Spirit the Church has remained the faithful spouse of her Lord and has never ceased to be the sign of salvation on earth, still she is very well aware that among her members,[143] both clerical and lay, some have been unfaithful to the Spirit of God during the course of many centuries. In the present age, too, it does not escape the Church how great a distance lies between the message she offers and the human failings of those to whom the gospel is entrusted.

Whatever be the judgment of history on these defects,[144] we ought to be conscious of them, and struggle against them energetically, lest they inflict harm on the spread of the gospel. The Church also realizes that in working out her relationship with the world she always has great need of the ripening which comes with the experience of the centuries. Led by the Holy Spirit, Mother Church unceasingly exhorts her sons "to purify and renew themselves so that the sign of Christ can shine more brightly on the face of the Church."[145]

THE HELP WHICH THE CHURCH RECEIVES FROM THE MODERN WORLD

44. Just as it is in the world's interest to acknowledge the Church as a historical reality, and to recognize her good in-

142. *Ibid., Art. 28: AAS loc. cit., pp. 35-36.*
143. *Cf. St. Ambrose, "De virginitate," Chapter VIII, Art. 48: ML 16, 278.*
144. Some Council Fathers would have preferred to have here an enumeration of some concrete historical instances. Even in this more general form, however, the present statement is important as a recognition of responsibility before the bar of history. In a similar vein is the candid admission of failings contained in the texts exchanged between Pope Paul and the Ecumenical Patriarch Athenagoras on Dec. 7, 1965.
145. *Cf. dogmatic constitution "Lumen Gentium," Chap. II, Art. 15: AAS 57 (1965), p. 20.*

fluence, so the Church herself knows how richly she has profited by the history and development of humanity.

Thanks to the experience of past ages, the progress of the sciences, and the treasures hidden in the various forms of human culture, the nature of man himself is more clearly revealed and new roads to truth are opened. These benefits profit the Church, too, For, from the beginning of her history, she has learned to express the message of Christ with the help of the ideas and terminology of various peoples, and has tried to clarify it with the wisdom of philosophers, too.

Her purpose has been to adapt the gospel to the grasp of all as well as to the needs of the learned, insofar as such was appropriate. Indeed, this accommodated preaching of the revealed Word ought to remain the law of all evangelization.[146] For thus each nation develops the ability to express Christ's message in its own way. At the same time, a living exchange is fostered between the Church and the diverse cultures of people.[147]

To promote such an exchange, the Church requires special help, particularly in our day, when things are changing very rapidly and the ways of thinking are exceedingly various. She must rely on those who live in the world, are versed in different institutions and specialties, and grasp their innermost significance in the eyes of both believers and unbelievers. With the help of the Holy Spirit, it is the task of the entire People of God, especially pastors and theologians, to hear, distinguish, and interpret the many voices of our age, and to judge them in the light of the divine Word. In this way, revealed truth can always be more deeply penetrated, better understood, and set forth to greater advantage.

Since the Church has a visible and social structure as a sign of her unity in Christ, she can and ought to be enriched by the development of human social life. The reason is not that the constitution given her by Christ is defective, but so that she may understand it more penetratingly, express it better, and adjust it more successfully to our times.

She gratefully understands that in her community life no

---

146. The principle of adaptation enunciated here is of vast significance not only for the missionary in the traditional sense of the term, but also for the theologian. The Church is "in" history and this means in turn that a sound theology is a living thing and one in touch with actualities of the age in which the Church finds itself. Hence, too, the necessity of calling on "the special help of those who live in the world."

147. Cf. dogmatic constitution "Lumen Gentium," Chapter II, Art. 13: AAS 57 (1965), p. 17.

less than in her individual sons, she receives a variety of helps from men of every rank and condition. For whoever promotes the human community at the family level, culturally, in its economic, social, and political dimensions, both nationally and internationally, such a one, according to God's design, is contributing greatly to the Church community as well, to the extent that it depends on things outside itself. Indeed, the Church admits that she has greatly profited and still profits from the antagonism of those who oppose or persecute her.[148]

CHRIST, THE ALPHA AND THE OMEGA

45. While helping the world and receiving many benefits from it, the Church has a single intention: that God's kingdom may come, and that the salvation of the whole human race may come to pass. For every benefit which the People of God during its earthly pilgrimage can offer to the human family stems from the fact that the Church is "the universal sacrament of salvation,"[149] simultaneously manifesting and exercising the mystery of God's love for man.

For God's Word, by whom all things were made, was Himself made flesh so that as perfect man He might save all men and sum up all things in Himself. The Lord is the goal of human history, the focal point of the longings of history and of civilization, the center of the human race, the joy of every heart, and the answer to all its yearnings.[150] He it is whom the Father raised from the dead, lifted on high, and stationed at His right hand, making Him Judge of the living and the dead. Enlivened and united in His Spirit, we journey toward the consummation of human history, one which fully accords with the counsel of God's love: "To re-establish all things in Christ, both those in the heavens and those on the earth" (Eph. 1:10).

The Lord Himself speaks: "Behold, I come quickly! And my reward is with me, to render to each one according to

---

148. *Cf. Justin, "Dialogus cum Tryphone," Chap. 110; MG 6, 729 (ed. Otto), 1897, pp. 391-393:* "...but the greater the number of persecutions which are inflicted upon us, so much the greater the number of other men who become devout believers through the name of Jesus." *Cf. Tertullian, Apologeticus, Chap. L, 13:* "Every time you mow us down like grass, we increase in number: the blood of Christians is a seed!" *Cf. dogmatic constitution "Lumen Gentium," Chap. II, Art. 9: AAS 57 (1965), p. 14.*
149. *Cf. dogmatic constitution "Lumen Gentium," Chap. II, Art. 15: AAS 57 (1965), p. 20.*
150. *Cf. Paul VI, address given on Feb. 3, 1965.*

his works. I am the Alpha and the Omega, the first and the last, the beginning and the end" (Apoc. 22:12-13).

PART II

SOME PROBLEMS OF SPECIAL URGENCY

PREFACE

46. This Council has set forth the dignity of the human person and the work which men have been destined to undertake throughout the world both as individuals and as members of society. There are a number of particularly urgent needs characterizing the present age, needs which go to the roots of the human race. To a consideration of these in the light of the gospel and of human experience, the Council would now direct the attention of all.

Of the many subjects arousing universal concern today, it may be helpful to concentrate on these: marriage and the family, human culture, life in its economic, social, and political dimensions, the bonds between the family of nations, and peace.[151] On each of these may there shine the radiant ideals proclaimed by Christ. By these ideals may Christians be led, and all mankind enlightened, as they search for answers to questions of such complexity.

---

151. As debate in the Council hall and other reports indicated, the Fathers manifested by their comments and criticisms the greatest interest in three of these pressing issues: marriage, atheism in modern culture, and war.

CHAPTER I

FOSTERING THE NOBILITY OF MARRIAGE AND THE FAMILY

MARRIAGE AND FAMILY IN THE MODERN WORLD

47. The well-being of the individual person and of human and Christian society is intimately linked with the healthy condition of that community produced by marriage and family. Hence Christians and all men who hold this community in high esteem sincerely rejoice in the various ways by which men today find help in fostering this community of love[152] and perfecting its life, and by which spouses and parents are assisted in their lofty calling. Those who rejoice in such aids look for additional benefits from them and labor to bring them about.

Yet the excellence of this institution is not everywhere reflected with equal brilliance. For polygamy, the plague of divorce, so-called free love, and other disfigurements have an obscuring effect. In addition, married love is too often profaned by excessive self-love, the worship of pleasure, and illicit practices against human generation. Moreover, serious disturbances are caused in families by modern economic conditions, by influences at once social and psychological, and by the demands of civil society. Finally, in certain parts of the world problems resulting from population growth are generating concern.

All these situations have produced anxious consciences. Yet, the power and strength of the institution of marriage and family can also be seen in the fact that time and again, despite the difficulties produced, the profound changes in modern society reveal the true character of this institution in one way or another.

---

152. A notable feature of the Council's teaching on Christian marriage is the repeated emphasis on the centrality of conjugal love. It is important, of course, to recall that Pius XI made much the same emphasis in a less-known passage of his encyclical "Casti Connubii." The present treatment is nonetheless remarkable.

Therefore, by presenting certain[153] key points of Church doctrine in a clearer light, this Council wishes to offer guidance and support to those Christians and other men who are trying to keep sacred and to foster the natural dignity of the married state and its superlative value.

THE SANCTITY OF MARRIAGE AND THE FAMILY

48. The intimate partnership of married life and love has been established by the Creator and qualified by His laws. It is rooted in the conjugal covenant of irrevocable personal consent. Hence, by that human act whereby spouses mutually bestow and accept each other, a relationship arises which by divine will and in the eyes of society too is a lasting one. For the good of the spouses and their offspring as well as of society, the existence of this sacred bond no longer depends on human decisions alone.

For God Himself is the author of matrimony, endowed as it is with various benefits and purposes.[154] All of these have a very decisive bearing on the continuation of the human race, on the personal development and eternal destiny of the individual members of a family, and on the dignity, stability, peace, and prosperity of the family itself and of human society as a whole. By their very nature, the institution of matrimony itself and conjugal love are ordained for the procreation and education of children,[155] and find in them their ultimate crown.

Thus a man and a woman, who by the marriage covenant of conjugal love "are no longer two, but one flesh" (Mt. 19:6), render mutual help and service to each other through an intimate union of their persons and of their actions. Through this union they experience the meaning of their oneness and attain to it with growing perfection day by day. As

153. It is important to an understanding of the entire section on Christian marriage and family life to realize that the Council intends to discuss "certain" key points only and not to give an exhaustive treatment of all matters in this area. Thus, it clearly intended to leave untouched those aspects of birth control and related themes that are under debate in the special commission set up by Paul VI to study them.

154. *Cf. St. Augustine, "De bono coniugii": PL 40, 375-376 and 394; St. Thomas, "Summa Theol.," Suppl. Quaest. 49, Art. 3 ad 1; Decretum pro Armenis: Denz.-Schoen. 1327; Pius XI, encyclical letter "Casti Connubii": AAS 22 (1930), pp. 547-548; Denz.-Schoen. 3703-3714.*

155. Here, as elsewhere when the question arises, the Council sedulously avoids the terminology of primary and secondary ends of marriage. It insists on the natural ordering of marriage and conjugal love to procreation but without recourse to such formulations. The same teaching is repeated in Art. 50, and the Council's care to avoid distinguishing "primary" and "secondary" is again evident.

a mutual gift of two persons, this intimate union, as well as the good of the children, imposes total fidelity on the spouses and argues for an unbreakable oneness between them.[156]

Christ the Lord abundantly blessed this many-faceted love, welling up as it does from the fountain of divine love and structured as it is on the model of His union with the Church. For as God of old made Himself present[157] to His people through a covenant of love and fidelity, so now the Savior of men and the Spouse[158] of the Church comes into the lives of married Christians through the sacrament of matrimony. He abides with them thereafter so that, just as He loved the Church and handed Himself over on her behalf,[159] the spouses may love each other with perpetual fidelity through mutual self-bestowal.

Authentic married love is caught up into divine love and is governed and enriched by Christ's redeeming power and the saving activity of the Church. Thus this love can lead the spouses to God with powerful effect and can aid and strengthen them in the sublime office of being a father or a mother.[160]

For this reason, Christian spouses have a special sacrament by which they are fortified and receive a kind of consecration in the duties and dignity of their state.[161] By virtue of this sacrament, as spouses fulfill their conjugal and family obligations, they are penetrated with the spirit of Christ. This spirit suffuses their whole lives with faith, hope, and charity. Thus they increasingly advance their own perfection, as well as their mutual sanctification, and hence contribute jointly to the glory of God.

As a result, with their parents leading the way by example and family prayer, children and indeed everyone gathered around the family hearth will find a readier path to human maturity, salvation, and holiness. Graced with the dignity and office of fatherhood and motherhood, parents will energetically acquit themselves of a duty which devolves primarily

---

156. *Cf. Pius XI, encyclical letter "Casti Connubii": AAS 22 (1930), pp. 546-547;* Denz.-Schoen. 3706.
157. *Cf. Os. 2; Jer. 3. 6-13; Ezek. 16 and 23; Is. 54.*
158. *Cf. Mt. 9:15: Mk. 2:19-20; Lk. 5:34-35; Jn. 3:29; cf. also 2 Cor. 11:2; Eph. 5:27; Apoc. 19:7-8; 21:2 and 9.*
159. *Cf. Eph. 5:25.*
160. *Cf. Second Vatican Council, dogmatic constitution "Lumen Gentium": AAS 57 (1965), pp. 15-16; 40-41; 47.*
161. *Pius XI, encyclical letter "Casti Connubii": AAS 22 (1930), p. 583.*

on them,[162] namely education, and especially religious education.

As living members of the family, children contribute in their own way to making their parents holy. For they will respond to the kindness of their parents with sentiments of gratitude, with love and trust. They will stand by them as children should when hardships overtake their parents and old age brings its loneliness. Widowhood, accepted bravely as a continuation of the marriage vocation, will be esteemed by all.[163] Families will share their spiritual riches generously with other families too. Thus the Christian family, which springs from marriage as a reflection of the loving covenant uniting Christ with the Church,[164] and as a participation in that covenant, will manifest to all men the Savior's living presence in the world, and the genuine nature of the Church. This the family will do by the mutual love of the spouses, by their generous fruitfulness, their solidarity and faithfulness, and by the loving way in which all members of the family work together.

CONJUGAL LOVE

49. The biblical Word of God several times urges the betrothed and the married to nourish and develop their wedlock by pure conjugal love and undivided affection.[165] Many men of our own age also highly regard true love between husband and wife as it manifests itself in a variety of ways depending on the worthy customs of various peoples and times.

This love is an eminently human[166] one since it is directed from one person to another through an affection of the will. It involves the good of the whole person. Therefore it can enrich the expressions of body and mind with a unique dignity, ennobling these expressions as special ingredients and signs of the friendship distinctive of marriage. This love the Lord has judged worthy of special gifts, healing, perfecting, and exalting gifts of grace and of charity.

162. The Council speaks also of the primary right and duty of parents with respect to the education of their children in its Declaration on Christian Education.
163. Cf. 1 Tim. 5:3.
164. Cf. Eph. 5:32.
165. Cf. Gen. 2:22-24; Pr. 5:15-20; 31:10-31; Tob. 8:4-8; Cant. 1:2-3; 1:16; 4:16; 5:1; 7:8-14; 1 Cor. 7:3-6; Eph. 5:25-33.
166. The emphasis on conjugal love necessarily involves a strong personalist tone in this section of the Constitution and thus brings once more to the fore a major theme of the entire document.

Such love, merging the human with the divine, leads the spouses to a free and mutual gift of themselves, a gift proving itself by gentle affection and by deed. Such love pervades the whole of their lives.[167] Indeed, by its generous activity it grows better and grows greater. Therefore it far excels mere erotic inclination, which, selfishly pursued, soon enough fades wretchedly away.

This love is uniquely expressed and perfected through the marital act. The actions within marriage by which the couple are united intimately and chastely are noble and worthy ones. Expressed in a manner which is truly human, these actions signify and promote that mutual self-giving by which spouses enrich each other with a joyful and a thankful will.

Sealed by mutual faithfulness and hallowed above all by Christ's sacrament, this love remains steadfastly true in body and in mind, in bright days or dark. It will never by profaned by adultery or divorce. Firmly established by the Lord, the unity of marriage will radiate from the equal personal dignity of wife and husband, a dignity acknowledged by mutual and total love.

The steady fulfillment of the duties of this Christian vocation demands notable virtue. For this reason, strengthened by grace for holiness of life, the couple will painstakingly cultivate and pray for constancy of love, largeheartedness, and the spirit of sacrifice.

Authentic conjugal love will be more highly prized, and wholesome public opinion created regarding it, if Christian couples give outstanding witness to faithfulness and harmony in that same love, and to their concern for educating their children; also, if they do their part in bringing about the needed cultural, psychological, and social renewal on behalf of marriage and the family.

Especially in the heart of their own families, young people should be aptly and seasonably instructed about the dignity, duty, and expression of married love. Trained thus in the cultivation of chastity, they will be able at a suitable age to enter a marriage of their own after an honorable courtship.

THE FRUITFULNESS OF MARRIAGE

50. Marriage and conjugal love are by their nature ordained toward the begetting and educating of children. Children are

---

167. *Cf. Pius XI, encyclical letter "Casti Connubii": AAS (1930), p. 547 and 548; Denz-Schoen. 3707.*

really the supreme gift of marriage and contribute very substantially to the welfare of their parents. The God Himself who said, "It is not good for man to be alone" (Gen. 2:18) and "who made man from the beginning male and female" (Mt. 19:4), wished to share with man a certain special participation in His own creative work. Thus He blessed male and female, saying: "Increase and multiply" (Gen. 1:28).

Hence, while not making the other purposes of matrimony of less account,[168] the true practice of conjugal love, and the whole meaning of the family life which results from it, have this aim: that the couple be ready with stout hearts to cooperate with the love of the Creator and the Savior, who through them will enlarge and enrich His own family day by day.

Parents should regard as their proper mission the task of transmitting human life and educating those to whom it has been transmitted. They should realize that they are thereby cooperators with the love of God the Creator, and are, so to speak, the interpreters of that love. Thus they will fulfill their task with human and Christian responsibility. With docile reverence toward God, they will come to the right decision by common counsel and effort.

They will thoughtfully take into account both their own welfare and that of their children, those already born and those which may be foreseen. For this accounting they will reckon with both the material and the spiritual conditions of the times as well as of their state in life. Finally, they will consult the interests of the family group, of temporal society, and of the Church herself.

The parents themselves should ultimately make this judgment, in the sight of God. But in their manner of acting, spouses should be aware that they cannot proceed arbitrarily. They must always be governed according to a conscience dutifully conformed to the divine law itself, and should be submissive toward the Church's teaching office, which authentically interprets that law in the light of the gospel. That divine law reveals and protects the integral meaning of conjugal love, and impels it toward a truly human fulfillment.

---

168. The Commission charged with drafting this text made every effort to avoid any appearance of wishing to settle questions concerning a hierarchy of the "ends" of marriage. Thus, the passage includes a beautiful reference to children as "the supreme gift of marriage," but this sentence makes it clear that the present text cannot be read as a judgment on the relative importance or primacy of ends.

Since the clause has been phrased with so much care, it may be useful to cite the Latin: "non posthabitis ceteris matrimonii finibus."

Thus, trusting in divine Providence and refining the spirit of sacrifice,[169] married Christians glorify the Creator and strive toward fulfillment in Christ when, with a generous human and Christian sense of responsibility, they acquit themselves of the duty to procreate. Among the couples who fulfill their God-given task in this way, those merit special mention who with wise and common deliberation, and with a gallant heart,[170] undertake to bring up suitably even a relatively large family.[171]

Marriage to be sure is not instituted solely for procreation. Rather, its very nature as an unbreakable compact between persons, and the welfare of the children, both demand that the mutual love of the spouses, too, be embodied in a rightly ordered manner, that it grow and ripen. Therefore, marriage persists as a whole manner and communion of life, and maintains its value and indissolubility, even when offspring are lacking—despite, rather often, the very intense desire of the couple.

HARMONIZING CONJUGAL LOVE WITH RESPECT FOR HUMAN LIFE

51. This Council realizes that certain modern conditions often keep couples from arranging their married lives harmoniously, and that they find themselves in circumstances where at least temporarily the size of their families should not be increased. As a result, the faithful exercise of love and the full intimacy of their lives are hard to maintain. But where the intimacy of married life is broken off, it is not rare for its faithfulness to be imperiled and its quality of fruitfulness ruined. For then the upbringing of the children and the courage to accept new ones are both endangered.

To these problems there are those who presume to offer dishonorable solutions. Indeed, they do not recoil from the taking of life. But the Church issues the reminder that a true contradiction cannot exist between the divine laws pertaining to the transmission of life and those pertaining to the fostering of authentic conjugal love.

For God, the Lord of life, has conferred on men the surpassing ministry of safeguarding life—a ministry which must

169. Cf. 1 Cor. 7:5.
170. The following reference to a text of Pius XII could be confirmed by citing similar statements from John XXIII's addresses on a number of occasions.
171. Cf. Pius XII, Address "Tra le visite," Jan. 20, 1958: AAS 50 (1958), p. 91.

be fulfilled in a manner which is worthy of man. Therefore from the moment of its conception life must be guarded with the greatest care, while abortion and infanticide are unspeakable crimes. The sexual characteristics of man and the human faculty of reproduction wonderfully exceed the dispositions of lower forms of life. Hence the acts themselves which are proper to conjugal love and which are exercised in accord with genuine human dignity must be honored with great reverence.

Therefore when there is question of harmonizing conjugal love with the responsible transmission of life, the moral aspect of any procedure does not depend solely on sincere intentions or on an evaluation of motives. It must be determined by objective standards. These, based on the nature of the human person and his acts, preserve the full sense of mutual self-giving and human procreation in the context of true love. Such a goal cannot be achieved unless the virtue of conjugal chastity is sincerely practiced. Relying on these principles, sons of the Church may not undertake methods of regulating procreation which are found blameworthy by the teaching authority of the Church[172] in its unfolding of the divine law.[173]

Everyone should be persuaded that human life and the task of transmitting it are not realities bound up with this world alone. Hence they cannot be measured or perceived only in terms of it, but always have a bearing on the eternal destiny of men.

172. Widely published reports indicated that this passage and the official footnote appended to it were the subject of considerable debate within the drafting commission in the last days of the Council's fourth session. It seems certain that Pope Paul submitted a recommendation that the text take note explicitly of statements by his predecessors, Pius XI and Pius XII, on birth control. It is evident, however, that the reference in the present footnote in no way alters the state of debate that had existed in the Church since Paul VI's own announcement of June 23, 1964, of his creation of a commission to study the questions in dispute. The Council states clearly that, with matters standing thus, it has no intention of proposing concrete solutions here.

173. *Cf. Pius XI, encyclical letter "Casti Connubii": AAS 22 (1930), Denz-Schoen., 3716-3718; Pius XII, Allocutio Conventui Unionis Italicae inter Obstetrices, Oct. 29, 1951: AAS 43 (1951), pp. 835-854; Paul VI, address to a group of cardinals, June 23, 1964: AAS 56 (1964), pp. 581-589. Certain questions which need further and more careful investigation have been handed over, at the command of the Supreme Pontiff, to a commission for the study of population, family, and births, in order that, after it fulfills its function, the Supreme Pontiff may pass judgment. With the doctrine of the magisterium in this state, this holy Synod does not intend to propose immediately concrete solutions.* [In the Latin text this is footnote 14 of Chap. I, in Part 2 of the document.—Ed.]

ALL MUST PROMOTE THE GOOD ESTATE
OF MARRIAGE AND THE FAMILY

52. The family is a kind of school of deeper humanity. But if it is to achieve the full flowering of its life and mission, it needs the kindly communion of minds and the joint deliberation of spouses, as well as the painstaking cooperation of parents in the education of their children. The active presence of the father is highly beneficial to their formation. The children, especially the younger among them, need the care of their mother at home. This domestic role of hers must be safely preserved, though the legitimate social progress of women should not be underrated on that account.

Children should be so educated that as adults they can, with a mature sense of responsibility, follow their vocation, including a religious one, and choose their state of life. If they marry, they can thereby establish their family in favorable moral, social, and economic conditions. Parents or guardians should by prudent advice provide guidance to their young with respect to founding a family, and the young ought to listen gladly. At the same time no pressure, direct or indirect, should be put on the young to make them enter marriage or choose a specific partner.

Thus the family is the foundation of society. In it the various generations come together and help one another to grow wiser and to harmonize personal rights with the other requirements of social life. All those, therefore, who exercise influence over communities and social groups should work efficiently for the welfare of marriage and the family.

Public authority should regard it as a sacred duty to recognize, protect, and promote their authentic nature, to shield public morality, and to favor the prosperity of domestic life. The right of parents to beget and educate their children in the bosom of the family must be safeguarded. Children, too, who unhappily lack the blessing of a family should be protected by prudent legislation and various undertakings, and provided with the help they need.

Redeeming the present time,[174] and distinguishing eternal realities from their changing expressions, Christians should actively promote the values of marriage and the family, both by the example of their own lives and by cooperation with

174. *Cf. Eph. 5:16; Col. 4:5.*

other men of good will. Thus when difficulties arise, Christians will provide, on behalf of family life, those necessities and helps which are suitably modern. To this end, the Christian instincts of the faithful, the upright moral consciences of men, and the wisdom and experience of persons versed in the sacred sciences will have much to contribute.

Those, too, who are skilled in other sciences, notably the medical, biological, social, and psychological, can considerably advance the welfare of marriage and the family, along with peace of conscience, if by pooling their efforts they labor to explain more thoroughly the various conditions favoring a proper regulation of births.

It devolves on priests duly trained about family matters to nurture the vocation of spouses by a variety of pastoral means, by preaching God's Word, by liturgical worship, and by other spiritual aids to conjugal and family life; to sustain them sympathetically and patiently in difficulties, and to make them courageous through love. Thus families which are truly noble will be formed.

Various organizations, especially family associations, should try by their programs of instruction and action to strengthen young people and spouses themselves, particularly those recently wed, and to train them for family, social, and apostolic life.[175]

Finally, let the spouses themselves, made to the image of the living God and enjoying the authentic dignity of persons, be joined to one another[176] in equal affection, harmony of mind, and the work of mutual sanctification. Thus they will follow Christ who is the principle of life.[177] Thus, too, by the joys and sacrifices of their vocation and through their faithful love, married people will become witnesses of the mystery of that love which the Lord revealed to the world by His dying and His rising up to life again.[178]

175. Examples of such organizations are the Christian Family Movement and the various types of Cana and Pre-Cana Conference programs conducted in the United States.
176. Cf. Sacramentarium Gregorianum: PL 78, 262.
177. Cf. Rom. 5:15 and 18; 6:5-11; Gal. 2:20.
178. Cf. Eph. 5:25-27.

CHAPTER II

THE PROPER DEVELOPMENT OF CULTURE

INTRODUCTION

53. It is a fact bearing on the very person of man that he can come to an authentic and full humanity only through culture, that is, through the cultivation of natural goods and values. Wherever human life is involved, therefore, nature and culture are quite intimately connected.

The word "culture" in its general sense indicates all those factors by which man refines and unfolds his manifold spiritual and bodily qualities. It means his effort to bring the world itself under his control by his knowledge and his labor. It includes the fact that by improving customs and institutions he renders social life more human both within the family and in the civic community. Finally, it is a feature of culture that throughout the course of time man expresses, communicates, and conserves in his works great spiritual experiences and desires, so that these may be of advantage to the progress of many, even of the whole human family.

Hence it follows that human culture necessarily has a historical and social aspect and that the word "culture" often takes on a sociological and ethnological sense.[179] It is in this sense that we speak of a plurality of cultures.

Various conditions of community living, as well as various patterns for organizing the goods of life, arise from diverse ways of using things, of laboring, of expressing oneself, of practicing religion, of forming customs, of establishing laws and juridical institutions, of advancing the arts and sciences, and of promoting beauty. Thus the customs handed down to it form for each human community its proper patrimony. Thus, too, is fashioned the specific historical environment

---

179. The concept of "culture" as it is understood by sociologists and anthropologists is a relatively new one. It is not surprising, then, that Vatican II should find it necessary to spell out several definitions of the term.

which enfolds the men of every nation and age and from which they draw the values which permit them to promote human and civic culture.

Section 1: The Circumstances of Culture in the World Today

NEW FORMS OF LIVING

54. The living conditions of modern man have been so profoundly changed in their social and cultural dimensions, that we can speak of a new age in human history.[180] Fresh avenues are open, therefore, for the refinement and the wider diffusion of culture. These avenues have been paved by the enormous growth of natural, human, and social sciences, by progress in technology, and by advances in the development and organization of the means by which men communicate with one another.

Hence the culture of today possesses particular characteristics. For example, the so-called exact sciences sharpen critical judgment to a very fine edge. Recent psychological research explains human activity more profoundly. Historical studies make a signal contribution to bringing men to see things in their changeable and evolutionary aspects.[181] Customs and usages are becoming increasingly uniform. Industrialization, urbanization, and other causes of community living create new forms of culture (mass-culture), from which arise new ways of thinking, acting, and making use of leisure. The growth of communication between the various nations and social groups opens more widely to all the treasures of different cultures.

Thus, little by little, a more universal form of human culture is developing, one which will promote and express the unity of the human race to the degree that it preserves the particular features of the different cultures.

MAN THE AUTHOR OF CULTURE

55. In every group or nation, there is an ever-increasing number of men and women who are conscious that they

180. *Cf. introductory statement of this Constitution, Art. 4 ff.*
181. Here the Council takes account of the influence on the contemporary intellectual climate of Marx, Darwin, Freud, and the broad movements attaching to their names.

themselves are the artisans and the authors of the culture of their community. Throughout the world there is a similar growth in the combined sense of independence and responsibility. Such a development is of paramount importance for the spiritual and moral maturity of the human race.[182] This truth grows clearer if we consider how the world is becoming unified and how we have the duty to build a better world based upon truth and justice. Thus we are witnesses of the birth of a new humanism, one in which man is defined first of all by his responsibility toward his brothers and toward history.

PROBLEMS AND DUTIES

56. In these conditions, it is no wonder that, feeling his responsibility for the progress of culture, man nourishes higher hopes but also looks anxiously upon many contradictions which he will have to resolve:

What must be done to prevent the increased exchanges between cultures, which ought to lead to a true and fruitful dialogue between groups and nations, from disturbing the life of communities, destroying ancestral wisdom, or jeopardizing the uniqueness of each people?[183]

How can the vitality and growth of a new culture be fostered without the loss of living fidelity to the heritage of tradition? This question is especially urgent when a culture resulting from the enormous scientific and technological progress must be harmonized with an education nourished by classical studies as adapted to various traditions.[184]

As special branches of knowledge continue to shoot out so rapidly, how can the necessary synthesis of them be worked out, and how can men preserve the ability to contemplate and to wonder, from which wisdom comes?

What can be done to make all men on earth share in cul-

---

182. The Constitution recognizes that the general move toward awareness of personhood and of the self as a responsible agent is something that affects the thinking of whole peoples. The worldwide phenomenon of the "emerging nations" and the drive for national independence that has swept across the earth since the close of World War II are events that have had profound impact on the human spirit everywhere.

183. The danger here sometimes takes on the guise of a cultural neo-colonialism. Pope John XXIII had pointed to one aspect of this peril in his "Mater et Magistra" when he noted that economically advanced nations sometimes export false values with their economic and technical aid to others (176).

184. The writings of C. P. Snow have highlighted for English-speaking nations the tension and conflict here under discussion.

tural values, when the culture of the more sophisticated grows ever more refined and complex?[185]

Finally, how is the independence which culture claims for itself to be recognized as legitimate without the promotion of a humanism which is merely earth-bound, and even contrary to religion itself?

In the thick of these tensions, human culture must evolve today in such a way that it can develop the whole human person harmoniously and at the same time assist men in those duties which all men, especially Christians, are called to fulfill in the fraternal unity of the one human family.

Section 2: Some Principles of Proper Cultural Development

FAITH AND CULTURE

57. Christians, on pilgrimage toward the heavenly city, should seek and savor the things which are above.[186] This duty in no way decreases, but rather increases, the weight of their obligation to work with all men in constructing a more human world. In fact, the mystery of the Christian faith furnishes them with excellent incentives and helps toward discharging this duty more energetically and especially toward uncovering the full meaning of this activity, a meaning which gives human culture its eminent place in the integral vocation of man.

For when, by the work of his hands or with the aid of technology, man develops the earth so that it can bear fruit and become a dwelling worthy of the whole human family, and when he consciously takes part in the life of social groups, he carries out the design of God. Manifested at the beginning of time, the divine plan is that man should subdue[187] the earth, bring creation to perfection, and develop himself. When a man so acts he simultaneously obeys the great Christian commandment that he place himself at the service of his brother men.

185. Attention has been called by competent critics to the existence of a "culture explosion" in countries like the United States. At the same time, there remains some uncertainty as to whether the "explosion" is not accompanied by a widening of the gap between "mass" and "elite" cultures.
186. Cf. Col. 3:1-2.
187. Cf. Gen. 1:28.

Furthermore, when a man applies himself to the various disciplines of philosophy, of history, and of mathematical and natural science, and when he cultivates the arts, he can do very much to elevate the human family to a more sublime understanding of truth, goodness, and beauty, and to the formation of judgments which embody universal values. Thus mankind can be more clearly enlightened by that marvelous Wisdom which was with God from all eternity, arranging all things with Him, playing upon the earth, delighting in the sons of men.[188]

In this way, the human spirit grows increasingly free of its bondage to creatures and can be more easily drawn to the worship and contemplation of the Creator. Moreover, under the impulse of grace, man is disposed to acknowledge the Word of God. Before He became flesh in order to save all things and to sum them up in Himself, "He was in the world" already as "the true light that enlightens every man" (Jn. 1:9-10).[189]

No doubt today's progress in science and technology can foster a certain exclusive emphasis on observable data, and an agnosticism about everything else. For the methods of investigation which these sciences use can be wrongly considered as the supreme rule for discovering the whole truth. By virtue of their methods, however, these sciences cannot penetrate to the intimate meaning of things. Yet the danger exists that man, confiding too much in modern discoveries, may even think that he is sufficient unto himself and no longer seek any higher realities.

These unfortunate results, however, do not necessarily follow from the culture of today, nor should they lead us into the temptation of not acknowledging its positive values.[190] For among its values are these: scientific study and strict fidelity toward truth in scientific research, the necessity of working together with others in technical groups, a sense of international solidarity, an ever clearer awareness of the responsibility of experts to aid men and even to protect them,

188. Cf. Pr. 8:30-31.
189. Cf. St. Irenaeus, "Adversus haereses": III, 11, 8 (ed. Sagnard, p. 200; cf. ibid., 16, 6: pp. 290-292; 21, 10-22: pp. 370-372; 22, 3: p. 378; etc.).
190. The Council here carefully distinguishes between excesses associated with a spirit of "scientism" and the permanently valid achievements of the positive sciences over the past few centuries. In doing so, it remains faithful to the spirit of Leo XIII, Pius XII, and John XXIII, pontiffs who made notable efforts to establish fruitful contact and collaboration with the shapers of modern science and culture.

the desire to make the conditions of life more favorable for all, especially for those who are deprived of the opportunity to exercise responsibility or who are culturally poor.

All of these values can provide some preparation for the acceptance of the message of the gospel—a preparation which can be animated with divine love by Him who came to save the world.

THE MANY LINKS BETWEEN THE GOSPEL AND CULTURE

58. There are many links between the message of salvation and human culture. For God, revealing Himself to His people to the extent of a full manifestation of Himself in His Incarnate Son, has spoken according to the culture proper to different ages.

Living in various circumstances during the course of time, the Church, too, has used in her preaching the discoveries of different cultures to spread and explain the message of Christ to all nations, to probe it and more deeply understand it, and to give it better expression in liturgical celebrations and in the life of the diversified community of the faithful.

But at the same time, the Church, sent to all peoples of every time and place, is not bound exclusively and indissolubly to any race or nation, nor to any particular way of life or any customary pattern of living, ancient or recent. Faithful to her own tradition and at the same time conscious of her universal mission, she can enter into communion with various cultural modes, to her own enrichment and theirs too.

The good news of Christ constantly renews the life and culture of fallen man. It combats and removes the errors and evils resulting from sinful allurements which are a perpetual threat. It never ceases to purify and elevate the morality of peoples. By riches coming from above, it makes fruitful, as it were from within, the spiritual qualities and gifts of every people and of every age. It strengthens, perfects, and restores[191] them in Christ. Thus by the very fulfillment of her own mission[192] the Church stimulates and advances human

---

191. Cf. Eph. 1:10.
192. Cf. the words of Pius XI to Father M. D. Roland-Gosselin: "It is necessary never to lose sight of the fact that the objective of the Church is to evangelize, not to civilize. If it civilizes, it is for the sake of evangelization" (Semaines sociales de France, Versailles, 1936, pp. 461-462).

and civic culture. By her action, even in its liturgical form, she leads men toward interior liberty.

HARMONY BETWEEN
THE FORMS OF CULTURE

59. For the aforementioned reasons, the Church recalls to the mind of all that culture must be made to bear on the integral perfection of the human person, and on the good of the community and the whole of society. Therefore the human spirit must be cultivated in such a way that there results a growth in its ability to wonder, to understand, to contemplate, to make personal judgments, and to develop a religious, moral, and social sense.

Because it flows immediately from man's spiritual and social nature, culture has constant need of a just freedom if it is to develop. It also needs the legitimate possibility of exercising its independence according to its own principles.[193] Rightly, therefore, it demands respect and enjoys a certain inviolability, at least as long as the rights of the individual and of the community, whether particular or universal, are preserved within the context of the common good.

This sacred Synod, therefore, recalling the teaching of the first Vatican Council, declares that there are "two orders of knowledge" which are distinct, namely, faith and reason. It declares that the Church does not indeed forbid that "when the human arts and sciences are practiced they use their own principles and their proper method, each in its own domain." Hence, "acknowledging this just liberty," this sacred Synod affirms the legitimate autonomy of human culture and especially of the sciences.[194]

All these considerations demand too, that, within the limits of morality and the general welfare, a man be free to search for the truth, voice his mind, and publicize it;[195] that he be free to practice any art he chooses; and finally that he have

---

193. Throughout this passage, the Council refuses to lend support to any concept of art for the sake of ideology. If it therefore rejects efforts to dictate true "socialist" art, it also calls in question efforts to insist that the primary norm in artistic criticism should be "morality."

194. *First Vatican Council, Constitution on the Catholic Faith: Denz. 1795, 1799 (3015, 3019). Cf. Pius XI, encyclical letter "Quadragesimo Anno": AAS 23 (1931), p. 190.*

195. Here the Council defends the broad human freedom of inquiry and of expression in general society, along with the right to be informed about public events. In a subsequent passage (62), it will affirm explicitly the freedom of the scholar in the Church.

appropriate access to information about public affairs.[196]

It is not the function of public authority to determine what the proper nature of forms of human culture should be. It should rather foster the conditions and the means which are capable of promoting cultural life among all citizens and even within the minorities of a nation.[197] Hence in this matter men must insist above all else that culture be not diverted from its own purpose and made to serve political or economic interests.

Section 3: Some Especially Urgent Duties of Christians with Regard to Culture

RECOGNIZING AND IMPLEMENTING THE RIGHT TO CULTURE

60. The possibility now exists of liberating most men from the misery of ignorance. Hence it is a duty most befitting our times that men, especially Christians, should work strenuously on behalf of certain decisions which must be made in the economic and political fields, both nationally and internationally. By these decisions universal recognition and implementation should be given to the right of all men to a human and civic culture favorable to personal dignity and free from any discrimination on the grounds of race, sex, nationality, religious, or social conditions.

Therefore it is necessary to provide every man with a sufficient abundance of cultural benefits, especially those which constitute so-called basic culture. Otherwise, because of illiteracy and a lack of responsible activity, very many will be prevented from collaborating in a truly human manner for the sake of the common good.

Efforts must be made to see that men who are capable of higher studies can pursue them. In this way, as far as possible, they can be prepared to undertake in society those duties, offices, and services which are in harmony with their natural aptitude and with the competence they will have acquired.[198] Thus all the individuals and the social groups comprising a

---

196. *Cf. John XXIII, encyclical letter "Pacem in Terris": AAS 55 (1963), p. 260.*
197. *Cf. John XXIII, encyclical letter "Pacem in Terris": AAS 55 (1963), p. 283; Pius XII, radio address, Dec. 24, 1941: AAS 34 (1942), pp. 16-17.*
198. *John XXIII, encyclical letter "Pacem in Terris": AAS 55 (1963), p. 260.*

given people will be able to attain the full development of their culture, a development in accord with their qualities and traditions.

Energetic efforts must also be expended to make everyone conscious of his right to culture and of the duty he has to develop himself culturally and to assist others. For existing conditions of life and of work sometimes thwart the cultural strivings of men and destroy in them the desire for self-improvement. This is especially true of country people and laborers. They need to be provided with working conditions which will not block their human development but rather favor it.

Women are now employed in almost every area of life. It is appropriate that they should be able to assume their full proper role in accordance with their own nature. Everyone should acknowledge and favor the proper and necessary participation of women in cultural life.

CULTURAL EDUCATION

61. Today it is more difficult than ever for a synthesis to be formed of the various branches of knowledge and the arts. For while the mass and the diversity of cultural factors are increasing, there is a decline in the individual man's ability to grasp and unify these elements. Thus the ideal of "the universal man" is disappearing more and more.[199] Nevertheless, it remains each man's duty to preserve a view of the whole human person, a view in which the values of intellect, will, conscience, and fraternity are pre-eminent. These values are all rooted in God the Creator and have been wonderfully restored and elevated in Christ.

The family is, as it were, the primary mother and nurse of this attitude. There, in an atmosphere of love, children can more easily learn the true structure of reality. There, too, tested forms of human culture impress themselves upon the mind of the developing adolescent in a kind of automatic way.

Opportunities for the same kind of education can also be found in modern society, thanks especially to the increased

---

199. Perhaps this passage could have been rounded out by a consideration of the phenomenon of socialization and its application here. For the expansion and diversification of scientific and cultural achievement have been accompanied increasingly by a growth of interdependent effort in the fields of intellectual inquiry and scientific investigation. Today one can even speak of the rise of "interdisciplinary personalities."

circulation of books and to the new means of cultural and social communication. All such opportunities can foster a universal culture.

The widespread reduction in working hours, for instance, brings increasing advantages to numerous people. May these leisure hours be properly used for relaxation of spirit and the strengthening of mental and bodily health. Such benefits are available through spontaneous study and activity and through travel, which refines human qualities and enriches men with mutual understanding. These benefits are obtainable too from physical exercise and sports events, which can help to preserve emotional balance, even at the community level, and to establish fraternal relations among men of all conditions, nations, and races.

Hence let Christians work together to animate the cultural expressions and group activities characteristic of our times with a human and a Christian spirit.

All these benefits, however, cannot educate men to a full self-development unless at the same time deep thought is given to what culture and science mean in terms of the human person.

HARMONY BETWEEN CULTURE AND CHRISTIAN FORMATION

62. Although the Church has contributed much to the development of culture, experience shows that, because of circumstances, it is sometimes difficult to harmonize culture with Christian teaching.

These difficulties do not necessarily harm the life of faith. Indeed they can stimulate the mind to a more accurate and penetrating grasp of the faith. For recent studies and findings of science, history, and philosophy raise new questions which influence life and demand new theological investigations.[200]

Furthermore, while adhering to the methods and requirements proper to theology, theologians are invited to seek continually for more suitable ways of communicating doctrine to the men of their times. For the deposit of faith or revealed truths are one thing; the manner in which they are formu-

200. This statement reveals the Council's own conviction that the notion of a theological "aggiornamento" means more than a rephrasing of conventional theological teaching in contemporary terminology. This same view had been set forth by John XXIII as a salient point of the Council's program in his address of Oct. 11, 1962, at the initial public session of Vatican II.

lated without violence to their meaning and significance is another.[201]

In pastoral care, appropriate use must be made not only of theological principles, but also of the findings of the secular sciences, especially of psychology and sociology. Thus the faithful can be brought to live the faith in a more thorough and mature way.

Literature and the arts are also, in their own way, of great importance to the life of the Church. For they strive to probe the unique nature of man, his problems, and his experiences as he struggles to know and perfect both himself and the world. They are preoccupied with revealing man's place in history and in the world, with illustrating his miseries and joys, his needs and strengths, and with foreshadowing a better life for him. Thus they are able to elevate human life as it is expressed in manifold forms, depending on time and place.

Efforts must therefore be made so that those who practice these arts can feel that the Church gives recognition to them in their activities, and so that, enjoying an orderly freedom, they can establish smoother relations with the Christian community. Let the Church also acknowledge new forms of art which are adapted to our age and are in keeping with the characterictics of various nations and regions. Adjusted in their mode of expression and conformed to liturgical requirements, they may be introduced into the sanctuary when they raise the mind to God.[202]

In this way the knowledge of God can be better revealed. Also, the preaching of the gospel can become clearer to man's mind and show its relevance to the conditions of human life.

May the faithful, therefore, live in very close union with the men of their time. Let them strive to understand perfectly their way of thinking and feeling, as expressed in their culture. Let them blend modern science and its theories and the understanding of the most recent discoveries with Christian morality and doctrine. Thus their religious practice and morality can keep pace with their scientific knowledge and with an ever-advancing technology.[203] Thus too they will be

201. *Cf. John XXIII, speech delivered on Oct. 11, 1962, at the beginning of the Council: AAS 54 (1962), p. 792.*
202. *Cf. Constitution on the Sacred Liturgy, Art. 123: AAS 56 (1964), p. 131; Paul VI, discourse to the artists of Rome: AAS 56 (1964), pp. 439-442.*
203. Here, as elsewhere, it is easy to recognize the compatibility of insights developed by thinkers such as Teilhard de Chardin in his "Divine Milieu" (Harper,

able to test and interpret all things in a truly Christian spirit.

Through a sharing of resources and points of view, let those who teach in seminaries,[204] colleges, and universities try to collaborate with men well versed in the other sciences. Theological inquiry should seek a profound understanding of revealed truth without neglecting close contact with its own times. As a result, it will be able to help those men skilled in various fields of knowledge to gain a better understanding of the faith.

This common effort will very greatly aid in the formation of priests. It will enable them to present to our contemporaries the doctrine of the Church concerning God, man, and the world in a manner better suited to them, with the result that they will receive it more willingly.[205] Furthermore, it is to be hoped that many laymen will receive an appropriate formation in the sacred sciences, and that some will develop and deepen these studies by their own labors. In order that such persons may fulfill their proper function, let it be recognized that all the faithful,[206] clerical and lay, possess a lawful freedom of inquiry and of thought, and the freedom to express their minds humbly and courageously about those matters in which they enjoy competence.[207]

1960) with the fundamental outlook of the Council. In a sense, this statement of the Constitution ratifies the basic inspiration of the "nouvelle théologie" of the 1940's. For those familiar with some of the controversy over the "nouvelle théologie" at that time it may be of interest to note that several of its leading promoters, including Fathers Henri de Lubac, Jean Daniélou, and Yves Congar, served as expert consultants to the commission responsible for drafting this Constitution.

204. It is to be noted that the spirit of open inquiry and research praised and safeguarded in this passage is to influence the academic atmosphere of seminaries as well as universities. This recommendation of the Constitution is fully in accord with basic guidelines for seminaries laid down in the Council's Decree on Priestly Formation.

205. Cf. Second Vatican Council, Decree on Priestly Formation and Declaration on Christian Education.

206. The freedoms here guaranteed are to be exercised within the Church and thus one must understand that they extend to all the faithful. The duty to recognize these rights therefore rests on all ecclesiastical superiors.

207. Cf. dogmatic constitution "Lumen Gentium," Chap. IV, Art. 37: AAS 57 (1965), pp. 42-43.

CHAPTER III

SOCIO-ECONOMIC LIFE

SOME ASPECTS OF ECONOMIC LIFE

63. In the socio-economic realm, too, the dignity and total vocation of the human person must be honored and advanced along with the welfare of society as a whole. For man is the source, the center, and the purpose of all socio-economic life.

As in other areas of social life, modern economy is marked by man's increasing domination over nature, by closer and more intense relationships between citizens, groups, and countries and by their mutual dependence, and by more frequent intervention on the part of government. At the same time progress in the methods of production and in the exchange of goods and services has made the economy an apt instrument for meeting the intensified needs of the human family more successfully.

Reasons for anxiety, however, are not lacking. Many people, especially in economically advanced areas, seem to be hypnotized, as it were, by economics, so that almost their entire personal and social life is permeated with a certain economic outlook. These people can be found both in nations which favor a collective economy as well as in others.[208]

Again, we are at a moment in history when the development of economic life could diminish social inequalities if that development were guided and coordinated in a reasonable and human way. Yet all too often it serves only to intensify the inequalities. In some places it even results in a decline in the social status of the weak and in contempt for the poor.

While an enormous mass of people still lack the absolute necessities of life, some, even in less advanced countries, live sumptuously or squander wealth. Luxury and misery rub

---

208. The Council decries a basic moral flaw in the socio-economic thinking of many advocates of communism and capitalism alike. Similar observations have been made repeatedly in the social pronouncements of recent Popes.

shoulders. While the few enjoy very great freedom of choice, the many are deprived of almost all possibility of acting on their own initiative and responsibility, and often subsist in living and working conditions unworthy of human beings.

A similar lack of economic and social balance is to be noted between agriculture, industry, and the services, and also between different parts of one and the same country. The contrast between the economically more advanced countries and other countries is becoming more serious day by day, and the very peace of the world can be jeopardized in consequence.

Our contemporaries are coming to feel these inequalities with an ever sharper awareness. For they are thoroughly convinced that the wider technical and economic potential which the modern world enjoys can and should correct this unhappy state of affairs.[209] Hence, numerous reforms are needed at the socio-economic level, along with universal changes in ideas and attitudes.

Now in this area the Church maintains certain principles of justice and equity as they apply to individuals, societies, and international relations. In the course of the centuries and with the light of the gospel she has worked out these principles as right reason demanded. In modern times especially, the Church has enlarged upon them. This sacred Council wishes to re-enforce these principles according to the circumstances of the times and to set forth certain guidelines, primarily with regard to the requirements of economic development.[210]

Section 1: Economic Development

IN THE SERVICE OF MAN

64. Today, more than ever before, progress in the production of agricultural and industrial goods and in the rendering of services is rightly aimed at making provision for the growth

---

209. It has become a commonplace among economists that today man stands in the position, perhaps for the first time in human history, of being able to abolish hunger, want, and illiteracy throughout the world. Paradoxically, there is some reason to believe that the gap between haves and have-nots in some parts of the world grows greater every day.

210. *Cf. Pius XII, address on Mar. 23, 1952: AAS 44 (1953), p. 273; John XXIII, allocution to the Catholic Association of Italian Workers, May 1, 1959: AAS 51 (1959), p. 358.*

of a people and at meeting the rising expectations of the human race. Therefore, technical progress must be fostered, along with a spirit of initiative, an eagerness to create and expand enterprises, the adaptation of methods of production, and the strenuous efforts of all who engage in production—in a word, all the elements making for such development.

The fundamental purpose of this productivity must not be the mere multiplication of products. It must not be profit or domination. Rather, it must be the service of man, and indeed of the whole man, viewed in terms of his material needs and the demands of his intellectual, moral, spiritual, and religious life. And when we say man, we mean every man whatsoever and every group of men, of whatever race and from whatever part of the world. Consequently, economic activity is to be carried out according to its own methods and laws but within the limits of morality,[211] so that God's plan for mankind can be realized.[212]

UNDER MAN'S CONTROL

65. Economic development must be kept under the control of mankind. It must not be left to the sole judgment of a few men or groups possessing excessive economic power, or of the political community alone, or of certain especially powerful nations. It is proper, on the contrary, that at every level the largest possible number of people have an active share in directing that development. When it is a question of international developments, all nations should so participate. It is also necessary for the spontaneous activities of individuals and of independent groups to be coordinated with the efforts of public authorities. These activities and these efforts should be aptly and harmoniously interwoven.

Growth must not be allowed merely to follow a kind of automatic course resulting from the economic activity of individuals. Nor must it be entrusted solely to the authority of government. Hence, theories which obstruct the necessary reforms in the name of a false liberty must be branded as erroneous. The same is true of those theories which subordi-

---

211. *Cf. Pius XI, encyclical letter "Quadragesimo Anno": AAS 23 (1931), p. 190 ff. Pius XII, address of Mar. 23, 1952: AAS 44 (1952), p. 276 ff; John XXIII, encyclical letter "Mater et Magistra": AAS 53 (1961), p. 450; Vatican Council II, Decree "Inter Mirifica"* [on the Instruments of Social Communication], *Chapter I, Art. 6: AAS 56 (1964), p. 147.*
212. *Cf. Mt. 16:26; Lk. 16:1-31; Col. 3:17.*

nate the basic rights of individual persons and groups to the collective organization of production.[213]

Citizens, for their part, should remember that they have the right and the duty, which must be recognized by civil authority, to contribute according to their ability to the true progress of their own community. Especially in underdeveloped areas, where all resources must be put to urgent use, those men gravely endanger the public good who allow their resources to remain unproductive or who deprive their community of the material and spiritual aid it needs.[214] The personal right of migration, however, is not to be impugned.

REMOVING HUGE DIFFERENCES

66. If the demands of justice and equity are to be satisfied, vigorous efforts must be made, without violence to the rights of persons or to the natural characteristics of each country, to remove as quickly as possible the immense economic inequalities which now exist. In many cases, these are worsening and are connected with individual and group discrimination.

In many areas, too, farmers experience special difficulties in raising products or in selling them. In such cases, country people must be helped to increase and to market what they produce, to make the necessary advances and changes, and to obtain a fair return. Otherwise, as too often happens, they will remain in the condition of lower-class citizens. Let farmers, especially young ones, skillfully apply themselves to perfecting their professional competence. Without it, no agricultural progress can take place.[215]

Justice and equity likewise require that the mobility which is necessary in a developing economy be regulated in such a way as to keep the life of individuals and their families from becoming insecure and precarious. Hence, when workers come from another country or district and contribute by their labor to the economic advancement of a nation or region,

---

213. *Cf. Leo XIII, encyclical letter "Libertas," in Acta Leonis XIII, t. VIII, p. 220 ff; Pius XI, encyclical letter "Quadragesimo Anno": AAS 23 (1931), p. 191 ff; Pius XI, encyclical letter "Divini Redemptoris": AAS 39 (1937), p. 65 ff; Pius XII, Christmas message, 1941: AAS 34 (1942), p. 10 ff; John XXIII, encyclical letter "Mater et Magistra": AAS 53 (1961), pp. 401-464.*

214. This condemnation will be read most widely as a criticism of wealthy persons in some parts of Latin America and other economically underdeveloped areas who refuse to invest their wealth in the development of their native lands but bank it in Switzerland or other European financial centers.

215. *In reference to agricultural problems cf. especially John XXIII, encyclical letter "Mater et Magistra": AAS 53 (1961), p. 341 ff.*

all discrimination with respect to wages and working conditions must be carefully avoided.

The local people, moreover, especially public authorities, should all treat them not as mere tools of production but as persons, and must help them to arrange for their families to live with them and to provide themselves with decent living quarters. The natives should also see that these workers are introduced into the social life of the country or region which receives them. Employment opportunities, however, should be created in their own areas as far as possible.

In those economic affairs which are today subject to change, as in the new forms of industrial society in which automation,[216] for example, is advancing, care must be taken that sufficient and suitable work can be obtained, along with appropriate technical and professional formation. The livelihood and the human dignity of those especially who are in particularly difficult circumstances because of illness or old age should be safeguarded.

Section 2: Certain Principles Governing Socio-Economic Life as a Whole

LABOR AND LEISURE

67. Human labor which is expended in the production and exchange of goods or in the performance of economic services is superior to the other elements of economic life. For the latter have only the nature of tools.

Whether it is engaged in independently or paid for by someone else, this labor comes immediately from the person. In a sense, the person stamps the things of nature with his seal and subdues them to his will. It is ordinarily by his labor that a man supports himself and his family, is joined to his fellow men and serves them, and is enabled to exercise genuine charity and be a partner in the work of bringing God's creation to perfection. Indeed, we hold that by offering his labor to God a man becomes associated with the redemptive work itself of Jesus Christ, who conferred an eminent dignity on labor when at Nazareth He worked with His own hands.

216. The Council wisely refuses to render a technical or concrete ethical judgment on a complex economic development such as the very recent step-up in automation.

From all these considerations there arise every man's duty to labor faithfully and also his right to work. It is the duty of society, moreover, according to the circumstances prevailing in it, and in keeping with its proper role, to help its citizens find opportunities for adequate employment. Finally, payment for labor must be such as to furnish a man with the means to cultivate his own material, social, cultural, and spiritual life worthily, and that of his dependents. What this payment should be will vary according to each man's assignment and productivity, the conditions of his place of employment, and the common good.[217]

Since economic activity is generally exercised through the combined labors of human beings, any way of organizing and directing that activity which would be detrimental to any worker would be wrong and inhuman. It too often happens, however, even in our day, that in one way or another workers are made slaves of their work. This situation can by no means be justified by so-called economic laws. The entire process of productive work, therefore, must be adapted to the needs of the person and to the requirements of his life, above all his domestic life. Such is especially the case with respect to mothers of families, but due consideration must be given to every person's sex and age.

The opportunity should also be afforded to workers to develop their own abilities and personalities through the work they perform. Though they should apply their time and energy to their employment with a due sense of responsibility, all workers should also enjoy sufficient rest and leisure to cultivate their family, cultural, social, and religious life.[218] They should also have the opportunity to develop on their own the resources and potentialities to which, perhaps, their professional work gives but little scope.

ECONOMIC PARTICIPATION AND CONFLICT

68. In economic enterprises it is persons who work together,

---

217. Cf. Leo XIII, encyclical letter "Rerum Novarum": AAS 23 (1890-91), p. 649, p. 662; Pius XI, encyclical letter "Quadragesimo Anno": AAS 23 (1931), pp. 200-201; Pius XI, encyclical letter "Divini Redemptoris": AAS 29 (1937), p. 92; Pius XII, radio address on Christmas Eve, 1942: AAS 35 (1943), p. 20; Pius XII, allocution of June 13, 1943: AAS 35 (1943), p. 172; Pius XII, radio address to the workers of Spain, Mar. 11, 1951: AAS 43 (1951), p. 215; John XXIII, encyclical letter "Mater et Magistra": AAS 53 (1961), p. 419.

218. Unlike Pope John's encyclical "Mater et Magistra," which devoted a special section (248-253) to the defense of Sunday as a sacred day of rest, the Constitution does not involve itself in so concrete a detail.

that is, free and independent human beings created to the image of God. Therefore the active participation of everyone in the running of an enterprise should be promoted.[219] This participation should be exercised in appropriately determined ways. It should take into account each person's function, whether it be one of ownership, hiring, management, or labor. It should provide for the necessary unity of operations.

However, decisions concerning economic and social conditions, on which the future of the workers and their children depends, are rather often made not within the enterprise itself but by institutions on a higher level. Hence the workers themselves should have a share also in controlling these institutions, either in person or through freely elected delegates.[220]

Among the basic rights of the human person must be counted the right of freely founding labor unions. These unions should be truly able to represent the workers and to contribute to the proper arrangement of economic life. Another such right is that of taking part freely in the activity of these unions without risk of reprisal. Through this sort of orderly participation, joined with an ongoing formation in economic and social matters, all will grow day by day in the awareness of their own function and responsibility. Thus they will be brought to feel that according to their own proper capacities and aptitudes they are associates in the whole task of economic and social development and in the attainment of the universal common good.

When, however, socio-economic disputes arise, efforts must be made to come to a peaceful settlement. Recourse must always be had above all to sincere discussion between the parties. Even in present-day circumstances, however, the strike can still be a necessary, though ultimate, means for the defense of the workers' own rights and the fulfillment of their

219. *Cf. John XXIII, encyclical letter "Mater et Magistra": AAS 53 (1961), pp. 408, 424, 427; however, the word "curatione" has been taken from the Latin text of the encyclical letter "Quadragesimo Anno": AAS 23 (1931) p. 199. Under the aspect of the evolution of the question cf. also: Pius XII, allocution of June 3, 1950: AAS 42 (1950), pp. 485-488; Paul VI, allocution of June 8, 1964: AAS 56 (1964), pp. 574-579.*
220. The Constitution makes a further application, now within the economic order, of the basic principle of participation in government by all members of a community or group. Its comments on the necessity of permitting the workers to be represented by "freely elected" delegates have meaning not only for countries where there are no workers' associations, but also for countries which have them but, like Spain, do not yet allow for adequately free choice of representatives by the workers themselves.

just demands. As soon as possible, however, ways should be sought to resume negotiations and the discussion of reconciliation.

THE COMMON PURPOSE OF CREATED THINGS

69. God intended the earth and all that it contains for the use of every human being and people. Thus, as all men follow justice and unite in charity, created goods should abound for them on a reasonable basis.[221] Whatever the forms of ownership may be, as adapted to the legitimate institutions of people according to diverse and changeable circumstances, attention must always be paid to the universal purpose for which created goods are meant. In using them, therefore, a man should regard his lawful possessions not merely as his own but also as common property in the sense that they should accrue to the benefit of not only himself but of others.[222]

For the rest, the right to have a share of earthly goods sufficient for oneself and one's family belongs to everyone. The Fathers and Doctors of the Church held this view, teaching that men are obliged to come to the relief to the poor, and to do so not merely out of their superfluous goods.[223] If a person is in extreme necessity, he has the right to take from the riches of others what he himself needs.[224] Since

221. Cf. Pius XII, encyclical "Sertum Laetitiae": AAS 31 (1939), p. 642; John XXIII, consistorial allocution: AAS 52 (1960), pp. 5-11; John XXIII, encyclical letter "Mater et Magistra": AAS 53 (1961), p. 411.
222. Cf. St. Thomas, "Summa Theol.": II-II q. 32, a. 5 ad 2; ibid. q. 66, a. 2; cf. explanation in Leo XIII, encyclical letter "Rerum Novarum": AAS 23 (1890-91) p. 651; cf. also Pius XII, allocution of June 1, 1941: AAS 33 (1941), p. 199; Pius XII, Christmas radio address 1954: AAS 47 (1955), p. 27.
223. Cf. St. Basil, Hom. in illud Lucae "Destruam horrea mea," Art. 2 (PG 31, 263); Lactantius, Divinarum institutionum, lib. V. on justice (PL 6, 565 B); St. Augustine, In Ioann. Ev. tr. 50, Art. 6 (PL 35, 1760); St. Augustine, Enarratio in Ps. CXLVII, 12 (PL 37, 192); St. Gregory the Great, Homiliae in Ev., hom. 20 (PL 76 1165); St. Gregory the Great, Regulae Pastoralis liber, pars III, c. 21 (PL 77, 87); St. Bonaventure, In III Sent. d. 33, dub. 1 (ed. Quacracchi, III, 728); St. Bonaventure, In IV Sent. d. 15, p. II, a.2 q.1 (ed. cit. IV, 371b); q. de superfluo (ms. Assisi, Bibl. Comun. 186, ff. 112a-113a); St. Albert the Great, In III Sent., d. 33, a.3, sol. 1 (ed. Borgnet XXVIII, 611); Id. In IV Sent. d. 15, a. 16 (ed. cit. XXIX, 494-497). As for the determination of what is superfluous in our day and age, cf. John XXIII, radio-television message of Sept. 11, 1962: AAS 54 (1962) p. 682: "The obligation of every man, the urgent obligation of the Christian man, is to reckon what is superfluous by the measure of the needs of others, and to see to it that the administration and the distribution of created goods serve the common good."
224. In that case, the old principle holds true: "In extreme necessity all goods are common, that is, all goods are to be shared." On the other hand, for the order, extension, and manner by which the principle is applied in the proposed text, besides the modern authors: cf. St. Thomas, "Summa Theol." II-II, q. 66, a. 7.

there are so many people in this world afflicted with hunger, this sacred Council urges all, both individuals and governments, to remember the saying of the Fathers: "Feed the man dying of hunger, because if you have not fed him you have killed him."[225] According to their ability, let all individuals and governments undertake a genuine sharing of their goods. Let them use these goods especially to provide individuals and nations with the means for helping and developing themselves.

In economically less advanced societies, it is not rare for the communal purpose of earthly goods to be partially satisfied through the customs and traditions proper to a community. By such means the absolute essentials are furnished to each member. If, however, customs cannot answer the new needs of this age, an effort must be made to avoid regarding them as altogether unchangeable. At the same time, rash action should not be taken against worthy customs which, provided that they are suitably adapted to present-day circumstances, do not cease to be very useful.

Similarly, in highly developed nations a body of social institutions dealing with insurance and security can, for its part, make the common purpose of earthly goods effective. Family and social services, especially those which provide for culture and education, should be further promoted. Still, care must be taken lest, as a result of all these provisions, the citizenry fall into a kind of sluggishness toward society, and reject the burdens of office and of public service.[226]

DISTRIBUTION AND MONEY

70. The distribution of goods should be directed toward providing employment and sufficient income for the people of today and of the future. Whether individuals, groups, or public authorities make the decisions concerning this distribution and the planning of the economy, they are bound to keep these objectives in mind. They must realize their serious obligation of seeing to it that provision is made for

---

Obviously, for the correct application of the principle, all the conditions that are morally required must be met.

225. *Cf. Gratian, Decretum, C. 21, dist. LXXXVI (ed. Friedberg I, 302). This axiom is also found already in PL 54, 591 A (cf. in Antonianum 27 [1952], 349-366).*

226. The Council here recognizes the peril of a civic lassitude or irresponsibility that may grow in the atmosphere of a social welfare society, but it properly insists that such a threat need not materialize if care is exercised. The Council obviously does not believe the danger to be so great or inevitable that it makes it imperative to abandon welfare programs.

the necessities of a decent life on the part of individuals and of the whole community. They must also look out for the future and establish a proper balance between the needs of present-day consumption, both individual and collective, and the necessity of distributing goods on behalf of the coming generation. They should also bear constantly in mind the urgent needs of underdeveloped countries and regions. In financial transactions they should beware of hurting the welfare of their own country or of other countries. Care should also be taken lest the economically weak countries unjustly suffer loss from a change in the value of money.

OWNERSHIP AND PROPERTY

71. Ownership and other forms of private control over material goods contribute to the expression of personality. Moreover, they furnish men with an occasion for exercising their role in society and in the economy. Hence it is very important to facilitate the access of both individuals and communities to some control over material goods.

Private ownership or some other kind of dominion over material goods provides everyone with a wholly necessary area of independence, and should be regarded as an extension of human freedom.[227] Finally, since it adds incentives for carrying on one's function and duty, it constitutes a kind of prerequisite for civil liberties.[228]

The forms of such dominion or ownership are varied today and are becoming increasingly diversified. They all remain a source of security not to be underestimated, even in the face of the public funds, rights, and services provided by society. This is true not only of material goods but also of intangible goods, such as professional skills.

The right of private control, however, is not opposed to the right inherent in various forms of public ownership. Still,

227. The Council's discussion of the institution of private property follows along somewhat the same lines as that adopted by John XXIII in his "Mater et Magistra." Thus, the stress here is on the necessity of private property, at least in principle, as a defense of human freedom. Pope John had insisted that the existence of other guarantees of freedom and economic security in a society was not sufficient to render the right of private ownership completely unnecessary.

228. Cf. Leo XIII, encyclical letter "Rerum Novarum": AAS 23 (1890-91), pp. 643-646; Pius XI, encyclical letter "Quadragesimo Anno": AAS 23 (1931), p. 191; Pius XII, radio message of June 1, 1941: AAS 33 (1941), p. 199; Pius XII, radio message on Christmas Eve 1942: AAS 35 (1943), p. 17; Pius XII, radio message of Sept. 1, 1944: AAS 36 (1944), p. 253; John XXIII, encyclical letter "Mater et Magistra": AAS 53 (1961), pp. 428-429.

goods can be transferred to the public domain only by the competent authority, according to the demands and within the limits of the common good, and with fair compensation. It is a further right of public authority to guard against any misuse of private property which injures the common good.[229]

By its very nature, private property has a social quality deriving from the law of the communal purpose of earthly goods.[230] If this social quality is overlooked, property often becomes an occasion of greed and of serious disturbances. Thus, to those who attack the concept of private property, a pretext is given for calling the right itself into question.

In many underdeveloped areas there are large or even gigantic rural estates which are only moderately cultivated or lie completely idle for the sake of profit. At the same time the majority of the people are either without land or have only very small holdings, and there is evident and urgent need to increase land productivity.[231]

It is not rare for those who are hired to work for the landowners, or who till a portion of the land as tenants, to receive a wage or income unworthy of human beings, to lack decent housing, and to be exploited by middlemen. Deprived of all security, they live under such personal servitude that almost every opportunity for acting on their own initiative and responsibility is denied to them, and all advancement in human culture and all sharing in social and political life are ruled out.

Depending on circumstances, therefore, reforms must be instituted if income is to grow, working conditions improve, job security increase, and an incentive to working on one's own initiative be provided. Indeed, insufficiently cultivated estates should be distributed to those who can make these lands fruitful. In this case, the necessary ways and means, especially educational aids and the right facilities for cooperative organization, must be supplied. Still, whenever the common good requires expropriation, compensation must be

---

229. Cf. Pius XI, encyclical letter "Quadragesimo Anno": AAS 23 (1931), p. 214; John XXIII, encyclical letter "Mater et Magistra": AAS 53 (1961), p. 429.
230. Cf. Pius XII, radio message of Pentecost 1941: AAS 44 (1941), p. 199; John XXIII, encyclical letter "Mater et Magistra": AAS 53 (1961), p. 430.
231. The problem of land reform is one that assumes urgent proportions in many nations today. Inequities in land distribution threaten to become a self-perpetuating force making for increasing social and economic inequality, though they are perhaps not so clearly the key to all economic problems that some would want to believe.

reckoned in equity after all the circumstances have been weighed.

ECONOMICS AND CHRIST'S KINGDOM

72. Christians who take an active part in modern socio-economic development and defend justice and charity should be convinced that they can make a great contribution to the prosperity of mankind and the peace of the world.[232] Whether they do so as individuals or in association, let their example be a shining one. After acquiring whatever skills and experience are absolutely necessary, they should in faithfulness to Christ and His gospel observe the right order of values in their earthly activities. Thus their whole lives, both individual and social, will be permeated with the spirit of the beatitudes, notably with the spirit of poverty.

Whoever in obedience to Christ seeks first the kingdom of God will as a consequence receive a stronger and purer love for helping all his brothers and for perfecting the work of justice under the inspiration of charity.[233]

CHAPTER IV

THE LIFE OF THE POLITICAL COMMUNITY

MODERN POLITICS

73. Our times have witnessed profound changes too in the institutions of peoples and in the ways that peoples are joined together. These changes are resulting from the cultural, economic, and social evolution of these same peoples. The

232. This passage should remove any possible question about the Council's positive judgment on direct social action as a logical expression of Christian commitment in the contemporary world.
233. *For the right use of goods according to the doctrine of the New Testament, cf. Lk. 3:11; 10:30 ff; 11:41; 1 Pet. 5:3; Mk. 8:36; 12:39-41; Jas. 5:1-6; 1 Tim. 6:8; Eph. 4:28; 2 Cor. 8:13; 1 Jn. 3:17 ff.*

changes are having a great impact on the life of the political community, especially with regard to universal rights and duties both in the exercise of civil liberty and in the attainment of the common good, and with regard to the regulation of the relations of citizens among themselves, and with public authority.

From a keener awareness of human dignity there arises in many parts of the world a desire to establish a political-juridical order in which personal rights can gain better protection. These include the rights of free assembly, of common action, of expressing personal opinions, and of professing a religion both privately and publicly.[234] For the protection of personal rights is a necessary condition for the active participation of citizens, whether as individuals or collectively, in the life and government of the state.

Among numerous people, cultural, economic, and social progress has been accompanied by the desire to assume a larger role in organizing the life of the political community. In many consciences there is a growing intent that the rights of national minorities be honored while at the same time these minorities honor their duties toward the political community. In addition men are learning more every day to respect the opinions and religious beliefs of others. At the same time a broader spirit of cooperation is taking hold. Thus all citizens, and not just a privileged few, are actually able to enjoy personal rights.

Men are voicing disapproval of any kind of government which blocks civil or religious liberty, multiplies the victims of ambition and political crimes, and wrenches the exercise of authority from pursuing the common good to serving the advantage of a certain faction or of the rulers themselves. There are some such governments holding power in the world.

No better way exists for attaining a truly human political life than by fostering an inner sense of justice, benevolence, and service for the common good, and by strengthening basic beliefs about the true nature of the political community, and about the proper exercise and limits of public authority.

NATURE AND GOAL OF POLITICS

74. Individuals, families, and various groups which compose

234. This affirmation of religious freedom simply echoes Pope John's encyclical "Pacem in Terris."

the civic community are aware of their own insufficiency in the matter of establishing a fully human condition of life. They see the need for that wider community in which each would daily contribute his energies toward the ever better attainment of the common good.[235] It is for this reason that they set up the political community in its manifold expressions.

Hence the political community exists for that common good in which the community finds its full justification and meaning, and from which it derives its pristine and proper right. Now, the common good embraces the sum of those conditions of social life by which individuals, families, and groups can achieve their own fulfillment in a relatively thorough and ready way.[236]

Many different people go to make up the political community, and these can lawfully incline toward diverse ways of doing things. Now, if the political community is not to be torn to pieces as each man follows his own viewpoint, authority is needed. This authority must dispose the energies of the whole citizenry toward the common good, not mechanically or despotically, but primarily as a moral force which depends on freedom and the conscientious discharge of the burdens of any office which has been undertaken.

It is therefore obvious that the political community and public authority are based on human nature and hence belong to an order of things divinely foreordained. At the same time the choice of government and the method of selecting leaders is left to the free will of citizens.[237]

It also follows that political authority, whether in the community as such or in institutions representing the state, must always be exercised within the limits of morality and on behalf of the dynamically conceived common good, according to a juridical order enjoying legal status. When such is the case citizens are conscience-bound to obey.[238] This fact clearly reveals the responsibility, dignity, and importance of those who govern.

Where public authority oversteps its competence and oppresses the people, these people should nevertheless obey to the extent that the objective common good demands. Still it

---

235. Cf. John XXIII, encyclical letter "Mater et Magistra": AAS 53 (1961), p. 417.
236. Cf. John XXIII, ibid.
237. Cf. Rom. 13:1-5.
238. Cf. Rom. 13:5.

is lawful for them to defend their own rights and those of their fellow citizens against any abuse of this authority, provided that in so doing they observe the limits imposed by natural law and the gospel.[239]

The practical ways in which the political community structures itself and regulates public authority can vary according to the particular character of a people and its historical development. But these methods should always serve to mold men who are civilized, peace-loving, and well disposed toward all—to the advantage of the whole human family.

POLITICAL PARTICIPATION

75. It is in full accord with human nature that juridical-political structures should, with ever better success and without any discrimination,[240] afford all their citizens the chance to participate freely and actively in establishing the constitutional bases of a political community, governing the state, determining the scope and purpose of various institutions, and choosing leaders.[241] Hence let all citizens be mindful of their simultaneous right and duty to vote freely in the interest of advancing the common good. The Church regards as worthy of praise and consideration the work of those who, as a service to others, dedicate themselves to the welfare of the state and undertake the burdens of this task.

If conscientious cooperation between citizens is to achieve its happy effect in the normal course of public affairs, a positive system of law is required. In it should be established a division of governmental roles and institutions and, at the same time, an effective and independent system for the protection of rights. Let the rights of all persons, families, and associations, along with the exercise of those rights, be rec-

239. The reference to limits here suggests the usefulness of such classic concepts as that of the conditions for a just war. A key criterion would be the preservation of a true proportion between the good end to be sought and the amount of force to be employed. In our time it is clear that many would read the gospel as dictating recourse, wherever possible, to nonviolence.

240. The Constitution has already made it clear that there can be no identification of a single political system as the only choice open to a people as *the* requirement of human dignity (cf. Art. 74). This passage stresses, however, the full compatibility of maximal representative government with the dignity of the human person. Here is clearly an advance from the suspicions of democracy that found favor in so many areas of Catholic thought throughout the nineteenth and into the present century.

241. Cf. *Pius XII, radio message, Dec. 24, 1942: AAS 35 (1943), pp. 9-24; Dec. 24, 1944: AAS 37 (1945), pp. 11-17; John XXIII, encyclical letter "Pacem in Terris": AAS 55 (1963), pp. 263, 271, 277, and 278.*

ognized, honored, and fostered.[242] The same holds for those duties which bind all citizens. Among the latter should be remembered that of furnishing the commonwealth with the material and spiritual services required for the common good.

Authorities must beware of hindering family, social, or cultural groups, as well as intermediate bodies and institutions. They must not deprive them of their own lawful and effective activity, but should rather strive to promote them willingly and in an orderly fashion. For their part, citizens both as individuals and in association should be on guard against granting government too much authority and inappropriately seeking from it excessive conveniences and advantages, with a consequent weakening of the sense of responsibility on the part of individuals, families, and social groups.

Because of the increased complexity of modern circumstances, government is more often required to intervene in social and economic affairs, by way of bringing about conditions more likely to help citizens and groups freely attain to complete human fulfillment with greater effect. The proper relationship between socialization[243] on the one hand and personal independence and development on the other can be variously interpreted according to the locales in question and the degree of progress achieved by a given people.

When the exercise of rights is temporarily curtailed on behalf of the common good, it should be restored as quickly as possible after the emergency passes. In any case it harms humanity when government takes on totalitarian or dictatorial forms injurious to the rights of persons or social groups.

Citizens should develop a generous and loyal devotion to their country, but without any narrowing of mind. In other words, they must always look simultaneously to the welfare of the whole human family, which is tied together by the manifold bonds linking races, peoples, and nations.

Let all Christians appreciate their special and personal vocation in the political community. This vocation requires that they give conspicuous example of devotion to the sense of duty and of service to the advancement of the common good. Thus they can also show in practice how authority is to be harmonized with freedom, personal initiative with con-

242. Cf. Pius XII, radio message of June 7, 1941: AAS 33 (1941), p. 200: John XXIII, encyclical letter "Pacem in Terris": l. c., p. 273 and 274.
243. Cf. John XXIII, encyclical letter "Mater et Magistra": AAS 53 (1961), p. 416.

sideration for the bonds uniting the whole social body, and necessary unity with beneficial diversity.

Christians should recognize that various legitimate though conflicting views can be held concerning the regulation of temporal affairs. They should respect their fellow citizens when they promote such views honorably even by group action.[244] Political parties should foster whatever they judge necessary for the common good. But they should never prefer their own advantage over this same common good.

Civic and political education is today supremely necessary for the people, especially young people. Such education should be painstakingly provided, so that all citizens can make their contribution to the political community. Let those who are suited for it, or can become so, prepare themselves for the difficult but most honorable art of politics.[245] Let them work to exercise this art without thought of personal convenience and without benefit of bribery. Prudently and honorably let them fight against injustice and oppression, the arbitrary rule of one man or one party, and lack of tolerance. Let them devote themselves to the welfare of all sincerely and fairly, indeed with charity and political courage.

POLITICS AND THE CHURCH

76. It is highly important, especially in pluralistic societies, that a proper view exist of the relation between the political community and the Church. Thus the faithful will be able to make a clear distinction between what a Christian conscience leads them to do in their own name as citizens, whether as individuals or in association, and what they do in the name of the Church and in union with her shepherds.

The role and competence of the Church being what it is, she must in no way be confused with the political community, nor bound to any political system.[246] For she is at once

---

244. The Constitution here proposes a standard of respect for differences of viewpoint and expression that ought to be observed not merely by individual Christians but also by the political authority. This should mean, concretely, respect for what is known in the United States as real freedom of the press, of assembly, and of petition.

245. *Pius XI, allocution "Ai dirigenti della Federazione Universitaria Cattolica": Discorsi di Pio XI (ed. Bertetto), Turin, vol. 1 (1960), p. 743.*

246. It is important to note that the Church is here distinguishing itself sharply from the State or political community as such. Its relation to the general society is something else again and is a matter dealt with elsewhere in the Constitution. At one point the Church is seen as fulfilling a unique function with respect to human society and it should be said that it is thus distinct from society, but not separate from or outside of it.

a sign and a safeguard of the transcendence of the human person.

In their proper spheres, the political community and the Church are mutually independent and self-governing. Yet, by a different title, each serves the personal and social vocation of the same human beings. This service can be more effectively rendered for the good of all, if each works better for wholesome mutual cooperation, depending on the circumstances of time and place. For man is not restricted to the temporal sphere. While living in history he fully maintains his eternal vocation.

The Church, founded on the Redeemer's love, contributes to the wider application of justice and charity within and between nations. By preaching the truth of the gospel and shedding light on all areas of human activity through her teaching and the example of the faithful, she shows respect for the political freedom and responsibility of citizens and fosters these values.

The apostles, their successors, and those who assist these successors have been sent to announce to men Christ, the Savior of the world. Hence in the exercise of their apostolate they must depend on the power of God, who very often reveals the might of the gospel through the weakness of its witnesses. For those who dedicate themselves to the ministry of God's Word should use means and helps proper to the gospel. In many respects these differ from the supports of the earthly city.[247]

There are, indeed, close links between earthly affairs and those aspects of man's condition which transcend this world. The Church herself employs the things of time to the degree that her own proper mission demands. Still she does not lodge her hope in privileges conferred by civil authority. Indeed, she stands ready to renounce the exercise of certain legitimately acquired rights if it becomes clear that their use raises doubt about the sincerity of her witness or that new conditions of life demand some other arrangement.

But it is always and everywhere legitimate for her to preach the faith with true freedom, to teach her social doc-

---

247. The simplest interpretation of this statement would seem to be that the Church renounces as foreign to its mission the use of certain means or approaches that may have been employed in the past under varying historical circumstances. Without rendering judgment on the appropriateness of such past practices in their time, the Council insists here on commitment to those ways and means that are truly proper.

trine, and to discharge her duty among men without hindrance. She also has the right to pass moral judgments, even on matters touching the political order, whenever basic personal rights or the salvation of souls make such judgments necessary. In so doing, she may use only those helps which accord with the gospel and with the general welfare as it changes according to time and circumstance.[248]

Holding faithfully to the gospel and exercising her mission in the world, the Church consolidates[249] peace among men, to God's glory. For it is her task to uncover, cherish, and ennoble[250] all that is true, good, and beautiful in the human community.

CHAPTER V

THE FOSTERING OF PEACE AND THE PROMOTION OF A COMMUNITY OF NATIONS

INTRODUCTION

77. In our generation when men continue to be afflicted by acute hardships and anxieties arising from ongoing wars or the threat of them, the whole human family has reached an hour of supreme crisis in its advance toward maturity. Moving gradually together and everywhere more conscious already of its oneness, this family cannot accomplish its task of constructing for all men everywhere a world more genuinely human unless each person devotes himself with renewed de-

---

248. Since the Church recognizes that the effectiveness of its ministry depends both on fidelity to its own inner nature and on the credit it enjoys among men for disinterestedness, it stands ready to renounce anything that smacks of worldly ambition or self-seeking even though perfectly proper in itself.
249. *Cf. Lk. 2:14.*
250. *Cf. Second Vatican Council, dogmatic constitution "Lumen Gentium," Art. 13: AAS 57 (1965), p. 17.*

termination to the reality of peace. Thus it happens that the gospel message, which is in harmony with the loftier strivings and aspirations of the human race, takes on a new luster in our day as it declares that the artisans of peace are blessed, "for they shall be called children of God" (Mt. 5:9).

Consequently, as it points out the authentic and most noble meaning of peace and condemns the frightfulness of war, this Council fervently desires to summon Christians to cooperate with all men in making secure among themselves a peace based on justice and love, and in setting up agencies of peace.[251] This Christians should do with the help of Christ, the Author of peace.

THE NATURE OF PEACE

78. Peace is not merely the absence of war. Nor can it be reduced solely to the maintenance of a balance of power between enemies. Nor is it brought about by dictatorship. Instead, it is rightly and appropriately called "an enterprise of justice" (Is. 32:7). Peace results from that harmony built into human society by its divine Founder, and actualized by men as they thirst after ever greater justice.

The common good of men is in its basic sense determined by the eternal law. Still the concrete demands of this common good are constantly changing as time goes on. Hence peace is never attained once and for all, but must be built up ceaselessly. Moreover, since the human will is unsteady and wounded by sin, the achievement of peace requires that everyone constantly master his passions and that lawful authority keep vigilant.

But such is not enough. This peace cannot be obtained on earth unless personal values are safeguarded and men freely and trustingly share with one another the riches of their inner spirits and their talents. A firm determination to respect other men and peoples and their dignity, as well as the studied practice of brotherhood, are absolutely necessary for the establishment of peace. Hence peace is likewise the fruit of love, which goes beyond what justice can provide.

251. The choice of language in this passage sets the tone and manifests the intent of the entire section on war and peace. It is clear that the Council wishes to avoid academic discussions or the style of casuistic debate. It is also clear that the drafting of this section was influenced in both style and substance by John XXIII's "Pacem in Terris." The appositeness of Paul VI's address on Oct. 4, 1965, to the United Nations General Assembly in New York was recognized by the Council Fathers and provision was made, at the suggestion of many, to have the text of this speech inserted in the official "Acta" of the Council.

That earthly peace which arises from love of neighbor symbolizes and results from the peace of Christ who comes forth from God the Father. For by His cross the incarnate Son, the Prince of Peace, reconciled all men with God. By thus restoring the unity of all men in one people and one body, He slew hatred in His own flesh.[252] After being lifted on high by His resurrection, He poured the Spirit of love into the hearts of men.

For this reason, all Christians are urgently summoned "to practice the truth in love" (Eph. 4:15) and to join with all true peacemakers in pleading for peace and bringing it about.

Motivated by this same spirit, we cannot fail to praise those who renounce the use of violence in the vindication of their rights and who resort to methods of defense which are otherwise available to weaker parties too, provided that this can be done without injury to the rights and duties of others or of the community itself.[253]

Insofar as men are sinful, the threat of war hangs over them, and hang over them it will until the return of Christ. But to the extent that men vanquish sin by a union of love, they will vanquish violence as well, and make these words come true: "They shall beat their swords into plowshares and their spears into pruning hooks; one nation shall not raise the sword against another, nor shall they train for war again" (Is. 2:4).*

Section 1: The Avoidance of War

CURBING THE SAVAGERY OF WAR

79. In spite of the fact that recent wars have wrought physical and moral havoc on our world, conflicts still produce their devastating effect day by day somewhere in the world. Indeed, now that every kind of weapon produced by modern science is used in war, the fierce character of warfare threatens to lead the combatants to a savagery far surpassing that of the past. Furthermore, the complexity of the

---

252. Cf. Eph. 2:16; Col. 1:20-22.
253. Here, as in the following Article's reference to the treatment of conscientious objectors, the Constitution does not demand sacrifice of the principle or right of self-defense. Its language is strongly positive, however, in referring to those who espouse a policy of nonviolence.
*1961 CCD transl.—Ed.

modern world and the intricacy of international relations allow guerrilla warfare to be drawn out by new methods of deceit and subversion. In many cases the use of terrorism is regarded as a new way to wage war.[254]

Contemplating this melancholy state of humanity, the Council wishes to recall first of all the permanent binding force of universal natural law and its all-embracing principles. Man's conscience itself gives ever more emphatic voice to these principles. Therefore, actions which deliberately conflict with these same principles, as well as orders commanding such actions, are criminal. Blind obedience cannot excuse those who yield to them. Among such must first be counted those actions designed for the methodical extermination of an entire people, nation, or ethnic minority.[255] These actions must be vehemently condemned as horrendous crimes. The courage of those who openly and fearlessly resist men who issue such commands merits supreme commendation.

On the subject of war, quite a large number of nations have subscribed to various international agreements aimed at making military activity and its consequences less inhuman. Such are conventions concerning the handling of wounded or captured soldiers, and various similar agreements. Agreements of this sort must be honored. Indeed they should be improved upon so that they can better and more workably lead to restraining the frightfulness of war.

All men, especially government officials and experts in these matters, are bound to do everything they can to effect these improvements. Moreover, it seems right that laws make humane provisions for the case of those who for reasons of conscience refuse to bear arms, provided however, that they accept some other form of service to the human community.[256]

Certainly, war has not been rooted out of human affairs.

254. The Constitution simply points to a problem which has bedeviled the United Nations and world leaders for some years.
255. The reference here is unmistakably to genocide and the post-World War II controversy over responsibility for "war crimes" and the culpability of subordinates under a corrupt regime. There can be no justification of the conduct of an Eichmann on the score that he simply executed commands from higher authorities. The praise given those who resisted unjust commands comes appropriately in the context of a document that stresses so repeatedly the importance of human dignity and the responsibility of a free human person.
256. The Constitution is careful in its statement of concern in this passage. The text makes no judgment on the objective moral claim of the conscientious

As long as the danger of war remains and there is no competent and sufficiently powerful authority at the international level, governments cannot be denied the right to legitimate defense once every means of peaceful settlement has been exhausted.[257] Therefore, government authorities and others who share public responsibility have the duty to protect the welfare of the people entrusted to their care and to conduct such grave matters soberly.

But it is one thing to undertake military action for the just defense of the people, and something else again to seek the subjugation of other nations. Nor does the possession of war potential make every military or political use of it lawful. Neither does the mere fact that war has unhappily begun mean that all is fair between the warring parties.

Those who are pledged to the service of their country as members of its armed forces should regard themselves as agents of security and freedom on behalf of their people. As long as they fulfill this role properly, they are making a genuine contribution to the establishment of peace.

TOTAL WAR

80. The horror and perversity of war are immensely magnified by the multiplication of scientific weapons. For acts of war involving these weapons can inflict massive and indiscriminate destruction far exceeding the bounds of legitimate defense. Indeed, if the kind of instruments which can now be found in the armories of the great nations were to be employed to their fullest, an almost total and altogether reciprocal slaughter of each side by the other would follow, not to mention the widespread devastation which would take place in the world and the deadly aftereffects which would be spawned by the use of such weapons.

All these considerations compel us to undertake an evaluation of war with an entirely new attitude.[258] The men of

objector. It neither accepts nor rejects the arguments in support of such a position. It simply appeals in the name of equity for humane treatment under the law of those who experience difficulties of conscience with respect to bearing arms.
257. Here the Constitution makes it clear that the right of self-defense on the part of governments is also to be acknowledged. The text recalls the traditional moral demand that all means short of force be employed first, but it refuses to call for total renouncement of force by individual nations until an adequate international security force actually exists.
258. *Cf. John XXIII, encyclical letter "Pacem in Terris," Apr. 11, 1963: AAS 55 (1963), p. 291: "Therefore in this age of ours which prides itself on its atomic*

our time must realize that they will have to give a somber reckoning for their deeds of war. For the course of the future will depend largely on the decisions they make today.[259]

With these truths in mind, this most holy Synod makes its own the condemnations of total war already pronounced by recent Popes,[260] and issues the following declaration:

Any act of war aimed indiscriminately at the destruction of entire cities or of extensive areas along with their population is a crime against God and man himself. It merits unequivocal and unhesitating condemnation.

The unique hazard of modern warfare consists in this: it provides those who possess modern scientific weapons with a kind of occasion for perpetrating just such abominations. Moreover, through a certain inexorable chain of events, it can urge men on to the most atrocious decisions. That such in fact may never happen in the future, the bishops of the whole world, in unity assembled, beg all men, especially government officials and military leaders, to give unremitting thought to the awesome responsibility which is theirs before God and the entire human race.[261]

THE ARMS RACE

81. Scientific weapons, to be sure, are not amassed solely for use in war. The defensive strength of any nation is considered to be dependent upon its capacity for immediate retaliation against an adversary. Hence this accumulation of arms, which increases each year, also serves, in a way heretofore unknown, as a deterrent to possible enemy attack. Many regard this state of affairs as the most effective way by which peace of a sort can be maintained between nations at the present time.

Whatever be the case with this method of deterrence, men

power, it is irrational to believe that war is still an apt means of vindicating violated rights."

259. The "new attitude" spoken of in the Constitution is one that was concretized in Pope John's "Pacem in Terris" and given eloquent expression in Pope Paul's United Nations address. The following sentence contains one of the few uses of the term "condemnation" in the record of Vatican II. It is clear that the usage is a popular one.

260. *Cf. Pius XII, allocution of Sept. 30, 1954: AAS 46 (1954), p. 589; radio message of Dec. 24, 1954: AAS 47 (1955), pp. 15 ff; John XXIII, encyclical letter "Pacem in Terris": AAS 55 (1963), pp. 286-291; Paul VI, allocution to the United Nations, Oct. 4, 1965.*

261. One hears in these words an echo of the voices of Pius XII and John XXIII as they appealed to men of power to recall that everything is lost in war.

should be convinced that the arms race in which so many countries are engaged is not a safe way to preserve a steady peace. Nor is the so-called balance resulting from this race a sure and authentic peace. Rather than being eliminated thereby, the causes of war threaten to grow gradually stronger.

While extravagant sums are being spent for the furnishing of ever new weapons, an adequate remedy cannot be provided for the multiple miseries afflicting the whole modern world. Disagreements between nations are not really and radically healed. On the contrary other parts of the world are infected with them. New approaches initiated by reformed attitudes must be adopted to remove this trap and to restore genuine peace by emancipating the world from its crushing anxiety.

Therefore, it must be said again: the arms race is an utterly treacherous trap for humanity, and one which injures the poor to an intolerable degree.[262] It is much to be feared that if this race persists, it will eventually spawn all the lethal ruin whose path it is now making ready.

Warned by the calamities which the human race has made possible, let us make use of the interlude granted us from above and in which we rejoice. In greater awareness of our own responsibility let us find means for resolving our disputes in a manner more worthy of man. Divine Providence urgently demands of us that we free ourselves from the age-old slavery of war. But if we refuse to make this effort, we do not know where the evil road we have ventured upon will lead us.

THE TOTAL BANNING OF WAR, AND INTERNATIONAL ACTION FOR AVOIDING WAR

82. It is our clear duty, then, to strain every muscle as we work for the time when all war can be completely outlawed by international consent. This goal undoubtedly requires the establishment of some universal public authority acknowledged as such by all, and endowed with effective power to safeguard, on the behalf of all, security, regard for justice, and respect for rights.

But before this hoped-for authority can be set up, the highest existing international centers must devote themselves

262. In a world that has become increasingly conscious of the enormous economic and social inequalities that exist between groups and among nations, the perennial debate over "arms or butter" has become more urgent than ever.

vigorously to the pursuit of better means for obtaining common security. Peace must be born of mutual trust between nations rather than imposed on them through fear of one another's weapons. Hence everyone must labor to put an end at last to the arms race, and to make a true beginning of disarmament, not indeed a unilateral disarmament, but one proceeding at an equal pace according to agreement, and backed up by authentic and workable safeguards.[263]

In the meantime, efforts which have already been made and are still under way to eliminate the danger of war are not to be underrated. On the contrary, support should be given to the good will of the very many leaders who work hard to do away with war, which they abominate. Though burdened by the enormous preoccupations of their high office, these men are nonetheless motivated by the very grave peacemaking task to which they are bound, even if they cannot ignore the complexity of matters as they stand.

We should fervently ask God to give these men the strength to go forward perseveringly and to follow through courageously on this work of building peace with vigor. It is a work of supreme love for mankind. Today it most certainly demands that these leaders extend their thoughts and their spirit beyond the confines of their own nation, that they put aside national selfishness and ambition to dominate other nations, and that they nourish a profound reverence for the whole of humanity, which is already making its way so laboriously toward greater unity.[264]

The problems of peace and of disarmament have already been the subject of extensive, strenuous, and relentless examination. Together with international meetings dealing with these problems, such studies should be regarded as the first steps toward solving these serious questions. They should be promoted with even greater urgency in the hope that they will yield practical results in the future.

Nevertheless, men should take heed not to entrust themselves only to the efforts of others, while remaining careless about their own attitudes. For government officials, who must simultaneously guarantee the good of their own people and promote the universal good, depend on public opinion

---

263. Cf. John XXIII, encyclical letter "Pacem in Terris," where reduction of arms is mentioned: AAS 55 (1963), p. 287.
264. The Council Fathers recognize the dedicated spirit of men in authority in many nations. Throughout this chapter of the Constitution a ceaseless effort has been made to avoid any appearance of taking sides in political disputes.

and feeling to the greatest possible extent. It does them no good to work at building peace so long as feelings of hostility, contempt, and distrust, as well as racial hatred and unbending ideologies, continue to divide men and place them in opposing camps.

Hence arises a surpassing need for renewed education of attitudes and for new inspiration in the area of public opinion. Those who are dedicated to the work of education, particularly of the young, or who mold public opinion, should regard as their most weighty task the effort to instruct all in fresh sentiments of peace.[265] Indeed, every one of us should have a change of heart as we regard the entire world and those tasks which we can perform in unison for the betterment of our race.

But we should not let false hope deceive us. For enmities and hatred must be put away and firm, honest agreements concerning world peace reached in the future. Otherwise, for all its marvelous knowledge, humanity, which is already in the middle of a grave crisis, will perhaps be brought to that mournful hour in which it will experience no peace other than the dreadful peace of death.

But, while we say this, the Church of Christ takes her stand in the midst of the anxiety of this age, and does not cease to hope with the utmost confidence. She intends to propose to our age over and over again, in season and out of season, this apostolic message: "Behold, now is the acceptable time" for a change of heart; "behold, now is the day of salvation!"[266]

Section 2: Building Up the International Community

THE CAUSES AND CURES OF DISCORD

83. If peace is to be established, the primary requisite is to eradicate the causes of dissension between men. Wars thrive on these, especially on injustice. Many of these causes stem

265. This reference to the responsibilities toward world peace of those charged with educating the young or forming public opinion would indicate possible failures in the past. Certainly there must be a strong commitment to an international spirit imparted in any sound educational program. The press and other mass media of communications, particularly those sectors under religious direction, must examine their consciences on past performance in this area.
266. Cf. 2 Cor. 2:6.

from excessive economic inequalities and from excessive
slowness in applying the needed remedies. Other causes spring
from a quest for power and from contempt for personal
rights. If we are looking for deeper explanations, we can find
them in human jealousy, distrust, pride, and other egotistic
passions.

Man cannot tolerate so many breakdowns in right order.
What results is that the world is ceaselessly infected with
arguments between men and acts of violence, even when war
is not raging. Moreover, these same evils are found in relationships between nations. Hence, if such evils are to be
overcome or prevented, and violence kept from becoming
unbridled, it is altogether necessary that international institutions cooperate to a better and surer extent and that they be
coordinated. Also, unwearying efforts must be made to create
agencies for the promotion of peace.[267]

THE COMMUNITY OF NATIONS
AND INTERNATIONAL ORGANIZATIONS

84. Today the bonds of mutual dependence become increasingly close between all citizens and all the peoples of the
world. The universal common good needs to be intelligently
pursued and more effectively achieved. Hence it is now necessary for the family of nations to create for themselves an
order which corresponds to modern obligations, particularly
with reference to those numerous regions still laboring under
intolerable need.

For the attainment of these goals, agencies of the international community should do their part to provide for the
various necessities of men. In the field of social life this
means food, health, education, and employment. In certain
situations which can obtain anywhere, it means the general
need to promote the growth of developing nations, to attend
to the hardships of refugees scattered throughout the world,
or to assist migrants and their families.

The international agencies, both universal and regional,
which already exist assuredly deserve well of the human race.
These stand forth as the first attempts to lay international
foundations under the whole human community for the solv-

267. It was obviously part of Pope Paul's intention in visiting the United Nations
headquarters on Oct. 4, 1965, to promote the chief organization designed to foster
peace on the world scene. It will be recalled that he determined to make the visit
for this purpose, despite gloomy forecasts of failure and forebodings in some
high quarters.

ing of the critical problems of our age, the promotion of global progress, and the prevention of any kind of war. The Church rejoices at the spirit of true fraternity flourishing between Christians and non-Christians in all these areas. This spirit strives to see that ever more intense efforts are made for the relief of the world's enormous miseries.[268]

INTERNATIONAL COOPERATION AT THE ECONOMIC LEVEL

85. The modern interconnection between men also demands the establishment of greater international cooperation in the economic field. For although nearly all peoples have gained their independence, it is still far from true that they are free from excessive inequalities and from every form of undue dependence, or that they have put behind them danger of serious internal difficulties.

The development of any nation depends on human and financial assistance. Through education and professional formation, the citizens of each nation should be prepared to shoulder the various offices of economic and social life. Such preparation needs the help of foreign experts. When they render assistance, these experts should do so not in a lordly fashion, but as helpers and co-workers.

The developing nations will be unable to procure the necessary material assistance unless the practices of the modern business world undergo a profound change. Additional help should be offered by advanced nations, in the form of either grants or investments. These offers should be made generously and without avarice. They should be accepted honorably.

If an economic order is to be created which is genuine and universal, there must be an abolition of excessive desire for profit, nationalistic pretensions, the lust for political domination, militaristic thinking, and intrigues designed to spread and impose ideologies.

Proposals are made in favor of numerous economic and social systems. It is to be hoped that experts in such affairs will find common bases for a healthy world trade. This hope will be more readily realized if individuals put aside their personal prejudices and show that they are prepared to undertake sincere discussions.

---

268. This passage picks up the theme of interreligious cooperation enunciated in the Council's Declaration on the Relationship of the Church to Non-Christian Religions.

SOME USEFUL NORMS

86. The following norms would seem to be appropriate for this cooperation:

a) Developing nations should strongly desire to seek the complete human fulfillment of their citizens as the explicit and fixed goal of progress. Let them be mindful that progress begins and develops primarily from the efforts and endowments of the people themselves. Hence, instead of depending solely on outside help, they should rely chiefly on the full unfolding of their own resources and the cultivation of their own qualities and tradition. Those who have greater influence on others should be outstanding in this respect.

b) As for the advanced nations, they have a very heavy obligation to help the developing peoples in the discharge of the aforementioned responsibilities. If this world-wide collaboration is to be established, certain psychological and material adjustments will be needed among the advanced nations and should be brought about.

Thus these nations should carefully consider the welfare of weaker and poorer nations when negotiating with them. For such nations need for their own livelihood the income derived from the sale of domestic products.

c) The international community should see to the coordination and stimulation of economic growth. These objectives must be pursued in such a way, however, that the resources organized for this purpose can be shared as effectively and justly as possible. This same community should regulate economic relations throughout the world so that they can unfold in a way which is fair. In so doing, however, the community should honor the principle of subsidiarity.*

Let adequate organizations be established for fostering and harmonizing international trade, especially with respect to the less advanced countries, and for repairing the deficiencies

---

*The principle of subsidiarity formulated by Pope Pius XI in the encyclical letter "Quadragesimo Anno" reads: "This supremely important principle of social philosophy, one which cannot be set aside or altered, remains firm and unshaken: Just as it is wrong to withdraw from the individual and commit to the community at large what private enterprise and endeavor can accomplish, so it is likewise unjust and a gravely harmful disturbance of right order to turn over to a greater society of higher rank functions and services which can be performed by lesser bodies on a lower plane. For a social undertaking of any sort, by its very nature, ought to aid the members of the body social, but never to destroy and absorb them." AAS 23 (1931), p. 203; quoted by Pope John XXIII in encyclical letter "Mater et Magistra," AAS 53 (1961), p. 414.—Ed.

caused by an excessive disproportion in the power possessed by various nations. Such regulatory activity, combined with technical, cultural, and financial help, ought to afford the needed assistance to nations striving for progress, enabling them to achieve economic growth expeditiously.

d) In many instances there exists a pressing need to reform economic and social structures. But nations must beware of technical solutions immaturely proposed, especially those which offer men material advantages while militating against his spiritual nature and development. For, "Not by bread alone does man live, but by every word that comes forth from the mouth of God" (Mt. 4:4). Each branch of the human family possesses in itself and in its worthier traditions some part of the spiritual treasure entrusted by God to humanity, even though many do not know the source of this treasure.[269]

INTERNATIONAL COOPERATION IN THE MATTER OF POPULATION

87. International cooperation becomes supremely necessary with respect to those peoples who, in addition to many other problems, are today often enough burdened in a special way with the difficulties stemming from a rapid population growth. There is an urgent need for all nations, especially the richer ones, to cooperate fully and intensely in an exploration as to how there can be prepared and distributed to the human community whatever is required for the livelihood and proper training of men. Some peoples, indeed, would greatly better their conditions of life if they could be duly trained to abandon ancient methods of farming in favor of modern techniques. With necessary prudence they should adapt these techniques to their own situations. In addition they need to establish a better social order and regulate the distribution of land with greater fairness.

Within the limits of their own competence, government officials have rights and duties with regard to the population problems of their own nation, for instance, in the matter of social legislation as it affects families, of migration to cities, of information relative to the condition and needs of the nation. Since the minds of men are so powerfully disturbed about this problem, the Council also desires that, especially

---

269. This passage repeats a theme from the opening paragraphs of the conciliar Declaration on the Relationship of the Church to Non-Christian Religions.

in universities, Catholic experts in all these aspects should skillfully pursue their studies and projects and give them an ever wider scope.[270]

Many people assert that it is absolutely necessary for population growth to be radically reduced everywhere or at least in certain nations. They say this must be done by every possible means and by every kind of government intervention. Hence this Council exhorts all to beware against solutions contradicting the moral law, solutions which have been promoted publicly or privately, and sometimes actually imposed.

For in view of the inalienable human right to marry and beget children, the question of how many children should be born belongs to the honest judgment of parents. The question can in no way be committed to the decision of government. Now since the judgment of the parents supposes a rightly formed conscience, it is highly important that every one be given the opportunity to practice upright and truly human responsibility. This responsibility respects the divine law and takes account of circumstances and the times. It requires that educational and social conditions in various places be changed for the better, and especially that religious instruction or at least full moral training be provided.

Human beings should also be judiciously informed of scientific advances in the exploration of methods by which spouses can be helped in arranging the number of their children. The reliability of these methods should be adequately proven and their harmony with the moral order should be clear.[271]

THE DUTY OF CHRISTIANS TO PROVIDE SUPPORT

88. Christians should collaborate willingly and wholeheartedly in establishing an international order involving genuine respect for all freedoms and amicable brotherhood between

270. The tone of this passage is clearly different from that of the section in "Mater et Magistra" (188-192), dealing with population problems and birth control. The text admits the reasonableness of formulating an official policy on population growth in a nation. It can be noted that in the United States a small number of Catholic specialists have been at work for some time on the questions raised in this passage. Some systematic investigations have been conducted at Catholic universities, notably Georgetown and Notre Dame.
271. This sentence lends official sanction to such efforts as the family-planning clinics sponsored in a growing number of dioceses in the United States. The approval given here would obviously not extend to programs designed to encourage limitation of births by recourse to abortion or similar morally unacceptable methods.

all men. This objective is all the more pressing since the greater part of the world is still suffering from so much poverty that it is as if Christ Himself were crying out in these poor to beg the charity of the disciples.

Some nations with a majority of citizens who are counted as Christians have an abundance of this world's goods, while others are deprived of the necessities of life and are tormented with hunger, disease, and every kind of misery. This situation must not be allowed to continue, to the scandal of humanity. For the spirit of poverty and of charity are the glory and authentication of the Church of Christ.

Christians, especially young people, are to be praised and supported, therefore, when they volunteer their services to help other men and nations. Indeed, it is the duty of the whole People of God, following the word and example of the bishops, to do their utmost to alleviate the sufferings of the modern age. As was the ancient custom in the Church, they should meet this obligation out of the substance of their goods, and not only out of what is superfluous.

Without being inflexible and completely uniform, the collection and distribution of aid should be conducted in an orderly fashion in dioceses, nations, and throughout the entire world. (Wherever it seems appropriate, this activity of Catholics should be carried on in unison with other Christian brothers.272) For the spirit of charity does not forbid but rather requires that charitable activity be exercised in a provident and orderly manner. Therefore, it is essential for those who intend to dedicate themselves to the service of the developing nations to be properly trained in suitable institutions.

EFFECTIVE PRESENCE OF THE CHURCH ON THE INTERNATIONAL SCENE

89. In pursuit of her divine mission, the Church preaches the gospel to all men and dispenses the treasures of grace. Thus, by imparting knowledge of the divine and natural law, she everywhere contributes to strengthening peace and to placing brotherly relations between individuals and peoples on solid

272. The work of Catholic agencies such as the American Catholic Relief Services—NCWC, the German Catholic Misereor program, etc., would be a model for further efforts in this direction. It is a matter of record that in the field some of these agencies have been engaged rather extensively in ecumenical cooperation with other Christian bodies. The World Council of Churches at a meeting in Enugu, in January of 1965, spelled out a positive attitude toward systematic fostering of such cooperation.

ground. Therefore, to encourage and stimulate cooperation among men, the Church must be thoroughly present in the midst of the community of nations. She must achieve such a presence both through her public institutions and through the full and sincere collaboration of all Christians, a collaboration motivated solely by the desire to be of service to all.

This goal will come about more effectively if the faithful themselves, conscious of their responsibility as men and as Christians, strive to stir up in their own area of influence a willingness to cooperate readily with the international community. In both religious and civic education, special care must be given to the proper formation of youth in this respect.

THE ROLE OF CHRISTIANS IN INTERNATIONAL INSTITUTIONS

90. An outstanding form of international activity on the part of Christians undoubtedly consists in the cooperative efforts which, as individuals and in groups, they make to institutes established for the encouragement of cooperation among nations. The same is true of their efforts to establish such agencies. There are also various international Catholic associations which can serve in many ways to construct a peaceful and fraternal community of nations. These deserve to be strengthened by an increase in the number of well-qualified associates and in the needed resources. Let them be fortified too by a suitable coordination of their energies. For today effective action as well as the need for dialogue demand joint projects.

Moreover, such associations contribute much to the development of a universal outlook—something certainly appropriate for Catholics. They also help to form an awareness of genuine universal solidarity and responsibility.

Finally, this Council desires that by way of fulfilling their role properly in the international community, Catholics should seek to cooperate actively and in a positive manner both with their separated brothers, who together with them profess the gospel of love, and with all men thirsting for true peace.

In view of the immense hardships which still afflict the majority of men today, the Council regards it as most opportune that some agency of the universal Church be set up for the world-wide promotion of justice for the poor and of

Christ's kind of love for them. The role of such an organization will be to stimulate the Catholic community to foster progress in needy regions, and social justice on the international scene.[273]

CONCLUSION

THE ROLE OF INDIVIDUAL BELIEVERS AND DIOCESES

91. Drawn from the treasures of Church teaching, the proposals of this sacred Synod look to the assistance of every man of our time, whether he believes in God, or does not explicitly recognize Him. Their purpose is to help men gain a sharper insight into their full destiny, so that they can fashion the world more to man's surpassing dignity, search for a brotherhood which is universal and more deeply rooted, and meet the urgencies of our age with a gallant and unified effort born of love.

Undeniably this conciliar program is but a general one in several of its parts—and deliberately so, given the immense variety of situations and forms of human culture in the world. Indeed, while it presents teaching already accepted in the Church, the program will have to be further pursued and amplified, since it often deals with matters in a constant state of development. Still, we have relied on the Word of God and the spirit of the gospel. Hence we entertain the hope that many of our proposals will be able to bring substantial benefit to everyone, especially after they have been adapted to individual nations and mentalities by the faithful, under the guidance of their pastors.

DIALOGUE BETWEEN ALL MEN

92. By virtue of her mission to shed on the whole world the

---

273. Much of the initial support for this conciliar recommendation came from a handful of interested parties that included Bishop Edward Swanstrom, Father Arthur MacCormack, and James J. Norris. Mr. Norris, who has been associated for some years with the United States Catholic Relief Services organization, was also a lay auditor at the Council.

radiance of the gospel message, and to unify under one Spirit all men of whatever nation, race, or culture, the Church stands forth as a sign of that brotherliness which allows honest dialogue and invigorates it.

Such a mission requires in the first place that we foster within the Church herself mutual esteem, reverence, and harmony, through the full recognition of lawful diversity. Thus all those who compose the one People of God, both pastors and the general faithful, can engage in dialogue with ever-abounding fruitfulness.[274] For the bonds which unite the faithful are mightier than anything which divides them. Hence, let there be unity in what is necessary, freedom in what is unsettled, and charity in any case.

Our hearts embrace also those brothers and communities not yet living with us in full communion. To them we are linked nonetheless by our profession of the Father and the Son and the Holy Spirit, and by the bond of charity. We are mindful that the unity of Christians is today awaited and desired by many, too, who do not believe in Christ. For the further it advances toward truth and love under the powerful impulse of the Holy Spirit, the more this unity will be a harbinger of unity and peace for the world at large.

Therefore, by common effort and in ways which are today increasingly appropriate for seeking this splendid goal effectively, let us take pains to pattern ourselves after the gospel more exactly every day, and thus work as brothers in rendering service to the human family. For in Christ Jesus this family is called into the family of the sons of God.

We also turn our thoughts to all who acknowledge God, and who preserve in their traditions precious elements of religion and humanity. We want frank conversation to compel us all to receive the inspirations of the Spirit faithfully and to measure up to them energetically.

For our part, the desire for such dialogue, which can lead to truth through love alone, excludes no one, though an appropriate measure of prudence must undoubtedly be exer-

274. The goal of a true dialogue within the Church was a concern of Pope John XXIII, and there is reason to believe that he looked on the summoning of an Ecumenical Council as a means to that end. It is Pope Paul, however, in his encyclical "Ecclesiam Suam," who has spelled out in detail the nature and scope of such a dialogue: "We would have it responsive to all truth and virtue and to all the realities of our doctrinal and spiritual inheritance. Sincere and ready in genuine spirituality, ever ready to give ear to the manifold voice of the contemporary world, ever more capable of making Catholics truly good men, men wise, free, serene, and strong: that is what we earnestly desire our family conversation to be" (117).

cised. We include those who cultivate beautiful qualities of the human spirit, but do not yet acknowledge the Source of these qualities.

We include those who oppress the Church and harass her in manifold ways.[275] Since God the Father is the origin and purpose of all men, we are all called to be brothers. Therefore, if we have been summoned to the same destiny, which is both human and divine, we can and we should work together without violence and deceit in order to build up the world in genuine peace.

BUILDING UP THE WORLD AND FULFILLING ITS PURPOSE

93. Mindful of the Lord's saying: "By this will all men know that you are my disciples, if you have love for one another" (Jn. 13:35), Christians cannot yearn for anything more ardently than to serve the men of the modern world ever more generously and effectively. Therefore, holding faithfully to the gospel and benefiting from its resources, and united with every man who loves and practices justice, Christians have shouldered a gigantic task demanding fulfillment in this world. Concerning this task they must give a reckoning to Him who will judge every man on the last day.

Not everyone who cries, "Lord, Lord," will enter into the kingdom of heaven, but those who do the Father's will and take a strong grip on the work at hand. Now, the Father wills that in all men we recognize Christ our brother and love Him effectively in word and in deed. By thus giving witness to the truth, we will share with others the mystery of the heavenly Father's love. As a consequence, men throughout the world will be aroused to a lively hope—the gift of the Holy Spirit—that they will finally be caught up in peace and utter happiness in that fatherland radiant with the splendor of the Lord.

"Now, to him who is able to accomplish all things in a measure far beyond what we ask or conceive, in keeping with the power that is at work in us—to him be glory in the

---

275. It is worth calling attention to the fact that a tone of quiet dignity and a deliberate avoidance of all polemical tendencies has characterized this last of the great conciliar texts of Vatican II. In this respect the Fathers of the Council remained true to the end to the vision of John XXIII. The late Pope in his historic opening address to the Council on Oct. 11, 1962, had spoken of the Church in our time using the "medicine of mercy" rather than measures of stern harshness. In a true sense his words and the deeds of the Council have marvelously revealed a Church at work at its essential ministry of healing or reconciliation.

Church and in Christ Jesus down through all the ages of time without end. Amen" (Eph. 3:20-21).

Each and every one of the things set forth in this Pastoral Constitution has won the consent of the Fathers of this most sacred Council. We too, by the apostolic authority conferred on us by Christ, join with the Venerable Fathers in approving, decreeing, and establishing these things in the Holy Spirit, and we direct that what has thus been enacted in synod be published to God's glory.

Rome, at St. Peter's, December 7, 1965

I, Paul, Bishop of the Catholic Church

There follow the signatures of the Fathers.

A RESPONSE

It would have been possible for the Second Vatican Council to concern itself solely with internal affairs—the reform of the liturgy, a fresh look at seminary education, and so on—and it is highly significant that rather than doing so the Council also turned outward to examine the ways in which a Church subject to "reform and renewal" should relate to those beyond its walls.

It is symbolically important that the Pastoral Constitution on the Church in the Modern World and the Declaration on Religious Freedom were promulgated on the last working day of the Council, so that the Council concluded on a note of concern for others.

Furthermore, since "The Church in the Modern World" is addressed "not only to the sons of the Church and to all who invoke the name of Christ, but to the whole of humanity" (Art. 2), this Council document is in a unique way the property of all men, and its significance may well be measured more by the degree to which it draws men together to implement its concerns than by the specific content of its paragraphs. Thus a Protestant evaluation is less a treatment of what "they" wrote, than an examination of what the document calls upon "us" to do.

Before engaging in either of these tasks, however, it is important to clarify what we should and should not expect of such a document. Those who anticipated a clear-cut manifesto from the Council, offering specific answers to each of the world's ills, have of course been disappointed. But it should have been clear long since that such a manifesto was beyond both the intent and the competence of the Council. There is no "answer" to a given problem of economic organization, for example, that applies equally to Ghana, Ireland, the United States, and Communist China. And even though the document contains a number of "prophetic" utterances, it would have been wrong to expect a prophetic manifesto from a 2,300-man deliberative assembly; prophetism does not thrive on majorities.

Let it also be granted that the document on many occasions is far too prolix, too general, and therefore sometimes disappointing. But, particularly considering the conditions under which it had to be prepared, debated, and revised, and the consensus it had to reflect, there is cause for astonishment that it should be as clear, concise, and specific as on so many occasions it is. If it is not the last word on "the Church in the modern world," it is an immeasurably important first word on a subject to which Catholicism has given far too little attention in the past. The critic who is still unconvinced that the document ushers in a new era is invited to compare it with an earlier Catholic treatment of the same issues—the Syllabus of Errors—and see if he does not emerge from the comparison rejoicing.

"The Church in the Modern World" deserves, and will receive, whole volumes of commentary and critique. All that can be offered here is a sampling of reactions by one reader. As a Protestant studies this document, he finds many emphases that encourage him, and with which he can make common cause.

1. Most important is the positive attitude toward "the world" that is in evidence throughout the document. In the past, there has been much Protestant negativism toward the world and the flesh, and until very recently "secularism" was the favorite whipping boy of Catholic apologists—all of which was a denial of the goodness of creation, and much of which leaned perilously close to a kind of Manichean or gnostic dualism. But "The Church in the Modern World" adopts an affirmative stance from the beginning. To Christians, "nothing genuinely human fails to raise an echo in their hearts" (Art. 1; cf. also Art. 3). "Man is not allowed to despise his bodily life" (Art. 14). "Men are not deterred by the Christian message from building up the world . . ." (Art. 34).

This means, among other things, a willingness on the part of the Church to learn from the world, as well as speak to the world. This may have been even clearer in earlier drafts of the document (cf. the statement, "We should listen to the voice of God . . . in the voice of the times," in the draft debated at session three), but the concern exemplified by that statement is still present in the final document, with its assertion that Christians must "recognize and understand the world in which we live" (Art. 4), and in the importance for them "of scrutinizing the signs of the times and of interpreting them in the light of the gospel" (Art. 4). There are even occasional hints that the Council Fathers have listened to the gospel of Marx as well as the gospel of Mark (cf. Art. 30).

This positive view of the world has the further corollary

that all men must work together for the betterment of the human lot. There is, of course, a special opportunity for Christians to work together: "The Catholic Church gladly holds in high esteem the things which other Christian Churches or ecclesial communities have done or are doing cooperatively by way of achieving the same goal" (Art. 40). What begins as statement ends as exhortation: "Wherever it seems appropriate, this activity of Catholics [of collecting and distributing aids] should be carried on in unison with other Christian brothers" (Art. 88 and cf. Art. 90).

The widening circumference of cooperative possibilities is clarified in the closing paragraphs, where various arenas of dialogue and cooperation are delineated: (a) the dialogue within the Church, recognizing lawful diversity, (b) dialogue with "those brothers and communities not yet living with us in full communion," (c) with "all who acknowledge God," (d) with those "who cultivate beautiful qualities of the human spirit, but do not yet acknowledge the Source of these qualities," and finally (e) with "those who oppress the Church and harass her in manifold ways" (Art. 92). This openness extends even to atheists, for "while rejecting atheism, root and branch, the Church sincerely professes that all men, believers and unbelievers alike, ought to work for the rightful betterment of this world in which all alike live" (Art. 21).

Another corollary of this positive attitude is reflected in a new kind of openness. There is a recognition that "new forms of art . . . may be brought into the sanctuary," that the faithful should "blend modern science and its theories and the understanding of the most recent discoveries with Christian morality and doctrine," and that teachers of theology should "try to collaborate with men well-versed in the other sciences" (Art. 62, cf. also Art. 57).

This openness is likewise exemplified by certain things the Council did *not* say. It is significant that despite strong pressures the Council did not use the document as an occasion for another wholesale condemnation of communism. It is strikingly consistent with Pope John's initial concern that the Council not issue condemnations and anathemas, that the present document, rather than engaging in anti-Communist diatribes, seeks ways in which dialogue can be fostered between men of differing convictions.

2. Important also are the twin recognitions that the Church, along with all Christians, must bear a large measure

of responsibility for the present plight of the world, and that
rather than striving to rule in the affairs of men, the Church
must offer herself as a servant to men. The document is free
of the kind of "triumphalism" that has often characterized
Catholic (and also Protestant) ecclesiasticism. Rather than
placing all blame on atheists, for example, for their lack of
belief, the document acknowledges that "believers themselves
frequently bear some responsibility for this situation" (Art.
19). Since atheism often arises in reaction to deficiencies in
the "religious, moral or social life" of believers, the latter
"have more than a little to do with the birth of atheism"
(Art. 19).

In even more sweeping terms, lack of full fidelity to the
gospel on the part of Catholics is acknowledged as an important cause of man's unhappy condition today. "The
Church . . . is very well aware that among her members,
both clerical and lay, some have been unfaithful to the Spirit
of God during the course of many centuries. In the present
age, too, it does not escape the Church how great a distance
lies between the message she offers and the human failings
of those to whom the gospel is entrusted" (Art. 43).

The Church, in seeking to remedy this situation must offer
herself as the servant Church. An early paragraph sets the
tone for all that follows: "Inspired by no earthly ambition,
the Church seeks but a solitary goal: to carry forward the
work of Christ Himself under the lead of the befriending
Spirit. And Christ entered this world to give witness to the
truth, to rescue and not to sit in judgment, to serve and not
to be served" (Art. 3).

The overall principle is given explicit content later in the
document. The Church, it is asserted, "does not lodge her
hope in privileges conferred by civil authority. Indeed, she
stands ready to renounce the exercise of certain legitimately
acquired rights, if it becomes clear that their use raises doubt
about the sincerity of her witness or that new conditions
of life demand some other arrangement" (Art. 76).

3. In the light of the attention focused on religious liberty
at Vatican II, the buttressing given to this theme within the
present document is encouraging. Because of the "growing
awareness of the exalted dignity proper to the human person . . . there must be made available to all men everything
necessary for leading a life truly human . . . [including]
rightful freedom in matters religious too" (Art. 26). Again,
"Respect and love ought to be extended also to those who

think or act differently than we do in social, political, and religious matters too" (Art. 28). The specific implications of this are spelled out later on, in a guarantee of "the right of free assembly, of common action, of expressing personal opinions, and of professing a religion both privately and publicly" (Art. 73; cf. also Art. 28, with its echoing of *Pacem in Terris*).

4. The stress put upon lay activity and involvement is also important. While the Vatican Council did not achieve the full emancipation of the laity, it did register significant theological advances in the Constitution on the Church, some of which were consolidated in the Decree on the Apostolate of the Laity. But "The Church in the Modern World" may actually provide more leverage than the latter document.

If Article 43 seems almost to remove the priest from an active role in the life of the world, it at least opens the way clearly to the laity. There is an explicit denial that the seeking of a heavenly city can discharge from the Christian his responsibility to reshape the earthly one. And in this task, the layman is urged, in a crucial phrase, to "take on his own distinctive role" (Art. 43). It is even pointed out that the pastor's insights may not be distinctive or helpful, and that lay initiative, quite apart from what a pastor may suggest, is to be encouraged.

This gradual emergence of the layman, so much a theme of conciliar speeches and concerns, may turn out to be one of the most important advances registered by Vatican II, and "The Church in the Modern World" will be one of the documents most often cited in making the point.

5. One particular insight about the nature of humanity is worth underscoring. There has often been a tendency for Christians to exalt the individual and his rights in such a way that an individualist understanding of humanity emerges. "The Church in the Modern World," however, is very clear that man *qua* man must be understood in social terms. He is not an individual who becomes social; he is a being whose individuality can be understood only in and through his social relations.

"This social life," the document insists, "is not something added on to man" (Art. 25). For this reason, "Man's social nature makes it evident that the progress of the human person and the advance of society itself hinge on each other" (Art. 25). This is important not merely as an anthropological insight, but for its obvious corollaries in the field of social

action; it renders untenable the frequent attempt to describe
Christian ethical responsibility in purely individual terms
(e.g., "religion and politics don't mix") and underscores the
need for corporate human action on a large scale to help
large groups of people. The interdependence of all men and
societies can thus be stressed, and even the word "socialization," so often suspect in ecclesiastical circles, can be employed positively rather than pejoratively (Art. 25).

6. Space does not permit an extended analysis of the specific problems discussed in Part Two of the document. It
should be noted, however, that the best emphases of the
"social encyclicals" have been incorporated into the chapter
on "Economic and Social Life" (Art. 63-72), and that these
Articles are among the best in the entire document.

The reiteration of the rights of collective bargaining, of
unionizing and of striking, are set forth unambiguously, and
there are passages on the need for land reform that will be
helpful to Churches in underdeveloped areas and parts of
the world where feudal attitudes still prevail.

The material on war, while subject to much reworking
within the Council, and certainly unsatisfactory to pacifists,
does provide some checks on the inordinate use of power. Indeed, the fact that a small group of American bishops felt
the document too sweeping in its indictment of nuclear weapons is a left-handed tribute.

It would be a less than responsible critic who simply offered praise. If the document is to be a first rather than a last
word, we have an obligation to suggest areas in which further
clarification is needed. Again, only a sampling of such suggestions is possible.

1. The most obvious instance of this need is in the material
on marriage. The document does register one very important
advance, for it goes far beyond the traditional teaching that
the procreation and education of children are the primary
ends of marriage. Thanks to the interventions of such men as
Cardinals Léger and Suenens, the document stresses the importance of conjugal love. Sexual love between men and
women is clearly distinguished from "the dispositions of lower
forms of life" (Art. 51)—where one has a suspicion it often
used to linger in the thought of earlier moral theologians.
Pure conjugal love "involves the good of the whole person"
(Art. 49). In such statements the lie is given to the notion
that sex in marriage is evil, or only a concession to con-
cupiscence, or valid only for procreation.

But it must also be recorded that the section is deliberately ambiguous on the relation of this insight to birth control. At many points the document only reiterates "traditional" teaching, and pessimists (at least Protestant pessimists) will be inclined to read it exclusively in such terms. Actually, in spite of strong efforts to foreclose discussion of birth control, the Council deliberately left the matter open, and thus achieved at least a modest victory. The crucial "footnote 14" (173) of the chapter on marriage not only cites the traditional teaching of *Casti Connubii,* but also cites Paul VI's speech to the papal commission on birth control, noting that a fresh examination of the problem is called for. The Protestant commentator cannot underscore too strongly that the matter needs resolution, since not only Roman Catholics are affected by the matter, but other persons as well, for whom the denial of birth control information to non-Catholics desiring to have it constitutes a serious moral as well as social problem.

2. Having registered appreciation for the document's positive approach to the world, a caveat must now be entered. There is a danger that in the laudable desire to affirm the world, the document may affirm it too uncritically.

Although proper in the context in which it is cited, the statement that "the Church knows that her message is in harmony with the most secret desires of the human heart" (Art. 21), illustrates a temptation throughout the document to assume that the gospel crowns the life of natural man, rather than being, as well, a challenge to, and judgment upon, that life. The document minimizes the degree to which the gospel is also a scandal and a stumbling-block, by which men can be offended as well as uplifted. (At a number of the press conferences in Rome, one could detect a desire on the part of defenders of the *schema* to explain controversial portions in such a way that they would not seem "offensive.") The making of common cause with others must not be achieved at the price of blunting the uniqueness and distinctiveness of the Christian message.

In subsequent Catholic reflection upon this problem, then, it can be hoped that the brief references to the relationship of eschatology and ethics (cf. Art. 39) will be further developed. Similarly, although the final version is more realistic about man's sin than were earlier drafts, there needs to be more recognition of the pervasiveness of sin in men and human institutions, so that the hopes raised by the tone of the document will not be unnecessarily dimmed by the hard realities of the world. The ongoing power of evil is a theme to which more attention could have been given. If this be Protestant pessimism, it is at least a pessimism we have learned from Scripture and tradition as well as from the daily newspaper.

3. After urging Catholics to cooperate with all men, the document then suggests "that some agency of the universal Church be set up for the world-wide promotion of justice for the poor and of Christ's kind of love for them. The role of such an organization will be to stimulate the Catholic community to foster progress in needy regions, and social justice on the international scene" (Art. 90). Although it is hard to know toward what this broad description points, the non-Catholic will hope that after so many statements about working with separated brethren and all men of good will, the Catholic Church will not begin (as the quotation suggests) to set up new structures, parallel to and competing with those already existing. The quotation seems out of harmony with the rest of the document, and one hopes that the spirit of cooperation, stressed elsewhere, will prevail over it.

While hoping that the ongoing debate will point to further areas needing development and clarification, it must be stressed in conclusion that the document contains so many opportunities for ecumenical social involvement that it will be as important to implement the document's strong points as to improve its weak ones.

ROBERT MCAFEE BROWN

COMMUNICATIONS

THIS IS ONE of nine decrees passed by the Second Vatican Ecumenical Council. The others concerned relations with the Oriental Churches, priests, bishops, renewal of religious life, the apostolate of the laity, missionary activity, priestly formation, and ecumenism.

The decrees are documents with practical significance. They differ from the four constitutions, which are documents expressive of broad theological views, and from the three declarations, which are statements of particular principles.

This communications Decree is one of the first two documents approved by the Council. It was passed at the final meeting of the second session of the Council, on December 4, 1963, by a vote of 1,960 to 164. The other document approved on the same day was the Constitution on the Sacred Liturgy.

In approving and promulgating the Decree, Pope Paul said that it was "not of small value," and that it demonstrates the capacity of the Church "to unite the interior and the exterior life, contemplation and action, prayer and the active apostolate."

One can speculate, however, that, if this Decree had been discussed later in the Council, after the many sessions devoted to the Church in the modern world and to religious freedom, the texture of the Decree might have been somewhat richer. As it now stands, it seems somewhat ironic that the Church, which is basically concerned with communicating truth and life to the world, and has shown, especially in the period of the Council, an awareness of the importance of mass means of communication, issued the slightest document of the Council on the media of social communication.

The Decree, however, does mark the first time that a general Council of the Church addressed itself to the problem of communication. It is important for this more than for its content. The Decree also marks the first general mandate of the Church to the clergy and laity on the use of communications media.

The late Father Gustave Weigel, S.J., said at the United States Bishops' press panel session, November 14, 1963: "The Decree does not strike me as being very remarkable. It is not going to produce great changes. It does not contain novel positions, but gathers and officially states a number of points previously stated and taught on a less official level."

THOMAS J. M. BURKE, S.J.

Decree on the Instruments of Social Communication

PAUL, BISHOP
SERVANT OF THE SERVANTS OF GOD
TOGETHER WITH THE FATHERS OF THE SACRED COUNCIL
FOR EVERLASTING MEMORY

1. By divine favor, especially in modern times, human genius has produced from natural material astonishing inventions in the field of technology. Some of these have extraordinary bearing on the human spirit,[1] since they open up new and highly effective avenues of communication for all kinds of information, ideas, and directives.

As a Mother, the Church welcomes and watches such inventions with special concern. Chief among them are those which by their very nature can reach and influence not only individual men, but the masses themselves, even the whole of society. Such would be the press, the cinema, radio, television, and similar media,[2] which can be properly classified as instruments of social communication.[3]

1. Although the need for communication and the basic pattern of communication are as old as man himself, it could be argued that the omnipresence and increase in technical means of communication, especially in the more developed countries, are producing a change "in kind" in human communication and thus basically affecting the human spirit.
2. The listing of media given shows that the Decree is concerned with what are commonly classified as the mass media of communications. No significant attention is given directly in the decree to the forces which, in effect, program the mass media, for example, advertising, marketing, public relations, propaganda, and psychological operations.
3. It is of great importance that the Council uses the phrase "instruments of social communication." The radical importance of communication to man as a social being is perhaps being fully realized only in our time. In many previous historical statements, man's character as a social being was described in terms of groups such as the family, neighborhood, national society, etc. But the increase in technology has produced what might be called the

2. Mother Church, to be sure, recognizes that if these instruments are rightly used they bring solid nourishment to the human race. For they can contribute generously to the refreshment and refinement of the spirit, and to the spread and strengthening of God's own kingdom.

But the Church is also aware that men can employ these gifts against the mind of the divine Benefactor, and abuse them to their own undoing. In fact, the Church grieves with a motherly sorrow at the damage far too often inflicted on society by the perverse use of these media.

For all these reasons, this most sacred Synod follows the path of vigilance shown by Supreme Pontiffs and bishops in so weighty a matter, and regards it a duty to deal with the main problems presented by the instruments of social communication. Moreover, the Council feels sure that the principles and directives thereby proposed will foster not only the welfare of Christians but the advancement of the human family as a whole.

CHAPTER I

3. The Catholic Church has been commissioned by the Lord Christ to bring salvation to every man, and is consequently bound to proclaim the gospel. Hence she judges it part of her duty[4] to preach the news of redemption with the aid of the instruments of social communication, and to instruct mankind as well in their worthy use.

Therefore the Church claims as a birthright the use and possession of all instruments of this kind which are necessary or useful for the formation of Christians and for every activity undertaken on behalf of man's salvation.

On religious shepherds devolves the task of so training and directing the faithful that by the help of these instruments,

communications group, people affected by and joined together by particular communicators or particular organs and programs of communications media. The communication group is a prime socializing force; it can be at variance with, and more flexible than, the historic biological and social groups.
4. The first chapter, in its opening paragraphs, asserts, for the first time in a general document of the Church, the obligation and right of the Church to use the instruments of social communication.

too, they may pursue their own salvation and fulfillment, and that of the entire human family.

For the rest, it is the layman's particular obligation to animate these instruments with a humane and Christian spirit. Thus will they abundantly satisfy the high hopes of mankind and the will of God Himself.

4. If these instruments are to be properly employed, it is absolutely necessary that all who use them know the norms of morality and apply them faithfully in this field. They should, therefore, consider the subject matter, which each instrument will communicate in its own way. At the same time, they should thoughtfully weigh all those circumstantial elements which define an action of communication and can modify its moral quality or even reverse it entirely. These include questions of intention, audience, place, and time.[5]

Pertinent, too, is the characteristic way in which a given instrument achieves its effect. Its power may be so compelling that people, especially if they are caught off guard, may scarcely be able to appreciate it, to moderate it, or, when necessary, to reject it.[6]

5. A special need exists for everybody concerned to develop an upright conscience on the use of these instruments, particularly with respect to certain issues which are rather sharply debated in our times.

The first question pertains to what is called "information," i.e., the search for news and the publication of it. Indeed because of the advances of contemporary society and the closer bonds linking its members together, the information process has clearly grown very useful and generally necessary. For an

5. Note that the statement about the norms of morality is carefully restricted by the statement that the circumstantial elements of intention, audience, place, and time must be considered in judging the morality of a particular communication.
6. The phrase "to appreciate it" is literally "to perceive it" *(eamdem animadvertere).* This would seem to comprehend subliminal and subaudial projection of messages to audiences in television, radio, and the cinema. It is a documented fact that an audience because of pre-set attitudes can resist the formal message of a television or film or printed communication. What has not been investigated with any degree of thoroughness is the ability or inability of the same audience to reject or even be aware of indirect persuasion by means of casual comments, secondary characters, or the settings of the same communication, especially when such "indirect" persuasion is carried on for an extensive period. Important also to the estimate of the power of communications would be their emotional effects, which are scarcely mentioned in the document.

open and timely revelation of events and affairs provides
individuals with a grasp of them which is sustained and considerably detailed. As a result, men can actively contribute to
the common good and all can more easily foster the development of the whole civic community.

Hence there exists within human society a right to information about affairs which affect men individually or collectively,
and according to the circumstances of each.[7] The proper exercise of this right demands that the matter communicated always be true, and as complete as charity and justice allow.
The manner of communication should furthermore be honorable and appropriate; this means that in the gathering and
publication of news the norms of morality and the legitimate
rights and dignity of a man must be held sacred. For knowledge is sometimes unprofitable, "but charity edifies" (1 Cor.
8:1).[8]

6. The second question bears on the connection between what
is called art and the rights and norms of the moral law. The
increasing disputes on this subject frequently spring from
ethical and artistic theories which are false. Hence the Council asserts that the primacy of the objective moral order demands absolute allegiance, for this order alone excels and
rightly integrates all other fields of human concern, including art, however lofty their value. Only the moral order
touches man in his total nature as God's reasoning creature,
summoned heavenwards. If this order is fully and faithfully
respected, it leads a man to a rich measure of fulfillment
and happiness.[9]

7. Finally, with the help of the media of social communication
too, the narration, description, or portrayal of moral evil can

7. This paragraph contains what is probably the most important statement
of the document. It asserts the existence within human society of a right
to information about affairs which affect man individually or collectively.
This right is predicated in foregoing sentences on the ability which it gives
men to actively contribute to the common good and to the whole civic
community.
8. The reference to the First Epistle to the Corinthians is to St. Paul's
statement that "knowledge puffs up but charity edifies." In St. Paul's context
the word "knowledge" is used ironically. It pertains more closely to what
we would call sophistication. The contrast St. Paul is making could be
paraphrased as that between the blasé and the genuinely concerned. The
word "edifies" is a favorite of Paul's, derived from the Old Testament. It
means, literally, "to build up," and is connected with the notion that
humanity is building up the soul and the Church as God's temple.
9. In connection with Art. 6 and 7, it would be well to refer back to Art.
4 and also to much of the Declaration on Religious Freedom.

indeed serve to make man more deeply known and studied, and to reveal and enhance the grandeur of truth and goodness. Such aims are achieved by means of appropriately heightened dramatic effects. Still, moral norms must prevail if harm rather than spiritual profit is not to ensue. This requirement is especially needed when the subjects treated are entitled to reverence, or may all too easily trigger base desires in man, wounded as he is by original sin.

8. Today public opinion exerts massive force and authority over the private and public life of every class of citizen.[10] Hence the necessity arises for every member of society to do what justice and charity require in this matter. With the aid of these instruments, then, each man should strive to form and to voice worthy views on public affairs.

9. Special duties bind those readers, viewers, or listeners who personally and freely choose to receive what these media have to communicate. For good choosing dictates that ample favor be shown to whatever fosters virtue, knowledge, or art.[11] People should reject whatever could become a cause or an occasion of spiritual harm to themselves, whatever could endanger others through bad example, and whatever would impede good selections and promote bad ones. The last effect generally results when financial support is given to men who exploit these media for commercial reasons.

If those who use these media are to honor the moral law, they must not neglect to inform themselves in good time of the judgments made in these affairs by competent authority. These judgments they should respect according to the requirements of a good conscience. By taking pains to guide and settle their conscience with appropriate help, they will more readily thwart less honorable influences and amply support those which are worthy.

10. People, especially the young, should take care to de-

10. It would be well to consult many of the recognized works on the force of public opinion which have been written since the middle of the last century, and also many statements *passim* of Pope Pius XII on public opinion in the Church. A convenient summary is provided by the pastoral letter of Richard Cardinal Cushing, Archbishop of Boston, issued on Good Shepherd Sunday, April 19, 1963, entitled "The Church and Public Opinion."
11. This paragraph correlates with good choosing among the various media the necessity of showing favor to what fosters virtue, knowledge, or art, and the withholding of financial support from those who commercially exploit various media for bad reasons.

velop moderation and self-control in the use of these instruments. Their goal should be an ever more discerning grasp of what they see, hear, and read. Discussions with educators and appropriate experts will school them to make mature judgments.

Parents should be mindful of their duty to guard against shows, publications, and the like which would jeopardize faith or good morals. Let them see that such things never cross the thresholds of their homes and that their children do not encounter them elsewhere.

11. The chief moral duties respecting the proper use of instruments of social communication fall on newsmen, writers, actors, designers, producers, exhibitors, distributors, operators, and sellers, critics, and whoever else may have a part of any kind in making and transmitting products of communication.[12] For it is quite clear what heavy responsibilities are given to all such persons in the present state of affairs. By molding and activating the human race they can lead it upward or to ruin.

On these persons, then, will lie the task of regulating the commercial, political, and artistic aspects of these media in ways which will never conflict with the common good. They will merit praise if they aim to secure this goal more certainly by joining professional groups which expect from their members reverence for moral laws in the affairs and regulations of their art. If necessary, these associations should require adherence to a code of ethical conduct.

In any case, these responsible persons should never forget that much of their audience consists of young people who have need of literature and shows that can give them decent amusement and inspiration. They should also see to it that worthy and competent men are put in charge of religious features and that such matters are handled with proper reverence.

12. In this whole field, civil authority is bound by special duties in terms of the common good, to which these instru-

12. Art. 11 is important for placing the chief responsibility for proper use of these instruments upon the people who are actively engaged in their use rather than upon government. In some of the early unfavorable comments upon this document, the priority given to the professionals in the various media was not fully credited. The paragraph also gives approval to the role of professional groups and approves, if necessary, the codes of ethical conduct now developed or being developed by many professionals.

ments are subordinate.[13] This authority is duty bound to defend and protect a true and just availability of information; the progress of modern society utterly depends on this, especially as regards freedom of the press. This authority should foster religion,[14] culture, and fine arts;[15] it should protect consumers in the free exercise of their lawful rights. It should also assist the undertaking of projects which could not other-

13. Whereas professionals were listed as having the chief moral duties in respect to the proper use of these instruments, the civic authority is said to have special duties in terms of the common good. In consonance with the right of information averred earlier in the document, Art. 12 places as the first duty of civic authority to foster and protect a true and just availability of information, since the progress of modern society depends on it.

In this connection it is well to consult the text of the Freedom of Information bill passed by the United States Senate on Oct. 13, 1965. The bill was designed to strengthen the public's access to news about the activities of Federal departments and agencies. Especially instructive are the hearings held before the Subcommittee on Administrative Practice and Procedure of the Committee on the Judiciary of the United States Senate, which indicate both the necessity of government action to protect the right of the public to information about government and the difficulties of invasion of privacy and personal damage to be considered in legislating such disclosure.

The Senate Judiciary Committee in urging passage of its bill said that "although the theory of an informed electorate is vital to the proper operation of a democracy, there is now nowhere in our present law a statute which provides for that information."

Cf. also the Report of the Special Study of Securities Markets, issued in Oct., 1963, by the Securities and Exchange Commission, which has some important sections on the protection of the public's right to know.

Specifically with regard to protection of freedom of the press, cf. the libel decision of the Supreme Court on Mar. 9, 1964, which established in the case of Montgomery, Alabama (Police Commissioner L. B. Sullivan against the *New York Times)* that newspapers cannot be sued for libel in criticizing public acts of public officials, even if the criticisms are in error, unless actual malice can be proved.

On the general subject of the availability of information from civil authority, cf. the serious questions raised in many articles, from the time of the "Bay of Pigs" incident to the present, about manipulation of information by government to serve particular policies and the practice of closing traditional avenues of information to inquiring news people.

Cf. also the survey done by the Associated Press for publication on Jan. 3, 1965, which indicated the state of censorship, direct and indirect, in various countries around the world. The survey showed that apart from direct censorship—direct changes by government of correspondents' stories—censorship at the source, in which information is restricted which might prove embarrassing to a government, is quite widespread. This is over and above the restriction of military information, which is vital to defense. There also exists, rather widely, a censorship of "responsibility" under which correspondents can be criticized or expelled for filing stories considered unfavorable by particular officials of an administration in power.

14. On fostering religion, cf. the Council's Declaration on Religious Freedom.
15. On culture and the fine arts, cf. the discussion leading up to, and the texts establishing, in 1964, the National Foundation on the Arts and the Humanities.

wise be initiated, despite their extreme usefulness, especially for young people.

Finally public authority, which properly concerns itself with the health of its citizens, has the duty of seeing to it in a just and vigilant manner that serious danger to public morals and social progress do not result from a perverted use of these instruments. This goal should be achieved by enactment of laws and their energetic enforcement.[16] The freedom of individuals and groups is not at all infringed upon by such watchful care, especially if those who have taken on themselves the responsibility of using these media have failed to observe sensible cautions.

Particular effort should be expended to protect youngsters from literature and shows which would be injurious to them at their age.

CHAPTER II[17]

13. With common heart and mind, let all the sons of the Church strive immediately and most energetically to use the instruments of social communication effectively[18] in the many fields of the apostolate, as the circumstances and the times require. These efforts should head off hurtful enterprises, especially in those places where moral and religious needs dictate a more active zeal.

Religious shepherds should speedily fulfill their duties in this field, closely connected as it is with their normal preaching responsibilities. Laymen who have a role in using these instruments should be busy giving witness to Christ, especially by

16. There are in the United States certain legal restrictions on lobbying, and on propaganda activities by government toward its own people. These restrictions have never proved very effective. The present state of disagreement in society about public morals seems to impede at the moment any very effective use of law as called for in this Decree.

17. Chapter One dealt with the teaching of the Church. Chapter Two deals with the pastoral activity of the Church concerning the instruments of social communication.

18. Cf. Art. 3, which gives the basis for the detailed implications here explored. Note that, in the detailed consideration of various media, the obligation of professional skill is usually placed prior to apostolic ardor.

performing their duties skillfully and with apostolic ardor. In their own way, let them also lend direct aid to the pastoral action of the Church through their technical, economic, cultural, and artistic abilities.

14. First of all, worthy journalism should be encouraged. By way of thoroughly inculcating a Christian spirit in its readers, a Catholic press worthy of the name should also be established and supported. Whether it is published and run by direct ecclesiastical authority or by Catholic laymen, let it be clearly edited with this goal: that it may form,[19] strengthen, and spread public views which are in harmony with the natural law, and with Catholic teachings and precepts; let it publicize and correctly interpret facts which pertain to the life of the Church. The faithful should be advised of the necessity of reading and circulating the Catholic press if they are to make Christian evaluations of all that happens.

The production and showing of films which serve honest relaxation as well as culture and art, especially those meant for young people, should be promoted and guaranteed by every effective means. Catholics can see to this especially by supporting and even joining those forces and enterprises which involve honorable producers and distributors; by commending praiseworthy films through critical acclaim and awards; by patronizing theatres managed by upright Catholics and others —theatres which would do well to form associations.

Likewise, let effective backing be given to decent radio and television productions, particularly those which are proper family fare. Catholic features should be intelligently encour-

---

19. Cf. the editorial by John B. Sheerin, C.S.P., "The Communications Decree: Why the Dissent?" published in *The Catholic World,* Feb., 1964, especially p. 270, which dissents from the word "form" *(efformet).* There is no indication that the Council was encouraging Catholic papers any more than the general press to become "propaganda" organs. The appreciation of a desirable quest for objectivity in media, however, should not blind one to the realistic and active role of media in forming opinion. It is one thing to approach the formation of public views in the manner and after the example of a sound educator, and another to do it in the fashion of a "manipulator" of the public.

Pope John XXIII said, on Oct. 13, 1962, in an address to journalists covering the Council: ". . . though the press may have at one time reached no more than a select few, it is obvious that today it *directs* the thoughts and feelings and emotions of a great part of mankind. For this reason, the distortions of truth by the organs of information can have incalculable consequences. . . . By means of the conscientious fulfillment of your mission as reporters on the Council, we look forward, gentlemen, to very happy results as regards the attitude of world opinion toward the Catholic Church in general, her institutions, and her teachings" (emphasis added).

aged, that through them audiences may be led to participate in
the Church's life, and truths of religion may be instilled. When
the opportunity presents itself, efforts should be made to establish Catholic stations. It should be a matter of concern that
their offerings excel in professional quality and forcefulness.

Let efforts be expended to see that the noble and ancient
art of the theatre, now widely popularized through the instruments of social communication, serves the cultural and
moral development of audiences.

15. That the aforementioned needs be met, let priests, religious, and laymen be opportunely trained to bring the necessary skills to the apostolic use of these instruments.

First of all, laymen should be instructed in art, doctrine,
and ethics. Such a goal requires an increased number of
schools, faculties, and institutes in which movie, radio, and
television writers, journalists, and other concerned persons can
obtain rounded formation animated by a Christian spirit,
especially with regard to the Church's social doctrine. The-
atrical actors should be trained and helped so that by their
artistry they may enrich human culture with their own special
gifts. Finally, active preparation should be given to critics in
the literary, movie, radio and television, and other fields, so
that each may know his specialty superbly and be taught and
inspired to make judgments in which moral issues are always
presented in their proper light.

16. Instruments of social communication are available to audiences of various ages and cultural backgrounds. Hence the
right use of them requires theoretical and practical instruction adapted to particular types of audience. At every level
of Catholic schooling, therefore, in seminaries and in groups
of the lay apostolate, programs suited to the purpose, especially for the benefit of minors, should be encouraged, multiplied and structured according to principles of Christian behavior. To facilitate this objective, statements and explanations
of Catholic doctrine and discipline on this matter should be
included in catechetical instruction.

17. It would be dishonorable indeed if sons of the Church
sluggishly allowed the word of salvation to be silenced or impeded by the technical difficulties or the admittedly enormous expenses which are characteristic of these instruments.
Hence the sacred Synod admonishes these sons that they are

duty bound to uphold and assist Catholic newspapers, magazines, movie enterprises, and radio and television stations and programs whose main purpose is to spread and defend the truth and to strengthen the Christian texture of human society. This Council likewise urgently invites associations and individuals with great economic or technical prestige to give willingly and generously of their resources and talents to the truly cultural and apostolic potential of these instruments.

18. The Church's manifold apostolate regarding instruments of social communication calls for reinforced vigor. Under the guidance of its bishop, therefore, let every diocese of the world devote a day of each year to instructing the faithful in their duties on this subject. Let these faithful be urged to pray about the matter, and to make a contribution towards the sacred cause of supporting and fostering those institutes and enterprises established by the Church to meet the needs of the Catholic world in this field.

19. For the fulfillment of his supreme pastoral responsibility regarding instruments of social communication, the Sovereign Pontiff has at his disposal a special office of the Holy See.[20]

20. Bishops in their own dioceses have the duty to oversee activities and enterprises of this kind, to promote them, and to regulate them insofar as they affect the apostolate in a public manner. This duty extends to affairs under the control of members of exempt religious communities.

21. A successful apostolate for an entire nation calls for unity of planning and effort. Hence this Sacred Council decrees and directs that national offices be everywhere established and thoroughly supported for affairs of the press, motion pictures, radio and television. Such offices will have the special obligation of helping the faithful to form a true conscience about the use of these media, and of fostering and co-ordinating Catholic activities directed to this end.

---

20. *The Council Fathers, however, willingly acceding to the wish of the Secretariat for the Supervision of Publications and Entertainment, respectfully ask the Supreme Pontiff that the duties and competence of this office be extended to all the media of social communication, including the press, and that experts, including laymen, from various nations be named to it.* (This is the only official footnote accompanying the Decree. Pope Paul VI responded affirmatively to the request. The Secretariat is now known as the Pontifical Commission for Social Communications Media.—Ed.)

In each nation the direction of this office should be confided to a special commission of bishops or to some delegate-bishop. Each office, too, should make use of laymen who are skilled in Catholic doctrine and in these artistic fields.

22. Where the influence of these media extends beyond national borders and affects individual persons as citizens of human society as a whole, national enterprises should join together and take on international scope. The offices mentioned in Article 21 should diligently collaborate with international Catholic groups established in each country. These groups are only those lawfully endorsed by the Holy See and responsible to it.

CONCLUSION

23. It is the explicit will of this sacred Synod that a pastoral instruction be drawn up under the supervision of the Office of the Holy See mentioned in Article 19. Experts from various countries should assist in this effort. In this way, all the principles and norms enunciated by this Council concerning the instruments of social communication may achieve their effect.

24. For the rest, this sacred Synod trusts that all the sons of the Church will cordially welcome and religiously observe this program of precepts and guidelines. By so doing they will not only avoid harm in the use of these advantages, but they will season the earth as its salt, and illumine the world as its light.

The Council further entreats all men of good will, especially those who control these instruments, to strive to apply them solely for the good of mankind. The fate of humanity grows daily more dependent on the right use of these media. And so, as with ancient artistic achievements, the name of the Lord will be glorified by these modern inventions as well. Thus will be fulfilled that ideal of the Apostle: "Jesus Christ yesterday, today, yes, and forever" (Heb. 13:8).

Each and every one of the things set forth in this Decree

has won the consent of the Fathers of this most sacred Council. We too, by the apostolic authority conferred on us by Christ, join with the Venerable Fathers in approving, decreeing, and establishing these things in the Holy Spirit, and we direct that what has thus been enacted in synod be published to God's glory.

Rome, at St. Peter's, December 4, 1963

I, Paul, Bishop of the Catholic Church

There follow the signatures of the Fathers.

A RESPONSE

Although Father Burke's appraisal of this Decree as being "the slightest document of the Council" is entirely acceptable, and although his additional commentary helps to strengthen the document, nevertheless we are dealing here not with Father Burke's introduction or commentary but with the Decree which Pope Paul VI promulgated and which now represents the official position of the Roman Catholic Church on the subject of the instruments of social communication.

Unfortunately, this Decree falls far short of the high standard established by the other documents (perhaps with the exception of the one on education). It also presents several propositions which, if taken seriously, would disrupt, if not curtail, the chief aspects of Pope John's *aggiornamento*. As a Catholic editor has put it, "It is not only pre-*aggiornamento* but definitely pre-Pius XII."

If this Decree had come near the end of the Council, rather than as the second document to be voted upon, very likely it would have included what the twenty-five bishops of the Council pleaded for in a statement circulated on the steps of St. Peter's on November 25, 1963, and what three Catholic journalists (supported by four prominent theologians) proposed in a protest message sent to the Council Fathers.

The bishops (who, by the way, did not include a single one from the United States) declared in the statement headed "URGENTE" (calling for a *non placet* vote on the Communications schema) that the document "is hardly fitting for a conciliar decree" and it "by no means reflects the wishes of the people, and especially of experts in the field." They said that if the Decree is promulgated "the authority of the Council will be called into question."

The Catholic journalists, in their message of November 16, 1963, maintained that "where the document is not vague and banal, it reflects a hopelessly abstract view of the relationship of the Church and modern culture. It deals with a press that exists only in textbooks and is unrecognizable to us. . . . This document may seem to many a mere pastoral exhortation. But it is proposed as a solemn Decree of an Ecumenical Council. . . . No Decree which the Second Vatican Council has yet discussed could touch the lives of contemporary men so directly. And yet this Decree, as it now stands, may one day be cited as a classic example of how the Second Vatican Ecumenical Council failed to come to grips with the world around it."

The message was written, of course, before the relevant Pastoral Constitution on the Church in the Modern World; yet, because the Decree on the Instruments of Social Communication was adopted by a vote of *placet* (1,598, with 503 *non placet* votes) on November 25, 1963, and promulgated on December 4, 1963, it is now the official position of the Roman Catholic Church on the subject.

The opposition statements, which were timed to block a final vote on the Decree, point out that the text does not take into consideration the remarkable advances which have already been achieved in the area of mass communication. It also fails to bring the Church into this exceedingly relevant field in any realistic manner. Moreover, behind the puritanical and restrictive language there are outdated elements which, if forced to their ultimate conclusions, would condone censorship, favor management of news, and promote a purely "Catholic" religious philosophy of pre-Council isolationism.

This document, as it now stands, therefore, is directly opposed to the ecumenical spirit and practice of Vatican II.

It would require much more space than is available here to spell this out, yet it can be summarized in these few words: unlike other documents of the Council (especially the Declaration on Religious Freedom and the Constitution on the Church in the Modern World) this Decree looks backward rather than forward, inward rather than outward; it deals primarily with one Church rather than with Christianity at large; it relies upon outdated Catholic misconceptions rather than upon creative achievements of the secular mass communication profession and practice.

However, the Decree does offer a ray of hope, in reverse. It indicates that new organizations will be established within the Church to further the cause of social communication. If the document is to be considered as a starting point rather than an end in itself, it can, in the spirit of the Council, help to develop a truly ecumenical concept of social communication and contribute to the secular aspects of such public-opinion-making media as the theatre, mass advertising, and the policy machinery behind radio, TV, and the press. For our modern problem is not the firm control of mass media, but the creative and constructive development of its content. Our aim should not be to force mass media into a particular system but to release it from its own bonds and set it free. This cannot be accomplished by placing it in the exclusive mold of "Catholic" thinking and procedure.

If this Decree, in reverse, can serve as a springboard for a larger lay participation in the policy-making areas of mass communication within and without the Roman Catholic Church, if it can stimulate a new sense of responsibility for the secular development of a much higher level of communication, if it will encourage freedom of speech and the mutual support of such causes as world peace, racial justice, the war against poverty, the rights of man in a secular society, the championing of questioning youth, and if it will encourage the Catholic Church to cooperate fully with non-Catholic agencies in the development of a modern approach to the instruments of social communication, then this document may serve as a way to something far better and greater than it represents in and by itself.

It is therefore our hope that this Decree does not represent the final word. We note that the late Father Gustave Weigel, S.J., said in regard to the promulgation of this Decree that while it is the "official and authentic doctrine of the Church," it will not become the "irreformable and once-for-all-times doctrine of the Church."

It is because the instruments of social communication are so vital to the advancement of the Christian cause in the world, where they are needed most of all, that, although we cannot accept this Decree as it now stands, we do take courage in the fact that it is surrounded by the progressive spirit of the Council. Therefore its inherent dangers may in practice be eliminated and its preachments may in reality be developed to the benefit of all concerned.

The Second Vatican Council has received in the main a very good press—not only in Catholic channels of communication but also in the public media directed by non-Catholic and secular interests. The total coverage of the Council has been phenomenal. This has been due largely to the reform and renewal nature of the Council. If this same spirit is injected into the post-Council period (as far as the instruments of social communication are concerned) then the real achievements of the Council, as represented by the other documents in this book, will reach down into society and accomplish what Pope Paul declared to be his great desire at the close of the Council: the realization in the world of what had already taken place through the calling, and the historic achievements, of this greatest of all Councils.

The true basis of "authority" is to be found in the freedom of the press. Therefore, it is our sincere desire, keeping in mind the future of ecumenical relations, that the Catholic Church will progress beyond this Decree and put into practice the following propositions which apply directly to the instruments of social communication:

"Let the world know this: the Church looks at the world with profound understanding, with sincere admiration, and with the sincere intention not of conquering it but of serving it; not of despising it but of appreciating it; not of condemning it but of strengthening it."—Pope Paul VI.

Pope Pius XII, in an address to Catholic journalists in 1950, after telling them that their task was not to dictate or regiment public opinion but to serve it by reflecting sound public opinion, lashed out at abuses of power by mass organizations "which seize modern man in their complicated mechanism, strangling in stride all spontaneity of public opinion and reducing it to a blind conformity of thought and judgment."

Finally, the American bishops, in their 1957 statement, endorsed the American tendency to restrict the extent of civil-law guardianship of morals. The statement declared, "Our judicial system has been dedicated from the beginning to the principle of minimal restraint. Those who may become impatient with the reluctance of the State through its laws to curb and curtail human freedom should bear in mind that this is a principle which serves to safeguard all our vital freedoms . . . to hold for liberty over restraint."

We shall all rejoice in the day when the Catholic press (supported of course by the Roman Catholic hierarchy) will take leadership in clearing the instruments of social communication of crass commercialism and blindness toward high morality, and will open many windows so that Pope John's fresh air of creativity and renewal will blow vital life into what this Decree calls the "new and highly effective avenues of communication."

STANLEY I. STUBER

ECUMENISM

EACH YEAR IN JANUARY, for many decades, Roman Catholics have offered eight days of prayer for Church unity. Until 1959, the general idea behind those days of prayer, January 18-25, was the hope that Protestants would "return" to the one true Church, and that the Orthodox schism would end. Throughout those same decades, Protestants became more and more involved in what had come to be called the "ecumenical movement." The development of the World Council of Churches, the growth of national and world-wide groupings of Protestant churches, the mergers of Churches—all these expressed a groping toward unity. The Roman Catholic Church remained aloof. There were Catholic centers of study in Europe that watched developments, but, in general, the Church watched and prayed without joining in the dialogue and prayer of the Protestant Churches. Then came Pope John XXIII and, on January 25, 1959, the announcement of his intention to call an Ecumenical Council.

On that day Pope John declared that he wanted "an Ecumenical Council for the whole Church." He said it would be "not only for the spiritual good and joy of the Christian people"; he desired "to invite the separated Communities to seek again that unity for which so many souls are longing in these days throughout the world." Did he mean he would ask Protestants and Orthodox to sit down together with the world's Catholic bishops, to discuss how they could overcome their divisions? It was not that simple, not that direct. Much had to be done before a Council of that kind could be held. As it turned out, the Pope took a number of remarkable steps in that direction. He asked that observers be delegated by the Protestant and Orthodox Churches; he had them seated in St. Peter's across the aisle from the cardinals; he established a Secretariat for Promoting Christian Unity that would be at the service of the observers, and he gave it status equal to that of Council commissions. To head the new secretariat, Pope John made the providential choice of a biblical scholar, Augustin Cardinal Bea.

As the Pope explained in his first encyclical, *Ad Petri Cathedram* (June 29, 1959), the Catholic Church first had to renew herself. In the first part of that work of renewal, on the liturgy, the bishops, it soon became clear, had the ultimate hope of Christian unity very much in mind; again and again in the Council discussions they stressed what liturgical renewal could mean to those whom Pope John called "our separated brethren." The next subject taken up in the Council's first session, "The Sources of Revelation," had to be withdrawn for a complete revision largely because, as cardinals and bishops pointed out, the proposed text would not encourage dialogue with non-Catholics.

Several documents dealing with Christian unity then came before the Council Fathers. The Commission for the Eastern Churches had proposed a text on unity; the Theological Commission proposed a chapter on Protestants in the schema for a constitution on the Church; the Secretariat for Promoting Christian Unity was drafting a text on general ecumenical principles. On December 1, 1962, the Council decided, by a vote of 2,068 to 36, that all this material should be worked out in one conciliar Decree on Ecumenism, to be composed by Cardinal Bea's Secretariat.

Between the first and second sessions of the Council, Pope John died (June 3, 1963). But he had lived to see the first version of the Decree on Ecumenism; on April 22, he had ordered it sent around the world to the Council Fathers for their study and recommendations. Pope John's successor, Paul VI, opened the Council's second session on September 29, and he had a great deal to say about ecumenism in his address. The same spirit was at work; there was strong forward movement here. The Council was soon at work discussing the text proposed for a Decree on Ecumenism.

As the Archbishop of Rouen explained to the Council on behalf of the secretariat, it was necessary to give Catholics a better understanding of the nature, attitude, and providential significance of the ecumenical movement; it was of such importance that the Council could not pass over it in silence. From November 18 to December 2, 1963, the Council Fathers discussed the document. There were five chapters. The first three covered principles and practice of ecumenism and relations with Protestant and Orthodox Churches. The fourth

chapter was on relations with the Jews; the fifth was on religious freedom. A significant vote was taken on November
21, when the Moderators asked if the Council would accept
the first three chapters as a basis of discussion; 1,970 voted
in favor, and only 86 against. (For the history of the other
two chapters, see the introductions to the Declaration on the
Relationship of the Church to Non-Christian Religions and
the Declaration on Religious Freedom.)

During the third session of the Council, in 1964, the Decree was refined. Over a thousand proposed changes were
examined by the secretariat. The changes it decided upon
were approved by large majorities. The chapters were voted
through; only the final vote on the Decree as a whole remained. The day before that vote was to take place, Pope
Paul made nineteen changes in the text. (The papal changes
are noted in the commentary accompanying the translation,
and some observations are made on them.) A number of
bishops, and non-Catholic observers too, were irritated that
the Pope had proposed changes after it was too late for the
Council Fathers to discuss them or vote on them. The next
day, November 20, the Council voted on the whole text, including the papal changes. The vote was 2,054 for, · 64
against. On November 21, in the final ceremonial vote, only
eleven were against the Decree. The Decree was then promulgated by the Pope; the Roman Catholic Church was fully
involved in the ecumenical movement.

Many sentences and sections of Vatican II decrees are remarkable for the fact that they are there at all. It can truly
be said that the whole Decree on Ecumenism is remarkable
for that fact. In this Decree, the focus is more on a "pilgrim"
Church moving toward Christ than on a movement of "return" to the Roman Catholic Church. In this Decree, the
Council goes beyond the assertion that the Catholic Church
is the true Church to assert that Jesus, in His Spirit, is at
work in the Churches and Communities beyond the visible
borders of the Catholic Church; the Council asserts that believers in Christ who are baptized are truly reborn and truly
our brothers and that God uses their worship to sanctify and
save them.

Dr. Oscar Cullmann, a Protestant observer at the Council,
has rightly said of the Decree: "This is more than the opening of a door; new ground has been broken. No Catholic
document has ever spoken of non-Catholic Christians in this
way." Among other things, too, there is a remarkable ad-

mission of guilt; the Council says the divisions among Christians are the result of sin on both sides (Article 1 and Article 3).

The Council moves into action in this contrite spirit: all have an obligation to pray and work for the restoration of unity; all are called to dialogue according to their ability; all are called to further common efforts, again according to their ability, in prayer and in social action. These are not mere words and plans. This is a call to action. And one is always to remember the essential thing: change of heart.

With this breathtaking prospect opened before them, some Catholics responding to the Council's call might take an unthinking plunge. A paragraph from a pastoral letter about the Decree is worth recalling here: "At this time of increasing communications one could be tempted to forget our differences, to bypass questions of doctrine and authority, and simply to come together as friends. Two generations ago, when the ecumenical movement began in the Protestant and Anglican Churches, there were many voices suggesting that the question of truth did not matter. The slogan used in those days was that doctrine divides while service unites. Since that time, partially due to the entry of the Eastern Orthodox Churches into the ecumenical movement, these voices have become rare among our separated brethren. Today, Protestant, Anglican, and Lutheran Christians realize that such a pragmatic approach to Christian unity ultimately results in confusion" ("Ecumenism and Catholic Truth," Pastoral Letter of the Catholic Conference of Ontario Bishops, September 1, 1965). The Council's Decree on Ecumenism sounds the same warning. It is hopeful, in fact optimistic, but the Council is also realistic; it reminds us that imprudence will harm, not help, the cause of unity.

It has been well said that the Decree on Ecumenism is not an end but a new beginning full of hopes and promises. The Constitution on the Sacred Liturgy marked the arrival of the vernacular movement, but it was a beginning rather than an end. The Constitution on Divine Revelation marked the establishment of the kerygmatic movement—again a beginning rather than an end of a movement. The Decree on Ecumenism marks the full entry of the Roman Catholic Church into the ecumenical movement. It is evident that much has been accomplished by the Decree, but what counts more is what remains to be done.

If he had lived to see the end of the Council, Gustave Wei-

gel, S.J., would have been invited to contribute introduction
and commentary for this Decree. He worked long and hard
for its development. He was called to the Council to work
with the English-speaking Protestant and Orthodox observers. He gave them everything he had, and they testify still
that he had a great deal to give. Between the second and
third sessions of the Council, he worked almost as hard as
he had during the sessions, in dialogue with both Christians
and Jews. He died shortly after finishing a morning dialogue
session, while preparing for an afternoon session. These notes
are respectfully dedicated to his memory.

WALTER M. ABBOTT, S.J.

Decree on Ecumenism

PAUL, BISHOP
SERVANT OF THE SERVANTS OF GOD
TOGETHER WITH THE FATHERS OF THE SACRED COUNCIL
FOR EVERLASTING MEMORY

INTRODUCTION

1. Promoting the restoration of unity[1] among all Christians is one of the Chief concerns of the Second Sacred Ecumenical Synod of the Vatican. The Church established by Christ the Lord is, indeed, one and unique. Yet many Christian communions[2] present themselves to men as the true heritage of Jesus Christ. To be sure, all proclaim themselves to be disciples of the Lord, but their convictions clash and their paths diverge, as though Christ Himself were divided (cf. 1 Cor. 1:13). Without doubt, this discord openly contradicts the will of Christ, provides a stumbling block to the world,[3] and inflicts damage on the most holy cause of proclaiming the good news[4] to every creature.

Nevertheless, the Lord of Ages wisely and patiently follows out the plan of His grace on behalf of us sinners. In recent times He has begun to bestow more generously upon

---

1. The opening words of papal encyclicals are commonly used as their titles. This conciliar document may also be cited that way *(Unitatis Redintegratio,* "Restoration of Unity"), but it already has an official title: Decree on Ecumenism.
2. "Communions" is a general term used in this Decree to indicate various Christian bodies without being more precise about their nature, etc.
3. Christ prayed for unity for his followers in order that the world might believe God the Father had sent Him (Jn. 17:21). The frustration of this purpose is a serious matter, in fact a scandal (the Latin for "stumbling block" here is *scandalo*). In Art. 3 the Decree admits the Catholic Church shares in the responsibility.
4. *Evangelium*, the gospel.

divided Christians remorse over their divisions and a longing for unity.

Everywhere, large numbers have felt the impulse of this grace, and among our separated brethren also there increases from day to day a movement, fostered by the grace of the Holy Spirit, for the restoration of unity among all Christians. Taking part in this movement, which is called ecumenical, are those who invoke the Triune God and confess Jesus as Lord and Savior.[5] They join in not merely as individuals but also as members of the corporate groups in which they have heard the gospel, and which each regards as his Church and, indeed, God's. And yet, almost[6] everyone, though in different ways, longs that there may be one visible Church of God, a Church truly universal and sent forth to the whole world that the world may be converted to the gospel and so be saved, to the glory of God.

This sacred Synod, therefore, gladly notes all these factors. It has already declared its teaching on the Church,[7] and now, moved by a desire for the restoration of unity among all the followers of Christ, it wishes to set before all Catholics certain helps, pathways, and methods[8] by which they too can respond to this divine summons and grace.

5. The authors of the document had in mind here a description of the World Council of Churches as "a fellowship of churches which confess the Lord Jesus Christ as God and Savior according to the Scriptures and therefore seek to fulfill together their common calling to the glory of the one God, Father, Son, and Holy Spirit" (from the Third World Assembly of the WCC held in New Delhi, 1961).
6. Pope Paul added the word "almost," apparently because some Protestants deny that Christ founded a visible Church.
7. The Dogmatic Constitution on the Church, promulgated the same day as the Decree on Ecumenism (Nov. 21, 1964), is essential reading for anyone working with the Decree.
8. The Decree on Ecumenism supersedes various preconciliar directives (e.g., the June 5, 1948, monitum and the Dec. 20, 1949 instruction of the Holy Office) and some sections of the Code of Canon Law.

CHAPTER I

CATHOLIC PRINCIPLES ON ECUMENISM [9]

2. What has revealed the love of God among us is that the only-begotten Son of God has been sent by the Father into the world, so that, being made man, the Son might by His redemption of the entire human race give new life to it and unify it (cf. 1 Jn. 4:9; Col. 1:18-20; Jn. 11:52). Before offering Himself up as a spotless victim upon the altar of the cross, He prayed to His Father for those who believe: "That all may be one even as thou, Father, in me, and I in thee; that they also may be one in us, that the world may believe that thou hast sent me" (Jn. 17:21). In His Church He instituted the wonderful sacrament of the Eucharist by which the unity of the Church is both signified and brought about. He gave His followers a new commandment of mutual love (cf. Jn. 13:34), and promised the Spirit, their Advocate (cf. Jn. 16:7), who, as Lord and life-giver, would abide with them forever.

After being lifted up on the cross and glorified, the Lord Jesus poured forth the Spirit whom He had promised, and through whom He has called and gathered together the people of the New Covenant, who comprise the Church, into a unity of faith, hope, and charity. For, as the apostle teaches, the Church is: "one body and one Spirit, even as you were called in one hope of your calling; one Lord, one faith, one baptism" (Eph. 4:4-5). For "all you who have been baptized into Christ, have put on Christ . . . for you are all one in

9. Before this final version, the title of the chapter had been "Principles of Catholic Ecumenism." The change implies that the Council recognizes ecumenism as one movement for all Christian Churches and Communities. The goal for all is the same, unity in the Christian faith, but the way of conceiving that unity and faith may vary, and so one may speak of a Church having its own principles of ecumenism. The first section of Chapter I gives a brief statement of beliefs that Catholics bring with them to the dialogue.

Christ Jesus" (Gal. 3:27-28). It is the Holy Spirit, dwelling in those who believe, pervading and ruling over the entire Church, who brings about that marvelous communion of the faithful and joins them together so intimately in Christ that He is the principle of the Church's unity. By distributing various kinds of spiritual gifts and ministries (cf. 1 Cor. 12:4-11), He enriches the Church of Jesus Christ with different functions "in order to perfect the saints for a work of ministry, for building up the body of Christ" (Eph. 4:12).

In order to establish this holy Church of His everywhere in the world until the end of time, Christ entrusted to the College of the Twelve the task of teaching, ruling, and sanctifying (cf. Mt. 28:18-20, in conjunction with Jn. 20:21-23). Among their number He chose Peter. After Peter's profession of faith, He decreed that on him He would build His Church; to Peter He promised the keys of the kingdom of heaven (cf. Mt. 16:19, in conjunction with Mt. 18:18). After Peter's profession of love, Christ entrusted all His sheep to him to be confirmed in faith (cf. Lk. 22:32) and shepherded in perfect unity (cf. Jn. 21:15-17). Meanwhile, Christ Jesus Himself forever remains the chief cornerstone (cf. Eph. 2:20) and shepherd of our souls (cf. 1 Pet. 2:25).[10]

It is through the faithful preaching of the gospel by the apostles and their successors—the bishops with Peter's successor at their head—through their administration of the sacraments, and through their loving exercise of authority, that Jesus Christ wishes His people to increase under the influence of the Holy Spirit. Thereby too, He perfects His people's fellowship in unity: in the confession of one faith, in the common celebration of divine worship, and in the fraternal harmony of the family of God.

The Church, then, God's only flock, like a standard lifted high for the nations to see (cf. Is. 11:10-12), ministers the gospel of peace to all mankind (cf. Eph. 2:17-18, in conjunction with Mk. 16:15), as she makes her pilgrim way in hope toward her goal, the fatherland above (cf. 1 Pet. 1:3-9).

This is the sacred mystery of the unity of the Church, in Christ and through Christ, with the Holy Spirit energizing a variety of functions. The highest exemplar and source of this mystery is the unity, in the Trinity of Persons, of one God, the Father and the Son in the Holy Spirit.

10. *I Vatican Council, Sess. IV (1870), the constitution "Pastor Aeternus":* Coll. Lac. 7, 482 a.

3. From her very beginnings there arose in this one and only Church of God certain rifts (cf. 1 Cor. 11:18-19, Gal. 1:6-9; 1 Jn. 2:18-19), which the apostle strongly censures as damnable (cf. 1 Cor. 1:11 ff.; 11:22). But in subsequent centuries more widespread disagreements appeared and quite large Communities became separated from full communion with the Catholic Church—developments for which, at times, men of both sides were to blame. However, one cannot impute the sin of separation to those who at present are born into these Communities and are instilled therein with Christ's faith. The Catholic Church accepts them with respect and affection as brothers. For men who believe in Christ and have been properly[11] baptized are brought into a certain, though imperfect, communion with the Catholic Church.[12] Undoubtedly, the differences that exist in varying degrees between them and the Catholic Church—whether in doctrine and sometimes in discipline, or concerning the structure of the Church—do indeed create many and sometimes serious obstacles to full ecclesiastical communion. These the ecumenical movement is striving to overcome. Nevertheless, all those justified by faith through baptism are incorporated into Christ.[13] They therefore have a right to be honored by the title of Christian, and are properly regarded as brothers in the Lord by the sons of the Catholic Church.[14]

Moreover some, even very many, of the most significant elements or endowments which together go to build up and give life to the Church herself can exist outside the visible boundaries of the Catholic Church: the written word of God; the life of grace; faith, hope, and charity, along with other interior gifts of the Holy Spirit and visible elements. All of

11. "Properly" reminds the reader that Catholics hold there are necessary conditions for valid baptism.

12. The Decree stops short of saying outright that they are "members" of the Church, probably because of the sentence in Pope Pius XII's encyclical "Mystici Corporis" (The Mystical Body) issued in 1943: "Only those are to be included as real members of the Church who have been baptized and profess the true faith and have not been so unfortunate as to separate themselves from the unity of the Body or been excluded from it by legitimate authority for serious faults." Cardinal Bea and other theologians, however, have developed a great deal of thinking on the situation of those born and baptized outside the visible borders of the Catholic Church who have not knowingly or deliberately separated themselves from the unity of the Body. Cf. Constitution on the Church, Art. 14 and 22, for more on the topic.

13. *Cf. Council of Florence, Sess. VIII (1439), the decree "Exultate Deo": Mansi 31. 1055 A.*

14. *Cf. St. Augustine, "In Ps. 32," Enarr. II, 29: PL 36, 299.*

these, which come from Christ and lead back to Him, belong by right[15] to the one Church of Christ.

The brethren divided from us also carry out many of the sacred actions of the Christian religion. Undoubtedly, in ways that vary according to the condition of each Church or Community, these actions can truly engender a life of grace, and can be rightly described as capable of providing access to the community of salvation.

It follows that these separated Churches[16] and Communities, though we believe they suffer from defects already mentioned, have by no means been deprived of significance and importance in the mystery of salvation. For the Spirit of Christ has not refrained from using them as means of salvation which derive their efficacy from the very fullness of grace and truth entrusted to the Catholic[17] Church.

Nevertheless, our separated brethren, whether considered as individuals or as Communities and Churches, are not blessed with that unity which Jesus Christ wished to bestow on all those whom He has regenerated and vivified into one body and newness of life—that unity which the holy Scriptures and the revered tradition of the Church proclaim. For it is through Christ's Catholic Church alone, which is the all-embracing means of salvation,[18] that the fullness of the means of salvation can be obtained. It was to the apostolic college alone, of which Peter is the head, that we believe our Lord entrusted all the blessings of the New Covenant, in order to establish on earth the one Body of Christ into which all those should be fully incorporated who already belong in any way to God's People. During its pilgrimage on earth, this People, though still in its members[19] liable to sin, is growing in Christ and is being gently guided by God, according to His hidden designs, until it happily arrives at the fullness of eternal glory in the heavenly Jerusalem.

---

15. "By right" was added by Pope Paul. Compare the last sentence of the preceding paragraph on the right to the title of Christian, etc.
16. *Cf. IV Lateran Council (1215) Constitution IV: Mansi 22, 990; II Council of Lyons (1274), profession of faith of Michael Palaeologos: Mansi 24, 71 E; Council of Florence, Sess. VI (1439), definition "Laetentur caeli": Mansi 31, 1026 E.*
17. "Catholic" was inserted by order of Pope Paul.
18. The Decree uses a term *(generale auxilium salutis)* from a letter of the Holy Office to Archbishop (later Cardinal) Richard J. Cushing, Aug. 8, 1949, in which the stand of Fr. Leonard Feeney concerning salvation outside the Church was rejected.
19. Pope Paul added "in its members," and thus the sentence avoids saying that the Church is liable to sin.

4. Today, in many parts of the world, under the inspiring grace[20] of the Holy Spirit, multiple efforts are being expended through prayer, word, and action to attain that fullness of unity which Jesus Christ desires. This sacred Synod, therefore, exhorts all[21] the Catholic faithful to recognize the signs of the times and to participate skillfully[22] in the work of ecumenism.

The "ecumenical movement" means those activities and enterprises which, according to various needs of the Church and opportune occasions, are started and organized for the fostering of unity among Christians. These are: first, every effort to eliminate words, judgments, and actions which do not respond to the condition of separated brethren with truth and fairness and so make mutual relations between them more difficult;[23] then, "dialogue" between competent experts from different Churches and Communities. In their meetings, which are organized in a religious spirit, each explains the teaching of his Communion in greater depth and brings out clearly its distinctive features. Through such dialogue, everyone gains a truer knowledge and more just appreciation of the teaching and religious life of both Communions. In addition, these Communions cooperate more closely in whatever projects a Christian conscience demands for the common good. They also come together for common prayer, where this is permitted. Finally, all are led to examine their own faithfulness to Christ's will for the Church and, wherever necessary,[24] undertake with vigor the task of renewal and reform.

20. Pope Paul inserted this to replace "under the inspiration of the Holy Spirit," perhaps because the Latin *Spiritu Sancto afflante* might be too reminiscent of *Divino Afflante Spiritu* (the title of Pope Pius XII's encyclical of 1943), a term referring to the special kind of inspiration given to the human authors of the Bible.
21. The Decree calls all Catholics to ecumenical work (cf. also Art. 5). Ecumenism, therefore, is not simply a matter one may take or leave; it is a central concern for Catholics.
22. The translation of the Decree from Cardinal Bea's Secretariat (Jan., 1965) expands "skillfully" *(sollerter)* into "take an active and intelligent part" in the work of ecumenism. See Art. 5 and note for a qualification.
23. A still wider rule or norm on this matter is given at the beginning of Art. 11 (cf. note there).
24. It is evident from the immediately following sentence that the Decree here refers to "grass-roots" renewal and reform, i.e., of Church institutions right down to parish organizations and of individual members. The phrase "wherever necessary" is to be connected with "signs of the times" above, in the first paragraph of Art. 4. Renewal and reform, here mentioned for the first time in the Decree, include the *aggiornamento,* or "up-dating," that Pope John XXIII so often spoke about as a necessary task of the Council and of the faithful.

When such actions are carried out by the Catholic faithful with prudence, patience, and the vigilance of their spiritual shepherds, they contribute to the blessings of justice and truth, of concord and collaboration, as well as of the spirit of brotherly love and unity. The result will be that, little by little, as the obstacles to perfect ecclesiastical communion are overcome, all Christians will be gathered, in a common celebration of the Eucharist, into that unity of the one and only Church which Christ bestowed on His Church from the beginning. This unity, we believe, dwells in the Catholic Church as something she can never lose, and we hope that it will continue to increase until the end of time.

However, it is evident that the work of preparing and reconciling those individuals who wish for full Catholic communion[25] is of its nature distinct from ecumenical action. But there is no opposition between the two, since both proceed from the wondrous providence of God.[26]

In ecumenical work, Catholics must assuredly be concerned for their separated brethren, praying for them, keeping them informed about the Church, making the first approaches towards them. But their primary duty is to make an honest and careful appraisal of whatever needs to be renewed and achieved in the Catholic household itself, in order that its life may bear witness more loyally and luminously to the teachings and ordinances which have been handed down from Christ through the apostles.

For although the Catholic Church has been endowed with all divinely revealed truth and with all means of grace, her members fail to live by them with all the fervor they should. As a result, the radiance of the Church's face shines less brightly in the eyes of our separated brethren and of the world at large, and the growth of God's kingdom is retarded. Every Catholic must therefore aim at Christian perfection (cf. Jas. 1:4; Rom. 12:1-2) and, each according to his station, play his part so that the Church, which bears in her own body the humility and dying of Jesus (cf. 2 Cor. 4:10; Phil. 2: 5-8), may daily be more purified and renewed, against the

25. The Decree here refers to what are commonly called "converts" and "conversion," but, it will be noticed, the Decree itself does not use those words in this connection.
26. *Ex Dei mirabili dispositione,* a phrase replacing, at the request of Pope Paul, an expression that might be translated "since both are a work inspired by the Holy Spirit" (see note 20).

day when Christ will present her to Himself in all her glory, without spot or wrinkle (cf. Eph. 5:27).

While preserving unity in essentials, let all members of the Church, according to the office entrusted to each, preserve a proper freedom in the various forms of spiritual life and discipline, in the variety of liturgical rites, and even in the theological elaborations of revealed truth.[27] In all things let charity be exercised. If the faithful are true to this course of action, they will be giving ever richer expression to the authentic catholicity of the Church, and, at the same time, to her apostolicity.

On the other hand, Catholics must joyfully acknowledge and esteem the truly Christian endowments from our common heritage which are to be found among our separated brethren. It is right and salutary to recognize the riches of Christ and virtuous works[28] in the lives of others who are bearing witness to Christ, sometimes even to the shedding of their blood. For God is always wonderful in His works and worthy of admiration.

Nor should we forget that whatever is wrought by the grace of the Holy Spirit in the hearts of our separated brethren can contribute to our own edification. Whatever is truly Christian never conflicts with the genuine interests of the faith; indeed, it can always result in a more ample realization of the very mystery of Christ and the Church.

Nevertheless, the divisions among Christians prevent the Church from effecting the fullness of catholicity proper to her in those of her sons who, though joined to her by baptism, are yet separated from full communion with her.[29] Furthermore, the Church herself finds it more difficult to express in actual life her full catholicity in all its aspects.

This sacred Synod is gratified to note that participation by the Catholic faithful in ecumenical work is growing daily. It

---

27. Pope John, Cardinal Bea, and others had drawn to the attention of the Council Fathers the important distinction between the unchanging deposit of faith and the changing, changeable manner, mode, language, etc., in which it is presented to men. Cf. Pope John's address at the beginning of the Council: "The deposit of faith is one thing; the way that it is presented is another. For the truths preserved in our sacred doctrine can retain the same substance and meaning under different forms of expression." AAS 54 (1962), p. 792. Cf. Art. 6, par. 2.

28. This was "the gifts of the Holy Spirit," but Pope Paul made it simply "virtuous works" apparently because it is difficult to discern the gifts of the Spirit. Art. 3, par. 2, has already acknowledged that the gifts of the Spirit can be found outside the visible boundaries of the Catholic Church.

29. A key phrase of the Decree: *qui sibi quidem baptismate appositi, sed a sua plena communione seiuncti sunt.*

commends this work to bishops everywhere in the world for their skillful promotion and prudent guidance.[30]

CHAPTER II

THE PRACTICE OF ECUMENISM

5. Concern for restoring unity pertains to the whole Church, faithful and clergy alike. It extends to everyone, according to the potential[31] of each, whether it be exercised in daily Christian living or in theological and historical studies. This very concern already reveals to some extent the bond of brotherhood existing among all Christians, and it leads toward that full and perfect unity which God lovingly desires.

6. Every renewal of the Church[32] essentially consists in an increase of fidelity to her own calling. Undoubtedly this explains the dynamism of the movement toward unity.

Christ summons the Church, as she goes her pilgrim way, to that continual reformation of which she always has need, insofar as she is an institution of men here on earth. Therefore, if the influence of events or of the times has led to deficiencies in conduct, in Church discipline, or even in the formulation of doctrine (which must be carefully distinguished from the deposit itself of faith),[33] these should be appropriately rectified at the proper moment.

30. Many bishops have established diocesan ecumenical commissions. In addition, the U.S. bishops, while still in Rome at the third session of the Council, established a national ecumenical commission with Archbishop (later Cardinal) Lawrence J. Shehan, of Baltimore, as chairman. Within a few months, the commission had set up eight subcommissions to explore possibilities of formal conversations with Orthodox, Protestant, and Jewish bodies. The national office of the U.S. Bishops' Commission for Ecumenical Affairs is at 1312 Massachusetts Avenue, N.W., Washington, D.C.
31. *Virtutem:* potential, ability, talent.
32. *Cf. V Lateran Council, Sess. XII (1517), constitution "Constituti": Mansi 32, 988 B-C.*
33. It is remarkable, indeed, for an Ecumenical Council to admit the possible deficiency of previous doctrinal formulations. Cf. note 27.

Church renewal therefore has notable ecumenical importance. Already this renewal is taking place in various spheres
of the Church's life: the biblical and liturgical movements,
the preaching of the word of God, catechetics, the apostolate
of the laity, new forms of religious life and the spirituality of
married life, and the Church's social teaching and activity.
All these should be considered as favorable pledges and signs
of ecumenical progress in the future.

7. There can be no ecumenism worthy of the name without
a change of heart. For it is from newness of attitudes (cf.
Eph. 4:23), from self-denial and unstinted love, that yearnings for unity take their rise and grow toward maturity. We
should therefore pray to the divine Spirit for the grace to be
genuinely self-denying, humble, gentle in the service of others, and to have an attitude of brotherly generosity toward
them. The Apostle of the Gentiles says: "I, therefore, the
prisoner in the Lord, exhort you to walk in a manner worthy
of the calling with which you were called, with all humility
and meekness, with patience, bearing with one another in
love, careful to preserve the unity of the Spirit in the bond
of peace" (Eph. 4:1-3). This exhortation applies especially
to those who have been raised to sacred orders so that the
mission of Christ may be carried on. He came among us "not
to be served but to serve" (Mt. 20:28).

St. John has testified: "If we say that we have not sinned,
we make him a liar, and his word is not in us" (1 Jn. 1:10).
This holds good for sins against unity. Thus, in humble
prayer, we beg pardon of God and of our separated brethren, just as we forgive those who trespass against us.[34]

Let all Christ's faithful remember that the more purely
they strive to live according to the gospel, the more they are
fostering and even practicing Christian unity. For they can
achieve depth and ease in strengthening mutual brotherhood
to the degree that they enjoy profound communion with the
Father, the Word, and the Spirit.[35]

34. This phrase, reminiscent of the Lord's Prayer, was translated with a
certain ecumenical liturgical flavor by Cardinal Bea's Secretariat: "Just as
we forgive them that trespass against us."
35. It can be said that this paragraph means Catholics who participate in
the renewed liturgy are engaged in a basic ecumenical activity. By its Constitution on the Sacred Liturgy, promulgated at the close of the second session,
Dec. 4, 1963, the Council took steps to renewal of faith and holiness in the
Church that are needed for basic ecumenical progress.

8. This change of heart and holiness of life, along with public and private prayer for the unity of Christians, should be regarded as the soul of the whole ecumenical movement, and can rightly be called "spiritual ecumenism."

Catholics already have a custom of uniting frequently in that prayer for the unity of the Church with which the Savior Himself, on the eve of His death, appealed so fervently to His Father: "That all may be one" (Jn. 17:21).

In certain special circumstances, such as in prayer services "for unity" and during ecumenical gatherings, it is allowable, indeed desirable,[36] that Catholics should join in prayer with their separated brethren. Such prayers in common are certainly a very effective means of petitioning for the grace of unity, and they are a genuine expression of the ties which even now bind Catholics to their separated brethren. "For where two or three are gathered together for my sake, there am I in the midst of them" (Mt. 18:20).

As for common worship,[37] however, it may not be regarded as a means to be used indiscriminately for the restoration of unity among Christians. Such worship depends chiefly on two principles: it should signify the unity of the Church; it should provide a sharing in the means of grace. The fact that it should signify unity generally rules out common worship.[38] Yet the gaining of a needed grace sometimes commends it.[39]

The practical course to be adopted, after due regard has been given to all the circumstances of time, place, and per-

36. Thus common prayer is not only permitted but definitely encouraged. Before the Decree, the Lord's Prayer (Our Father) was commonly used for prayer at ecumenical gatherings. Now, in addition, it may be judged appropriate for Catholics to join in Psalms, full Bible services or "vigils," and spontaneous prayer at ecumenical gatherings. Pope Paul set an interesting example four days before the close of the Council (Dec. 4, 1965) when he participated in an interfaith prayer service for unity at the Basilica of St. Paul Outside the Walls (a church, not an auditorium), assisting (not presiding) with Protestant, Catholic, and Orthodox in a reading of Scripture lessons.

37. The Council here uses in a laudatory way an expression, *communicatio in sacris,* which, up to this time, had meant for students of canon law something simply prohibited (and, in fact, mentioned in tones akin to horror). The notion of worship connotes the official, public prayer of a Church or Community. Normally, it implies commitment to the faith or creed of that Church or Community.

38. *Significatio unitatis plerumque vetat communicationem.* The adverb *plerumque* has a wide range of meaning in Latin: often, commonly, for the most part, etc. The word "generally" reflects the prevailing tone of Council Fathers' speeches, interventions, etc.

39. *Gratia procuranda quandoque illam commendat.* From Council speeches, interventions, etc., it is evident that this sentence and the preceding sentence refer to our present context in the history of ecumenism.

sonage, is left to the prudent decision of the local episcopal authority, unless the Bishops' Conference according to its own statutes, or the Holy See, has determined otherwise.[40]

9. We must come to understand the outlook of our separated brethren. Study is absolutely required for this, and should be pursued with fidelity to truth and in a spirit of good will. When they are properly prepared for this study, Catholics need to acquire a more adequate understanding of the distinctive doctrines of our separated brethren, as well as of their own history, spiritual and liturgical life, their religious psychology and cultural background. Of great value for this purpose are meetings between the two sides, especially for discussion of theological problems, where each can deal with the other on an equal footing.[41] Such meetings require that those who take part in them under authoritative guidance be truly competent.[42] From dialogue of this sort will emerge still more clearly what the true posture of the Catholic Church is. In this way, too, we will better understand the attitude of our separated brethren and more aptly present our own belief.

10. Instruction in sacred theology and other branches of knowledge, especially those of a historical nature, must also be presented from an ecumenical point of view, so that at every point they may more accurately correspond with the facts of the case.

For it is highly important that future bishops and priests should have mastered a theology carefully worked out in this way and not polemically, especially in what concerns the relations of separated brethren with the Catholic Church. For it is upon the formation which priests receive that the necessary instruction and spiritual formation of the faithful and of religious depend so very greatly.

Moreover, Catholics engaged in missionary work, in the same territories as other Christians, ought to know, particu-

40. The U.S. Bishops' Commission for Ecumenical Affairs issued, on June 18, 1965, a statement entitled "Interim Guidelines for Prayer in Common and Communicatio in Sacris." Cf. "Catholic Mind," Oct., 1965, pp. 57-64.
41. "Ecumenical activity is possible only if we respect the consciences of our separated brethren and they respect our conscience." (Pastoral letter of the Catholic Conference of Ontario Bishops, Sept., 1965).
42. "In dialogue and in other ecumenical activities the individual participant does not speak or act simply in his own name; he always gives testimony as a responsible member of his Church." (Ibid.) Cf. also Art. 1, par. 3, of this Decree.

larly in these times, the problems and the benefits which affect their apostolate because of the ecumenical movement.

11. The manner and order in which Catholic belief is expressed should in no way become an obstacle to dialogue with our brethren. It is, of course, essential that doctrine be clearly presented in its entirety. Nothing is so foreign to the spirit of ecumenism as a false conciliatory approach[43] which harms the purity of Catholic doctrine and obscures its assured genuine meaning.

At the same time, Catholic belief needs to be explained more profoundly and precisely, in ways and in terminology which our separated brethren too can really understand.

Furthermore, Catholic theologians engaged in ecumenical dialogue, while standing fast by the teaching of the Church and searching together with separated brethren into the divine mysteries, should act with love for truth, with charity, and with humility. When comparing doctrines, they should remember that in Catholic teaching there exists an order or "hierarchy" of truths, since they vary in their relationship to the foundation of the Christian faith. Thus the way will be opened for this kind of fraternal rivalry to incite all to a deeper realization and a clearer expression of the unfathomable riches of Christ (cf. Eph. 3:8).

12. Before the whole world, let all Christians profess their faith in God, one and three, in the incarnate Son of God, our Redeemer and Lord. United in their efforts, and with mutual respect, let them bear witness to our common hope, which does not play us false. Since in our times cooperation in social matters is very widely practiced, all men without exception are summoned to united effort. Those who believe in God have a stronger summons, but the strongest claims are laid on Christians, since they have been sealed with the name of Christ.

Cooperation among all Christians vividly expresses that bond which already unites them, and it sets in clearer relief the features of Christ the Servant.[44] Such cooperation, which has already begun in many countries, should be ever increas-

---

43. *Irenismus,* often translated "irenicism," is from a Greek word meaning "peace."

44. The theme of service "in conformity with the example of the Divine Master" was sounded by the Second Vatican Council in its first public statement, "Message to Humanity," issued Oct. 20, 1962, and it runs through all the Council's decrees.

ingly developed, particularly in regions where a social and technical evolution is taking place. It should contribute to a just appreciation of the dignity of the human person, the promotion of the blessings of peace, the application of gospel principles to social life, and the advancement of the arts and sciences in a Christian spirit. Christians should also work together in the use of every possible means to relieve the afflictions of our times, such as famine and natural disasters, illiteracy and poverty, lack of housing, and the unequal distribution of wealth. Through such cooperation, all believers in Christ are able to learn easily how they can understand each other better and esteem each other more, and how the road to the unity of Christians may be made smooth.

CHAPTER III

CHURCHES AND ECCLESIAL COMMUNITIES[45] SEPARATED FROM THE ROMAN APOSTOLIC SEE

13. We now turn our attention to the two main kinds of rending which have damaged the seamless robe of Christ.

The first divisions occurred in the East, either because of disputes over the dogmatic pronouncements of the Councils

---

45. The whole phrase is an attempt to convey what the French, for example, mean by the words *ecclesiastique* and *ecclesial*. Implicit in the use of these terms, and in the Decree, is the idea that the more a Church has of the essential structures of the Catholic Church, the more it approaches the ideal of the Church. On this institutional scale of measurement, some are more properly called Churches than others, and the Decree regards Eastern Churches as practically sister Churches of the Roman Catholic Church. (Cf. Art. 14, par. 1 and par. 2). Another reason, of course, for the expression "ecclesial Communities" and the word "Communities" throughout the Decree is that some Christian bodies do not wish to be called "Church."

of Ephesus[46] and Chalcedon,[47] or later by the breakdown[48] of ecclesiastical communion between the Eastern Patriarchates and the Roman See.

Still other divisions arose in the West[49] more than four centuries afterwards. These stemmed from a series of happenings commonly referred to as the Reformation. As a result, many Communions, national or denominational, were separated from the Roman See. Among those in which some Catholic traditions and institutions continue to exist, the Anglican Communion occupies a special place.

These various divisions, however, differ greatly from one another not only by reason of their source, location, and age, but especially in their view of the nature and importance of issues bearing on belief and Church structure.[50] Therefore, neither minimizing the differences between the various Christian bodies, nor overlooking the bonds which continue to exist among them in spite of divisions, this sacred Synod has

46. The Council of Ephesus (431) defined as matters of faith a number of doctrines about Jesus Christ (that He was both God and man, but one divine person, with divine and human natures joined in a special union called "hypostatic") and solemnly proclaimed His Mother Mary to be the holy Mother of God. The Council deposed Nestorius, Patriarch of Constantinople, for having held opposing doctrines. Followers of Nestorius' ideas (e.g., that God merely dwelt in the human nature assumed by Him in the womb of Mary) formed their own Church and came to be called Nestorians. There are some thousands of them still in the Middle East.

47. The Council of Chalcedon (451) defined that Jesus was perfect God and perfect man, in (not of) two natures, without confusion, without change (against the Monophysites), without separation, without division, both natures being united in one person and one "hypostasis."

48. *Solutionem,* sometimes translated "dissolving." For centuries, the year 1054 has been taken as symbolic of one of history's most divisive events: the tragic rupture between Eastern and Western Christendom. On July 16 of that year, in the name of Pope Leo IX (who had been dead for three months), the papal legate Humbert hurled on the altar of Hagia Sophia in Constantinople a document excommunicating Patriarch Michael Cerularius. In turn, the Patriarch excommunicated the papal delegation.

Neither the See of Rome nor that of Constantinople anathematized each other's followers; the excommunications were personal. By a sad and muddled interpretation of history, however, partisans of East and West focused on this event as marking the moment of definitive schism. In any case, the discourteous language of both anathemas ("wild pigs," "cockle of heresy," "impious men," and the like) went far to deepen the estrangement.

Just before the close of Vatican Council II, Pope Paul and Patriarch Athenagoras made deeply Christian gestures of reconciliation. On Dec. 7, 1965, in solemn ceremonies at St. Peter's and at the Patriarch's cathedral in Istanbul, the nine-century-old anathemas were nullified and the way dramatically opened for accepting the breath of the Holy Spirit.

49. Before Pope Paul's last-minute change, the text here read: "in the Western Church itself."

50. *Fidem et structuram ecclesiasticam,* sometimes translated "faith and order in the Church" or "faith and Church order."

decided to propose the following considerations for prudent ecumenical action.

The Special Position of the Eastern Churches

14. For many centuries, the Churches of the East and of the West went their own ways, though a brotherly communion of faith and sacramental life bound them together. If disagreements in belief and discipline[51] arose among them, the Roman See acted by common consent as moderator.

This most sacred Synod gladly reminds all of one highly significant fact among others: in the East there flourish many particular or local Churches; among them the Patriarchal Churches[52] hold first place; and of these, many glory in taking[53] their origins from the apostles themselves.[54] As a result, there prevailed and still prevails among Orientals an eager desire to perpetuate in a communion of faith and charity those family ties which ought to thrive between local Churches, as between sisters. It is equally worthy of note that from their very origins the Churches of the East have had a treasury from which the Church of the West has amply drawn for its liturgy, spiritual tradition, and jurisprudence. Nor must we underestimate the fact that basic dogmas of the Christian faith concerning the Trinity and God's Word made flesh of the Virgin Mary[55] were defined in Ecumenical Councils held in the East.[56] To preserve this faith, these Churches have suffered much, and still do so.

However, the heritage handed down by the apostles was

---

51. *Fidem vel disciplinam,* also translated "faith and order."
52. I.e., Constantinople, Antioch, Alexandria, Jerusalem (Greek tradition); Moscow, Serbia, Bulgaria (Slavic tradition). The Patriarchate of Rumania and the Church of Georgia are related to both traditions. In the Greek tradition there are also the "autocephalous" Churches of Greece and Cyprus. The "autocephalous" Churches of Poland, Czechoslovakia, and Finland are in the Slavic tradition.
53. A phrase added by Pope Paul to replace "many took their origins . . ."
54. We read in the Acts of the Apostles and St. Paul's Epistles that James the Less was at Jerusalem (Gal. 1:18-19), Peter at Antioch (Gal. 2:11-14), Paul at Cyprus and Athens (Acts 13:4-12; 17:16-34). Alexandria was traditionally held to be the see of Mark.
55. Pope Paul simplified the text here, which read: "from the Virgin Mother of God."
56. The first seven Ecumenical Councils were held in, or not far from, Constantinople: Nicaea I (325), Constantinople I (381), Ephesus (431), Chalcedon (451), Constantinople II (533), Constantinople III (680), Nicaea II (787).

received in different forms and ways, so that from the very beginnings of the Church it has had a varied development in various places, thanks to a similar variety of natural gifts and conditions of life. Added to external causes, and[57] to mutual failures in understanding and charity, all these circumstances set the stage for separations.

Therefore, this sacred Synod urges all, but especially those who plan to devote themselves to the work of restoring the full communion that is desired[58] between the Eastern Churches and the Catholic Church, to give due consideration to these special aspects of the origin and growth of the Churches of the East, and to the character of the relations which obtained between them and the Roman See before the separation, and to form for themselves a correct evaluation of these facts.[59] If these recommendations are carefully carried out, they will make a very great contribution to any proposed dialogues.

15. Everybody also knows with what love the Eastern Christians enact the sacred liturgy, especially the celebration of the Eucharist, which is the source of the Church's life and the pledge of future glory. In this celebration the faithful, united with their bishop and endowed with an outpouring of the Holy Spirit, gain access to God the Father through the Son, the Word made flesh, who suffered and was glorified. And so, made "partakers of the divine nature" (2 Pet. 1:4), they enter into communion with the most holy Trinity. Hence, through the celebration of the Eucharist of the Lord in each of these Churches, the Church of God is built up and grows in stature,[60] while through the rite of concelebration their bond with one another is made manifest.

In this liturgical worship, the Christians of the East pay high tribute, in very beautiful hymns, to Mary ever Virgin, whom the Ecumenical Synod of Ephesus solemnly proclaimed to be God's most holy Mother so that, in accord with the Scriptures, Christ may be truly and properly acknowledged as Son of God and Son of Man. They also give homage to

---

57. By inserting the word "etiam" (propter defectum etiam mutuae comprehensionis et caritatis), Pope Paul stressed the word "mutual."
58. Pope Paul inserted "that is desired."
59. The general reader will perhaps find it useful to consult the compact (192 p.) work by Hubert Jedin, "Ecumenical Councils of the Catholic Church" (Paulist Press, 95¢).
60. Cf. St. John Chrysostom, "In Ioannem Homilia XLVI," PG 59, 260-262.

the saints, including Fathers of the universal Church.[61]

Although these Churches are separated from us, they possess true sacraments, above all—by apostolic succession—the priesthood and the Eucharist, whereby they are still joined to us in a very close relationship. Therefore, given suitable circumstances and the approval of Church authority, some worship in common is not merely possible but is recommended.[62]

Moreover, in the East are to be found the riches of those spiritual traditions to which monasticism gives special expression. From the glorious days of the holy Fathers, there flourished in the East that monastic spirituality which later flowed over into the Western world, and there provided a source from which Latin monastic life took its rise and has often drawn fresh vigor ever since. Therefore Catholics are strongly urged to avail themselves more often[63] of these spiritual riches of the Eastern Fathers, riches which lift up the whole man to the contemplation of divine mysteries.

All should realize that it is of supreme importance to understand, venerate, preserve, and foster the exceedingly rich liturgical and spiritual heritage of the Eastern Churches, in order faithfully to preserve the fullness of Christian tradition, and to bring about reconciliation between Eastern and Western Christians.

16. From the earliest times, moreover, the Eastern Churches followed their own disciplines, sanctioned by the holy Fathers, by synods, even ecumenical Councils. Far from being an obstacle to the Church's unity, such diversity of customs and observances only adds to her comeliness, and contributes greatly to carrying out her mission, as has already been recalled. To remove any shadow of doubt, then, this sacred Synod solemnly declares that the Churches of the East, while keeping in mind the necessary unity of the whole Church, have the power[64] to govern themselves according to their

61. Basil, Gregory of Nyssa, Gregory of Nazianzen, John Chrysostom, Athanasius, Ephrem.
62. Fuller instruction on this point is set forth in the Council's Decree on Catholic Eastern Churches, promulgated Nov. 21, 1964 (Art. 26-29).
63. Pope Paul added the phrase "more often," perhaps because, without it, the sentence might be taken to mean that Catholics had ignored the spiritual riches of the Eastern Fathers.
64. There is dispute among scholars about the significance of a change Pope Paul made here, from "have the right and duty" (*ius et officium*) to "have the power" (*facultatem*). Some argue the change weakens the text; others point out that in canon law *facultas* means *ius et officium*. Cf. Decree on Eastern Catholic Churches, Art. 5.

own disciplines, since these are better suited to the temperament of their faithful and better adapted to foster the good of souls. Although it has not always been honored, the strict observance of this traditional principle is among the prerequisites for any restoration of unity.[65]

17. What has already been said about legitimate variety we are pleased to apply to differences in theological expressions of doctrine. In the investigation of revealed truth, East and West have used different methods and approaches in understanding and proclaiming divine things. It is hardly surprising, then, if sometimes one tradition has come nearer than the other to an apt appreciation of certain aspects of a revealed mystery, or has expressed them in a clearer manner. As a result, these various theological formulations are often[66] to be considered as complementary rather than conflicting. With regard to the authentic theological traditions of the Orientals, we must recognize that they are admirably rooted in holy Scripture, fostered and given expression in liturgical life, and nourished by the living tradition of the apostles and by the writings of the Fathers and spiritual authors of the East; they are directed toward a right ordering of life, indeed, toward a full contemplation of Christian truth.

While thanking God that many Eastern sons of the Catholic Church, who are preserving this heritage and wish to express it more faithfully and completely in their lives, are already living in full communion[67] with their brethren who follow the tradition of the West, this sacred Synod declares that this entire heritage of spirtuality and liturgy, of discipline and theology, in their various traditions, belongs to the full catholic and apostolic character of the Church.

18. After taking all these factors into consideration, this sacred Synod confirms what previous Councils and Roman Pontiffs have proclaimed: in order to restore communion and unity or preserve them, one must "impose no burden beyond what is indispensable" (Acts 15:28). It is the Coun-

---

65. The Decree stresses that unity does not mean uniformity. The Eastern Churches are here assured that diversity of rite among the Churches in union with Rome is guaranteed.

66. The text read "considered more as . . ." before Pope Paul changed "more" to "often."

67. This is a reference to those who are often called "Uniates." The Decree does not use the term—a tactful decision, since the term has had a history of derogatory use among the Orthodox.

cil's urgent desire that every effort should henceforth be made toward the gradual realization of this goal in the various organizations and living activities of the Church,[68] especially by prayer and by fraternal dialogue on points of doctrine and the more pressing pastoral problems of our time. Similarly, to the pastors and faithful of the Catholic Church, it recommends close relationships with those no longer living in the East but far from their homeland, so that friendly collaboration with them may increase in a spirit of love, without quarrelsome rivalry. If this task is carried on wholeheartedly, this sacred Synod hopes that with the removal of the wall dividing the Eastern and Western Church[69] there may at last be but the one dwelling, firmly established on the cornerstone, Christ Jesus, who will make both one.[70]

The Separated Churches and Ecclesial Communities in the West

19. The Churches and ecclesial Communities* which were separated from the Apostolic See of Rome during the very serious crisis that began in the West at the end of the Middle Ages, or during later times, are bound to the Catholic Church by a special affinity and close relationship in view of the long span of earlier centuries when the Christian people lived in ecclesiastical communion.

Since in origin, teaching, and spiritual practice, these

68. Earlier attempts at restoration of unity between the Churches of East and West (the Council of Lyons and the Council of Florence) ended in failure. Among the reasons for the failure, historians give prominent place to lack of understanding and cooperation among the people. In this sentence and in the following sentence, therefore, the Second Vatican Council stresses the need for prayer and dialogue in parish organizations, etc.

69. On Feb. 15, 1965, Pope Paul VI welcomed two Greek Orthodox envoys sent by Orthodox Ecumenical Patriarch Athenagoras of Constantinople and his Synod to carry out the mandate given Athenagoras by the Pan-Orthodox Conference held at Rhodes in Nov., 1964. The envoys, Metropolitan Meliton of Heliopolis and Theira and Metropolitan Chrysostomos of Myra, told the Pope the Conference of 14 Churches had decided unanimously that further preparation was necessary for a dialogue between the Orthodox and Catholic Churches, and the Conference would work for the success of such a dialogue "through creating favorable circumstances and by study of the various subjects of this dialogue." This day, the Pope said, might be regarded as the end of centuries of history and the beginning of new relations between the Catholic Church and the Orthodox East.

70. Cf. Council of Florence, Sess. VI (1439), definition "Laetentur caeli": Mansi 31, 1026 E.

*On the terminology, cf. note 45.

Churches and ecclesial Communities differ not only from us
but also among themselves to a considerable degree, the task
of describing them adequately is very difficult; we do not
propose to do it here.[71]

Although the ecumenical movement and the desire for
reconciliation with the Catholic Church have not yet grown
universally strong, it is our hope that the ecumenical spirit
and mutual esteem will gradually increase among all men.

At the same time, however, one should recognize that between these Churches and Communities on the one hand,
and the Catholic Church on the other, there are very weighty
differences not only of a historical, sociological, psychological,
and cultural nature, but especially in the interpretation of
revealed truth. That ecumenical dialogue may be more easily
undertaken, despite these differences, we desire to propose in
what follows some considerations which can and ought to
serve as a basis and motivation for such dialogue.

20. Our thoughts are concerned first of all with those Christians who openly confess Jesus Christ as God and Lord and
as the sole Mediator between God and man unto the glory
of the one God, Father, Son, and Holy Spirit. We are indeed
aware that among them views are held considerably different
from the doctrine of the Catholic Church even concerning
Christ, God's Word made flesh, and the work of redemption,
and thus concerning the mystery and ministry of the Church
and the role of Mary in the work of salvation. But we rejoice to see our separated brethren looking to Christ as the
source and center of ecclesiastical communion. Inspired by
longing for union with Christ, they feel compelled to search
for unity ever more ardently, and to bear witness to their
faith among all the peoples of the earth.

21. A love, veneration, and near cult of the sacred Scriptures
lead our brethren to a constant and expert[72] study of the
sacred text. For the gospel "is the power of God unto salva-

---

71. This short paragraph and the following one interrupt the logical flow
somewhat. The reason is that they are insertions (not by Pope Paul but by
the Secretariat for Promoting Christian Unity) to take care of questions
readers may ask when going through this Decree: Why aren't the separated
Churches and Communities identified or described? Do the Council Fathers
think all Churches other than the Catholic Church are dedicated to the
ecumenical movement?

72. *Constans et sollers . . . studium. Sollers,* often mistranslated "diligent,"
means clever, skillful, expert, intelligent, etc. What is stressed here is that
Protestants know the Bible.

tion to everyone who believes, to Jew first and then to Greek" (Rom. 1:16).

Calling upon the Holy Spirit, they seek in these sacred Scriptures God as He speaks to them in Christ,[73] the One whom the prophets foretold, God's Word made flesh for us. In the Scriptures they contemplate the life of Christ, as well as the teachings and the actions of the Divine Master on behalf of men's salvation, in particular the mysteries of His death and resurrection.

But when Christians separated from us affirm the divine authority of the sacred Books, they think differently from us —different ones in different ways—about the relationship between the Scriptures and the Church. In the Church, according to Catholic belief, an authentic teaching office plays a special role in the explanation and proclamation of the written word of God.

Nevertheless, in dialogue itself, the sacred utterances are precious instruments in the mighty hand of God for attaining that unity which the Savior holds out to all men.[74]

22. By the sacrament of baptism, whenever it is properly conferred in the way the Lord determined, and received with the appropriate dispositions of soul, a man becomes truly incorporated into the crucified and glorified Christ and is reborn to a sharing of the divine life, as the apostle says: "For you were buried together with him in Baptism, and in him

73. Until almost the last moment, the text here read: "At the prompting of the Holy Spirit, they find God in the Holy Scriptures, who speaks to them in Christ." Pope Paul VI called for the change. Early translations of the final Decree read: "While invoking the Holy Spirit, they seek in these very Scriptures God, as it were, speaking to them in Christ," and: "At the call of the Holy Spirit they look in the Holy Scriptures for God, who in some manner speaks to them in Christ." The translation we are using clears up problems caused by misplaced commas and a misunderstood Latin word: *quasi*. Early translators apparently took *quasi sibi loquentem in Christo* to mean "as if He were speaking in Christ." *Quasi* would have that meaning "as if" with a subjunctive, but not with the participle it accompanies here. The text of the Decree actually affirms a real manner in which God speaks to those who seek Him in the Bible. The sentence certainly does not contradict the immediately preceding affirmation that the gospel "is the power of God unto salvation to everyone who believes. . . ."

74. This very thought has been at the heart of the movement for a "common Bible," i.e., a faithful translation accepted for use by Catholic and Protestant Churches, especially in the dialogue. The possibility of such a Bible became evident when objective scholarship led Catholic and Protestant scholars again and again to the same results (cf. Walter M. Abbott, S.J., "The Bible Is a Bond," *America*, Oct. 24, 1959, pp. 100-102). The Second Vatican Council endorsed the idea in the Constitution on Divine Revelation, Art. 22.

also rose again through faith in the working of God who raised him from the dead" (Col. 2:12; cf. Rom. 6:4).

Baptism, therefore, constitutes a sacramental bond of unity linking all who have been reborn by means of it. But baptism, of itself, is only a beginning, a point of departure, for it is wholly directed toward the acquiring of fullness of life in Christ. Baptism is thus oriented toward a complete profession of faith, a complete incorporation into the system of salvation such as Christ Himself willed it to be, and finally, toward a complete participation in Eucharistic communion.

The ecclesial Communities separated from us lack that fullness of unity with us which should flow from baptism, and we believe that especially because of the lack of the sacrament of orders they have not preserved the genuine and total[75] reality of the Eucharistic mystery. Nevertheless, when they commemorate the Lord's death and resurrection in the Holy Supper, they profess that it signifies life in communion with Christ and they await His coming in glory. For these reasons, dialogue should be undertaken concerning the true meaning of the Lord's Supper, the other sacraments, and the Church's worship and ministry.

23. The Christian way of life of these brethren is nourished by faith in Christ. It is strengthened by the grace of baptism and the hearing of God's Word. This way of life expresses itself in private prayer, in meditation on the Bible, in Christian family life, and in services of worship offered by Communities assembled to praise God. Furthermore, their worship sometimes displays notable features of an ancient, common liturgy.

The faith by which they believe in Christ bears fruit in praise and thanksgiving for the benefits received from the hands of God. Joined to it are a lively sense of justice and a true neighborly charity. This active faith has produced many organizations for the relief of spiritual and bodily distress, the education of youth, the advancement of humane social conditions, and the promotion of peace throughout the world.[76]

---

75. Pope Paul changed the text from *plenam realitatem Mysterii eucharistici* to *genuinam atque integram substantiam Mysterii eucharistici* (from "full reality of the Eucharistic mystery" to "genuine and total reality of the Eucharistic mystery").
76. Again, a second time in this Decree, the text stresses the connection between the spiritual life and social action. Cf. Art. 14.

And if in moral matters there are many Christians who do not always understand the gospel in the same way as Catholics, and do not admit the same solutions for the more difficult problems of modern society, nevertheless they share our desire to cling to Christ's word as the source of Christian virtue and to obey the apostolic command: "Whatever you do in word or in work, do all in the name of the Lord Jesus,* giving thanks to God the Father through him" (Col. 3:17). Hence, the ecumenical dialogue could start with discussions concerning the application of the gospel to moral questions.

24. So, after this brief exposition of the circumstances within which ecumenical activity has to operate and of the principles by which it should be guided, we confidently look to the future.[77] This most sacred Synod urges the faithful to abstain from any superficiality or imprudent zeal, for these can cause harm to true progress towards unity. Their ecumenical activity must not be other than fully and sincerely Catholic, that is, loyal to the truth we have received from the apostles and the Fathers,[78] and in harmony with the faith which the Catholic Church has always professed, and at the same time tending toward that fullness with which our Lord wants His body to be endowed in the course of time.

This most sacred Synod urgently desires that the initiatives of the sons of the Catholic Church, joined with those of the separated brethren, go forward without obstructing the ways of divine Providence and without prejudging the future inspiration of the Holy Spirit.[79] Further, this Synod declares

---

*The Latin adds "Christ."—Ed.

77. By this Decree, the Roman Catholic Church established its position in the ecumenical movement without becoming a member of the World Council of Churches. However, less than two months after promulgation of the Decree, the World Council's Central Committee, meeting at Enugu, Nigeria, approved a proposal to form an eight-member working group for discussions with the Catholic Church. In Rome, a spokesman for the Secretariat for Promoting Christian Unity called the decision "a concrete result of the Decree on Ecumenism" and said it "could lead to further development of ecumenical dialogue." On Feb. 18, 1965, Augustin Cardinal Bea, president of the Secretariat, announced at the World Council's headquarters in Geneva that the Holy See "greets with joy and fully accepts" the World Council's invitation "to explore together the possibilities of dialogue and cooperation." The Cardinal added that the Holy See wished "to develop direct contacts with individual Churches or federations of Churches, in the East and in the West, as well as contacts with the World Council of Churches as such."

78. I.e., the ancient Fathers of the Church.

79. It is surely not an exaggeration to say that the Council here adopts an open and forward-looking attitude, and expects there will be need of updating again in the future—methods and approaches of today may soon be out of date.

its realization that the holy task of reconciling all Christians in the unity of the one and only Church of Christ transcends human energies and abilities. It therefore places its hope entirely in the prayer of Christ for the Church, in the love of the Father for us, and in the power of the Holy Spirit. "And hope does not disappoint, because the charity of God is poured forth in our hearts by the Holy Spirit who has been given to us" (Rom. 5:5).

Each and every one of the things set forth in this Decree has won the consent of the Fathers. We, too, by the apostolic authority conferred on us by Christ, join with the Venerable Fathers in approving, decreeing, and establishing these things in the Holy Spirit, and we direct that what has thus been enacted in synod be published to God's glory.

Rome, at St. Peter's, November 21, 1964

I, Paul, Bishop of the Catholic Church

There follow the signatures of the Fathers.

A RESPONSE

Unless all signs fail, the Decree on Ecumenism marks the beginning of a new era in the relation of the Churches to one another—an era that can truly be called ecumenical. Although an ecumenical movement had been developing outside of Roman Catholicism for fifty years prior to the summoning of Vatican Council II by Pope John XXIII, it was truncated by the lack of Catholic participation. The convening of the Council awakened hopes that there might be a change in Catholic attitude. Those hopes have now been fulfilled far beyond all expectations.

The promise of a new era is especially evident in the new way in which the Decree speaks of non-Catholic Christians. No one can read it without being impressed by the respect shown for those outside the Roman obedience and by the care which is taken to understand their position and to state it fairly. Moreover, instead of dogmatically insisting on their return to Rome as the only possible movement toward unity, the Decree is concerned with a movement toward Christ. From a Protestant angle, this fresh orientation is of the highest consequence and is pregnant with creative possibilities.

The significance of the Decree stands out vividly when it is read side by side with the encyclical *Mortalium Animos* of 1928 and the *Monitum* of the Holy Office in 1948. These represented such an isolated aloofness that the door appeared to be closed against any effective dialogue between Roman Catholics and non-Roman Christians. Today the door is wide open.

The Decree's recognition of the "truly Christian endowments" which are to be formed among the non-Roman bodies is crucial. The ecumenical dialogue is lifted to a new level when it is acknowledged that they "have by no means been deprived of significance and importance in the mystery of salvation" and that the work of God's grace in them could result in "a more ample realization of the very mystery of Christ and the Church" (4). The assumption that the Holy Spirit is at work in "ecclesial communities" outside the Roman Catholic Church is very different from the previous way of treating non-Roman Christians merely as individuals and ignoring their corporate life and structure.

Another seminal point is the stress on "the task of re-

newal and reform" as essential to ecumenical advance. To
Protestants it is especially gratifying to read that "Christ
summons the Church, as she goes on her pilgrim way, to that
continual reformation of which she always has need" (6).
This is in accord with a fundamental principle of the Protestant Reformation, and the recognition of it by Vatican
Council II will surely make for better understanding.

Another noteworthy aspect of the Decree, closely related
to the foregoing, is the frank statement that for the divisions
of Christendom "men of both sides were to blame." The accent on the need for common penitence and mutual forgiveness (7) should go far to develop a new atmosphere of ecclesiastical relations, very different from the polemical self-
righteousness which has often characterized discussions between Catholics and Protestants in the past.

The reference to the difference between Catholic and
Protestant thinking about "the relationship between the
Scriptures and the Church" (21) reminds us that the argu-
ment over the source of revelation has not been resolved.
But the strong emphasis on Scripture, with an implied as-
sumption of the centrality of Scripture in tradition, narrows
the distance between Catholic and Protestant viewpoints.
There is reason to be grateful also for the manifestation of
Catholic concern for biblical studies unhampered by dog-
matic considerations.

The decision that "in certain special circumstances" it is
"allowable, indeed desirable," that Catholics "join in prayer
with their separated brethren" (8) is likely to have the most
far-reaching influence. Even though prayer together is restricted to "special circumstances" and the practice of it controlled by local bishops, it may be expected to keep the coming dialogue at a deep spiritual level and save it from becoming over-intellectualized. Prayer together will often be the
simplest expression of a new ecclesiastical relationship in the
local community and also the most convincing evidence of
it. It is a cause for rejoicing that Pope Paul VI has himself
set the example by joining with Protestant and Orthodox
participants in a service of prayer for unity in Rome during
the last week of the Council.

The commendation of "cooperation among all Christians"
and the suggestion that it be "increasingly developed" in relation to problems of modern society (12) is warmly welcomed. Already there are concrete evidences that this is being translated into action, and we may rightly expect that, as

we serve together in tasks to which Christ calls us both, we shall come to a greater awareness of our oneness in Him and so be better prepared to deal with the differences that separate us in the realm of doctrine. For this reason, the decision of the World Council of Churches and of the Holy See to establish a working group, both for considering the possibilities of cooperation in common concerns and for dialogue on differences, is to be hailed with enthusiasm. There is good reason to hope that through such an instrumentality, paralleled by such regional arrangements as have already been developed in the United States between the National Council of Churches and the Bishops' Commission for Ecumenical Affairs, the Decree on Ecumenism will be practically implemented in steadily increasing ways.

While clearly committing the Catholic Church to ecumenical dialogue and action, the Decree wisely warns against "a false conciliatory approach" (11). Such an approach, it is rightly affirmed, would be "foreign to the spirit of ecumenism." When we are really trying to see things through the eyes of another, we may be tempted to be so amiable that differences are obscured or blurred. For genuine and fruitful dialogue candor is as essential as respect.

With this in mind, I suggest that the Decree does not really reconcile its ecumenical outlook with its assumption that the Roman Catholic is the only true Church. This assumption is explicit in the statement that "it is through Christ's Catholic Church alone, which is the all-embracing means of salvation, that the fullness of the means of salvation can be obtained" (3). Associated with this is the further assumption of the primacy of Peter and of his jurisdiction over the whole Church. These assumptions seem to indicate that the Roman Catholic understanding of ecumenism is unchangeably Rome-centered. If so, how far can the Roman Catholic Church go in ecumenical relations with those whose ecumenism has no center but Christ?

Another way of approaching this issue is to ask how much is involved in the Decree's reference to Protestant bodies as "ecclesial communities." On the one hand, this seems to imply a modification of the traditional Catholic attitude. At least, it suggests that the corporate life of Protestants has some kind of churchly reality. But, on the other hand, the hesitation in speaking of non-Catholic bodies as Churches apparently implies a difference between "Church" and "ecclesial community." What is this difference? Non-Catholics still need further light as to how far the Catholic Church goes in acknowledging the reality of the Church beyond its own borders.

Whatever may happen in future ecumenical dialogue about ecclesiology, there is every reason to believe that the Roman Catholic Church and the non-Roman Churches can now live and work together in Christian fellowship. For this happy prospect we can all be grateful—Protestant and Catholic alike—to the Vatican Council's Decree on Ecumenism.

The test of the Decree will be found in what now happens in local communities. It is there that the full meaning of it will be explored and discovered. The great thing to be desired at this juncture is that Christian congregations of every name begin to move forward in both dialogue and concrete measures of cooperation such as the Decree recommends. The inherited patterns of separateness and suspicion will not be overcome easily, but Vatican Council II is a challenge to all Christians to follow the more excellent way.

SAMUEL MCCREA CAVERT

EASTERN CHURCHES

THIS DECREE SHOULD be considered as a complement to the Decree on Ecumenism.

Before the beginning of the Council, the Commission for the Eastern Churches had drafted a schema entitled, "That All May Be One." It was presented to the Council Fathers on December 1, 1962, but was rejected and sent to a mixed commission composed of members of the Theological Commission, the Commission for the Eastern Churches, and the Secretariat for Promoting Christian Unity. Between the first and the second sessions, the Secretariat for Promoting Christian Unity drafted its first schema on ecumenism. The Commission for the Eastern Churches then restricted its studies to those Eastern Churches in union with the Holy See, and drafted a new schema. This new text met with much criticism and could not be discussed during the second session. Between the second and third sessions, the text was improved. Finally, it was submitted to the Council Fathers on October 15, 1964. When a vote was taken, 1,920 *modi* (reservations or proposals for amendment) were expressed by the Council Fathers.

The text was again revised by the commission and, on November 21, when the final vote was taken in the presence of the Holy Father, 2,110 Fathers voted *placet* and only thirty-nine voted *non placet*.

The decree has brought most valuable clarifications in several fields concerning the Catholic Eastern Churches. (1) It expresses unequivocally the position and the rights of the Eastern communities in the Catholic Church and re-establishes privileges and customs which have been abolished in the past. (2) It clearly manifests the hope of the Council for a corporate reunion of the Eastern Churches presently not in union with the Church of Rome.

Two commentaries on the Decree have been published in English: the first, in *The Jurist* (April, 1965; Volume XXV #2), was written by the Rev. Meletius Wojnar, O.S.B.M.; the second appears in a separate volume by Msgr. Victor J. Pospishil, J.C.D. (John XXIII Center for Eastern Christian Studies, Fordham University, New York).

There are six main Eastern Catholic rites: the Chaldean, Syrian, Maronite, Coptic, Armenian, and Byzantine rites. There are about one million Catholics of Eastern rites in the United States.

PAUL MAILLEUX, S.J.

Decree on Eastern Catholic¹ Churches

PAUL, BISHOP
SERVANT OF THE SERVANTS OF GOD
TOGETHER WITH THE FATHERS OF THE SACRED COUNCIL
FOR EVERLASTING MEMORY

INTRODUCTION

1. The Catholic Church holds in high esteem the institutions of the Eastern Churches, their liturgical rites, ecclesiastical traditions, and Christian way of life. For, distinguished as they are by their venerable antiquity, they are bright with that tradition² which was handed down from the apostles through the Fathers,³ and which forms part of the divinely revealed and undivided heritage of the universal Church.

This sacred and ecumenical Synod, therefore, in its concern for the Eastern Churches which bear living witness to this tradition, and in its desire that they may flourish and execute with new apostolic vigor the task entrusted to them, has determined to lay down a number of principles beyond those which relate to the universal Church. Other particulars are left to the care of the Eastern synods and of the Apostolic See.⁴

---

1. The word "Catholic" has been unduly omitted in many translations. The word is essential because the Decree is not directly intended for the Eastern Churches that are not united with Rome.
2. *Leo XIII, apostolic letter "Orientalium dignitas," Nov. 30, 1894: Leonis XIII Acta, XIV, 201-202.*
3. I.e., the ancient Fathers of the Church.—Ed.
4. The Council itself admits that its work is unfinished; this Decree needs to be completed and adapted by the Holy See and by local particular synods.

The Individual Churches or Rites

2. That Church, Holy and Catholic, which is the Mystical Body of Christ, is made up of the faithful who are organically united in the Holy Spirit through the same faith, the same sacraments, and the same government and who, combining into various groups held together by a hierarchy, form separate Churches or rites. Between these, there flourishes such an admirable brotherhood that this variety within the Church in no way harms her unity, but rather manifests it. For it is the mind of the Catholic Church that each individual Church or rite retain its traditions whole and entire, while adjusting its way of life to the various needs of time and place.[5]

3. Such individual Churches, whether of the East or of the West, although they differ somewhat among themselves in what are called rites (that is, in liturgy, ecclesiastical discipline, and spiritual heritage)[6] are, nevertheless, equally entrusted to the pastoral guidance of the Roman Pontiff, the divinely appointed successor of St. Peter in supreme governance over the universal Church. They are consequently of equal dignity,[7] so that none of them is superior to the others by reason of rite. They enjoy the same rights and are under

5. *Leo IX, "In terra pax" (1053): "Ut enim"; Innocent III, IV Lateran Synod (1215), chap. IV: "licet Graecos"; letter "Inter quatuor," Aug. 2, 1206: "Postulasti postmodum"; Innocent IX, letter "Cum de cetero," Aug. 27, 1247; letter "Sub catholicae," Mar. 6, 1254, intro.; Nicholas III, letter "Istud est memoriale," Oct. 9, 1278; Leo X, apostolic letter "Accepimus nuper," May 18, 1521; Paul III, apostolic letter § 5; Clement VIII, constitution "Magnus Dominus," Dec. 23, 1595, § 10; Paul V, constitution "Solet circumspecta," Dec. 10, 1615, § 3; Benedict XIV, encyclical letter "Allatae sunt," June 26, 1755, §§ 3, 6-19, 32; Pius VI, encyclical letter "Catholicae communionis," May 24, 1787; Pius IX, letter "In suprema," Jan. 6, 1848, § 3; apostolic letter "Ecclesiam Christi," Nov. 26, 1853; constitution "Romani Pontificis," Jan. 6, 1862; Leo XIII, apostolic letter "Praeclara," June 20, 1894, no. 7; apostolic letter "Orientalium dignitas," Nov. 30, 1894, intro; etc.*
6. The word "rite" means more than liturgical customs. It could be called the style of Christian life of a community which, according to the Decree on Ecumenism (Art. 15, 16, 17) is to be found in the particularities of worship, of canon law, of asceticism and monasticism and also in the peculiar theological system. The consideration of the Church for the Eastern rites is emphasized in the Decree on Ecumenism, Art. 14.
7. By stressing the equal dignity of the different Catholic rites, the Council condemns clearly the theory of those who, mostly in the 18th century, taught that the Roman rite enjoyed some kind of precedence over the others. In the past, the apostolate in the missions has been conducted exclusively in the Latin rite. This practice has been resented by some Easterners, mostly in India where the priests of the ancient Malabar rite were always obliged to adopt the Roman rite to undertake missionary apostolate.

the same obligations, even with respect to preaching the gospel to the whole world (cf. Mk. 16:15) under the guidance of the Roman Pontiff.

4. Therefore, attention should everywhere be given to the preservation and growth of each individual Church. For this purpose, parishes and a special hierarchy should be established for each where the spiritual good of the faithful so demands.[8] The Ordinaries of the various individual Churches which have jurisdiction in the same territory should, by taking common counsel in regular meetings, strive to promote unity of action. Through common endeavor let them sustain common tasks, the better to further the good of religion and the more effectively to safeguard clerical discipline.[9]

All clerics and those aspiring to sacred orders should be well instructed in various rites and especially in the principles which are involved in interritual questions. As part of their catechetical education, the laity, too, should be taught about these rites and their rules.

Finally, each and every Catholic, as also the baptized number of every non-Catholic Church or community who enters into the fullness of Catholic communion, should everywhere retain his proper rite,[10] cherish it, and observe it to the best of his ability.[11] This rule does not deny the right whereby

8. In the United States and Canada proper eparchies (Eastern term for dioceses) have been established for Eastern Catholics: seven for the Ukrainians (four in Canada and three in the United States) and two for the Ruthenians. Besides, 110 parishes have been organized for less numerous Eastern groups; they are committed to the local Latin rite bishops.
9. *Pius XII, motu proprio "Cleri sanctitati," June 2, 1957, can. 4.*
10. The Council wishes unequivocally that every Eastern Christian who is received into the Catholic Church retain his original rite. Does it make invalid his reception into the Latin rite—without dispensation of the Holy See? The canonists do not agree in their answer. That point will have to be clarified. It may be of major importance in some marriage cases. Let us suppose, for instance, that a young Greek who was baptized in the Orthodox Church becomes formally the member of a Latin rite Catholic parish without any dispensation. Later, he meets a Greek Orthodox girl and marries her in an Orthodox Church. If he has remained of the Byzantine rite, his marriage is valid; if he has effectively gone over to the Latin rite, his marriage is invalid. See Art. 18.
It may be appropriate here to remember that the regulations established earlier for North America remain in force, particularly in cases of marriages between Catholics of different rites; the marriage must be celebrated in the rite of the bridegroom, and the children belong to the rite of their father.
11. *Pius XII, motu proprio "Cleri Sanctitati," June 2, 1957, can. 8: "without the permission of the Holy See," following the practice of preceding centuries. In the same manner, concerning baptized non-Catholics we read in can. 11 that "they may adopt the rite which they prefer." In the text offered here the observance of the rite is regulated in a positive way for all and everywhere in the world.*

persons, communities, or areas may in special cases have recourse to the Apostolic See, which, as the supreme judge of interchurch relations, will directly or through other authorities meet the needs of the occasion in an ecumenical spirit and issue opportune directives, decrees, or rescripts.

Preservation of the Spiritual Heritage of the Eastern Churches

5. History, tradition, and numerous ecclesiastical institutions manifest luminously how much the universal Church is indebted to the Eastern Churches.[12] This sacred Synod, therefore, not only honors this ecclesiastical and spiritual heritage with merited esteem and rightful praise, but also unhesitatingly looks upon it as the heritage of Christ's universal Church.[13] For this reason, it solemnly declares that the Churches of the East, as much as those of the West, fully enjoy the right, and are in duty bound, to rule themselves. Each should do so according to its proper and individual procedures, inasmuch as practices sanctioned by a noble antiquity harmonize better with the customs of the faithful and are seen as more likely to foster the good of souls.

6. All Eastern rite members should know and be convinced that they can and should always preserve their lawful liturgical rites and their established way of life, and that these should not be altered except by way of an appropriate and organic development. Easterners themselves should honor all these things with the greatest fidelity. Besides, they should acquire an ever greater knowledge and a more exact use of them. If they have improperly fallen away from them because of circumstances of time or personage, let them take pains to return to their ancestral ways.

Those who, by reason of their office or an apostolic assignment, are in frequent communication with the Eastern Churches or their faithful should, in proportion to the gravity of their task, be carefully trained to know and respect the rites, discipline, doctrine, history, and characteristics of East-

12. *Cf. Leo XIII, apostolic letter "Orientalium dignitas," Nov. 30, 1894; "Praeclara gratulationis," June 20, 1894, and the documents listed in note 5.*
13. In many instances, the traditions of the Western and the Eastern Churches are complementary.

erners.[14] Religious societies and associations of the Latin rite working in Eastern countries or among Eastern faithful are earnestly counseled to multiply the success of their apostolic labors by founding houses or even provinces of Eastern rite, as far as this can be done.[15]

Eastern Rite Patriarchs[16]

7. The institution of the patriarchate has existed in the Church from the earliest times and was recognized by the first ecumenical Synods.[17]

By the name Eastern Patriarch is meant the bishop who has jurisdiction over all bishops (including metropolitans), clergy, and people of his own territory or rite, in accordance with the norms of law and without prejudice to the primacy of the Roman Pontiff.[18]

Wherever an Ordinary of any rite is appointed outside the territorial bounds of its patriarchate, he remains attached to the hierarchy of the patriarchate of that rite, in accordance with the norm of law.[19]

8. Though some of the patriarchates of the Eastern Churches are of later origin than others, all are equal in patriarchal dignity. Still the honorary and lawfully established order of precedence among them is to be preserved.[20]

9. In keeping with the most ancient tradition of the Church,

14. Cf. Benedict XV, motu proprio "Orientis catholici," Oct. 15, 1917; Pius XI, encyclical letter "Rerum orientalium," Sept. 8, 1929; etc.
15. The practice of the Catholic Church in the time of Pius XI, Pius XII, and John XXIII abundantly demonstrates this movement.
16. The following declarations of the Decree about the Patriarchs have not answered the expectations of many Eastern Fathers. They decided nevertheless to vote for the Decree because they considered that it was preferable to have the present Decree promulgated, even if not perfect, than to have no decree at all.
17. Cf. I Nicene Synod, can. 6; I Constantinople, can. 2 and 3; Chalcedon, can. 28; can. 9; IV Constantinople, can. 17; can. 21; IV Lateran, can. 5; can. 30; Florence, decree pro Graecis; etc.
18. Cf. I Nicene Synod, can. 6; I Constantinople, can. 3; IV Constantinople, can. 17; Pius XII, motu proprio "Cleri sanctitati," can. 216, § 2, 1°.
19. It follows that the Patriarchs are not entitled to nominate bishops for the faithful of their rite established in America or Australia without the approval of the Holy See.
20. In ecumenical councils: I Nicea, can. 6; I Constantinople, can. 3; IV Constantinople, can. 21; IV Lateran, can. 5; Florence, decree pro Graecis, July 6, 1439, § 9 Cf. Pius XII, motu proprio "Cleri sanctitati," June 2, 1957, can. 219, etc.

the Patriarchs of the Eastern Churches are to be accorded exceptional respect, since each presides over his patriarchate as father and head.

This sacred Synod, therefore, decrees that their rights and privileges should be re-established in accord with the ancient traditions of each Church and the decrees of the ecumenical Synods.[21]

The rights and privileges in question are those which flourished when East and West were in union, though they should be somewhat adapted to modern conditions.

The Patriarchs with their synods constitute the superior authority for all affairs of the patriarchate, including the right to establish new eparchies[22] and to nominate bishops of their rite within the territorial bounds of the patriarchate, without prejudice to the inalienable right of the Roman Pontiff to intervene in individual cases.[23]

10. What has been said of Patriarchs applies as well, under the norm of law, to major archbishops, who preside over the whole of some individual Church or rite.[24]

11. Inasmuch as the patriarchal office is a traditional form of government in the Eastern Church, this Sacred and Ecumenical Council earnestly desires that where needed, new patriarchates should be erected.[25] The establishment of such is reserved to an ecumenical Synod or to the Roman Pontiff.[26]

21. Cf. supra, note 17.
22. "Eparchies": cf. note 8.—Ed.
23. The motu proprio "Cleri sanctitati" of Pius XII (1957), can. 395, stipulated that the patriarchal synods had first to submit the names of the candidates to the Holy See for approval. The Council has restored the Patriarchs' greater independence.
24. Cf. Synod of Ephesus, can. 8; Clement VIII, "Romanum Pontificem," Feb. 28, 1596; Pius VII, apostolic letter "In universalis Ecclesiae," Feb. 22, 1807; Pius XII, motu proprio "Cleri sanctitati," June 2, 1957, can. 324-327; Synod of Carthage (419), can. 17.
25. There are presently in the Catholic Church six Eastern Patriarchs: the Coptic Patriarch of Alexandria; the Melkite Patriarch of Antioch, who has also the title of Alexandria and Jerusalem; the Syrian and the Maronite Patriarchs, who have the title of Antioch; the Armenian and the Chaldean Patriarchs.
26. Synod of Carthage (419), can. 17 and 57; Chalcedon (451), can. 12; St. Innocent I, letter "Et onus et honor," (ca. 415): "Nam quid sciscitaris": St. Nicholas I, letter "Ad consulta vestra," Nov. 13, 866: "A quo autem"; Innocent III, letter "Rex regum," Feb. 25, 1204; Leo XII, apostolic constitution "Petrus Apostolorum Princeps," Aug. 15, 1824; Leo XIII, apostolic letter "Christi Domini" (1895); Pius XII, motu proprio "Cleri sanctitati," June 2, 1957, can. 1959.

Rules Concerning the Sacraments

12. This sacred Ecumenical Synod endorses and lauds the ancient discipline of the sacraments existing in the Eastern Churches, as also the practices connected with their celebration and administration, and ardently wishes that they be restored where circumstances warrant.

13. With respect to the minister of holy chrism (confirmation), let that practice be fully restored which existed among Easterners in most ancient times.[27] Priests, therefore, can validly confer this sacrament, provided they use chrism blessed by a Patriarch or bishop.[28]

14. In conjunction with baptism or otherwise, all Eastern Rite priests can confer this sacrament validly on all the faithful of any rite, including the Latin; licitly, however, only if the regulations of both common and particular law are observed.[29] Priests of the Latin rite, to the extent of the faculties they enjoy for administering this sacrament, can confer it also on the faithful of Eastern Churches, without prejudice to rite. They do so licitly if the regulations of both common and particular law are observed.[30]

27. By going back to the primitive tradition, the Council very fortunately settles once and for all a question which has raised many conflicts in the past. In the apostolic letter "Ea Semper" of 1907, the Holy See had deprived the Byzantine rite priests in the United States of their right to administer the sacrament of confirmation, but the opposition was so great that it had to be tacitly restored seven years later. Before the Second Vatican Council, the Maronite, Italo-Greek, and Malabar priests had lost that right.
28. Cf. Innocent III, letter "Ad episcopum Primatem Bulgarorum," Feb. 27, 1203; Innocent IV, letter "Sub catholicae," Mar. 6, 1254, § 3, no. 4; II Lyons (1274), profession of faith of Michael Palaeologus given to Gregory X; Eugene IV, in the Synod of Florence, constitution "Exsultate Deo," Nov. 22, 1439, § 11; Clement VIII, instruction "Sanctissimus," Aug. 31, 1595; Benedict XIV, constitution "Etsi pastoralis," May 26, 1742, § II, no. 1, § III, no. 1, etc.; Synod of Laodicea (347/381), can. 48; Syn. Sisen. Armenorum (1342); Syn. Libanen. Maronitarum (1736), P. II, chap. III, no. 2; and other particular synods.
29. Cf. Sacred Cong. of the Holy Office, instruction ad Ep. Scepusien. (1783); Sacred Cong. for the Propagation of the Faith (pro Coptis), Mar. 15, 1790, no. XIII; decree of Oct. 6, 1863, C, a; Sacred Cong. for the Oriental Churches, May 1, 1948; Sacred Cong. of the Holy Office, reply of Apr. 22, 1896, and letter of May 19, 1896.
30. Code of Canon Law, can. 782, § 4; Sacred Cong. for the Oriental Churches, decree "de Sacramento Confirmationis administrando etiam fidelibus orientalium a presbyteris latini ritus, qui hoc indulto gaudeant pro fidelibus sui ritus," May 1, 1948.

15. The faithful are bound on Sundays and feast days to attend the divine liturgy or, according to the regulations or custom of their own rite, the celebration of the Divine praises.[31] That the faithful may be able to satisfy their obligation more easily, it is decreed that this obligation can be fulfilled from the Vespers of the vigil to the end of the Sunday or the feast day.[32] The faithful are earnestly exhorted to receive holy Communion on these days, and indeed more frequently—even daily.[33]

16. Because of the everyday intermingling of the communicants of diverse Eastern Churches in the same Eastern region or territory, the faculty for hearing confession, duly and unrestrictedly granted by his proper bishop to a priest of any rite, is applicable to the entire territory of the grantor, also to the places and the faithful belonging to any other rite in the same territory,[34] unless an Ordinary of the place explicitly decides otherwise with respect to the places pertaining to his rite.[35]

17. In order that the ancient discipline of the sacrament of orders may flourish again in the Eastern Churches, this sacred Synod ardently desires that where it has fallen into disuse the office of the permanent diaconate[36] be restored.[37] The leg-

---

31. *Cf. Synod of Laodicea (347/381), can. 29; St. Nicephorus CP., chap. 14; Syn. Duinen. Armenorum (719), can. 31; St. Theodorus Studita, sermo 21; St. Nicholas I, "Ad consulta vestra," Nov. 13, 886: "In quorum Apostolorum"; "Nos cupitis"; "Quod interrogatis"; "Praeterea consulitis"; "Si die Dominico"; and particular synods.*

32. *Something new, at least where there is an obligation of hearing the divine liturgy; for the rest, it is consistent with the liturgical day among the Eastern Christians.*

33. *Cf. Canones Apostolorum, 8 and 9; Synod of Antioch (341), can. 2; Timothy of Alexandria, interrogat. 3; Innocent III, constitution "Quia divinae," Jan. 4, 1215; and many particular synods of the Oriental Churches in more recent times.*

34. The former legislation led sometimes to unbelievable situations. A priest of the Archdiocese of New York, for example, could not hear confessions inside the Ukrainian church of the city; he had to walk outside the church with the penitent to absolve him. The new legislation puts the Eastern priests of America in a privileged position: any priest who has faculties to hear confessions in the Ruthenian eparchies of Pittsburgh and Passaic will "ipso facto" have faculties for all the churches of the United States.

35. *While preserving the territoriality of jurisdiction, the norm intends, for the good of souls, to provide for a plurality of jurisdiction in the same territory.*

36. The permanent diaconate has fallen into disuse in all the Eastern Catholic communities, partly because, under Western influence, priests have been allowed to officiate as deacons in liturgical services. In the West, permanent deacons are wanted mostly for pastoral activity; in the East, for liturgical celebrations.

37. *Cf. I Nicene Synod, can. 18; Synod of Neocaesarea (314/325), can. 12; Synod of Sardica (343), can. 8; St. Leo I, letter "Omnium quidem," Jan. 13, 444; Synod of Chalcedon, can. 6; IV Constantinople, can. 23, 26, etc.*

islative authority of each individual church should decide about the subdiaconate and the minor orders,[38] including their rights and obligations.[39]

18. By way of preventing invalid marriages between Eastern Catholics and baptized Eastern non-Catholics, and in the interests of the permanence and sanctity of marriage and of domestic harmony, this sacred Synod decrees that the canonical "form" for the celebration of such marriages obliges only for lawfulness. For their validity, the presence of a sacred minister suffices,[40] as long as the other requirements of law are honored.[41]

Divine Worship

19. Henceforth, it will be the exclusive right of an ecumenical Synod or the Apostolic See to establish, transfer, or suppress feast days common to all the Eastern Churches. To establish, transfer, or suppress feast days for any of the individual Churches is within the competence not only of the Apostolic See but also of a patriarchal or archiepiscopal synod, provided due consideration is given to the entire region and to other individual Churches.[42]

38. *In several Oriental Churches, the subdiaconate is considered a minor order, but the obligations of major orders are prescribed for it by the motu proprio of Pius XII, "Cleri sanctitati." The norm returns to the ancient discipline of the individual Churches with regard to obligations of subdeacons, derogating from the common law of "Cleri sanctitati."*
39. The motu proprio "Cleri sanctitati" had enforced celibacy for the Eastern subdeacons. The Decree here restores the discipline which had prevailed in the East for many centuries.
40. "Cleri sanctitati" had extended to Eastern Catholics the obligation to contract their marriage in the presence of their pastor or his delegate. This requirement entailed invalidity of many marriages, because in the Near East local customs often make it nearly impossible for Catholic girls to have their marriages celebrated in another church than the church of their fiancé. This is why many Easterners asked the Second Vatican Council to restore the ancient discipline.
41. *Cf. Pius XII, motu proprio "Crebrae allatae," Feb. 22, 1949, can. 32, § 2, 5° (the faculty of Patriarchs to dispense from the form); Pius XII, motu proprio "Cleri sanctitati," June 2, 1957, can. 267 (the faculty of Patriarchs to grant a "sanatio in radice,"); the Sacred Cong. of the Holy Office and the Sacred Cong. for the Oriental Churches in 1957 granted the faculty of dispensing from the form and sanating "ob defectum formae" ("ad quinquennium"): "extra patriarchatus, Metropolitis ceterisque Ordinariis locorum . . . qui nullum habent Superiorem infra Sanctam Sedem."*
42. *Cf. St. Leo I, letter "Quod saepissime," Apr. 15, 454: "Petitionem autem"; St. Nicephorus, CP., chap. 13; Synod of the Patriarch Sergius, Sept. 18, 1596, can. 17; Pius VI, apostolic letter "Assueto paterne," Apr. 8, 1775; etc.*

20. Until such time as all Christians desirably concur on a fixed day for the celebration of Easter,[43] and with a view meantime to promoting unity among the Christians of a given area or nation, it is left to the Patriarchs or supreme authorities of a place to reach a unanimous agreement, after ascertaining the views of all concerned, on a single Sunday for the observance of Easter.[44]

21. With respect to rules concerning sacred seasons, individual faithful dwelling outside the area or territory of their own rite may conform completely to the established custom of the place where they live. When members of a family belong to different rites, they are all permitted to observe sacred seasons according to the rules of any one of these rites.[45]

22. From ancient times the Divine Praises have been held in high esteem among all Eastern Churches. Eastern clerics and religious should celebrate these Praises as the laws and customs of their own traditions require.[46] To the extent they can, the faithful too should follow the example of their forbears by assisting devoutly at the Divine Praises.

23. It is the right of a Patriarch with his synod, or of the supreme authority of each Church with its council of Ordinaries, to regulate the use of languages in sacred liturgical functions and, after making a report to the Apostolic See, to approve translations of texts into the vernacular.[47]

43. Due to the different rules for computing Easter, the feast is celebrated in some years on the same Sunday in both the East and the West; in some years it is one week later in the East; and in some other years it may be as many as five weeks later. It may not be easy to come to the desired general agreement, because there is no central authority among the Eastern Christians not united with Rome to make a decision for all.
44. Cf. II Vatican Synod; Constitution on the Sacred Liturgy, Dec. 4, 1963.
45. Cf. Clement VIII, instruction "Sanctissimus," Aug. 31, 1595, § 6: "Si ipsi graecis"; Sacred Cong of the Holy Office, June 7, 1673, ad 1, 3; Mar. 13, 1727, ad 1; Sacred Cong. for the Propagation of the Faith, decree of Aug. 18, 1913, art. 33; decree of Aug. 14, 1914, art. 27; decree of Mar. 27, 1916, art. 14; Sacred Cong. for the Oriental Churches, decree of Mar. 1, 1929, art. 36; decree of May 4, 1930, art. 41.
46. Cf. Synod of Laodicea (347/381), can. 18; Syn. Mar Isaaci Chaldaeorum (410), can. 15; St. Nerses Glaien. Armenorum (1166); Innocent IV, letter "Sub catholicae," Mar. 6, 1254, § 8; Benedict XIV, constitution "Etsi pastoralis," May 26, 1742, § 7, no. 5; instruction "Eo quamvis tempore," May 4, 1745, §§ 42 ss.; and more recent particular synods of the Armenians (1911), Copts (1898), Maronites (1736), Rumanians (1872), Ruthenians (1891), Syrians (1888).
47. From the Eastern tradition.

Relations with the Brethren of Separated Churches

24. The Eastern Churches in communion with the Apostolic See of Rome have a special role to play in promoting the unity of all Christians, particularly Easterners, according to the principles of this sacred Synod's Decree on Ecumenism: first of all by prayer, then by the example of their lives, by religious fidelity to ancient Eastern traditions,[48] by greater mutual knowledge, by collaboration, and by a brotherly regard for objects[49] and attitudes.[50]

25. If any separated Eastern Christian should, under the guidance of grace of the Holy Spirit, join himself to Catholic unity, no more should be required of him than what a simple profession of the Catholic faith demands. A valid priesthood is preserved among Eastern clerics. Hence, upon joining themselves to the unity of the Catholic Church, Eastern clerics are permitted to exercise the orders they possess,[51] in accordance with the regulations established by the competent authority.[52]

26. Divine Law forbids any common worship (communicatio in sacris) which would damage the unity of the Church, or involve formal acceptance of falsehood or the danger of deviation in the faith, of scandal, or of indifferentism.[53] At the same time, pastoral experience clearly shows that with respect to our Eastern brethren there should and can be taken into consideration various circumstances affecting individuals, wherein the unity of the Church is not jeopardized nor are intolerable risks involved, but in which salvation itself

48. A specific task of the Catholic Eastern Churches is to manifest to the separated brethren that Church unity can be effected without the particular Churches losing their individual characteristics.
49. Literally "things" ("rerum"), which might include sacred objects (e.g., ikons). The word for "attitudes" ("animorum") includes feelings, etc.—Ed.
50. *According to the text of the papal bull of reunion given to the different Eastern Catholic Churches.*
51. What is said here of the priesthood should apply also of course to baptism and confirmation. An Eastern Christian who is received into the Catholic Church should not be baptized or confirmed unless the former administration of those sacraments in an Orthodox Church cannot be established.
52. *Synodal obligation for the separated Eastern Brethren and for the orders of every degree of divine and ecclesiastical law.*
53. *This doctrine is also common to the separated Churches.*

and the spiritual profit of souls are urgently at issue.[54]

Hence, in view of special circumstances of time, place, and personage, the Catholic Church has often adopted and now adopts a milder policy, offering to all the means of salvation and an example of charity among Christians through participation in the sacraments and in other sacred functions and objects. With these considerations in mind, and "lest because of the harshness of our judgment we prove an obstacle to those seeking salvation,"[55] and in order to promote closer union with the Eastern Churches separated from us, this sacred Synod lays down the following policy:

27. In view of the principles recalled above, Eastern Christians who are separated in good faith from the Catholic Church, if they ask of their own accord and have the right dispositions, may be granted the sacraments of penance, the Eucharist, and the anointing of the sick. Furthermore, Catholics may ask for these same sacraments from those non-Catholic ministers whose Churches possess valid sacraments, as often as necessity or a genuine spiritual benefit recommends such a course of action, and when access to a Catholic priest is physically or morally impossible.[56]

28. Again, in view of these very same principles, Catholics may for a just cause join with their separated Eastern brethren in sacred functions, things, and places.[57]

29. This more lenient policy with regard to common worship involving Catholics and their brethren of the separated Eastern Churches is entrusted to the care and execution of the

---

54. At the present time, the great majority of Eastern Christians find themselves living under atheistic regimes or in countries where Christians (Orthodox and Catholics together) constitute less than one tenth of the predominantly Moslem population. In Siberia, for example, there are thousands of Catholics, but there is not a single priest authorized by the Soviet authorities to hear confessions or to say Mass. In these regions cooperation between all Christians is often an imperative for survival. For this reason, the Second Vatican Council wanted to relax rules of human institution that prevented collaboration. Of course, in North America, where Orthodox and Catholic priests can be found in most cities, the situation is different. (Cf. note 58.)

55. St. Basil the Great, "Epistula canonica ad Amphilochium," PG 32, 669 B.

56. The basis for mitigation is considered to be: (1) validity of the sacraments; (2) good faith and disposition; (3) necessity of eternal salvation; (4) absence of one's own priest; (5) exclusion of the dangers to be avoided and of formal adhesion to error.

57. This article is about the so-called "extra-sacramental worship in common" ("communicatio in sacris extrasacramentalis"). The Council here concedes a mitigation, "servatis servandis" [i.e., with the required prudence].

local Ordinaries so that, by taking counsel among themselves and, if circumstances warrant, after consultation also with the Ordinaries of the separated Churches, they may govern relations between Christians by timely and effective rules and regulations.[58]

CONCLUSION

30. This Sacred Council feels great joy in the fruitful and zealous collaboration between the Eastern and the Western Catholic Churches, and at the same time declares that all these directives of law are laid down in view of the present situation, until such time as the Catholic Church and the separated Eastern Churches come together into complete unity.

Meanwhile, however, all Christians, Eastern as well as Western, are earnestly asked to pray to God fervently and insistently, indeed daily, that with the aid of the most holy Mother of God, all may become one. Let them pray also that the strength and the consolation of the Holy Spirit may descend copiously upon all those many Christians of whatsoever Church who endure suffering and deprivations for their unwavering loyalty to the name of Christ.

---

58. The Council wishes that the bishops of the separated Churches be consulted. In fact, the Standing Conference of the American Orthodox Bishops in its meeting of Jan. 22, 1965, took a courteous negative attitude toward the decision of the Council. "Eucharistic mystery," declared the Orthodox bishops, "is the end of unity, not a means to that end." They seem to have misinterpreted the intention of the Council, which did not want to use intercommunion as a means toward visible unity. The Catholic Church, acting in the spirit of the tradition rather than according to the letter, simply believes that in the situation of emergency which obtains in some regions (cf. note 54) baptized Christians who remain in good faith outside her visible unity should not be treated with the same severity as those who left her with malice.

In a matter of this kind, Catholics should follow strictly the rules established in each region by the bishop lest they antagonize their Orthodox brethren. Still, in hospitals, prisons, on the battlefield, and in remote regions, situations may become rather similar to that which obtains in Siberia or in the Near East. In those cases, Catholic chaplains or missionaries should know that the Church wishes them to assist their isolated Eastern brethren in the best way possible.

"Love one another with brotherly affection; outdo one another in showing honor" (Rom. 12:10).[59]

Each and every one of the things set forth in this Decree has won the consent of the Fathers. We too, by the Apostolic authority conferred on Us by Christ, join with the Venerable Fathers in approving, decreeing, and establishing these things in the Holy Spirit, and we direct that what has thus been enacted in synod be published to God's glory.

Rome, at St. Peter's, November 21, 1964

I, Paul, Bishop of the Catholic Church.

There follow the signatures of the Fathers.

Notice: The Supreme Pontiff has ordered that the legal force of the Decree on Eastern Catholic Churches be deferred for a period of two months. However, he authorizes the Patriarchs to reduce or prolong the time for a just reason.

PERICLE FELICI
Titular Archbishop of Samosata
Secretary General of the Second
Vatican Council

---

59. The translation is from the Revised Standard Version, clearer here than older translations (e.g., Confraternity, 1941: "Love one another with fraternal charity, anticipating one another with honor").—Ed.

A RESPONSE

It is not easy for an Orthodox to express his views on this particular Decree for the simple yet important reason that the very existence of the "Uniate" Eastern Catholic Churches has always been considered by the Orthodox as one of the major obstacles to any sincere theological confrontation with the Roman Catholic Church.

The Orthodox appreciate, to be sure, the efforts made in these last years by some spiritual leaders of these communities to represent and voice within the Roman Catholic Church the Eastern tradition as a whole, efforts which were especially obvious at the Council itself and which no doubt greatly contributed to the basic orientation of the present Decree. But for the sake of true ecumenical understanding, it must be stressed that for the Orthodox there remains in this whole question of uniatism a deep ambiguity, to which all Orthodox are extremely sensitive and which must have a high priority on the ecumenical agenda of the future.

There can be no doubt as to the positive, irenic, and constructive intentions of the Decree as a whole. It is one more step, and a decisive one, toward the recognition of the Eastern tradition as "equal in dignity" to that of the West. Of utmost importance is its emphasis on the temporary character of its provisions—"until such time as the Catholic Church and the separated Eastern Churches come together into complete unity." This seems to indicate a rather significant shift in the very understanding of the function of the Eastern Catholic communities called now to serve as bridges to, rather than substitutes for, the Orthodox East.

Certain important reservations must, however, be made. First of all, the Decree seems to "take for granted" and to perpetuate the reduction of the differences between the East and the West to the sole area of rites, discipline, and "way of life." But it is precisely this reduction which forms the basis of "uniatism" that the Orthodox reject, for they affirm that the liturgical and canonical tradition of the East cannot be isolated from doctrinal principles which it implies and which constitute the real issue between Roman Catholicism and Eastern Orthodoxy.

The decree solemnly proclaims the *equality* of the Eastern tradition yet, at the same time, formulates and regulates it in terms of a Western and even juridical ecclesiology hardly adequate to its spirit and orientations. To a great degree it remains thus a *Latin* text about the Eastern tradition. The institution of Patriarchates, for example, is not only given an importance it does not have, in fact, in the Eastern Church, but is also defined as a personal jurisdiction of the Patriarch over other bishops, which is alien to the Eastern canonical tradition, where the Patriarch or any other Primate is always a *primus inter pares*.

Finally, one word about the *communicatio in sacris*. In regard to this painful and complex problem, the Decree shows great tact and caution. An Orthodox commentator must stress, however, that even a partial solution of this problem must be a bilateral action and that, given its crucial importance, it must express, on the Orthodox side, the consensus of all Orthodox Churches.

ALEXANDER SCHMEMANN

BISHOPS

IN A PERSONAL letter to each bishop, written two weeks before the Council began, Pope John XXIII appealed to his brothers: "A bishop who is himself holy will most certainly have a following of holy priests, whose holiness will in turn redound to the religious perfection of the whole diocese." Several months later in a Council speech, Cardinal Montini, soon to be John's successor, traced a good bishop's influence to its source; he must be "the image of the Father and the image of Christ." For both Popes, the thrust of the Council had to be decidedly pastoral.

The First Vatican Council has been called "the Council of the Pope"; the Second "The Council of the bishops." This is over-simplified, but the episcopacy was surely the bridge on which the two Councils met. The theology of the episcopacy was expressed in the Constitution on the Church (Chapter III). Then, following the Popes' guideline, the Fathers moved on to the pastoral, practical Decree on the Bishops' Pastoral Office in the Church. It became one of four closely related documents (the others: on priests, religious, laity) that flowed from the restored concept of the Church as the People of God.

Although the bishops' future tasks are involved in every aspect of the conciliar teaching—the Word of God and His worship, the formation of priests, the scope of the Church's mission and the broader dimensions of ecumenism, religious liberty and the agony of today's world—it is to the document on the Church that the Christian must turn for the nature and role of the episcopacy, and to that on the pastoral office of bishops for the practical application.

Every document of the Council picked its way through the rocky fields of preparation and debate (with a crossfire of criticism, amendments, rejection or qualified approval) to the final conciliar approval and promulgation. During the four

sessions, the schema on bishops was given a new proportion, a new tone, and a new name. It absorbed most of an
early schema, "On the Care of Souls," and became a corollary, not a competitor of Chapter III in the Constitution on
the Church. Moving forward, the schema cut across the preserve guarded by the Roman Curia, and welcomed a tiny
path of fairly recent date, the national episcopal conference.
It suffered detours at the hands of its opponents, and triviali-
ties from friends. But when it was promulgated, October 28,
1965, it stood out as a broad authentic highway bearing
much that was new or rediscovered to the vast area of the
Church's universal and pastoral responsibility.

CONTENTS

The new Decree opens with a preface that flows directly
from the papal primacy and infallibility defined by the Council of 1869-70: ". . . the Roman Pontiff, as successor of
Peter, enjoys supreme, full, immediate, and universal authority over the care of souls by divine institution . . . a
primacy of ordinary power over all churches [i.e., dioceses]."
Then the Fathers of 1962-65 picked up what Paul VI called
"the broken threads of the First Vatican Council." Having
clarified the bishops' role in the Constitution on the Church,
they repeated it here: "The bishops, having been appointed
by the Holy Spirit, are successors of the apostles as pastors
of souls. Together with the Supreme Pontiff and under his
authority, they are sent to continue throughout the ages the
work of Christ, the eternal pastor. . . . Bishops have been
made true and authentic teachers of the faith, pontiffs, and
pastors through the Holy Spirit who has been given to them."

The decree on bishops applies this doctrine in three chapters: the bishops' relation (a) to the universal Church; (b)
to their own particular churches; and (c) to the coordinated
programs of the dioceses in a region. There is a compelling
logic in this arrangement; this was lacking in the earlier
drafts.

Each chapter has both its central thesis and its apex of
high controversy. First, the universal concern of each bishop
for all the churches—and the insistence on a reorganized, internationalized Roman Curia. Second, the diocese itself where
the Church of Christ is truly present and operative—and a
new orientation for priests of religious orders, who "in a certain genuine sense must be said to belong to the clergy of the
diocese." And finally the communion of bishops in charity for

the needs of a particular region—and the extent of an episcopal conference's authority.

But dozens of other subjects are in this decree: the bishop as teacher, priest, and pastor; assistants to the bishops (especially the unfamiliar offices of episcopal vicar and a pastoral commission); close ties with priests, their "sons and friends"; with the laity sharing in church affairs; with separated brethren, the non-baptized and the lapsed Catholics; new methods of religious and social research; the restructuring of dioceses, provinces, and regions; critical problems of contemporary society; granting of permissions, resignation of bishops, and so on.

There is a page-after-page reminder of the bishops' responsibilities and duties, almost nothing of prerogatives and rights. Priests and laymen will find here, as Father Bernard Haering did, "a conscience which gives a decisive 'yes' to the challenge of self-denial and the abandonment of a power mentality. In short, it is a 'yes' to selfless service."

The new blueprint has been drawn to secure for bishops not power or prestige, but that people might hear in them the words of Christ, "I came not to be ministered to, but to minister."

THROUGH THE CENTURIES

"The right time has come . . . a brilliant hour has shone upon us," said Pope Paul after the collegiality of the bishops and the Pope had been defined. He continued, in words that would have to be shared with the fourth session's decree on the pastoral office of the bishops:

"An hour, we say, whose past approach was gradual, whose brilliance shines forth today, whose salvific power will surely enrich the future life of the Church with a new growth in doctrine, with increased powers, with better-suited means and instruments."

The development of the doctrinal and pastoral concepts of the episcopacy was indeed gradual, but it was steady. The scriptural base was Jesus' appointment of the Twelve with Peter as head, and their commission to teach, sanctify, and govern the Church which He built upon the rock, Peter, and this until the end of time. Among many New Testament citations, that of Matthew (18:18-20) is the most succinct. The twelve apostles had been eyewitnesses of the Risen Lord. They appointed men like Barnabas, Titus, and Timothy as "delegated apostles"; other men like James of Jerusalem, Ignatius of Antioch, and Clement of Rome appeared as "superintendents" of the local churches. The terms were not precisely distinguished nor were those of "bishop" or "priest," but the practice of the early Church pointed to a true succession from the Twelve as a body or college. Cyprian, for example, wrote in the early third century: "The Church wholly one is not divided up into sections, but forms one whole of which the unison of the bishops is the bond." The first Christian centuries are witness to the collegial structure of the Church.

This evidence pointed to the pastoral side as well as the doctrinal. The thinking of both St. Paul and St. John coalesced as the decades went by: Paul stressed the local community, the "building up of the Body of Christ" by all, while John emphasized the local bishop as an incarnation of unity, a living image of the Church's vigor.

How could the bishops' collegiality and the pastoral implications become so obscured, "a forgotten idea for fifteen centuries," as Father Yves Congar put it? Formidable reasons come to mind at once: the Constantine centralization, the growing authority of patriarchs and metropolitan archbishops, the misunderstanding of certain passages in St. Jerome. Yet despite all of these, and the increased centralization brought about by the Popes of the early Middle Ages, the episcopal responsibility survived, especially in the liturgical texts of a bishop's consecration. Even the motive of the Gregorys (I and VII), in their determination to reinforce papal supremacy, was partly to raise bishops from the low level to which local administration had fallen during those bleak centuries.

But the bishops' significance suffered after the break between the Christian East and West in the eleventh century. Western Christianity became more concentrated in Rome. Abortive efforts by independent bishops raised the threat of interposition, i.e., a council of bishops placing itself between the Pope and his increased authority. This came to a head at the Council of Constance (1414-18). Cardinal Koenig has shown how this Council quieted immediate crises, but left unanswered many questions demanded by the conciliarists. As their desire for autonomy grew, they drifted into the ill-fated Council of Basle.

All this produced within the Church an extremely defensive reaction to such trends as Gallicanism, Jansenism, and the Protestant proposals. The Council of Trent in the 16th century was the climax, with its interpretation of the papacy as the very essence of the Church. Such extremism, as Koenig wisely warns, always involves impoverishment.

Recent studies by Guiseppe Alberigo show that the doctrinal and pastoral status of the bishops, although curtailed, never vanished. Both at the Council of Trent and the First Vatican Council, some of the most ardent centralists accepted the dignity of the episcopacy as a fact and even used the collegial nature of the hierarchy as a point of reference from which papal authority could be derived. But the First Vatican Council ended so abruptly and unsatisfactorily that German bishops, as well as others, declared that their role in union with the Pope was based on divine authority, nor were they mere agents or delegates of the Pope. Both Pius IX and Leo XIII pronounced this declaration correct.

FROM 1962 TO 1965

This long, tortuous ordeal of episcopal theology brought Popes and bishops to a threshold of decision in 1962. John XXIII, well acquainted with the tradition of the Eastern Churches, also sensed the need in the writings of contemporary Catholic theologians in the West. In his motu proprio of June 5, 1960, he announced the conciliar commissions; that on bishops and diocesan government was second only to the Theological Commission.

This schema did not come up for debate until the second session, early in November, 1963. But the Fathers received in April that year the first draft. It consisted of five chapters about the bishops: their relations with the Curia, the functions of coadjutors and auxiliaries, national conferences, boundaries of diocese and province, and the establishment of parishes.

Meanwhile, in the "mother schema" on the Church, Chapter III on the hierarchy was sharply debated on the last four days of the first session and all through October in the second. Practically every Council leader, pro or con, spoke. The famous vote on the key questions, October 30, 1963, brought an overwhelming affirmation to the scriptural interpretation of the episcopal college, i.e., collegiality. On the outcome would depend the success of the bishops' own draft.

But when the debate on bishops and diocesan government opened on November 5, the proposed text met vigorous charges of tampering. Four members of the commission it-self held that it was not the original schema they had origi-nally prepared. They stated that a meeting in March (1963), attended only by bishops and experts in and near Rome, had deleted much material, leaving it "one-sided" and "out of harmony with the intentions of those who prepared it." They were rebutted by warnings of "radical change," "genuine threat," "dangerous waters," and the familiar "let us take care!" The high points of the debate included a dramatic encounter between Cardinals Frings and Ottaviani over the powers and methods of the Curia, and the public conflict of four American cardinals over the extent of authority the episcopal conference should have. The debate closed on No-vember 15, 1963.

An entirely new schema was sent to the bishops in the spring of 1964 under the title, "On the Pastoral Office of Bishops." The new name and order of chapters were signifi-cant. Absorbing much of the earlier schema "On the Care of Souls," and linked to the teaching on collegiality soon to be promulgated, the new draft breathed with a new spirit. It echoed Pope Paul's insistence that the national episcopal con-ference's function was "nearly indispensable"; and that epis-copal consecration has the force of a sacrament. The new draft foreshadowed the Pope's opening address in the fall. Speaking to the bishops, he urged this accurate paradox: "You need a unifying center . . . the Holy See needs you, Venerable Brethren."

In the third session, voting continued on amendments pre-sented to meet the four hundred changes submitted by the Fathers. The pastoral document enjoyed the same sweep of majorities that was making the schema "On the Church" a reality of the 1964 session. Even in such touchy areas as the reorganization of the Roman Curia, exempt religious, and the powers of the episcopal conference, the approval was overwhelming.

A few refinements were made, and voting continued dur-ing October, 1965. Then, on the seventh anniversary of Pope John's election, October 28, 1965, the solemn vote and pro-mulgation took place. Cardinal Marella's commission, the speakers in the aula, other bishops and periti, and finally Pope Paul himself had produced a conciliar document of genuine pastoral content. The final approving vote: *Placet*— 2,319; *Non Placet*—2; Void—1; Total voting—2,322.

TODAY'S PROMISE

The Church's pursuit of pastoral goals can be no exercise in pragmatism, no mere incident in activism. The sacred deposit of Christian doctrine must be guarded and taught. As John XXIII said, the substance of the deposit of faith is one thing, but *"the way in which it is presented* is another." As collegiality of Pope and bishops continues to grow, so should the "collegial" relations of bishop and priests, of priests and laity increase. Every page in the Decree on the Bishops' Pastoral Office in the Church inspires this hope. So do the facts of 1962 and the ensuing years.

The new Apostolic Synod planned by Paul VI should point the way to more consultations by all pastors with God's people. The liturgical experience of episcopal conferences throughout the world will probably encourage the hierarchy to broaden these important instruments. The restoration of faculties from the Curia to residential bishops can be a sign of more holy liberty in the bishops' own dealings with priests and people. The evidences for hope are all around us. But they can be stifled if God's people grow weary again, if God's leaders become complacent.

Historically judged, this *can* happen because it *has* happened. Only if we plant and nourish the seeds of the Vatican renewal will God give the increase. Father Karl Rahner, as the Council closes, speaks confidently: "The Christian of the future will not feel himself reduced in stature or oppressed by his bishop. . . . He will know that even in the community of the faithful there must be those who are responsible for binding decisions and action, and the spirit of Christ which animates all will be with such men. As for the bishop, there will be nothing else for him, as in the ancient Church of the martyrs, but continually to invite such voluntary obedience and understanding for his decisions, in love and humility."

"For you, I am a bishop," said St. Augustine to his people, "but *with* you I am a Christian. The first is an office accepted, the second a grace received; one a danger, the other safety. If, then, I am gladder by far to be redeemed *with you* than I am to be placed *over you,* I shall, as the Lord commanded, be more completely your servant."

The good bishop is the good pastor, the good servant. Anything less is unworthy of the charge given by Christ.

✠ PAUL J. HALLINAN

Decree on the Bishops' Pastoral Office in the Church

PAUL, BISHOP
SERVANT OF THE SERVANTS OF GOD
TOGETHER WITH THE FATHERS OF THE SACRED COUNCIL
FOR EVERLASTING MEMORY

PREFACE[1]

1. Christ the Lord, Son of the living God, came that He might save His people from their sins[2] and that all men might be made holy. Just as He Himself was sent by the Father, so He also sent His apostles.[3] Therefore, He sanctified them, conferring on them the Holy Spirit, so that they too might glorify the Father upon earth and save men, "for the building up of the body of Christ" (Eph. 4:12), which is the Church.

---

1. The link between the two Vatican Councils is clearly demonstrated by their references to Pope and bishops. In 1870, the stress was on the unique role of the Pope and his authority, although it was stated that bishops appointed by the Holy Spirit are true successors of the apostles, and this until the end of time. But in 1965 the emphasis has shifted to the bishops. Christ is present in them as they stand "in the midst of those who believe." They are true and authentic teachers in union with their head, the Pope; ministers of grace and shepherds for the earthly pilgrimage. Theirs is the full power of the priesthood, transmitted to them by their episcopal consecration. This Pope-bishop relationship is the Church's solid tradition, from the apostles and Church Fathers, down through Trent, to Popes John and Paul. There is no break in continuity. As Pope Paul said at the close of the third session of Vatican II (Nov. 21, 1964): "What the Church has taught for centuries is what we teach. The only difference is that something that up to now could be found only in the vital activity of the Church is now clearly expressed as doctrine."
2. Cf. Mt. 1:21.
3. Cf. Jn. 20:21.

2. In this Church of Christ the Roman Pontiff is the successor of Peter, to whom Christ entrusted the feeding of His sheep and lambs. Hence by divine institution he enjoys supreme, full, immediate, and universal authority over the care of souls. Since he is pastor of all the faithful, his mission is to provide for the common good of the universal Church and for the good of the individual churches. He holds, therefore, a primacy of ordinary power over all the churches.[4]

For their part, the bishops too have been appointed by the Holy Spirit, and are successors of the apostles as pastors of souls.[5] Together with the Supreme Pontiff and under his authority, they have been sent to continue throughout the ages the work of Christ, the eternal pastor.[6] Christ gave the apostles and their successors the command and the power to teach all nations, to hallow men in the truth, and to feed them. Hence, through the Holy Spirit who has been given to them, bishops have been made true and authentic teachers of the faith, pontiffs, and shepherds.[7]

3. Sharing in solicitude for all the churches, bishops exercise this episcopal office of theirs, received through episcopal consecration,[8] in communion with and under the authority of the Supreme Pontiff. All are united in a college[9] or body

4. The terms describing different levels of authority fall into three categories: (1) that of the Pope; (2) that of the college of bishops; (3) that of individual bishops in their own dioceses. The Pope in his own right has authority that is *supreme*—over all the churches; *full*—over everything pertaining to them; *immediate*—over all members, including bishops, without intermediary; and *ordinary*—by the very reason of his office (not delegated). The college of bishops, together with its head the Pope and never without him, has this same authority over the universal Church. In his own diocese the local bishop has the same power, but it is *particular* to a given diocese, and *subordinate* (as Karl Rahner puts it) to the supreme authority because the universal Church as an event is manifested in a particular diocese, and the bishop embodies the universal Church whose unity is embodied in the Pope.

5. *Cf. First Vatican Council, fourth session, part 1 of Dogmatic Constitution on the Church of Christ, c. 3, Denz. 1828 (306).*

6. *First Vatican Council, fourth session, Introduction to Dogmatic Constitution on the Church of Christ, Denz. 1821 (3050).*

7. *Cf. Second Vatican Council, Dogmatic Constitution on the Church, Chap. 3, Art. 21, 24, and 25: AAS 57 (1965) pp. 24-25, 29-31.*

8. *Cf. Second Vatican Council, Dogmatic Constitution on the Church, Chap. 3, Art. 21: AAS 57 (1965), pp. 24-25.*

9. "Collegiality" is no innovation in the Church as the Constitution on the Church demonstrates (III, Art. 22). But the term has not been familiar to Catholics. It pertains to the "college" or "body" of bishops acting as a union. "The Roman Pontiff, the successor of Peter, and the bishops, the successors of the apostles joined together . . . as in the Gospel, the Lord so disposing, St. Peter and the other apostles constitute one apostolic college." In Art. 22 and 23 collegiality is summarized: its historical course; and the

with respect to teaching the universal Church of God and governing her as shepherds.

They exercise this office individually over the portions of the Lord's flock assigned to them, each one taking care of the particular church[10] committed to him. On occasion some of them jointly provide for certain common needs of their various dioceses.

This most sacred Synod, therefore, attentive to the developments in human relations which have brought about a new order of things[11] in our time,[12] and wishing to determine more exactly the pastoral office of bishops, issues the following decrees.

CHAPTER I

THE RELATIONSHIP OF BISHOPS TO THE UNIVERSAL CHURCH

I. The Role of the Bishops in the Universal Church [13]

4. By virtue of sacramental consecration and hierarchical communion with the head and other members of the college,

episcopal relationships to the Pope, the local churches and the universal churches.

10. "Particular church" or "local church" refers today to the diocese entrusted to a residential bishop. It has early Christian overtones, especially in St. Paul's letters, where "church" referred at times to the whole mystical body of Christ, at others to a local congregation.

11. The phrase "a new order of things" is taken directly from John XXIII's proclamation of the Second Vatican Council (Dec. 25, 1961). It sums up the urgent reasons why its purpose must be mainly pastoral. Society is "seriously disturbed," glorying "in its recent scientific and technological advances, yet suffering damage to its social order." The Church stands ready with its "perennial, vital divine power of the gospel." Here the phrase places upon the bishops' shoulders the urgency of their pastoral role.

12. Cf. John XXIII, apostolic constitution "Humanae Salutis," Dec. 25, 1961: AAS 54 (1962), p. 6.

13. Considerable material from the earlier schema, "On the Care of Souls," was included in the decree on bishops, in accordance with a decision reached

a bishop becomes a part of the episcopal body.[14] "The order of bishops is the successor to the college of the apostles in teaching authority and pastoral rule; or, rather, in the episcopal order the apostolic body continues without a break. Together with its head, the Roman Pontiff, and never without this head, the episcopal order is the subject of supreme and full power over the universal Church. But this power can be exercised only with the consent of the Roman Pontiff."[15] This power "is exercised in a solemn manner in an Ecumenical Council."[16] Therefore, this most sacred Synod decrees that all bishops who are members of the episcopal college have the right to be present at an Ecumenical Council.

"The same collegiate power can be exercised in union with the Pope by the bishops living in all parts of the world, provided that the head of the college calls them to collegiate action, or provided that at least he so approves or freely accepts the united action of the dispersed bishops that it is made a true collegiate act."[17]

5. Bishops from various parts of the world, chosen through ways and procedures established or to be established by the Roman Pontiff, will render especially helpful assistance to the supreme pastor of the Church in a council[18] to be known by the proper name of Synod of Bishops.[19] Since it will be

by the Council's Coordinating Commission, and sent to the commission working on the schema, "On Bishops and Diocesan Government" in January, 1964. A new draft, predominantly pastoral, was to be drawn up, leaving juridical matters to the post-conciliar reform of canon law. The earlier material is evident in the treatment of bishops' solicitude for all the churches, and in those parts relating to a bishop's duties in his diocese, and to pastors and religious.

14. *Cf. Second Vatican Council, Dogmatic Constitution on the Church, Chap. 3, Art. 22: AAS 57 (1965), pp. 25-27.*
15. *Ibid.*
16. *Ibid.*
17. *Ibid.*
18. The Synod of Bishops (Apostolic Synod) was formally announced by Paul VI at the beginning of the fourth session in the motu proprio, "Apostolica Sollicitudo" (Sept. 15, 1965). At least 85% of those taking part are to be elected by the episcopate. The Pope will convoke the Synod and provide its agenda. The old tensions of the past are being harmonized in the spirit of Pope Gregory the Great who said: "My honor is the honor of the universal Church. My honor is the stout energy of my brothers. When each is accorded the honor due him, then I am honored." This has been echoed frequently by Pope Paul, and finds an episcopal response in Bishop Manuel Larrain of Chile, president of the Latin American Bishops' Conference, who has stated: "The more you affirm collegiality, so much the more do you exalt the importance of the head of the college, who is the Roman Pontiff." The advocates of both exaggerated centralization and decentralization will find no comfort in the present Pope or the Council at which he presided.
19. *Cf. Paul VI, motu proprio "Apostolica Sollicitudo," Sept. 15, 1965.*

acting in the name of the entire Catholic episcopate, it will
at the same time demonstrate that all the bishops in hierarchical communion share in the responsibility for the universal Church.[20]

6. As lawful successors of the apostles and as members of the
episcopal college, bishops should always realize that they are
linked one to the other, and should show concern for all the
churches.[21] For by divine institution and the requirement of
their apostolic office, each one in concert with his fellow
bishops is responsible for the Church.[22] They should be especially concerned about those parts of the world where the
Word of God has not yet been proclaimed or where, chiefly
because of the small number of priests, the faithful are in
danger of departing from the precepts of the Christian life,
and even of losing the faith itself.

Let bishops, therefore, make every effort to have the faithful actively support and promote works of evangelization and
the apostolate. Let them strive, moreover, to see to it that
suitable sacred ministers as well as assistants, both religious
and lay, are prepared for the missions and other areas suffering from a lack of clergy. As far as possible, they should
also arrange for some of their own priests to go to such
missions or dioceses to exercise the sacred ministry permanently or at least for a set period of time.

Moreover, in administering ecclesiastical assets, bishops
should think not only of the needs of their own dioceses, but
of other ones as well, for these too are part of the
one Church of Christ. Finally, in proportion to their means,
bishops should give attention to relieving the disasters which
afflict other dioceses and regions.[23]

20. Cf. Second Vatican Council, Dogmatic Constitution on the Church, Chap.
3, Art. 23: AAS 57 (1965), pp. 27-28.
21. A bishop's responsibility is never limited to the diocese entrusted to
him. As part of the episcopal college, his concern must run with the
world-wide boundaries of the Church. The root of this concept is the supreme
and full authority of the College (with its head, and never without it) over
the universal Church. The branches are the broad responsibilities and hearty
solicitude of all the bishops for all the churches.
22. Cf. Pius XII, encyclical letter "Fidei Donum," Apr. 21, 1957; AAS 49
(1957), p. 27 ff.; also, cf. Benedict XV, apostolic letter "Maximum Illud,"
Nov. 30, 1919; AAS 11 (1919), p. 440; Pius XI, encyclical letter "Rerum
Ecclesiae," Feb. 28, 1926; AAS 18 (1926), p. 68.
23. Like St. Paul, each bishop should have a practical care for all the
churches. The contemporary view of the Church's wide mission must not
obscure the help needed by the struggling churches of newly emerging
nations, ancient lands of Asia and Africa, and areas like Latin America. In
recent times, the messages of Pius XI and Pius XII, "Rerum Ecclesiae," and

7. Above all, let them unite themselves in brotherly affection with those bishops who, for the sake of Christ, are harassed by false accusations and by restrictions, detained in prisons, or prevented from exercising their ministry.[24] They should take an active fraternal interest in them so that their sufferings may be assuaged and alleviated through the prayers and good works of their confreres.

II. Bishops and the Apostolic See

8. (a) As successors of the apostles, bishops automatically enjoy in the dioceses entrusted to them all the ordinary, proper, and immediate authority required for the exercise of their pastoral office. But this authority never in any instance infringes upon the power which the Roman Pontiff has, by virtue of his office, of reserving cases to himself or to some other authority.

(b) Except when it is a question of matters reserved to the supreme authority of the Church, the general law of the Church gives each diocesan bishop the faculty to grant dispensations in particular cases to the faithful over whom he exercises authority according to the norm of law,[25] provided he judges it helpful for their spiritual welfare.

9. In exercising supreme, full, and immediate power over the universal Church, the Roman Pontiff makes use of the de-

"Fidei Donum," have amplified the great apostolic letter of Benedict XV, "Maximum Illud," which drew up a modern charter for the missionary apostolate. Certainly, Catholic bishops have become more alert to missionary needs. The present situation in Latin America is but one of many examples of a widespread solicitude for a region short of priests and religious teachers as well as laymen skilled in the work of welfare, healing, social and economic planning. Cf. AAS 18 (1926); 49 (1957); 11 (1919).

24. Joyous ovations were given by the Council Fathers to two prominent Catholic bishops who arrived in Rome from Communist prisons: Archbishop Josyf Slipyi of Lvov in the Ukraine, and Archbishop Josef Beran of Czechoslovakia. The Council's abstaining from explicit condemnation of communism has indicated what would be called on the political level, "an opening to the left." This is a delicate and difficult movement which must await the judgment of history. But it has not lessened the episcopate's high admiration for their brothers "harassed by false accusations, and restrictions, detained in prisons, or prevented from exercising their ministries."

25. After the close of the Council's session, Pope Paul issued a motu proprio, "Pastorale Munus," which extended to bishops a wider use of their authority without recourse to the Apostolic See. Included are forty "faculties" (permissions) relating to sucn matters as the time and place of Mass, the fast for the Eucharist, the Divine Office; and eight "privileges" (personal permissions, not to be delegated) dealing with the simplification of blessings and other subjects. Cf. AAS Jan., 64.

partments of the Roman Curia.[26] These, therefore, perform their duties in his name and with his authority for the good of the churches and in the service of the sacred pastors.

The Fathers of this most sacred Council, however, strongly desire that these departments—which have rendered exceptional assistance to the Roman Pontiff and to the pastors of the Church—be reorganized and better adapted to the needs of the times, and of various regions and rites.[27] This task should give special thought to their number, name, competence, and particular method of procedure, as well as to the coordination of their activities.[28] The Fathers also eagerly desire that, in view of the pastoral role proper to bishops, the office of legates of the Roman Pontiff be more precisely determined.

10. Furthermore, since these departments are established for the good of the universal Church, this Council wishes that their members, officials, and consultors, as well as legates of the Roman Pontiff, be drawn more widely from various geographical areas of the Church, insofar as it is possible. In such a way the offices and central agencies of the Catholic Church will exhibit a truly universal character.

It is also desired that into the membership of these departments there be brought other bishops, especially diocesan ones, who can more adequately apprise the Supreme Pontiff of the thinking, the desires, and the needs of all the churches.

Finally, the Fathers of the Council believe it would be

26. The Curia and its affiliated branches are the central administrative body of the Church, a staff composed of congregations, tribunals, and other offices. Cardinals, bishops, priests, and laymen constitute its membership. In the words of Paul VI, it is "an instrument which the Pope needs and which he uses to fulfill his own divine mandate." It dates back to 1588, when Pope Sixtus V established it in its present form. In our times it was updated by St. Pius X and formalized in the Code of Canon Law in 1917.
27. Both Pope Paul and the Council Fathers agreed on the need for the Curia to be reorganized and internationalized. In a firm, yet tactful, address to the members, Sept. 21, 1963, the Pope stated that the new reforms should be "drawn up according to venerable and reasonable traditions on the one hand, and according to the needs of the time on the other." Two years later, after the decree on the bishops had been promulgated, he announced broad changes in both the name and methods of the Congregation of the Holy Office. Other moves in keeping with the opinions of the Council Fathers are certain to be made.

"It is understandable," the Pope told the Curia in 1963, "how such an establishment would have grown ponderous with its own venerable age . . . how it feels the need of being simplified and decentralized . . . broadened and made fit for new functions." ("Address to Curia," Sept. 21, 1963; and the motu proprio, "Integrae Servandae," Dec. 7, 1965.)
28. *Cf. Paul VI, allocution to the cardinals, prelates, and various officials of the Roman Curia, Sept. 21, 1963: AAS 55 (1963), p. 793 ff.*

most advantageous if these same departments would give a greater hearing to laymen who are outstanding for their virtue, knowledge, and experience. Thus they, too, will have an appropriate share in Church affairs.[29]

CHAPTER II

BISHOPS AND THEIR PARTICULAR CHURCHES OR DIOCESES

I. Diocesan Bishops

11. A diocese is that portion of God's people which is entrusted to a bishop to be shepherded by him with the cooperation of the presbytery. Adhering thus to its pastor and gathered together by him in the Holy Spirit through the gospel and the Eucharist, this portion constitutes a particular church in which the one, holy, catholic, and apostolic Church of Christ is truly present and operative.

The individual bishops, to each of whom the care of a particular church has been entrusted, are, under the authority of the Supreme Pontiff, the proper, ordinary and immediate pastors of these churches. They feed their sheep in the name of the Lord, and exercise in their regard the office of teaching, sanctifying, and governing. Yet they should acknowledge the rights which lawfully belong to patriarchs[30] and other hierarchical authorities.[31]

29. The advice of the Council Fathers to the Curia "to give a greater hearing to laymen who are outstanding for their virtue, knowledge, and experience" is applied equally to themselves in their own diocesan administration. The ideas contained in the Decree on the Apostolate of the Laity, and in Chapter III, of the Constitution on the Church, are readily applied here. A good example is the encouragement to draw the laity into the apostolate of teaching, and good works, representation in the diocesan curia and pastoral commission.
30. The Decree on Eastern Catholic Churches devotes one section to the subject of the patriarchs. The allusion in this Decree is simply an instance of the renewed solicitude of the Church for the hierarchy, clergy, and faithful of these rites which constitute a large part of the Catholic world. Cf. also Chap. II, Art. 23 of this Decree.
31. *Cf. Second Vatican Council, Decree on Eastern Catholic Churches, Nov. 21, 1964, Art. 7-11: AAS 57 (1965), pp. 29 ff.*

Bishops should dedicate themselves to their apostolic office as witnesses of Christ before all men. Not only should they look after those who already follow the Prince of Pastors, but they should also devote themselves wholeheartedly to those who have strayed in any way from the path of truth or who are ignorant of the gospel of Christ and His saving mercy. Their ultimate goal as bishops is that all men may walk "in all goodness and justice and truth" (Eph. 5:9).

12. In exercising their duty of teaching, they should announce the gospel of Christ to men, a task which is eminent among the chief duties of bishops.[32] They should, in the power of the Spirit, summon men to faith or confirm them in a faith already living. They should expound the whole mystery of Christ to them, namely, those truths the ignorance of which is ignorance of Christ. At the same time they should point out the divinely revealed way to give glory to God and thus attain to everlasting bliss.[33]

They should show, moreover, that earthly goods and human institutions structured according to the plan of God the Creator are also related to man's salvation, and therefore can contribute much to the upbuilding of Christ's Body.[34]

Hence let them teach with what seriousness the Church believes these realities should be regarded:[35] the human person with his freedom and bodily life, the family and its unity

---

32. *Cf. Council of Trent, fifth session, Decree "De Reform.," c. 2, Mansi 33, 30: 24th session, Decree "De Reform.," c. Mansi 33, 159 (cf. Second Vatican Council, Dogmatic Constitution on the Church, Chap. 3, Art. 25: AAS 57 (1965), p. 29 ff.)*

33. *Cf. Second Vatican Council, Dogmatic Constitution on the Church, Chap. 3, Art. 25: AAS 57 (1965), pp. 29-31.*

34. Three extended paragraphs are devoted to a bishop's chief tasks, to teach and to preach. The mystery of Christ and the means of salvation must be the main issue of our instruction, in keeping with the reform decrees of the Council of Trent, and the Constitution on the Church, of Vatican II.

But the fabric of the gospel does not end with these. The Council Fathers stress the "realities" of human institutions and earthly goods, and the concrete application of religious norms to society's problems. That these are proper subject matter for preaching is attested by Pope John's encyclicals "Pacem in Terris" and "Mater et Magistra," and by Pope Paul in his first encyclical, "Ecclesiam Suam," in which he stated: "The world cannot be saved from the outside . . . the Church should enter into dialogue with the world in which it exists and labors. The Church has something to say."

35. The subjects listed in this paragraph are almost a catalog of the problems treated in the Pastoral Constitution on the Church in the Modern World. The slow beginning of this schema and its multitude of drafts and interventions finally led to a courageous document that might be termed a "position paper" or (in more popular terms) a first hesitant plunge into cold waters. The preacher, whether bishop or not, must frequently read over this text so that his teaching voice will echo both the Church's wisdom and the world's problems.

and stability, the procreation and education of children, civil
society with its laws and professions, labor and leisure, the
arts and technical inventions, poverty and affluence. Finally,
they should set forth the ways by which are to be solved the
very grave questions concerning the ownership, increase, and
just distribution of material goods, peace and war, and brotherly relations among all peoples.[36]

13. The bishops should present Christian doctrine in a manner adapted to the needs of the times, that is to say, in a
manner corresponding to the difficulties and problems by
which people are most vexatiously burdened and troubled.
They should also guard that doctrine, teaching the faithful
to defend and spread it. In propounding it, bishops should
manifest the Church's maternal solicitude for all men, believers or not. With a special concern they should attend upon
the poor and the lower classes to whom the Lord sent them
to preach the gospel.

Since it is the mission of the Church to converse with the
human society in which she lives,[37] bishops especially are
called upon to approach men, seeking and fostering dialogue
with them. These conversations on salvation ought to be distinguished for clarity of speech as well as for humility and
gentleness so that truth may always be joined with charity,
and understanding with love. Likewise they should be characterized by due prudence allied, however, with that trustful-
ness which fosters friendship and thus is naturally disposed
to bring about a union of minds.[38]

They should also strive to use the various means at hand
today for making Christian doctrine known: namely, first of
all, preaching and catechetical instruction which always hold
pride of place, then the presentation of this doctrine in
schools, academies, conferences, and meetings of every kind,
and finally its dissemination through public statements made
on certain occasions and circulated by the press and various
other media of communication, which should certainly be
used to proclaim the gospel of Christ.[39]

36. *Cf. John XXIII, encyclical letter "Pacem in Terris," Apr. 11, 1963,
passim: AAS 55 (1965), pp. 257-304.*
37. *Cf. Paul VI, encyclical letter "Ecclesiam Suam," Aug. 6, 1964: AAS 56
(1964), p. 639.*
38. *Cf. Paul VI, encyclical letter "Ecclesiam Suam," Aug. 6, 1964: AAS 56
(1964), pp. 644-645.*
39. *Cf. Second Vatican Council, Decree on the Instruments of Social Communication, Dec. 4, 1963: AAS 56 (1964), pp. 145-153.*

14. Catechetical training is intended to make men's faith become living, conscious, and active, through the light of instruction. Bishops should see to it that such training be painstakingly given to children, adolescents, young adults, and even grownups. In this instruction a proper sequence should be observed as well as a method appropriate to the matter that is being treated and to the natural disposition, ability, age, and circumstances of life of the listener. Finally, they should see to it that this instruction is based on sacred Scripture, tradition, the liturgy, the teaching authority, and life of the Church.

Moreover, they should take care that catechists be properly trained for their task, so that they will be thoroughly acquainted with the doctrine of the Church and will have both a theoretical and a practical knowledge of the laws of psychology and of pedagogical methods.

Bishops should also strive to reestablish or better adapt the instruction of adult catechumens.

15. In fulfilling their duty to sanctify, bishops should be mindful that they have been taken from among men and appointed their representatives before God in order to offer gifts and sacrifices for sins. Bishops enjoy the fullness of the sacrament of orders, and all priests as well as deacons are dependent upon them in the exercise of authority. For the "presbyters" are prudent fellow workers of the episcopal order and are themselves consecrated as true priests of the New Testament, just as deacons are ordained for service and minister to the People of God in communion with the bishop and his presbytery. Therefore bishops are the principal dispensers of the mysteries of God,[40] just as they are the governors, promoters, and guardians of the entire liturgical life in the church committed to them.[41]

40. The tremendous responsibility of the bishop can be sensed in the words of the chapter on the "Promotion of Liturgical Life," in the Constitution on the Sacred Liturgy: "The bishop is to be considered as the high priest of his flock, from whom the life in Christ of his faithful is in some way derived and dependent." Surely this concept dramatizes the description as "governors, promoters, and guardians of the entire liturgical life in the church [diocese] committed to them." They dispense the divine mysteries either personally or through their priests. But the Council Fathers also glimpse a scriptural vision, now almost mystical. The liturgical constitution sees the pre-eminent manifestation of the Church "in the liturgical life of the diocese centered around the bishop, especially in his cathedral church: the full, active participation of all God's holy people . . . especially in the same Eucharist, in a single prayer, at one altar, at which the bishop presides surrounded by his college of priests, and by his ministers."
41. Cf. Second Vatican Council, Constitution on the Sacred Liturgy, Dec. 4,

Hence, they should constantly exert themselves to have the faithful know and live the paschal mystery more deeply through the Eucharist and thus become a firmly knit body in the solidarity of Christ's love.[42] "Intent upon prayer and the ministry of the word" (Acts 6:4), they should devote their labor to this end, that all those committed to their care may be of one mind in prayer[43] and through the reception of the sacraments may grow in grace and be faithful witnesses to the Lord.

As those who lead others to perfection, bishops should be diligent in fostering holiness among their clerics, religious, and laity according to the special vocation of each.[44] They should also be mindful of their obligation to give an example of holiness through charity, humility, and simplicity of life.[45] Let them so hallow the churches entrusted to them that the true image of Christ's universal Church may shine forth fully in them. For that reason they should foster priestly and religious vocations as much as possible, and take a special interest in missionary vocations.

16. (a)* In exercising his office of father and pastor,[46] a bishop should stand in the midst of his people as one who serves.[47] Let him be a good shepherd who knows his sheep and whose sheep know him. Let him be a true father who

---

1963: AAS 56 (1964), p. 97 ff.; Paul VI, motu proprio "Sacram Liturgiam," Jan. 25, 1964: AAS 56 (1964), p. 139 ff.
42. Cf. Pius XII, encyclical letter "Mediator Dei," Nov. 20, 1947; AAS 39 (1947), p. 97 ff.; Paul VI, encyclical letter "Mysterium Fidei," Sept. 3, 1965.
43. Cf. Acts 1:14 and 2:46.
44. Cf. Second Vatican Council; Dogmatic Constitution on the Church, Chap. 6, Art. 44 and 45: AAS 57 (1965), pp. 50-52.
45. During the Council, there was much criticism of the signs of pomp and wealth seen in the lives of bishops. The subject was as delicate as the proper age for episcopal retirement. But as the fourth session closed, Paul VI made an adroit gesture, full of his own generosity, but pointedly symbolic of this "humility and simplicity of life." He gave each bishop a ring, simple in form and tasteful in design, bearing no jewel nor decoration except a small engraved miter. The ring spoke more eloquently than a hundred decrees.
*The paragraphs of this Article were not in correct order in some early translations. The letters a-f (not in the Latin text) indicate the correct order.—Ed.
46. The pastoral tone of this Decree, in contrast with the legal precisions found in the documents of earlier Councils, is nowhere more impressive than right here. In this paragraph and in paragraph 2 of Art. 23, we find the delineation of "The Compleat Bishop." He must be one who serves. He must be in the midst of his people. He must be a good shepherd, a true father. He must personally perform his proper functions, and direct the works of the apostolate. There are many other facets of a bishop's life detailed in the body of Vatican II's renewal. But those listed here are the measure of his worth.
47. Cf. Lk. 22:26-27.

excels in the spirit of love and solicitude for all and to whose divinely conferred authority all gratefully submit themselves. Let him so gather and mold the whole family of his flock that everyone, conscious of his own duties, may live and work in the communion of love.

(b) To accomplish these things effectively, a bishop, "ready for every good work" (2 Tim. 2:21) and "enduring all things for the sake of the chosen ones" (2 Tim. 2:10), should arrange his life in such a way as to accommodate it to the needs of the time.

(c) A bishop should always welcome priests with a special love since they assume in part the bishop's duties and cares and carry the weight of them day by day so zealously. He should regard his priests as sons and friends.[48] Thus by his readiness to listen to them and by his trusting familiarity, a bishop can work to promote the whole pastoral work of the entire diocese.

(d) He should be concerned about the spiritual, intellectual, and material condition of his priests, so that they can live holy and pious lives and fulfill their ministry faithfully and fruitfully. For this reason, he should encourage institutes and hold special meetings in which priests can gather from time to time for the performance of lengthier spiritual exercises by way of renewing their lives and for the acquisition of deeper knowledge of ecclesiastical subjects, especially sacred Scripture and theology, the social questions of major importance, and the new methods of pastoral activity.[49] With active mercy a bishop should attend upon priests who are in any sort of danger or who have failed in some respect.

(e) In order to be able to consult more suitably the welfare of the faithful according to the condition of each one, a bishop should strive to become duly acquainted with their needs in the social circumstances in which they live. Hence, he ought to employ suitable methods, especially social re-

48. Cf. Jn. 15:15.
49. Like many other things in the Church today, pastoral methods are undergoing radical changes. Here social research is an important key. Describing the present scene in which "sociological factors reshape outworn structures, with a definite impact upon religious life," Archbishop Antonio Riberi, papal nuncio to Spain, continued: "Pastoral organization and effort are impossible if we do not understand each and every personal and environmental facet of the situation in which we live." The Decree urges exactly that. In his diocese, the bishop is encouraged to employ suitable methods, "especially social research." In forming the apostolate, not only spiritual and moral, but social, demographic, and economic conditions, must be considered. The Council does not want the wine of renewal to be put into old bottles.

search. He should manifest his concern for all, no matter what their age, condition, or nationality, be they natives, strangers, or foreigners. In exercising this pastoral care he should preserve for his faithful the share proper to them in Church affairs; he should also recognize their duty and right to collaborate actively in the building up of the Mystical Body of Christ.

(f) He should deal lovingly with the separated brethren,[50] urging the faithful also to conduct themselves with great kindness and charity in their regard, and fostering ecumenism as it is understood by the Church.[51] He should also have the welfare of the non-baptized at heart so that upon them too there may shine the charity of Christ Jesus, to whom the bishop is a witness before all men.

17. Various forms of the apostolate should be encouraged, and in the whole diocese or in given areas of it the coordination and close interconnection of all apostolic works should be fostered under the direction of the bishop. In this way, all undertakings and organizations, whether catechetical, missionary, charitable, social, family, educational, or any other program serving a pastoral goal, will be brought into harmonious action. At the same time the unity of the diocese will thereby be made more evident.

The faithful should be vigorously urged to assume their duty of carrying on the apostolate, each according to his state in life and his ability. They should be invited to join or assist the various works of the lay apostolate, especially Catholic Action. Those associations should also be promoted and supported which either directly or indirectly pursue a supernatural goal, for example, attaining a saintlier life, spreading the gospel of Christ to all men, promoting Chris-

---

50. Here the Decree singles out a vital part of the apostolate—the cause of unity. Like the liturgical reform, the changing relationship with Churches of other faiths is puzzling to many Catholics. The history of the Catholic part in ecumenism, as well as in her relations with the non-baptized, began only recently. It is not therefore surprising that Catholics are unprepared for the kind of fellowship, dialogue, and unity now being encouraged. The bishops' task is crucial: to deal lovingly with the separated brethren and the non-baptized, urge the faithful to do the same, and promote ecumenism in the framework of the Decree on Ecumenism and the Declaration on the Relationship of the Church to Non-Christian Religions. The unswerving ecumenical example of both Popes of the Council was climaxed by the Bible vigil service at St. Paul's Basilica. Pope Paul took part with Protestant and Orthodox churchmen in this program of prayer for the intention of religious unity.
51. *Cf. Second Vatican Council, Decree on Ecumenism, Nov. 21, 1964; AAS 57 (1965), pp. 90-107.*

tian doctrine or the liturgical apostolate, pursuing social aims, or performing works of piety and charity.

The forms of the apostolate should be properly adapted to current needs not only in terms of spiritual and moral conditions, but also of social, demographic, and economic ones. Religious and social surveys, made through offices of pastoral sociology, contribute greatly to the effective and fruitful attainment of that goal, and they are cordially recommended.

18. Special concern should be shown for those among the faithful who, on account of their way or condition of life, cannot sufficiently make use of the common and ordinary pastoral services of parish priests or are quite cut off from them. Among this group are very many migrants, exiles and refugees, seamen, airplane personnel, gypsies, and others of this kind. Suitable pastoral methods should also be developed to sustain the spiritual life of those who journey to other lands for a time for the sake of recreation.[52]

Episcopal conferences, especially national ones, should pay energetic attention to the more pressing problems confronting the aforementioned groups. Through common agreement and united efforts, such conferences should look to and promote the spiritual care of these people by means of suitable methods and institutions. They should first bear in mind the special rules already laid down or due to be laid down by the Apostolic See.[53] These can be suitably adapted to the circumstances of time, place, and persons.

19. In discharging their apostolic office, which concerns the salvation of souls, bishops of themselves enjoy full and perfect freedom, and independence from any civil authority.[54]

---

52. Pius XII established norms for the care of exiles, refugees, migrants, and seamen in two documents: the apostolic constitution, "Exsul Familia" in 1952 and a summary of regulations for the Apostolate of the Sea in 1957. Cf. AAS 54 (1952); 50 (1958).

53. Cf. St. Pius X, motu proprio "Iampridem," Mar. 19, 1914; AAS 6 (1914), p. 174 ff.; Pius XII, apostolic constitution "Exsul Familia," Aug. 1, 1952: AAS 54 (1952), p. 652 ff.; "Leges Operis Apostolatus Maris," compiled under the authority of Pius XII, Nov. 21, 1957: AAS 50 (1958), p. 375 ff.

54. A healthy balance is advocated in the solution of the Church-State issue. The Church must have full and perfect freedom and independence from the state in "the things of God," those duties related to the salvation of souls. On the other hand, the state is entitled to the Church's support in "the things of Caesar," that is, bishops should take their proper episcopal position, advocating "obedience to just laws and reverence for legitimately constituted authorities." The Church serves human society as a conscience. It is not a

Hence, the exercise of their ecclesiastical office may not be hindered, directly or indirectly, nor may they be forbidden to communicate freely with the Apostolic See, with ecclesiastical authorities, or with their subjects.

Assuredly, while sacred pastors devote themselves to the spiritual care of their flock, they are also in fact having regard for social and civil progress and prosperity. According to the nature of their office and as behooves bishops, they collaborate actively with public officials for this purpose, and advocate obedience to just laws and reverence for legitimately constituted authorities.

20. Since the apostolic office of bishops was instituted by Christ the Lord and serves a spiritual and supernatural purpose, this most sacred Ecumenical Synod declares that the right of nominating and appointing bishops belongs properly, peculiarly, and of itself exclusively to the competent ecclesiastical authority.[55]

Therefore, for the purpose of duly protecting the freedom of the Church and of promoting more suitably and efficiently the welfare of the faithful, this most holy Council desires that in the future no rights or privileges of election, nomination, presentation, or designation for the office of bishop be any longer granted to civil authorities. Such civil authorities, whose favorable attitude toward the Church this most sacred Synod gratefully acknowledges and very warmly appreciates, are most kindly requested to make a voluntary renunciation of the above-mentioned rights and privileges which they presently enjoy by reason of a treaty or custom. The matter, however, should first be discussed with the Apostolic See.

policeman for the state, blindly enforcing its edicts whether right or wrong. Nor is it a public enemy, claiming for itself an unwarranted competence in all public issues, whether spiritual or temporal. Today the involvement of the Church in such affairs as civil rights and foreign policy demands prudent judgment. There is a moral core to each of these problems, but the implementation rests essentially with the public authorities. The Church is a conscience of human society.

55. The anomaly of the state selecting bishops by "election, nomination, presentation, or designation" is an accident of history. It flourished under public authorities eager to crush the Church or to absorb it by patronage. Surely, it fails to fit the bishops' office, which must be "spiritual and supernatural." The Church in this paragraph declares her independence of civil power. The Council Fathers speak gently ("the Council desires. . . . public authorities are most kindly requested to make a voluntary renunciation"), but quite firmly: "the Ecumenical Synod declares that the right of nominating and appointing bishops belongs properly, peculiarly, and of itself exclusively, to the competent ecclesiastical authority."

21. Since the pastoral office of bishops is so important and weighty, when diocesan bishops and others, regarded in law as their equals, have become less capable of fulfilling their duties properly because of the increasing burden of age or some other serious reason, they are earnestly requested to offer their resignation from office either on their own initiative or upon invitation from the competent authority. If the competent authority accepts the resignation, it will make provision for the suitable support of those who have resigned and for special rights to be accorded them.

II. Diocesan Boundaries

22. For a diocese to fulfill its purpose, the nature of the Church must be clearly evident to the People of God who belong to that diocese. Likewise, bishops must be able to carry out their pastoral duties effectively among their people. Finally, the welfare of the People of God must be served as perfectly as possible.

These requirements, then, demand a proper determination of the boundaries of dioceses and a distribution of clergy and resources which is reasonable and in keeping with the needs of the apostolate. All these things will truly benefit not only the clergy and Christian people directly involved, but also the entire Catholic Church.

Concerning diocesan boundaries, therefore, this most sacred Synod decrees that, to the extent required by the good of souls, a fitting revision of diocesan boundaries be undertaken prudently and as soon as possible. This mandate can be met by dividing, dismembering, or uniting dioceses, or by changing their boundaries, or by determining a better place for the episcopal see or, finally, by providing them with a new internal organization, especially when they are composed of rather large cities.

23. In revising diocesan boundaries, the very first concern must be with the organic unity of each diocese, whose personnel, offices, and institutions must operate like a properly functioning body. In individual cases, all circumstances should be carefully studied and the general criteria which follow should be kept in mind.

1.) In fixing a diocesan boundary, as much consideration as possible should be given to the variety in composition of the People of God. Such provision can contribute greatly to a more effective exercise of the pastoral office. At the same time, population clusterings, together with the civil jurisdictions and social institutions which give an organic structure, should be preserved as units to the extent possible. For this reason the territory of each diocese should be continuous.

Provision should also be made, if necessary, for civil boundaries and the special characteristics of regions and peoples. They may be psychological, economic, geographic and historical.

2.) The extent of the diocesan boundaries and the number of its inhabitants should generally be such that, on the one hand, though he may be helped by others, the bishop can exercise his pontifical functions and suitably carry out pastoral visitations, can properly direct and coordinate all the works of the apostolate in his diocese, be especially well acquainted with his priests and with the religious and laity who have some part in diocesan enterprises. On the other hand, an adequate and suitable area should be provided so that bishop and clergy can usefully devote all their energies to the ministry, while the needs of the Church at large are not overlooked.

3.) Finally, in order that the ministry of salvation be more suitably carried out in each diocese, each diocese should regularly have clergy of at least sufficient number and quality for the proper care of the People of God. Also, there should be no lack of the offices, institutions, and organizations which are proper to the particular church and which experience has shown necessary for its efficient government and apostolate; finally, resources for the support of personnel and institutions should be on hand or at least should be prudently foreseen as available elsewhere.

For the same reasons, where there are faithful of a different rite, the diocesan bishop should provide for their spiritual needs either through priests or parishes of that rite or through an episcopal vicar endowed with the necessary faculties. Wherever it is fitting, the latter should also have episcopal rank. Or, the Ordinary himself may perform the office of an Ordinary of different rites. If for certain reasons, these arrangements are not feasible in the eyes of the Apostolic See, then a proper hierarchy for the different rites is to be established.[56]

56. *Cf. Second Vatican Council, Decree on Eastern Catholic Churches, Nov. 21, 1964, Art. 4: AAS 57 (1965), p. 77.*

Also, in similar circumstances, provision should be made for the faithful of different language groups, either through priests or parishes of the same language, or through an episcopal vicar well versed in the language, and, if need be, endowed with the episcopal dignity; or, in some other more appropriate way.

24. By way of effecting the changes and alterations in dioceses, as set forth in Articles 22 and 23, and without prejudice to the discipline of the Oriental Churches, it is desirable that the competent episcopal conferences examine these matters, each for its respective territory. If deemed opportune, a special episcopal commission may be employed for this purpose. But account must always be taken of the opinions of the bishops of the provinces or regions concerned. Finally, these conferences should propose their recommendations and wishes to the Apostolic See.

III. Those Who Cooperate with the Diocesan Bishop in His Pastoral Task

1. COADJUTOR AND AUXILIARY BISHOPS

25. In the government of dioceses, the welfare of the Lord's flock must be the prime concern in any provisions relating to the pastoral office of bishops. That this welfare may be duly secured, auxiliary bishops must frequently be appointed because the diocesan bishop cannot personally fulfill all his episcopal duties as the good of souls demands. The problem may be the vast extent of the diocese, the great number of its inhabitants, the special nature of the apostolate, or other reasons of a different nature. Sometimes, in fact, a particular need requires that a coadjutor bishop be appointed to assist the diocesan bishop.[57] Coadjutor and auxiliary bishops should be granted those faculties necessary for rendering their work more effective and for safeguarding the dignity

---

57. A coadjutor bishop with the right to succeed the residential bishop, at the latter's death or retirement, is named to a diocese for some particular need, e.g., the ill health or advanced age of the incumbent. He must be named vicar general by the diocesan bishop; in some cases, he may be granted more extensive faculties by the competent authority. An auxiliary (assistant) bishop has no right of succession, but he should be named vicar general or at least an episcopal vicar, and be empowered with faculties needed to render his work effective and his episcopal dignity safeguarded.

proper to bishops. These purposes should always be accomplished without detriment to the unity of the diocesan administration and the authority of the diocesan bishop.

Since coadjutor and auxiliary bishops are called to share part of the burden of the diocesan bishop, they should exercise their office in such a way that they may proceed in all matters in single-minded agreement with him. In addition, they should always manifest obedience and reverence toward the diocesan bishop. He, in turn, should have a fraternal love for coadjutor and auxiliary bishops and hold them in esteem.

26. When the good of souls demands, the diocesan bishop should not decline to ask the competent authority for one or more auxiliaries who will be appointed for the diocese without the right of succession.

If there is no provision for it in the letter of nomination, the diocesan bishop should appoint his auxiliary or auxiliaries as vicars general or at least as episcopal vicars. They shall be dependent upon his authority only, and he may wish to consult them in examining questions of major importance, especially of a pastoral nature.

Unless competent authority has otherwise determined, the powers and faculties which auxiliary bishops have by law do not cease when the administration of a diocesan bishop comes to an end. Unless some serious reasons persuade otherwise, it is also desirable that when the See is vacant the office of ruling the diocese should be committed to the auxiliary bishop or, when there are more than one, to one of the auxiliaries.

A coadjutor bishop, appointed with the right of succession, must always be named vicar general by the diocesan bishop. In particular cases the competent authority can grant him even more extensive faculties.

In order to provide as far as possible for the present and future good of the diocese, the diocesan bishop and his coadjutor should not fail to consult with one another on matters of major importance.

2. THE DIOCESAN CURIA AND COUNCILS

27. The most important office in the diocesan curia is that of vicar general. However, as often as the proper government

of the diocese requires it, one or more episcopal vicars[58] can be named by the bishop. These automatically enjoy for a certain part of the diocese, or for a determined type of activity, or for the faithful of a determined rite, the same authority which the common law grants the vicar general.

Included among the collaborators of the bishop in the government of the diocese are those priests who constitute his senate or council, such as the cathedral chapter, the board of consultors, or other committees established according to the circumstances or nature of various localities. To the extent necessary, these institutions, especially the cathedral chapters, should be reorganized in keeping with present-day needs.

Priests and lay people who belong to the diocesan curia should realize that they are making a helpful contribution to the pastoral ministry of the bishop.

The diocesan curia should be so organized that it is an appropriate instrument for the bishop, not only for administering the diocese but also for carrying out the works of the apostolate.

It is highly desirable that in each diocese a pastoral council be established over which the diocesan bishop himself will preside and in which specially chosen clergy, religious, and lay people will participate. The function of this council will be to investigate and to weigh matters which bear on pastoral activity, and to formulate practical conclusions regarding them.

3. THE DIOCESAN CLERGY

28. All priests, both diocesan and religious, participate in and exercise with the bishop the one priesthood of Christ and are thereby meant to be prudent cooperators of the episcopal order. In securing the welfare of souls, however, the first place is held by diocesan priests who are incardinated or attached to a particular church, and who fully dedicate themselves to its service by way of pasturing a single

---

58. In the description of the administrative staff of the diocese, two new terms appear: (1) *episcopal vicars* empowered by the bishop with the authority of a vicar general, but only for a certain part of the diocese, for a determined type of activity, or for the faithful of a particular rite; (2) the *pastoral commission* of the diocese composed of specially chosen clergy, religious and laity, presided over by the bishop. It is the duty of this commission to evaluate matters of pastoral activity and to formulate practical conclusions regarding them. These offices do not set limits to the use of other departments, commissions, or boards, since the diocesan curia must be "an appropriate instrument for the bishop" in both the administration and apostolate of the diocese.

portion of the Lord's flock. In consequence, they form one presbytery and one family, whose father is the bishop. In order to distribute the sacred ministries more equitably and properly among his priests, the bishop should possess a necessary freedom in assigning offices and benefices. Therefore, rights or privileges which in any way limit this freedom are to be suppressed.

The relationships between the bishop and his diocesan priests should rest above all upon the bonds of supernatural charity so that the harmony of the will of the priests with that of their bishop will render their pastoral activity more fruitful. Hence, for the sake of greater service to souls, let the bishop engage in discussion with his priests, even collectively, especially about pastoral matters. This he should do not only occasionally but, as far as possible, at fixed intervals.

Furthermore, all diocesan priests should be united among themselves and thereby develop a pressing concern for the spiritual welfare of the whole diocese. They should also be mindful that the benefits which they receive by reason of their ecclesiastical office are closely bound up with their sacred work. Therefore, they should contribute generously according to their means to the material needs of the diocese as the bishop's program provides for them.

29. Collaborating even more closely with the bishop are those priests charged with a pastoral office or apostolic works of a supraparochial nature, whether in a certain area of the diocese or among special groups of the faithful or with respect to a specific kind of activity.

Priests assigned by the bishop to various works of the apostolate, whether in schools or in other institutions or associations, contribute an exceedingly valuable assistance. Those priests also who are engaged in supradiocesan works are commended to the special consideration of the bishop in whose diocese they reside, for they perform outstanding works of the apostolate.

30. Pastors,[59] however, cooperate with the bishop in a very

---

59. More than a dozen paragraphs in this Decree deal with pastors and assistant pastors. This is not surprising, because priests "associated with their bishop in a spirit of trust and generosity make him present in a certain sense in the individual local congregations . . . and they make the universal Church visible in their own locality" (Constitution on the Church, Chap. III, Art. 28). The bishop in his pastoral role is multiplied by the effective apostolate of his pastors and other priests.

special way, for as shepherds in their own right they are entrusted with the care of souls in a certain part of the diocese under the bishop's authority.

1.) In exercising this care of souls, pastors and their assistants should so fulfill their duty of teaching, sanctifying, and governing that the individual parishioners and the parish communities will really feel that they are members of the diocese and of the universal Church. To this end, they should collaborate with other pastors, and with priests who exercise a pastoral office in the area (such as vicars forane and deans), as well as with those engaged in works of a supra-parochial nature. In this way the pastoral work in the diocese will be unified and made more effective.

Moreover, the care of souls should always be infused with a missionary spirit so that it reaches out in the proper manner to everyone living within the parish boundaries. If the pastor cannot contact certain groups of people, he should seek the help of others, including laymen, who can assist him in the apostolate.

To render the care of souls more efficacious, community life for priests is strongly recommended, especially for those attached to the same parish. While this way of living encourages apostolic action, it also affords an example of charity and unity to the faithful.

2.) In the exercise of their teaching office it is the duty of pastors to preach God's word to all the Christian people so that, rooted in faith, hope, and charity, they may grow in Christ, and that the Christian community may bear witness to that charity which the Lord commended.[60] Pastors should bring the faithful to a full knowledge of the mystery of salvation through a catechetical instruction which is adapted to each one's age. In imparting this instruction, they should seek not only the assistance of religious but also the cooperation of the laity, and should establish the Confraternity of Christian Doctrine.

In discharging their duty to sanctify their people, pastors should arrange for the celebration of the Eucharistic Sacrifice to be the center and culmination of the whole life of the Christian community. They should labor to see that the faithful are nourished with spiritual food through the devout and frequent reception of the sacraments and through intelligent and active participation in the liturgy. Pastors should also be mindful of how much the sacrament of penance contributes

60. *Cf. Jn. 13:35.*

to developing the Christian life and, therefore, should make themselves available to hear the confessions of the faithful. If necessary, they should invite the assistance of priests who are experienced in various languages.

In fulfilling the office of shepherd, pastors should first take pains to know their own flock. Since they are the servants of all the sheep, they should foster growth in Christian living among the individual faithful and also in families, in associations especially dedicated to the apostolate, and in the whole parish community. Therefore, they should visit homes and schools to the extent that their pastoral work demands. They should pay special attention to adolescents and youth, devote themselves with a paternal love to the poor and the sick, and have a particular concern for workingmen. Finally, they should encourage the faithful to assist in the works of the apostolate.

3.) As cooperators with the pastor, assistant pastors make an outstanding and active contribution to the pastoral ministry under the authority of the pastor. Therefore, there should always be fraternal association, mutual charity, and respect between the pastor and his assistants. They should assist one another with counsel, help, and example, furthering the welfare of the parish with united purpose and energy.

31. In making a judgment on the suitability of a priest for the administration of any parish, the bishop should take into consideration not only his knowledge of doctrine but also his piety, apostolic zeal, and other gifts and qualities necessary for the proper exercise of the care of souls.

The parish exists solely for the good of souls. Therefore, by way of enabling the bishop to provide more easily and effectively for pastorates, all rights whatsoever of presentation, nomination, reservation are to be suppressed, including any general or particular law of concursus.[61] The rights of religious, however, are to be maintained.

Pastors should enjoy in their respective parishes that stability of office which the good of souls demands. Hence, although the distinction between removable and irremovable

---

61. "Concursus" in canon law refers to a competitive examination held to determine qualifications of applicants for appointments to parochial office in general or to a particular pastorate. The office or offices are conferred per se in the order of suitability as manifested by the examination. In the United States the system is not in use; suitability of priests for offices is determined by the bishop, assisted, insofar as necessary, by officials deputed for examination of the clergy ("synodal examiners"). Cf. CIC, can. 459.

pastors is to be abrogated, the procedure for transferring and removing pastors is to be re-examined and simplified. In this way, while natural and canonical equity are preserved, the bishop can better provide for the needs of the good of souls.

Pastors who are unable to fulfill their office properly and fruitfully because of the increasing burden of age or some other serious reason are urgently requested to tender their resignation voluntarily or upon invitation from the bishop. The bishop should see to the suitable support of those who have resigned.

32. Finally, the same concern for souls should be the basis for determining or reconsidering the erection or suppression of parishes and any other changes of this kind, which the bishop will be able to bring about on his own authority.

4. RELIGIOUS[62]

33. All religious have the duty, each according to his proper vocation, of cooperating zealously and diligently in building up and increasing the whole Mystical Body of Christ and for the good of the particular churches. (In this section of the present document, it should be noted, the word religious includes members from other institutes who make a profession of the evangelical counsels.)

It is their duty to foster these objectives primarily by means of prayer, works of penance, and the example of their own life. This most sacred Synod strongly urges them ever to increase their esteem and zeal for these means. With due consideration for the character proper to each religious community, they should also enter more vigorously into the external works of the apostolate.

34. Religious priests are consecrated for the office of the presbyterate so that they may be the prudent cooperators of the episcopal order. Today they can be of even greater help to bishops in view of the mounting needs of souls. Therefore, in a certain genuine sense they must be said to belong to the clergy of the diocese inasmuch as they share in the care of

---

62. Men and women who are members of religious communities do not occupy an intermediate place between clergy and laity. Rather they are called by God from both states of life to bind themselves by vows to the three evangelical counsels: poverty, chastity, and obedience. The chapter on religious in the Constitution on the Church (III) treats of the internal elements of the religious state; in this decree on the bishops, the external works of the apostolate are considered.

souls and in carrying out works of the apostolate under the authority of the sacred prelates.

Other members of religious communities, both men and women, also belong in a special way to the diocesan family and offer great assistance to the sacred hierarchy. With the increasing demands of the apostolate, they can and should offer that assistance more every day.

35. In order that the works of the apostolate be carried out harmoniously in individual dioceses and that the unity of diocesan discipline be preserved intact, these principles are established as fundamental:[63]

1.) Religious should always attend upon bishops, as upon successors of the apostles, with devoted deference and reverence. Whenever they are legitimately called upon to undertake works of the apostolate, they are obliged to discharge their duties in such a way that they may be available and docile helpers to bishops.[64] Indeed, religious should comply promptly and faithfully to the requests and desires of the bishops in order that they may thereby assume an even more extensive role in the ministry of human salvation. They should act thus with due respect for the character of their institute and in keeping with their constitutions which, if need be, should be adapted to this goal in accord with the principles of this conciliar Decree.

Especially in view of the urgent need of souls and the

63. The history of religious communities has been a long narrative of dedicated prayer and service. Their role: building up and increasing the whole Mystical Body of Christ. Their relation to the local bishops has not always been smooth, as ecclesiastical law and history attest. Tensions can often arise between adherence to a particular rule and practice, and service in a diocese. In a desire, mutually shared by the communities and the episcopate, to insure a proper harmony, the Council has established certain norms.

The Council Fathers showed a good sense of balance. The community ideal is affirmed: the particular character and spirit of each is affirmed with full observance of the rule and obedience to superiors. But the "mounting need of souls" has opened up today new avenues of activity under the direction of the bishops. Accordingly, religious may be said "in a real sense to belong to the clergy of the diocese inasmuch as they share in the care of souls and in carrying out works of the apostolate under the authority of the sacred prelates." These works include preaching, divine worship, care of souls, religious and moral education. The local Ordinary has charge of matters concerning clerical decorum and prescriptions of episcopal councils and conferences intended for all priests.

Bishops, for their part, must keep in mind the particular character of a community, and impress its members with the duty of fidelity and obedience to it. To assure a right harmony, bishops and religious superiors should meet when necessary for mutual consultation.

64. Cf. Pius XII, allocution of Dec. 8, 1950: AAS 43 (1951), p. 28; cf. also Paul VI, allocution of May 23, 1964: AAS 56 (1964), p. 571.

scarcity of diocesan clergy, religious communities which are not dedicated exclusively to the contemplative life can be called upon by the bishops to assist in various pastoral ministries. The particular character of each community should, however, be kept in mind. Superiors should encourage this work to the utmost, even by accepting parishes on a temporary basis.

2.) Religious engaged in the active apostolate, however, should be imbued with the spirit of their religious community, and remain faithful to the observance of their rule and to submissiveness toward their own superiors. Bishops should not neglect to impress this obligation upon them.

3.) The privilege of exemption,[65] by which religious are called to the service of the Supreme Pontiff or other ecclesiastical authority and are withdrawn from the jurisdiction of bishops, applies chiefly to the internal order of their communities so that in them all things may be more aptly coordinated and the growth and depth of religious life better served.[66] These communities are also exempt in order that the Supreme Pontiff may make use of them for the good of the universal Church[67] or that any other competent authority may do so for the good of the churches under its own jurisdiction.

This exemption, however, does not exclude religious in individual dioceses from the jurisdiction of the bishop in accordance with the norm of law, insofar as the performance of his pastoral office and the right ordering of the care of souls require.[68]

4.) All religious, exempt and non-exempt, are subject to the authority of the local Ordinaries in those things which

---

65. "Exempt religious" are those communities withdrawn from the authority of the local ordinary and subject to the Pope alone. The purpose is "to more fully provide for the necessities of the entire flock of the Lord and in consideration of the common good." The decree on bishops explains that this special status "applies chiefly to the internal order of their communities, so that in them all things may be properly coordinated and the growth and perfection of religious life promoted . . . this exemption, however, does not exclude religious in individual dioceses from the jurisdiction of the bishop in accordance with the norm of law, insofar as the performance of his pastoral office and the right ordering of the care of souls require."

This conciliar formula for the fruitful harmony of the hierarchy and the religious communities has been drawn from historical precedent and canonical practice, especially expressed in the teaching of Leo XIII, Pius XII, and the present Pontiff.

66. *Cf. Leo XIII, apostolic constitution "Romanos Pontifices," May 8, 1881; Acta Leonis XIII, vol. 2, 1882, p. 234.*

67. *Cf. Paul VI, allocution of May 23, 1964: AAS 56 (1965), pp. 570-571.*

68. *Cf. Pius XII, allocution of Dec. 8, 1950, loc. cit.*

pertain to the public exercise of divine worship (except where differences in rites are concerned), the care of souls, sacred preaching intended for the people, the religious and moral education of the Christian faithful, especially of children, catechetical instruction, and liturgical formation. Religious are subject to the local Ordinary also in matters of proper clerical decorum as well as in the various works which concern the exercise of the sacred apostolate. Catholic schools conducted by religious are also subject to the authority of the local Ordinaries as regards general policy and supervision, but the right of religious to direct them remains intact. Religious also are bound to observe all those things which episcopal councils or conferences legitimately prescribe for universal observance.

5.) A well-ordered cooperation is to be encouraged between various religious communities, and between them and the diocesan clergy. There should also be a very close coordination of all apostolic works and activities. This depends especially on a supernatural attitude of hearts and minds, an attitude rooted in and founded upon charity. The Apostolic See is competent to supervise this coordination for the universal Church; bishops are competent in their own respective dioceses: and patriarchal synods and episcopal conferences in their own territory.

With respect to those works of the apostolate which religious are to undertake, bishops or episcopal conferences, religious superiors or conferences of major religious superiors should take action only after mutual consultations.

6.) In order to foster harmonious and fruitful relations between bishops and religious, at stated times and as often as it is deemed opportune, bishops and religious superiors should be willing to meet for discussion of those affairs which pertain generally to the apostolate in their territory.

CHAPTER III

CONCERNING THE COOPERATION OF BISHOPS FOR THE COMMON GOOD OF MANY CHURCHES

I. Synods, Councils, and Especially Episcopal Conferences [69]

36. From the very first centuries of the Church the bishops who were placed over individual churches were deeply influenced by the fellowship of fraternal charity and by zeal for the universal mission entrusted to the apostles. And so they pooled their resources and unified their plans for the common good and for that of the individual churches. Thus there were established synods, provincial councils, and plenary councils in which bishops legislated for various churches a common pattern to be followed in teaching the truths of faith and ordering ecclesiastical discipline.

This sacred Ecumenical Synod earnestly desires that the venerable institution of synods and councils flourish with new vigor. Thus, faith will be spread and discipline preserved more fittingly and effectively in the various churches, as the circumstances of the times require.

37. Nowadays especially, bishops are frequently unable to

---

69. The Council urges the increased use of synods and councils, not only because of the contemporary need for such assemblies, but because of their venerable origin. Since the first centuries of Christianity, bishops have "pooled their resources" and effected "a holy union of energies." Synods and councils of various kinds are as old as the Church. An American example is the series of "Baltimore Councils" held in 1852, 1866, and 1884.

The episcopal conference is of later origin. The Plenary Council of Latin America launched in 1899 a prototype of the modern conference, the Latin American Episcopal Conference (CELAM), which has continued a program aimed at the study and coordinated solutions of common problems. France, Spain, and the United States established similar conferences on a national basis after World War I.

fulfill their office suitably and fruitfully unless they work more harmoniously and closely every day with other bishops. Episcopal conferences, already established in many nations, have furnished outstanding proofs of a more fruitful apostolate. Therefore, this most sacred Synod considers it supremely opportune everywhere that bishops belonging to the same nation or region form an association and meet together at fixed times. Thus, when the insights of prudence and experience have been shared and views exchanged, there will emerge a holy union of energies in the service of the common good of the churches.

Wherefore, this sacred Synod issues the following decrees concerning episcopal conferences:

38. 1.) An episcopal conference is a kind of council in which the bishops of a given nation or territory jointly exercise their pastoral office by way of promoting that greater good which the Church offers mankind, especially through forms and programs of the apostolate which are fittingly adapted to the circumstances of the age.

2.) Members of the episcopal conference are all local Ordinaries of every rite, coadjutors, auxiliaries, and other titular bishops who perform a special work entrusted to them by the Apostolic See or the episcopal conferences. Vicars general are not members. *De jure* membership belongs neither to other titular bishops nor, in view of their particular assignment in the area, to legates of the Roman Pontiff.

Local Ordinaries and coadjutors hold a deliberative vote. Auxiliaries and other bishops who have a right to attend the conference will exercise either a deliberative or a consultative vote, as the statutes of the conference determine.

3.) Each episcopal conference is to draft its own statutes, to be reviewed by the Apostolic See. In these statutes, among other agencies, offices should be established which will aid in achieving the conference's purpose more efficaciously: for example, a permanent board of bishops, episcopal commissions, and a general secretariat.

4.) Decisions of the episcopal conference,[70] provided they have been made lawfully and by the choice of at least two-

---

70. This Decree provides for more than a coordinating agency. In certain cases the conference may exercise juridical authority by majority vote, namely, in cases prescribed by common law, or determined by special mandate of the Apostolic See, given spontaneously or in response to a petition from the conference itself. Thus both the proper authority of the local bishop and the common good of an entire region are safeguarded.

thirds of the prelates who have a deliberative vote in the conference, and have been reviewed by the Apostolic See, are to have juridically binding force in those cases and in those only which are prescribed by common law or determined by special mandate of the Apostolic See, given spontaneously or in response to a petition from the conference itself.

5.) Wherever special circumstances require and the Apostolic See approves, bishops of many nations can establish a single conference.

Moreover, contacts between episcopal conferences of different nations should be encouraged in order to promote and safeguard their higher welfare.

6.) It is highly recommended that when prelates of the Oriental Churches promote in synod the discipline of their own churches and more efficaciously foster works for the good of religion, they take into account also the common good of the whole territory where many churches of different rites exist. They should exchange views on this point at inter-ritual meetings held in accord with the norms to be given by the competent authority.

II. The Boundaries of Ecclesiastical Provinces and the Establishment of Ecclesiastical Regions

39. The welfare of souls requires appropriate boundaries not only for dioceses but also for ecclesiastical provinces; indeed, it sometimes counsels the establishment of even wider ecclesiastical units. Thus the needs of the apostolate will be better provided for according to social and local circumstances. Thus, too, relations can be made more smooth and productive between individual bishops, or between bishops and their metropolitans or other bishops of the same country, or between bishops and civil authorities.

40. Therefore, in order to accomplish these aims, this most sacred Synod decrees as follows:

1.) The boundaries of ecclesiastical provinces are to be submitted to an early review, and the rights and privileges of metropolitans are to be defined according to new and suitable norms.

2.) As a general rule all dioceses and other territorial divisions which are by law equivalent to dioceses should be attached to an ecclesiastical province. Therefore dioceses which are now directly subject to the Apostolic See and not united to any other are either to be brought together to form a new ecclesiastical province, if that be possible, or else attached to that province which is nearer or more convenient. They are to be made subject to the metropolitan jurisdiction of the archbishop, in keeping with the norms of common law.

3.) Wherever advantageous, ecclesiastical provinces should be grouped into ecclesiastical regions, for the organization of which provision is to be made by law.

41. It is fitting that the competent episcopal conferences examine the question of the boundaries of such provinces or the establishment of such regions, in keeping with the norms given with respect to diocesan boundaries in Articles 23 and 24. They are then to submit their suggestions and wishes to the Apostolic See.

III. Bishops with an Interdiocesan Office

42. Since pastoral needs increasingly require that some pastoral undertakings be directed and carried forward as joint projects, it is fitting that certain offices be created for the service of all or many dioceses of a determined region or nation. These offices can even be filled by bishops.

This sacred Synod recommends that between the prelates or bishops serving in these offices on the one hand and the diocesan bishops and the episcopal conferences on the other, there always exist fraternal association and harmonious cooperation in matters of pastoral concern. These relationships should also be defined by common law.

43. Because of the special conditions of the way of life of military personnel, their spiritual care requires extraordinary consideration. Hence, there should be established in every nation, if possible, a military vicariate. Both the military vicar and the chaplains should devote themselves unsparingly to this difficult work in harmonious cooperation with the diocesan bishops.[71]

71. *Cf. Sacred Consistorial Congregation's Instruction to Military Ordinariates,*

Diocesan bishops should release to the military vicar a sufficient number of priests who are qualified for this serious work. At the same time they should promote all enterprises on behalf of improving the spiritual welfare of military personnel.[72]

General Directive [73]

44. This most sacred Synod prescribes that in the revision of the Code of Canon Law suitable laws be drawn up in keeping with the principles stated in this Decree. Due consideration should also be given to observations made by individual commissions or Fathers of this Council.

This sacred Synod also prescribes that general directories be drawn up concerning the care of souls, for the use of both bishops and pastors. In this way, shepherds can be provided with sure methods designed to help them discharge their particular pastoral office with greater facility and success.

There should also be prepared individual directories concerning the pastoral care of special groups of the faithful, as the different circumstances of particular nations or regions require. Another directory should be composed with respect to the catechetical instruction of the Christian people, and should deal with the fundamental principles of such instruc-

Apr. 23, 1951: AAS 43 (1951), pp. 562-565; Formula Regarding the Conferring of the Status of Military Ordinariates, Oct. 20, 1956: AAS 49 (1957), pp. 150-163; Decree on Ad Limina Visits of Military Ordinariates, Feb. 28, 1959; AAS 51 (1959), pp. 272-274; Decree on the Granting of Faculties for Confessions to Military Chaplains, Nov. 27, 1960: AAS 53 (1961), pp. 49-50. Also cf. Congregation of Religious' Instruction on Religious Military Chaplains, Feb. 2, 1955: AAS 47 (1955), pp. 93-97.

72. Cf. *Sacred Consistorial Congregation, letter to the cardinals, archbishops, and bishops of Spanish-speaking nations, June 27, 1951: AAS 43 (1951), p. 566.*

73. The Decree closes on a strong note of practicality: the necessary revision of certain elements in the new Code of Canon Law, publication of directories (i.e., manuals or guides, for the care of souls), catechetical instruction, and apostolic activity among special groups of the faithful.

The practical treatment of episcopal duties, especially those of a pastoral nature, together with the widening concern for the universal Church, form the recurring theme of the entire decree on the bishops. The episcopal conference at home, the curial reorganization in Rome, and a new bridge in the Apostolic Synod are prophetic steps in making collegiality work. When the Council Fathers approved these instruments and Pope Paul heartily concurred in them, one of the most dynamic developments of the Second Vatican Council took place. The office of the bishop in the renewal of the Church is evolving from the juridical concept of administrator to the pastoral office of "good shepherd . . . true father."

tion, its arrangement, and the composition of books on the subject. In the preparation of these directories, too, special attention is to be given to the views which have been expressed by individual commissions and Fathers of the Council.

In the name of the most holy and undivided Trinity, the Father and the Son and the Holy Spirit.

The Decree on the Bishops' Pastoral Office in the Church has won the consent of the Fathers in this most sacred and universal Second Vatican Synod that has been legitimately convoked.

We too, by the apostolic authority conferred on us by Christ, join with the Venerable Fathers in approving, decreeing, and establishing these things in the Holy Spirit, and we direct that what has thus been enacted in synod be published to God's glory.

Rome, at St. Peter's, October 28, 1965

I, Paul, Bishop of the Catholic Church

There follow the signatures of the Fathers.

A RESPONSE

While one may have assumed that the Second Vatican Council's Decree on the Bishops' Pastoral Office in the Church would be technical and professional, it turned out to be, in fact, as practical as the Pastoral Constitution on the Church in the Modern World, and from the standpoint of Church renewal and Christian unity it is as relevant and important.

The central concern in current discussions on Church unity is the place, work, and nature of the episcopacy. Protestant proposals for uniting the denominations now recognize that some form of episcopacy must be provided in the polity of a united Church. Thus, from the standpoint of the second major objective of the Second Vatican Council, namely Church unity, this Decree speaks to a pressing concern.

Apart from its New Testament origin and its historic place in Church government, the office of a bishop appears to have validated itself in the divine economy of the Church in the modern world. It has proved its value by its works and justifies its claim to be of God by its fruits. A world Church must have a functional and historic governing and administrative organization which unites and holds together her parts. She must have a voice that can speak for all the Church to all the world. The latest major proposal for Protestant Church union, though congregational governed Churches are included in it, proposes an episcopacy. Protestants, therefore, are studying the Decree on the Bishops' Pastoral Office in the Church with interest rather than with curiosity, because a doctrine of the episcopacy is now recognized to be basic in the concept of Christians as "one people and one Church."

The nature and function of the episcopacy are questions on which the Church bodies interested in union have not come to an agreement. But a major step forward has been made in the recognition of the necessity of the principle of the episcopacy in a united Christendom.

The Decree commends itself to the modern Church world because it is practical and pastoral. It interprets traditional authority in terms of current necessity. It succeeds in returning the episcopacy to its original vocation in the Church, while closing the gap now existing between bishop, clergy, and laity through a renewed dedication to the teaching, evangelizing, and pastoral office of a bishop.

The authors of the Decree have made it truly ecumenical in terms which relate the office of a bishop to the origin of the Church and outline its functions in the universal fellowship in Christ.

Specifically, the Decree speaks to all bishops, Roman Catholic and non-Roman Catholic. By New Testament standards, it points out that charity, simplicity, holiness, and humility are the qualities of a true bishop of the Church. It deals with the teaching, preaching, and leadership responsibilities peculiar to the office of a bishop. It recalls that the prototype of our modern episcopacy was known for humility and accessibility. It challenges the bishops to accept their responsibility by exercising their Godly authority. It points out that the office of a bishop has lost some of its functions through its willingness to avoid responsibility by delegating its powers to other bodies. It warns that a bishop is a shepherd and a pastor, and not a computer or a kind of ecclesiastical univac. While not mentioning St. John by name, it holds up the image of a people seeking the blessing and benediction of a bishop through whom the love of God is kindled in their hearts.

The Second Vatican Council's word to its own bishops is a message to all bishops.

The Decree speaks to the clergy, recalling to them the consciousness of their pastoral function in an age of automation and anonymity. It lifts up the unity and fellowship of the pastoral vocations, which unite the clergy to each other and to the bishop and to their people. It says a timely word concerning the spiritual need of the confessional, which is as spiritually needed for Protestants as for Catholics, and which the Protestant fathers retained in adapted forms. Teaching, sanctifying, and governing are the key words in a modern pastoral ministry to a congregation.

The Decree speaks to the state, declaring a right which the Church cannot surrender without destroying herself. It is the right of freedom from civil authority and resistance to the state's intrusion in ecclesiastical appointments. This phase of the Decree has implications for the free world as well as for the totalitarian world and will require a rethinking of both Church and state in their relation especially to "the established Church" in the modern world.

In a more technical sense, the Decree speaks to the questions of effective diocesan administration, what the bishop's special responsibilities are within his diocese—a ministry to all, including the poor; a ministry of participation in community affairs, and not a policy of withdrawal; the obligation of the supervision and promotion of catechetical training— and the limitation in the size of dioceses, which makes all of this possible for the bishop and his auxiliaries to perform. In short, the bishop must become a "person" in the dioceses and not simply a kind of impersonal power. The Decree speaks of Church organization and the necessity of using the laity and the parish and diocesan organizations or curia, following the example of Pope Paul in his new pattern of collegiality in administration. It deals also with the location of authority, which is so inherent in all life that it cannot be avoided in the Church. The basis of orderly and progressive existence must have authority morally, spiritually, and intelligently exercised. The Church, too, must have its doctrine of authority, its chain of responsibility, and its levels of decision.

The so-called authoritarianism of the Roman Catholic Church is assumed by many to be one of the most difficult barriers to remove in order to achieve Church unity. While its difficulty is apparent, its consideration cannot be avoided. Every Church has its center of ultimate and final authority. In some it is decentralized to the point of residing in the local congregation, while in others, like the Methodist Church, it is centralized in a judicial council of nine persons elected by the Church's representative body called the General Conference. The trend now appears to be toward centralization of authority with a large measure of local flexibility. The place to begin such a discussion, however, is the fact of authority and not the method of authority. Many of what appeared to the separated brethren to be arbitrary procedures in the exercise of Roman Catholic authority have been removed by the Pope and the Second Vatican Council, indicating that authority, rights, and freedom within the Church are not incompatible.

In summary, the Decree on the Bishops' Pastoral Office in the Church seeks to make the episcopacy effective in the twofold purpose of the Second Vatican Council: to renew the Church and to advance Christian unity. Its practical approach justifies the hope that it will make the administration of the Church more acceptable and more effective.

But just as the image of the Church as expressed in the work and personality of Pope John and Pope Paul created the trust and confidence as well as the pattern needed for the success of the Second Vatican Council, so their dedicated example as the chief shepherd has both humanized and spiritualized the episcopal office and re-established it not only in the respect but also in the love of the people.

The Decree of the Council and the example of Pope John and Pope Paul have made sure the place of the Christlike bishop in the modern world.

The Decree envisages a conference of Catholic bishops— why not, for the sake of all of Christ's sheep, a conference of all chief pastors and shepherds of His Flock?

BISHOP FRED PIERCE CORSON

PRIESTLY FORMATION

IT HAS BECOME common practice for anyone discussing a Conciliar document to maintain that it is "one of the most important documents of the Council." Without going that far, I would like to point out that the Decree on Priestly Formation is an essential part of the twofold vision which is at the very heart of the Council.

As the Council progressed, what began as a series of separate and almost unrelated documents slowly took on organic unity. The key word *aggiornamento,* coined by Pope John, began to express itself as a new self-awareness of the Church. The Constitution on the Church thus became the touchstone of reform. Here the mission, the nature, the mystery of the Church were examined and held up to the mirror of the gospel of Christ and the spirit of Christ. But it was not enough to consider the Church only in herself; she had to be studied in her concrete and historical character in her continued incarnation in the world and in time. Therefore, the Pastoral Constitution on the Church in the Modern World became the second key document of the Council, especially in the presentation of general principles in the first part of the document.

From this twofold aspect of the study of the Church flow all the other documents, and each traces its genesis and even its final form to the basic positions to be found there. The Decree on Priestly Formation breathes the spirit of Vatican II, just as much as the great documents on the liturgy and revelation or the timely statements on ecumenism, religious freedom, and the attitude of the Church toward non-Christian religions.

This Decree was prepared with Vatican II in mind. Because the members of the Commission did not have to introduce their subject until last year, they had time to catch the spirit abroad among the Fathers. Therefore, they had two full years to learn from the manhandling received by documents which had failed to take into account the reforming mentality of the Council. This explains why, from the beginning, the present Decree received gentle treatment. It was immediately accepted in principle with only forty-seven negative votes. Even the qualified approvals for the whole text (which were called "juxta modum" approvals) were relatively few and consisted in large part in a desire that the study of philosophy not be limited to Thomism.

In other words, the bishops found the essential link between the Decree offered for the training of priests and the concern of the Council for the true image of the Church. To understand this Decree and read between all of its lines, one must understand the Constitution on the Church. One must read the beautiful and lofty thoughts on the nature and mission of the priest both in that Constitution and in the document which deals specifically with the priesthood. One must read the guidelines of the Church in the Modern World, in which a real effort is made to do away with any supposed dichotomy between the doctrine of the Church and her practical involvement in time and space and action. To be in the world is of the very nature of the Church. So, too, to live in the world and to be an instrument there of Christ is the very nature of the priesthood.

The training of the priest in this concept called for adaptation and reform. Regardless of all the criticism which the new wave suddenly produced, our seminaries had already begun to seek to adjust to the pastoral needs of the day. It is true that they were hampered by a very tight control from the Congregation for Seminaries and Universities. Four hundred years ago, the Council of Trent established the norms for seminaries as we know them today. In that time and at that moment of history, a highly centralized organism was necessary. Clergy morale and, often, morality were at a low ebb. Institutionally, the Church was in the doldrums and was being torn apart by schism and separation. Often priests were ordained with little or no theology; equally lacking was spiritual training. Candidates for holy orders were taught by individuals in a priest's home. There was little effort to find a common method or criterion for discerning vocations and preparing the candidate carefully for the role he was to fill in the Church. The reforming regulations laid down by the Council of Trent were, therefore, a blessing. Nor has seminary training remained static since Trent. The Holy See from time to time has issued directives always aimed at strengthening the work of the seminary and producing the type of priest who could truly preside over the People of God, announce the living and ever-contemporary truth of the gospel, and unite the faithful in the sacrifice and banquet of the Eucharist.

With the new insights of the Second Vatican Council, with the social and economic revolution of our age, with the Church's new awareness of her mission, it is evident that the training of a priest must undergo change. His training must be at once doctrinal and pastoral. The theology he is taught will be an organic reflection of the Church both in its mission and nature and in the impact it must exercise in the world at this moment of history. The decentralization which marks other fields contemplated by the Council applies here, too, as the local church comes back into its full focus. There will always be a basic unity in the deep reality underlying all good seminary training, but the pastoral preparation must take into account the specific environment in which the young priest will begin his ministry. By the same token, just as the responsibility which bishops share for the universal Church has been underlined in this Council, so too the need for training priests who share this vision and are willing to serve anywhere will find its expression in this Decree.

With this in mind, read the document. Do not look for a detailed plan. A seminary is not a lumber mill or a smelter. It cannot take a raw youth and, after subjecting him to a few approved processes, turn out a neatly fashioned or keenly honed priest. The Decree on Priestly Formation will give directives and, in some cases, counsel and suggestions. In its spirit, bishops, seminary staffs, diocesan priests, and religious priests—all who have a part to play in discerning and developing vocations—but most of all the seminarians themselves must use their ingenuity and will and must respond to the grace of Christ to work out the solution. Their willingness and faithfulness in adhering to the spirit of this Decree will determine much of the future of the Church.

✠ ALEXANDER CARTER

Decree ₁on Priestly Formation

PAUL, BISHOP
SERVANT OF THE SERVANTS OF GOD
TOGETHER WITH THE FATHERS OF THE SACRED COUNCIL
FOR EVERLASTING MEMORY

PREFACE

This sacred Synod well knows that the wished-for renewal of
the whole Church depends in large measure on a ministry of
priests which is vitalized by the spirit of Christ.[2] Hence it
proclaims the extreme importance of priestly formation and
affirms certain basic principles pertaining to it. These principles
will strengthen laws which have already proven their value
through the experience of centuries, and will provide for
the addition of new laws which reflect the Constitutions

1. The Second Vatican Council has used different terms to signify different
types of documents; hence some are called Constitutions, others Declarations.
At other times the Council sent a Message. This document was first presented
as "Propositiones" (proposals) and finally became a Decree, i.e., an authoritative statement of directives and counsels.
2. *How very greatly the progress of the entire People of God depends on
the ministry of priests, as Christ himself has willed it, is evident from the
words by which the Lord made the apostles and their successors and helpers
preachers of the gospel, the selected leaders of a new people, and the dispensers of the mysteries of God; it is also confirmed by the writings of the
Fathers and of the saints, as well as in many papal documents.*
  See especially:
    St. Pius X, exhortation to the clergy "Haerent Animo," Aug. 4, 1908:
S. Pii X Acta IV, pp. 237-264.
    *Pius XI, encyclical letter "Ad Catholici Sacerdotii," Dec. 20, 1935: AAS
28 (1936), especially pp. 37-52.*
    *Pius XII, apostolic exhortation "Menti Nostrae," Sept. 23, 1950: AAS
42 (1950), pp. 657-702.*
    *John XXIII, encyclical letter "Sacerdotii Nostri Primordia," Aug. 1,
1959: AAS 51 (1959), pp. 545-579.*
    *Paul VI, apostolic letter "Summi Dei Verbum," Nov. 4, 1963: AAS 55
(1963), pp. 979-995.*

and Decrees of this holy Council, as well as the changed conditions of our times. In view of the very unity of the Catholic priesthood, this priestly training is a necessity for all priests of either[3] clergy and of whatever rite. Therefore, while these regulations directly concern the diocesan clergy, they should be adapted for all others to the extent that corresponding situations require.

CHAPTER I

PROGRAM OF PRIESTLY FORMATION TO BE UNDERTAKEN BY INDIVIDUAL COUNTRIES

1. Since the variety of peoples and places is so great, only general rules can be legislated. Hence in each nation or particular rite a "Program of Priestly Formation" should be undertaken.[4] It should be drawn up by the Episcopal Conferences,[5] revised at definite intervals, and approved by the Apostolic See. By it, universal laws are to be adapted to the special circumstances of time and place, so that priestly formation will always answer the pastoral needs of the area in which the ministry is to be exercised.

3. I.e., diocesan clergy and priests who are members of religious orders, congregations, and other societies.
4. Without impinging on the supervisory authority of the Holy See, the very first statement calls for a decentralization. It is now for the first time the Episcopal Conferences of the various countries or groups of countries which will adjust priestly training to local pastoral needs and conditions. This is a very important paragraph. It is a key implementation of the spirit of the Council.
5. *The entire formation of priests, that is, the arrangement of the seminary, its spiritual instruction, its curriculum, the common life and discipline of the students, and its pastoral training, should be adapted to the various circumstances of regions. And this adaptation, since it deals with very important principles, is to be carried out both according to common norms for secular clergy set up by the Bishops' Conferences, and in agreement with the rules made by competent superiors for the regular clergy (cf. the general statutes joined to the apostolic constitution "Sedes Sapientiae," Art. 19).*

CHAPTER II

THE INTENSIFIED ENCOURAGEMENT OF PRIESTLY VOCATIONS

2. The task of fostering vocations[6] devolves on the whole Christian community, which should do so in the first place by living in a fully Christian way. Outstanding contributions are made to this work by families which are alive with the spirit of faith, love, and reverence and which serve as a kind of introductory seminary; and by parishes in whose pulsing vitality young people themselves have a part.

Teachers and all others, especially Catholic associations, who in any capacity provide for the training of boys and young men should strive so to develop those entrusted to them that these young people will be able to recognize a divine calling and willingly answer it. To the greatest possible extent every priest should manifest the zeal of an apostle in fostering vocations. Let him attract the hearts of young people to the priesthood by his own humble and energetic life, joyfully pursued, and by love for his fellow priests and brotherly collaboration with them.

It is the bishop's duty to make his people active in promoting vocations and to see to it that all vocational resources and activities are closely coordinated. As a father he should make every sacrifice to help those whom he judges to be called to the Lord's service.

Such an active partnership between the whole People of God in the work of encouraging vocations corresponds to the

---

6. *Among the principal hardships with which the Church is today afflicted, that of the very small supply of vocations stands out almost everywhere.*

See: Pius XII, apostolic exhortation, "Menti Nostrae": ". . . the number of priests, both in Catholic areas and in missionary territories, is for the most part unequal to the ever-increasing needs." (AAS 42 (1950), p. 682.)

John XXIII: "The problem of ecclesiastical and religious vocations is a daily concern of the Pope . . . , it is the subject of his prayer, the ardent hope of his soul." (From his allocution to the First International Congress on Vocations to the States of Perfection, Dec. 16, 1961: "L'Osservatore Romano," Dec. 17, 1961.)

activity of divine Providence.[7] For God properly endows and aids with His grace those men divinely chosen to share in Christ's hierarchical priesthood. To the lawful ministers of the Church He confides the work of calling proven candidates whose fitness has been acknowledged and who seek so exalted an office with the right intention and full freedom. Her ministers exercise the further commission of consecrating such men with the seal of the Holy Spirit to the worship of God and the service of the Church.[8]

This holy Synod gives primary commendation to the traditional means of joint effort, such as persistent prayer and Christian mortification; also, a formation of the faithful which grows more penetrating every day, and which is imparted either through preaching or catechetical instruction, or even by the various media of social communication. In all these means of formation the necessity, nature, and excellence of the priestly vocation should be made clear. The Council also directs that in accord with pontifical documents on the subject all pastoral activity on behalf of vocations should be systematically handled and unified by vocational organizations already established or due to be established in the territories of each diocese, region, or nation. These groups should foster such activity with equal discretion and zeal, and should neglect no appropriate helps which modern psychology and sociology can offer.[9]

Efforts on behalf of vocations should be largehearted enough to transcend the boundaries of each diocese, nation, religious community, and rite. Responding to the needs of the whole Church, these efforts should give special help to those

7. Some wanted a theological definition of a vocation. The Council preferred to describe in a very general way how vocations are discerned and fostered. In keeping with the new stress on the involvement of the whole People of God in the mission of the Church, the responsibility is placed in varying degrees, but in a real way for all, on the entire community.
8. Pius XII, apostolic constitution "Sedes Sapientiae," May 31, 1956: AAS 48 (1956), p. 357.
   Paul VI, apostolic letter "Summi Dei Verbum," Nov. 4, 1963: AAS 55 (1963), pp. 984 ff.
9. See especially: Pius XII, motu proprio "Cum Nobis," "Concerning the Pontifical Work of Priestly Vocations Established in the Sacred Congregation in Charge of Seminaries and Universities," Nov. 4, 1941: AAS 33 (1941), p. 479; along with the statutes and norms promulgated by the same Congregation on Sept. 8, 1943. Motu proprio, "Cum Supremae," "Concerning the Distinguished Pontifical Work on Religious Vocations," Feb. 11, 1955: AAS 47 (1955), p. 266; also the connected statutes and norms promulgated by the Sacred Congregation of Religious (ibid., pp. 298-301); the Decree of the Second Vatican Council: On the Appropriate Renewal of the Religious Life, Art. 24; also the Decree: On the Bishops' Pastoral Office in the Church, Art. 15.

places where workers for the Lord's vineyard are more urgently called for.

3. In minor seminaries, which are built to nurture the seeds of a vocation, students can be conditioned to follow Christ the Redeemer with a generous and pure heart. The means should be a special religious formation which gives first place to spiritual direction. Under the fatherly guidance of superiors and with appopriate cooperation of parents, the students should lead a life which is suited to the age, mentality, and developmental stage of young men, and which fully conforms to the laws of a healthy psychology. The students should be suitably involved in normal human activities, and have frequent contact with their own families.[10] To the extent that they apply to the goal and program of minor seminaries, the following decrees on major seminaries should be adapted to minor ones. In any case, the course of studies ought to be so arranged that students can continue them elsewhere without disadvantage if they choose another state of life. Equal care should be expended on fostering the seeds of a vocation among adolescents and young men attending institutes which under the circumstances also serve the purposes of a minor seminary. The same applies to those who are being trained in different schools or by other means of education.[11] Let active concern be shown for schools and other projects designed for men who pursue a vocation at a later time of life.

10. *Cf. Pius XII, apostolic exhortation "Menti Nostrae," Sept. 23, 1950: AAS 42 (1950), p. 685.*
11. The question of minor seminaries is a complex one, and there is some difference of opinion concerning their advisability or the form they should take. Wisely, the bishops do not try to settle any arguments. Starting from the fact that minor seminaries exist and may be necessary in some places, the document clearly states that the young people should not be given the "hothouse" treatment. They should have normal social contacts for their age, and their studies should be such as to fit them for life in any other capacity, should they decide against the priesthood. An even greater development, perhaps, should have been presented here: the need to seek out vocations in public schools and other institutions, and the late vocations to be found in universities and elsewhere. At least the richest field has been mentioned in this article.

CHAPTER III

THE PROGRAMMING OF MAJOR SEMINARIES

4. Major seminaries are necessary for priestly formation.[12] In them the whole training of students ought to provide for the development of true shepherds of souls after the model of our Lord Jesus Christ, who was Teacher, Priest, and Shepherd.[13]

Let these students, then, be readied for the ministry of the word, so that they may always grow in their understanding of God's revealed word, may know how to grasp it through meditation, and express it through word and conduct.

Let them be readied for the ministry of worship and sanctification, that by their prayers and participation in sacred liturgical ceremonies, they may know how to exercise the work of salvation through the Eucharistic Sacrifice and the other sacraments.

Let them be readied for the ministry of a shepherd. They should know how to represent Christ before men. He did not "come to be served but to serve, and to give his life as a ransom for many" (Mk. 10:45; cf. Jn. 13:12-17). Becoming the servants of all, let them win over that many more (cf. 1 Cor. 9:19).

Therefore, every program of instruction, whether spiritual, intellectual, or disciplinary, should be joined with practical implementation and directed toward the aforementioned pastoral goal. In loyal obedience to the authority of the bishop, let all directors and teachers energetically and harmoniously bend their efforts to the pursuit of this objective.

5. Since the training of seminarians hinges, to a very large extent, on wise regulations and on suitable teachers, seminary

12. This paragraph is important not only for what it says but for the fact that it is there. It is a clear recognition of the need for major seminaries—a point which needed restatement at this time.
13. *Cf. Second Vatican Council, Dogmatic Constitution on the Church, Art. 28: AAS 57 (1965), p. 34.*

directors and professors should be chosen from among the best,[14] and be painstakingly prepared by solid doctrine, appropriate pastoral experience, and special spiritual and pedagogical training. Hence encouragement deserves to be given to institutes conducted to this end, or at least to suitably programmed courses, and to meetings of seminary moderators held at set intervals.

For directors and teachers need to be keenly aware of how greatly the outcome of seminary formation depends on their own manner of thinking and acting. Under their rector's lead, they should create the strictest harmony in spirit and behavior. Among themselves and with their students they should constitute the kind of family which answers the Lord's prayer "that they may be one" (cf. Jn. 17:11) and which intensifies in each student the joy of his calling. With active and loving concern, the bishop ought to inspire those who work in the seminary, and show himself to be a true father in Christ to its students. Finally, let every priest regard the seminary as the heart of the diocese, gladly offering the help of his own service.[15]

6. Depending on the age of each seminarian and his state of progress, careful inquiry should be made concerning the rightness of his intention and the freedom of his choice,[16] his spiritual, moral, and intellectual fitness, the suitability of his bodily and mental health, and any tendencies he might have inherited from his family. His ability to bear priestly burdens and exercise pastoral duties must also be weighed.[17]

---

14. *Cf. Pius XI, encyclical letter "Ad Catholici Sacerdotii," Dec. 20, 1935: AAS 28 (1936), p. 37: "Be careful especially in the choice of moderators and teachers . . . and assign to sacred colleges of this type priests endowed with the greatest virtue; and do not hesitate to remove them from duties which, though in appearance of much greater import, can in no way be compared with this foremost duty, whose elements are supplied by nothing else." This principle of selecting the best men is reiterated by Pius XII in his apostolic letters sent to the Ordinaries of Brazil on Apr. 23, 1947: "Discorsi e Radiomessaggi," IX, pp. 579-580.*
15. *Concerning the common duty for seminaries to undertake supplementary work, see Paul VI, apostolic letter "Summi Dei Verbum," Nov. 4, 1963: AAS 55 (1963), p. 984.*
16. In the succeeding paragraphs, continuing the teaching of the recent Popes, great stress is laid on the freedom of choice, spiritual training, and insistence that the need for priests must not affect the necessary judgment on the quality of candidates for the priesthood. Importance is given to a family spirit and individual responsibilty.
17. *Cf. Pius XII, apostolic exhortation "Menti Nostrae," Sept. 23, 1950: AAS 42 (1950), p. 684; also see: The Sacred Congregation of Sacraments, the general letter to the Ordinaries of territories, "Magna Equidem," Dec.*

In all selection and testing of seminarians, necessary standards must always be firmly maintained, even when there exists a regrettable shortage of priests.[18] For God will not allow His Church to lack ministers if worthy candidates are admitted while unsuited ones are speedily and paternally directed towards the assuming of other tasks and are encouraged to take up the lay apostolate readily, in a consciousness of their Christian vocation.

7. Where individual dioceses are not equal to establishing an adequate seminary of their own, seminaries serving several dioceses, a whole national section, or a nation itself should be set up and fostered. In this way the solid formation of seminarians, which must be regarded as the supreme law in this matter, will be more successfully provided for. When such seminaries are regional or national, they should be governed according to the statutes which have been decreed by the bishops affected[19] and endorsed by the Apostolic See.

In seminaries where the student body is large, uniformity should be maintained in discipline and professional training, but students should be intelligently arranged into smaller groups so that their personal development can be given better attention.

CHAPTER IV

THE DEEPENING OF SPIRITUAL FORMATION

8. Spiritual formation should be closely linked with doctrinal

---

27, 1935, Art. 10. For religious see: "Statuta Generalia," added to the apostolic constitution "Sedes Sapientiae," May 31, 1956, Art. 33.

Paul VI, apostolic letter, "Summi Dei Verbum," November 4, 1963: AAS 55 (1963), pp. 987 ff.

18. Cf. Pius XI, encyclical letter "Ad Catholici Sacerdotii," Dec. 20, 1935: AAS 28 (1936), p. 41.

19. It is established that in the determining of the statutes of regional or national seminaries all bishops concerned should take part, and the prescript of canon 1357, par. 4 of the Code of Canon Law is repealed.

and pastoral training.[20] Especially with the help of the spiritual director,[21] such formation should help seminarians learn to live in familiar and constant companionship with the Father, through Jesus Christ His Son, in the Holy Spirit. By sacred ordination they will be molded in the likeness of Christ the Priest. As friends they should be used to loyal association with Him through a profound identification of their whole lives with His.[22] They should live His paschal mystery in such a way that they know how to initiate into it the people entrusted to them. They should be taught to look for Christ in many places: in faithful meditation on God's word, in active communion with the most holy mysteries of the Church, especially in the Eucharist and the divine Office,[23] in the bishop who sends them, and in the people to whom they are sent, especially the poor, the young, the sick, the sinful, and the unbelieving. With the trust of a son, they should love and honor the most Blessed Virgin Mary, who was given as a mother to His disciple by Christ Jesus as He hung dying on the cross.

Let them earnestly practice those exercises of piety recommended by the venerable usage of the Church, though care should be taken to keep spiritual formation from consisting solely in these things, and from producing unsubstantial religious feelings. Seminarians should learn rather to live according to the gospel and to grow strong in faith, hope, and char-

20. The influence of the Constitution on the Church and the Constitution on the Sacred Liturgy is very evident in the directives given for the spiritual training of seminarians. The Word of God and the paschal mystery are to be focal points of their meditation and spiritual life. Attention is drawn to the community aspect of union with their bishop and with the People of God, especially those in need. Notice how this spiritual training is expected to prepare them for a hard choice: a life of service and self-denial with no illusions about their calling. It is also destined to allow them to develop a true, dignified, and personal acceptance of loving obedience to the Holy Father and their bishop, and a spirit of open and loyal cooperation with their fellow priests.
21. Cf. Pius XII, apostolic exhortation "Menti Nostrae," Sept. 23, 1950: AAS 42 (1950), p. 674; Sacred Congregation of Seminaries and Universities, "La Formazione spirituale del candidato al sacerdozio," Vatican City, 1965.
22. Cf. St. Pius X, exhortation to the Catholic clergy "Haerent Animo," Aug. 4, 1908: S. Pii X Acta, IV, pp. 242-244; Pius XIII, apostolic exhortation "Menti Nostrae," Sept. 23, 1950: AAS 42 (1950), pp. 659-661; John XXIII, encyclical letter "Sacerdotii Nostri Primordia," Aug. 1, 1959; AAS 51 (1959), pp. 550 f.
23. Cf. Pius XII, encyclical letter "Mediator Dei," Nov. 20, 1947: AAS 39 (1947), pp. 547 ff. and 572 f.; John XXIII, apostolic exhortation "Sacrae Laudis," Jan. 6, 1962: AAS 54 (1962), p. 69; Second Vatican Council, Constitution on the Sacred Liturgy, Art. 16 and 17: AAS 56 (1964), pp. 104 f.; Sacred Congregation of Rites, "Instructio ad exsecutionem Constitutionis de Sacra Liturgia recte ordinandam," Sept. 26, 1964, Art. 14-17: AAS 56 (1964), pp. 880 f.

ity. By exercising these virtues they will develop the spirit of prayer,[24] secure strength and protection for their vocation, promote the vitality of the other virtues, and grow in the desire to win all men to Christ.

9. Seminarians should be thoroughly penetrated by the mystery of the Church, especially as it has been presented with new clarity by this holy Synod. Thus, bound even now to Christ's Vicar with humble and filial love, attached after ordination to their own bishop as loyal assistants, and working in concert with their brother priests, they will give witness to that unity by which men are attracted to Christ.[25] Let them learn to share largeheartedly in the whole life of the Church according to the spirit of St. Augustine's saying: "A man possesses the Holy Spirit to the measure of his love for Christ's Church."[26] Seminarians should understand very plainly that they are called not to domination or to honors, but to give themselves over entirely to God's service and the pastoral ministry. With special care they must be trained in priestly obedience, in a program of humble living, and in the spirit of self-denial.[27] As a result, even in matters which are lawful but not expedient, they will be accustomed to make prompt renunciation and to imitate Christ crucified.

Seminarians should be informed about the obligations they must undertake, and no hardship of the priestly life should go unmentioned—not that they should see practically nothing but the element of peril in the busy life which lies ahead, but rather that they may be confirmed in the spiritual life, which will be strengthened in the greatest measure by pastoral activity itself.

10. Students who, according to the holy and fixed laws of their own rite, follow the revered tradition of priestly celibacy should be very carefully trained for this state.[28] By it they re-

24. Cf. John XXIII, encyclical letter "Sacerdotii Nostri Primordia": AAS 51 (1959), pp. 559 f.
25. Cf. Second Vatican Council, Dogmatic Constitution on the Church, Art. 28: AAS 57 (1956), pp. 35 f.
26. St. Augustine, "In Ioannem Tract." 32, 8: PL 35, 1646.
27. Cf. Pius XII, apostolic exhortation "Menti Nostrae": AAS 42 (1950), pp. 662 f., 685, 690; John XXIII, encyclical letter "Sacerdotii Nostri Primordia": AAS 51 (1959), pp. 551-553 and 556 f.; Paul VI, encyclical letter "Ecclesiam Suam," Aug. 6, 1964: AAS 56 (1964), pp. 634 f.; Second Vatican Council, Dogmatic Constitution on the Church, esp. Art. 8: AAS 57 (1956), p. 12.
28. In a key passage, the Council treats the much discussed question of clerical celibacy. Note the motivation offered and the reasons restated. It is

nounce the companionship of marriage for the sake of the kingdom of heaven (cf. Mt. 19:12); they devote themselves to the Lord with an undivided love[29] which is profoundly proper to the new covenant; they bear witness to the state which the resurrection will bring about in the world to come (cf. Lk. 20:36); [30] and they gain extremely appropriate help for exercising that perfect and unremitting love by which they can become all things to all men through their priestly ministration.[31] May they deeply sense how gratefully this state deserves to be undertaken—not only as a requisite of Church law but as a precious gift which should be humbly sought of God and to which they should freely and generously hasten to respond through the energizing and fortifying grace of the Holy Spirit.

Seminarians should be duly aware of the duties and dignity of Christian marriage, which bodies forth the love between Christ and the Church (cf. Eph. 5:32 f.). Let them perceive as well the superiority of virginity consecrated to Christ,[32] so that by a choice which is maturely thought out and magnanimous they may attach themselves to God by a total gift of body and soul.

Let them be warned of the very severe dangers with which their chastity will be confronted in present-day society.[33] Aided by appropriate helps, both divine and human, may they learn so to integrate the renunciation of marriage into their life and activity that these will not suffer any detriment from celibacy; rather, that they themselves may achieve a greater mastery of soul and body, and added growth in maturity; and may comprehend more profoundly the blessedness promised by the gospel.

11. The norms of Christian education are to be religiously

not a hysterical refusal of sex as something basically repugnant or belittling. The beauty and dignity of Christian marriage are recognized, but consecrated virginity is chosen for its own even greater dignity and beauty. Priestly celibacy is referred to the renunciation for the kingdom of heaven of which Matthew speaks—to an undivided love of the Savior—and it is given its eschatological meaning. Finally, this gift of God is shown as a kind of freedom at the service of charity.

29. Cf. Pius XII, encyclical letter "Sacra Virginitas," Mar. 25, 1954: AAS 46 (1954), pp. 165 ff.
30. Cf. St. Cyprian, "De habitu virginum," 22: PL 4, 475; St. Ambrose, "De Virginibus" I, 8, 52: PL 16, 202 f.
31. Cf. Pius XII, apostolic exhortation "Menti Nostrae": AAS 42 (1950), p. 663.
32. Cf. Pius XII, encyclical letter "Sacra Virginitas," loc. cit., pp. 170-174.
33. Cf. Pius XII, apostolic exhortation "Menti Nostrae," loc. cit., pp. 664 and 690 f.

maintained, and should be properly complemented by the latest findings in sound psychology and pedagogy.[34] By wisely planned training there should also be developed in seminarians a due degree of human maturity, attested to chiefly by a certain emotional stability, by an ability to make considered decisions, and by a right manner of passing judgment on events and people. They should be practiced in an intelligent organization of their proper talents; they should be trained in what strengthens character; and, in general, they should learn to prize those qualities which are highly regarded among men and speak well of a minister of Christ.[35] Such are sincerity of heart, a constant concern for justice, fidelity to one's word, courtesy of manner, restraint, and kindliness in speech.

The discipline required by seminary life should not be regarded merely as a strong support of community life and of charity. For it is a necessary part of the whole training program designed to provide self-mastery, to foster solid maturity of personality, and to develop other traits of character which are extremely serviceable for the ordered and productive activity of the Church.[36]

Let discipline be exercised, then, in a way which will develop in the students an internal attitude by which the authority of superiors will be accepted through an act of personal conviction, that is, conscientiously (cf. Rom. 13:5) and for supernatural reasons. The rules of discipline should be applied in accord with the age of the students so that they can gradually learn to govern themselves, to make wise use of their freedom, to act on their own initiative and energetically,[37] and can know how to work along with their confreres and lay people as well.

The whole seminary program, permeated with a cultivation of reverence and silence and with a concern for mutual help, should be structured as a kind of introduction into the life which the seminarian will lead as a priest.

12. It belongs to bishops to establish an appropriate period of time for more intense spiritual apprenticeship, so that spiritual training can rest upon a firmer basis and students can embrace

---

34. The positive and pastoral tone of the Council recurs in these directives on education. The priest must be a man—mature, with human and social virtues—not a clerical caricature.
35. *Cf. Paul VI, apostolic letter "Summi Dei Verbum," Nov. 4, 1963: AAS 55 (1963), p. 991.*
36. The accent on discipline is constructive, suggesting an adult and responsible approach to the whole question.
37. *Cf. Pius XII, apostolic exhortation "Menti Nostrae," loc. cit., p. 686.*

their vocation with a decision maturely weighed. It is also for them to consider the opportuneness of deciding on a certain interruption of studies or arranging for a suitable pastoral apprenticeship so that a more rounded test can be made of priestly candidates.[38] It is likewise the concern of bishops to decide, in view of the circumstances of individual regions, that the age currently required by general law for holy orders be raised and to weigh the suitability of legislating that after seminarians complete their theological course they exercise the diaconate for an appropriate length of time before being advanced to the priesthood.

CHAPTER V

THE REVISION OF ECCLESIASTICAL STUDIES[39]

13. Before seminarians take up those sacred studies which are properly ecclesiastical, they should be equipped with the humanistic and scientific training which in their own countries enables young people to undertake higher studies. In addition, they should acquire a command of Latin which will enable them to understand and use the source material of so many sciences, and the documents of the Church as well.[40] The study of the liturgical language proper to each rite is to be regarded as necessary, while a suitable knowledge of the languages of sacred Scripture and of the sources of tradition should be strongly encouraged.

14. In the revision of ecclesiastical studies, the first object in

---

38. A new element appears here. Some bishops had already experimented with the ordination of third-year theologians as deacons, enabling them to gain experience during vacations. Now the bishop may, if he chooses, interrupt theological studies to test the candidates, or have them serve as deacons for a period after their studies. Presumably the bishop may do this in all or only in some specific cases.

39. Chap. V is one of the key chapters of the whole Decree. The theme of the Council recurs, as we shall see in the development.

40. Cf. Paul VI, apostolic letter "Summi Dei Verbum," loc. cit., p. 993.

view must be a better integration of philosophy and theology. These subjects should work together harmoniously to unfold ever increasingly to the minds of the seminarians the mystery of Christ, that mystery which affects the whole history of the human race,[41] influences the Church continuously, and is mainly exercised by the priestly ministry.[42]

That this understanding may be communicated to students from the very start of their training, ecclesiastical studies should begin with an introductory course of suitable duration. In this initiation, the mystery of salvation should be presented in such a way that the students will see the meaning of ecclesiastical studies, their interrelationship, and their pastoral intent. They will be helped thereby to root their whole personal lives in faith and to permeate them with it. They will be strengthened to embrace their vocation with personal commitment and a joyful heart.

15. Philosophy should be taught in such a way that students will be led to acquire a solid and coherent understanding of man, of the world, and of God. Basing themselves on a philosophic heritage which is perennially valid,[43] students should also be conversant with contemporary philosophical investigations, especially those exercising special influence in their own country, and with recent scientific progress.[44] In this way, thanks to a correct understanding of the character of modern times, students will be properly prepared for dialogue with the men of their own day.[45]

The history of philosophy should be so taught that by coming to grasp the basic principles of the various systems, students will hold what is shown to be true among them, and be able to detect the roots of errors and disprove them.

The very manner of teaching should inspire in students a love for seeking, honoring, and defending the truth vigorously,

---

41. Not only is greater cohesion called for in the teaching of philosophy and theology but the mystery of salvation becomes the unifying element in the spiritual life of the seminarian as well as in his studies.
42. Cf. Second Vatican Council, Dogmatic Constitution on the Church, Art. 7 and 28: AAS 57 (1965), pp. 9-11 and 33 f.
43. Cf. Pius XII, encyclical letter "Humani Generis," Aug. 12, 1950: AAS 42 (1950), pp. 571-575.
44. Without detracting from the value of the perennial philosophy, the document provides here a needed assertion of the true nature of philosophical studies and stresses the need to be conversant with contemporary writings. This will undoubtedly be a liberalizing influence in most seminaries.
45. Cf. Paul VI, encyclical letter "Ecclesiam Suam," Aug. 6, 1964: AAS 56 (1964), pp. 637 ff.

along with an honest recognition of the limitations of human understanding. The link between philosophy and the true problems of life should be carefully pointed out, as well as the relationship of philosophy to the questions which stir the students' minds. Students should also be helped to see the connections between philosophical argument and the mysteries of salvation, matters which are treated in theology under the superior light of faith.

16. Under the light of faith and with the guidance of the Church's teaching authority,[46] theology should be taught in such a way that students will accurately draw Catholic doctrine from divine revelation, understand that doctrine profoundly, nourish their own spiritual lives with it,[47] and be able to proclaim it, unfold it, and defend it in their priestly ministry.[48]

In the study of sacred Scripture, which ought to be the soul of all theology,[49] students should be trained with special diligence. After a suitable introduction to it, they should be accurately initiated into exegetical method, grasp the pre-eminent themes of divine revelation, and take inspiration and nourishment from reading and meditating on the sacred books day by day.[50]

Dogmatic theology should be so arranged that the biblical

---

46. *Cf. Pius XII, encyclical letter "Humani Generis," Aug. 12, 1950: AAS 42 (1950), pp. 567-569; allocution "Si diligis," May 31, 1954: AAS 46 (1954), pp. 314 f.; Paul VI, allocution delivered in the Pontifical Gregorian University of Studies, Mar. 12, 1964: AAS 56 (1964), pp. 364 f.; Second Vatican Council, Dogmatic Constitution on the Church, Art. 25: AAS 57 (1965), pp. 29-31.*

47. *Cf. St. Bonaventure, "Itinerarium mentis in Deum," Prologue, Art 4: "Let no one believe that it is enough to read without unction, to speculate without devotion, to investigate without wonder, to observe without joy, to act without godly zeal, to know without love, to understand without humility, to study without divine grace, or to reflect as a mirror without divinely inspired wisdom" (St. Bonaventure, "Opera Omnia," V, Quaracchi, 1891, p. 296.*

48. If intelligently interpreted and applied, the directives on theological studies will completely renew the theology course. The theology of renewal is recognized and acclaimed. Recent developments in the study of Scripture and in the whole catechetical and liturgical movement find their place here. The mystery of Christ, the history of salvation, is made the center of all theological studies. Moral theology must be restated, and canon law and Church history must be taught in that context. A double note of ecumenism is sounded: the contribution of the Greek Fathers and the Eastern Church is recognized, and the students are to acquire a real knowledge of other religions.

49. *Cf. Leo XIII, encyclical "Providentissimus Deus," Nov. 18, 1893: AAS 26 (1893-94), p. 283.*

50. *Cf. Pontifical Biblical Commission, "Instructio de Sacra Scriptura recte docenda," May 13, 1950: AAS 42 (1950), p. 502*

themes are presented first. Students should be shown what the Fathers of the Eastern and Western Church contributed to the fruitful transmission and illumination of the individual truths of revelation, and also the later history of dogma and its relationship to the general history of the Church.[51] Then, by way of making the mysteries of salvation known as thoroughly as they can be, students should learn to penetrate them more deeply with the help of speculative reason exercised under the tutelage of St. Thomas.[52] Students should learn too how these mysteries are interconnected, and be taught to recognize their presence and activity in liturgical actions[53] and in the whole life of the Church. Let them learn to search for solutions to human problems with the light of revelation, to apply eternal truths to the changing conditions of human affairs, and to communicate such truths in a manner suited to contemporary man.[54]

Other theological disciplines should also be renewed by livelier contact with the mystery of Christ and the history of salvation. Special attention needs to be given to the development of moral theology. Its scientific exposition should be more thoroughly nourished by scriptural teaching. It should show the nobility of the Christian vocation of the faithful, and their obligation to bring forth fruit in charity for the life of the world. Again, in the explanation of canon law and Church history, the mystery of the Church should be kept in mind, as it was set forth in the Dogmatic Constitution on the Church, promulgated by this holy Synod. Sacred liturgy, which must

51. *Cf. Pius XII, encyclical letter "Humani Generis," Aug. 12, 1950: AAS 42 (1950), pp. 568 f.: ". . . the sacred disciplines are always rejuvenated by the study of the sacred fonts; while on the contrary, speculation that neglects a further examination of the sacred deposit (of faith) becomes sterile, as we know from experience."*

52. *Cf. Pius XII, discourse to seminarians, June 24, 1939; AAS 31 (1939), p. 247: "By recommending the teaching of St. Thomas, eagerness for the discovery of truth and the diffusion of it is not suppressed, but rather is stimulated and provided with a safe guide." Paul VI, allocution delivered in the Pontifical Gregorian University of Studies, Mar. 12, 1964: AAS 56 (1964), p. 365: "Let teachers reverently pay heed to the voice of the Doctors of the Church, among whom St. Thomas holds the principal place; for the Angelic Doctor's force of genius is so great, his love of truth so sincere, and his wisdom in investigating, illustrating, and collecting the highest truths in a most apt bond of unity so great, that his teaching is a most efficacious instrument not only in safeguarding the foundations of the faith, but also in profitably and surely reaping the fruits of its sane progress." Cf. also his allocution before the 6th International Thomistic Congress, Sept. 10, 1965.*

53. *Cf. Second Vatican Council, Constitution on the Sacred Liturgy, Art. 7 and 16: AAS 56 (1964), pp. 100 f. and 104 f.*

54. *Cf. Paul VI, encyclical letter "Ecclesiam Suam," Aug. 6, 1964: AAS 56 (1964), pp. 640 f.; Second Vatican Council, schema of the Pastoral Constitution on the Church in the Modern World (1965).*

be regarded as the primary and indispensable source of a truly Christian spirit, should be taught according to the prescriptions of Articles 15 and 16 of the Constitution on the Sacred Liturgy.[55]

According to an opportune evaluation of the conditions of various regions, students should be led to a more adequate understanding of the Churches and ecclesial Communities separated from the Roman, Apostolic See. Thus the students can contribute to the restoration of unity among all Christians according to the directives of this sacred Synod.[56]

They should also be introduced to a knowledge of the other religions which are more widely spread through individual areas. In this way, they can better understand the elements of goodness and truth which such religions possess by God's Providence, and will learn how to disprove the errors in them, and to share the full light of truth with those who lack it.

17. Since doctrinal training ought not to aim at a mere communication of ideas, but at a genuine and deep formation of students, teaching methods should be revised as they apply to lectures, discussions, and seminars and with respect to the promotion of study among students, whether individually or in small groups.

The unified and substantial quality of all this training should be carefully provided for; hence excessive multiplying of subjects and classes is to be avoided. Those questions should be omitted which retain scarcely any significance, or which should be left for higher academic studies.

18. Bishops should see that young men suitably fitted by temperament, virtue, and talent are sent to special schools, faculties, colleges, or universities, so that there will be a supply of priests versed in the higher scientific method of sacred sciences and other sciences which may appear serviceable. Such priests will be able to meet the various needs of the apostolate. The spiritual and pastoral training of these students must by no means be neglected, especially if they have not yet been ordained.

55. *Second Vatican Council, Constitution on the Sacred Liturgy, Art. 10, 14, 15, 16; Sacred Congregation of Rites, "Instructio ad exsecutionem Constitutionis de Sacra Liturgia recte ordinandam," Sept. 26, 1964, Art. 11 and 12: AAS 56 (1964), pp. 879 f.*
56. *Cf. Second Vatican Council, Decree on Ecumenism, Art. 1, 9, 10: AAS 57 (1965), pp. 90 and 98 f.*

CHAPTER VI

THE PROMOTION OF STRICTLY PASTORAL TRAINING

19. That pastoral concern which should thoroughly penetrate the entire training of seminarians[57] also requires that they be carefully instructed in those matters which have a special bearing on the sacred ministry, especially catechetics, preaching, liturgical worship, the conferral of the sacraments, works of charity, the duty of seeking out the straying sheep and unbelievers, and other pastoral obligations.[58] Let them receive careful instruction in the art of guiding souls, so that they can lead all sons of the Church, before everything else, to a Christian life which is fully conscious and apostolic, and to a fulfillment of the duties of their state. With equal thoroughness they should learn to assist men and women religious to persevere in the grace of their vocation and to make progress according to the spirit of their various communities.[59]

57. *The perfect ideal of a pastor can be deduced from the documents of recent Popes which distinctly treat of the life, the qualities, and the institution of the priesthood, especially:*

> *St. Pius X, exhortation to the clergy "Haerent Animo," S. Pii X Acta, IV, pp. 237 ff.*
>
> *Pius XI, encyclical letter "Ad Catholici Sacerdotii": AAS 28 (1936), pp. 5 ff.*
>
> *Pius XII, apostolic exhortation "Menti Nostrae": AAS 52 (1950), pp. 657 ff.*
>
> *John XXIII, encyclical letter "Sacerdotii Nostri Primordia": AAS 51 (1959), pp. 545 ff.*
>
> *Paul VI, apostolic letter "Summi Dei Verbum": AAS 55 (1963), pp. 979 ff.*
>
> *Much pastoral formation is found also in the encyclical letters "Mystici Corporis" (1943), "Mediator Dei" (1947), "Evangelii Praecones" (1951), "Sacra Virginitas" (1954), "Musicae Sacrae Disciplina" (1955), "Princeps Pastorum" (1959), and also in the apostolic constitution "Sedes Sapientiae" (1956) for religious.*
>
> *Pius XII, John XXIII, and Paul VI also very often illustrate the ideal of a good pastor in their allocutions to seminarians and priests.*

58. The decree ends, as might be expected, with a return to the pastoral note which has dominated its thinking. Students are to be initiated into pastoral duties even during the course of their studies. They are to be taught the need for and value of dialogue to prepare them for their ministry.

59. *Concerning the importance of the state of life that is constituted by the profession of the evangelical counsels, cf. Second Vatican Council, Dogmatic*

In general, there should be developed in seminarians the abilities most appropriate for the promotion of dialogue with men, such as a capacity to listen to other people and to open their hearts in a spirit of charity to the various circumstances of human need.[60]

20. Let them be taught to use, in a proper manner and according to the norms of Church authority, the helps which pedagogy, psychology, and sociology can offer.[61] Again, they should be trained with exactness to ignite and fan the apostolic activity of laymen,[62] and to promote the various and more successful forms of the apostolate. They need to be penetrated with that truly Catholic spirit by which they can transcend the borders of their own diocese, nation, or rite, be accustomed to consulting the needs of the whole Church, and be ready in spirit to preach the gospel everywhere.[63]

21. Seminarians need to learn the art of exercising the apostolate not only in theory but also in practice. They have to be able to pursue their assignments both on their own initiative and in concert with others. Hence, even during their course of studies, and also during holidays, they should be introduced into pastoral practice by appropriate undertakings. Depending on the age of the seminarians and the local conditions, and given the prudent approval of their bishops, such programs should be pursued in a methodical way and under the guidance of men experienced in pastoral matters. The surpassing value of supernatural helps should, however, always be kept in mind.[64]

Constitution on the Church, Chap. VI: AAS 57 (1965), pp. 49-53; Decree on the Appropriate Renewal of the Religious Life.
60. Cf. Paul VI, encyclical letter "Ecclesiam Suam," Aug. 6, 1964: AAS 56 (1964) passim, esp. pp. 635 f. and 640 ff.; Second Vatican Council, schema of the Pastoral Constitution on the Church in the Modern World (1965).
61. Cf. esp. John XXIII, encyclical letter "Mater et Magistra," May 15, 1961: AAS 53 (1961), pp. 401 ff.
62. Cf. principally Second Vatican Council, schema of the Decree on the Apostolate of the Laity (1965), Art. 25 and 30, pp. 54 and 62.
63. Cf. Second Vatican Council, Dogmatic Constitution on the Church, Art. 17: AAS 57 (1965), pp. 20 f.; schema of the Decree on the Church's Missionary Activity (1965), esp. Art. 36 and 37, pp. 25 f.
64. Many papal documents warn against the danger of neglecting the supernatural end in pastoral action and the danger of making little of supernatural helps, at least in practice; cf. esp. the documents cited in note 41.

CHAPTER VII

THE REFINEMENT OF TRAINING AFTER THE COURSE OF STUDIES

22. Especially because of the circumstances of modern society, priestly training should be pursued and perfected even after the seminary course of studies has been completed.[65] Hence, Episcopal Conferences ought to make use in their individual countries of the more effective means to this end,[66] such as pastoral institutes involving aptly chosen parishes, conferences held at set times, and fitting projects designed to afford the younger clergy a gradual introduction into the priestly life and apostolic activity under their spiritual, intellectual, and pastoral aspect, and calculated to help young priests renew and develop this life and activity more intensely every day.

CONCLUSION

The Fathers of this sacred Synod, furthering the work begun by the Council of Trent, trustingly confide to seminary direc-

---

65. *More recent documents of the Holy See urge that particular care be taken for newly ordained priests. These especially should be noted:*
   Pius XII, motu proprio "Quandoquidem," Apr. 2, 1949: AAS 41 (1949), pp. 165-167; the apostolic exhortation "Menti Nostrae," Sept. 23, 1950: AAS 42 (1950); the apostolic constitution (for religious) "Sedes Sapientiae," May 31, 1956, and the general statutes attached to it; the allocution to priests "Convictus Barcinonensis," June 14, 1957, "Discorsi e Radiomessaggi," XIX, pp. 271-273.
   Paul VI, allocution before the priests of the Gian Matteo Giberti Institute of the diocese of Verona, Mar. 11, 1964.
66. On the Episcopal Conferences devolves the responsibility for setting up ways and means of continuing clerical training and formation after ordination. This is to be done by means of institutes, conferences, meetings, and other initiatives which can be and must be adapted to the particular environment in which the priest is called to serve.

tors and teachers the duty of forming Christ's future priests in the spirit of that renewal which this most sacred Synod has fostered. At the same time, it urgently entreats those who are readying themselves for the priestly ministry to realize clearly that the hope of the Church and the salvation of souls are being entrusted to them. Embracing the directives of this Decree with a willing heart, let them bear most abundantly that fruit which remains forever.

Each and every one of the things set forth in this Decree has won the consent of the Fathers of this most sacred Council. We, too, by the apostolic authority conferred on us by Christ, join with the Venerable Fathers in approving, decreeing, and establishing these things in the Holy Spirit, and we direct that what has thus been enacted in synod be published to God's glory.

Rome, at St. Peter's, October 28, 1965[67]

I, Paul, Bishop of the Catholic Church

There follow the signatures of the Fathers.

---

67. After the document there is printed an announcement entitled "A Suspension of Law" (*Vacatio legis*): "With respect to the new laws contained in this promulgated decree, the Most Holy Father grants a suspension until June 29, 1966, the feast of Sts. Peter and Paul. In the meantime, the Supreme Pontiff will issue norms for the implementation of the aforementioned laws. Rome, October 28, 1965. ✠ Pericle Felici, Titular Archbishop of Samosata, Secretary General of the Most Holy Council."—Ed.

A RESPONSE

All who have followed the proceedings of the Second Vatican Council have been impressed by the freshness and vitality of its work. The Constitutions on the Liturgy, the Church, and the Church in the Modern World, the Decree on Ecumenism, and the Declarations on Religious Freedom and on Non-Christian Religions open the possibility of a new situation within the Roman Catholic Church, in its relations to other Churches, and in its relation to the world. Not least in importance in channeling the contribution of these documents into the life of the church is the Decree on Priestly Formation. Whether the vision of Vatican II becomes a reality or a lost opportunity depends to a large extent on the way it is realized in the seminaries and among the leaders of the Church.

The reader who shares the theological perspective of the Reformation finds many impressive features in this document. He notes first the emphasis upon the Word of God as the foundation and center of the theological curriculum. The study of the Scriptures thus becomes the formative factor in the life of the student, and everything else is to find its proper place in relation to the mystery of Christ, the history of salvation. With biblical themes at the center, the other disciplines must be rethought in this light. This calls for a restatement of moral theology, the teaching of Church history and canon law in the light of the mystery of the Church, and a continuing examination of the relationship between biblical theology, liturgy, and life. This program alone, if intelligently carried out, can bring about a renewal of seminary education.

A second notable feature is the stress upon adaptation to local conditions. This recognizes the fact of social change in the contemporary world and the necessity for the Church to relate herself to it intelligently in order to proclaim the gospel effectively. The repeated instruction that seminaries are to learn from modern sociology, psychology, and pedagogy prods theologians to grapple with the problem of communication and forbids them contentment with repetition of theological formulas. The directive to adapt seminary education to local situations holds great promise for enrichment of the Church through diversification and through development of the distinctive emphases and charisms of national or regional groups. The unity of the Church does not demand uniformity, but rather the growth and sharing of the great variety of God's gifts to his Church. Vesting of Episcopal Conferences with authority should encourage more effective encounter with local problems. The program for revision at definite intervals, if followed up, should help prevent ossification in any one set of educational formulas.

The new ecumenical climate brought about by the Council is not only acknowledged but brought into the educational process. Students "should be led to a more adequate understanding of the Churches and Ecclesial Communities separated from the Roman Apostolic See," so that they "can contribute to the restoration of unity among all Christians." The study of non-Christian religions is also prescribed, in keeping with the declaration on non-Christian religions. Here, however, one questions whether the happiest formulation has been achieved. As it stands, it suggests a somewhat mechanical and argumentative approach, understanding "elements of truth and goodness" and disproving errors. Even the generous disposition to share the "full light of truth" with those who lack it sounds somewhat patronizing in this context. On the other hand, one may wonder whether either the declaration on non-Christian religions or the paragraph relating to it in this Decree faces up adequately to the dangers of syncretism.

The stress upon a "genuine and deep formation of students" is a welcome contribution to the discussion of seminary education. While the language is unfamiliar to American Protestants, its concern is one they can share. Recent attempts to reassess theological education in America have called attention to the dangers of treating theology as though it were only a body of knowledge or a collection of techniques. The integration of theological education into the total life and mission of the Church is both highly desirable and especially difficult, as is also the reorganization of the theological curriculum to avoid multiplication of subjects and classes and to provide the proper perspective for the whole enterprise. It is altogether praiseworthy that a student be helped to understand that he is not called to dominion or honors, and that he be trained in priestly obedience, humility, and self-denial, as other religious communities can also appreciate. But should not the document have spoken somewhere of the freedom and dignity of the individual and of the desirability of developing the diversity of the Spirit's gifts even among members of the sacramental priesthood? At this point the Decree reads too much like a composition of bishops for bishops, absent-mindedly withholding from their brother priests what they generously allow to laymen and even to those outside the Church.

The prescription of a historical approach to dogmatic theology is an especially important point. The Council's will to relate to the contemporary world will be set forward more by taking this seriously than by anything else which could be mentioned. Theologians willing to learn from scientists, historians, and philosophers have discovered the high cost of taking the world with full seriousness. It is nothing less than the recognition that God Himself has in the Incarnation accepted the hazards of historical existence, a full involvement in the relativities of human life and history. This means that the events of salvation history, including Jesus Christ Himself, are bound up with the historical relativities of their time and that all of Scripture and all of theology are similarly involved.

If the impressive theological resources of the Roman Catholic Church can be mobilized for this program, it will mean great stress but also a great contribution to the missionary task of the Church in the world. But the repeated assertion of the perennial character of the thought of St. Thomas makes one wonder whether those who framed the Decree understand what a radical and strenuous task they have assigned to their theological faculties. If the historical approach is taken seriously, there will be no shelter behind the walls of a perennial philosophy or theology. The task should be undertaken, for its benefits will be greater than its cost, and even the actual achievement of St. Thomas will in no way be diminished though quite radically reinterpreted.

There are two points where one wishes that the Decree spoke more fully. Virtually nothing is said about a most important tool of theological education, the library. If the Council's impulse for the renewal of the Church is to be realized, students must certainly have access not only to their own heritage but also to the theological interpretations of other traditions and even to the questions raised by earnest men who belong to no Church. It is rumored that not all bishops are poignantly aware of the importance of libraries, so some specifics on this topic could be helpful.

A second topic calling for fuller treatment is the faculty.

It is good that the seminary is characterized as the heart of the diocese, and that bishops are urged to choose their ablest and best-prepared men for the task of priestly formation. It is good that faculties are encouraged to become the kind of family which answers the Lord's prayer that "they may be one." But in view of the regrettable tendency of theological faculties to be cautious rather than adventurous, to be Thomists rather than Thomases, there could well have been some encouragement of experiment in education and communication. It is the function of the bishop to preserve the heritage of the Church. He may be most ably assisted in this work by theologians who remember that the new wine requires new wine skins.

WARREN A. QUANBECK

RELIGIOUS LIFE

INTRODUCTION

THE AIM OF Vatican Council II is stated in the words of Pope John XXIII: to invoke a new Pentecost, calling for renewal of the Church in her head and in all her members, for her reformation in the reflection of Christ in the Gospels. This ardent desire of enabling the Church in an ever more perfect manner to live as the Bride of Christ was, of course, felt in a special manner by those who, in accordance with their very vocation, dedicate themselves entirely to the loving service of Christ in the Church. Owing particularly to their active and fruitful collaboration, Pope Paul VI could, during the fourth Council session, promulgate in his own name and in that of the Council Fathers, the decree concerning the adaptation and renovation of religious institutes, not excluding cloistered and contemplative orders.

REASONS FOR RENEWAL

To anyone who knows the history of the Church it is obvious that the Holy Spirit has at all times raised in the Church men and women who, under His guidance and in correspondence to the needs of the Church, have initiated spiritual movements which were then continued and expanded by the religious families they founded. But it is not less clear that the same Spirit who continues to evoke new spiritual movements in the People of God is also constantly urging those religious who already have dedicated their lives to a certain type of service in the Church, to reflect seriously and actively so as to discover how their institute could and should be adapted ever more perfectly to the continuously changing circumstances of their own times.

WHAT RENEWAL INVOLVES: FUNDAMENTAL CRITERIA

The answer to renewal is not just change of religious dress. Nor is it sweeping adaptation to the spirit of our times. Therefore the decree on religious very wisely puts forward two fundamental norms which, like beacon-lights, signal to all religious bodies the direction which change and reformation should take. The first norm, the ultimate norm of every institute, must be the following of Christ as set down in the luminous pages of the Gospel. The second norm, particular to each individual institute, reflects the spirit of the founder as revealed in the rules and apostolate peculiar to the respective order or congregation.

CHRIST AND HIS DISCIPLES

In the incandescent light of the New Testament we clearly observe the first Christian community, its life, its light, and its charity—Christ and His disciples. Under that light, rules can be studied to determine whether any should be changed or dropped. More often perhaps, under the inspiration of the Gospels, it is not the multiplication of rules that will be seen as necessary, but rather the living evangelical spirit of the rules made operative today. Only by the closest study of the life of Christ with His apostles and disciples will renovation of rule, customs and good works be conceived and perfected. The Gospels remain the fountainhead of all renewal.

For this reason the Decree states right from the beginning that "all those who are called by God to practice the evangelical counsels, and who do so faithfully, devote themselves in a special way to the Lord. They imitate Christ the virgin and the poor man, who, by an obedience which carried Him even to death on the cross, redeemed men and made them holy. As a consequence, impelled by a love which the Holy Spirit has poured into their hearts, these Christians spend themselves ever increasingly for Christ, and for His body the Church (cf. Col. 1:24)" (Article 1). Bearing this in mind, it is easy to understand why the heart of the Decree is to be found in the Articles dealing with the religious vows (Articles 12-14) and with life in community (Article 15). These Articles contain an inspiring description of the manner in which this life of union with Christ should be brought about in practice through the vows and the holocaust made by them of what constitutes some precious and profound natural aspirations of man.

THE SPIRIT OF THE FOUNDER

The amazing variety of religious communities enables the Church to engage in every good work. This variety is due to founders of religious institutes who wrote different rules, composed constitutions, and pinpointed exact areas of apostolate. Into their spiritual families, by the sanctification of the Holy Spirit, they infused some aspect or feature of Christ's own zeal, love, and spirit. This inspiration of the founder was then sealed by papal brief and chartered for the ministry of the Church. So when the question arises of adapting religious life and customs to the needs of Holy Mother the Church today, we have first to assess the astonishing revolutions and discoveries of science and the social and cultural pattern of our astonishing times, and then to examine how the religious institutes can meet contemporary demands in the light of the Gospels and the peculiar spirit and mission of each individual institute. Unless these unfailing guideposts mark the road of renovation and adaptation, our efforts will result in unwanted consequences or fruitless novelties.

A NECESSARY DISTINCTION: RENEWAL—ADAPTATION

It would not be right to focus our attention primarily or even solely on external changes of religious life in the Church. One of the basic points for a proper assessment of this conciliar Decree consists precisely in the clear distinction between *adaptation* and *renewal:* the former term is concerned with changes that are necessary on behalf of external contemporary needs and the outward circumstances of our times, whereas the term *renewal* refers to interior renovation of the spirit by which the very essence of religious life, that is, the deeper association with and consecration of man to our suffering Redeemer, should be lived ever more profoundly. "Since the religious life is intended above all else to lead those who embrace it to an imitation of Christ and to union with God through the profession of the evangelical counsels, the fact must be honestly faced that even the most desirable changes made on behalf of contemporary needs will fail of their purpose unless a renewal of spirit gives life to them. Indeed such an interior renewal must always be accorded the leading role even in the promotion of exterior works" (Article 2e).

Only from this deepened spiritual insight and life of the religious calling may we expect authentic renewal and adaptation of religious institutes to the peculiar necessities of the Church in our modern world. If the religious life is understood and lived in the spirit of the gospel and in accordance with the intention of those whom the Spirit of God moved to found a religious family, the legitimate need of renewal and adaptation will be felt spontaneously and carried out in a responsible and efficacious manner. Doubtlessly some daring experiments and perhaps even some drastic changes will have to be made by competent authorities, and we should not be afraid of engaging in them, even though some initial difficulties and failings may have to be overcome. The conciliar document indicates the general lines of this adaptation without, naturally, entering into such details as can—in view of the great variety in religious life—only be worked out by the general chapter of each particular institute.

The concrete application of this Decree will therefore demand some time, most careful study, arduous labor and, particularly, prayer and generous sacrifice. But the Council, which on various occasions has publicly and in a solemn manner stated its highest esteem for the religious life and recognized its urgent need for our present times, is fully confident that the spirit of renewal and adaptation that already so clearly manifests itself in countless ways will continue to make of the religious institutes a most fertile and indispensable element not only in the spiritual life of the Church but also in its manifold apostolic activities in the dioceses and missions all over the world, and indeed in all the inward and outward manifestations of her vitality.

✠ JOHN J. McELENEY, S.J.

Decree on the Appropriate Renewal¹ of the Religious Life

PAUL, BISHOP

SERVANT OF THE SERVANTS OF GOD

TOGETHER WITH THE FATHERS OF THE SACRED COUNCIL

FOR EVERLASTING MEMORY

1. In its Constitution which begins, "The Light of the World,"² this most sacred Synod has already pointed out how the teaching and example of the Divine Master laid the foundation for a pursuit of perfect charity³ through the exercise of the evangelical counsels,⁴ and how such a pursuit serves as a blazing emblem of the heavenly kingdom. In this present document, the Synod intends to deal with the life and rules of those institutes whose members profess chastity, poverty, and obedience, and to make provisions for their needs as the tenor of the times indicates.⁵

From the very infancy of the Church, there have existed men and women who strove to follow Christ more freely and imitate Him more nearly by the practice of the evangelical

---

1. *De accommodata renovatione*, often translated "on the adaptation and renewal." The Decree will clarify the two points involved. See, for example, Art. 2.
2. The Dogmatic Constitution on the Church, promulgated Nov. 21, 1964. Ch. 6 of that Constitution should be read first by anyone studying this Decree.
3. In the official Latin, the Decree begins with this phrase: *Perfectae caritatis* ("perfect charity," "complete love"), a very appropriate opening. See Art. 15 for extended treatment of the topic.
4. Evangelical counsels: these have been traditionally associated with poverty, chastity, and obedience, as the concrete realization of our Lord's invitation found in the Gospel according to St. Matthew (19:21; 19:10-12). Cf. Constitution on the Church, Art. 43.
5. *Prout tempora nostra suadent*. The Decree here touches on the theme of updating or modernization, which will recur throughout the document. See especially the beginning of Art. 2 and its section d.

counsels. Each in his own way, these souls have led a life dedicated to God. Under the influence of the Holy Spirit, many of them pursued a solitary life,[6] or founded religious families to which the Church willingly gave the welcome and approval of her authority.

And so it happened by divine plan that a wonderful variety of religious communities grew up. This variety contributed mightily toward making the Church experienced in every good deed (cf. 2 Tim. 3:17) and ready for a ministry of service[7] in building up Christ's body (cf. Eph. 4:12). Not only this, but adorned by the various gifts of her children, the Church became radiant like a bride made beautiful for her spouse (cf. Apoc. 21:2); and through her God's manifold wisdom could reveal itself (cf. Eph. 3:10).

But whatever the diversity of their spiritual endowments, all who are called by God to practice the evangelical counsels, and who do so faithfully, devote themselves in a special way to the Lord. They imitate Christ the virgin and the poor man (cf. Mt. 8:20; Lk. 9:58), who, by an obedience which carried Him even to death on the cross (cf. Phil. 2:8), redeemed men and made them holy. As a consequence, impelled by a love which the Holy Spirit has poured into their hearts (cf. Rom. 5:5), these Christians spend themselves ever increasingly for Christ, and for His body the Church (cf. Col. 1:24).

Hence the more ardently they unite themselves to Christ through a self-surrender involving their entire lives, the more vigorous becomes the life of the Church and the more abundantly her apostolate bears fruit.

A life consecrated by a profession of the counsels is of surpassing value. Such a life has a necessary role to play in the circumstances of the present age. That this kind of life and its contemporary role may achieve greater good for the Church, this sacred Synod issues the following decrees. They concern only the general principles which must underlie an appropriate renewal of the life and rules of religious communities. These principles apply also to societies living a community life without the exercise of vows,[8] and to secular

6. The reference is to those who lived as hermits.
7. A constant theme of the Second Vatican Council, and a basic theme of Christianity.
8. These organizations (e.g., Sulpicians, Maryknollers) are often called "societies of common life."

institutes,[9] though the special character of both groups is to be maintained. After the Council, the competent authority will be obliged to enact particular laws opportunely spelling out and applying what is legislated here.

2. The appropriate renewal[10] of religious life involves two simultaneous processes: (1) a continuous return to the sources of all Christian life and to the original inspiration behind a given community[11] and (2) an adjustment of the community to the changed conditions of the times. It is according to the following principles that such renewal should go forward under the influence of the Holy Spirit and the guidance of the Church.

a) Since the fundamental norm of the religious life is a following of Christ as proposed by the gospel, such is to be regarded by all communities as their supreme law.

b) It serves the best interests of the Church for communities to have their own special character and purpose. Therefore loyal recognition and safekeeping should be accorded to the spirit of founders, as also to all the particular goals and wholesome traditions which constitute the heritage of each community.

c) All communities should participate in the life of the Church. According to its individual character, each should make its own and foster in every possible way the enterprises and objectives of the Church in such fields as these: the scriptural, liturgical, doctrinal, pastoral, ecumenical, missionary, and social.

d) Communities should promote among their members a suitable awareness of contemporary human conditions and of the needs of the Church. For if their members can combine the burning zeal of an apostle with wise judgments, made in

9. Secular institutes are associations of priests or laity or both. Their members live the life of the vows or promises of poverty, chastity and obedience without the protections of religious habit, cloistered room, or spiritual exercises in common. Secular institutes differ from Third Order groups, Sodalities, and Catholic Action organizations because the institutes involve profession of poverty, chastity, and obedience and have been given a special place in the canonical structure of the Church.
10. As indicated by Pope John in originally summoning the Council, this renewal was primarily a "New Pentecost." The "fresh air" he longed to see within the Church was chiefly the breath of the Holy Spirit in renewal.
11. "Institutes" is a more literal translation of the word used in the Latin text here. "Community" is widely used by religious congregations to mean what the technical word "institute" stands for, i.e., a whole order, society, or congregation (as is clear from Art. 13, speaking of "provinces and houses of a religious community").—Ed.

the light of faith, concerning the circumstances of the modern world, they will be able to come to the aid of men more effectively.

e) Since the religious life is intended above all else to lead those who embrace it to an imitation of Christ and to union with God through the profession of the evangelical counsels, the fact must be honestly faced that even the most desirable changes made on behalf of contemporary needs will fail of their purpose unless a renewal of spirit gives life to them.[12] Indeed such an interior renewal must always be accorded the leading role even in the promotion of exterior works.

3. The manner of living, praying, and working should be suitably adapted to the physical and psychological conditions of today's religious and also, to the extent required by the nature of each community, to the needs of the apostolate, the requirements of a given culture,[13] the social and economic circumstances anywhere, but especially in missionary territories.

The way in which communities are governed should also be re-examined in the light of these same standards.

For this reason constitutions, directories, custom books,[14] books of prayers and ceremonies, and similar compilations are to be suitably revised and brought into harmony with the documents of this sacred Synod. This task will require the suppression of outmoded regulations.

4. Successful renewal and proper adaptation cannot be achieved unless every member of a community cooperates.[15]

In the work of appropriate renewal, it is the responsibility of competent authorities alone, especially of general chapters,[16] to issue norms, to pass laws, and to allow for a right

12. A key sentence of the Decree, and, in fact, a key principle of the whole spiritual life.
13. Adaptation of the religious life to the local culture is vital, especially in missionary work. The failure of some missionary activity is due precisely to neglect of this adaptation.
14. Custom books are handbooks of observances approved in a province or region of a religious order.
15. Art. 4 touches on the proper relationship between authorities and members in religious communities. Note that the Decree, consistent with the Council's teaching on authority as a role of service, does not call religious men and women "subjects" but *sodales*, i.e., fellow members. There is much more on the topic in Art. 14.
16. In the spirit of the Decree, a number of religious orders (e.g., Jesuits, Franciscans) even before the end of the Council announced plans for the meeting of their general chapter or congregation to work out appropriate renewal for their communities.

amount of prudent experimentation, though in all such matters, according to the norm of law, the approval of the Holy
See and of local Ordinaries must be given when it is required.
In decisions which involve the future of an institute as a
whole, superiors should in appropriate manner consult the
members and give them a hearing.

For the suitable renewal of convents of nuns, their wishes
and recommendations can also be ascertained from meetings
of federations or from other assemblies lawfully convoked.

Let all bear in mind, however, that the hope of renewal
must be lodged in a more diligent observance of rule and of
constitution rather than in a multiplication of individual laws.

5. The members of each community should recall above everything else that by their profession of the evangelical counsels they have given answer to a divine call to live for God
alone not only by dying to sin (cf. Rom. 6:11) but also by
renouncing the world. They have handed over their entire
lives to God's service in an act of special consecration which
is deeply rooted in their baptismal consecration and which
provides an ampler manifestation of it.

Inasmuch as their self-dedication has been accepted by the
Church, they should realize that they are committed to her
service as well.

The fact that they are in God's service should ignite and
fan within them the exercise of virtues, especially humility,
obedience, courage, and chastity. Through them they share
spiritually in Christ's self-surrender (cf. Phil. 2:7-8) and in
His life (cf. Rom. 8:1-13).

Therefore, in fidelity to their profession and in renunciation of all things for the sake of Christ (cf. Mk. 10:28), let
religious follow Him (cf. Mt. 19:21) as their one necessity
(cf. Lk. 10:42). Let them listen to His words (cf. Lk. 10:
39) and be preoccupied with His work (cf. 1 Cor. 7:32).

To this end, as they seek God before all things and only
Him, the members of each community should combine contemplation with apostolic love. By the former they adhere
to God in mind and heart; by the latter they strive to associate themselves with the work of redemption and to spread
the Kingdom of God.

6. Those who profess the evangelical counsels love and seek
before all else that God who took the initiative in loving us
(cf. 1 Jn. 4:10); in every circumstance they aim to develop

a life hidden with Christ in God (cf. Col. 3:3). Such dedication gives rise and urgency to the love of one's neighbor for the world's salvation and the upbuilding of the Church. From this love the very practice of the evangelical counsels takes life and direction.

Therefore, drawing on the authentic sources of Christian spirituality, let the members of communities energetically cultivate the spirit of prayer and the practice of it. In the first place they should take the sacred Scriptures in hand each day by way of attaining "the excelling knowledge of Jesus Christ" (Phil. 3:8) through reading these divine writings and meditating on them. They should enact the sacred liturgy, especially the most holy mystery of the Eucharist, with hearts and voices attuned to the Church; here is a most copious source of nourishment for the spiritual life.

Fed thus at the table of the divine law and of the sacred altar, they can bring a brother's love to the members of Christ, and a son's love to their revered pastors; thus they can live and think with the Church[17] to an ever-increasing degree, and spend themselves completely on her mission.

7. Members of those communities which are totally dedicated to contemplation give themselves to God alone in solitude and silence and through constant prayer and ready penance.[18] No matter how urgent may be the needs of the active apostolate, such communities will always have a distinguished part to play in Christ's Mystical Body, where "all members have not the same function" (Rom. 12:4). For they offer God a choice sacrifice of praise. They brighten God's people with the richest splendors of sanctity. By their example they motivate this people; by imparting a hidden, apostolic fruitfulness, they make this people grow. Thus they are the glory of the Church and an overflowing fountain of heavenly graces. Nevertheless, their manner of living should be revised according to the aforementioned principles and standards of appropriate renewal, though their withdrawal from the world and the practices of their contemplative life should be maintained at their holiest.

8. There exist within the Church a great number of clerical

---

17. The phrase "think with the Church" will recall to many readers the "Rules for Thinking with the Church" at the end of St. Ignatius Loyola's Spiritual Exercises. The Council expresses the idea in connection with the Bible and the liturgy (at the beginning of the sentence).
18. E.g., Carthusians, Cistercians (Trappists), Carmelites of the Strict Observance.

and lay institutes devoted to various aspects of the aposto-late.[19] They have contributions to make which are as various as the graces given them: some exercise a ministry of service, some teach doctrine, some encourage through exhortation, some give in simplicity, or bring cheerfulness to the sorrowful[20] (cf. Rom. 12:5-8). "Now there are varieties of gifts, but the same Spirit" (1 Cor. 12:4).

In such communities the very nature of the religious life requires apostolic action and services, since a sacred ministry and a special work of charity have been consigned to them by the Church and must be discharged in her name. Hence the entire religious life of the members of these communities should be penetrated by an apostolic spirit, as their entire apostolic activity should be animated by a religious spirit.[21] Therefore, in order that members may above all respond to their vocation of following Christ and may serve Christ Himself in His members, their apostolic activity should result from an intimate union with Him. In this way it will happen that love for God and neighbor will itself be nurtured.

These communities, then, should skillfully harmonize their observances and practices with the needs of the apostolate to which they are dedicated. But inasmuch as the religious life which is committed to apostolic works takes on many forms, a necessary diversity will have to distinguish its path to a suitable renewal, and members of the various communities will have to be sustained in living for Christ's service by means which are proper and fitting for themselves.

9. In the East and in the West, the venerable institution of monastic life should be faithfully preserved, and should grow ever-increasingly radiant with its own authentic spirit. Through the long course of the centuries, this institution has proved its merits splendidly to the Church and to human society.[22] The main task of monks is to render to the Divine Majesty a service at once simple and noble, within the monastic confines. This they do either by devoting themselves entirely to divine worship in a life that is hidden, or by lawfully taking up some apostolate or works of Christian charity.

19. The reference is to orders, congregations and societies of priests, brothers and sisters engaged in a wide variety of work: parishes, schools, retreats, etc.
20. *Qui miseretur in hilaritate:* almost inevitably one thinks of St. Philip Neri, the "jolly" saint, and of Pope John XXIII.
21. Again the interpenetration of action and contemplation.
22. The following sentences of the Decree give a description of the monastic life (as found, for example, in the Benedictine Order).

While safeguarding the proper identity of each institution, let monasteries be renewed in their ancient and beneficial traditions, and so adapt them to the modern needs of souls that monasteries will be seedbeds of growth[23] for the Christian people.

There are religious communities which by rule or constitution closely join the apostolic life with choral prayer and monastic observances.[24] Let these groups, too, so harmonize their manner of life with the requirements of the apostolate belonging to them that they still faithfully preserve their form of life, for it is one which serves the highest welfare of the Church.

10. The lay religious life, for both men and women, constitutes a state which of itself is one of total dedication to the profession of the evangelical counsels.[25] This sacred Synod highly esteems such a life, since it serves the pastoral work of the Church so usefully by educating the young, caring for the sick, and discharging other services. The Council supports such religious in their vocation, and entreats them to adapt their life to modern needs.

This sacred Synod declares that there is no objection to religious congregations of brothers admitting some members to holy orders, to supply needed priestly ministrations for their own houses, provided that the lay character of the congregation remains unchanged and that it is the general chapter that makes the decision.

11. Secular institutes are not religious communities but they carry with them in the world a profession of the evangelical counsels which is genuine and complete, and recognized as such by the Church.[26] This profession confers a consecration on men and women, laity and clergy, who reside in the world. For this reason they should chiefly strive for total self-dedica-

23. *Seminaria sint aedificationis*, "institutions of edification," in the terminology of many classical works on the subject.
24. Many Catholic girls and women are familiar with this type of community in the Religious of the Society of the Sacred Heart and other dedicated women who conduct academies and colleges around the world.
25. The Council warmly commends the work of religious brothers and sisters.
26. Secular institutes differ from religious institutes in this: their profession of poverty, chastity, and obedience is by some act other than *public* vows, and community of life is not required. This form of the life of evangelical perfection in the world was first given official recognition by the Holy See in the constitution *Provida Mater* (Feb. 2, 1947). The secular institute form of life should not be confused with either the religious life or lay apostolates such as Catholic Action.

tion to God, one inspired by perfect charity. These institutes should preserve their proper and particular character, a secular one, so that they may everywhere measure up successfully to that apostolate which they were designed to exercise, and which is both in the world and, in a sense, of the world.[27]

Yet they should surely realize that they cannot acquit themselves of so immense a task unless their members are skillfully trained in matters both human and divine, and can thus be a genuine leaven in the world for strengthening and enlarging Christ's body. Therefore directors should give especially serious care to the spiritual training of members and to the promotion of more advanced formation as well.

12. That chastity which is practiced "on behalf of the heavenly Kingdom" (Mt. 19:12), and which religious profess, deserves to be esteemed as a surpassing gift of grace. For it liberates the human heart in a unique way (cf. 1 Cor. 7:32-35) and causes it to burn with greater love for God and all mankind. It is therefore an outstanding token of heavenly riches, and also a most suitable way for religious to spend themselves readily in God's service and in works of the apostolate. Religious thereby give witness to all Christ's faithful of that wondrous marriage between the Church and Christ her only spouse, a union which has been established by God and will be fully manifested in the world to come.

Hence, as they strive to live their profession faithfully, religious do well to lodge their faith in the words of the Lord; trusting in God's help rather than presuming on their own resources, let them practice mortification and custody of the senses. They should take advantage of those natural helps which favor mental and bodily health. As a result they will not be influenced by those erroneous claims[28] which present complete continence as impossible or as harmful to human development. In addition a certain spiritual instinct should lead them to spurn everything likely to imperil chastity. Above all, everyone should remember—superiors especially

27. *In saeculo ac veluti ex saeculo.* The word "secular" in the term "secular institute" is based on the Latin word for "world"; as the Decree itself here stresses, that word properly distinguishes these institutes from others.
28. This is the nearest the Decree comes to language of condemnation. The Council here confronts a recurring objection made by some people in the world. Firmly (but also gently, in the spirit of Pope John) the Council takes a stand.

—that chastity has stronger safeguards in a community when true fraternal love thrives among its members.[29]

Since the observance of total continence intimately involves the deeper inclinations of human nature, candidates should not undertake the profession of chastity nor be admitted to its profession except after a truly adequate testing period[30] and only if they have the needed degree of psychological and emotional maturity. They should not only be warned of the dangers confronting chastity, but be trained to make a celibate life consecrated to God part of the richness of their whole personality.

13. Poverty voluntarily embraced in imitation of Christ provides a witness which is highly esteemed, especially today.[31] Let religious painstakingly cultivate such poverty, and give it new expressions if need be. By it a man shares in the poverty of Christ, who became poor for our sake when before He had been rich, that we might be enriched by His poverty (cf. 2 Cor. 8:9; Mt. 8:20).

Religious poverty requires more than limiting the use of possessions to the consent of superiors; members of a community ought to be poor in both fact and spirit, and have their treasures in heaven (cf. Mt. 6:20).

In discharging his duty, each religious should regard himself as subject to the common law of labor. While making necessary provisions for their livelihood and undertakings, religious should brush aside all undue concern and entrust themselves to the providence of the heavenly Father (cf. Mt. 6:25).

In their constitutions, religious communities can allow their members to renounce any inheritance which they have acquired or are due to acquire.[32]

Depending on the circumstances of their location, communities as such should aim at giving a kind of corporate witness to their own poverty. Let them willingly contribute something from their own resources to the other needs of

29. The sentence expresses a valuable insight. See the end of the next paragraph for another important insight.
30. This testing period usually has two parts, postulancy (a short initial period) and noviceship (one or two years in duration). At the end of noviceship (novitiate), the promises or vows are pronounced. During the noviceship period the candidate examines the life of the institute and superiors examine the candidate (to judge, among other things, the psychological and emotional maturity to which the Decree refers here).
31. I.e., by those (the Council Fathers, et al.) who understand what has been handed down from sacred Scripture on the subject.
32. Until promulgation of this Decree, renunciation of inheritance had been a distinguishing mark of final and solemn vows as distinguished from temporary and simple vows.

the Church, and to the support of the poor, whom religious
should love with the tenderness of Christ (cf. Mt. 19:21;
25:34-46; Jas. 2:15-16; 1 Jn. 3:17). Provinces and houses
of a religious community should share their resources with
one another, those which are better supplied assisting those
which suffer need.

To the degree that their rules and constitutions permit,
religious communities can rightly possess whatever is necessary for their temporal life and their mission. Still, let them
avoid every appearance of luxury, of excessive wealth, and
accumulation of possessions.

14. Through the profession of obedience, religious offer to
God a total dedication of their own wills as a sacrifice of
themselves; they thereby unite themselves with greater steadi-
ness and security to the saving will of God. In this way they
follow the pattern of Jesus Christ, who came to do the Father's will (cf. Jn. 4:34; 5:30; Heb. 10:7; Ps. 39:9). "Taking
the nature of a slave" (Phil. 2:7), He learned obedience
from His sufferings (cf. Heb. 5:8). Under the influence of
the Holy Spirit, religious submit themselves to their superiors,
whom faith presents as God's representatives, and through
whom they are guided into the service of all their brothers
in Christ. Thus did Christ Himself out of submission to the
Father minister to the brethren and surrender His life as a
ransom for many (cf. Mt. 20:28; Jn. 10:14-18). In this way,
too, religious assume a firmer commitment to the ministry
of the Church and labor to achieve the mature measure of
the fullness of Christ (cf. Eph. 4:13).

Therefore, in a spirit of faith and of love for God's will,
let religious show humble obedience to their superiors in accord with the norms of rule and constitution. Realizing that
they are giving service to the upbuilding of Christ's body according to God's design, let them bring to the execution of
commands and to the discharge of assignments entrusted to
them the resources of their minds and wills, and their gifts
of nature and grace. Lived in this manner, religious obedience will not diminish the dignity of the human person but
will rather lead it to maturity in consequence of that enlarged
freedom which belongs to the sons of God.

For his part, as one who will render an account for the
souls entrusted to him (cf. Heb. 13:17), each superior should
himself be docile to God's will in the exercise of his office.
Let him use his authority in a spirit of service for the breth-

ren, and manifest thereby[33] the charity with which God loves them. Governing his subjects as God's own sons, and with regard for their human personality, a superior will make it easier for them to obey gladly. Therefore he must make a special point of leaving them appropriately free with respect to the sacrament of penance and direction of conscience. Let him give the kind of leadership which will encourage religious to bring an active and responsible obedience to the offices they shoulder and the activities they undertake. Therefore a superior should listen willingly to his subjects and encourage them to make a personal contribution to the welfare of the community and of the Church. Not to be weakened, however, is the superior's authority to decide what must be done and to require the doing of it.

Let chapters[34] and councils faithfully acquit themselves of the governing role given to them; each should express in its own way the fact that all members of the community have a share in the welfare of the whole community and a responsibility for it.

15. The primitive Church provided an example of community life when the multitude of believers were of one heart and one mind (cf. Acts 4:32), and found nourishment in the teaching of the gospel and in the sacred liturgy, especially the Eucharist. Let such a life continue in prayerfulness and a sharing of the same spirit (cf. Acts 2:42). As Christ's members living fraternally together, let them excel one another in showing respect (cf. Rom. 12:10), and let each carry the other's burdens (cf. Gal. 6:2). For thanks to God's love poured into hearts by the Holy Spirit (cf. Rom. 5:5), a religious community is a true family gathered together in the Lord's name and rejoicing in His presence (cf. Mt. 18:20). For love is the fulfillment of the law (cf. Rom. 13:10) and the bond of perfection (cf. Col. 3:14); where it exists we know we have been taken from death to life (cf. 1 Jn. 3:14). In fact, brotherly unity shows that Christ has come (cf. Jn. 13:35; 17:21); from it results great apostolic influence.

To strengthen the bond of brotherhood between members of a community, those who are called lay brothers, assist-

33. In the following phrase the Decree touches on one of the profound theological truths that lie behind the theme of service.
34. Some religious orders have other terms to denote these bodies of delegates who legislate for the whole community or institute (e.g., the Jesuits have a General Congregation).

ants, or some other name,[35] should be brought into the heart of its life and activities. Unless the state of affairs suggests otherwise, care must be taken to produce in women's communities a single category of sister. Then there may be retained only such distinction between persons as is demanded by the diversity of the works for which sisters are destined by a special call from God or by particular aptitude.

According to the norms of their constitutions, monasteries and communities of men which are not exclusively lay in their character can admit both clergy and laity on the same basis and with equal rights and duties, excepting those which result from ordination.

16. The papal cloister[36] for nuns totally dedicated to contemplation is to be retained. Still, it should be modified according to the conditions of time and place, and outdated customs done away with. In such matters, consideration should be given to the wishes of the monasteries themselves.

Other nuns institutionally devoted to external works of the apostolate should be exempt from papal cloister so that they can better discharge the apostolic tasks assigned to them. They should, however, maintain the kind of cloister required by their constitutions.

17. Since they are signs of a consecrated life, religious habits[37] should be simple and modest, at once poor and becoming. They should meet the requirements of health and be suited to the circumstances of time and place as well as to the services required by those who wear them. Habits of men and women which do not correspond to those norms are to be changed.

18. The suitable renewal of religious communities depends very largely on the training of their members. Therefore religious men other than clerics, and religious women as well, should not be assigned to apostolic works immediately after the novitiate. In suitable residences and in a fitting manner, let them continue their training in the religious life and the

35. E.g., coadjutor brothers.
36. Cloister, i.e., the fact and rules of enclosure (known to monastery and convent visitors chiefly as designation of an area they may not enter) are regulated by the Holy See for the nuns referred to here (Carmelites, Poor Clares, etc.).
37. Habits, i.e., the garb of religious priests, brothers, and sisters.

apostolate, in doctrine and technical matters, even to the extent of winning appropriate degrees.[38]

Lest the adaptations of religious life to the needs of our time be merely superficial, and lest those who by constitution pursue the external apostolate prove unequal to the fulfillment of their task, religious should be properly instructed, according to the intellectual gifts and personal endowments of each, in the prevailing manners of contemporary social life, and in its characteristic ways of feeling and thinking. If such training is harmoniously coordinated it will contribute to integrity of life on the part of religious.

Throughout their lives religious should labor earnestly to perfect their spiritual, doctrinal, and professional development. As far as possible, superiors should provide them with the opportunity, the resources, and the time to do so.

It also devolves upon superiors to see that the best persons are chosen for directors, spiritual guides, and professors, and that they are carefully trained.

19. When there is a question of establishing new communities,[39] serious thought must be given to the need for them, or at least to their eminent usefulness, and also to the likelihood that they will prosper. Otherwise, lack of caution will give rise to communities which serve no purpose or are deprived of sufficient vitality.

Where the Church has newly taken root, special attention should be given to the establishment and development of fresh forms of religious life. These should take into account the natural endowments and the manners of the people, and also local customs and circumstances.

20. Communities should faithfully maintain and fulfill their proper activities. Yet, they should make adjustments in them according to the needs of time and place and in favor of what will benefit the universal Church and individual dioceses.[40] To this end they should resort to suitable techniques,

38. *Titulis*, educational degrees or other certificates and titles (e.g., apprentice) that are relevant to the work of religious men and women.
39. New communities: not new houses or schools but new institutes, congregations, or societies. As the next paragraph shows, the Council here takes a long forward look into the future.
40. The apostolate of religious carried out in particular dioceses is also the proper concern of the local bishop. Therefore, in these adaptations it would be proper for religious to consult the bishops for advice as to what may be to the best interest of the local church.

including modern ones,[41] and abandon whatever activities are today less in keeping with the spirit of the community and its authentic character.

The missionary spirit should be thoroughly[42] maintained in religious communities, and, according to the character of each one, given a modern expression. In this way the preaching of the gospel among all peoples can be done more successfully.

21. If after consulting the appropriate Ordinaries, the Holy See decides that certain communities or monasteries no longer offer any reasonable hope of flourishing, these should be forbidden thereafter to accept novices. If it can be done, they should be absorbed by a more vigorous community or monastery which approximates their own purpose and spirit.

22. Where opportunity and the Holy See permit, independent communities and monasteries should work towards making a federation of themselves if they belong in some sense to the same religious family; or, if their constitutions and customs are practically the same and a kindred spirit animates them, they should try to form a union, especially when of themselves they are excessively small; or let them enter into an association if they engage in external activities of an identical or similar nature.

23. Favor is to be shown to conferences or councils of major superiors[43] which have been established by the Holy See. These can make splendid contributions to several goals: helping individual communities fulfill their purpose more adequately; fostering more successful cooperation on behalf of the Church; distributing workers in a given territory more advantageously; and working on affairs of common concern to religious communities.

Where the exercise of the apostolate is involved, appropriate coordination and collaboration with episcopal conferences should be established.

Similar conferences can also be set up for secular institutes.

41. *Etiam novis mediis:* perhaps "even though modern."—Ed.
42. *Omnino,* often translated "by all means."—Ed.
43. Participation in such conferences or councils, especially in the case of smaller religious groups of men or women, serves to widen the apostolic horizons of particular religious institutes and can be a useful line of communication with the regional conferences of bishops.

24. Priests and Catholic teachers should make serious efforts[14] on behalf of religious vocations, so that a new supply may be at hand for meeting the Church's needs adequately.[45] Candidates should be appropriately and carefully selected. Ordinary sermons should treat more often of the evangelical counsels and the choice of the religious state. Parents should develop and protect religious vocations in the hearts of their children by training them to behave like Christians.

Communities have the right to spread knowledge of themselves by way of attracting vocations, and to seek out candidates as well. Only, they should do so with proper prudence, adhering to the norms set down by the Holy See and the local bishop.

Religious should not forget that the good example of their own lives affords the highest recommendation for their community, and the most appealing invitation to embrace the religious life.

25. The communities for which these norms of appropriate renewal are decreed should react with a willing spirit to their divine calling and their contemporary mission in the Church. This sacred Synod has high regard for the character of their life—virginal, poor, and obedient—of which Christ the Lord Himself is the model. The Council places steady hope in the immense fruitfulness of their labors, both the unseen ones and the obvious.

Let all religious therefore spread throughout the whole world the good news of Christ by the integrity of their faith, their love for God and neighbor, their devotion to the Cross, and their hope of future glory. Thus will their witness be seen by all, and our Father in heaven will be glorified (cf. Mt. 5:16). Thus, too, with the prayerful aid of that most loving Virgin Mary, God's Mother, "whose life is a rule of life for all,"[46] religious communities will experience a daily growth

44. Orders of priests, brothers, and sisters have rightly established the office of vocation director, vocation recruiter, etc.
45. The first task of the vocation director is to *discover* the invitation of the Holy Spirit. The director will often meet candidates who are directed by the Holy Spirit to serve in the diocesan clergy or in some congregation other than his own. In such a case it will be his function to encourage such a candidate to follow this invitation—an attitude that will promote the ultimate well-being of his own institute and the entire Church.
46. *St. Ambrose, "De Virginitate," 1, II, c. n. 15.* (This is the only non-biblical reference in the Decree.—Ed.)

in numbers, and will yield a richer harvest of fruits that bring salvation.

Each and every one of the things set forth in this Decree has won the consent of the Fathers of this most sacred Council. We, too, by the apostolic authority conferred on us by Christ, join with the Venerable Fathers in approving, decreeing, and establishing these things in the Holy Spirit, and we direct that what has thus been enacted in synod be published to God's glory.

Rome, at St. Peter's, October 28, 1965*

I, Paul, Bishop of the Catholic Church

There follow the signatures of the Fathers.

---

*Following the Decree there is an announcement entitled "A Suspension of Law" (*Vacatio legis*): "With respect to the new laws contained in this promulgated Decree, the Most Holy Father grants a suspension until June 29, 1966, that is, until the feast of Sts. Peter and Paul next year. In the meantime the Supreme Pontiff will issue norms for the implementation of the aforementioned laws. Rome, October 28, 1965. ✠Pericle Felici, Titular Archbishop of Samosata, Secretary General of the Most Holy Council."—Ed.

A RESPONSE

For the doctrinal basis of the Decree on the Appropriate Renewal of the Religious Life we must look to the foundational text of the Council, the Constitution on the Church. The Constitution declares that *everyone* in the Church is called to holiness in his own state of life, not merely certain Christians who have been set apart in monasteries and convents.

The point is important, for it meets a Protestant criticism of Western monasticism which has sometimes appeared to hold that the monastic way was a higher way, and especially that the celibate life was essentially superior to the married state. The Constitution explains that holiness appears in a special way through the practice of the counsels customarily called "evangelical." These counsels are chastity dedicated to God, and poverty, and obedience—based upon the words and examples of the Lord. The counsels may, under the impulse of the Holy Spirit, be practiced privately or in a religious community or order.

The practice of the evangelical counsels, however, is properly subordinated by the Constitution to the saving mission of the Church, which is the overriding goal and task of all Christian people. The spiritual life of persons who profess the counsels is to be devoted to the welfare of the whole Church. From this fact arises their duty of working to implant and strengthen the kingdom of Christ through prayer or active works of the apostolate. Furthermore, profession of the evangelical counsels is understood to be a sign that should attract all the members of the Church to the fulfillment of the duties of their own Christian vocation.

All this is important, for it meets questions of Protestants about the place of religious orders in the economy of the Church's mission. Sometimes religious orders have seemed to be preoccupied with themselves. Now they are summoned to live for Christ *and* for His body the Church. It remains to be seen, of course, to what extent these teachings of Vatican II will make headway in the religious orders themselves.

The Decree on the "religious" life is itself given over to general principles or norms for the adaptation and renewal of the life and discipline of the orders. It is impossible to comment upon the details of the proposed renovation, but certain appreciations will be in order.

At the outset, the document speaks of the "wonderful variety" of religious communities. Protestants are increasingly impressed with the adaptability of the religious order throughout history. New forms of monastic life have arisen in every age to meet new needs. There were the hermits of old, who protested by means of the state of their life against an increase of worldliness in the Church; the friars of the Middle Ages, who appeared to preach the gospel to the people when zeal for preaching seemed to have diminished in the Church; and there are the modern "secular" institutes, in which men and women bind themselves to a rule but retain secular jobs, hoping to permeate modern societal structures with the liberating gospel.

Alongside the relatively unchanging diocesan structure of the Church (and partly perhaps because of it), the religious orders provide not only flexibility of ministry but also mobility. Often exempted from the jurisdiction of the diocesan bishop, and committed to vows of obedience, members of orders may freely be sent, sometimes through the intervention of authorities in Rome who know of needs, to any part of the world. At first glance this appears to be merely a practical arrangement, but such flexibility and mobility is also a response to the nature of the Church as the People of God on pilgrimage, in a certain sense free from the things of the world and *sent* to preach the gospel to the corners of the earth.

These appreciations, as well as the recognized need for clear examples of the true nature of Christian community, have brought the beginnings of a revival of religious orders in Protestant Churches. The idea of monasticism and its special place in the Church is still foreign to most Protestants, and certainly the Protestant reformers of the 16th century severely criticized the monasteries of their time, but the revival is making headway. The Eastern Orthodox, of course, have always valued the monastic life, and in the Anglican Communion the revival of monastic life began in the 19th century.

If, as the Decree proposes, the adaptation and renewal of Roman Catholic religious orders is centered in a constant return to the source of all Christian life, the holy Scripture, and if Protestants, too, constantly return to the Gospels as they profess to do, monasticism may no longer be a bone of contention but a means to the recomposition of all Christians in unity. Evidence already exists to show that this may be so, for encounters between members of religious orders and Protestant Christians are multiplying. The prayer of the monasteries will surely have its place, as will contemplation and the study of Scripture, theology, and contemporary social life. Not least in its effects will be our common obedience to Christ in the service of man.

WILLIAM A. NORGREN

LAITY

ALTHOUGH a "lay apostolate" has existed in the Church since the days of our Lord in Jerusalem, it was not until the Second Vatican Council that the Church's official thinking on the matter was stated in a conciliar decree. As one layman put it pungently, "The lay apostolate has been simmering on the 'back burner' of the Church's apostolic life for nearly two thousand years, and finally the Fathers of this Council moved it up to the 'front burner' and turned the heat up all the way." Everyone hopes it will 'come to a boil' soon because so much of the Church's mission depends on an apostolic laity. Indeed, the renewal of the Church, called for by the documents of the Council, depends in great part on a laity that fully understands not only these documents but also their own co-responsibility for the mission of Christ in the Church and in the world.

The Decree on the Apostolate of the Laity is by no means the only document that directly refers to the laity and, therefore, it should not be read or studied in isolation. For example, this Decree is based on the theology of the Church set forth in the Constitution on the Church, especially in the chapters on the People of God and the laity. In addition, the Decree finds its primary fulfillment in the Pastoral Constitution on the Church in the Modern World. Other documents, too, are important, if we are to know what Vatican II has asked of the laity. Such pronouncements as those on Ecumenism, Missionary Life, Christian Education, and the Liturgy speak to the laity of their role in various areas of the Church's mission.

The history of the Decree on the Apostolate of the Laity is an indication of the close relationship between the layman's role in the Church's mission and the vital issues that so concerned the Second Vatican Council. The final Decree is the product of more than five years' intensive work on the part of the preconciliar Preparatory Commission and the actual Council Commission itself.

The document began as a draft of considerable length which comprehensively examined all aspects of the lay apostolate. By the end of the first session, well over half of the document had been excised and handed over to other Council Commissions, to whose work the excised sections were specifically related. For example, much that had been prepared on the layman's task in the Christianization of the temporal order was reserved for the Constitution on the Church in the Modern World; another part was included in the Decree on the Church's Missionary Activity; a third part was contained in the Decree on Ecumenism; and so forth. In addition, specific theological treatment of the laity was reserved to the commission working on the doctrinal text that dealt with the nature of the Church; the latter document, if it were to be comprehensive, required a statement of the theology of the lay members of the Church.

This extensive editing of the text, and the transfer of parts of it to other documents, were inevitable because the laity are involved in some way in the total mission of Christ and His Church. Furthermore, to place the laity in the context of the issue discussed in a specific document was preferable to attempting to say everything about the laity in a single document. Eventually, through a series of constantly improved drafts, the present Decree came into existence as the official teaching of the Church, established by the highest authoritative body within the Church, namely, the bishops of the world, gathered in Council, with the Pope, and promulgated by him.

It was a difficult document to write, not only because the subject matter was so all-encompassing but also because there was no precedent to follow, no model to imitate. Much had been written by recent Popes; many theologians had been studying and treating of the subject in past years; but no Council had ever before attempted to set forth official teaching on the lay apostolate. When work began in the Preparatory Commission, no conciliar theology of the laity was available. When the Commission on Morals and Doctrine finished its work on the theology of the laity, this new theology had to be integrated into the existing draft on the lay apostolate.

Despite these difficulties, it was a document that simply had to be written by the Council—not only because "it was long overdue," not merely because, as the result of a shortage of priests, the Church urgently needed the laity to help the bishops in their apostolate. It had to be written because the laity are the People of God. They are the Church—co-responsible with bishops, priests, and religious for Christ's mission on earth. This sense of co-responsibility is vital because of the widening gap between the modern world and the message of the gospel. The growth of an educated laity and the developing variety of apostolic activity made it essential that the Fathers of the Council speak on the lay apostolate.

It had to be written, most of all, because as the Decree itself states: "Modern conditions demand that their apostolic activity be more intense and broader." These modern conditions exist in a secular world which, if not the exclusive area of the layman, is certainly his primary responsibility in the apostolate. It is becoming clearer that it is the layman who must bring Christianity into the marketplace; he is the Church's "bridge to the modern world," as Paul VI so eloquently said.

Because of these situations, the Fathers of the Council felt the need to speak of the lay apostolate. The Decree, in their own words, "seeks to delineate the nature, character, and variety of the lay apostolate, as well as to state its basic principles and offer pastoral directives for its more effective exercise."

The Decree will require study and considerable reflection because it has much to say, and because, like all other Council documents, it is written for the universal Church and for all forms of the apostolate. Such study and reflection are extremely important both for the individual and the group. Approached with humility and with a strong desire to learn the mind of the Church today on the nature and obligations of lay Christians, it will produce the renewed lay apostolate that is so essential to a renewed Church.

MARTIN H. WORK

Decree on the Apostolate of the Laity[1]

PAUL, BISHOP
SERVANT OF THE SERVANTS OF GOD
TOGETHER WITH THE FATHERS OF THE SACRED COUNCIL
FOR EVERLASTING MEMORY

INTRODUCTION

1. Wishing to intensify the apostolic activity of the People of God,[2] this most holy Synod earnestly addresses itself to the laity, whose proper and indispensable role in the mission of the Church it has already called to mind in other documents.[3] The layman's apostolate derives from his Christian vocation, and the Church can never be without it. Sacred Scripture clearly shows how spontaneous and fruitful such activity was at the very beginning of the Church (cf. Acts 11:19-21; 18:26; Rom. 16:1-16; Phil. 4:3).

1. Suggestions were made by some Council Fathers to change this title to "The Participation of the Laity in the Mission of the Church." The Commission decided to retain the former title because it had become "an almost consecrated" expression in the terminology of the Council.
2. Cf. John XXIII, apostolic constitution "Humani Salutis" Dec. 25, 1961: AAS 54 (1962), pp. 7-10.
3. Cf. Second Vatican Council, Dogmatic Constitution on the Church, Art. 33 ff.: AAS 57 (1965), pp. 39 ff.: cf. also Constitution on the Sacred Liturgy, Art. 26-40: AAS 56 (1964), pp. 107-111; Decree on the Instruments of Social Communication: AAS 56 (1964), pp. 145-158; Decree on Ecumenism: AAS 57 (1965), pp. 90-107; Decree on the Bishops' Pastoral Office in the Church, Art. 16, 17, 18; Declaration on Christian Education, Art. 3, 5, 7; Decree on Missionary Activity of the Church, Art. 15, 21, 41; Decree on Priestly Life and Ministry, Art. 9.
   Although this Decree contains all the essential principles for the apostolate, it is essential to study many of the other documents in order to be familiar with all the Council has said concerning the laity—especially Chapter IV, "On the Laity," in the Constitution on the Church.

Our own times require of the laity no less zeal. In fact, modern conditions demand that their apostolate be thoroughly broadened and intensified. The constant expansion of population, scientific and technical progress, and the tightening of bonds between men have not only immensely widened the field of the lay apostolate, a field which is for the most part accessible only to them. These developments have themselves raised new problems which cry out for the skillful concern and attention of the laity. This apostolate becomes more imperative in view of the fact that many areas of human life have become very largely autonomous. This is as it should be, but it sometimes involves a certain withdrawal from ethical and religious influences and a serious danger to Christian life. Besides, in many places where priests are very few or, in some instances, are deprived of due freedom in their ministry, the Church could scarcely be present and functioning without the activity of the laity.

An indication of this manifold and pressing need is the unmistakable work of the Holy Spirit in making the laity today even more conscious of their own responsibility [4] and inspiring them everywhere to serve Christ and the Church.[5]

In this decree the Council seeks to describe the nature, character, and diversity of the lay apostolate, to state its basic principles, and to give pastoral directives for its more effective exercise. All these should be regarded as norms in the revision of canon law as it pertains to the lay apostolate.[6]

---

4. Emphasis on the special responsibility of the laity to be Christian witnesses in the temporal order is constantly repeated whenever the laity's role in the mission of the Church is discussed. It is most fully treated in the Pastoral Constitution on the Church in the Modern World.

5. Cf. Pius XII, allocution to cardinals, Feb. 18, 1946: AAS 38 (1946), pp. 101-102; sermon to young Catholic workers, Aug. 25, 1957: AAS 49 (1957), p. 843.

6. The commission for the revision of canon law will have this responsibility. All of canon law will have to be updated in order to bring it into conformity with conciliar documents. At the present time, very little is contained in canon law that pertains to the lay apostolate as we know it today.

THE LAYMAN'S CALL
TO THE APOSTOLATE

2. For this the Church was founded: that by spreading the kingdom of Christ everywhere for the glory of God the Father, she might bring all men to share in Christ's saving redemption;[7] and that through them the whole world might in actual fact be brought into relationship with Him. All activity of the Mystical Body directed to the attainment of this goal is called the apostolate, and the Church carries it on in various ways through all her members. For by its very nature the Christian vocation is also a vocation to the apostolate. No part of the structure of a living body is merely passive but each has a share in the functions as well as in the life of the body. So, too, in the body of Christ, which is the Church, the whole body, "according to the functioning in due measure of each single part, derives its increase" (Eph. 4:16). Indeed, so intimately are the parts linked and interrelated in this body (cf. Eph. 4:16) that the member who fails to make his proper contribution to the development of the Church must be said to be useful neither to the Church nor to himself.

In the Church, there is diversity of service but unity of purpose. Christ conferred on the apostles and their successors the duty of teaching, sanctifying, and ruling in His name and power. But the laity, too, share in the priestly, prophetic, and royal office of Christ and therefore have their own role to play in the mission of the whole People of God in the Church and in the world.[8]

They exercise a genuine apostolate by their activity on behalf of bringing the gospel and holiness to men, and on behalf of penetrating and perfecting[9] the temporal sphere of things through the spirit of the gospel. In this way, their temporal

7. *Cf. Pius XI, encyclical "Rerum Ecclesiae": AAS 18 (1926), p. 65.*
8. *Cf. Second Vatican Council, Dogmatic Constitution on the Church, Art. 31: AAS 57 (1965), p. 37.*
9. The twofold distinction is used to indicate that the laity has the double responsibility of teaching the gospel and holiness and also of bringing a

activity can openly bear witness to Christ and promote the salvation of men. Since it is proper to the layman's state in life for him to spend his days in the midst of the world and of secular transactions, he is called by God to burn with the spirit of Christ and to exercise his apostolate in the world as a kind of leaven.

3. The laity derive the right and duty with respect to the apostolate from their union with Christ their Head. Incorporated into Christ's Mystical Body through baptism and strengthened by the power of the Holy Spirit through confirmation, they are assigned to the apostolate by the Lord himself. They are consecrated into a royal priesthood and a holy people (cf. 1 Pet. 2:4-10) in order that they may offer spiritual sacrifices through everything they do, and may witness to Christ throughout the world. For their part, the sacraments, especially the most holy Eucharist, communicate and nourish that charity which is the soul of the entire apostolate.[10]

The apostolate is carried on through the faith, hope, and charity which the Holy Spirit diffuses in the hearts of all members of the Church. Indeed, the law of love, which is the Lord's greatest commandment, impels all the faithful to promote God's glory through the spread of His kingdom and to obtain for all men that eternal life which consists in knowing the only true God and Him whom He sent, Jesus Christ (cf. Jn. 17:3). On all Christians therefore is laid the splendid burden of working to make the divine message of salvation known and accepted by all men throughout the world.

For the exercise of this apostolate, the Holy Spirit who sanctifies the People of God through the ministry and the sacraments gives to the faithful special gifts as well (cf. 1 Cor. 12:7), "allotting to everyone according as he will" (1 Cor. 12:11). Thus may the individual, "according to the gift that each has received, administer it to one another" and become "good stewards of the manifold grace of God" (1 Pet. 4:10), and build up thereby the whole body in charity (cf. Eph. 4:16). From the reception of these charisms or gifts, including those which are less dramatic, there arise for each believer the right and duty to use them in the Church and in the world for the good of mankind and for the upbuilding of the Church. In so doing, believers need to enjoy the freedom of

Christian influence to bear on society and its institutions toward the same end—namely, the salvation of men.
10. Cf. ibid., Art. 33, p. 39; also Art. 10, p. 14.

the Holy Spirit who "breathes where he wills" (Jn. 3:8).[11] At the same time, they must act in communion with their brothers in Christ, especially with their pastors. The latter must make a judgment about the true nature and proper use of these gifts, not in order to extinguish the Spirit, but to test all things and hold fast to what is good (cf. 1 Th. 5:12, 19, 21).[12]

4. Since Christ in His mission from the Father is the fountain and source of the whole apostolate of the Church, the success of the lay apostolate depends upon the laity's living union with Christ. For the Lord has said, "He who abides in me, and I in him, he bears much fruit: for without me you can do nothing" (Jn. 15:5). This life of intimate union with Christ in the Church is nourished by spiritual aids which are common to all the faithful, especially active participation in the sacred liturgy.[13] These are to be used by the laity in such a way that while properly fulfilling their secular duties in the ordinary conditions of life, they do not disassociate union with Christ from that life. Rather, by performing their work according to God's will they can grow in that union. In this way must the laity make progress in holiness, showing a ready and happy spirit, and trying prudently and patiently to overcome difficulties.[14] Neither family concerns nor other secular affairs should be excluded from their religious program of life. For as the Apostle states, "Whatever you do in word or work, do all in the name of the Lord Jesus Christ,* giving thanks to God the Father through him" (Col. 3:17).

Such a life requires a continual exercise of faith, hope, and charity.

Only by the light of faith and by meditation on the word of God can one always and everywhere recognize God in whom "we live, and move, and have our being" (Acts 17:28), seek His will in every event, see Christ in all men whether they be close to us or strangers, and make correct judgments about the true meaning and value of temporal things, both in themselves and in their relation to man's final goal.

---

11. *Cf.* Chap. IV of the Constitution on the Church for a fuller treatment of what has been called the "apostolate of public opinion in the Church." The theological basis for improved communication and dialogue among bishops, priests, and laity will be found there.
12. *Cf. ibid.,* Art. 12, p. 16.
13. *Cf. Second Vatican Council, Constitution on the Sacred Liturgy, Chap. 1, Art. 11: AAS 56 (1964), pp. 102-103.*
14. *Cf. Second Vatican Council, Dogmatic Constitution on the Church, Art. 32: AAS 57 (1965), p. 38; cf. also Art. 40-41: ibid., pp. 45-47.*
*Like most Greek texts, the CCD version omits "Christ."—Ed.

They who have this faith live in the hope of what will be revealed to the sons of God and bear in mind the cross and resurrection of the Lord.

In the pilgrimage of this life, hidden with Christ in God and free from enslavement to wealth, they aspire to those riches which remain forever, and generously dedicate their entire selves to spreading God's Kingdom and to fashioning and perfecting the sphere of earthly things according to the spirit of Christ. Among the struggles of this life, they find strength in hope, convinced that "the sufferings of the present time are not worthy to be compared with the glory to come that will be revealed in us" (Rom. 8:18).

Impelled by divine charity, they do good to all men, especially to those of the household of the faith (cf. Gal. 6:10), laying aside "all malice and all deceit and pretense, and envy, and all slander" (1 Pet. 2:1), and thereby they draw men to Christ. This charity of God, which "is poured forth in our hearts by the Holy Spirit who has been given to us" (Rom. 5:5), enables the laity to express the true spirit of the beatitudes in their lives. Following Jesus who was poor, they are neither depressed by the lack of temporal goods nor puffed up by their abundance. Imitating Christ who was humble, they have no obsession for empty honors (cf. Gal. 5:26) but seek to please God rather than men, ever ready to leave all things for Christ's sake (cf. Lk. 14:26) and to suffer persecution for justice' sake (cf. Mt. 5:10). For they remember the words of the Lord, "If anyone wishes to come after me, let him deny himself, and take up his cross, and follow me" (Mt. 16:24). Promoting Christian friendship among themselves, they help one another in any kind of necessity.

The layman's religious program of life should take its special quality from his status as a married man and a family man, or as one who is unmarried or widowed, from his state of health, and from his professional and social activity. He should not cease to develop earnestly the qualities and talents bestowed on him in accord with these conditions of life, and he should make use of the gifts which he has received from the Holy Spirit.[15]

Furthermore, the laity who in pursuit of their vocation have become members of one of the associations or institutes approved by the Church are trying faithfully to adopt the

---

15. Chap. VI, "Training for the Apostolate," further amplifies this treatment of lay spirituality. The distinction between so-called "monastic" spirituality and "lay" spirituality is implicitly but clearly made.

special characteristics of the spiritual life which are proper
to these as well. They should also hold in high esteem professional skill, family and civic spirit, and the virtues relating
to social behavior, namely, honesty, justice, sincerity, kindness, and courage, without which there can be no true Christian life.

The perfect example of this type of spiritual and apostolic
life is the most Blessed Virgin Mary, Queen of Apostles.
While leading on earth a life common to all men, one filled
with family concerns and labors, she was always intimately
united with her Son and cooperated in the work of the Savior
in a manner altogether special. Now that she has been taken
up into heaven, "with her maternal charity she cares for these
brothers of her Son who are still on their earthly pilgrimage
and are surrounded by dangers and difficulties; she will care
until they are led into their blessed fatherland." [16] All should
devoutly venerate her and commend their life and apostolate
to her motherly concern.

CHAPTER II

THE GOALS TO BE ACHIEVED

5. Christ's redemptive work, while of itself directed toward
the salvation of men, involves also the renewal of the whole
temporal order. Hence the mission of the Church is not only
to bring to men the message and grace of Christ, but also to
penetrate and perfect the temporal sphere with the spirit of
the gospel. In fulfilling this mission of the Church, the laity,
therefore, exercise their apostolate both in the Church and in
the world, in both the spiritual and the temporal orders. These
realms, although distinct, are so connected in the one plan of
God that He Himself intends in Christ to appropriate the
whole universe into a new creation, initially here on earth,
fully on the last day. In both orders, the layman, being simul-

16. *Ibid., Art. 62, p. 63; also Art. 65, pp. 64-65.*

taneously a believer and a citizen, should be constantly led
by the same Christian conscience.

6. The mission of the Church concerns the salvation of men,
which is to be achieved by belief in Christ and by His grace.
Hence the apostolate of the Church and of all her members is
primarily designed to manifest Christ's message by words
and deeds and to communicate His grace to the world. This
work is done mainly through the ministry of the Word and
of the sacraments, which are entrusted in a special way to the
clergy. But the laity too have their very important roles to
play if they are to be "fellow-workers for the truth" (3 Jn.
8). It is especially on this level that the apostolate of the
laity and the pastoral ministry complement one another.

There are innumerable opportunities open to the laity for
the exercise of their apostolate of making the gospel known
and men holy. The very testimony of their Christian life,
and good works done in a supernatural spirit, have the power
to draw men to belief and to God; for the Lord says, "Even
so let your light shine before men, in order that they may see
your good works and give glory to your Father in heaven"
(Mt. 5:16).

However, an apostolate of this kind does not consist only
in the witness of one's way of life; a true apostle looks for
opportunities to announce Christ by words addressed either to
non-believers with a view to leading them to faith, or to believers with a view to instructing and strengthening them, and
motivating them toward a more fervent life. "For the love of
Christ impels us" (2 Cor. 5:14), and the words of the Apostle
should echo in every Christian heart: "For woe to me if I do
not preach the gospel" (1 Cor. 9:16).[17]

Since, in this age of ours, new problems are arising and
extremely serious errors are gaining currency which tend to
undermine the foundations of religion, the moral order, and
human society itself, this sacred Synod earnestly exhorts laymen, each according to his natural gifts and learning, to be
more diligent in doing their part according to the mind of the
Church, to explain and defend Christian principles, and to apply them rightly to the problems of our era.[18]

17. *Cf. Pius XI, encyclical "Ubi Arcano," Dec. 23, 1922: AAS 14 (1922),
p. 659; Pius XII, encyclical "Summi Pontificatus," Oct. 20, 1939: AAS 31
(1939), pp. 442-443.*
18. The "passive" apostolate of merely leading the "good life" is not
sufficient for lay Christians today. They must "preach" the gospel to
Christian and non-Christian alike, as the opportunity presents itself. The

7. God's plan for the world is that men should work together to restore the temporal sphere of things and to develop it unceasingly.

Many elements make up the temporal order: namely, the good things of life and the prosperity of the family, culture, economic affairs, the arts and professions, political institutions, international relations, and other matters of this kind, as well as their development and progress. All of these not only aid in the attainment of man's ultimate goal but also possess their own intrinsic value. This value has been implanted in them by God, whether they are considered in themselves or as parts of the whole temporal order. "God saw all that he had made, and it was very good" (Gen. 1:31). This natural goodness of theirs takes on a special dignity as a result of their relation to the human person, for whose service they were created. Last of all, it has pleased God to unite all things, both natural and supernatural, in Christ Jesus "that in all things he may have the first place" (Col. 1:18). This destination, however, not only does not deprive the temporal order of its independence, its proper goals, laws, resources, and significance for human welfare but rather perfects the temporal order in its own intrinsic strength and excellence and raises it to the level of man's total vocation upon earth.[19]

In the course of history, temporal things have been foully abused by serious vices. Affected by original sin, men have frequently fallen into multiple errors concerning the true God, the nature of man, and the principles of the moral law. The result has been the corruption of morals and human institutions and not rarely contempt for the human person himself. In our own time, moreover, those many who have trusted excessively in the advances of the natural sciences and of technology have fallen into an idolatry of temporal things and have become their slaves rather than their masters.

It is the task of the whole Church to labor vigorously so that men may become capable of constructing the temporal order rightly and directing it to God through Christ. Her pastors must clearly state the principles concerning the pur-

laity must be able to defend Christian belief in the face of atheism, materialism, and general amoral or immoral philosophies.

19. This section clarifies the Church's teaching on the essential goodness of the things of this world and acknowledges that they have true value in themselves and their own proper laws. It thus lays the foundation for the Christian renewal of the temporal order. The age-old detachment of the Church from the "evil world" is no longer valid. Christian laymen must engage in the world, contribute to the perfection of its own values, and enlighten it with the truths of the gospel.

pose of creation and the use of temporal things, and must make available the moral and spiritual aids by which the temporal order can be restored in Christ.

The laity must take on the renewal of the temporal order as their own special obligation. Led by the light of the gospel and the mind of the Church, and motivated by Christian love, let them act directly and definitively in the temporal sphere. As citizens they must cooperate with other citizens, using their own particular skills and acting on their own responsibility. Everywhere and in all things they must seek the justice characteristic of God's kingdom. The temporal order must be renewed in such a way that, without the slightest detriment to its own proper laws, it can be brought into conformity with the higher principles of the Christian life and adapted to the shifting circumstances of time, place, and person. Outstanding among the works of this type of apostolate is that of Christian social action. This sacred Synod desires to see it extended now to the whole temporal sphere, including culture.[20]

8. While every exercise of the apostolate should take its origin and power from charity, some works by their very nature can become especially vivid expressions of this charity. Christ the Lord wanted these works to be signs of His messianic mission (cf. Mt. 11:4-5).

The greatest commandment in the law is to love God with one's whole heart and one's neighbor as oneself (cf. Mt. 22:37-40). Christ made this commandment of love of neighbor His own and enriched it with a new meaning. For He wanted to identify Himself with His brethren as the object of this love when He said, "As long as you did it for one of these, the least of my brethren, you did it for me" (Mt. 25:40). Taking on human nature, He bound the whole human race to Himself as a family through a certain supernatural solidarity and established charity as the mark of His disciples, saying, "By this will all men know that you are my disciples, if you have love for one another" (Jn. 13:35).

In her very early days, the holy Church added the "agape"[21] to the Eucharistic Supper and thus showed herself to be wholly united around Christ by the bond of charity. So, too, in every era she is recognized by this sign of love, and

20. Cf. Leo XIII, encyclical "Rerum Novarum": AAS 23 (1890-91), p. 47; Pius XI, encyclical "Quadragesimo Anno": AAS 23 (1931), p. 190; Pius XII, radio message of June 1, 1941: AAS 33 (1941), p. 207.
21. The agape was a quasi-liturgical fraternal love feast intended to strengthen the bond of unity among the faithful.

while she rejoices in the undertakings of others, she claims works of charity as her own inalienable duty and right.[22] For this reason, pity for the needy and the sick, and works of charity and mutual aid intended to relieve human needs of every kind are held in special honor by the Church.[23]

At the present time, when the means of communication have grown more rapid, the distances between men have been overcome in a sense, and the inhabitants of the whole world have become like members of a single family, these actions and works have grown much more urgent and extensive. These charitable enterprises can and should reach out to absolutely every person and every need. Wherever there are people in need of food and drink, clothing, housing, medicine, employment, education; wherever men lack the facilities necessary for living a truly human life or are tormented by hardships or poor health, or suffer exile or imprisonment, there Christian charity should seek them out and find them, console them with eager care and relieve them with the gift of help. This obligation is imposed above all upon every prosperous person and nation.[24]

That the exercise of such charity may rise above any deficiencies in fact and even in appearance, certain fundamentals must be observed. Thus attention is to be paid to the image of God in which our neighbor has been created, and also to Christ the Lord to whom is really offered whatever is given to a needy person. The freedom and dignity of the person being helped should be respected with the utmost delicacy, and the purity of one's charitable intentions should not be stained by a quest for personal advantage or by any thirst for domination.[25] The demands of justice should first be satisfied, lest the giving of what is due in justice be represented as the offering of a charitable gift. Not only the effects but also the causes of various ills must be removed. Help should be given in such a way that the recipients may gradually be freed from dependence on others and become self-sufficient.

Therefore, the laity should hold in high esteem and, according to their ability, aid the works of charity and projects for social assistance, whether public or private, including inter-

---

22. Here, as in a number of other documents, the Church shows its concern for the poor and sick by singling out the charitable apostolate for special mention. It makes no distinction between public and private aid, or between persons or needs. It urges cooperation with all men of good will.
23. Cf. John XXIII, encyclical "Mater et Magistra": AAS 53 (1961), p. 402.
24. Cf., ibid., pp. 440-441.
25. Cf., ibid., pp. 442-443.

national programs whereby effective help is given to needy
individuals and peoples. In so doing, they should cooperate
with all men of good will.[26]

CHAPTER III

THE VARIOUS FIELDS
OF THE APOSTOLATE

9. The laity carry out their manifold apostolate both in the
Church and in the world. In both areas there exists a variety
of opportunities for apostolic activity. We wish to list here
the more important fields of action: namely, church communities, the family, youth, the social milieu, and national and
international affairs. Since in our times women have an ever
more active share in the whole life of society, it is very important that they participate more widely also in the various
fields of the Church's apostolate.[27]

10. As sharers in the role of Christ the Priest, the Prophet,
and the King, the laity have an active part to play in the life
and activity of the Church. Their activity is so necessary within church communities that without it the apostolate of the
pastors is generally unable to achieve its full effectiveness. In
the style of the men and women who helped Paul to spread
the gospel (cf. Acts 18:18, 26; Rom. 16:3), the laity with
the right apostolic attitude supply what is lacking to their

26. Cf. Pius XII, allocution to "Pax Romana," Apr. 25, 1957: AAS 49 (1957),
pp. 298-299; and especially John XXIII, "Ad Conventum Consilii," Food
and Agriculture Organization, Nov. 10, 1959: AAS 51 (1959), pp. 856-866.
27. This statement was inserted during the final drafting. It is one of the
few places in all of the Council documents where special attention is given
to the contribution of women to the mission of the Church. However, it
was clearly the mind of the Council that they were included and eminently
so, whenever the general role of the laity was discussed. It is interesting to
note that by the time the Council ended twelve laywomen and ten religious
women were present as "auditrices." Mrs. Joseph McCarthy and Sister Mary
Luke, S.L., joined laymen James Norris and Martin Work as official representatives from the United States.

brethren, and refresh the spirit of pastors and of the rest of the faithful (cf. 1 Cor. 16:17-18). Strengthened by active participation in the liturgical life of their community, they are eager to do their share in the apostolic works of that community. They lead to the Church people who are perhaps far removed from it, earnestly cooperate in presenting the word of God especially by means of catechetical instruction, and offer their special skills to make the care of souls and the administration of the temporalities of the Church more efficient.

Offering an obvious example of the apostolate on the community level is the parish, inasmuch as it brings together the many human differences found within its boundaries and draws them into the universality of the Church.[28] The laity should accustom themselves to working in the parish in close union with their priests,[29] bringing to the church community their own and the world's problems as well as questions concerning human salvation, all of which should be examined and resolved by common deliberation. As far as possible, the laity ought to collaborate energetically in every apostolic and missionary undertaking sponsored by their local parish.

They should constantly foster a feeling for their own diocese, of which the parish is a kind of cell, and be ever ready at their bishop's invitation to participate in diocesan projects. Indeed, if the needs of cities and rural areas[30] are to be met, laymen should not limit their cooperation to the parochial or diocesan boundaries but strive to extend it to interparochial, interdiocesan, national, and international fields,[31] the more so because the daily increase in population mobility, the growth of mutual bonds, and the ease of communication no longer allow any sector of society to remain closed in upon itself. Thus they should be concerned about the needs of the People

---

28. *Cf. St. Pius X, apostolic letter "Creationis Duarum Novarum Paroeciarum," June 1, 1905: AAS 38 (1905), pp. 65-67; Pius XII, allocution to faithful of parish of St. Saba, Jan. 11, 1953: Discourses and Radio Messages of His Holiness Pius XII, 14 (1952-53), pp. 449-454; John XXIII, allocution to clergy and faithful of suburbicarian diocese of Albano, "Ad Arcem Gandulfi Habita," Aug. 26, 1962: AAS 54 (1962), pp. 656-660.*
29. *Cf. Leo XIII, allocution Jan. 28, 1894: Acta, 14 (1894), pp. 424-425.*
30. *Cf. Pius XII, allocution to pastors, etc., Feb. 6, 1951: Discourses and Radio Messages of His Holiness Pius XII, 12 (1950-51), pp. 437-443; 852: ibid., 14 (1952-53), pp. 5-10; Mar. 27, 1953: ibid., 15 (1953-54), pp. 27-35; Feb. 28, 1954: ibid., pp. 585-590.*
31. This direction to the laity parallels what is said in other documents, especially in the Constitution on the Church and the Decree on the Bishops' Pastoral Office, concerning the necessity for cooperation at all levels of the Church's life and the co-responsibility of bishops, priests, and laity for the total life of the Church.

of God dispersed throughout the world. They should above all make missionary activity their own by giving material or even personal assistance, for it is a duty and honor for Christians to return to God a part of the good things they receive from Him.

11. Since the Creator of all things has established the conjugal partnership as the beginning and basis of human society and, by His grace, has made it a great mystery in Christ and the Church (cf. Eph. 5:32), the apostolate of married persons and of families is of unique importance for the Church and civil society.

Christian husbands and wives are cooperators in grace and witnesses of faith on behalf of each other, their children, and all others in their household. They are the first to communicate the faith to their children and to educate them; by word and example they train their offspring for the Christian and apostolic life. They prudently help them in the choice of their vocation and carefully promote any religious calling which they may discern in them.

It has always been the duty of Christian couples, but today it is the supreme task of their apostolate, to manifest and prove by their own way of life the unbreakable and sacred character of the marriage bond, to affirm vigorously the right and duty of parents and guardians to educate children in a Christian manner, and to defend the dignity and lawful independence of the family. They and the rest of the faithful, therefore, should cooperate with men of good will[32] to ensure the preservation of these rights in civil legislation, and to make sure that attention is paid to the needs of the family in government policies regarding housing, the education of children, working conditions, social security, and taxes; and that in decisions affecting migrants their right to live together as a family is safeguarded.[33]

The family has received from God its mission to be the

---

32. This is just one of the many places in this Decree where Catholics are urged to cooperate with men of good will wherever possible, especially in matters related to the good of society as a whole.

33. Cf. Pius XI, encyclical "Casti Connubii": AAS 22 (1930), p. 554; Pius XII, Radio Messages, Jan. 1, 1941: AAS 33 (1941), p. 203; to delegates of the convention of the members of the International Union to Protect the Rights of Families, Sept. 20, 1949: AAS 41 (1949), p. 552; to heads of families on pilgrimage from France to Rome, Sept. 18, 1951: AAS 43 (1951), p. 731; Christmas Radio Message of 1952: AAS 45 (1953), p. 41; John XXIII, encyclical "Mater et Magistra," May 15, 1961: AAS (1961), pp. 429, 439.

first and vital cell of society. It will fulfill this mission if it shows itself to be the domestic sanctuary of the Church through the mutual affection of its members and the common prayer they offer to God, if the whole family is caught up in the liturgical worship of the Church, and if it provides active hospitality and promotes justice and other good works for the service of all the brethren in need. Among the multiple activities of the family apostolate may be enumerated the following: the adoption of abandoned infants, hospitality to strangers, assistance in the operation of schools, helpful advice and material assistance for adolescents, help to engaged couples in preparing themselves better for marriage, catechetical work, support of married couples and families involved in material and moral crises, help for the aged not only by providing them with the necessities of life but also by obtaining for them a fair share of the benefits of economic progress.[34]

At all times and places but particularly in areas where the first seeds of the gospel are being sown, or where the Church is still in her infancy or is involved in some serious difficulty, Christian families give priceless testimony to Christ before the world by remaining faithful to the gospel and by providing a model of Christian marriage throughout their lives.[35]

It can help them achieve the goals of their apostolate more easily if families organize themselves into groups.[36]

12. Young persons exert very substantial influence on modern society.[37] There has been a complete change in the circumstances of their lives, their mental attitudes, and their relationships with their own families. Frequently they move too quickly into new social and economic conditions. While their social and even their political importance is growing from day to day, they seem to be unable to cope adequately with the new burdens imposed upon them.[38]

---

34. The truly "pastoral" character of this Decree is most evident in the discussion of the family apostolate. Note the practical suggestions for Christian family activity, and the encouragement of the development of the so-called "couple" movements, such as the Christian Family Movement, Cana Conferences, and others of a similar nature.

35. Cf. Pius XII, encyclical "Evangelii Praecones," June 2, 1951: AAS 43 (1951), p. 514.

36. Cf. Pius XII, to delegates to the convention of members of the International Union for the Defense of Family Rights, Sept. 20, 1949: AAS 41 (1949), p. 552.

37. Cf. St. Pius X, allocution to Association of French Catholic Youth on piety, knowledge, and action, Sept. 25, 1904: AAS 37 (1904-05), pp. 296-300.

38. This special section on youth was inserted at the request of many bishops who felt that early drafts had not adequately treated of the great importance

Their heightened influence in society demands of them a proportionately active apostolate. Happily, their natural qualities fit them for this activity. As they become more conscious of their own personality, they are impelled by a zest for life and abounding energies to assume their own responsibility, and they yearn to play their part in social and cultural life. If this zeal is imbued with the spirit of Christ and is inspired by obedience to and love for the shepherds of the Church, it can be expected to be very fruitful. They themselves ought to become the prime and direct apostles of youth, exercising the apostolate among themselves and through themselves and reckoning with the social environment in which they live.[39]

Adults ought to engage in friendly discussion with young people so that both groups, overcoming the age barrier, can become better acquainted and can share the special benefits each generation has to offer the other. Adults should attract young persons to the apostolate first by good example, and, if the opportunity presents itself, by offering them balanced advice and effective assistance. For their part, young people would be wise to cultivate toward adults respect and trust. Although the young are naturally attracted to new things, they should exercise an intelligent regard for worthwhile traditions.

Children also have their own apostolic work to do. In their own way, they can be true living witnesses to Christ among their companions.

13. The apostolate of the social milieu, that is, the effort to infuse a Christian spirit into the mentality, customs, laws, and structures of the community in which a person lives, is so much the duty and responsibility of the laity that it can never be properly performed by others. In this area the laity can exercise the apostolate of like toward like. It is here that laymen add to the testimony of life the testimony of their speech[40]; it is here in the arena of their labor, profession, studies, residence, leisure, and companionship that laymen have a special opportunity to help their brothers.

To fulfill the mission of the Church in the world, the laity

of youth in the apostolate. This also was one of the two sections in which "day of voting" changes were made by the commission to clarify and strengthen the section.

39. Cf. Pius XII, letter "Dans Quelques Semaines" to Archbishop of Montreal, Canada, to be relayed to the Assemblies of Canadian Young Christian Workers, May 24, 1947: AAS 39 (1947), p. 257; radio message to Young Christian Workers, Brussels, Sept. 3, 1950: AAS 42 (1950), pp. 640-641.

40. Cf. Pius XI, encyclical "Quadragesimo Anno," May 15, 1931: AAS 23 (1931), pp. 225-226.

have certain basic needs. They need a life in harmony with
their faith, so they can become the light of the world. They
need that undeviating honesty which can attract all men to
the love of truth and goodness, and finally to the Church and
to Christ. They need the kind of fraternal charity which will
lead them to share in the living conditions, labors, sorrows,
and hope of their brother men, and which will gradually and
imperceptibly dispose the hearts of all around them for the
saving work of grace. They need a full awareness of their role
in building up society, an awareness which will keep them
preoccupied with bringing Christian largeheartedness to the
fulfillment of their duties, whether family, social, or professional. If laymen can meet all these needs, their behavior will
have a penetrating impact, little by little, on the whole circle
of their life and labors.

This apostolate should reach out to all men wherever they
can be found; it should not exclude any spiritual or temporal
benefit which can possibly be conferred. True apostles, however, are not content with this activity alone, but look for the
opportunity to announce Christ to their neighbors through the
spoken word as well. For there are many persons who can
hear the gospel and recognize Christ only through the laity
who live near them.

14. A vast field for the apostolate has opened up on the national and international levels where most of all the laity are
called upon to be stewards of Christian wisdom. In loyalty
to their country and in faithful fulfillment of their civic obligations, Catholics should feel themselves obliged to promote
the true common good. Thus, they should make the weight of
their opinion felt, so that civil authority may act with justice,
and laws may conform to moral precepts and the common
good. Catholics skilled in public affairs and adequately enlightened in faith and Christian doctrine should not refuse to
administer public affairs, since by performing this office in a
worthy manner they can simultaneously advance the common
good and prepare the way for the gospel.[41]

Catholics should try to cooperate with all men and women
of good will to promote whatever is true and just, whatever
is holy and worth loving (cf. Phil. 4:8). They should hold
discussions with them, excelling them in prudence and cour-

41. Note the strong endorsement of the value of Christian participation in
political and civic life, and the admonition that the common good is always
to be respected in public affairs.

tesy, and initiate research on social and public practices which can be improved in the spirit of the gospel.

Among the signs of our times, the irresistibly increasing sense of solidarity among all peoples is especially noteworthy. It is a function of the lay apostolate to promote this awareness zealously and to transform it into a sincere and genuine sense of brotherhood. Furthermore, the laity should be informed about the international field and about the questions and solutions, theoretical as well as practical, which arise in this field, especially with respect to developing nations.[42]

All who work in or give help to foreign nations must remember that relations among peoples should be a genuine fraternal exchange in which each party is at the same time a giver and a receiver. Whether their purpose is international affairs, private business, or leisure, traveling Christians should remember that they are journeying heralds of Christ wherever they go, and should act accordingly.

CHAPTER IV

THE VARIOUS METHODS OF THE APOSTOLATE

15. The laity can engage in their apostolic activity either as individuals or as members of various groups or associations.

16. The individual apostolate, flowing generously from the wellspring of a truly Christian life (cf. Jn. 4:14), is the origin and condition of the whole lay apostolate, even in its organized expression, and admits of no substitute.

Regardless of circumstance, all lay persons (including those who have no opportunity or possibility for collaboration in associations) are called to this type of apostolate and obliged

42. Cf. John XXIII, encyclical "Mater et Magistra," May 15, 1961: AAS 53 (1961), pp. 448-450.

to engage in it. Such an apostolate is useful at all times and places, but in certain circumstances it is the only one appropriate and feasible.[43]

There are many forms of the apostolate in which the laity build up the Church, sanctify the world, and give it life in Christ.

A particular form of the individual apostolate, as well as a sign especially suited to our times, is the testimony of a layman's entire life as it develops out of faith, hope, and charity. This form manifests Christ living in those who believe in Him. Then by the apostolate of the word, which is utterly necessary under certain circumstances, lay people announce Christ, explain and spread His teaching according to their situation and ability, and faithfully profess it.

Furthermore, in collaborating as citizens of this world in whatever pertains to the upbuilding and operation of the temporal order, the laity should, under the light of faith, seek for loftier motives of action in their family, professional, cultural, and social life, and make them known to others when the occasion arises. Let them be aware that by so doing they are cooperating with God the Creator, Redeemer, and Sanctifier and are giving praise to Him.

Finally, the laity should vivify their lives with charity and express it as best they can in their works.

Let each one remember that he can have an impact on all men and contribute to the salvation of the whole world by public worship and prayer as well as by penance and voluntary acceptance of the labors and hardships of life. By such means does the Christian grow in likeness to the suffering Christ (cf. 2 Cor. 4:10; Col. 1:24).

17. There is a very urgent need for this individual apostolate in places where the freedom of the Church is seriously restricted.[44] In exceedingly trying circumstances, the laity do what they can to take the place of priests, risking their freedom and sometimes their lives to teach Christian doctrine to those around them, to train them in a religious way of life and

43. This is the second essential division of the apostolate that the Decree develops: the individual or "unorganized" apostolate, in addition to the group, or "organized" apostolate.
44. This paragraph grew out of Council discussions on how the lay apostolate functioned in Communist-dominated countries where the official Church is severely restricted, and in cultures where Catholics were in a very definite minority.

in a Catholic mentality, to lead them to receive the sacraments frequently, and to develop their piety, especially toward the Eucharist.[45] This most sacred Synod heartily thanks God for continuing in our times to raise up lay persons of heroic fortitude in the midst of persecutions, and it embraces them with fatherly affection and gratitude.

The individual apostolate has an area of special opportunity wherever Catholics are few in number and widely dispersed. Here the laity who engage in the apostolate only as individuals, whether for the reasons already mentioned or for special reasons including those deriving from their own professional activity, can still usefully gather into small discussion groups lacking the more formal kind of establishment or organization. In this way an indication of the community of the Church can always be apparent to others as a true witness of love. Moreover, by giving spiritual help to one another through friendship and the sharing of experiences, they gain strength to overcome the disadvantages of an excessively isolated life and activity, and to make their apostolate more productive.

18. The faithful are called upon to engage in the apostolate as individuals in the varying circumstances of their life. They should remember, nevertheless, that man is naturally social and that it has pleased God to unite those who believe in Christ in the People of God (cf. 1 Pet. 2:5-10) and into one body (cf. 1 Cor. 12:12). Hence the group apostolate of Christian believers happily corresponds to a human and Christian need and at the same time signifies the communion and unity of the Church in Christ, who said, "Where two or three are gathered together for my sake, there am I in the midst of them" (Mt. 18:20).

For this reason the faithful should exercise their apostolate by way of united effort.[46] Let them be apostles both in their family communities and in their parishes and dioceses, which themselves express the community nature of the apostolate, as well as in voluntary groups which they decide to join.

The group apostolate is highly important also because the apostolate must often be implemented through joint action, in both the church communities and various other spheres. For the associations established to carry on the apostolate in com-

---

45. Cf. Pius XII, allocution to the first convention of laymen representing all nations on the promotion of the apostolate, Oct. 15, 1951: AAS 43 (1951), p. 788.
46. Cf., ibid., pp. 787-788.

mon sustain their members, form them for the apostolate, and rightly organize and regulate their apostolic work so that much better results can be expected than if each member were to act on his own.

In the present circumstances, it is quite necessary that, in the area of lay activity, the united and organized form of the apostolate be strengthened.[47] In fact, only the close pooling of resources is capable of fully achieving all the aims of the modern apostolate and firmly protecting its interests.[48] Here it is especially important that the apostolate concern itself too with the common attitudes and social background of those members for whom it is designed. Otherwise, those engaged in the apostolate will often be unequal to the pressure of public opinion or of social institutions.

19. There is a great variety of associations in the apostolate.[49] Some set before themselves the broad apostolic purpose of the Church; others aim to evangelize and sanctify in a special way. Some propose to infuse a Christian spirit into the temporal order. Others bear witness to Christ in a particular way through works of mercy and charity.

Among these associations, those which promote and encourage a closer harmony between the everyday life of the members and their faith must be given primary consideration. Associations are not ends unto themselves; rather they should serve to fulfill the Church's mission to the world. Their apostolic dynamism depends on their conformity with the goals of the Church as well as on the Christian witness and evangelical spirit of the individual member and of the association as a whole.

Now, in view of the progress of social institutions and the fast-moving pace of modern society, the global nature of the Church's mission requires that apostolic enterprises of Catholics should increasingly develop organized forms at the international level. Catholic international organizations will more effectively achieve their purpose if the groups comprising them, as well as their members, are involved more closely and individually in these international organizations.

---

47. This strong statement on the need for the united and organized apostolate balances nicely the previous remarks on the individual apostolate and should help settle the debate about which is the truer and more important apostolate.
48. Cf. Pius XII, encyclical "Le Pelerinage de Lourdes," July 2, 1957: AAS 49 (1957), p. 615.
49. Cf. Pius XII, allocution to the assembly of the International Federation of Catholic Men, Dec. 8, 1956: AAS 49 (1957), pp. 26-27.

As long as the proper relationship is kept to Church authorities,[50] the laity have the right to found[51] and run such
associations and to join those already existing. Yet the scattering of energies must be avoided. This waste occurs when
new associations and projects are promoted without a sufficient reason, or if antiquated associations or methods are retained beyond their period of usefulness. Nor is it always fitting to make an indiscriminate transfer to other nations of
forms of the apostolate that have been used in one nation.[52]

20. More than a few decades ago the laity in many nations
began to dedicate themselves increasingly to the apostolate.
They grouped themselves into various kinds of activities and
societies which, in rather close union with the hierarchy,
pursued and continue to pursue goals which are properly apostolic. Among these associations, or even among similar but
older ones, those are especially noteworthy which followed
different methods of operation and yet produced excellent results for Christ's kingdom, and were deservedly recommended
and promoted by the Popes and many bishops. From these
they received the title of "Catholic Action." This was very
often described as involving the collaboration of the laity in
the apostolate of the hierarchy.[53]
    Whether these forms of the apostolate have the name of
"Catholic Action" or some other title, they exercise an apostolate of great value for our times and are composed of the
combined and simultaneous possession of the following characteristics:
a) The immediate aim of organizations of this kind is the
Church's apostolic aim, that is, to make the gospel known
and men holy, and to form in them a Christian conscience so
that they can infuse the spirit of the gospel into the various
communities and spheres of life.
b) Cooperating with the hierarchy in their own way, the laity
contribute the benefit of their experience to the running of
these organizations, to the weighing of the conditions in
which the pastoral activity of the Church has to be conducted,

50. Cf., infra, Chap. 5, Art. 24.
51. Cf. Sacred Congregation of the Council, concerning the dissolution of the
Corrientes diocese in Argentina, Nov. 13, 1920: AAS 13 (1921), p. 139.
52. Cf. John XXIII, encyclical "Princeps Pastorum," Dec. 10, 1959: AAS 51
(1959), p. 856.
53. Cf. Pius XI, letter "Quae Nobis" to Cardinal Bertram, Nov. 13, 1928:
AAS 20 (1928), p. 385. Cf. also Pius XII, allocution to Italian Catholic
Action, Sept. 4, 1940: AAS 32 (1940), p. 362.

and to the hammering out and carrying out of a program of action. In all such matters, they assume responsibility.

c) The laity act together in the manner of an organic body so that the community nature of the Church is more fittingly symbolized and the apostolate rendered more effective.

d) Whether they offer themselves spontaneously or are invited to act and to cooperate directly with the apostolate of the hierarchy, the laity function under the higher direction of the hierarchy itself, and the latter can sanction this cooperation by an explicit mandate.

Organizations in which, in the opinion of the hierarchy, the ensemble of these characteristics is realized, must be considered to be Catholic Action even though they take on various forms and titles because of the needs of different regions and peoples.[54]

This most holy Council earnestly endorses these associations, which surely answer the needs of the apostolate of the Church among many peoples. It invites the clergy and laity working in them to develop the aforementioned characteristics to an ever greater degree, and to cooperate at all times fraternally with all other forms of the apostolate in the Church.

21. All associations of the apostolate must be given due appreciation. Those, however, which the hierarchy has praised or recommended as responsive to the needs of time and place, or has directed to be established as particularly urgent, must be held in highest esteem by priests, religious, and laity and promoted according to each one's ability. Among these associations, moreover, international associations or groups of Catholics must be especially prized today.

22. Deserving of special honor and commendation in the Church are those lay people, single or married, who devote themselves and their professional skill either permanently or temporarily, to the service of associations and their activities.

54. "Catholic Action" was the subject of great debate in the Council and in the commission. The term has special significance for Italy and the many Latin countries that follow the strict organizational formula of Italian Catholic Action. It also has political implications in some countries. Throughout it was a question of how much emphasis to place on this particular form of the apostolate, which some maintain is so closely related to the hierarchy that it cannot be truly called "lay." The present statement is a compromise and leaves the use of the name and the organizational structure free. At the same time, it gives special honor to those groups that fulfill the four marks. The term is not popular in the United States, though many groups would qualify as possessing the required marks.

The Church derives great joy from the fact that every day an increasing number of lay persons offer their personal service to apostolic associations and activities, either within the limits of their own nation or in the international field, or especially in Catholic mission communities and in regions where the Church has only recently been implanted.

The pastors of the Church should gladly and gratefully welcome these lay persons and make sure that their situation meets the demands of justice, equity, and charity to the fullest possible extent, particularly as regards proper support for them and their families. Pastors should also see to it that these lay people enjoy the necessary formation, spiritual consolation, and incentive.

CHAPTER V

THE PRESERVATION OF GOOD ORDER

23. Whether the lay apostolate is exercised by the faithful as individuals or as members of organizations, it should be incorporated into the apostolate of the whole Church according to a right system of relationships. Indeed, union with those whom the Holy Spirit has assigned to rule God's Church (cf. Acts 20:28) is an essential element of the Christian apostolate. No less necessary is cooperation among various projects of the apostolate, which have to be suitably coordinated by the hierarchy.

Indeed, if spirit of unity is to be promoted so that fraternal charity may be resplendent in the whole apostolate of the Church, common goals attained, and destructive rivalries avoided, there must exist mutual esteem between all forms of the apostolate in the Church and, with due respect for the particular character of each organization, proper coordination.[55] Such esteem and coordination are most fitting, since any particular activity in the Church requires harmony and

55. Cf. Pius XI, encyclical "Quamvis Nostra," Apr. 30, 1936: AAS 28 (1936), pp. 160-161.

apostolic cooperation on the part of both branches of the clergy,[56] as well as the religious, and the laity.

24. The hierarchy should promote the apostolate of the laity, provide it with spiritual principles and support, direct the exercise of this apostolate to the common good of the Church, and attend to the preservation of doctrine and order.

Depending on its various forms and goals, the lay apostolate admits of different types of relationships with the hierarchy.

For in the Church there are many apostolic undertakings which are established by the free choice of the laity and regulated by their prudent judgment. The mission of the Church can be better accomplished in certain circumstances by undertakings of this kind, and therefore they are frequently praised or recommended by the hierarchy.[57] No project, however, may claim the name "Catholic" unless it has obtained the consent of the lawful Church authority.[58]

Certain forms of the apostolate of the laity are given explicit recognition by the hierarchy, though in various ways.

Because of the demands of the common good of the Church, moreover, ecclesiastical authority can select and promote in a particular way some of the apostolic associations and projects which have an immediately spiritual purpose, thereby assuming in them a special responsibility. Thus, making various dispositions of the apostolate according to circumstances, the hierarchy joins some particular form of it more closely with its own apostolic function. Yet the proper nature and individuality of each apostolate must be preserved, and the laity must not be deprived of the possibility of acting on their own accord. In various Church documents, this procedure of the hierarchy is called a mandate.

Finally, the hierarchy entrusts to the laity some functions which are more closely connected with pastoral duties, such as the teaching of Christian doctrine, certain liturgical actions, and the care of souls. By virtue of this mission, the laity

56. I.e., diocesan clergy and regular clergy (priests who are members of religious orders, congregations, etc.).
57. Cf. Sacred Congregation of the Council on the dissolution of the diocese of Corrientes, Argentina, Nov. 13, 1920; AAS 13 (1921), pp. 137-140.
58. The question of freedom of decision and action of various types of the lay apostolate is established. This section grants the right of organizations and admits the importance of independent apostolic undertakings. However, it warns that such groups cannot use the name "Catholic" without permission of lawful authority. The closer the apostolate moves from the strictly temporal to the more directly spiritual, the closer it is subject to the direction of the hierarchy.

are fully subject to higher ecclesiastical direction in the performance of such work.

As regards activities and institutions in the temporal order, the role of the ecclesiastical hierarchy is to teach and authentically interpret the moral principles to be followed in temporal affairs. Furthermore, it has the right to judge, after careful consideration of all related matters and consultation with experts, whether or not such activities and institutions conform to moral principles. It also has the right to decide what is required for the protection and promotion of values of the supernatural order.

25. Bishops, pastors of parishes, and other priests of both branches of the clergy should keep in mind that the right and duty to exercise the apostolate is common to all the faithful, both clergy and laity, and that the laity also have their own proper roles in building up the Church.[59] For this reason, they should work fraternally with the laity in and for the Church and take special care of the lay persons engaged in apostolic works.[60]

Particular attention must be paid to the selection of priests who are capable of promoting particular forms of the apostolate of the laity and are properly trained.[61] By virtue of the mission they receive from the hierarchy, those who are engaged in this ministry represent the hierarchy by their pastoral activity. Always adhering faithfully to the spirit and teaching of the Church, they should promote proper relations between laity and hierarchy. They should devote themselves to nourishing the spiritual life and an apostolic mentality in the Catholic societies entrusted to them; they should contribute their wise counsel to the apostolic activity of these associations and promote their undertakings. Through continuous dialogue with the laity, these priests should carefully search for the forms which make apostolic activity more fruitful. They should promote the spirit of unity within the association as well as between it and others.

Finally, religious brothers and sisters should esteem the apostolic works of the laity and, according to the spirit and

59. Cf. Pius XII, allocution to the second convention of laymen representing all nations on the promotion of the apostolate, Oct. 5, 1957: AAS 49 (1957), p. 927.
60. Cf. Second Vatican Council, Dogmatic Constitution on the Church, Art. 37: AAS 57 (1965), pp. 442-443.
61. Cf. Pius XII, apostolic exhortation "Menti Nostrae," Sept. 23, 1950: AAS 42 (1950), p. 660.

norms of their communities, willingly devote themselves to promoting lay enterprises.[62] They should also strive to support, uphold, and complement priestly functions.

26. In dioceses, as far as possible, there should be councils which assist the apostolic work of the Church either in the field of making the gospel known and men holy, or in the charitable, social, or other spheres.[63] To this end, clergy and religious should appropriately cooperate with the laity. While preserving the proper character and autonomy of each organization, these councils will be able to promote the mutual coordination of various lay associations and enterprises.[64]

Councils of this type should be established as far as possible also on the parochial, interparochial, and interdiocesan level as well as in the national or international sphere.[65]

Some special secretariat, moreover, should be established at the Holy See for the service and encouragement of the lay apostolate. It can serve as a center well-equipped for communicating information about the various apostolic programs of the laity, promoting research into modern problems arising in this field, and assisting with its advice the hierarchy and laity in their apostolic works. The various movements and projects of the apostolate of the laity throughout the world should also be represented in this secretariat, and here clergy and religious also are to cooperate with the laity.[66]

27. The common heritage of the gospel and the common duty of Christian witness resulting from it recommend and frequently require the cooperation of Catholics with other Christians, a cooperation exercised on the part of individuals and communities within the Church, either in activities or in associations, and on the national or international level.[67]

62. Cf. Second Vatican Council, Decree on the Appropriate Renewal of the Religious Life, Art. 8.

63. The Decree is here suggesting a form of coordination that is exemplified to a great degree in the National Councils of Catholic Men and Women in the United States, and their diocesan and parochial counterparts.

64. Cf. Benedict XIV, On the Diocesan Synod, I, 3, Chap. 9, Art. 7.

65. Cf. Pius XI, encyclical "Quamvis Nostra," Apr. 30, 1936: AAS 28 (1936), pp. 160-161.

66. This will call for a new organization at the Holy See, for neither of the two existing over-all international lay bodies, namely, the Conference of International Catholic Organizations and the Permanent Committee for the World Congress of the Lay Apostolate, fulfills the requirements for the Secretariat. In a very limited sense this Secretariat can be considered a "Synod of the Laity" similar to that announced for the bishops by the Holy Father during the last session of the Council.

67. Cf. John XXIII, encyclical "Mater et Magistra," May 15, 1961: AAS

Likewise, common human values not infrequently call for cooperation between Christians pursuing apostolic aims and men who do not profess Christ's name but acknowledge these values.

By this dynamic and prudent cooperation,[68] which is of special importance in temporal activities, the laity bear witness to Christ, the Savior of the world, as well as to the unity of the human family.[69]

CHAPTER VI

FORMATION FOR THE APOSTOLATE

28. The apostolate can attain maximum effectiveness only through a diversified and thorough formation. Such training is demanded not only by the continuous spiritual and doctrinal progress of the lay person himself but also by the need to adapt his activity to circumstances which vary according to the affairs, persons, and duties involved. This formation for the apostolate should rest upon those fundamentals which have been defended and proclaimed by this most holy Council in other documents.[70] In addition to the formation which is common for all Christians, many forms of the apostolate require a specific and particular formation as well, because of the variety of persons and circumstances.

29. Since laymen share in their own way in the mission of the Church, their apostolic formation takes its special flavor

53 (1961), pp. 456-457. Cf. Second Vatican Council, Decree on Ecumenism, Art. 12: AAS 57 (1965), pp. 99-100.
68. Cf. Second Vatican Council, Decree on Ecumenism, Art. 12: AAS 57 (1965), p. 100; also cf. Dogmatic Constitution on the Church, Art. 15: AAS 57 (1965), pp. 19-20.
69. This section contains the ecumenical principles that are to specifically guide the lay apostolate. The Decree on Ecumenism has much to say on this subject as well.
70. Cf. Second Vatican Council, Dogmatic Constitution on the Church, Chaps. 2, 4, and 5: AAS 57 (1965), pp. 12-21, 37-49; also cf. Decree on Ecumenism, Art. 4, 6, 7, and 12: AAS 57 (1965), pp. 94, 96, 97, 99, 100; cf. also above Art. 4.

from the distinctively secular quality of the lay state and from its own form of spirituality.[71]

Formation for the apostolate means a certain human and well-rounded formation adapted to the natural abilities and circumstances of each lay person. Well-informed about the modern world, the lay person should be an active member of his own society and be adjusted to its culture.

Above all, however, the lay person should learn to advance the mission of Christ and the Church by basing his life on belief in the divine mystery of creation and redemption, and by being sensitive to the movement of the Holy Spirit, who gives life to the People of God and who would impel all men to love God the Father as well as the world and mankind in Him. This formation should be deemed the basis and condition for every successful apostolate.

In addition to spiritual formation, there is needed solid doctrinal instruction in theology, ethics, and philosophy, instruction adjusted to differences of age, status, and natural talents. The importance of acquiring general culture along with practical and technical training should not be overlooked in the least.

For the cultivation of good human relations, truly human values must be fostered, especially the art of living fraternally with others, cooperating with them, and initiating conversation with them.

Since formation for the apostolate cannot consist in merely theoretical instruction, from the very beginning of their formation the laity should gradually and prudently learn how to view, judge, and do all things in the light of faith as well as to develop and improve themselves and others through action, thereby entering into the energetic service of the Church.[72] This formation, always in need of improvement because of the increasing maturity of the human person and the unfolding of problems, requires an ever deeper knowledge and the adjustment of activities. In the fulfillment of all the demands of formation, the unity and integrity of the human personality

71. The length and completeness of this full chapter on formation clearly indicate where the bishops wished to place their greatest emphasis. Great care has been taken to be certain that it was directed toward the formation of the laity and not of religious and priests; and that responsibility for apostolic formation was made the charge of all those persons and institutions responsible for education generally.

72. Cf. Pius XII, allocution to the first international Boy Scouts Congress, June 6, 1952: AAS 44 (1952), pp. 579-580; John XXIII, encyclical "Mater et Magistra," May 15, 1961: AAS 53 (1961), p. 456.

must be kept in mind at all times, so that its harmony and balance may be safeguarded and enhanced.

In this way the lay person will throw himself wholly and energetically into the reality of the temporal order and effectively assume his role in conducting its affairs. At the same time, as a living member and witness of the Church, he will make the Church present and active in the midst of temporal affairs.[73]

30. Training for the apostolate should start with a child's earliest education. In a special way, however, adolescents and young adults should be initiated into the apostolate and imbued with its spirit. This formation must be perfected throughout their whole lives in keeping with the demands of new responsibilities. It is evident, therefore, that those who have the obligation to provide for Christian education also have the duty to provide for formation in the apostolate.

In the family, parents have the task of training their children from childhood to recognize God's love for all men. Especially by example they should teach them little by little to show concern for the material and spiritual needs of their neighbor. The whole of family life, then, would become a sort of apprenticeship for the apostolate.

Children must also be educated to transcend the family circle, and to open their minds to ecclesiastical and temporal communities. They should be so involved in the local community of the parish that they will acquire a consciousness of being living and active members of the People of God. In their catechetical instructions, their ministry of the word, their direction of souls, and in their other pastoral services, priests should be preoccupied with forming apostles.

Schools, colleges, and other Catholic educational institutions also have the duty to develop a Catholic sense and apostolic activity in young people. If young people lack this formation either because they do not attend these schools or because of any other reason, parents, pastors of souls, and apostolic organizations should attend to it all the more. Teachers and educators, who carry on a distinguished form of the apostolate of the laity by their vocation and office, should be equipped with the learning and pedagogical skill needed for imparting such apostolic training effectively.

73. Cf. *Second Vatican Council, Dogmatic Constitution on the Church,* p. 33: *AAS* 57 (1965), p. 39.

In keeping with their purpose and according to their measure, lay groups and associations dedicated to the apostolate or to other supernatural goals should carefully and persistently promote formation for the apostolate.[74] Frequently these groups are the ordinary vehicle of harmonious formation for the apostolate since they provide doctrinal, spiritual, and practical formation. Their members meet in small groups with their associates or friends, examine the methods and results of their apostolic activity, and measure their daily way of life against the gospel.

Formation of this type must be designed to take into account the whole lay apostolate, which is to be carried on not only among the organized groups themselves but also in all circumstances of a man's life, especially his professional and social life. Indeed, everyone should painstakingly ready himself personally for the apostolate, especially as an adult. For the advance of age brings with it better self-knowledge, thus enabling each person to evaluate more accurately the talents with which God has enriched his soul and to exercise more effectively those charismatic gifts which the Holy Spirit has bestowed on him for the good of his brothers.

31. Some types of the apostolate demand very special formation.

a) When the apostolate is one of making the gospel known and men holy, the laity must be specially formed to engage in conversation with others, believers or non-believers, in order to manifest Christ's message to all men.[75]

Since in our times, variations of materialism are rampant everywhere, even among Catholics, the laity should not only learn doctrine more carefully, especially those main points which are the subjects of controversy, but should also provide the witness of an evangelical life in contrast to all forms of materialism.

b) With respect to the Christian renewal of the temporal order, laymen should be instructed in the true meaning and value of temporal things, both in themselves and in their relation to the total fulfillment of the human person. They should be trained in the right use of things and the organization of

---

74. Cf. John XXIII, encyclical "Mater et Magistra," May 15, 1961: AAS 53 (1961), p. 455.
75. Cf. Pius XII, encyclical "Sertum Laetitiae," Nov. 1, 1939: AAS 31 (1939), pp. 653-654; to graduates of Italian Catholic Action, May 24, 1953.

institutions, attentive always to the common good as related
to the principles of the moral and social teaching of the
Church. Laymen should above all learn the principles and
conclusions of this social doctrine so as to become capable of
doing their part to advance this doctrine and of rightly applying these same principles and conclusions to individual cases.[76]
c) Since the works of charity and mercy afford the most striking testimony of the Christian life, apostolic formation should
lead also to the performance of these works so that the faithful may learn from childhood to have compassion for their
brothers and to be generous in helping those in need.[77]

32. There already exist many aids for lay persons devoted to
the apostolate, namely, study sessions, congresses, periods of
recollection, spiritual exercises, frequent meetings, conferences, books, and periodicals. All these are directed toward
the acquisition of a deeper knowledge of sacred Scripture and
Catholic doctrine, the nourishment of spiritual life, an appreciation of world conditions, and the discovery and development of suitable methods.[78]

These formative aids take into account the various types of
the apostolate, according to the milieu in which it is to be
exercised.

For this purpose also, centers or advanced institutes have
been erected, and have already proved highly successful.

This most holy Council rejoices over projects of this kind
which are already flourishing in certain areas, and it desires
that they may be promoted also in other areas where they
are needed.

Furthermore, centers of documentation and study not only
in theology but also in anthropology, psychology, sociology,
and methodology should be established for all fields of the
apostolate, for the better development of the natural capacities of laymen and laywomen, whether they be young persons
or adults.

76. Cf. Pius XII, allocution to the universal congress of the World Federation
of Young Catholic Women, Apr. 18, 1952: AAS 42 (1952), pp. 414-419;
allocution to the Christian Association of Italian Workers, May 1, 1955: AAS
47 (1955), pp. 403-404.
77. Cf. Pius XII, to delegates of the Assembly of Charity Associations, Apr.
27, 1952: pp. 470-471.
78. Cf. John XXIII, encyclical "Mater et Magistra," May 15, 1961: AAS 53
(1961), p. 454.

33. This most sacred Council, then, earnestly entreats in the Lord that all laymen give a glad, generous, and prompt response to the voice of Christ, who is giving them an especially urgent invitation at this moment, and to the impulse of the Holy Spirit. Younger people should feel that this call has been directed to them in particular, and they should respond to it eagerly and magnanimously. Through this holy Synod, the Lord Himself renews His invitation to all the laity to come closer to Him every day, and, recognizing that what is His is also their own (Phil. 2:5), to associate themselves with Him in His saving mission. Once again He sends them into every town and place where He Himself will come (cf. Lk. 10:1). Thus they can show that they are His co-workers in the various forms and methods of the Church's one apostolate, which must be constantly adapted to the new needs of the times. May they always abound in the works of God, knowing that they will not labor in vain when their labor is for Him (cf. 1 Cor. 15:58).

Each and every one of the things set forth in this Decree has won the consent of the Fathers of this most sacred Council. We, too, by the apostolic authority conferred on us by Christ, join with the Venerable Fathers in approving, decreeing, and establishing those things in the Holy Spirit, and we direct that what has been thus enacted in synod be published to God's glory.

Rome, at St. Peter's, November 18, 1965*

I, Paul, Bishop of the Catholic Church

There follow the signatures of the Fathers.

*Following the Decree there is an announcement entitled "A Suspension of Law" (Vacatio legis), naming June 29, 1966 as the effective date for laws contained in this Decree. For text, see footnote at end of preceding Decree.—Ed.

A RESPONSE

In considering the massive challenges facing the Christian Church in the fast-moving, urban, technological world of today, there is ground for the thesis that nothing is more urgent for the renewal of the Church than a radical look at the apostolate of the laity. This is equally true of all churches —Protestant, Orthodox, and Catholic. In spite of external differences and variations in doctrinal statements, the past and present attitudes of the Churches toward their lay members are surprisingly alike.

During the long centuries of Christian history, following the first apostolic period when functions of various members of the Body of Christ were fairly fluid, a strikingly similar pattern appears in all the manifestations of the Church. Through most of these centuries few people were educated; political and social life was clearly hierarchical; everyone had his place, knew it, and accepted it. Life for the vast majority of mankind was an unending struggle to meet basic needs. A measure of protection and a civil or religious leadership which fostered the maintenance of family and simple community life was all that could be expected. Participation in the rule of Church or State was beyond the abilities or the imagination of most men—and totally beyond the wildest dreams of women!

Under these conditions it was inevitable that in all Churches the clergy, with assigned responsibility for the institutional life of the Church and its work, accepted the tasks of leadership and decision making. The pattern of Church life was paternalism—as a rule thoroughly benevolent. This was consistent with paternalistic political, social, and family life.

It is only within the past century and a half that the conditions which required paternalism have gradually but completely changed. To catalogue the changes would require a volume. One need only mention the explosion of knowledge; the spread of education; technological and scientific developments which have overturned old beliefs, produced abundance in the material realm, revolutionized communication and transportation, to remind us that we live in a world radically different from that of our fathers. The effects of all these changes on the individual and on social organization are profound. One need not agree entirely with a phrase such as Bonhoeffer's "man come of age" to recognize that it is a way of describing the profound changes which have taken place in the minds and hearts of people.

Modern man is rebelling against paternalism in every sphere of life. This can be seen in the racial revolution of our day, and in the fierce nationalism of former colonial lands. It can be seen in less violent forms in new concepts of educational methods, and in present-day management of business and industry where participation in decision making is shared as widely as possible. Governmental and private organizations dedicated to helping the unfortunate or the poor are discovering that they must learn to work *with* rather than *for* those whom they would serve.

In view of this, it is not surprising that most Churches are taking a new look at the place and role of the laity. As this Decree on the Apostolate of the Laity clearly recognizes, the Church's mission of evangelizing the world in order that all men may share in God's redemption cannot possibly be carried out in the modern world unless the entire membership of the Church shares actively in that mission. And modern lay men and women will not be moved to an active apostolate if they feel that theirs is a secondary or derivative role.

Awareness of this fact has been growing in all the Churches in recent years. Books on the laity have been published in increasing numbers. The World Council of Churches Department on the Laity has stimulated widespread discussion among and about laity in all parts of the world. In the present ecumenical climate, non-Catholics have eagerly awaited this Decree as one more document which we might study and discuss together. To me, as a Protestant, it makes very rewarding reading. I would like to comment on every paragraph. But I will limit myself to comments on a few portions, which I found of very special interest.

The Decree, in its first chapter, states unequivocally the fact that the Church is the People of God—all of them. A Protestant reader can rejoice in phrases like "a diversity of ministry but oneness of mission," and "the laity likewise share in the priestly, prophetic, and royal office of Christ." The deeply biblical nature of this chapter is also helpful to a Protestant. It would not have been difficult for the writers of the document to have found good quotations in many earlier papal or other Church documents to support many of their points, but they have chosen to base it directly on Scripture. Among other things, this will make it extremely fruitful for joint Catholic-Protestant study and discussion. The only portion of the first chapter which will trouble the Protestant reader is the final paragraph on the Virgin Mary—which is the only one that quotes an authority other than the Bible!

I found the second chapter, on objectives, the single most helpful part of the document. It makes clear statements about many of the complex questions relating to the laity—the fact that their ministry must include work in the Church and outside the institutional Church in the temporal world. The paragraph in this chapter on the intrinsic worth and value of all those things which make up the temporal order is beautifully done. The challenge to the lay person in our time, when new problems are arising and ideas are abroad which can undermine religion and human society itself, to prepare himself to explain and defend his faith is another excellent note. The exhortation to traditional works of charity is linked with a strong statement about working to remove the causes of poverty, injustice, and suffering—and the laity are urged to do this in cooperation with all men of good will.

The third chapter, on the various fields of the apostolate, expands the discussion of the layman's role both in the Church and in the world. A Protestant misses here a stronger emphasis on a share in the actual government of the Church. This may be an area where the Catholic Church will have to gradually make some changes. There is, however, a warm recognition of the fact that lay people have many skills which can be useful within the life of the Church.

The paragraphs on the family and on young people seem less relevant to the realities of today's world than other parts of the document. I found myself saying "Yes, but how?" to many of the statements there. It is not a fault of this document alone, however. None of us in the Churches have as yet discovered what to say in these areas of our common life. We are still caught in old patterns of thought and cannot take fully into account the changes which are coming in family life, and in the widening gap between the generations.

In the fourth chapter, I missed something which has been at the forefront of Protestant thinking about the apostolate of the laity, and that is a serious discussion of the dilemmas of the modern Christian in his daily work. He is exhorted to be a Christian in all that he does, but there is little overt recognition of the fact that this is often perplexing advice. The Bible and Church tradition have little to say about the kinds of problems faced by a modern business man. I wondered, as I read this, how many lay people actually engaged in secular occupations shared in the drafting of the document. In this chapter, however, I found helpful the discussion of the perennial problem of the lay person witnessing and serving as an individual or as a member of an organization. This question troubles Protestants too.

Chapter five deals mainly with the organization of lay work in the Roman Catholic Church. We Protestants are often amazed at the number and variety of Catholic lay organizations, and it is interesting to see the efforts at coordination suggested in the Decree. The establishment of a special secretariat at the Vatican is indicative of the seriousness with which the Council looks upon the apostolate of the laity. We Protestants can learn from our Catholic brethren something of the value of international lay organizations, which are specially stressed in the Decree. We have almost nothing of this kind within the Churches. Perhaps we should.

The final chapter, entitled "Formation for the Apostolate" sounds very familiar, except that we find the world "formation" a strange one. We are more likely to talk about "Lay Training," but we mean the same thing. How, in the modern over-busy, over-specialized world, can a lay person know enough about the Bible and Christian doctrine to be able to "think theologically" about all the areas of his life in which he should act in a Christian way? We have tried all the things the Decree suggests—"study sessions, congresses, periods of recollection, spiritual exercises, frequent meetings, conferences, books and periodicals." But we know we reach only a small proportion of our laity. Perhaps this is one of the areas in which Catholics and Protestants can fruitfully work together.

With a very few exceptions, this entire document reflects the thinking, the theological background, and the practical problems faced by the Protestant and Orthodox Churches as they struggle with questions of the ministry of the laity. Surely this is an area in which we can all gain through common study and action. After all, Catholic and Protestant lay people share a common life in communities and in the world of work. As they learn to serve and witness together, the mission of Christ in the world can be greatly strengthened.

Mrs. Theodore O. Wedel

PRIESTS

THERE HAD BEEN among the early documents handed to the bishops from the beginning of the Council and intended for conciliar consideration one entitled "On the Care of Souls," which, of course, had bearing on the priesthood. But it was never tabled.

In brief outline, the story of the Council's Decree on the Ministry and Life of Priests began in the Second Session, 1963, when the Constitution on the Church was under discussion. Voices were raised on the floor of the Council criticising the reference to priests in this Constitution as too meager and calling for more adequate treatment of these men of the Church, on whose work and dedication she is so dependent. At the end of this Session the text of a special message to all priests was circulated for the acceptance of the Fathers, but it was rejected as falling short of expectations.

In the Third Session (1964), a rather bare list of propositions on the priesthood was brought before the Council, not because of lack of appreciation of the sacred dignity and role of the priest in the Church, but in an effort to keep the Council's agenda within manageable limits. However, the bishops overrode this consideration and sent the skeleton back to the relevant commission to be fleshed out into a vital document on the ministry and life of priests.

In the Fourth Session (1965), a draft decree came forward for debate, and the text, after revision in the light of the debate, was resubmitted to the Council. After further voting and modifications, Pope Paul together with the Fathers of the Council promulgated it on December 7th, 1965.

In this Decree, Vatican II gives fuller and more positive teaching on the ministry and life of priests than any preceding Council. It enlarges our vision of the priesthood: no longer is the focus almost exclusively on the priest as the "cult man," as the representative standing apart from the community at the altar.

The pivotal principle on which the Council's teaching turns is that the priest is a man drawn from the ranks of the People of God to be made, in the very depths of his being, like to Christ, the Priest of mankind. He is consecrated by a special seal of the Holy Spirit. In virtue of this consecration, he acts in the person of Christ, and, as a minister of Christ, the Head, he is deputed to serve the People of God. Through him Christ continues and fulfills that mission which He received from the Father.

The teaching of Vatican II corrects an off-balance view of the priesthood that we have had, at least in the West, for centuries. Looking at the sacrament of orders, the tendency has been to see the priesthood as the point of departure to which the episcopate added an extension of jurisdiction plus extra sacramental powers. This Decree takes as its perspective the uniqueness and unity of the priestly consecration and mission of Christ and then sees in the first place the episcopate as the full and highest participation in that consecration and mission through the sacrament of orders. In his turn, the bishop communicates in a subordinate degree to priests this consecration and mission. Thus they become his co-workers and extension.

Bishops and priests, being united in their participation in the one priesthood and ministry of Christ, although hierarchically graded, fundamentally are brothers. This brotherhood is not a mere communion of mind and heart, but is a sacramental reality. Its intimacy is especially close among the priests of a diocese forming one body (the one *presbyterium*) under the leadership of the bishop.

In its teaching on the relationship between the bishop and his priests, the Decree draws strong, clear, doctrinal guidelines, but it does not provide a detailed vade mecum for the immediate solution of the not inconsiderable problem of the limits of freedom, initiative, and obedience experienced by many excellent priests in our time.

On the one hand, the Decree teaches unequivocally that the bishop fully possesses (in the sacramental order) the priesthood of Christ, while the priest participates in that priesthood in a derived and dependent manner. The bishop alone is the direct and immediate sign of Christ to his flock, while the priest is a sign, not directly of Christ the Priest, but of his bishop. In some way it is the bishop whom the priest immediately makes present to the community over which he presides. The bishop, limited by time and space, cannot be everywhere at once, and this is why he has a body of co-workers, extensions of himself, the priests who teach, sanctify, and rule in his name. Hence the duty of loyalty and obedience that the priests have to the bishop.

On the other hand, the Council wants priests to be mature human beings. In its Decree on Priestly Formation there is a strong emphasis on the training of future priests to maturity, that they may be men having the power of decision and judgment. The priests, too, are sharers in the freedom of the sons of God that is postulated so strongly for the laity in the Decree on the Apostolate of the Laity. Not only by baptism but by the fuller consecration of ordination, priests are personally responsible for the good and growth of the Church. Bishops are exhorted to treat their priests as their helpers, counsellors, brothers, and, indeed, friends.

On the basis of this teaching, definite patterns will have to be drawn for the priest-bishop relationship so that the initiative, zeal, and competence of our priests may be more fully released and stimulated for the building up of the Body of Christ. The provision in the Decree for some kind of representative body of priests assisting the bishop in his work for the diocese gives a lead in this direction.

The Council's insistence on the common priesthood of all the faithful and the participation of all in the mission of the Church to the world recurs again at the very beginning of this Decree, but this teaching is not allowed to obscure the distinct nature of the ministerial priesthood, its sacred power, the public office it performs, and the special value of its apostolate. The priest, however, is kept deeply rooted in the Christian community and, indeed, in the human family from which his priestly consecration does not separate him, but rather to the service of which it the more completely commits him.

The idea of a priestly caste, an ingrown professional group, is excluded in the very first chapter. The priest remains a "disciple of the Lord"; he belongs to the People of God; he is to be "as a brother among brothers" vis-a-vis the laity. The priest, of course, has his special duties, his own way of life, and his special sacramental grace with a consequent definite quality of priestly holiness, but the virtues that are first listed in the Decree to be his are significantly those of any authentic Christian: "kindliness of heart, sincerity, strength of soul and constancy, assiduous regard for justice, and urbanity." And a theme returning frequently—about ten times in the first part of the Decree—is "service," service of God and of the family of God. This but re-echoes St. Paul's conviction of what was especially required of him as a Christian called and empowered to be an apostle.

This service of the People of God is specified in Chapter 2. The priest is the minister of God's Word, of the sacraments and the Eucharist, and the leader of His People. All these functions find their "source and summit" in the celebration of the Eucharist. To form a community, with a deep sense of its own identity, not static and hidebound by a constricting parochialism, but open in love and action to the wider community of the whole Church and the world—this is the challenge the Council throws down to her priests. To train men and women to Christian maturity that will flow over into free, loving action in the community of their fellow men, and to recognize the gifts and insights freely dispensed by God to all, laity as well as priests—this should be the goal of the exercise of priestly authority and spiritual power. Thus the Council breaks the possibility of the deadening grip of a monopolistic clericalism.

Although the "root and hinge" of the Christian community is the celebration of the Eucharist over which the priest presides, it is the ministry of the Word of the living God that is his first duty. In announcing that Word, by catechesis and instruction and by the living of it, the priest gathers together a people for God and nourishes their living faith above all in the Liturgy of the Word at Mass. This Word must be preached, not in generalities and abstractions, but concretely and with a psychological and social relevance to 20th-century man.

Emerging from the doctrine firmly set in the first part, the teaching on priestly holiness in Chapter 3 goes far toward dissolving the tensions and antinomies which priests experience between their action and spirituality. Here, too, the priest is kept closely tied to the Christian community, for he is reminded that, although he is called in a special way to Christian perfection, it is that perfection to which he, together with all the faithful, is called by baptismal consecration itself.

Under the pressure of the activities in which his ministry increasingly involves the priest of today, he must not be torn by the dichotomy of work and spirituality. It is in and

through his ministry that Christ lives and acts in him and he
grows in Christ—this is his road to Christian perfection. In
his ministry of the Word, the living God not only speaks daily
to the priest, but in the very act of giving it to others he is
more intimately united with Christ the Master and led by
His Spirit. There is caught up into his daily offering of the
Sacrifice of the Mass his asceticism, which is his total dedication of himself to the service of men in the Spirit of Christ
in his workaday life.

This unity of action and spirituality is not achieved in glu-
ing the external works of his ministry to his interior life by
mere practices of piety, although, of course, they help considerably. It is Christ alone who fuses the two into one
through the dynamic of a "pastoral charity" flowing mightily
from the Eucharistic Sacrifice, the "center and root" of the
whole life of the priest. Plunged into a diversity of problems
and duties in today's world, the priest surmounts the area of
tension between action and spirituality in the serene polarity
of giving himself, united to Christ, in the service of his
people.

A life whose texture is "pastoral charity" is the Council's
portrayal of priestly holiness, but in the catalogue of the
virtues that are woven into this whole, those specifically
named are humility, obedience, perfect continence, a liberating spirit of detachment and poverty. Germinal ideas are
sown about the interlocking of obedience with mature liberty,
initiative, frank outspokenness to superiors, and an active responsibility for the needs of the flock. Structures will have to
be erected on which these ideas can grow into strong, obedient actions and policies.

To a world cynical of man's capability of virtuous sex, and
cynical even of its desirability, the Church calmly restates
the high value she places on the centuries-old tradition of
perfect continence for her priests. Sign and incentive of pastoral charity and a special source of spiritual fecundity in
the world, celibacy, nevertheless, is not demanded by the
priesthood. This Decree in no way wishes to change the legitimate practice of the Eastern Churches, where there are
married priests to be duly honored.

For many reasons, perfect continence harmonizes beautifully with the Christian priesthood. These reasons are not
first and foremost or merely pragmatic, but are rooted in the
mystery of Christ and His mission. The priest's manhood,
consecrated by the seal of the Spirit in ordination, is in a

new way consecrated by celibacy. This consecration draws its
meaning and value from the fact that it manifests the
priest's undivided dedication to his mission—the service of
the new humanity, which Christ, the conqueror of death,
raises up through His Spirit in the world, and which is born
"not of blood, nor of the will of man, but of God." By this
consecration he stands in the midst of the faithful showing
forth to them that it is his mission to espouse the Church, the
Virgin Bride, to the one Bridegroom Christ. Through his
celibate consecration, he evokes the divine marriage of God
with man, and he is a living sign of that future world toward which he leads his people on their pilgrim way and in
which the children of the resurrection will neither marry nor
be given in marriage.

Supreme is the Council's confidence that, although perfect
continence is not a covenanted gift necessarily meshed with
the vocation to priesthood, this gift will be given by God to
her priests because of its fittingness and at the prayer of the
priests themselves and the Church.

With brief but penetrating glances at the aids to the spiritual life, study, equitable remuneration and the establishment
of common funds for priests in need, for diocesan works and
poorer sister Churches, the Council brings her Decree to an
end, gracefully thanking the Church's priests for their zeal
and labor, and asks them to laugh in joyous confidence
amidst the enveloping pessimism of our world, for the victory
is Christ's.

The comments accompanying the text are meant only as
sign posts. They keep as close as possible to the points made
by the bishops in their discussion in Council and to the
thoughts expressed by the Commission entrusted with the
more detailed shaping of the Decree. The commentary is not
a theology developing and synthesizing this great document's
doctrine on the priesthood. That work remains for theological reflection on the part of the fine minds of the Church
through the coming years.

✠ GUILFORD C. YOUNG

Decree on the Ministry and Life of Priests [1]

PAUL, BISHOP
SERVANT OF THE SERVANTS OF GOD
TOGETHER WITH THE FATHERS OF THE SACRED COUNCIL
FOR EVERLASTING MEMORY

PREFACE

1. The excellence of the order of priests in the Church has already been recalled several times to the minds of all by this most sacred Synod.[2] Since, however, in the renewal of Christ's Church[3] tasks of the greatest importance and of ever-increasing difficulty are being assigned to this order, it has seemed eminently useful to treat of the subject of priests at greater length and depth. What is said here applies to all priests, especially those devoted to the care of souls, though suitable adaptations are to be made for priests who are religious.

1. For the Council's complete and integrated teaching on the priesthood, this Decree has to be collated with other conciliar documents, viz., Constitution on the Sacred Liturgy, Dogmatic Constitution on the Church, Decree on the Pastoral Office of Bishops, and Decree on Priestly Formation, together with valuable sections scattered throughout some of the other documents, e.g., Pastoral Constitution on the Church in the Modern World.
2. *Second Vatican Council, Constitution on the Sacred Liturgy, Dec. 4, 1963; AAS 56 (1964), p. 97 ff.; dogmatic constitution "Lumen Gentium" Nov. 21, 1964; AAS 57 (1965), p. 5 ff.; decree "Christus Dominus" on the Bishops' Pastoral Office in the Church, Oct. 28, 1965; Decree on Priestly Formation, Oct. 28, 1965.*
3. The Council, in writing this Decree, was primarily motivated by the basic purpose of the Council: the renewal of the Church, because of the momentous role to be played by priests.

By sacred ordination and by the mission they receive from their bishops, priests are promoted to the service of Christ, the Teacher, the Priest, and the King.[4] They share in His ministry of unceasingly building up the Church on earth into the People of God, the Body of Christ, and the Temple of the Holy Spirit.

Now, the pastoral and human circumstances of the priesthood have in very many instances been thoroughly changed.[5] Therefore, in order that the ministry of priests may be carried on more effectively and their lives better provided for, this most sacred Synod declares and decrees as follows.

CHAPTER I

THE PRIESTHOOD IN
THE MISSION OF THE CHURCH

2. The Lord Jesus, "whom the Father has made holy and sent into the world" (Jn. 10:36), has made His whole Mystical Body share in the anointing by the Spirit with which He Himself has been anointed.[6] For in Him all the faithful are made a holy and royal priesthood.[7] They offer spiritual sacrifices to God through Jesus Christ, and they proclaim the perfections of Him who has called them out of darkness into

---

4. From the very outset there is mention of the priest's mission and the threefold ministry by which he discharges this mission: he serves Christ the Teacher (ministry of the Word), Christ the Priest (ministry of the sacraments and the Eucharist), Christ the King (ministry of ruling the People of God). This is developed in Chap. 2.

5. The central idea of the whole Council, adaptation to modernity, "aggiornamento," is sounded so that the priesthood may move effectively into the 20th Century.

6. Cf. Mt. 3:16; Lk. 4:18; Acts 4:27; 10:38.

7. The nature of the priesthood emerges from a consideration of the mission given by Christ to the whole Church and the common priestly status, dignity, and function of all members of the Mystical Body, the Church. All the baptized and confirmed are consecrated into a holy and royal priesthood: all have a share in the mission of the whole Body. Cf. Decree on the Apostolate of the Laity, Chap. 1.

His marvelous light.[8] Hence, there is no member who does not have a part in the mission of the whole Body. Rather, each one ought to hallow Jesus in his heart[9] and bear witness to Jesus in the spirit of prophecy.[10]

Now, the same Lord has established certain ministers among the faithful in order to join them together in one body where "all the members have not the same function" (Rom. 12:4).[11] These ministers in the society of the faithful would be able by the sacred power of their order to offer sacrifice and to remit sins.[12] They would perform their priestly office publicly for men in the name of Christ.

So it was that Christ sent the apostles just as He Himself had been sent by the Father.[13] Through these same apostles He made their successors, the bishops,[14] sharers in His consecration and mission. Their ministerial role has been handed down[15] to priests in a limited degree.[16] Thus established in the order of the priesthood, they are co-workers of the episcopal order[17] in the proper fulfillment of the apostolic mission entrusted to the latter order by Christ.

8. Cf. 1 Pet. 2:5, and 9.
9. Cf. 1 Pet. 3:15.
10. Cf. Apoc. 19:10; Second Vatican Council, dogmatic constitution "Lumen Gentium." Nov. 21, 1964, Art. 35: AAS 57 (1965), pp. 40-41.
11. From this basic affirmation there is the transition to the ministerial priesthood of those faithful who have received the sacrament of orders. In these days of emphasis on the apostolate of the laity, the Council teaches the distinctive character of the priests' apostolate. Priests have a sacred power and exercise a "public" priestly office for men.
12. Council of Trent, 23rd session, Chap. 1, c. 1: Denz. 957 and 961 (1764 and 1771).
13. Cf. Jn. 20:21; Second Vatican Council, dogmatic constitution "Lumen Gentium," Nov. 21, 1964, Art. 18: AAS 57 (1965), pp. 21-22.
14. Cf. Second Vatican Council, dogmatic constitution "Lumen Gentium," Nov. 21, 1964, Art. 22: AAS 57 (1965), pp. 33-36.
15. Cf. ibid.
16. The progression is from Christ to the apostles to the bishops to the priests. There is but one eternal priesthood and one mission: that received by Christ from the Father. Christ made the apostles sharers in His priesthood and divine mission. Bishops, as successors of the apostles, participate fully (in the sacramental order) therein. Priests participate to a lesser degree in the fullness of the bishop's priesthood and mission: they are derived from, and dependent on, him. Note as an example of the Council's scrupulous use of words the passive "has been handed down" (traditum est). The previous unrevised draft had the active form (tradiderunt). But this touched on the debated question whether the priesthood (not the episcopacy) was instituted by the apostles or by the Church, which the Decree did not wish to solve. Hence the verbal change in the definitive text.
17. Cf. Roman Pontifical, "Ordination of Priests," preface. These words are already found in the Verona Sacramentary (ed. L. C. Moehlberg, Rome, 1956, p. 122); also in Frankish Missal (ed. L. C. Moehlberg, Rome, 1957, p. 9) and in the Book of Sacramentaries of the Roman Church (ed. L. C.

Inasmuch as it is connected with the episcopal order, the priestly office shares in the authority by which Christ Himself builds up, sanctifies, and rules His Body. Therefore, while it indeed presupposes the sacraments of Christian initiation, the sacerdotal office of priests is conferred by that special sacrament through which priests, by the anointing of the Holy Spirit, are marked with a special character[18] and are so configured to Christ the Priest that they can act in the person of Christ the Head.[19]

Since in their own measure priests participate in the office of the apostles, God gives them the grace to be ministers of Christ Jesus among the people. They shoulder the sacred task of the gospel, so that the offering of the people can be made acceptable through the sanctifying power of the Holy Spirit.[20] For, through the apostolic proclamation of the gospel, the People of God is called together and assembled so that when all who belong to this People have been sanctified by the Holy Spirit, they can offer themselves as "a sacrifice, living, holy, pleasing to God" (Rom. 12:1). Through the ministry of priests, the spiritual sacrifice of the faithful is made perfect in union with the sacrifice of Christ, the sole Mediator.[21] Through the hands of priests and in the name of the whole Church, the Lord's sacrifice is offered in the Eucharist in an unbloody and sacramental manner until He Himself returns.[22]

The ministry of priests is directed toward this work and is perfected in it. For their ministry, which takes its start from the gospel message, derives its power and force from the sacrifice of Christ. Its aim is that "the entire common-

Moehlberg, Rome, 1960, p. 25) and Roman-German Pontificals (ed. Vogel-Elze, Vatican City, 1963, vol. 1, p. 34).
18. The ministerial priesthood derives from a special sacrament conferring a distinctive consecration, by which the priest's manhood is sealed by the Holy Spirit and he is made like Christ, the Priest. Thereby he is empowered to act in the person of Christ, precisely as Head of the Mystical Body.
19. *Cf. Second Vatican Council, dogmatic constitution "Lumen Gentium," Nov. 21, 1964, Art. 10: AAS 57 (1965), pp. 14-15.*
20. *Cf. Rom. 15:16 (Greek)*
21. Thus distinctively consecrated, the priests exercise within the Church a function that is a participation in the very function exercised by the apostles. They are empowered to perform the ministry of the Word, by which men are formed into the People of God. They catch up and draw into the Eucharistic Sacrifice the spiritual sacrifice of the common priesthood of the faithful.
22. *Cf. 1 Cor. 11:26.*

wealth of the redeemed, that is, the community and society of the saints, be offered as a universal sacrifice to God through the High Priest who in His Passion offered His very Self for us that we might be the body of so exalted a Head."[23]

The purpose, therefore, which priests pursue by their ministry and life is the glory of God the Father as it is to be achieved in Christ. That glory consists in this: that men knowingly, freely, and gratefully accept what God has achieved perfectly through Christ, and manifest it in their whole lives. Hence, whether engaged in prayer and adoration, preaching the Word, offering the Eucharistic sacrifice, ministering the other sacraments, or performing any of the works of the ministry for men, priests are contributing to the extension of God's glory as well as to the development of divine life in men.[24] Since all of these activities result from Christ's Passover, they will be crowned in the glorious return of the same Lord when He Himself hands over the kingdom to His God and Father.[25]

3. Priests are taken from among men and appointed for men in the things which pertain to God, in order to offer gifts and sacrifices for sins.[26] Hence they deal with other men as with brothers. This was the way that the Lord Jesus, the Son of God, a man sent by the Father to men, dwelt among us and willed to become like His brothers in all things except sin.[27] The holy apostles imitated Him; and blessed Paul, the teacher of the Gentiles, who was "set apart for the gospel of God" (Rom. 1:1), declares that he became all things to all men that he might save all.[28]

By their vocation and ordination, priests of the New Testament are indeed set apart in a certain sense within the midst of God's people. But this is so, not that they may be sepa-

23. St. Augustine, "De Civitate Dei" 10, 6: PL 41, 284.
24. There is no dichotomy between the priest's adoration and service of God and his service to his fellow men. Both sides of his total ministry are intimately and unbreakably united.
25. Cf. 1 Cor. 15:24.
26. Cf. Heb. 5:1.
27. Cf. Heb. 2:17; 4:15.
28. Cf. 1 Cor. 9:19-23 (Vg.)
29. Having glimpsed something of the divine mystery of the priesthood within the transcendental dimensions of the soaring mystery of Christ, the

rated from this people or from any man,[29] but that they may be totally dedicated to the work for which the Lord has raised them up.[30] They cannot be ministers of Christ unless they are witnesses and dispensers of a life other than this earthly one. But they cannot be of service to men if they remain strangers to the life and conditions of men.[31] Their ministry itself by a special title forbids them to be conformed to this world.[32] Yet at the same time this ministry requires that they live in this world among men, and that as good shepherds they know their sheep. It requires that they seek to lead those who are not of this sheepfold so that they too may hear the voice of Christ and that there may be one fold and one Shepherd.[33]

Council hastens to state that the priest is deeply involved in our human condition. The priest, although totally consecrated to the mission of Christ, is not separated thereby from his fellowmen, but rather is thereby the more fully committed to them. It is because his total consecration is for them, and for this reason only, that he cannot be a conformist to the world. It is in this sense that we speak of him as a man set apart. He must live with his fellowmen as a brother with brothers; nothing truly human is alien to him. To the extent that he became one of a special caste, an in-member of a closed group, to that extent would he betray his mission. Hence this human involvement flows, not from a mere sociological requirement, but from the very heart of his divine mission. The Decree in this whole section leans heavily on Pope Paul's encyclical "Ecclesiam Suam," of Aug. 6th, 1964.

30. Cf. Acts 13:2.

31. "In the pursuit of this kind of religious and moral perfection, the Church is stimulated by circumstances outside herself. Indeed, she cannot remain unaffected by changes in the human condition; she cannot be indifferent to them. They surround her, and they have considerable influence on her way of doing things; they affect her manner of life and they place conditions on it. It is quite evident that the Church is not cut off from the doings of men. She is immersed in them, and therefore her children are drawn to the same things and influenced by the same things; they breathe the culture of the world, accept its laws, absorb its customs. This contact of the Church with the life of man continually brings up difficult problems, and today they are extremely difficult. . . . the Apostle of the Gentiles thus exhorted the Christians of his time: 'Do not bear the yoke with unbelievers. For what has justice in common with iniquity? Or what fellowship has light with darkness? . . . Or what part has the believer with the unbeliever?' (2 Cor. 6:14-15). For this reason today's educators and teachers in the Church must advise Catholic youth of their privileged situation and of the duty, which flows from it, of living in this world, not in the manner of the world but in a way conformed to this prayer that Jesus said for His disciples: 'I do not pray that thou take them out of the world, but that thou keep them from evil. They are not of the world, even as I am not of the world' (Jn. 17:15-16). This distinction, however, is not the same as a separation; it does not mean neglecting the world, fearing it, or despising it. When the Church makes a distinction between herself and the race of mankind, she does so not to put herself in opposition to it but to be the more joined to it." Paul VI, encyclical "Ecclesiam Suam," Aug. 6, 1964: AAS 56 (1964), pp. 627 and 638.

32. Cf. Rom. 12:2.

33. Cf. Jn. 10:14-16.

In the achievement of these goals, priests will find great help in the possession of those virtues which are deservedly esteemed in human affairs, such as goodness of heart, sincerity, strength and constancy of character, zealous pursuit of justice, civility, and those other traits which the Apostle Paul commends, saying: "Whatever things are true, whatever honorable, whatever just, whatever holy, whatever lovable, whatever of good repute, if there be any virtue, if anything worthy of praise, think upon these things" (Phil. 4:8).[34]

CHAPTER II

THE MINISTRY OF PRIESTS

I. Priestly Functions

4. The People of God finds its unity first of all through the Word of the living God,[35] which is quite properly sought from the lips of priests.[36] Since no one can be saved who has not first believed,[37] priests, as co-workers with their bishops, have as their primary duty the proclamation[38] of the

---

34. Cf. St. Polycarp, Epist. ad Philippenses, 6, 1 (ed. F. X. Funk, Apostolic Fathers, I, p. 303): "Priests should be inclined to sympathize, to show mercy to all, to bring back those who have wandered astray, to visit all the sick. They should not neglect the widow, the orphan, the pauper. Their concern should always be to do good before God and men; they should always refrain from anger, from discrimination, from unjust judgment; they should have nothing to do with avarice; they should be slow to believe anything unfavorable about anyone; they should not be too harsh in judging; they should know that we are all sinners."
35. Cf. 1 Pet. 1:23; Acts 6:7; 12:24. "(The apostles) preached the word of truth and founded Churches." (St. Augustine, On Psalms, 44, 23; PL 36, 508.)
36. Cf. Mal. 2:7; 1 Tim. 4:11-13; 1 Tim. 1:9.
37. Cf. Mk. 16:16.
38. Cf. 2 Cor. 11:7. All that has been said regarding bishops also applies to priests inasmuch as they are cooperators of the bishops. Cf. "Statuta Ecclesiae Antiqua," c. 3 (ed. Ch. Munier, Paris, 1960, p. 79); "Decree of Gratian," c. 6, D. 88 (ed. Friedberg, 1, 307); Council of Trent, Decree

gospel of God to all.[39] In this way they fulfill the Lord's command: "Go into the whole world and preach the gospel to every creature" (Mk. 16:15).[40] Thus they establish and build up the People of God.

For through the saving Word the spark of faith is struck in the hearts of unbelievers, and fed in the hearts of the faithful. By this faith the community of the faithful begins and grows. As the Apostle says: "Faith depends on hearing and hearing on the word of Christ" (Rom. 10:17).

Toward all men, therefore, priests have the duty of sharing the gospel truth[41] in which they themselves rejoice in the Lord. And so, whether by honorable behavior among the nations they lead them to glorify God,[42] whether by openly preaching they proclaim the mystery of Christ to unbelievers, whether they hand on the Christian faith or explain the Church's teaching, or whether in the light of Christ they strive to deal with contemporary problems, the task of priests is not to teach their own wisdom but God's Word, and to summon all men urgently to conversion and to holiness.[43]

No doubt, priestly preaching is often very difficult in the circumstances of the modern world. If it is to influence the mind of the listener more fruitfully, such preaching must not

---

"De Reform.," Session 5, c. 2, n. 9 (Ecumenical Council Decrees, ed. Herder, Rome, 1963, p. 645); Session 24, c. 4 (p. 739); Second Vatican Council, dogmatic constitution "Lumen Gentium," Nov. 21, 1964, Art. 25: AAS 57 (1965), pp. 29-31.

39. Here once again the Council brings back into the forefront of the Church's life the Word of God. In the first document it promulgated, the Constitution on the Sacred Liturgy, and in place after place in subsequent documents, the power and the role of God's revealed Word in the saving of man recurs. Later in this Decree, Art. 18, comes the lapidary phrase that stands like a monument of Vatican II's meditation on the Word: "The faithful of Christ are nourished by the Word of God from the twofold table of sacred Scripture and the Eucharist."

40. Cf. "Constitutiones Apostolorum" II, 26, 7: "(Priests) are teachers of sacred science as the Lord Himself commanded when He said: 'Going, therefore, teach. etc.'" (ed. F. X. Funk, "Didascalia et Constitutiones Apostolorum," 1, Paderborn, 1905, p. 105); Leonine Sacramentary and other sacramentaries up to the Roman Pontifical, preface of the ordination of priests: "By this providence, Lord, You have added to the apostles of your Son fellow teachers of the faith through whom the apostles have filled the whole world with their teaching." Ordo Book of the Mozarabic Liturgy, preface to the ordination of priests: "Teacher of peoples and ruler of subjects, he keeps intact the Catholic faith and announces true salvation to all." (ed. M. Ferotin, Paris, 1904, col. 55.)

41. Cf. Gal. 2:5.

42. Cf. 1 Pet. 2:12.

43. Cf. Rite of priestly ordination in the Alexandrian Jacobite Church: ". . . Gather your people to the word of doctrine like a fostermother who nourishes her children" (Denz., "Oriental Rites," Book 11, Wurzburg, 1863, p. 14).

present God's Word in a general and abstract fashion only, but it must apply the perennial truth of the gospel to the concrete circumstances of life.

Thus the ministry of the Word is carried out in many ways, according to the various needs of those who hear and the special gifts of those who preach. In areas or communities which are non-Christian, the gospel message draws men to faith and the sacraments of salvation.[44] In the Christian community itself, especially among those who seem to understand or believe little of what they practice, the preaching of the Word is needed for the very administration of the sacraments.[45] For these are sacraments of faith, and faith is born of the Word and nourished by it.[46]

Such is especially true of the Liturgy of the Word during the celebration of Mass.[47] In this celebration, the proclamation of the death and resurrection of the Lord is inseparably joined to the response of the people who hear, and to the very offering whereby Christ ratified the New Testament in His blood. The faithful share in this offering both by their prayers and by their recognition of the sacrament for what it is.[48]

---

44. Cf. Mt. 28:19; Mk. 16:16; Tertullian, "On Baptism," 14, 2 (The Body of Christians, Latin Series, I, p. 289, 11-13); St. Athanasius, "Against the Arians," 2, 42 (PG 26, 237); St. Jerome, "On Matthew," 28, 19 (PL 26, 218 BC): "First let them teach all nations, and then pour water on those who have learned. It cannot be that the body receive the sacrament of baptism unless the soul first has received the truth of faith"; St. Thomas, "Exposition of the first decretal," Art. 1: "Sending His disciples to preach, our Savior enjoined on them three things: first, that they teach the faith; second, that they confer the sacraments on believers . . ." (ed. Marietti, "Opuscula Theologica," Taurini-Rome, 1954, 1138).

45. Note that while the People of God are assembled, gathered together, in the first place by the Word of the living God, this is only an initiating action that has to be completed by the priest's sacramental ministry, for they have not been incorporated into Christ until they have been baptized. Having become God's People, their living faith still needs to be nourished by the announcing of the Word, by instruction, by application of it to the questions of the day, by preaching that is not a mouthing of abstractions and generalities but concrete and adapted to the psychological and social conditions of the modern audience. And the Word he speaks must flow over into the life of the priest; it is thus he brings unbelievers to the acknowledgment of God.

46. Cf. Second Vatican Council, Constitution on the Sacred Liturgy, Dec. 4, 1963, Art. 35, 2: AAS 56 (1964), p. 109.

47. The dynamic thrust (the eschatological dimension) of all the priest's action, which is demanded by the very concept of the pilgrim Church moving always forward to its final destination and perfection, is exemplified and realized in the celebration of the Mass. Here in the Liturgy of the Word his ministry of the Word reaches its high point.

48. Cf. ibid., Art. 33, 35, 48, 52 (pp. 108-109, 113, 114).

5. God, who alone is holy and bestows holiness, willed to raise up for Himself as companions and helpers men who would humbly dedicate themselves to the work of sanctification. Hence, through the ministry of the bishop, God consecrates priests so that they can share by a special title in the priesthood of Christ. Thus, in performing sacred functions they can act as the ministers of Him who in the liturgy continually exercises his priestly office on our behalf by the action of His Spirit.[49]

By baptism men are brought into the People of God. By the sacrament of penance sinners are reconciled to God and the Church. By the oil of the sick the ailing find relief. And, especially by the celebration of Mass, men offer sacramentally the sacrifice of Christ. In administering all the sacraments, as St. Ignatius Martyr already bore witness in the days of the primitive Church,[50] priests by various titles are bound together hierarchically with the bishop.[51] Thus in a certain way they make him present in every gathering of the faithful.[52]

The other sacraments, as well as every ministry of the Church and every work of the apostolate,[53] are linked with the holy Eucharist and are directed toward it.[54] For the most blessed Eucharist contains the Church's entire spiritual wealth,[55] that is, Christ Himself, our Passover and living bread. Through His very flesh, made vital and vitalizing by the Holy Spirit, He offers life to men. They are thereby invited and led to offer themselves, their labors, and all created things together with Him.

---

49. *Cf. ibid., Art. 7 (pp. 100-101); Pius XII, encyclical letter "Mystici Corporis,"* June 29, 1943: *AAS* 35 (1943), p. 230.

50. *St. Ignatius Martyr, "Smyrn.,"* 8, 1-2 (ed. F. X. Funk, p. 282, 6-15); *"Constitutions of the Apostles,"* VIII, 12, 3 (ed. F. X. Funk, p. 496); VIII, 29, 2 (p. 532).

51. This whole section should be read with the Constitution on the Sacred Liturgy on hand. The priest is, above all, Christ's minister, presiding over the worshiping and sanctifying action of Christ in the liturgy. Because he is derived from and, in all his priestly activity, dependent on the bishop, the priest, in administering the sacraments and celebrating the Eucharist, makes the bishop present to his congregation.

52. *Cf. Second Vatican Council, dogmatic constitution "Lumen Gentium,"* Nov. 21, 1964, Art. 28: *AAS* 57 (1965), pp. 33-36.

53. All the priest's functions and the work and life of the community which he serves have their source in the celebration of the Eucharist—the hub on which everything centers and in which multiplicity is reduced to unity.

54. *"The Eucharist indeed is a quasi consummation of the spiritual life, and the goal of all the sacraments"* (St. Thomas, *"Summa Theol.,"* III, q. 73, a. 3 c); *cf. "Summa Theol.,"* III, q. 65, a. 3.

55. *Cf. St. Thomas, "Summa Theol.,"* III, q. 65, a. 3, ad 1; q. 79, a. 1, c, and ad 1.

Hence the Eucharist shows itself to be the source and the apex of the whole work of preaching the gospel. Those under instruction are introduced by stages to a sharing in the Eucharist. The faithful, already marked with the sacred seal of baptism and confirmation, are through the reception of the Eucharist fully[56] joined to the Body of Christ.

Thus the Eucharistic Action is the very heartbeat of the congregation of the faithful over which the priest presides. So priests must instruct them to offer to God the Father the divine Victim in the sacrifice of the Mass, and to join to it the offering of their own lives.[57] In the spirit of Christ the Shepherd, priests should train them to submit their sins with a contrite heart to the Church in the sacrament of penance. Thus, mindful of the Lord's words: "Repent, for the kingdom of God is at hand" (Mt. 4:17), the people will be drawn ever closer to Him each day.

Priests should likewise teach them to participate in the celebrations of the sacred liturgy in such a way that they can rise to sincere prayer during them. They must lead the faithful along to an ever-improved spirit of prayer offered throughout the whole of life according to the graces and needs of each.[58] They must persuade everyone to the discharge of the duties of his proper state in life, and bring the saintlier ones to an appropriate exercise of the evangelical counsels. They must show the faithful how to sing to the Lord hymns and spiritual songs in their hearts, always giving thanks to God the Father for all things in the name of our Lord, Jesus Christ.[59]

Priests themselves extend to the different hours of the day the praise and thanksgiving of the Eucharistic celebration by

56. A small but very significant adverb was inserted here in the revised definitive text—"plene" (fully) in place of "plenius" (more fully)—to point up the truth that it is participation in the Eucharist that fully incorporates us into Christ. Cf. the Pastoral Constitution on the Church in the Modern World, Art. 38, for a vision of the vast sweep of the Eucharistic action. In it (the Eucharist) the elements of nature, transformed by the work of man, are changed into the glorified Body and Blood of Christ and a love feast of men made brothers is celebrated in anticipation of the heavenly banquet to which men are destined.
57. In the Sacrifice of the Mass the faithful offer not only their own lives; they really offer to the Father the divine Victim. This is one of many examples in the Council's teaching of the influence of the magisterial work of Pope Pius XII. The bishops who had this written into the Decree invoked Pius XII's encyclical "Mediator Dei."
58. The Decree deliberately does not make a distinction between "mental" prayer on the one hand and "vocal" or "liturgical" prayer on the other, because genuine liturgical prayer is at the same time both mental and vocal.
59. Cf. Eph. 5:19-20.

reciting the Divine Office. Through it they pray to God in the name of the Church on behalf of the whole people entrusted to them and indeed for the whole world.[60]

In the house of prayer the most Holy Eucharist is celebrated and preserved. There the faithful gather, and find help and comfort through venerating the presence of the Son of God our Savior,[61] offered for us on the sacrificial altar. This house must be well kept and suitable for prayer and sacred functions.[62] There, pastors and the faithful are called to respond with grateful hearts to the gift of Him who through His humanity constantly pours divine life into the members of His Body.[63]

Let priests take care to cultivate an appropriate knowledge and facility in the liturgy, so that by their own liturgical ministry, the Christian communities entrusted to them may ever more adequately give praise to God, the Father and the Son and the Holy Spirit.[64]

6. To the degree of their authority and in the name of their bishop,[65] priests exercise the office of Christ the Head and the Shepherd. Thus they gather God's family together as a brotherhood of living unity, and lead it through Christ and in the Spirit to God the Father.[66] For the exercise of this ministry, as for other priestly duties, spiritual power is con-

60. Thus the Divine Office is intimately united to the celebration of the Eucharist and its special value, as the prayer of the priest in the name of the Church for his people, is highlighted.
61. By an exact choice of phrase the particular manner of the divine presence in our churches is stated: the divine presence is the presence of Christ the God-Man, and it is related to the Sacrifice of the Mass.
62. Cf. St. Jerome, Epistles, 114, 2 (PL 22, 934) ". . . the holy chalices and holy vestments and the rest that pertains to the cult of the Lord's Passion . . . from their connection with the body and blood of the Lord these things should be venerated as one would venerate His body and blood." See Second Vatican Council, Constitution on the Sacred Liturgy, Dec. 4, 1963, Art. 122-127: AAS 56 (1964), pp. 130-132.
63. "Moreover, in the course of the day the faithful should not omit to visit the Blessed Sacrament, which according to the liturgical laws must be kept in the churches with the greatest possible reverence and in a most honorable location. Such visits are a proof of gratitude, an expression of love to Christ the Lord present in the sacrament, and a duty of the adoration we owe." Paul VI, encyclical letter "Mysterium Fidei," Sept. 3, 1965: AAS 57 (1965), p. 771.
64. A new era of great liturgical art, after years of artistic penury and debasement, could be opened by these few words.
65. So that it would be clear that the bishop's action in ruling the community is a continuing action even after he has appointed a priest to a charge, the phrase, "in the name of the bishop," was purposely chosen.
66. Cf. Second Vatican Council, dogmatic constitution "Lumen Gentium," Nov. 21, 1964, Art. 28: AAS 57 (1965), pp. 33-36.

ferred upon them for the upbuilding of the Church.[67]

In achieving this goal, priests must treat all with outstanding humanity, in imitation of the Lord. They should act toward men, not as seeking to win their favor[68] but in accord with the demands of Christian doctrine and life. They should teach and admonish men[69] as dearly beloved sons,[70] according to the words of the Apostle: "Be urgent in season, out of season; reprove, entreat, rebuke with all patience and teaching." (2 Tim. 4:2).[71]

Therefore, as educators in the faith, priests must see to it, either by themselves or through others, that the faithful are led individually in the Holy Spirit to a development of their own vocation as required by the gospel, to a sincere and active charity,[72] and to that freedom with which Christ has made us free.[73] Ceremonies however beautiful, or associations however flourishing, will be of little value if they are not directed toward educating men in the attainment of Christian maturity.[74]

To further this goal, priests should help men see what is required and what is God's will in the great and small events of life. Christians should also be taught that they do not live for themselves alone, but, according to the demands of the new law of charity, every man must administer to others the grace he has received.[75] In this way all will discharge in a Christian manner their duties within the community of men.

Although he has obligations toward all men, a priest has

---

67. *Cf. 2 Cor. 10:8; 13:10.*
68. *Cf. Gal. 1:10.*
69. Into this section is introduced the concept of the "father" relationship of the priest to his people. In the Constitution on the Church, Art. 28, the foundation of this relationship, viz., the priest's spiritual generation of the faithful by baptism and teaching, is established by quoting St. Paul and St. Peter (1 Cor. 4:15; 1 Pet. 1:23).
70. *Cf. 1 Cor. 4:14.*
71. *Cf. "Didascalia," II, 34, 3; II, 46, 6; II, 47, 1; "Constitutions of the Apostles," II, 47, 1 (ed. F. X. Funk, "Didascalia and Constitutions," I. pp. 116, 142, and 143).*
72. Later in this section there is emphasis on the priest's duty of forming a community. Here his duty to each one of his people, human persons in all their variety, is underlined. Each personality has to be cultivated to active charity—an essential requirement of the Christian; to authentic liberty in the Holy Spirit (there is further development of this in Art. 9); and to Christian maturity. The nature of Christian maturity is sketched in a few words. The interdependence of and responsibility for one another within the community are firmly stated.
73. *Cf. Gal. 4:3; 5:1 and 13.*
74. *Cf. St. Jerome, Epistles, 58, 7 (PL 22, 584): "Of what use is it if the walls gleam with jewels and Christ dies in a poor man?"*
75. *Cf. 1 Pet. 4:10 ff.*

the poor and the lowly entrusted to him in a special way. The Lord Himself showed that He was united to them,[76] and the fact that the gospel was preached to them is mentioned as a sign of Messianic activity.[77] With special diligence, priests should look after youth, as well as married people and parents. It is desirable that each of these groups join together in friendly associations and thereby help one another act more easily and adequately as Christians in a condition of life which is often demanding.

Priests should remember that all religious, both men and women, who have a distinguished place indeed in the house of the Lord, deserve special care in their pursuit of spiritual progress for the good of the whole Church.[78] Finally and above all, priests must be solicitous for the sick and the dying, visiting them and strengthening them in the Lord.[79]

The office of pastor is not confined to the care of the faithful as individuals, but is also properly extended to the formation of a genuine Christian community.[80] If community spirit is to be duly fostered, it must embrace not only the local Church but the universal Church. The local community should not only promote the care of its own faithful, but filled with a missionary zeal, it should also prepare the way to Christ for all men. To this community in a special way are entrusted catechumens and the newly baptized, who must be gradually educated to recognize and lead a Christian life.

No Christian community, however, can be built up unless it has its basis and center in the celebration of the most Holy Eucharist.[81] Here, therefore, all education in the spirit of community must originate.[82] If this celebration is to be sin-

---

76. *Cf. Mt. 25:34-45.*

77. *Cf. Lk. 4:18.*

78. A heavy demand is made on priests to help brothers and sisters to advance in the spiritual life. A similar obligation vis-a-vis those of the laity who are called to a higher spiritual life appears in Art. 9.

79. *Other categories could be named, e.g., migrants, nomads, etc. The Decree on the Bishops' Pastoral Office in the Church, Oct. 28, 1965, treats of these.*

80. The community which the priest forms must not be turned in upon itself, but, universal in spirit and outlook, turned outward as a community to the diocese, the universal Church, the city, the nation, and the world. This outgoing spirit is beautifully developed in the Pastoral Constitution on the Church in the Modern World.

81. Once again the celebration of the Eucharist is shown as the mainspring of the communitarian spirit, and a Christianity that is reduced to a mere fidelity to Mass-going is definitely rejected.

82. *Cf. "Didascalia," II, 59, 1-3 (ed. F. X. Funk, I, p. 170): "Teach them. Tell the people to come to church and not to stay away. Tell them to come to-*

cere and thorough, it must lead to various works of charity and mutual help, as well as to missionary activity and to different forms of Christian witness.

Moreover, by charity, prayer, example, and works of penance,[83] the Church community exercises a true motherhood toward souls who are to be led to Christ. For this community constitutes an effective instrument by which the path to Christ and to His Church is pointed out and made smooth for unbelievers, and by which the faithful are aroused, nourished, and strengthened for spiritual combat.

In building the Christian community, priests are never to put themselves at the service of any ideology or human faction. Rather, as heralds of the gospel and shepherds of the Church, they must devote themselves to the spiritual growth of the Body of Christ.

II. Priests as Related to Others

7. All priests, together with bishops, so share in one and the same priesthood and ministry of Christ that the very unity of their consecration and mission requires their hierarchical communion with the order of bishops.[84] At times they express this communion in a most excellent manner by liturgical concelebration.[85] At every Mass, however, they openly acknowledge that they celebrate the Eucharistic Action in union with the episcopate.[86] Therefore, by reason of the gift

gether always and not to constrict the church by staying away and making the body of Christ that much without a member. . . . do not let yourselves be separated from the church by not being united into one, for you are members of Christ. When you have Christ the Head present, according to His own promise, and communicating to you, do not neglect the Savior, do not cut Him off from His members, do not cut or scatter His body. . . ." Paul VI, allocution to Italian clergy present at the 13th week-long congress at Orvieto on pastoral aggiornamento, Sept. 6, 1963; AAS 55 (1963), pp. 750 ff.
83. For a world cushioned with increasing affluence and gadgets, special mention is made of the practice of penance, and the powerful effectiveness of a really-lived Christian life for the winning of others to Christ is recalled.
84. Cf. Second Vatican Council, dogmatic constitution "Lumen Gentium," Nov. 21, 1964, Art. 28: AAS 57 (1965), p. 35.
85. It is in concelebrating Mass that the bishop and his priests best show forth that intimate communion which is theirs because of their sharing in the one and the same priesthood and ministry of Christ, not to the same degree, of course, but in a hierarchical order.
86. Cf. cited "Ecclesiastical Constitution of the Apostles," XVIII: "Presbyteri sunt symmystai et synepimachoi Episcoporum" (ed. Th. Schermann, "Die allgemeine Kirchenordnung," I, Paderborn, 1914, p. 26; A. Harnack, T. u. U., II, 4, p. 13, Art 18 and 19); Pseudo-Jerome, "The Seven Orders of the Church," "in benedictione cum episcopis consortes mysteriorum sunt" (ed. A. W. Kalff, Wurzburg, 1937, p. 45); St. Isidore of Hispali, "Ecclesiastical Offices," c. VII (PL 83, 787); "Praesunt enim Ecclesiae Christi et in confectione Corporis et

of the Holy Spirit which is given to priests in sacred ordination, bishops should regard them as necessary helpers and counselors[87] in the ministry and in the task of teaching, sanctifying, and nourishing the People of God.[88]

Already in the ancient days of the Church we find liturgical texts proclaiming this relationship with insistence, as when they solemnly called upon God to pour out upon the candidate for priestly ordination "the spirit of grace and counsel so that with a pure heart he may help and govern the People [of God],"[89] just as in the desert the spirit of Moses was extended to the minds of seventy prudent men,[90] "and using them as helpers, he easily governed countless multitudes among the people."[91]

Therefore, on account of this communion in the same priesthood and ministry,[92] the bishop should regard priests as his brothers and friends.[93] As far as in him lies, he should

Sanguinis consortes cum episcopis sunt, similiter et in doctrina populorum et in officio praedicandi."

87. In stating that priests are "necessary helpers and counselors," the Decree wants to make clear that such priestly help and counsel are not a kind of extrinsic luxury at the whim of the bishop to use or not, nor can this priestly help and counsel be substituted by any other.

88. Cf. "Didascalia," II, 28, 4 (ed. F. X. Funk, p. 108); "Constitutions of the Apostles," II, 28, 4; II, 34, 3 (ibid., pp. 109 and 117).

89. "Constitutions of the Apostles," VIII, 16, 4 (ed. F. X. Funk, I, p. 522, 13); cf. "Epitome of the Constitutions of the Apostles," VI (ibid., II, p. 80, 3-4); "Testamentum Domini," (transl. I. E. Rahmani, Moguntiae, 1899, p. 69) ". . . give him the Spirit of grace, counsel, and magnanimity, the spirit of the priesthood . . . for helping and governing thy people in deed, in fear, in purity of heart." Also in "Trad. Apost." (ed. B. Botte, "La Tradition Apostolique," Munster, i.w. 1963, p. 20).

90. Cf. Num. 11:16-25.

91. Roman Pontifical, "Ordination of Priests," preface: these words are also found in the Leonine Sacramentary, the Gelasian Sacramentary, and the Gregorian Sacramentary. Similar words can be found in the Oriental Liturgies: cf. "Trad. Apost.": (ancient Latin version of Verona, ed. B. Botte, "La Tradition Apostolique de St. Hippolyte. Essai de reconstruction," Munster, i.w. 1963, p. 20); "Constitutions of the Apostles," VIII, 16, 4 (ed. F. X. Funk, I, p. 522, 16-17); "Epitome on the Constitutions of the Apostles," 6 (ed. F. X. Funk, II, p. 20, 5-7); "Testamentum Domini" (transl. I. E. Rahmani, Moguntiae, 1899, p. 69); "Euchologium Serapionis," XXVII (ed. F. X. Funk, "Didascalia and Constitutions," II, p. 190, 1-7); Maronite Rite of Ordination (Denz., "Rites of the Orientals," II, Wurzburg, 1863, p. 161). Among the Fathers can be cited: Theodore of Mopsuestia, "On First Timothy," 3, 8 (ed. Swete, II, pp. 119-121); Theodoretus, "Questions on Numbers," XVIII (PG 80, 372 b).

92. The foundation of the brother-relationship between the bishop and his priests is their common sharing in the one priesthood and ministry of Christ. The duty of priestly obedience is taught as being rooted in the priest's participation in the fullness of the bishop's ministry. Because of this hierarchic, subordinate participation, as the opening paragraph of this numbered section states, there is a necessary relationship of obedience of priest to bishop.

93. Cf. Second Vatican Council, dogmatic constitution "Lumen Gentium," Nov. 21, 1964, Art. 28: AAS 57 (1965), p. 35.

have at heart the material and especially spiritual welfare of his priests. For above all, upon the bishop rests the heavy responsibility[94] for the sanctity of his priests.[95] Hence, he should exercise the greatest care on behalf of the continual formation of his priests.[96] He should gladly listen to them, indeed, consult them,[97] and have discussions with them about those matters which concern the necessities of pastoral work and the welfare of the diocese.

In order to put these ideals into effect, a group or senate[98] of priests representing the presbytery should be established. It is to operate in a manner adapted to modern circumstances and needs[99] and have a form and norms to be determined by law.[100] By its counsel, this body will be able to

94. This insistence on the supreme duty of the bishop's spiritual formation of his priests is in line with St. Thomas's teaching (e.g., De Perfectione Vitae Spiritualis, cc. 17-18).
95. *Cf. John XXIII, encyclical letter "Sacerdotii Nostri Primordia," Aug. 1, 1959: AAS 51 (1959), p. 576; St. Pius X, exhortation to the clergy "Haerent Animo," Aug. 4, 1908; Acts of St. Pius X, vol. IV (1908), pp. 237 ff.*
96. *Cf. Second Vatican Council, Decree on the Bishops' Pastoral Office in the Church, Oct. 28, 1956, Art. 15 and 16.*
97. It is not said that the bishop has to consult all his priests about everything.
98. *St. Ignatius Martyr, "Magn." 6, 1: (ed. F. X. Funk, p. 234, 10-13): "Take care, I urge you, to do everything in the harmony of God, with the bishop presiding and taking the place of God, and the priest taking the place of the apostolic senate, and the deacons (who have a very special place in my heart) having entrusted to them the ministry of Jesus Christ who before all time was with the Father and has appeared at the end." St. Ignatius Martyr, "Trall.," 3, 1 (ibid., p. 244, 10-12): "Let all revere the deacon as Jesus Christ, just as we revere the bishop, who is a type of the Father, and the priests, whom we revere as the senate of God and the council of the apostles—without them it is not called a church." St. Jerome, "On Isaiah," II, 3 (PL 24, 61 A): "And we have our senate in the Church, the corps of priests (coetum presbytero-rum)."*
99. *The Cathedral Chapter is already found in established law, as the "senate and assembly" of the bishop (Code of Canon Law. c. 391), or if there is not one, an assembly of diocesan consultors (cf. Code of Canon Law, cc. 423-428). It is our desire to give recognition to such institutions so that modern circumstances and necessities may better be provided for. As is evident, this synod of priests differs from the pastoral "consilium" spoken of in the Decree on the Bishops' Pastoral Office of Oct. 28, 1965 (Art. 27), of which the laity can also be members, and whose function is mainly to map out a plan of action for pastoral work. Concerning priests as counselors of the bishops, one may refer to the "Didascalia," II, 28, 4 (ed. F. X. Funk, 1, p. 108); also "Constitutions of the Apostles," II, 28, 4 (ed. F. X. Funk, I, p. 109); St. Ignatius Martyr, "Magn." 6, 1 (ed. F. X. Funk, p. 234, 10-16); "Trall.," 3, 1 (ed. F. X. Funk, p. 244, 10-12); Origen, "Against Celsus," 3, 30: "Priests are counselors or 'bouleytai' " (PG 11, 957 d-960 a).*
100. Some indication of the nature of this representative body of priests is given in the Decree on the Bishops' Pastoral Office in the Church, Art. 27, but it will be the task of the commission now engaged on the revision of the Code of Canon Law to provide detailed norms. Remember also that provision has been made by the Ecumenical Council for a pastoral council embracing lay members and religious as well as priests to assist the bishop in his pastoral work.

give effective assistance to the bishop in his government of the diocese.

Keeping in mind the fullness of the sacrament of orders which the bishop enjoys, priests must respect in him the authority of Christ, the chief Shepherd. They must therefore stand by their own bishop in sincere charity and obedience.[101] This priestly obedience animated with a spirit of cooperation is based on the very sharing in the episcopal ministry which is conferred on priests both through the sacrament of orders and the canonical mission.[102]

This union of priests with their bishops is all the more necessary today since in our present age for various reasons apostolic activities are required not only to take on many forms, but to extend beyond the boundaries of one parish or diocese.[103] Hence no priest can in isolation or singlehandedly accomplish his mission in a satisfactory way. He can do so only by joining forces with other priests under the direction of Church authorities.

8. Established in the priestly order by ordination, all priests are united among themselves in an intimate sacramental brotherhood.[104] In a special way they form one presbytery[105] in a diocese to whose service they are committed under their own bishop. For even though priests are assigned to different duties they still carry on one priestly ministry on behalf of men.

All priests are sent forth as co-workers in the same undertaking, whether they are engaged in a parochial or supra-

101. Cf. Paul VI, allocution to the family heads of Rome and Lenten speakers, Mar. 1, 1965, in the Sistine Hall: AAS 57 (1965), p. 326.

102. Cf. "Constitutions of the Apostles," VIII 47, 39: (ed. F. X. Funk, p. 577): "Priests . . . should do nothing without agreement of the bishop, for he is the one to whose charge the people of God have been given, and from him will be demanded an accounting of their souls."

103. Cognizance is taken here of today's sociological factors which are cutting across the parochial unit and giving rise to large communities that are supra or interparochial, although the parish will certainly continue as the indispensable center of pastoral life.

104. By careful wording the Decree keeps the distinction between that union existing among priests in the total ambience of the Church and that which exists between priests of a diocese: the former is of divine ordinance, the latter is immediately of ecclesiastical law.

105. It is difficult to translate the word "Presbyterium." The Council consciously refused to use "college of priests" so that there would be no suggestion of any parallel between the diocesan "Presbyterium" and the "College of Bishops." The "College of Bishops" is an institution of divine law; the diocesan "Presbyterium" is an institution of ecclesiastical law. This "Presbyterium" is not the body of priests considered apart from the bishop. He is the very "raison d'etre" of the "Presbyterium": it is the priests together with, and under, the bishop. Cf. Constitution on the Church, Art. 28.

parochial ministry, whether they devote their efforts to scientific research[106] or teaching, whether by manual labor they share in the lot of the workers themselves—if there seems to be need for this and competent authority approves[107]—or whether they fulfill any other apostolic tasks or labors related to the apostolate.[108] All indeed are united in the single goal of building up Christ's Body, a work requiring manifold roles and new adjustments, especially nowadays.

Hence it is very important that all priests, whether diocesan or religious, always help one another to be fellow workers on behalf of truth.[109] Each one therefore is united by special bonds of apostolic charity, ministry, and brotherhood with the other members of this presbytery.

This fact has been manifested from ancient times in the liturgy, when the priests present at an ordination are invited to join with the ordaining bishop in imposing hands on the new candidate, and when priests concelebrate the sacred Eucharist in unity of heart. Each and every priest, therefore, is joined to his brother priests by a bond of charity, prayer, and every kind of cooperation. In this manner, they manifest that unity with which Christ willed His own to be perfectly one, so that the world might know that the Son has been sent by the Father.[110]

Consequently, older priests should receive younger priests as true brothers and give them a hand with their first undertakings and assignments in the ministry. They should likewise

106. Because the Council saw the search for truth in all spheres of science as a service to mankind and the increasing of God's glory among men, it refused to limit the priest's ministry in this regard to the sacred sciences, although it made sure to imply that such study had to be ordered to the apostolate: the priest must never forget that he is always a priest, divinely and totally committed to the ministry of Christ.
107. Conciliar recognition is given to the special apostolate of the "working" priest which is exercised by some in the Western Church and by certain Eastern rite priests. Because of its pioneering character and the difficulties, dangers, and controversy surrounding it, the Council hedges this form of priestly apostolate with the qualification that competent authority has to approve it: more than the normal mission and approval necessary for all priestly ministry are required in this case.
108. This whole paragraph aims to lessen the tensions that have come into the "Presbyterium" because our age demands an increasing number of "specialists." "Specialist" priests must not be considered as fish out of water. The love, prayer, and cooperation of the whole "Presbyterium" must enfold them. This mutual love and cooperation is non-exclusive. All priests, diocesan and those of religious congregations, are brought into its warm unity.
109. Cf. 3 Jn. 8.
110. Cf. Jn. 17:23.

try to understand the mentality of younger priests, even though it be different from their own, and should follow their projects with good will.[111] For his part, a young priest should respect the age and experience of his seniors. He should discuss plans with them, and willingly cooperate with them in matters which pertain to the care of souls.

Inspired by a fraternal spirit, priests will not neglect hospitality,[112] but cultivate kindliness and share their goods in common.[113] They will be particularly solicitous for priests who are sick, afflicted, overburdened with work, lonely, exiled from their homeland, or suffering persecution.[114] They will readily and joyfully gather together for recreation,[115] remembering the Lord's own invitation to the weary apostles: "Come apart into a desert place and rest a while" (Mk. 6:31).

Furthermore, in order that priests may find mutual assistance in the development of their spiritual and intellectual lives, that they may be able to cooperate more effectively in their ministry and be saved from the dangers which may arise from loneliness, let there be fostered among them some kind or other of community life. Such a life can take on several forms according to various personal or pastoral needs: for instance, a shared roof where this is feasible, or a common table, or at least frequent and regular gatherings.

Worthy too of high regard and zealous promotion are those associations whose rules have been examined by competent Church authority,[116] and which foster priestly holiness in the exercise of the ministry through an apt and properly approved rule of life and through brotherly assistance. Thus these associations aim to be of service to the whole priestly order.

Finally, by reason of the same communion in the priest-

111. There is a major problem about the best use of the energy, maturity, and talent of the younger priests in the Church, when in many dioceses they have to remain assistant priests (curates) for years. This paragraph touches on a few basic things that can be done at the present juncture, but by no means gives an adequate solution.
112. *Cf. Heb. 13:1-2.*
113. *Cf. Heb. 13:16.*
114. *Cf. Mt. 5:10.*
115. Again the idea of community is put forward. It is good to see recreation, joy, and laughter so written into a solemn Council document by our Mother, the Church.
116. With sensitive consideration for the personal life of the priest and his legitimate freedom, these priests' associations are not juridically placed under the bishops or episcopal conferences. Generally, of course, their statutes have to be approved by the competent ecclesiastical authority.

hood, priests should realize that they have special obligations toward priests who labor under certain difficulties. They should give them timely help[117] and also, if necessary, admonish them prudently. Moreover, they should always treat with fraternal charity and magnanimity those who have failed in some way, offering urgent prayers to God for them and continually showing themselves to be true brothers and friends.

9. In virtue of the sacrament of orders, priests of the New Testament exercise the most excellent and necessary office of father and teacher among the People of God and for them. They are nevertheless, together with all of Christ's faithful, disciples of the Lord, made sharers in His kingdom by the grace of God who calls them.[118] For priests are brothers among brothers[119] with all those who have been reborn at the baptismal font.[120] They are all members of one and the same body of Christ, whose upbuilding is entrusted to all.[121]

Priests therefore should preside in such a way that they seek the things of Jesus Christ,[122] not the things which are their own. They must work together with the lay faithful and conduct themselves in their midst after the example of their Master, who among men "has not come to be served but to serve, and to give his life as a ransom for many" (Mt. 20:28).[123]

Priests must sincerely acknowledge and promote the dignity of the laity and the role which is proper to them in the

117. Here the Church's heart and mind go out to the shepherds wandering in the mist, and she appeals to priests not to let a tempted brother priest drift too far, but to act in time and not let the bishop be the last one to know that a tragedy is imminent.

118. *Cf. 1 Th. 2:12; Col. 1:13.*

119. Rightly, much is made of the brother-relationship of the priest with the other members of the Christian community in this section, but, at the outset, the truth that he is their father and teacher is firmly planted. This ambivalence, that the priest is both father and brother, is, of course, expressed again and again in the Epistles of St. Paul. Priestly consecration does not nullify but intensifies that primary relationship of brotherhood established by baptism.

120. *Cf. Mt. 23:8.* Also Paul VI, encyclical letter "Ecclesiam Suam," Aug. 6, 1964: AAS 58 (1964), p. 647: *"In the very act of trying to make ourselves pastors, fathers and teachers of men, we must make ourselves their brothers."*

121. *Cf. Eph. 4:7 and 16; "Constitutions of the Apostles," VIII, 1, 20: (ed. F. X. Funk, I, p. 467): The bishop should not lord it over deacons or priests, and priests should not lord it over the people, for they both enter into the very makeup of the body.*

122. *Cf. Phil. 2:21.*

123. Read this whole section with Chap. 4 of the Constitution on the Church and the Decree on the Apostolate of the Laity.

mission of the Church.[124] They should scrupulously honor that just freedom which is due to everyone in this earthly city. They should listen to the laity willingly, consider their wishes in a fraternal spirit, and recognize their experience and competence in the different areas of human activity, so that together with them they will be able to read the signs of the times.

While testing spirits to see if they be of God,[125] priests should discover with the instinct of faith, acknowledge with joy, and foster with diligence the various humble and exalted charisms of the laity. Among the other gifts of God which are found in abundance among the faithful, those are worthy of special attention which are drawing many to a deeper spiritual life. Priests should also confidently entrust to the laity duties in the service of the Church, allowing them freedom and room for action. In fact, on suitable occasions, they should invite them to undertake works on their own initiative.[126]

Finally, priests have been placed in the midst of the laity to lead them to the unity of charity, that they may "love one another with fraternal charity, anticipating one another with honor" (Rom. 12:10). It is their task, therefore, to reconcile differences of mentality in such a way that no one will feel himself a stranger in the community of the faithful. Priests are defenders of the common good, with which they are charged in the name of the bishop. At the same time, they are strenuous defenders of the truth, lest the faithful be tossed about by every wind of opinion.[127] To their special concern are committed those who have fallen away from the use of the sacraments, or perhaps even from the faith. As good shepherds, they should not cease from going after them.

---

124. Practical recognition has to be given to the human dignity of the laity and their own proper role in the mission of the Church. They should open their minds, express their needs and desires freely and confidently. (Cf. Constitution on the Church, Art. 37.) And the priest is to be a good listener, recognizing their experience, competence, and the special gifts given them by God. Freedom and room for movement should be left them when they are given a task, and they should be encouraged to act on their own initiative. According to the Decree on the Apostolate of the Laity, Art. 26, diocesan, parochial, and interparochial councils consisting of the clergy, religious, and laity are to be set up, if possible, to assist in the apostolic work of the Church.
125. Cf. 1 Jn. 4:1.
126. Cf. Second Vatican Council, dogmatic constitution "Lumen Gentium," Nov. 21, 1964, Art. 37: AAS 57 (1965), pp. 42-43.
127. Cf. Eph. 4:14.

Mindful of this Council's directives on ecumenism,[128] let them not forget their brothers who do not enjoy full ecclesiastical communion with us.[129]

Finally, to them are commended all those who do not recognize Christ as their Savior.

The Christian faithful, for their part, should realize their obligations toward their priests and with filial love they should follow them as their shepherds and fathers.[130] Likewise sharing their cares, they should help their priests by prayer and work to the extent possible, so that their priests can more readily overcome difficulties and be able to fulfill their duties more fruitfully.[131]

III. The Distribution of Priests and Priestly Vocations

10. The spiritual gift which priests received at their ordination prepares them not for any limited and narrow mission but for the widest scope of the universal mission of salvation "even to the very ends of the earth" (Acts 1:8). For every priestly ministry shares in the universality of the mission entrusted by Christ to His apostles. The priesthood of Christ, in which all priests truly share, is necessarily intended for all peoples and all times. It is bound by no limits of blood, nationality, or time, a fact already mysteriously prefigured in the person of Melchisedech.[132]

Let priests remember then, that they must have at heart the care of all the churches.[133] Hence priests belonging to dioceses which are rich in vocations should show themselves willing and ready, with the permission or at the urging of

---

128. *Second Vatican Council, Decree on Ecumenism, Nov. 21, 1964: AAS 57 (1965), pp. 90 ff.*
129. A priest's concern extends wider than the care of his flock: it goes out to our brothers in Christ who are not in full communion with the Church, and to agnostics, atheists, etc.
130. As it began so this section ends with the figure of the priest as pastor and father for whom his people show a practical filial love.
131. *Cf. Second Vatican Council, dogmatic constitution "Lumen Gentium," Nov. 21, 1964, Art. 37: AAS 57 (1965), pp. 42-43.*
132. *Cf. Heb. 7:3.*
133. Channels are opened in this number for the stimulated flow of priests from the better staffed dioceses to the priest-starved areas of the Church. The Decree on the Bishops' Pastoral Office in the Church, Arts. 33-35, draws priests of religious congregations into this urgent operation challenging the modern Church.

their own bishop, to exercise their ministry in other regions, missions, or activities which suffer from a shortage of clergy.

In addition, the norms of incardination and excardination should be so revised that while this ancient practice remains intact it will better correspond to today's pastoral needs. Where an apostolic consideration truly requires it, easier procedures should be devised, not only for the appropriate distribution of priests, but for special pastoral objectives on behalf of diverse social groups, whether these goals are to be achieved in a given area, a nation, or anywhere on earth.

To these ends, therefore, there can be usefully established certain international seminaries, special dioceses, or personal prelatures and other agencies of this sort. In a manner to be decreed for each individual undertaking, and without prejudice to the rights of local Ordinaries, priests can thereby be assigned or incardinated for the general good of the whole Church.

As far as possible, priests should not be sent singly to a new field of labor, especially to one in whose language and customs they are not yet well versed. Rather, after the example of the disciples of Christ,[134] they should be sent in at least twos or threes so that they may be mutually helpful to one another. Likewise, thoughtful care should be given to their spiritual life as well as their mental and bodily strength. As far as possible the locale and circumstances of work should be adapted to the personal situation of each priest assigned.

At the same time it will be highly advantageous if those priests who seek to work in a nation new to them take care not only to know well the language of that place but also the psychological and social characteristics peculiar to the people they wish to serve in humility. Thus they will be able to communicate with them as successfully as possible and thereby imitate St. Paul, who could say of himself: "For, free though I was as to all, unto all I have made myself a slave that I might gain the more converts. And I have become to the Jews a Jew that I might gain the Jews" (1 Cor. 9:19-20).

11. The Shepherd and Bishop of our souls[135] so constituted His Church that the people whom He chose and purchased

---

134. *Cf. Lk. 10:1.*
135. *Cf. 1 Pet. 2:25.*

by His blood[136] would be due to have its priests always and to the end of time, lest Christians should ever be like sheep without a shepherd.[137] Acknowledging Christ's desire and inspired by the Holy Spirit, the apostles considered it their duty to select ministers "who shall be competent in turn to teach others" (2 Tim. 2:2). This duty then is a part of the priestly mission by which every priest is made a partaker in the care of the whole Church, so that workers may never be lacking for the People of God on earth.

Since, however, "a common concern unites the captain of a ship with its passengers,"[138] the whole Christian people should be taught that it is their duty to cooperate in one way or another, by constant prayer and other means at their disposal,[139] so that the Church may always have the necessary number of priests to carry out her divine mission. In the first place, therefore, by the ministry of the Word and by the personal testimony of a life radiant with the spirit of service and true pascal joy, priests should have it dearly at heart to demonstrate to the faithful the excellence and necessity of the priesthood.

Sparing neither care nor inconvenience, let priests assist those young men or adults whom they prudently judge to be fit for so great a ministry, that they may prepare themselves properly and then at last with full external and internal freedom be able to be called by the bishop. In this effort, careful and prudent spiritual direction is of the greatest value.

Parents and teachers and all who are in any way engaged in the education of boys and young men should so prepare them that, recognizing the Lord's concern for His flock and considering the needs of the Church, they will be ready to respond generously to our Lord if He should call, and will say with the prophet: "Lo, here am I, send me" (Is. 6:8).

This voice of the Lord in summons, however, is never to be looked for as something which will be heard by the ears of future priests in any extraordinary manner. It is rather to be detected and weighed in the signs by which the will of God is customarily made known to prudent Christians. These indications should be carefully noted by priests.[140]

---

136. *Cf. Acts 20:28.*
137. *Cf. Mt. 9:36.*
138. *Roman Pontifical, "Ordination of Priests."*
139. *Cf. Second Vatican Council, Decree on Priestly Formation, Oct. 28, 1965, Art 2.*
140. *"The voice of God that calls is expressed in two different ways, won-*

Vocational projects, therefore, whether diocesan or national, are warmly recommended to priests.[141] In sermons, in catechetical instructions, and in written articles, priests should eloquently set forth the needs of the Church both local and universal, putting into vivid light the nature and excellence of the priestly ministry. In this ministry, weighty responsibilities are mixed with profound joys. In it especially, as the Fathers of the Church teach, a supreme testimony of love can be given to Christ.[142]

CHAPTER III

THE LIFE OF PRIESTS

I. The Priestly Call to Perfection

12. By the sacrament of orders priests are configured to Christ the Priest so that as ministers of the Head and co-workers of the episcopal order they can build up and establish His whole Body which is the Church. Already indeed, in the consecration of baptism, like all Christians, they received

drous and converging: the one interior, that of grace, that of the Holy Spirit, the inexpressible way of that interior charm exercised by the silent and powerful voice of the Lord in the unsearchable depths of the human soul; the other exterior, human, perceivable, social, juridical, concrete, that of the qualified minister of the word of God, that of the apostle, that of the hierarchy, the indispensable instrument instituted and willed by Christ, as the vehicle charged with translating into perceptible language the message of the divine word and command. Catholic doctrine so teaches with St. Paul: 'How are they to hear, if no one preaches. . . . Faith then depends on hearing' (Rom. 10:14 and 17). Paul VI, allocution of May 5, 1965: L'Osservatore Romano, May 6, 1965, p. 1. In the official footnote, the quotation from Pope Paul's allocution is given in Italian, which makes this footnote quite unusual among the Council documents.—Ed.
141. Cf. Second Vatican Council, Decree on Priestly Formation, Oct. 28, 1965, Art. 2.
142. The Fathers teach this in their explanations of Christ's words to Peter: "Do you love me? . . . Feed my sheep." (Jn. 21:17); thus St. John Chrysostom, "On the Priesthood," II, 1-2 (PG 47-48, 633); St. Gregory the Great, "Reg. Past. Liber," P. I. c. 5 (PL 77, 19 a).

the sign and the gift of so lofty a vocation and a grace that
even despite human weakness[143] they can and must pursue
perfection according to the Lord's words: "You therefore are
to be perfect, even as your heavenly Father is perfect" (Mt.
5:48).[144]

To the acquisition of this perfection priests are bound by
a special claim, since they have been consecrated to God in
a new way by the reception of orders. They have become living instruments of Christ the eternal priest, so that through
the ages they can accomplish His wonderful work of reunit-
ing the whole society of men with heavenly power.[145]
Therefore, since every priest in his own way represents the
person of Christ Himself, he is also enriched with special
grace. Thus, serving the people committed to him and the
entire People of God, he can more properly imitate the perfection of Him whose part he takes. Thus, too, the weakness
of human flesh can be healed by the holiness of Him who
has become for our sake a high priest "holy, innocent, undefiled, set apart from sinners" (Heb. 7:26).

Christ, whom the Father sanctified and consecrated, and
sent into the world,[146] "gave himself for us that he might
redeem us from all iniquity and cleanse for himself an acceptable people, pursuing good works" (Tit. 2:14). And so He
entered into His glory through His Passion.[147] Likewise,
consecrated by the anointing of the Holy Spirit and sent by
Christ, priests mortify in themselves the deeds of the flesh
and devote themselves entirely to the service of men.[148]

---

143. *Cf. 2 Cor. 12:9.*
144. Already in the Constitution on the Church (Chap. 5), the Council has
taught that all in the Church, the laity and hierarchy without distinction, are
destined for holiness, the perfection of charity. Again it is repeated here
in tune with this Decree's continuous effort to insure that priests are
not separated from the Christian community. Their priestly ordination,
presupposing their baptismal consecration and call to sanctity, binds them
by a new consecration to its attainment. Because of the role allotted to
them as living instruments for the continuation of Christ's redemption of
man, they are enriched with particular grace so that in and through their
service of their people and the Church universal they can strive after the
sanctity of Christ.
145. *Cf. Pius XI, encyclical letter "Ad Catholici Sacerdotii," Dec. 20,
1935: AAS 28 (1936), p. 10.*
146. *Cf. Jn. 10:36.*
147. *Lk. 24:26.*
148. See introductory essay for the way in which the priest's holiness is
related to his ministry. He is primarily made holy through his ministry
exercised in the Spirit of Christ. This, of course, does not imply for a
moment that there is no need of constant, personal, interior, conscious
effort. This is why the Council inserted the phrase "they mortify in themselves the works of the flesh."

Thus they can grow in the sanctity with which they are endowed in Christ, to the point of perfect manhood.[149]

And so it is that they are grounded in the life of the Spirit while they exercise the ministry of the Spirit and of justice,[150] as long as they are docile to Christ's Spirit, who vivifies and leads them. For by their everyday sacred actions themselves, as by the entire ministry which they exercise in union with the bishop and their fellow priests, they are being directed toward perfection of life.

Priestly holiness itself contributes very greatly to a fruitful fulfillment of the priestly ministry. True, the grace of God can complete the work of salvation even through unworthy ministers. Yet ordinarily God desires to manifest His wonders through those who have been made particularly docile to the impulse and guidance of the Holy Spirit. Because of their intimate union with Christ and their holiness of life, these men can say with the Apostle: "It is now no longer I that live, but Christ lives in me" (Gal. 2:20).

This most holy Synod desires to achieve its pastoral goals of renewal within the Church, of the spread of the gospel throughout the world, and of dialogue with the modern world. Therefore it fervently exhorts all priests to use the appropriate means endorsed by the Church[151] as they ever strive for that greater sanctity which will make them increasingly useful instruments in the service of all of God's People.

13. Priests will attain sanctity in a manner proper to them if they exercise their offices sincerely and tirelessly in the Spirit of Christ.[152]

Since they are ministers of God's Word, they should every day read and listen to that Word which they are required to

---

149. *Cf. Eph. 4:13.*
150. *Cf. 2 Cor. 3:8-9.*
151. *Cf. among others:*
   St. Pius X, exhortation to the clergy "Haerent animo," Aug. 4, 1908: *St. Pius X, AAS 4 (1908), pp. 237 ff.*
   Pius XI, encyclical letter "Ad Catholici Sacerdotii," Dec. 20, 1935; *AAS 28 (1936).*
   Pius XII apostolic exhortation "Menti nostrae," Sept. 23, 1950: *AAS (1950), pp. 657 ff.*
   John XXIII, encyclical letter "Sacerdoti Nostri primordia," Aug. 1, 1959: *AAS 51 (1959), pp. 545 ff.*
152. This article shows that the tonality of Christian holiness that is especially priestly is determined by the threefold ministry to which the priest is consecrated: the ministry of the Word, the ministry of the sacraments and the Eucharist, and the ministry of ruling and pasturing the People of God. Priestly sanctity is not only a requirement of this service, which is his total committal, but is nourished and perfected by it.

teach to others. If they are at the same time preoccupied with welcoming this message into their own hearts, they will become ever more perfect disciples of the Lord.[153] For as the Apostle Paul wrote to Timothy: "Meditate on these things, give thyself entirely to them, that thy progress may be manifest to all. Take heed to thyself and to thy teaching, be earnest in them. For in so doing thou wilt save both thyself and those who hear thee" (1 Tim. 4:15-16).

As priests search for a better way to share with others the fruits of their own contemplation,[154] they will win a deeper understanding of "the unfathomable riches of Christ" (Eph. 3:8) as well as the manifold wisdom of God.[155] Remembering that it is the Lord who opens hearts[156] and that sublime utterance comes not from themselves but from God's power,[157] in the very act of preaching His word they will be united more closely with Christ the Teacher and be led by His Spirit. Thus joined to Christ, they will share in God's love, whose mystery, hidden for ages,[158] has been revealed in Christ.

As ministers of sacred realities, especially in the Sacrifice of the Mass, priests represent the person of Christ in a special way. He gave Himself as a victim to make men holy. Hence priests are invited to imitate the realities they deal with. Since they celebrate the mystery of the Lord's death, they should see to it that every part of their being is dead to evil habits and desires.[159]

Priests fulfill their chief duty in the mystery of the Eucharistic Sacrifice. In it the work of our redemption continues to be carried out.[160] For this reason, priests are strongly urged to celebrate Mass every day,[161] for even if the faithful

---

153. Speaking the Word of the living God, he is at the same time both teacher and disciple of the Lord. No mere verbal performance, no matter how learned, this utterance of the living Word, but, in its perfection, a communication of the mystery of Christ that the priest, through his contact with Christ the Teacher and His Spirit, makes the very texture of his life.
154. Cf. St. Thomas "Summa Theol.," II-II, q. 188, a. 7.
155. Cf. Heb. 3:9-10.
156. Acts 16:14.
157. Cf. 2 Cor. 4:7.
158. Cf. Eph. 3:9.
159. Cf. Roman Pontifical, "Ordination of Priests."
160. Cf. Roman Missal, Prayer over the Offerings of the Ninth Sunday after Pentecost.
161. In earnestly commending the daily celebration of the Mass to priests, even if it is not possible to have the people present, the Council gives the reason for it, viz., because it is always the great action of Christ and the Church. The Council says no more than this. Further explanation is left to the theologians, but the Council intends all to keep in mind the

are unable to be present, it is an act of Christ and the Church.[162]

So it is that while priests are uniting themselves with the act of Christ the Priest, they are offering their whole selves every day to God. While being nourished by the Body of Christ, their hearts are sharing in the love of Him who gives Himself as food for His faithful ones.

In a similar way, they are joined with the intention and love of Christ when they administer the sacraments. Such is especially the case when they show themselves entirely and always ready to perform the office of the sacrament of penance as often as the faithful reasonably request it. By reciting the Divine Office, they lend their voice to the Church as in the name of all humanity she perseveres in prayer along with Christ, who "lives always to make intercession for us" (Heb. 7:25).

Guiding and nourishing God's People, they are inspired by the love of the Good Shepherd to give their lives for their sheep.[163] They are ready to make the supreme sacrifice, following the example of those priests who even in our time have not refused to lay down their lives.

Since they are teachers in the faith, they themselves "are free to enter the Holies in virtue of the blood of Christ" (Heb. 10:19) and approach God "with a true heart in fullness of faith" (Heb. 10:22). They can build up a firm hope concerning their people.[164] Those who are in any distress they can console with the encouragement by which God encourages them.[165]

As rulers of the community, they ideally cultivate the as-

relevant doctrine of the Constitution on the Sacred Liturgy, Art. 26 and 27, especially that celebration of the Mass in which the people actively participate is to be preferred to a private celebration.

162. "A priest may offer a Mass in private, but no Mass is a private thing; it is an act of Christ and of the Church. In offering this sacrifice, the church learns to offer herself as a sacrifice for all, and she applies the single, boundless, redemptive power of the sacrifice of the cross for the salvation of the entire world. The fact is that every Mass which is celebrated is offered not for the salvation of ourselves alone but for the salvation of the whole world. . . . Therefore, from a paternal and solicitous heart we earnestly recommend to priests, who are our special joy and our crown in the Lord, that . . . they worthily and devoutly offer Mass each day." Paul VI, encyclical letter "Mysterium Fidei," Sept. 3, 1965: AAS 57 (1965), pp. 761-762. Cf. Second Vatican Council, Constitution on the Sacred Liturgy, Dec. 4, 1963, Art. 26 and 27; AAS 56 (1964), p. 107.

163. Cf. Jn. 10:11.
164. Cf. 2 Cor. 1:7.
165. Cf. 2 Cor. 1:4.

ceticism proper to a pastor of souls, renouncing their own conveniences,[166] seeking what is profitable for the many and not for themselves, so that the many may be saved.[167] They are always going to greater lengths to fulfill their pastoral duties more adequately. Where there is' need, they are ready to undertake new pastoral approaches under the lead of the loving Spirit who breathes where He will.[168]

14. In today's world men have so many obligations to fulfill. There is, too, such a great diversity of problems vexing them, and often enough, they have to attend to them hastily. As a result they are sometimes in danger of scattering their energies in many directions.

For their part, priests, who are already involved in and distracted by the very numerous duties of their office, cannot without anxiety seek for a way which will enable them to unify their interior lives with their program of external activities. No merely external arrangement of the works of the ministry, no mere practice of religious exercises can bring about this unity of life, however much these things can help foster it. But priests can truly build up this unity by imitating Christ the Lord in the fulfillment of their ministry,[169] His food was to do the will of Him who sent Him to accomplish His work.[170]

In very fact Christ works through His ministers to achieve unceasingly in the world that same will of the Father by means of the Church. Hence Christ forever remains the source and origin of their unity of life. Therefore priests attain to the unity of their lives by uniting themselves with Christ in acknowledging the Father's will and in the gift of themselves on behalf of the flock committed to them.[171]

---

166. The asceticism proper to the priest is his day-to-day service as pastor of his people, which involves the giving of himself to their needs, his own convenience taking second place.
167. Cf. 1 Cor. 10:33.
168. Cf. Jn. 3:8.
169. See introductory essay for comment on this Article, which shows how and why the priest's holiness flows from his ministry. In these few paragraphs unity and harmony are brought into the life and work of the priest, who today has to be involved, as Art. 3 teaches, for otherwise he could not serve modern man in a world of frightening, frenetic activity. Christ is his life's fulcrum and it is from the taproot of the Eucharistic Sacrifice that he draws into his life that pastoral charity which is his bond of perfection. His fidelity to Christ is indivisible from his fidelity to his Church, which fidelity once again evokes the communitarian, ecclesial theme running through the Decree, for it involves intimate communion with the bishops and their other brothers in the priesthood.
170. Cf. Jn. 4:34.
171. Cf. 1 Jn. 3:16.

Thus, by assuming the role of the Good Shepherd, they will find in the very exercise of pastoral love the bond of priestly perfection which will unify their lives and activities. This pastoral love[172] flows mainly from the Eucharistic Sacrifice, which is therefore the center and root of the whole priestly life. The priestly soul strives thereby to apply to itself the action which takes place on the altar of sacrifice. But this goal cannot be achieved unless priests themselves penetrate ever more deeply through prayer into the mystery of Christ.

That they may be able to verify the unity of their lives in concrete situations too, they should subject all their undertakings to the test of God's will,[173] which requires that projects should conform to the laws of the Church's evangelical mission. For loyalty toward Christ can never be divorced from loyalty toward His Church.

Hence pastoral love requires that a priest always work in the bond of communion with the bishop and with his brother priests, lest his efforts be in vain.[174] If he acts in this way, a priest will find the unity of his own life in the very unity of the Church's mission. Thus he will be joined with the Lord, and through Him with the Father in the Holy Spirit. Thus he will be able to be full of consolation and to overflow with joy.[175]

II. Special Spiritual Needs of the Priestly Life

15. Among the virtues most necessary for the priestly ministry must be named that disposition of soul by which priests are always ready to seek not their own will, but the will of Him who sent them.[176] For the divine work which the Holy Spirit has raised them up[177] to fulfill transcends all human energies and human wisdom: ". . . the foolish things of the world has God chosen to put to shame the 'wise' " (1 Cor. 1:27).

Therefore, conscious of his own weakness, the true minister of Christ labors in humility, testing what is God's will.[178]

172. *"May it be a duty of love to feed the Lord's flock"* (St. Augustine, *"Tract on John,"* 123, 5: PL 35, 1967).
173. *Cf. Rom. 12:2.*
174. *Cf. Gal. 2:2.*
175. *Cf. 2 Cor. 7:4.*
176. *Cf. Jn. 4:34; 5:30; 6:38.*
177. *Cf. Acts 13:2.*
178. *Cf. Eph. 5:10.*

In a kind of captivity to the Spirit[179] he is led in all things by the will of Him who wishes all men to be saved. He can detect and pursue this will in the circumstances of daily life by humbly serving all those who are entrusted to him by God through the office assigned to him and through the various happenings of his life.

Since the priestly ministry is the ministry of the Church herself, it can be discharged only by hierarchical communion with the whole body. Therefore pastoral love demands that acting in this communion, priests dedicate their own wills through obedience[180] to the service of God and their brothers. This love requires that they accept and carry out in a spirit of faith whatever is commanded or recommended by the Sovereign Pontiff, their own bishop, or other superiors.

Let them very gladly spend themselves and be spent[181] in any task assigned to them, even the more lowly and poor ones. For in this way they will preserve and strengthen the necessary unity with their brothers in the ministry, most of all with those whom the Lord has appointed the visible rulers of His Church. Thus too they will work to build up Christ's Body, which grows "through every joint of the system."[182]

This obedience leads to the more mature freedom[183] of God's sons. Of its nature it demands that in the fulfillment of their duty priests lovingly and prudently look for new avenues for the greater good of the Church. At the same time, it demands that they confidently propose their plans and urgently expose the needs of the flock committed to them, while remaining ready to submit to the judgment of those who exercise the chief responsibility for governing the Church of God.

By such responsible and voluntary humility and obedience,

179. *Cf. Acts 20:22.*
180. The obedience of the priest springs from several sources. It is postulated by the very nature of his ministry, which, in so far as it is a ministry inserted into an ordered hierarchic whole, involves obedience. Because the priestly ministry is the work of the whole Church, unity of action is demanded and therefore obedience. Finally, that charity which is the source of all virtues and the spur of the whole ministry of the priest requires that he act in communion with his superiors.
181. *Cf. 2 Cor. 12:15.*
182. *Cf. Eph. 4:11-16.*
183. The priest's obedience does not lead to infantilism nor make him a cautious yes-man, but rather enables him to breathe more fully the free air of the sons of God. It does not make him a puppet without initiative of his own, but, indeed, demands that in the fulfilling of his office he search out new ways for the building of the kingdom of Christ, frankly and fully open his mind and bring to the notice of superiors the needs of his people, always, of course, with the serenity engendered by his obedience.

priests make themselves like Christ, having in themselves the attitude which was in Christ Jesus, who "emptied himself, taking the nature of a slave . . . becoming obedient to death" (Phil. 2:7-9). By such obedience Christ overcame and redeemed the disobedience of Adam. For as the Apostle gave witness: "By the disobedience of the one man the many were constituted sinners, so also by the obedience of the one the many will be constituted just" (Rom. 5:19).

16. With respect to the priestly life, the Church has always held in especially high regard perfect and perpetual continence[184] on behalf of the kingdom of heaven. Such continence was recommended by Christ the Lord[185] and has been gladly embraced and praiseworthily observed down through the years and in our day too by many Christians. For it simultaneously signifies and stimulates pastoral charity and is a special fountain of spiritual fruitfulness on earth.[186] It is not, indeed, demanded by the very nature of the priesthood, as is evident from the practice of the primitive Church[187] and from the tradition of the Eastern Churches. In these Churches, in addition to all bishops and those others who by a gift of grace choose to observe celibacy, there also exist married priests of outstanding merit.

While this most sacred Synod recommends ecclesiastical celibacy, it in no way intends to change that different discipline which lawfully prevails in Eastern Churches. It lovingly exhorts all those who have received the priesthood after marriage to persevere in their sacred vocation, and to continue to spend their lives fully and generously for the flock committed to them.[188]

Celibacy accords with the priesthood on many scores. For the whole priestly mission is dedicated to that new humanity which Christ, the conqueror of death, raises up in the world through His Spirit. This humanity takes its origin "not of blood, nor of the will of the flesh, nor of the will of man, but of God" (Jn. 1:13). Through virginity or celibacy observed for the sake of the kingdom of heaven,[189] priests are

---

184. See the comment on priestly celibacy in the introductory essay.
185. *Cf. Mt. 19:12.*
186. *Cf. Second Vatican Council, dogmatic constitution "Lumen Gentium," Nov. 21, 1964, Art. 42: AAS 57 (1965), pp. 47-49.*
187. *Cf. 1 Tim. 3:2-5: Tit. 1:6.*
188. *Cf. Pius XI, encyclical letter "Ad Catholici Sacerdotii," Dec. 20, 1935: AAS 28 (1936), p. 28.*
189. *Cf. Mt. 19:12.*

consecrated to Christ in a new and distinguished way. They more easily hold fast to Him with undivided heart.[190] They more freely devote themselves in Him and through Him to the service of God and men. They more readily minister to His kingdom and to the work of heavenly regeneration, and thus become more apt to exercise paternity in Christ, and do so to a greater extent.

Hence in this way they profess before men that they desire to dedicate themselves in an undivided way to the task assigned to them, namely, to betroth the faithful to one man, and present them as a pure virgin to Christ.[191] They thereby evoke that mysterious marriage which was established by God and will be fully manifested in the future, and by which the Church has Christ as her only spouse.[192] Moreover, they become a vivid sign of that future world which is already present through faith and charity, and in which the children of the resurrection will neither marry nor take wives.[193]

For these reasons, which are based on the mystery of the Church and her mission, celibacy was at first recommended to priests. Then, in the Latin Church, it was imposed by law on all who were to be promoted to sacred orders. This legislation, to the extent that it concerns those who are destined for the priesthood, this most holy Synod again approves and confirms. It trusts in the Spirit that the gift of celibacy, which so befits the priesthood of the New Testament, will be generously bestowed by the Father, as long as those who share in Christ's priesthood through the sacrament of orders, and indeed the whole Church, humbly and earnestly pray for it.

This holy Synod likewise exhorts all priests who, trusting in God's grace, have freely undertaken sacred celibacy in imitation of Christ to hold fast to it magnanimously and wholeheartedly. May they persevere faithfully in this state, and recognize this surpassing gift which the Father has given them, and which the Lord praised so openly.[194] Let them keep in mind the great mysteries which are signified and fulfilled in it.

---

190. *Cf. 1 Cor. 7:32-34.*
191. *Cf. 2 Cor. 11:2.*
192. *Cf. Second Vatican Council, dogmatic constitution "Lumen Gentium," Nov. 21, 1964, Art. 42 and 44: AAS 57 (1965), pp. 47-49 and 50-51; Decree on the Appropriate Renewal of Religious Life, Oct. 28, 1965, Art. 12.*
193. *Cf. Lk. 20:35-36; Pius XI, encyclical letter "Ad Catholici Sacerdotii," Dec. 20, 1935, AAS 28 (1936) pp. 24-28; Pius XII, encyclical letter "Sacra Virginitas," Mar. 25, 1954, AAS 46 (1954), pp. 169-172.*
194. *Cf. Mt. 19:11.*

Many men today call perfect continence impossible. The more they do so, the more humbly and perseveringly priests should join with the Church in praying for the grace of fidelity. It is never denied to those who ask. At the same time let priests make use of all the supernatural and natural helps which are available to all. Let them not neglect to follow the norms, especially the ascetical ones, which have been tested by the experience of the Church and which are by no means less necessary in today's world. And so this most holy Synod beseeches not only priests, but all the faithful to have at heart this precious gift of priestly celibacy. Let all beg of God that He may always lavish this gift on His Church abundantly.

17. By friendly and fraternal dealings among themselves and with other men, priests can learn to cultivate human values and to esteem created goods as gifts of God.[195] Still as they go about in this world they should always realize that according to the word of our Lord and Master they are not of this world.[196] Therefore, using the world as though they used it not,[197] they will attain to that liberty which will free them from all excessive concern and make them docile to the divine voice which makes itself heard in everyday life.[198]

From this freedom and docility will grow a spiritual discernment through which a proper relationship to the world and its goods will be worked out. Such a relationship is highly important for priests, since the Church's mission is fulfilled in the midst of the world and since created goods are altogether necessary for the personal development of a man. Let them therefore be grateful for everything which the heavenly Father gives them for leading their lives properly. Nevertheless they ought to evaluate in the light of faith everything which comes their way. Thus they can be led to a right use of goods corresponding to God's will, and can reject whatever would be harmful to their mission.

The Lord is "the portion and the inheritance" (Num. 18:20) of priests. Hence they should use temporal goods only

---

195. There is in this Article, first, a consideration of the priest's right Christian use of temporal goods and then the question of voluntary poverty.
196. *Cf. Jn. 17:14-16.*
197. *Cf. 1 Cor. 7:31.*
198. A positive attitude, free of any taint of Manicheism, is inculcated in regard to human values and the good things of God's creation, but the priest must not be the prisoner of what the world has to offer, because his consecration demands that he especially be a free man.

for those purposes to which it is permissible to direct them
according to the teaching of Christ the Lord and the regulations of the Church.

With all possible help from experienced laymen,[199] priests
should manage those goods which are, strictly speaking, ecclesiastical as the norms of Church law and the nature of
the goods require. They should always direct them toward
the goals in pursuit of which it is lawful for the Church to
possess temporal goods. Such are: the arrangement of divine
worship, the procuring of an honest living for the clergy, and
the exercise of works of the sacred apostolate or of charity,
especially toward the needy.[200]

Without prejudice to particular law,[201] priests and bishops[202]
should devote primarily to their decent livelihood and to the
fulfillment of the duties of their proper state the benefits which
they receive when they exercise some church office. What remains beyond that they should devote to the good of the
Church or to works of charity. Therefore they should not
regard an ecclesiastical office as a source of profit,[203] nor
should they spend the revenue accruing to it for the advantage of their own families.[204] Hence by never attaching
their hearts to riches,[205] priests will always avoid any greedi-
ness and carefully abstain from any appearance of merchan-
dising.

Indeed, they are invited to embrace voluntary poverty.
By it they will be more clearly likened to Christ and will become more devoted to the sacred ministry. For Christ became poor for our sakes, whereas He had been rich, so that
we might be enriched by His poverty.[206] By their own example the apostles gave witness that God's free gift must be

---

199. Here the Council clearly opens the way for the priest's fuller employment of the often much greater competence of the laity in the handling
of ecclesiastical property, strictly so called.
200. *Council of Antioch, can. 25: Mansi 2, 1328; "Decree of Gratian,"
c. 23, c. 12 q. 1 (ed. Friedberg, I, pp. 684-685).*
201. *This is to be understood especially with regard to the laws and customs
prevailing in the Eastern Churches.*
202. It is worth noting here that the bishops in Council wanted mention
made of themselves together with their priests in this context. They considered it useful for the priest to know that they were imposing on themselves the same obligation they were putting on the priests.
203. The enriching of themselves and their relatives with money that
comes from their office is forbidden.
204. *Council of Paris a, 829, can. 15: M.G.H. Sect. III, "Concilia," t. 2,
para. 6 622; Council of Trent, Session XXV, "De Reform.," Chap 1.*
205. *Ps. 62:11 (Vg. 61).*
206. *Cf. 2 Cor. 8:9.*

freely given.[207] They knew how to abound and how to suffer want.[208]

After the example of that communion of goods which was praised in the history of the primitive Church,[209] some common use of things can pave the way to pastoral charity in an excellent manner.[210] Through this form of living, priests can laudably reduce to practice the spirit of poverty recommended by Christ.

Led, therefore, by the Lord's Spirit, who anointed the Savior and sent Him to preach the gospel to the poor,[211] priests as well as bishops will avoid all those things which can offend the poor in any way. More than the other followers of Christ, priests and bishops should spurn any type of vanity in their affairs. Finally, let them have the kind of dwelling which will appear closed to no one and which no one will fear to visit, even the humblest.[212]

III. The Means of Support for Priestly Life

18. That priests may be able to foster union with Christ in all the circumstances of life, they enjoy, in addition to the conscious exercise of their ministry, those means, common and particular, new and old, which the Spirit of God never ceases to stir up in the People of God and which the Church commends and indeed at times commands for the sanctification of her members.[213] Of all spiritual helps, those acts are outstanding by which the faithful receive nourishment from God's Word at the twofold table[214] of sacred Scripture and

207. *Cf. Acts 8:18-25.*
208. *Cf. Phil. 4:12.*
209. *Cf. Acts 2:42-47.*
210. Inviting priests to embrace voluntary poverty, the Decree boldly suggests to the priests of the 20th century something similar to a practice of the early Church, which involves a common sharing of goods.
211. *Cf. Lk. 4:18.*
212. While ordering priests and also bishops not to live in such a way that the poor are embarrassed to come to their homes and even feel repelled, the Council refused to lose sight of the fact that the Church's priests and bishops are also responsible for the affluent and, consequently, would not allow this text to be given a one-sided emphasis. There is a balance to be observed.
213. *Cf. Code of Canon Law, 125 ff.*
214. Having taught in Art. 13 that the priest's own proper way to holiness is in and through the sincere and indefatigable exercise, in the Spirit of Christ, of his ministry, the Decree now considers some of the more important aids to his sanctification. In continuity with the doctrine of its Dogmatic Constitution on Divine Revelation, the Council places the highest value on

the Eucharist.[215] It is obvious how important for the proper sanctification of priests is the energetic and frequent exercise of such acts.

To Christ the Savior and Shepherd, ministers of sacramental grace are intimately united through the fruitful reception of the sacraments, especially the repeated sacramental act of penance. For this sacrament, prepared for by a daily examination of conscience, greatly fosters the necessary turning of the heart toward the love of the Father of mercies. With the light of a faith nourished by spiritual reading, priests can carefully detect the signs of God's will and the impulses of His grace in the various happenings of life, and thus can become more docile day by day to the mission they have undertaken in the Holy Spirit.

They can always find a wondrous model of such docility in the Blessed Virgin Mary. Led by the Holy Spirit, she devoted herself entirely to the mystery of man's redemption.[216] With the devotion and veneration of sons, priests should lovingly honor this mother of the supreme and eternal Priest, this Queen of the Apostles and protectress of their ministry.[217]

That they may discharge their ministry with fidelity, they should prize daily conversation with Christ the Lord in visits of personal devotion to the most Holy Eucharist. They should gladly undertake spiritual retreats and highly esteem spiritual direction. In manifold ways, especially through approved methods of mental prayer and various voluntary forms of prayer, priests should search for and earnestly beg of God that Spirit of genuine adoration by which they themselves, along with the people entrusted to them, can unite themselves intimately with Christ the Mediator of the New Testament. Thus, as sons of adoption, they will be able to cry out: "Abba, Father" (Rom. 8:15).[218]

those acts of priestly piety which revolve around the two poles of the Church's life, the Bible and the Eucharist.
215. Cf. Second Vatican Council, Decree on the Appropriate Renewal of Religious Life, Oct. 28, 1965, Art. 6; Dogmatic Constitution on Divine Revelation, Nov. 18, 1965, Art. 21.
216. Cf. Second Vatican Council, dogmatic constitution "Lumen Gentium," Nov. 21, 1964, Art. 65: AAS 57 (1965), pp. 64-65.
217. Among the practices enumerated, one at first sight could be surprised by the omission of the Rosary, but remember that this is a document intended for the priests of the whole Church, and in the Eastern Churches our Lady is honored by other prayer forms.
218. No one school of spirituality is canonized in the Decree, as was made clear by the commission responsible for it.

19. In the sacred rite of ordination the bishop admonishes priests to be "mature in knowledge," and to make their doctrine "a spiritual medicine for God's People."[219] The knowledge of a sacred minister should be sacred, since it is drawn from a sacred fountain and is directed to a sacred goal. Hence that knowledge should be drawn primarily from reading and meditating on the sacred Scriptures.[220] But it should also be fruitfully nourished by a study of the Holy Fathers and Doctors and other annals of tradition.

In addition, that they may be able to provide proper answers to the questions discussed by the men of this age, priests should be well acquainted with the documents of the Church's teaching authority and especially of Councils and the Roman Pontiffs. They should consult, too, the best, approved writers in theological science.

Since in our times human culture and the sacred sciences are making new advances, priests are urged to develop their knowledge of divine and human affairs[221] aptly and uninterruptedly. In this way they will prepare themselves more appropriately to undertake discussions with their contemporaries.

That priests may more easily pursue their studies and learn methods of evangelization and of the apostolate to better effect, every care should be taken to provide them with opportune aids. Such would be the instituting of courses or of congresses, according to the conditions of each region, the establishment of centers dedicated to pastoral studies, the setting up of libraries, and appropriate programs of study conducted by suitable persons.

Bishops, moreover, as individuals or jointly, should consider working out some easier way for their priests to attend courses giving them the opportunity to acquire a better grasp of pastoral methods and theological science, to strengthen their spiritual lives, and to share their apostolic experiences with their brothers.[222] Such courses should be held at set

---

219. *Roman Pontifical, "Ordination of Priests."*
220. *Cf. Second Vatican Council, Dogmatic Constitution on Divine Revelation, Nov. 18, 1965, Art. 25.*
221. This section on study, although strongly encouraging priests to study both the sacred and other sciences and indicating practical provisions to help them thereto, does not conceive of the priest-student as aloof in an ivory tower of inconsequence. His study of Scripture, for example, must also be a meditation on God's Word, thus making it the fiber of his being. And he always has in view a sacred end: the purpose of entering more deeply into dialogue with contemporary man.
222. *Second Vatican Council, Decree on the Bishops' Pastoral Office in the Church, Oct. 28, 1965, Art. 16.*

times, especially a few years after ordination.[223] By these
and other appropriate helps newly appointed pastors and
those who are assigned to a new pastoral activity can be assisted with special care. The same is true of those who are
sent to another diocese or country.

Finally, bishops must be concerned that some persons dedicate themselves to a more profound knowledge of theological
matters. Thus there will never be any lack of suitable teachers to train clerics, and the rest of the clergy as well as the
faithful can be assisted in providing themselves with the
needed teaching. Thus, too, will be fostered that wholesome
advancement in the sacred disciplines which is altogether
necessary for the Church.

20. Dedicated to serving God through the discharge of the
task assigned to them, priests are worthy of receiving a just
recompense.[224] For, "the laborer deserves his wages" (Lk.
10:7),[225] and "the Lord directed that those who preach the
gospel should have their living from the gospel" (1 Cor.
9:14). Hence, where a fitting recompense of priests is not
otherwise provided for, the faithful themselves are bound by
a genuine obligation to see that the needed means can be
procured for them to lead a respectable and worthy life.
For it is in behalf of the welfare of the faithful that priests
labor.

Bishops are obliged to remind the faithful of their duty.
They should see to it either individually for their own dioceses or, better, through several bishops acting simultaneously for a common territory, that norms are set up by which a
decent upkeep can be duly provided for those who perform
some function in the service of God's People, or have done
so.

Depending on the nature of the office itself and the conditions of place and time, the recompense should be fundamentally the same for all those operating in the same circumstances. It should be adjusted to their situation and

223. *This course is not the same as the pastoral course which is to be under-*
taken immediately after ordination, spoken of in the Decree on Priestly
Training, Oct. 28, 1965, Art. 22.
224. A spirit of detachment from this world's goods and the excellence of
voluntary poverty have already been treated. Now the Council reminds us
that the Church's priests are worthy of equitable remuneration and places
squarely on the bishop the responsibility of keeping before the faithful
their obligation in this regard. The Council declares for a fundamental
equality of income for priests.
225. *Cf. Mt. 10:10; 1 Cor. 9:7; 1 Tim. 5:18.*

should also allow them to make a suitable return to those who dedicate themselves to the service of priests. It should also enable them to give some kind of personal assistance to the needy. From her earliest beginnings the Church has always held this ministry toward the poor in high regard.

Moreover, this recompense should be such as to allow priests a requisite and sufficient vacation each year. Bishops should see to it that priests can have a vacation of this sort.

The chief emphasis should be given to the office which sacred ministers fulfill. Hence the so-called benefice system should be abandoned or at least it should be reformed in such a way that the beneficiary aspect, that is, the right to revenues accruing to an endowed office, will be treated as secondary, and the main consideration in law will be accorded to the ecclesiastical office itself. From now on such an office should be understood as any function which has been permanently assigned and is to be exercised for a spiritual purpose.

21. The example should never be overlooked of the believers in the primitive Church at Jerusalem. There "they had all things in common" (Acts 4:32) and "distribution was made to each, according as anyone had need" (Acts 4:35). Accordingly it is supremely appropriate that at least in areas where clerical support depends entirely or largely on the offerings of the faithful, some kind of diocesan agency should collect the offerings made for this purpose.[226] The bishop is to administer it with the help of delegated priests and, where it may be useful, laymen skilled in economic affairs.

It is also desirable, to the extent possible, that in individual dioceses or regions a common fund be established out of which bishops can satisfy different obligations to persons serving the Church, and to meet various diocesan needs. Through it, also, wealthier dioceses can help poorer ones, providing for the wants of the latter out of their abundance.[227] This common fund should be drawn primarily from the offerings of the faithful, but can derive from other sources too, as determined by law.

---

226. It is strongly recommended that a common fund for the sustentation of priests be instituted in the diocese, to be administered by the bishop with the help of priest-delegates and, when useful, of lay experts in finance. The Council also desires the establishing of a common fund as a pool for diocesan works, and even a fund shared by several dioceses so that the richer can come to the aid of the poorer.
227. Cf. 2 Cor. 8:14.

In some nations social security is not yet properly organized toward the support of the clergy. In such places Episcopal Conferences should see to it that under the vigilance of the hierarchy sufficient provision is made for an appropriate program of preventive medicine and so-called health benefits, and for the necessary support of priests burdened by infirmity, ill health, or old age. To this end there can be set up diocesan programs—and these can be amalgamated—or programs simultaneously instituted for various dioceses, or associations initiated for a whole territory. In any case, pertinent ecclesiastical and civil laws should always be taken into account.

Motivated by a spirit of solidarity with their brothers and sharing in their trials,[228] priests should support these arrangements after they have been established. At the same time they should consider that they can thereby give themselves over entirely to the welfare of souls and practice poverty in a readier evangelical sense without anxiety about their future. Let those concerned be preoccupied that such associations in various nations be interrelated. In this way they can gain strength more surely and be more widely established.

CONCLUSION AND EXHORTATION

22. While contemplating the joys of priestly life, this most holy Synod cannot overlook the difficulties which priests experience in the circumstances of contemporary life.[229] For it realizes how deeply economic and social conditions and even the customs of men are being transformed, and how profoundly scales of value are being changed in the estimation of man.

As a result, the ministers of the Church and even, at times, the faithful themselves feel like strangers in this world, anx-

228. *Cf. Phil. 4:14.*
229. In this final word to her priests, Vatican Council II speaks realistically enough about the difficulties caused by the radical and rapid social and moral revolution of their world. But the tone is one of optimism. The world is not all bad. There are exciting new avenues to be explored by modern priestly initiative. No priest is alone in the struggle: the power of God is with him, and his brother priests and a great faithful people are of his company. God's saving plan for man, the mystery of Christ, is but gradually realized in history. Above all, faith will give them a sustaining vision and confidence in the victory of Christ.

iously looking for appropriate ways and words with which
to communicate with it. For the modern obstacles blocking
faith, the seeming sterility of their past labors, and also the
bitter loneliness they experience can lead them to the danger
of becoming depressed in spirit.

The world which is entrusted today to the loving ministry
of the pastors of the Church is that world which God so
loved that He gave His only Son for it.[230] The truth is that
though entangled indeed in many sins this world is also endowed with great talents and provides the Church with the
living stones[231] to be built up into the dwelling place of
God in the Spirit.[232] Impelling the Church to open new avenues of approach to the world of today, this same Holy Spirit
is suggesting and fostering fitting adaptations in the ministry
of priests.

Priests should remember that in performing their tasks they
are never alone. Relying on the power of Almighty God and
believing in Christ Who called them to share in His priesthood, they should devote themselves to their ministry with
complete trust, knowing that God can intensify in them the
ability to love.[233]

Let them be mindful too that they have as partners their
brothers in the priesthood and indeed the faithful of the entire world. For all priests cooperate in carrying out the
saving plan of God. This plan is the mystery of Christ, the
sacrament hidden from the ages in God.[234] It is brought to fulfillment only by degrees, through the collaboration of many
ministries in the upbuilding of Christ's Body until the full
measure of His manhood is achieved.

Since all of these realities are hidden with Christ in
God[235] they can be best grasped by faith. For the leaders of
the People of God must walk by faith, following the example
of the faithful Abraham, who in faith "obeyed by going out
into a place which he was to receive for an inheritance; and
he went out, not knowing where he was going" (Heb. 11:8).
The dispenser of the mysteries of God can be truly compared
to the man who sowed his field and of whom the Lord said:

230. *Cf. Jn. 3:16.*
231. *Cf. 1 Pet. 2:5.*
232. *Cf. Eph. 2:22.*
233. *Cf. Roman Pontifical, "Ordination of Priests."*
234. *Cf. Eph. 3:9.*
235. *Cf. Col. 3:3.*

"Then he slept and rose, night and day. And the seed sprouted and grew without his knowing it" (Mk. 4:27).[236]

As for the rest, the Lord Jesus Who said: "Take courage, I have overcome the world" (Jn. 16:33), did not by these words promise His Church a perfect victory in this world.

This most holy Synod truly rejoices that the earth has been sown with the seed of the Gospel and now bears fruit in many places under the influence of the Lord's Spirit. He it is who fills the whole earth and has stirred up a true missionary spirit in the hearts of many priests and faithful. For all of these blessings, this most holy Synod gives most loving thanks to all the priests of the world.

"Now to him who is able to accomplish all things in a measure far beyond what we ask or conceive, in keeping with the power that is at work in us—to him be glory in the Church and in Christ Jesus" (Eph. 3:20-21).

Each and every one of the things set forth in this Decree has won the consent of the Fathers of this most sacred Council. We too, by the Apostolic authority conferred on Us by Christ, join with the Venerable Fathers in approving, decreeing and establishing these things in the Holy Spirit, and we direct that what has thus been enacted in synod be published to God's glory.

Rome, at St. Peter's, December 7, 1965*

I, Paul, Bishop of the Catholic Church

There follow the signatures of the Fathers.

---

236. To clarify the sense of its use here, this section of Mark's Gospel is rendered in the indicative mood—Ed.

*Following the Decree there is an announcement entitled "A Suspension of the law" (Vacatio legis), declaring that June 29, 1966 is the effective date for laws contained in this Decree. The text is the same as that given in note 67 at the end of the Decree on Priestly Formation.—Ed.

A RESPONSE

When all Christendom today is told in new terms that "baptism is the ordination of the layman," the question leaps up naturally as to what more, then, is the ordination of the clergyman? In its Decree on the Ministry and Life of Priests, the Council boldly and winsomely opens up striking vistas of freedom here, classically restates the hallowed chain-of-command claims regarding ordination which the Reformation most violently rejected, and poignantly, prophetically, lifts up the servant role of the man of God in modern life.

From the start, a fresh and exciting note of the Decree is its repeatedly commending a new, unseparated, brotherly relation on the part of the priest—with his fellow-clergymen (particularly bishops and needy colleagues), with laymen in his congregation, and with secular-minded people in the world. The over-all mood is: "Come out of your solitary Masses, your prelatical doting upon rank or affluence, your privileged station at altar or confessional—and identify radiantly, humbly, with everyman!" Again and again the 1 Peter 2:9 calling of the whole People of God to be "a royal priesthood" is underlined, much as it might be in Protestant and especially Quaker appeals. And even though this window-opening, wide franchise must be variously withdrawn at other points in the document, there is here an amazing openness and "all ye are brethren" atmosphere for discussion.

A similar pervasive emphasis, which parallels the most sensitive Protestant accounts of the ministry today, is the earnest story here of what the priest is called actually to do and be in his daily task and witness. He is bidden to serve eagerly those in want. He is to identify, even radically, with the poor and the poor in spirit. He is sternly to discipline his selfish desires and to keep his devotions without fail. His delight is to "bring the saintlier ones to an appropriate exercise of the evangelical counsels," and to "show the faithful how to sing to the Lord hymns and spiritual songs." Here is no authoritarian cleric prompting sentimental veneration or advertising novenas with guaranteed benefits, moving among mere communicants in haughty eminence: he is the gracious, unassuming, joyful, completely honest and dependable servant of God and of common folk. He does hold in his hands the grace of the Eucharist, but the fire and healing of the preached and acted-out Word are his also. He preaches, directly and urgently, from Scripture. For an affluent age, with power and the panoply of war and stridency of bigness all about us, what prophetic limning out of the task of the clergyman!

The actual freedom of this contemporary priest, as person and apostle, is only touched upon—especially in his relation to bishop and hierarchy and superior. As Archbishop Young remarks in his introduction to this section, much more filling in is needed here. Priestly freedom has become a particularly crucial principle for American parish pastors, teachers, and clergy in orders, as there have been various tests of authority in recent years. The Decree, despite the insistence upon structured accountability which could be expected of authors who are bishops, repeatedly insists that brotherly understanding and not subservience should be the basic guide for authority.

Turning to specifically Protestant reactions to the document, we find emerging at once the Reformation claim as to what ordination does mean. The Council's necessary presupposition is of course plain: that our Lord appointed certain persons "who would be able by the sacred power of their order to offer sacrifice and to remit sins. . . . Christ sent the apostles just as He Himself had been sent by the Father. Through these same apostles He made their successors, the bishops, sharers in His consecration and mission. Their ministerial role has been handed down to priests in a limited degree" (Article 2). In Archbishop Young's rephrasing, the Council is saying that the priest thus "acts *in the person of* Christ." Once this interpretation of New Testament history is accepted, there is some basis for the whole structure of authority. But the Protestant's question, obviously, is whether this apostle or (the Hebrew term) *shaliach* or surrogate was appointed in any except an informal and spiritual sense. In the appointing, was there conceivably involved any "right of succession"? Was Paul, never so commissioned, thus a true apostle? Was "bishop" in any way distinct from "pastor" before 160 A.D.? Could not any believer, in the earliest time, serve the Communion? Was not "forgiving one another," in New Testament terms, only a two-way relationship? Undoubtedly the most sweeping claim of all, with which some Protestants would also hotly disagree, is that in the New Testament even the term or role of "priest" is renounced by all the apostles themselves and apparently by our Lord. At such points as these, the Decree makes clear the fact that it follows a wholly different principle of historicity, and a sharply contrasting hypothesis regarding "spiritual succession" in the Church, vis-a-vis the Reformation thinker—however amicable both sides may be.

A second broadly Protestant reservation involves the "perfection" which is enjoined among priests, to a degree or of a sort not normally expected of laymen. Sometimes the Decree merges the two, even though not quite echoing the comforting man-in-the-street assurance that "a clergyman is just an ordained layman"! Yet at other places the doctrine appears that clergy are by definition committed to a higher set of standards, commending and achieving a piety not really available to laymen. Certainly the special commendation accorded to clerical celibacy is in this category. Here Protestants assert that there is actually no "second-class citizenship" in piety or good works or acceptability before God: all must live by both "the precepts" and "the counsels." Illogically perhaps, these same Protestants do expect their ministers to "be good" or at least to "be pious" beyond the laymen's average, but the principle is not written into their theology. One point is clear: if clerical piety as outlined and commended in the Decree did lay hold upon men of the cloth in every communion, the Church would rapidly be unrecognizable!

We do well to look beyond such real and honest disagreement, to the spirit and tenor of the whole Decree noted at the start: evangelical concern which is both Catholic and Protestant for the ministry of the whole Church in the whole world. The moving phrases of the Conclusion and Exhortation are a recalling of the bonds which unite us: ". . . the ministers of the Church and even at times the faithful themselves, feel like strangers, anxiously looking for appropriate ways and words with which to communicate with it." Every contemporary apostle, whether in slum or suburb or classroom or mission outpost, knows too "the modern obstacles blocking faith, the seeming sterility of their past labors, and also the bitter loneliness. . . ." Yet the Decree exults in wonder that "the earth has been sown with the seed of the gospel and now bears fruit in many places under the influence of the Lord's Spirit." This is a startling, imminent ministry which we all share.

JOHN OLIVER NELSON

MISSIONS

IT IS WORTH noting that the Decree on the Missionary Activity of the Church *(Ad Gentes)* and the basic decree of Vatican II, the Constitution on the Church *(Lumen Gentium)*, both begin with a reference to the same passage from Isaiah which presents the People of God as being sent into the world to be the light and salvation of the unbelieving nations—the *gentes*. The connection between these two documents, however, goes much deeper than the similarity of the initial words; there is a substantial connection between the two.

Both documents illustrate the rediscovery of the true biblical nature of the Church and its mission to unbelievers. The mission of the Church to "those without," as belonging to the essential nature of the People of God, receives major stress in the Constitution on the Church; the Church has been sent to unbelievers to be the "sacrament of unity of the whole human race." The decree on the missions continues this theme, not merely by way of repeating it, but by locating this mission within the history and geography of the globe and in specifying its yet unaccomplished task in the context of the modern world.

Certainly, one of the major concerns of Vatican II was that it be an ecumenical Council—ecumenical in the sense of world-wide or global in concern. For understandable reasons, most Councils in the past millennium have been marked by a pronounced Western orientation. In Vatican II, despite its world-wide episcopal representation and the movement of contemporary secular osciety toward world-consciousness and community, there was some disposition to think that the mission of the Church would be completely fulfilled by the important task of making the Church a living presence in the de-Christianized society of the West. The Decree on the missions added a necessary and universal dimension to this mission by pointing to areas of the globe, in Asia and Africa especially, whose diverse cultures and teeming populations have not yet been penetrated by the gospel. "The Church sent by Christ to manifest the love of God for all men and nations understands missionary work as its immense task still to be performed," says the Decree.

Since these unbelieving nations are *gentes* in the scriptural sense of the term as opposed to unbelievers in a de-Christianized society, this work of the missions, involving as it does the preaching of the gospel for the first time and the building up of the Body of Christ to its full stature, is called by the Council "the greatest and holiest work of the Church." Against the background, too, of modern man's search for world unity it also heightens the relevance of the Church's mission to contemporary society.

In the decidedly scriptural approach which the mission Decree takes toward the problem of the missions, the master idea is one taken from the Pauline description of the Father's plan for the whole of humanity—"his loving design, centered in Christ to give history its fulfillment, by resuming everything in him, all that is in heaven, all that is on earth, summed up in him" (Eph. 1:9-11). "The essential reason for missionary activity is in summary deduced from that plan of God," it asserts. "It is God's plan that the whole body of men which makes up the human race should form one People of God, should be joined in one Body of Christ, should be built up together in one Temple of the Holy Spirit. . . . In respect to the accomplishment of this plan of God, the missionary activity of the Church must be declared absolutely necessary. In no other way but through it is the plan of God sedulously accepted and obediently carried into operation for the glory of God."

The task of carrying out this plan of God in all its magnificence and universality is the work, not of a few professional missionaries, but of the whole Church—all the People of God. "The whole Church is missionary," declares the Decree. This assertion, it should be pointed out, has to be understood not in the general sense that the Church has a mission to mankind but in the restricted meaning which the Decree gives to the term "missionary activity." It defines missionary work as that which is undertaken by the Church in favor of nations or peoples who have not yet heard the gospel and into whose non-Christian culture the gospel message has never been implanted, in other words, the modern *gentes,* the more than two billion non-Christian peoples of the world who live especially, but not exclusively, in Asia, Africa, and Oceania. Efforts to expand this definition to include some de-Christianized areas of the West where the number of unbelievers and half-believers is large were rejected by the Council as rendering the term "missions" unbiblical and meaningless. This, then, is the meaning of the Council's statement that "the whole Church is missionary"—this and the added fact that this missionary work is the task of the entire People of God.

Indeed, as the Decree points out, the task of reaching these people with the gospel message is a "fundamental duty" of all Christians. To dispel any possible doubt that might exist about this duty the Decree continues: "The sacred Synod, therefore, summons all to a deep internal renewal" in regard to the importance for all of missionary work. This renewal must be regarded as an essential part of the *aggiornamento* envisioned by the Council. "Everyone," it says, "should have a vivid realization of his personal responsibility for the spread of the gospel and should play his part in missionary work among non-Christians." The faithful expression of this fundamental duty results in what "is nothing less than the manifestation or epiphany of God's plan in the world and in history."

The universality of this plan in time and space, applying as it does to all cultures and all peoples of the world, is something which the Synod especially calls all Christians to lift up their minds and hearts to, as a necessary condition for their renewal and for the manifestation of God's plan in the world. "Of this People of God," it declares, "it was prophetically said: 'Extend the dimensions of your tents and stretch the canvas of your tabernacles. Don't be constricted'" (Is. 54:2). It insists that all the sons of the Church should have a vivid realization of "their responsibility for the world"; they should preserve in themselves a fervent "catholic," or universal, spirit and should devote themselves to the work of evangelization according to their state. For this reason, it adds: "All the Christian faithful should have a clear knowledge of the present state of the Church in the world and should give ear to the voice of the multitudes crying out 'Help us'" (Acts. 16:9).

Not only individuals but Christian communities also should manifest and make visible their essential missionary character. "The grace of renewal cannot increase in these communities unless one enlarges the extent of its charity to the ends of the earth and has a solicitude for far-off peoples like the one it has for its own members."

Although the Decree on the Missionary Activity of the Church is obviously directed toward all the People of God, it does contain many elements which apply, in the first place, to active missionaries and to the Church in the missions and only secondarily to the rest of the faithful. Among these elements, two should be pointed out briefly since they underline the direction which modern missionary work is taking in response both to the past progress of the missions and the movement of history.

As is quite evident throughout the text, the focus of missionary activity today is less on territorial expansion, which has been virtually achieved, than on making the Church an *active* presence within and native to the diverse and developing non-Christian cultures in which it exists. Hence the emphasis on dialogue with non-Christians, adaptation to local conditions, and participation in community and national life.

Coincident with this cultural and social outreach, there is also to be an intensification of consciousness on the part of the local community of its existence as a *church,* existing not on the margin but within the unity of the universal Church and through the cooperation and communion of the churches both contributing and receiving in an interchange of life which builds up the Body of Christ and gives witness to this divine presence in the world as the sacrament of the unity of mankind.

CALVERT ALEXANDER, S.J.

Decree on the Missionary Activity of the Church

PAUL, BISHOP

SERVANT OF THE SERVANTS OF GOD

TOGETHER WITH THE FATHERS OF THE SACRED COUNCIL

FOR EVERLASTING MEMORY

PREFACE

1. The Church has been divinely sent to all nations that she might be "the universal sacrament of salvation."[1] Acting out of the innermost requirements of her own catholicity and in obedience to her Founder's mandate (cf. Mk. 16:16), she strives to proclaim the gospel to all men.[2] For the Church was founded upon the apostles, who, following in the footsteps of Christ, "preached the message of truth and begot Churches."[3] Upon their successors devolves the duty of perpetuating this work through the years. Thus "the word of God may run and be glorified" (2 Th. 3:1) and God's kingdom can be everywhere proclaimed and established.

The present historical situation is leading humanity into a new stage.[4] As the salt of the earth and light of the world

---

1. *Dogmatic constitution "Lumen Gentium," 48.*
2. Of the two motives for the necessity of proclaiming the gospel to *all* men, namely, the command "Go into the whole world . . . ,'' and the demands made by the very nature of the Church's universality, the latter receives the major emphasis in this modern approach to the problem of the missions.
3. *St. Augustine, "Exposition on Psalm 44," 23 (PL 36, 508; CChr 38, 510).* *The 1941 CCD transl. has "the Lord" for "God."—Ed.
4. The "new" condition of man which makes world-wide evangelization "more urgent" today is, as the Constitution on the Church *(Lumen Gentium)* points out, the movement of modern man toward world community and the effective unity of mankind.

(cf. Mt. 5:13-14), the Church is summoned with special urgency to save and renew every creature. In this way all things can be restored in Christ, and in Him mankind can compose one family and one people.

Hence this holy Synod gives thanks to God for the splendid accomplishments already achieved through the noble energy of the whole Church. At the same time she wishes to sketch the principles of missionary activity and to marshal the forces of all the faithful. Her intention is that God's people, undertaking the narrow way of the cross, may spread everywhere the kingdom of Christ, the Lord and Overseer of the ages (cf. Sir. 36:19), and may prepare the way for His coming.

CHAPTER I

DOCTRINAL PRINCIPLES

2. The pilgrim Church is missionary by her very nature.[5] For it is from the mission of the Son and the mission of the Holy Spirit that she takes her origin, in accordance with the decree of God the Father.[6]

This decree flows from "that fountain of love" or charity within God the Father. From Him, who is "the origin without origin," the Son is begotten and the Holy Spirit proceeds through the Son. Freely creating us out of His surpassing and merciful kindness, and graciously calling us moreover to communicate in life and glory with Himself, He has generously poured out His divine goodness and does not cease to do so. Thus He who made all things may at last be "all in

---

5. The theological reasons why the Church on earth is missionary of its very nature, which are given here and in the subsequent paragraphs, are basically the same as those given in *Lumen Gentium,* with perhaps a greater insistence on the universality and comprehensiveness of God's plan for man's redemption and elevation which the Church is sent to carry out within the context of human history. It should be pointed out that the great contribution of *Lumen Gentium* to "the missions" was to locate the activity of the Church within the center of the Church's life instead of on its periphery.

6. *Cf. Dogmatic constitution "Lumen Gentium," 1.*

all" (1 Cor. 15:28), procuring at one and the same time His own glory and our happiness.

But it has not pleased God to call men to share His life merely as individuals without any mutual bonds. Rather, He wills to mold them into a people in which His sons, once scattered abroad, can be gathered together (cf. John 11:52).

3. This universal design of God for the salvation of the human race is not carried out exclusively in the soul of a man, with a kind of secrecy. Nor is it achieved merely through those multiple endeavors, including religious ones, by which men search for God, groping for Him that they may by chance find Him (though He is not far from any one of us) (cf. Acts 17:27). For these attempts need to be enlightened and purified, even though, through the kindly workings of Divine Providence, they may sometimes serve as a guidance course toward the true God, or as a preparation for the gospel.[7]

In order to establish peace or communion between sinful human beings and Himself, as well as to fashion them into a fraternal community, God determined to intervene in human history in a way both new and definitive. For He sent His Son, clothed in our flesh, in order that through this Son He might snatch men from the power of darkness and of Satan (cf. Col. 1:13; Acts 10:38) and that in this Son He might reconcile the world to Himself (cf. 2 Cor. 5:19). Through Him, God made all orders of existence.[8] God further appointed Him heir of all things, so that in the Son He might restore them all (cf. Eph. 1:10).

For Jesus Christ was sent into the world as a real Mediator between God and men. Since he is God, all divine fullness dwells bodily in Him (Col. 2:9). According to His human nature, He is the new Adam, made head of a renewed humanity, and full of grace and of truth (Jn. 1:14). Therefore the Son of God walked the ways of a true Incarnation

---

7. *Cf. St. Irenaeus, "Against Heretics," III, 18, 1: "The word existing with God, by whom all things were made, and who always stood by the human race . . ." (PG 7, 932); id. IV, 6, 7: "From the beginning the Son, His own creation, reveals the Father to all to whom He wills, and when He wills, and as the Father wills it." (ibid. 990); cf. IV, 20, 6 and 7 (ibid. 1037); Demonstration No. 34 (Eastern Fathers, XII, 773; "Sources Chretiennes," 62, Paris, 1958, p. 87; Clement of Alexandria, "Protrept." 112, 1 (GCS Clement I, 79); "Strom." VI, 6, 44, 1 (GCS Clement II, 453); 13, 106, 3 and 4 (ibid. 485). For the doctrine itself, cf. Pius XII, radio messages, Dec. 31, 1952; Dogmatic constitution "Lumen Gentium," 16.*
8. *Cf. Heb. 1:2; Jn. 1:3, and 10; 1 Cor. 8:6; Col. 1:16.*

that He might make men sharers in the divine nature. He became poor for our sakes, though He had been rich, in order that His poverty might enrich us (2 Cor. 8:9). The Son of Man came not that He might be served, but that He might be a servant, and give His life as a ransom for the many—that is, for all (cf. Mk. 10:45).

The sainted Fathers of the Church firmly proclaim that what was not taken up by Christ was not healed.[9] Now, what He took up was our entire human nature such as it is found among us in our misery and poverty, though without our sin (cf. Heb. 4:15; 9:28). For Christ said concerning Himself, whom the Father made holy and sent into the world (cf. Jn. 10:36): "The Spirit of the Lord is upon me because he anointed me; to bring good news to the poor he sent me, to heal the broken-hearted,* to proclaim to the captives release, and sight to the blind" (Lk. 4:18). And again: "The Son of Man came to seek and to save what was lost" (Lk. 19:10).

But what was once preached by the Lord, or what was once wrought in Him for the saving of the human race, must be proclaimed and spread abroad to the ends of the earth (Acts 1:8), beginning from Jerusalem (cf. Lk. 24:47). Thus, what He once accomplished for the salvation of all may in the course of time come to achieve its effect in all.

4. To accomplish this goal, Christ sent the Holy Spirit from the Father. The Spirit was to carry out His saving work inwardly and to impel the Church toward her proper expansion. Doubtless, the Holy Spirit was already at work in the world before Christ was glorified.[10] Yet on the day of Pente-

---

9. *Cf. St. Athanasius, "Letter to Epictetus," 7 (PG 26, 1060); St. Cyril of Jerusalem, "Catech." 4, 9 (PG 33, 465); Marius Victorinus, "Against Arius," 3, 3 (PL 8, 1101); St. Basil, Letter 261, 2 (PG 32, 969); St. Gregory Nazianzan, Letter 101 (PG 37, 181); St. Gregory of Nyssa, "Antirrheticus, Against Apollinaris," 17 (PG 45, 1156); St. Ambrose Letter 48, 5 (PL 16, 1153); St. Augustine, "On John's Gospel" tract XXIII, 6 (PL 35, 1585; CChr 36, 236); moreover, he proves that the Holy Spirit did not redeem us, from this fact, that He did not become incarnate: "On the Agony of Christ," 22, 24 (PL 40, 302); St. Cyril of Alexandria, "Against Nestorius," I, 1 (PG 76, 20); St. Fulgentius, Letter 17, 3, 5 (PL 65, 454); "Ad Trasimundum," III, 21 (PL 65, 284: on sorrow and fear).*

*The phrase "to heal the broken-hearted" is omitted by the CCD and other versions.—Ed.

10. *It is the Spirit who has spoken through the Prophets; Creed of Constantinople (Denzinger-Shoenmetzer, 150); St. Leo the Great, Sermon 76 (PL 54, 405-406): "When on the day of Pentecost the Holy Spirit filled the disciples of the Lord, it was not so much the beginning of a gift as it was the completion of one already bountifully possessed: because the patriarchs,*

cost, He came down upon the disciples to remain with them forever (cf. Jn. 14:16). On that day the Church was publicly revealed to the multitude, the gospel began to spread among the nations by means of preaching, and finally there occurred a foreshadowing of that union of all peoples in a universal faith.

That union was to be achieved by the Church of the New Covenant, a Church which speaks all tongues, which lovingly understands and accepts all tongues, and thus overcomes the divisiveness of Babel.[11] For it was from Pentecost that the "Acts of the Apostles" took their origin. In a similar way Christ was conceived when the Holy Spirit came upon the Virgin Mary. Thus too Christ was impelled to the work of His ministry when the same Holy Spirit descended upon Him at prayer.[12]

Now, before freely giving His life for the world, the Lord Jesus so arranged the ministry of the apostles and so promised to send the Holy Spirit, that both they and the Spirit were to be associated in effecting the work of salvation always and everywhere.[13] Throughout all ages, the Holy Spirit gives the entire Church "unity in fellowship and in service; He furnishes her with various gifts, both hierarchical and charismatic."[14] He vivifies ecclesiastical institutions as a kind

---

the prophets, the priests, and all the holy men who preceded them were already quickened by the life of the same Spirit . . . although they did not possess his gifts to the same degree." Also Sermon 77, 1 (PL 54, 412); Leo XIII, encyclical "Divinum Illud" (AAS 1897, 650-651). Also St. John Chrysostom, although he insists on the newness of the Holy Spirit's mission on Pentecost; "On Eph." c. 4, Homily 10, 1 (PG 62, 75).

11. The holy Fathers often speak of Babel and Pentecost; Origen, "On Genesis," c. 1 (PG 12, 112); St. Gregory Naz., Oration 41, 16 (PG 36, 449); St. John Chrysostom, Homily 2 on Pentecost, 2 (PG 50, 467); "On the Acts of the Apostles" (PG 44); St. Augustine, "Exposition on Psalm 54," 11 (PL 36, 636; CChr 39, 664 ff.); Sermon 271: (PL 38, 245); St. Cyril of Alexandria, Glaphyra on Genesis II (PG 69, 79); St. Gregory the Great, "Homily on the Gospels," Book 2, Homily 30, 4 (PL 76, 1222); St. Bede, "In Hexaem." Book 3 (PL 91, 125). See also the image in St. Mark's Basilica in Venice.

The Church speaks all languages, and thus gathers all in the catholicity of the faith: St. Augustine, Sermons 267, 268, 269 (PL 38, 1225-1237); Sermon 175, 3 (PL 38, 946); St. John Chrysostom, "On the First Epistle to the Corinthians," Homily 35 (PG 61, 296); St. Cyril of Alexandria, fragment on the Acts (PG 74, 758); St. Fulgentius, Sermon 8, 2-3 (PL 65, 743-744).

Concerning Pentecost as a consecration of the apostles to their mission, cf. J. A. Cramer, "Catena in Acta Apostolorum," Oxford, 1838, pp. 24 ff.

12. Cf. Lk. 3:22; 4:1; Acts 10:38.

13. Cf. Jn. c. 14-17; Paul VI, allocution during the Council, Sept. 14, 1964 (AAS 1964, 807).

14. Cf. Dogmatic constitution "Lumen Gentium," 4.

of soul[15] and instills into the hearts of the faithful the same mission spirit which motivated Christ Himself. Sometimes He visibly anticipates the apostles' action,[16] just as He unceasingly accompanies and directs it in different ways.[17]

5. From the very beginning, the Lord Jesus "called to him men of his own choosing. . . . And he appointed twelve that they might be with him, and that he might send them forth to preach" (Mk. 3:13; cf. Mt. 10:1-42). Thus the apostles were the first members of the New Israel, and at the same time the beginning of the sacred hierarchy.

By His death and His resurrection the Lord completed once for all in Himself the mysteries of our salvation and of the renewal of all things. He had received all power in heaven and on earth (cf. Mt. 28:18). Now, before He was taken up into heaven (cf. Acts 1:11), He founded His Church as the sacrament of salvation, and sent His apostles into all the world just as He Himself had been sent by His Father (cf. Jn. 20:21). He gave them this command: "Go, therefore, and make disciples of all nations, baptizing them in the name of the Father, and of the Son, and of the Holy Spirit, teaching them to observe all that I have commanded you" (Mt. 28:19 f.). "Go into the whole world; preach the gospel to every creature. He who believes and is baptized shall be saved, but he who does not believe shall be condemned" (Mk. 16:15 f.).

Since then the duty has weighed upon the Church to spread the faith and the saving work of Christ. This duty exists not only in virtue of the express command which was inherited from the apostles by the order of bishops, assisted by priests and united with the successor of Peter and supreme shepherd of the Church. It exists also in virtue of that life which flows from Christ into His members: "From him the whole body (being closely joined and knit together through every joint of the system according to the functioning in due measure of each single part) derives its increase to the building up of itself in love" (Eph. 4:16).

The mission of the Church, therefore, is fulfilled by that activity which makes her fully present to all men and nations.

15. *St. Augustine, Sermon 267, 4 (PL 38, 1231). "The Holy Spirit does in the whole church what the soul does in all the members of one body." Cf. Dogmatic constitution "Lumen Gentium," 7 (with note 8).*
16. *Cf. Acts 10:44-47; 11:15; 15:8.*
17. *Cf. Acts 4:8; 5:32; 8:26, 29, 39; 9:31; 10; 11:24-28; 13:2, 4, 9; 16:6-7; 20:22-23; 21:11; etc.*

She undertakes this activity in obedience to Christ's command and in response to the grace and love of the Holy Spirit. Thus, by the example of her life and by her preaching, by the sacraments and other means of grace, she can lead them to the faith, the freedom, and the peace of Christ. Thus there lies open before them a free and trustworthy road to full participation in the mystery of Christ.

This mission is a continuing one. In the course of history it unfolds the mission of Christ Himself, who was sent to preach the gospel to the poor. Hence, prompted by the Holy Spirit, the Church must walk the same road which Christ walked: a road of poverty and obedience, of service and self-sacrifice to the death, from which death He came forth a victor by His resurrection. For thus did all the apostles walk in hope. On behalf of Christ's body, which is the Church, they supplied what was wanting of the sufferings of Christ by their own many trials and sufferings (cf. Col. 1:24). Often, too, the blood of Christians was like a seed.[18]

6. This duty must be fulfilled by the order of bishops, whose head is Peter's successor, and with the prayer and cooperation of the whole Church. This duty is one and the same everywhere and in every situation, even though the variety of situations keeps it from being exercised in the same way. Hence, the differences to be found in this activity of the Church do not result from the inner nature of her mission itself, but are due rather to the circumstances in which this mission is exercised.[19]

These circumstances depend sometimes on the Church, sometimes on the peoples or groups or individuals to whom the mission is directed. For although the Church includes within herself the totality or fullness of the means of salvation, she does not and cannot always and instantly bring all of them into action.

Rather, she knows what it means to make beginnings and to advance step by step in the work by which she strives to

18. *Tertullian, "Apologeticum," 50, 13 (PL 1, 534; CChr. 1, 171).*
19. This section is important since it rather accurately defines "missionary activity." While insisting that the mission of the Church is one, in the exercise of the mission certain differences are to be acknowledged. These differences arise chiefly from the condition of the peoples *for* whom the mission is exercised, the faithful or unbelievers; they also may arise by a specific designation by the Church. "Missionary activity" is then defined as that which is carried on in favor of peoples or nations that do not yet believe in Christ and whose culture has not been transformed and elevated by the gospel. These are the *gentes* of sacred Scripture.

make God's plan a reality. In fact, there are times when, after a happy beginning, she must lament another setback, or is at least detained in a certain state of partial and insufficient fulfillment. As for the men, groups, and peoples concerned, only by degrees does she touch and pervade them, and thus take them up into full catholicity. The appropriate actions and tools must be brought to bear on any given circumstance or situation.

"Missions" is the term usually given to those particular undertakings by which the heralds of the gospel are sent out by the Church and go forth into the whole world to carry out the task of preaching the gospel and planting the Church among peoples or groups who do not yet believe in Christ. These undertakings are brought to completion by missionary activity and are commonly exercised in certain territories recognized by the Holy See.

The specific purpose of this missionary activity is evangelization and the planting of the Church among those peoples and groups where she has not yet taken root.[20] Thus from the seed which is the Word of God, particular native Churches can be adequately established and flourish the world over, endowed with their own vitality and maturity. Thus too, sufficiently provided with a hierarchy of their own which is joined to a faithful people, and adequately fitted out with requisites for living a full Christian life, they can make their contribution to the good of the Church universal.

The chief means of this implantation is the preaching of the gospel of Jesus Christ. The Lord sent forth His disciples into the whole world to preach this gospel. Thus reborn by the Word of God (cf. 1 Pet. 1:23), men may through baptism be joined to that Church which, as the body of the

---

20. *Already St. Thomas Aquinas speaks of the apostolic duty of "planting" the Church; cf. "Sent." Book I, Dist. 16, q. 1, 2 ad 2 and ad 4; a. 3 sol.; "Summa Theol." 1, q. 43, a. 7 ad 6; I, II, q. 106 a. 4 ad 4. Cf. Benedict XV, "Maximum Illud" Nov. 30, 1919 (AAS 1919, 445 and 453); Pius XI, "Rerum Ecclesiae," Feb. 28, 1926 (AAS 1926, 74); Pius XII, Apr. 30, 1939, to the directors of the Pontifical Missionary Societies; id., June 24, 1944, to the directors of the Pontifical Missionary Societies (AAS 1944, 210; again in AAS 1950, 727 and 1951, 508); id., June 29, 1948, to the native clergy (AAS 1948, 374); id., "Evangelii Praecones," June 2, 1951 (AAS 1951, 507); id., "Fidei Donum," Jan. 15, 1957 (AAS 1957, 236); John XXIII, "Princeps Pastorum," Nov. 28, 1959 (AAS 1959, 835); Paul VI, homily Oct. 18, 1964 (AAS 1964, 911).*
The Supreme Pontiffs as well as the Fathers and scholastics have spoken of the expansion of the Church: St. Thomas Aquinas, commentary on Mt. 16:28; Leo XIII, encyclical "Sancta Dei Civitas" (AAS 1880, 241); Benedict XV, encyclical "Maximum Illud" (AAS 1919, 442); Pius XI, encyclical "Rerum Ecclesiae" (AAS 1926, 65).

Word Incarnate, is nourished and lives by the Word of God and by the Eucharistic Bread (cf. Acts 2:43).

In this missionary activity of the Church various stages are sometimes found side by side: first, that of the beginning or planting, then that of newness or youth. When these stages have passed, the Church's missionary activity does not cease. Rather, there lies upon the particular Churches which are already set up the duty of continuing this activity and of preaching the gospel to those still outside.

Moreover, the groups among which the Church dwells often undergo radical changes for one reason or other, and an entirely new set of circumstances can arise. Then the Church must deliberate whether these conditions call for a renewal of her missionary activity. Besides, circumstances are sometimes such that, for the time being, there is no possibility of expounding the gospel directly and immediately. Then, missionaries can and must at least bear witness to Christ by charity and by works of mercy, with all patience, prudence, and great confidence. Thus they will prepare the way for the Lord and make Him present in some manner.

It is plain, then, that missionary activity wells up from the Church's innermost nature and spreads abroad her saving faith. It perfects her Catholic unity by expanding it. It is sustained by her apostolicity. It gives expression to the collegial awareness of her hierarchy. It bears witness to her sanctity while spreading and promoting it.

Thus, missionary activity among the nations differs from pastoral activity exercised among the faithful, as well as from undertakings aimed at restoring unity among Christians. And yet these two other activities are most closely connected with the missionary zeal of the Church,[21] because the division among Christians damages the most holy cause of preaching the gospel to every creature[22] and blocks the way to the faith for many. Hence, by the same mandate which makes missions necessary, all the baptized are called to be gathered into one flock, and thus to be able to bear unanimous witness

---

21. *In this notion of missionary activity, as is evident, according to the circumstances, even those parts of Latin America are included in which there is neither a hierarchy proper to the region, nor maturity of Christian life, nor sufficient preaching of the gospel. Whether or not such territory de facto is recognized as missionary by the Holy See does not depend on this Council. Therefore, regarding the connection between the notion of missionary activity and a certain territory, it is wise to say that this activity "in the majority of cases" is exercised in certain territories recognized by the Holy See.*
22. *Decree "Unitatis Redintegratio" (Decree on Ecumenism) 1.*

before the nations to Christ their Lord. And if they are not yet capable of bearing full witness to the same faith, they should at least be animated by mutual esteem and love.

7. This missionary activity finds its reason in the will of God, "who wishes all men to be saved and to come to the knowledge of the truth. For there is one God, and one Mediator between God and men, himself man, Christ Jesus, who gave himself a ransom for all" (1 Tim. 2:4-5), "neither is there salvation in any other" (Acts 4:12).[23]

Therefore, all must be converted to Him as He is made known by the Church's preaching. All must be incorporated into Him by baptism, and into the Church which is His body. For Christ Himself "in explicit terms . . . affirmed the necessity of faith and baptism (cf. Mk. 16:16; Jn. 3:5) and thereby affirmed also the necessity of the Church, for through baptism as through a door men enter the Church. Whosoever, therefore, knowing that the Catholic Church was made necessary by God through Jesus Christ, would refuse to enter her or to remain in her could not be saved."[24]

Therefore, though God in ways known to Himself can lead those inculpably ignorant of the gospel to that faith without which it is impossible to please Him (Heb. 11:6), yet a necessity lies upon the Church (cf. 1 Cor. 9:16), and at the same time a sacred duty, to preach the gospel. Hence missionary activity today as always retains its power and necessity.

By means of this activity, the Mystical Body of Christ unceasingly gathers and directs its forces toward its own growth (cf. Eph. 4:11-16). The members of the Church are impelled to carry on such missionary activity by reason of the love with which they love God and by which they desire to share with all men in the spiritual goods of both this life and the life to come.

Finally, by means of this missionary activity, God is fully glorified, provided that men consciously and fully accept His work of salvation, which He has accomplished in Christ.

23. The ultimate reason for the necessity of missionary activity in favor of non-Christian peoples is the universality and comprehensiveness of God's plan for mankind's salvation and elevation. Although individual non-Christians can be and are saved without baptism and die in friendship with God, neither unbelievers nor unbelieving nations can live and develop in the fullness of divine life which God has destined for all men in Christ without being incorporated into His Body and becoming one People of God.
24. Cf. Dogmatic constitution "Lumen gentium," 14.

Through this activity that plan of God is thus fulfilled to which Christ was obediently and lovingly devoted for the glory of the Father who sent Him.[25] According to this plan, the whole human race is to form one people of God, coalesce into the one body of Christ, and be built up into one temple of the Holy Spirit. Since it concerns brotherly concord, this design surely corresponds with the inmost wishes of all men.

And so the plan of the Creator, who formed man to His own image and likeness, will be realized at last when all who share one human nature, regenerated in Christ through the Holy Spirit and beholding together the glory of God, will be able to say "Our Father."[26]

8. Missionary activity is closely bound up too with human nature itself and its aspirations. By manifesting Christ, the Church reveals to men the real truth about their condition and their total vocation. For Christ is the source and model of that renewed humanity, penetrated with brotherly love, sincerity, and a peaceful spirit, to which all aspire.[27] Christ and the Church, which bears witness to Him by preaching the gospel, transcend every particularity of race or nation and therefore cannot be considered foreign anywhere or to anybody.[28] Christ Himself is the Truth and the Way. The

---

25. *Cf. Jn. 7:18; 8:30 and 44; 8:50; 17:1.*
26. *On this synthetic idea, see teaching of St. Irenaeus, "De Recapitulatione." Cf. also Hippolytus, "De Antichristo," 3: "Wishing all, and desiring to save all, wishing all the excellence of God's children, and calling all the saints in one perfect man . . ." (PG 10, 732; GCS Hippolyt I 2 p. 6); "Benedictiones Iacob," 7 (T.U., 38-1, p. 18, lin. 4 ss.); Origen, "In Ioann." Tom. I, no. 16: "Then there will be one action of knowing God on the part of all those who have attained to God, under the leadership of the Word who is with God, that thus all sons may be correctly instructed in the knowledge of the Father, as now only the Son knows the Father" (PG 14, 49; GCS Orig. IV 20); St. Augustine, "De Sermone Domini in monte," I 41: "Let us love what can lead us to that kingdom where no one says, 'My Father,' but all say to the one God: 'Our Father' ": (PL 34, 1250); St. Cyril Alex., "In Ioann." I: "For we are all in Christ, and the common person of humanity comes back to life in him. That is why he is also called the New Adam . . . For he dwelt among us, who by nature is the Son of God; and therefore in his Spirit we cry out: Abba, Father! But the Word dwells in all, in one temple, namely, that which he assumed for us and from us, that having us all in himself, he might, as Paul says, reconcile all in one body to the Father" (PG 73, 161-164).*
27. Missionary activity, as the *kerygma* of salvation, affects man in his historical condition, answering the deepest aspirations of his created nature and making them realizable in a divine manner in the forward thrust of mankind toward ultimate development.
28. Benedict XV, *"Maximum Illud" (AAS 1919, 445): "For as the Church of God is Catholic and is foreign to no people or nation . . ." Cf. John XXIII, "Mater et Magistra": "By divine right the Church belongs to all nations . . . since she has, as it were, transfused her enrgy into the veins of a people,*

preaching of the gospel opens them up to all when it proclaims to all these words of the same Christ: "Repent, and
believe in the gospel" (Mk. 1:15).

Now, since he who does not believe is already judged (cf.
Jn. 3:18), the words of Christ are at one and the same time
words of judgment and of grace, of death and of life. For it
is only by putting to death what is old that we are able to
come to a newness of life. This fact applies first of all to persons, but it holds also for the various goods of this world,
which bear the mark both of man's sin and of God's blessing;
for "all have sinned and have need of the glory of God"
(Rom. 3:23). By himself and by his own power, no one is
freed from sin or raised above himself, or completely rid of
his sickness or his solitude or his servitude.[29] On the contrary, all stand in need of Christ, their Model, their Mentor,
their Liberator, their Savior, their Source of life.

The gospel has truly been a leaven of liberty and progress
in human history, even in its temporal sphere, and always
proves itself a leaven of brotherhood, of unity, and of peace.
Therefore, not without cause is Christ hailed by the faithful
as "the expected of the nations, and their Savior."[30]

9. And so the time for missionary activity extends between
the first coming of the Lord and the second.[31] Then from
the four winds the Church will be gathered like a harvest
into the kingdom of God.[32] For the gospel must be preached
to all nations before the Lord returns (cf. Mk. 13:10).

Missionary activity is nothing else and nothing less than a
manifestation or epiphany of God's will, and the fulfillment
of that will in the world and in world history. In the course
of this history God plainly works out the history of salvation
by means of mission. By the preaching of the word and by
the celebration of the sacraments, whose center and summit
is the most holy Eucharist, missionary activity brings about
the presence of Christ, the Author of salvation.

But whatever truth and grace are to be found among the

she neither is nor considers herself an institution imposed on that people from
without . . . And hence whatever seems to her good and noble, that they
confirm and perfect" (namely, those reborn in Christ) (AAS 1961, 444).
29. Cf. Irenaeus, "Against Heretics" III, 15, no. 3 (PG 7, 919): "They were
preachers of truth and apostles of liberty."
30. Antiphon O for Dec. 23.
31. It is particularly in the eschatological perspective presented here that the
necessary function of missionary activity in bringing to historical completion
and fullness what God has willed for all men stands out most emphatically.
32. Cf. Mt. 24:31; Didache, 10, 5 (Funk I, p. 32).

nations, as a sort of secret presence of God, this activity frees from all taint of evil and restores to Christ its maker, who overthrows the devil's domain and wards off the manifold malice of vice. And so, whatever good is found to be sown in the hearts and minds of men, or in the rites and cultures peculiar to various peoples, is not lost. More than that, it is healed, ennobled, and perfected for the glory of God, the shame of the demon, and the bliss of men.[33]

Thus, missionary activity tends toward the fulfillment which will come at the end of time.[34] For by it the People of God advances toward that degree of growth and that time of completion which the Father has fixed in His power (cf. Acts 1:7). To this people it was said in prophecy: "Enlarge the space for your tent, spread out your tent cloths unsparingly"* (Is. 54:2).[35] By missionary activity, the mystical body grows to the mature measure of the fullness of Christ (cf. Eph. 4:13). The spiritual temple, where God is adored in spirit and in truth (cf. Jn. 4:23), grows and is built up upon the foundation of the apostles and prophets with Christ Jesus Himself remaining the chief cornerstone (Eph. 2:20).

CHAPTER II

MISSION WORK ITSELF

10. Sent by Christ to reveal and to communicate the love of God to all men and nations, the Church is aware that there

33. *Dogmatic constitution "Lumen Gentium," 17. St. Augustine, 7, "City of God," 1917 (PL 41, 646). Instruction of the Sacred Congregation for the Propagation of the Faith (Collectanea I, no. 35, p. 42).*
34. *According to Origen, the gospel must be preached before the end of this world: Homily on Luke XXI (GCS, Origen IX, 136, 21 ff.); "Commentary on Matthew" 39 (XI 75 25 ff.; 76, 4 ff.); Homily on Jeremiah III, 2 (VIII 308, 29 ff.); St. Thomas "Summa Theol." Ia, IIae q. 106, a. 4, ad 4.*
*1960 CCD transl.—Ed.
35. *Hilary of Poitiers, "On the Psalms" 14 (PL 9, 301); Eusebius of Caesarea, "On Isaiah" 54, 2-3 (PG 24, 462-463); Cyril of Alexandria, "On Isaiah V," chap. 54, 1-3 (PG 70, 1193).*

still remains a gigantic missionary task for her to accomplish. For the gospel message has not yet been heard, or scarcely so, by two billion human beings.[36] And their number is increasing daily. These are formed into large and distinct groups by permanent cultural ties, by ancient religious traditions, and by firm bonds of social necessity.

Some of these men are followers of one of the great religions, others remain strangers to the very notion of God, while still others expressly deny His existence, and sometimes even attack it. In order to be able to offer all of them the mystery of salvation and the life brought by God, the Church must become part of all these groups for the same motive which led Christ to bind Himself, in virtue of His Incarnation, to the definite social and cultural conditions of those human beings among whom He dwelt.

ART. 1: CHRISTIAN WITNESS

11. The Church must be present in these groups of men through those of her children who dwell among them or are sent to them.[37] For, wherever they live, all Christians are bound to show forth, by the example of their lives and by the witness of their speech, that new man which they put on at baptism, and that power of the Holy Spirit by whom they were strengthened at confirmation. Thus other men, observing their good works, can glorify the Father (cf. Mt. 5:16) and can better perceive the real meaning of human life and the bond which ties the whole community of mankind together.

That they may be able to give this witness to Christ fruitfully, let them be joined to those men by esteem and love, and acknowledge themselves to be members of the group of men among whom they live. Let them share in cultural and social life by the various exchanges and enterprises of human living. Let them be familiar with their national and religious

36. The chief *locus* of missionary activity is given here, namely, the two billion non-Christian peoples in Africa, Asia, and Oceania whose diverse cultures and the vast majority of whose immense population have yet to be markedly affected by the gospel.

37. The manner in which the evangelization of these peoples is to proceed is incarnational—"the same way that Christ is bound Himself by the social and cultural conditions of the persons with whom He conversed." Due to the past progress of the missions in setting up the Church virtually everywhere in the globe, the focus of missionary activity in our era is less on geographical expansion and more on making the Church a living and active presence within and native to the various cultures of non-Christian peoples. Dialogue and cultural adapation are given more than usual emphasis in what follows.

traditions, gladly and reverently laying bare the seeds of the Word which lie hidden in them.

At the same time, however, they should look to the profound changes which are taking place among nations. They should exert themselves lest modern man, overly intent on the science and technology of today's world, become a stranger to things divine. Rather, let them awaken in him a fiercer yearning for that truth and charity which God has revealed.

Christ Himself searched the hearts of men, and led them to divine light through truly human conversation. So also His disciples, profoundly penetrated by the Spirit of Christ, should know the people among whom they live, and should establish contact with them. Thus they themselves can learn by sincere and patient dialogue what treasures a bountiful God has distributed among the nations of the earth. But at the same time, let them try to illumine these treasures with the light of the gospel, to set them free, and to bring them under the dominion of God their Savior.

12. The presence of the Christian faithful in these human groups should be animated by that charity with which God has loved us, and with which He wills that we should love one another (cf. 1 Jn. 4:11). Christian charity truly extends to all, without distinction of race, social condition, or religion. It looks for neither gain nor gratitude. For as God has loved us with a spontaneous love, so also the faithful should in their charity care for the human person himself by loving him with the same affection with which God sought out man.

Christ went about all the towns and villages, curing every kind of disease and infirmity as a sign that the kingdom of God had come (cf. Mt. 9:35 ff.; Acts 10:38). So also the Church, through her children, is one with men of every condition, but especially with the poor and the afflicted. On their behalf she gladly spends herself (cf. 2 Cor. 12:15). For she shares in their joys and sorrows, knows their longings and problems, suffers with them in the throes of death. To those in quest of peace, she wishes to answer in fraternal dialogue, bringing to them the peace and light of the gospel.

Let the faithful labor and collaborate with all others in the proper regulation of the affairs of economic and social life. With special care, let them devote themselves to the education of children and young people by means of different kinds of schools. These schools should be considered not only as an outstanding means for forming and developing Christian youth, but also as a service of supreme value to men, especially in the developing nations, a service elevating the level of human dignity, and preparing the way for living conditions which are more humane.

Furthermore, let the faithful take part in the strivings of those peoples who are waging war on famine, ignorance, and disease and thereby struggling to better their way of life and to secure peace in the world. In this activity, the faithful should be eager to offer their prudent aid to projects sponsored by public and private organizations, by governments, by international agencies, by various Christian communities, and even by non-Christian religions.

However, the Church in no way desires to inject herself into the government of the earthly city. She claims no other authority than that of ministering to men with the help of God, in a spirit of charity and faithful service (cf. Mt. 20:26; 23:11).[38]

Closely united with men in their life and work, Christ's disciples hope to render to others true witness of Christ, and to work for their salvation, even where they are not able to proclaim Christ fully. For they are not seeking a mere material progress and prosperity for men, but are promoting their dignity and brotherly union, teaching those religious and moral truths which Christ illumined with His light. In this way, they are gradually opening up a wider approach to God. Thus too they help men to attain to salvation by love for God and neighbor. And the mystery of Christ begins to shine forth. In this mystery the new man has appeared, created according to God (cf. Eph. 4:24). In it the love of God is revealed.

ART. 2: PREACHING THE GOSPEL AND GATHERING GOD'S PEOPLE TOGETHER

13. Wherever God opens a door of speech for proclaiming the mystery of Christ (cf. Col. 4:3), there should be announced (cf. 1 Cor. 9:15; Rom. 10:14) to all men (cf. Mk. 16:15) with confidence and constancy (cf. Acts 4:13, 29, 31; 9:27, 28; 13:46; 14:3; 19:8; 26:26; 28:31; 1 Th. 2:2; 2 Cor. 3:12; 7:4; Phil. 1:20; Eph. 3:12; 6:19, 20) the living God, and He whom He has sent for the salvation of all, Jesus Christ (cf. 1 Th. 1:9-10; 1 Cor. 1:18-21; Gal.

38. Cf. Allocution of Paul VI of Nov. 21, 1964 in council (AAS 1964, 1013).

1:31; Acts 14:15-17; 17:22-31). Thus, when the Holy Spirit opens their heart (cf. Acts 16:14) non-Christians may believe and be freely converted to the Lord, and may sincerely cling to Him who, as "the way, the truth, and the life" (Jn. 14:6), fulfills all their spiritual expectations, and even infinitely surpasses them.

This conversion, to be sure, must be regarded as a beginning. Yet it is sufficient that a man realize that he has been snatched away from sin and led into the mystery of the love of God, who has called him to enter into a personal relationship with Him in Christ. For, by the workings of divine grace, the new convert sets out on a spiritual journey. Already sharing through faith in the mystery of Christ's death and resurrection, he journeys from the old man to the new one, perfected in Christ (cf. Col. 3:5-10; Eph. 4:20-24).

This transition, which brings with it a progressive change of outlook and morals, should manifest itself through its social effects, and should be gradually developed during the time of the catechumenate. Since the Lord he believes in is a sign of contradiction (cf. Lk. 2:34; Mt. 10:34-39), the convert often experiences human breaks and separations. But he also tastes the joy which God gives without measure (cf. 1 Th. 1:6).

The Church strictly forbids forcing anyone to embrace the faith, or alluring or enticing people by unworthy techniques. By the same token, she also strongly insists on a person's right not to be deterred from the faith by unjust vexations on the part of others.[39]

In accord with the Church's very ancient custom, a convert's motives should be looked into, and if necessary, purified.

14. Those who, through the Church, have accepted from God a belief in Christ[40] should be admitted to the catechumenate by liturgical rites. The catechumenate is not a mere expounding of doctrines and precepts, but a training period for the whole Christian life. It is an apprenticeship of appropriate length, during which disciples are joined to Christ their Teacher. Therefore, catechumens should be properly instructed in the mystery of salvation and in the practice of

---

39. *Cf. Declaration on Religious Freedom 2, 4, 10; Constitution on the Church in the Modern World.*
40. *Cf. Dogmatic constitution "Lumen Gentium," 17.*

gospel morality. By sacred rites which are to be held at successive intervals,[41] they should be introduced into the life of
faith, liturgy, and love, which God's People lives.

Then, when the sacraments of Christian initiation have
freed them from the power of darkness (cf. Col. 1:13),[42]
having died with Christ, been buried with Him, and risen
with Him (cf. Rom. 6:4-11; Col. 2:12-13; 1 Pet. 3:21-22;
Mk. 16:16), they receive the Spirit (cf. 1 Th. 3:5-7; Acts
8:14-17) who makes them adopted sons, and celebrate the
remembrance of the Lord's death and resurrection together
with the whole People of God.

It is the desire of this Council that the liturgy of the Lent-
en and Easter seasons be restored in such a way as to dispose the hearts of the catechumens to celebrate the paschal
mystery at whose solemn ceremonies they are reborn to
Christ through baptism.

But this Christian initiation through the catechumenate
should be taken care of not only by catechists or priests, but
by the entire community of the faithful, especially by the
sponsors. Thus, right from the outset the catechumens will
feel that they belong to the People of God. Since the life of
the Church is an apostolic one, the catechumens should also
learn to cooperate actively, by the witness of their lives and
by the profession of their faith, in the spread of the gospel
and in the upbuilding of the Church.

Finally, the juridical status of catechumens should be
clearly defined in the new code of canon law. For since they
are joined to the Church,[43] they are already of the household of Christ.[44] In many cases they are already leading a
life of faith, hope, and charity.

ART. 3: FORMING THE CHRISTIAN COMMUNITY

15. The Holy Spirit, who calls all men to Christ by the seeds
of the Word and by the preaching of the gospel, stirs up in
their hearts the obedience of faith. When in the womb of
the baptismal font He begets to a new life those who believe in Christ, He gathers them into the one People of God

41. Cf. *Constitution on the Sacred Liturgy, 64-65.*
42. *Concerning this liberation from the slavery of the devil and the powers of
darkness, in the gospel, cf. Mt. 12:28; Jn. 8:44; 12:31 (Cf. 1 Jn. 3:8; Eph.
2:1-2). In liturgy of baptism, cf. Roman Ritual.*
43. Cf. *Dogmatic constitution "Lumen Gentium," 14.*
44. Cf. *St. Augustine, "Tract on John" 11, 4 (PL 35, 1476).*

which is "a chosen race, a royal priesthood, a holy nation, a purchased people" (1 Pet. 2:9).[45]

Therefore, let missionaries as God's co-workers (cf. 1 Cor. 3:9), raise up congregations of the faithful who will walk in a manner worthy of the vocation to which they have been called (cf. Eph. 4:1), and will exercise the priestly, prophetic, and royal office which God has entrusted to them. In this way, the Christian community becomes a sign of God's presence in the world. For by reason of the Eucharistic Sacrifice, this community is ceaselessly on the way with Christ to the Father.[46] Carefully nourished on the Word of God,[47] it bears witness to Christ.[48] And, finally, it walks in love and glows with an apostolic spirit.[49]

From the very start, the Christian community should be so formed that it can provide for its own necessities insofar as this is possible.

This congregation of the faithful, endowed with the riches of its own nation's culture, should be deeply rooted in the people. Let families flourish which are penetrated with the spirit of the gospel[50] and let them be assisted by suitable schools. Let associations and groups be organized through which the lay apostolate will be able to permeate the whole of society with the spirit of the gospel. Finally, let charity shine out between Catholics of different rites.[51]

The ecumenical spirit too should be nurtured in the neophytes. They should rightly consider that the brethren who believe in Christ are Christ's disciples, reborn in baptism, sharers with the People of God in very many riches. Insofar as religious conditions allow, ecumenical activity should be furthered in such a way that without any appearance of indifference or of unwarranted intermingling on the one hand, or of unhealthy rivalry on the other, Catholics can cooperate in a brotherly spirit with their separated brethren, according to the norms of the Decree on Ecumenism.

To the extent that their beliefs are common, they can make before the nations a common profession of faith in God and in Jesus Christ. They can collaborate in social and in technical projects as well as in cultural and religious ones.

45. Cf. Dogmatic constitution "Lumen Gentium," 9.
46. Cf. Dogmatic constitution "Lumen Gentium," 10, 11, 34.
47. Cf. Dogmatic Constitution on Divine Revelation, 21.
48. Cf. Dogmatic constitution "Lumen Gentium," 12, 35.
49. Cf. Ibid., 23, 36.
50. Cf. Ibid., 11, 35, 41.
51. Cf. Decree on Eastern Catholic Churches, 30.

Let them work together especially for the sake of Christ, their common Lord. Let His Name be the bond that unites them! This cooperation should be undertaken not only among private persons, but also, according to the judgment of the local Ordinary, among Churches or ecclesial Communities and their enterprises.

The Christian faithful, gathered together in the Church out of all nations, "are not marked off from the rest of men by their government, nor by their language, nor by their political institutions."[52] So they should live for God and Christ by following the honorable customs of their own nation. As good citizens, they should practice true and effective patriotism. At the same time, let them altogether avoid racial prejudice and bitter nationalism, fostering instead a universal love for man.

In the attainment of all these goals, laymen have the greatest importance and deserve special attention. These are those Christians who have been incorporated into Christ by baptism and who live in the world. For it is up to them, imbued with the spirit of Christ, to be a leaven animating temporal affairs from within, disposing them always to become as Christ would wish them.[53]

But it is not enough for the Christian people to be present and organized in a given nation. Nor is it enough for them to carry out an apostolate of good example. They are organized and present for the purpose of announcing Christ to their non-Christian fellow-citizens by word and deed, and of aiding them toward the full reception of Christ.

Now, if the Church is to be planted and the Christian community grow, various ministries are needed. These are raised up by divine vocation from the midst of the faithful, and are to be carefully fostered and cultivated by all. Among these are the offices of priests, deacons, and catechists, as well as Catholic action. By their prayers and by their active labors, religious men and women play an indispensable role too in rooting and strengthening the kingdom of Christ in souls, and in causing it to expand.

16. With great joy the Church gives thanks for the priceless gift of the priestly calling which God has granted to so

---

52. *Epistle to Diognetus*, 5 (PG 2, 1173); Cf. *Dogmatic constitution "Lumen Gentium,"* 38.
53. Cf. *Dogmatic constitution "Lumen Gentium,"* 32; *Decree on the Apostolate of the Laity.*

many youthful members of those peoples recently converted to Christ. For the Church is more firmly rooted in any given sector of the human family when the various groupings of the faithful draw from their own members ministers of salvation in the orders of bishop, priest, and deacon. As these come to serve their brethren, the new Churches gradually acquire a diocesan structure equipped with its own clergy.

What this Council has decreed concerning priestly vocations and formation should be religiously observed where the Church is first planted, and among the young Churches. The greatest attention must be paid to what was said about closely joining spiritual formation with the doctrinal and pastoral; about living a life patterned after the gospel, without concern for personal or family advantage; about cultivating an intimate appreciation for the mystery of the Church. From all this, seminarians will learn extraordinarily well how to dedicate themselves wholly to the service of the Body of Christ and to the work of the gospel, how to stand by their own bishop as his faithful co-workers, and to cooperate with their colleagues.[54]

By way of achieving this general goal, the whole training of students should be planned in the light of the mystery of salvation as it is revealed in the Scriptures. This mystery of Christ and of man's salvation they should discover and live in the liturgy.[55]

These common requirements of priestly training, including the pastoral and practical ones prescribed by the Council,[56] should be combined with an attempt on the students' part to make contact with the particular way of thinking and acting characteristic of their own people. Therefore, let the minds of the students be kept open and attuned so that they can be versed in the culture of their people and be able to evaluate it. In their philosophical and theological studies, let them consider the points of contact between the traditions and religion of their homeland and the Christian religion.[57] Likewise, priestly training should have an eye to the pastoral needs of a given region.

The students should learn the history, aim, and method of the Church's missionary activity, and the special social, economic, and cultural conditions of their own people. Let them

---

54. *Cf. Decree on Priestly Formation, 4, 8, 9.*
55. *Cf. Constitution on the Sacred Liturgy, 17.*
56. *Cf. Decree on Priestly Formation, 1.*
57. *Cf. John XXIII, "Princeps Pastorum" (AAS 1959, 843-844).*

be educated in the ecumenical spirit, and duly prepared for fraternal dialogue with non-Christians.[58] All these objectives require that seminarians pursue their priestly studies, as far as possible, while associating and living together with their own people.[59] Finally, let care be taken that students are trained in orderly ecclesiastical administration, even in its economic aspect.

Moreover, after gaining some pastoral experience, suitable priests should be chosen to pursue higher studies in universities, even abroad and especially in Rome, as well as in other institutes of learning. In this way, the young Churches will have at hand men from among the local clergy equipped with the learning and skill needed for discharging more difficult ecclesiastical duties.

Where Episcopal Conferences deem it opportune, the order of the diaconate should be restored as a permanent state of life, according to the norms of the Constitution on the Church.[60] For there are men who are actually carrying out the functions of the deacon's office, either by preaching the Word of God as catechists, or by presiding over scattered Christian communities in the name of the pastor and the bishop, or by practicing charity in social or relief work. It will be helpful to strengthen them by that imposition of hands which has come down from the apostles, and to bind them more closely to the altar. Thus they can carry out their ministry more effectively because of the sacramental grace of the diaconate.

17. Likewise worthy of praise are the ranks of men and women catechists, to whom missionary work among the nations owes so very much. Animated with an apostolic spirit, they by their immense efforts make an outstanding and altogether necessary contribution to the spread of the faith and of the Church.

In our time, when there are few clerics to preach the gospel to such great numbers and to exercise the pastoral ministry, the role of catechists is of maximum importance. Therefore, their training must be so thorough and so well adapted to cultural advances that, as powerful co-workers of the priestly order, they can perform their task as superbly as can be, even though it is weighed down with new and expanding burdens.

58. Cf. Decree on Ecumenism, 4.
59. Cf. John XXIII, "Princeps Pastorum" (AAS 1959, 842).
60. Cf. Dogmatic constitution "Lumen Gentium," 29.

There should, then, be an increase in the number of schools, both on the diocesan and on the regional levels, in which future catechists can study Catholic doctrine, especially in the fields of Scripture and the liturgy, as well as catechetical method and pastoral practice. Let there be more schools in which they can develop Christian habits in themselves[61] and can devote themselves tirelessly to cultivating piety and sanctity of life.

Moreover, gatherings or courses should be held in which at certain times catechists can be refreshed in the disciplines and skills useful for their ministry, and in which their spiritual life can be nourished and strengthened. In addition, for those who dedicate themselves entirely to this work, a decent standard of living and social security should be provided through a just salary.[62]

This Council desires that special funds from the Sacred Congregation for the Propagation of the Faith provide for the due training and support of catechists. If it seems necessary and fitting, let an association for catechists be founded.

Moreover, the Churches should gratefully acknowledge the noble work being done by auxiliary catechists, whose help they will need. These preside over prayers in their communities and teach sacred doctrine. Their doctrinal and spiritual training should be properly seen to. Besides, it is to be hoped that, where it seems opportune, catechists who are duly trained will receive a "canonical mission" in a publicly celebrated liturgical ceremony. In this way they can serve the faith with greater authority in the eyes of the people.

18. Right from the planting stage of the Church, the religious life should be carefully fostered. This not only confers precious and absolutely necessary assistance on missionary activity. By a more inward consecration made to God in the Church, it also luminously manifests and signifies the inner nature of the Christian calling.[63]

Working to plant the Church, and thoroughly enriched with the treasures of mysticism adorning the Church's religious tradition, religious communities should strive to give expression to these treasures and to hand them on in a manner harmonious with the nature and the genius of each na-

---

61. Cf. John XXIII, "Princeps Pastorum" (AAS 1959, 855).
62. The reference is to expressions of this kind: "catechistes a plein temps," "full-time catechists."
63. Cf. Dogmatic constitution "Lumen Gentium," 31, 44.

tion. Let them reflect attentively on how Christian religious life may be able to assimilate the ascetic and contemplative traditions whose seeds were sometimes already planted by God in ancient cultures prior to the preaching of the gospel.

Various forms of religious life should be cultivated in a young Church, so that they can display different aspects of Christ's mission and the Church's life, can devote themselves to various pastoral works, and can prepare their members to exercise them rightly. Still, bishops in their Conference should take care that congregations pursuing the same apostolic aims are not multiplied to the detriment of the religious life and the apostolate.

Worthy of special mention are the various projects aimed at helping the contemplative life take root. There are those who while retaining the essential elements of monastic life are bent on implanting the very rich traditions of their own order. Others are returning to simpler forms of ancient monasticism. But all are striving to work out a genuine adaptation to local conditions. For the contemplative life belongs to the fullness of the Church's presence, and should therefore be everywhere established.

CHAPTER III

PARTICULAR CHURCHES

19. The work of planting the Church in a given human community reaches a kind of milestone when the congregation of the faithful, already rooted in social life and considerably adapted to the local culture, enjoys a certain stability and firmness. This means that the congregation is now equipped with its own supply, insufficient though it be, of local priests, religious, and laymen. It means that it is endowed with those ministries and institutions which are necessary if the People of God are to live and develop its life under the guidance of its own bishop.

In such new Churches,[64] the life of God's People must mature in all those areas of Christian living which are to be renewed according to the norms of this Council. The congregations of the faithful must every day become increasingly aware and alive as communities of faith, liturgy, and love. The laity must strive by their civic and apostolic activity to set up a public order based on love and justice. The means of social communication must be used prudently and opportunely.

By a truly Christian life, families must become nurseries of the lay apostolate and of vocations to the priesthood and the religious life. Finally, the faith must be taught by an adequate catechesis celebrated in a liturgy which harmonizes with the genius of the people, and introduced into upright institutions and local customs by appropriate canonical legislation.

The bishop, in turn, together with his own college of priests, must become increasingly animated with the mind of Christ and of the Church, and must think and live in union with the universal Church. Let the young Churches preserve an intimate communion with the Church universal. They should embed her traditions in their own culture, thereby increasing the life of the Mystical Body by a certain mutual exchange of energies.[65] Hence, stress should be laid on those theological, psychological, and human elements which can contribute to fostering this sense of communion with the universal Church.

But these Churches, most often located in the poorer parts of the world, are generally suffering from a very serious lack of priests and of material support. Therefore, they desperately require that the continued missionary activity of the whole Church furnish them with those subsidies which principally serve the growth of the local Church and the maturity of Christian life. This mission action should furnish help also

---

64. The treatment in this section of the "young Churches" also marks a relatively new and necessary development in missionary activity. Instead of treating Christian communities only as "missions" existing someplace on the perimeter of the Church, they are to be regarded as Churches existing and developing within the universal Christian community, both receiving and contributing to the unity and diversity of the Body of Christ through active intercommunion between the Churches. This may involve considerable adjustment in thinking and acting on the part of "foreign missionaries" and those who assist the young Churches as well as on the part of the young Churches themselves.

65. Cf. John XXIII, "Princeps Pastorum" (AAS 1959, 838).

to those Churches, founded long since, which are in a certain state of regression or weakness.

Yet these same Churches should launch a common pastoral effort and suitable projects in favor of increasing the number of vocations to the diocesan clergy and to religious congregations, of discerning them more readily, and training them more efficiently.[66] Thus, little by little, these Churches will be able to provide for themselves and to bring aid to others.

20. Since particular Churches are bound to mirror the universal Church as perfectly as possible, let them rightly realize that they have been sent to those also who are living in the same territory with it, and who do not yet believe in Christ. By the living witness of each one of the faithful and of the whole community, let the particular Church be a sign which points out Christ to others.

Furthermore, there is need for the ministry of the Word, if the gospel is to reach all. The bishop should be first and foremost a herald of the faith, leading new disciples to Christ.[67] In order that he may properly fulfill this outstanding task, let him be thoroughly aware of the conditions of his flock, and the innermost views of his countrymen concerning God. He should also take careful note of those changes introduced by so-called urbanization, migrations, and religious indifferentism.

The local priests in the young Churches should zealously address themselves to the work of spreading the gospel by joining forces with the foreign missionaries who form with them one college of priests, united under the authority of the bishop. This they should do, not only with a view to feeding the faithful flock and celebrating divine worship, but also to preaching the gospel to those outside. When the occasion presents itself, let them with a willing heart offer themselves to the bishop for the undertaking of missionary work in distant and forsaken areas of their own diocese or of other dioceses. In any case, priests should show themselves ready to make the offer.

Let religious men and women, and the laity too, burn with the same zeal toward their countrymen, especially the poor.

Episcopal Conferences should see to it that biblical, theo-

---

66. Cf. Decree on the Ministry and Life of Priests, 11; Decree on Priestly Formation, 2.
67. Dogmatic constitution "Lumen Gentium," 25.

logical, spiritual, and pastoral refresher courses are held at fixed intervals. Their purpose should be to provide the clergy with a more adequate knowledge of the theological sciences and of pastoral methods. For priests must carry out their tasks in a variety of circumstances and amid many changing conditions.

For the rest, those things should be religiously observed which this Council has laid down, particularly in the Decree on the Ministry and Life of Priests.

If this missionary work of the particular Church is to be accomplished, there is need of qualified ministers. These must be seasonably prepared in a way suited to the conditions of each Church. Now, since men are increasingly banding together into groups, it is very fitting that Episcopal Conferences should form a common plan concerning the dialogue to be held with such groups.

If in certain regions, groups of men are to be found who are kept away from embracing the Catholic faith because they cannot adapt themselves to the peculiar form which the Church has taken on there, it is the desire of this Council that such a condition be provided for in a special way,[68] until such time as all the Christians concerned can gather together in one community. Let individual bishops call to their dioceses the missionaries whom the Holy See may have on hand for this purpose; or let them receive such missionaries gladly, and support their undertakings effectively.

In order that this missionary zeal may flourish among their native members, it is very fitting that the young Churches should participate as soon as possible in the universal missionary work of the Church. Let them send their own missionaries to proclaim the gospel all over the world, even though they themselves are suffering from a shortage of clergy. For their communion with the universal Church reaches a certain measure of perfection when they themselves take an active part in missionary zeal toward other nations.

21. The Church has not been truly established, and is not yet fully alive, nor is it a perfect sign of Christ among men, unless there exists a laity worthy of the name working along with the hierarchy. For the gospel cannot be deeply im-

---

68. *Cf. Decree on the Ministry and Life of Priests, 10, where in order to render particular pastoral labors easier for various social groups, provision is made for establishment of personal prelatures insofar as this is called for by sound procedure in exercising the apostolate.*

printed on the talents, life, and work of any people without the active presence of laymen. Therefore, even in the very founding of a Church, the greatest attention is to be paid to raising up a mature Christian laity.

For the lay faithful fully belong at one and the same time both to the People of God and to civil society. They belong to the nation in which they were born. They have begun to share in its cultural treasures by means of their education. They are joined to its life by manifold social ties. They are cooperating in its progress by their individual efforts, each in his own profession. They feel its problems as their very own, and they are trying to solve them.

They also belong to Christ, because they were regenerated in the Church by faith and by baptism. Thus they are Christ's in newness of life and work (cf. 1 Cor. 15:23), so that in Christ, all things may be made subject to God, and finally God will be all in all (cf. 1 Cor. 15:28).

Their main duty, whether they are men or women, is the witness which they are bound to bear to Christ by their life and works in the home, in their social group, and in their own professional circle. For in them there must appear the new man created according to God in justice and true holiness (cf. Eph. 4:24). But they must give expression to this newness of life in the social and cultural framework of their own homeland, according to their own national traditions. They must be acquainted with this culture. They must heal it and preserve it. They must develop it in accordance with modern conditions, and finally perfect it in Christ. Thus the faith of Christ and the life of the Church will no longer be something extraneous to the society in which they live, but will begin to permeate and transform it.

Let them be one with their fellow countrymen in sincere charity, so that there may appear in their way of life a new bond of unity and of universal solidarity, drawn from the mystery of Christ. Let them also spread the faith of Christ among those with whom they live or have professional connections. This obligation is all the more urgent, because very many men can hear of the gospel and recognize Christ only by means of the laity who are their neighbors. In fact, wherever possible, the laity should be prepared, in more immediate cooperation with the hierarchy, to fulfill a special mission of proclaiming the gospel and communicating Christian teachings. Thus they can add vigor to the developing Church.

Let the clergy highly esteem the arduous apostolate of the

laity. Let them train the laity to become conscious of the responsibility which as members of Christ they bear for all men. Let them instruct them deeply in the mystery of Christ, introduce them to practical methods, and be at their side in difficulties, according to the tenor of this Council's Constitution on the Church *(Lumen Gentium)* and its Decree on the Apostolate of the Laity *(Apostolicam Actuositatem)*.

While pastors and laymen, then, retain each their own due functions and their own responsibilities, the whole young Church should render one vital and firm witness to Christ, and thus become a shining beacon of the salvation which comes to us in Christ.

22. The seed which is the Word of God sprouts from the good ground watered by divine dew. From this ground the seed draws nourishing elements which it transforms and assimilates into itself. Finally it bears much fruit. Thus, in imitation of the plan of the Incarnation, the young Churches, rooted in Christ and built up on the foundation of the apostles, take to themselves in a wonderful exchange all the riches of the nations which were given to Christ as an inheritance (cf. Ps. 2:8). From the customs and traditions of their people, from their wisdom and their learning, from their arts and sciences, these Churches borrow all those things which can contribute to the glory of their Creator, the revelation of the Savior's grace, or the proper arrangement of Christian life.[69]

If this goal is to be achieved, theological investigation must necessarily be stirred up in each major socio-cultural area, as it is called. In this way, under the light of the tradition of the universal Church, a fresh scrutiny will be brought to bear on the deeds and words which God has made known, which have been consigned to sacred Scripture, and which have been unfolded by the Church Fathers and the teaching authority of the Church.

Thus it will be more clearly seen in what ways faith can seek for understanding in the philosophy and wisdom of these peoples. A better view will be gained of how their customs, outlook on life, and social order can be reconciled with the manner of living taught by divine revelation. As a result, avenues will be opened for a more profound adaptation in the whole area of Christian life. Thanks to such a procedure, every appearance of syncretism and of false par-

69. *Cf. Dogmatic constitution "Lumen Gentium," 13.*

ticularism can be excluded, and Christian life can be accommodated to the genius and the dispositions of each culture.[70]

Particular traditions, together with the individual patrimony of each family of nations, can be illumined by the light of the gospel, and then be taken up into Catholic unity. Finally, the individual young Churches, adorned with their own traditions, will have their own place in the ecclesiastical communion, without prejudice to the primacy of Peter's See, which presides over the entire assembly of charity.[71]

And so, it is to be hoped and is altogether fitting that Episcopal Conferences within the limits of each major socio-cultural territory will be so united among themselves that they will be able to pursue this program of adaptation with one mind and with a common plan.

CHAPTER IV

MISSIONARIES[72]

23. Every disciple of Christ has the obligation to do his part in spreading the faith.[73] Yet Christ the Lord always calls whoever He chooses from among the number of His disciples, to be with Him and to be sent by Him to preach to the nations (cf. Mk. 3:13 f.). Therefore, through the Holy Spirit, who distributes His charismatic gifts as He wills for

70. *Cf. Allocution of Paul VI at the canonization of the Uganda Martyrs (AAS 1964, 908).*

71. *Cf. Dogmatic constitution "Lumen Gentium," 13.*

72. The portrait of the modern missionary that is drawn in this chapter is largely, as it should be, a portrait of Christ, who, being sent by the Father, "emptied Himself and took the form of a servant" in order to devote Himself totally to the announcement of the good news to mankind. Notably absent from it are the romantic elements which for so long have clung to the popular ideal of the missionary as an explorer, a discoverer of new peoples and continents, a far-ranging and hardy pioneer. The persistence of such an ideal in the world already discovered and explored may have caused the missionary to lose his "privileged position" in the Church. In this chapter, that position is restored in the only way it can be done, by stressing closeness to the essentially missionary character of the world's Savior.

73. *Dogmatic constitution "Lumen Gentium," 17.*

the common good (1 Cor. 12:11), Christ inspires the missionary vocation in the hearts of individuals. At the same time He raises up in the Church certain groups[74] which take as their own special task that duty of preaching the gospel which weighs upon the whole Church.

For there are certain priests, religious, and laymen who are prepared to undertake mission work[75] in their own countries or abroad, and who are endowed with the appropriate natural dispositions, character, and talents. These souls are marked with a special vocation. Sent by legitimate authority, they go out faithfully and obediently to those who are far from Christ. They are set apart for the work to which they have been called (cf. Acts 13:2) as ministers of the gospel, so "that the offering up of the Gentiles may become acceptable, being sanctified by the Holy Spirit" (Rom. 15:16).

24. Yet a man must so respond to God's call that, without consulting flesh and blood (cf. Gal. 1:16), he can devote himself wholly to the work of the gospel. This response, however, can be made only when the Holy Spirit gives His inspiration and strength. For he who is sent enters upon the life and mission of Him who "emptied himself, taking the nature of a slave" (Phil. 2:7). Therefore, he must be ready to stand by his vocation for a lifetime, and to renounce himself and all those whom he thus far considered as his own, and instead to become "all things to all men" (1 Cor. 9:22).

Announcing the gospel among the nations, he confidently makes known the mystery of Christ, whose ambassador he is. Thus in Christ he dares to speak as he ought (cf. Eph. 6:19 f.; Acts 4:31), and is not ashamed of the scandal of the Cross. Following in his Master's footsteps, meek and humble of heart, he shows that His yoke is easy and His burden light (Matt. 11:29 f.). By a truly evangelical life,[76] in much patience, in long-suffering, in kindness, in unaffected love (cf. 2 Cor. 6:4 f.), he bears witness to his Lord, if need be, to the shedding of his blood. He will ask of God power and strength, so that he may come to know that abounding joy can be found even while he undergoes severe trials and the depths of poverty (cf. 2 Cor. 8:2). Let him be convinced

74. *"Institutes" refers to orders, congregations, institutions, and associations which work in the missions.*
75. *Cf. Pius XI, "Rerum Ecclesiae" (AAS 1926, 69-7); Pius XII, "Saeculo Exeunte" (AAS 1940, 256); "Evangelii Praecones" (AAS 1951, 506).*
76. *Cf. Benedict XV, "Maximum Illud" (AAS 1919, 449-450).*

that obedience is the hallmark of the servant of Christ, who redeemed the human race by His obedience.

Lest the heralds of the gospel neglect the grace which is in them, they should be renewed day by day in spirit and in mind (cf. 1 Tim. 4:14; Eph. 4:23; 2 Cor. 4:16). Their Ordinaries and superiors should gather the missionaries together at fixed times to strengthen them in the hope of their calling and renew them in the apostolic ministry. Houses should even be built for this purpose.

25. For such an exalted task, the future missionary is to be prepared by a special spiritual and moral training.[77] For he must be ready to take initiatives, constant in the execution of projects, persevering in difficulties, patient and strong of heart in bearing with solitude, fatigue, and fruitless labor. He must bring an open mind and heart to men, and gladly shoulder the duties entrusted to him. He needs a noble spirit for adapting himself to strange customs and changing circumstances. He needs a sympathetic mind and a responsive heart for cooperating with his brethren and with all who dedicate themselves to a common task. Thus, together with the faithful, missionaries will be of one heart and mind (cf. Acts 2:42; 4:32), in imitation of the apostolic community.

Even during a missionary's training period, these attitudes should be earnestly practiced and developed. For its part, his spiritual life should ennoble and nourish them. Imbued with a living faith and a hope that never fails, the missionary should be a man of prayer. He should glow with a spirit of strength and of love and of self-discipline (cf. 2 Tim. 1:7). Let him learn to be resourceful in every circumstance (cf. Phil. 4:11). Let him in the spirit of sacrifice always bear about in himself the dying of Jesus, so that the life of Jesus may work in those to whom he is sent (cf. 2 Cor. 4:10 ff.). Out of zeal of souls, let him gladly spend all and be spent himself for souls (cf. 2 Cor. 12:15 f.): so that "by the daily exercise of his duty he may grow in the love of God and neighbor."[78] Thus, joined with Christ in obedience to the will of the Father, he will continue His mission under the

---

77. Cf. Benedict XV, "Maximum Illud" (AAS 1919, 448-449); Pius XII, "Evangelii Praecones" (AAS 1951, 507). In the formation of priests to be missionaries consideration is also to be given to those things established in the Decree on Priestly Formation of the Second Vatican Council.
78. Dogmatic constitution "Lumen Gentium," 41.

hierarchical authority of the Church and cooperate in the mystery of salvation.

26. As good ministers of Christ, those who are going to be sent to various nations should be nourished with the "words of faith and of good doctrine" (1 Tim. 4:6). These they should draw principally from the sacred Scriptures as they study the mystery of Christ, whose heralds and witnesses they will be.

Therefore, all missionaries—priests, brothers, sisters, and laymen—each according to his own state, need preparation and training if they are not to be found unequal to the demands of their future work.[79] From the very beginning, their doctrinal training should be so planned that it takes into account both the universality of the Church and the diversity of the world's nations. This requirement holds for all the studies by which they are prepared for the exercise of the ministry, as also for the other branches of learning which it would be useful for them to master. They will thereby gain a general knowledge of peoples, cultures, and religions, a knowledge that looks not only to the past, but to the present as well. For anyone who is going to encounter another people should have a great esteem for their patrimony and their language and their customs.

It is above all necessary for the future missionary to devote himself to missiological studies: that is, to know the teachings and norms of the Church concerning missionary activity, the roads which the heralds of the gospel have traversed in the course of the centuries, the present condition of the missions, and the methods now considered especially effective.[80]

But even though this entire training program is imbued with pastoral considerations, a special and organized apostolic training ought to be given. It should consist of both teaching and practical exercises.[81]

As many brothers and sisters as possible should be well instructed and prepared in the catechetical art, so that they

79. Cf. Benedict XV, "Maximum Illud" (AAS 1919, 440); Pius XII, "Evangelii Praecones" (AAS 1951, 507).
80. Benedict XV, "Maximum Illud" (AAS 1919, 448); Decree S.C.P.F., May 20, 1923 (AAS 1923, 369-370); Pius XII "Saeculo Exeunte" (AAS 1940, 256); "Evangelii Praecones" (AAS 1951, 507); John XXIII, "Princeps Pastorum" (AAS 1959, 843-844).
81. Decree on Priestly Formation, 19-21; apostolic constitution "Sedes Sapientiae," with general statutes.

can collaborate in the apostolate to an even greater extent.

Even those who are to take only a temporary part in missionary activity need to acquire a training which is sufficient for their purposes.

These types of formation should be completed in the lands to which missionaries will be sent. Thus they will gain a more thorough knowledge of the history, social structures, and customs of the people. They will ascertain their system of moral values and their religious precepts, and the innermost ideas which, according to their sacred traditions, they have formed concerning God, the world, and man.[82] Let missionaries learn languages to the extent of being able to use them in a fluent and polished manner. Thus they will find more easy access to the minds and the hearts of men.[83] Furthermore, they should be properly introduced into special pastoral problems.

Some should receive an especially thorough preparation in missiological institutes or in other faculties or universities. As a result they will be able to discharge special duties more effectively[84] and to be a help, by their learning, to other missionaries in carrying on missionary work. In our time especially, this work presents very many difficulties and opportunities.

It is also highly desirable that regional Episcopal Conferences should have available an abundance of such experts, and that in meeting the needs of their office bishops should make fruitful use of the knowledge and experience of these men. There should be no lack either of persons who are perfectly skilled in the use of practical instruments and the means of social communication. The importance of these tools should be greatly appreciated by all.

27. While all these requirements are thoroughly necessary for each and every person sent to the nations, they can in reality scarcely be met by individual missionaries. Since experience teaches too that mission work itself cannot be accomplished by lone individuals, a common calling has gathered individuals together into communities. In these, thanks to united effort, they can be properly trained and will be

---

82. *Pius XII, "Evangelii Praecones" (AAS 1951, 523-524).*
83. *Benedict XV, "Maximum Illud" (AAS 1919, 448); Pius XII, "Evangelii Praecones" (AAS 1951, 507).*
84. *Cf. Pius XII, "Fidei Donum" (AAS 1957, 234).*

able to carry out this work in the name of the Church and at the direction of the hierarchy.

For many centuries now, these communities have borne the burden of the day and the heat, devoting themselves to missionary labor either entirely or in part. Often, vast territories were committed to them by the Holy See for evangelization, and there they gathered together a new people for God, a local Church loyal to its own shepherds. These communities have founded Churches by their own sweat, and even their blood. In the future they will serve these Churches with their zeal and experience in a spirit of brotherly cooperation. This they can do by undertaking the normal care of souls or by discharging special assignments on behalf of the common good.

Sometimes, throughout the entire extent of some region, they will take certain more pressing tasks upon themselves; for example, the evangelization of groups or peoples who perhaps for special reasons have not yet accepted the gospel message, or who have thus far resisted it.[85]

If need be, let them be ready to use their experience to help and train those who will devote themselves temporarily to missionary activity.

For these reasons, and since there are still many nations to be led to Christ, such communities remain especially necessary.

CHAPTER V

PLANNING MISSIONARY ACTIVITY

28. Since Christians have different gifts (cf. Rom. 12:6), each one must collaborate in the work of the gospel according to his own opportunity, ability, charismatic gifts, and call to service (cf. 1 Cor. 3:10). Hence all alike, those who sow and those who reap (cf. Jn. 4:37), those who plant and

85. *Cf. Decree on the Ministry and Life of Priests, 10, where reference is made to dioceses and personal prelatures and the like.*

those who irrigate, must be united (cf. 1 Cor. 3:8). Thus, "in a free and orderly fashion cooperating toward a common goal,"[86] they can spend their forces harmoniously for the upbuilding of the Church.

Therefore, the labors of the gospel heralds and the help given by the rest of the Christian faithful must be so directed and intertwined that "all things [may] be done . . . in order" (1 Cor. 14:40) in every area of missionary activity and co-operation.

29. The responsibility to proclaim the gospel throughout the world falls primarily on the body of bishops.[87] Now the Synod of Bishops is a "stable council of bishops concerned with the entire Church."[88] Hence among its affairs of general concern,[89] it should give special consideration to missionary activity. For this is a supremely great and sacred task of the Church.[90]

For all missions and for the whole of missionary activity, there should be only one competent Curial office, namely, that of the "Propagation of the Faith." This office should direct and coordinate missionary work itself as well as missionary cooperation throughout the world. However, the law of the Oriental Churches is to remain untouched.[91]

The Holy Spirit uses manifold means to arouse the mission spirit in the Church of God, and often anticipates the action of those whose task it is to rule the life of the Church. Still, for its part, this aforementioned office should promote missionary vocations and spirituality as well as zeal and prayer for the missions, and should produce authentic and adequate reports about them.

Let it raise up missionaries and distribute them according to the more urgent needs of various areas. Let it arrange for an orderly plan of action, issue directives and principles suited to the work of evangelization, and give that work impetus. Let it take care of activating and coordinating an effective collection of funds. These are to be distributed on

---

86. *Cf. Dogmatic constitution "Lumen Gentium,"* 18.
87. *Cf. Dogmatic constitution "Lumen Gentium,"* 23.
88. *Cf. Motu proprio "Apostolica Sollicitudo,"* Sept. 15, 1965.
89. *Cf. Paul VI, allocution Nov. 21, 1964, in Council (AAS 1964).*
90. *Cf. Benedict XV, "Maximum Illud" (AAS 1919, 39-40).*
91. *If any missions, for special reasons, are still temporarily subject to other curial offices, it is expedient that these offices be in contact with the Sacred Congregation for the Propagation of the Faith, in order that an altogether constant and uniform policy and regulation may be maintained in the planning and direction of all missions.*

the basis of necessity and usefulness, the extent of the territory in question, the number of believers and unbelievers, of projects and institutes, of auxiliaries and missionaries.

In coordination with the Secretariat for Promoting Christian Unity, it should search out ways and means for bringing about and directing fraternal cooperation as well as harmonious living with the missionary undertakings of other Christian communities. Thus, as far as possible, the scandal of division can be removed.

Therefore, this office must be both an administrative instrument and an agency of dynamic direction. As such it should make use of scientific methods and of means suited to the conditions of modern times. It should certainly take into consideration present-day research in theology, methodology, and missionary pastoral procedure.

In the direction of this office, an active role with a deliberative vote should be exercised by selected representatives of all those who cooperate in missionary work.[92] The latter include the bishops of the whole world (whose Episcopal Conferences will have to be heard from in this matter), as well as the moderators of papal institutes and activities whose representatives will be chosen in ways and under conditions to be determined by the Roman Pontiff. All these representatives will be called together at fixed times and will exercise supreme control of all mission work, under the authority of the Supreme Pontiff.

This office should have available a permanent group of expert consultors, of proven knowledge or experience. Their duty it will be, among other things, to gather pertinent information about local conditions in various regions, the outlook of various groups of men, and the means of evangelization to be used. They will then propose scientifically based conclusions for mission work and cooperation.

Communities of religious women, regional undertakings on behalf of the missions, and lay organizations (especially international ones) should be suitably represented.

30. In order for the proper goals and results to be obtained in the actual exercise of mission activity itself, all missionary

92. It is to be noted that the reform of the Congregation of the Propagation of the Faith is based on the principle of collegiality which underlines the co-responsibility of the bishops with the Pope for the universal Church and especially for the missions. Residential bishops from all over the world will have an active part in the government of the missions. This is a change of far-reaching importance.

workers should have but "one heart and one soul" (Acts 4:32).

It is the role of the bishop, as the ruler and center of unity in the diocesan apostolate, to promote missionary activity, to direct it, and to coordinate it, but always in such a way that the spontaneous zeal of those who share in the work will be preserved and fostered. All missionaries, even exempt Religious, are subject to his power in the various works which involve the exercise of the sacred apostolate.[93]

To improve coordination, let the bishop set up, insofar as possible, a pastoral council. In this council, clergy, religious, and laity can have a part through the medium of selected delegates. Moreover, let him take care that apostolic activity not be limited to those only who have already been converted. A fair proportion of personnel and funds should be assigned to the evangelization of non-Christians.

31. Episcopal Conferences should take common counsel to deal with weightier questions and urgent problems, without however overlooking their own local differences.[94] Lest an insufficient supply of men and means be dissipated, or lest projects be multiplied without necessity, it is recommended that these Conferences pool their resources to found projects which will serve the good of all: as for instance, seminaries, schools of higher learning and of technology; pastoral, catechetical, and liturgical centers, as well as communications centers.

Such cooperation, when indicated, should also be initiated between different Episcopal Conferences.

32. It will also be helpful to coordinate the activities which are being carried on by ecclesiastical institutes and associations. All these, of whatever kind, should defer to the local Ordinary in everything concerning missionary activity itself. Therefore it will be highly beneficial if contracts are drawn up governing the relations between local Ordinaries and the moderator of such an institute.

When a territory has been committed to a certain religious community, both the ecclesiastical superior and the community must be concerned to direct everything to this objective, namely, that the new Christian community may grow into a

---

93. *Cf. Decree on the Bishops' Pastoral Office in the Church, 35, 4.*
94. *Cf. Decree on the Bishops' Pastoral Office in the Church, 36-38.*

local Church, which will in due time be directed by its own pastor with his clergy.

When the commission given to communities over certain territories expires, a new state of affairs begins. Then the Episcopal Conferences and the communities in joint deliberation should lay down norms governing the relations between local Ordinaries and the communities.[95] It will be the role of the Holy See to outline the general principles according to which regional and even particular agreements are to be drawn up.

The communities should be prepared to continue the work which they have begun, by cooperating in the ordinary ministry of the care of souls. Yet, as the local clergy increases, care should be taken that, insofar as this is in agreement with its purpose, the community should remain faithful to the diocese by generously shouldering special works or assuming responsibility for some part of it.

33. Communities engaged in missionary activity in the same territory should find ways and means of coordinating their work. Therefore, extreme usefulness recommends conferences of religious men and unions of religious women, in which all communities working in the same country or region can take part. These conferences should try to discover what things can be done by combined efforts, and should be in close touch with the Episcopal Conferences.

With equal reason, all these recommendations can be appropriately extended to include the cooperation of missionary communities in the home lands. Thus common problems and projects can be handled more easily and with less expense: for instance, the doctrinal formation of future missionaries, courses for present missionaries, relations with public authorities and with international or supranational organizations.

34. The proper and orderly exercise of missionary activity requires that those who labor for the gospel be scientifically prepared for their task, especially for dialogue with non-Christian religions and cultures. It requires that they be effectively assisted in the carrying out of this task. Hence this Council desires that, for the sake of the missions, fraternal and generous collaboration exist on the part of scientific institutes specializing in missiology and in other sciences and

95. *Cf. Decree on the Bishops' Pastoral Office in the Church, 35, 5-6.*

arts useful for the missions. Such would be ethnology and linguistics, the history and science of religions, sociology, pastoral skills, and the like.

CHAPTER VI

MISSIONARY COOPERATION

35. Since the whole Church is missionary, and the work of evangelization is a basic duty of the People of God, this sacred Synod summons all to a deep interior renewal. Thus, from a vivid awareness of their own responsibility for spreading the gospel, they will do their share in missionary work among the nations.

36. As members of the living Christ, all the faithful have been incorporated into Him and made like unto Him through baptism, confirmation, and the Eucharist. Hence all are duty-bound to cooperate in the expansion and growth of His Body, so that they can bring it to fullness as swiftly as possible (Eph. 4:13).

Therefore, all sons of the Church should have a lively awareness of their responsibility to the world. They should foster in themselves a truly catholic spirit. They should spend their energies in the work of evangelization.

Yet, let all realize that their first and most important obligation toward the spread of the faith is this: to lead a profoundly Christian life. For their fervor in the service of God and their charity toward others will cause new spiritual inspiration to sweep over the whole Church. Then she will appear as a sign lifted up among the nations (cf. Is. 11:12), "the light of the world" (Mt. 5:14) and "the salt of the earth" (Mt. 5:13). This living testimony will more easily achieve its effect if it is given in unison with other Christian communities, according to the norms of the Decree on Ecumenism, 12.[96]

96. *Cf. Decree on Ecumenism, 12.*

From this renewed spirit, prayer and works of penance will be spontaneously offered to God that He may make the work of missionaries fruitful by His grace. Then missionary vocations will be generated, and the resources which missions need will be forthcoming.

Each and every one of the Christian faithful needs to be fully acquainted with the present condition of the Church in the world, and to hear the voice of the multitudes who cry: "Help us!" (cf. Acts 16:9). Hence modern means of social communication should also be used to furnish the kind of mission information which will make the faithful feel that mission work is their very own, will make them open their hearts to such vast and profound human needs, and enable them to come to the relief of these needs.

Also needed is coordination of such information, and cooperation with national and international agencies.

37. But since the People of God lives in communities, especially in dioceses and parishes, and becomes visible in them in a certain way, it also devolves on these to witness Christ before the nations.

The grace of renewal cannot flourish in communities unless each of them extends the range of its charity to the ends of the earth, and devotes to those far off a concern similar to that which it bestows on those who are its own members.

Thus the whole community prays, collaborates, and exercises activity among the nations through those of its sons whom God chooses for this most excellent task.

Provided the universal scope of mission work is not thereby neglected, it will be very useful for a community to maintain contact with missionaries who came from its ranks, or with some parish or diocese in the missions. In this way the bond between communities will be made visible, and will provide mutual edification.

38. As members of the body of bishops which succeeds the College of Apostles, all bishops are consecrated not just for some one diocese, but for the salvation of the entire world. Christ's mandate to preach the gospel to every creature (Mk. 16:15) primarily and immediately concerns them, with Peter and under Peter. From this fact arises that communion and cooperation between Churches which is so necessary today for carrying on the work of evangelization.[97] In virtue

97. Communion and cooperation *between the Churches,* mentioned in this

of this communion, individual Churches carry a responsibility for all the others. They make their necessities known to one another, and keep one another mutually informed regarding their affairs. For the extension of the Body of Christ is the duty of the whole College of Bishops.[98]

In his own diocese, with which he comprises a single unit, the bishop stimulates, promotes, and directs the work for the missions. Thus he makes the mission spirit and zeal of the People of God present and, as it were, visible, so that the whole diocese becomes missionary.

It will be the bishop's task to raise up from among his own people, especially the sick and those oppressed by hardship, souls who will offer prayers and penance to God with a generous heart for the evangelization of the world. The bishop will also gladly foster vocations to mission communities among young people and clerics. He will react with a grateful spirit if God should call some of them to engage in the missionary activity of the Church.

The bishop will exhort and help the diocesan congregations to play a role of their own in the missions. He will promote the works of mission institutes among his own faithful, but especially the papal mission societies. For it is only right to give these works pride of place, since they are the means of imbuing Catholics from their very infancy with a genuinely universal and missionary outlook. They are also the means for undertaking an effective collection of funds to subsidize all missions, each according to its needs.[99]

The need for workers in the vineyard of the Lord grows from day to day, while diocesan priests have expressed the wish to play an ever greater part in the evangelization of the world. Hence this sacred Synod desires that in view of the critical shortage of priests which is hindering the evangelization of many areas, bishops should send some of the better priests who offer themselves for mission work to those dio-

paragraph and specified in the previous section as a community-to-community relationship, restores to the Church an ancient practice which is involved in the doctrine of collegiality. This Church-to-Church relationship for assistance to the missions is not a substitute for aid on the more common vertical axis, from bishops-to-Pope-to-missions, but operates simultaneously with it and under the direction of the Supreme Pontiff. Already highly developed in some European countries, it is destined for even greater development since, as the Decree states, it is today so necessary for the effective spreading of the gospel.

98. *Cf. Dogmatic constitution "Lumen Gentium," 23-24.*
99. *Cf. Benedict XV, "Maximum Illud" (AAS 1919, 453-454); Pius XI, "Rerum Ecclesiae" (AAS 1926, 71-73); Pius XII, "Evangelii Praecones" (AAS 1951, 525-526); Id. "Fidei Donum" (AAS 1957, 241.)*

ceses which are lacking in clergy. After due preparation, they can exercise there a missionary ministry in the spirit of service at least for a time.[100]

In order that the missionary activity of individual bishops on behalf of the whole Church may be expressed more effectively, it will be helpful for Episcopal Conferences to regulate those affairs which concern the orderly cooperation of their own region.

In their Conferences, bishops should deliberate about dedicating to the evangelization of the nations some priests from among the diocesan clergy. They should deal with the definite offering which in proportion to its resources each diocese is obliged to set aside annually for the work of the missions.[101] They should consider how to direct and organize the ways and means by which the missions receive direct help. They should weigh the matter of assisting and if need be, founding, missionary institutes and seminaries for diocesan mission clergy, and promoting closer relations between such institutes and the dioceses.

It likewise pertains to the Episcopal Conferences to found and promote projects for providing a brotherly welcome and due pastoral care for those who immigrate from mission lands for the sake of studying or working. For through them, faraway peoples become neighbors in a certain sense. An excellent opportunity is offered to communities which have long been Christian to converse with nations which have not yet heard the gospel, and to show them the genuine face of Christ[102] through their own offices of love and assistance.

39. Priests represent Christ, and are collaborators with the order of bishops in that threefold sacred task which by its very nature bears on the mission of the Church.[103] Therefore, they should fully understand that their life has also been consecrated to the service of the missions. By means of their own ministry, which deals principally with the Eucharist as the source of perfecting the Church, they are in communion with Christ the Head and are leading others to this communion. Hence they cannot help realizing how much is yet wanting to the fullness of that Body, and how much therefore must be done if it is to grow from day to day.

100. Cf. Pius XII, "Fidei Donum" (AAS 1957, 245-246).
101. Decree on the Bishops' Pastoral Office in the Church, 6.
102. Cf. Pius XII, "Fidei Donum" (AAS 1957, 245).
103. Cf. Dogmatic constitution "Lumen Gentium," 28.

They will consequently organize their pastoral activity in such a way that it will serve to spread the gospel among non-Christians.

In that pastoral activity, priests should stir up and preserve amid the faithful a zeal for the evangelization of the world. This they can do by instructing them in catechism classes and in sermons about the Church's task of announcing Christ to all nations; by teaching Christian families about the necessity and the honor of fostering missionary vocations among their own sons and daughters; by promoting mission fervor among young people who attend schools and Catholic associations so that among them there may arise future heralds of the gospel. Let priests train the faithful to pray for the missions, and let them not be ashamed to ask alms of them for this purpose, becoming like beggars for Christ and for the salvation of souls.[104]

Seminary and college professors should teach young people the true state of the world and of the Church, so that the necessity of a more intense evangelization of non-Christians will become clear to them and will nurture their zeal. In teaching the dogmatic, biblical, moral, and historical branches, they should bring to light the missionary aspects contained therein. In this way a missionary awareness can be formed in future priests.

40. Religious communities of the contemplative and of the active life have so far played, and still do play, a very great role in the evangelization of the world. This sacred Synod gladly acknowledges their merits and thanks God for all that they have done for the glory of God and the service of souls. It exhorts them to go on untiringly in the work which they have begun, since they know that the virtue of charity impels and obliges them to a spirit and an effort which is truly Catholic.[105] By their vocation they are bound to practice this charity with a special degree of perfection.

By their prayers, works of penance, and sufferings, contemplative communities have a very great importance in the conversion of souls. For it is God who sends workers into His harvest when He is asked to do so (cf. Mt. 9:38), who opens the minds of non-Christians to hear the gospel (cf. Acts 16:14), and who makes the word of salvation fruitful

104. *Cf. Pius XI, "Rerum Ecclesiae" (AAS 1926, 72).*
105. *Cf. Dogmatic constitution "Lumen Gentium," 44.*

in their hearts (cf. 1 Cor. 3:7). In fact, these communities are urged to found houses in mission areas, as not a few of them have already done. Thus living out their lives in a manner accommodated to the truly religious traditions of the people, they can bear splendid witness there among non-Christians to the majesty and love of God, as well as to man's brotherhood in Christ.

Whether they pursue a strictly mission goal or not, communities dedicated to the active life should sincerely ask themselves in the presence of God, whether they cannot broaden their activity in favor of expanding God's kingdom among the nations; whether they might not leave certain ministries to others so that they themselves can spend their energies on the missions; whether they can undertake work among the missions, adapting their constitutions if necessary, but according to the spirit of their founder; whether their members are involved as much as possible in missionary activity; and whether their type of life bears to the gospel a witness which is accommodated to the character and condition of the people.

Thanks to the inspiration of the Holy Spirit, secular institutes are increasing every day in the Church. Under the authority of the bishop, their programs can be fruitful in the missions in many ways as a sign of complete dedication to the evangelization of the world.

41. Laymen cooperate in the Church's work of evangelization. As witnesses and at the same time as living instruments, they share in her saving mission.[106] This is especially so if they have been called by God and have been accepted by the bishop for this work.

In those lands which are already Christian, laymen cooperate in the work of evangelization by nurturing in themselves and in others a knowledge and love of the missions; by stimulating vocations in their own family, in Catholic societies, and in the schools; by providing subsidies of every kind, so that they can offer to others that gift of faith which they have freely received.

But in mission lands, let laymen, whether foreigners or natives, teach in schools, administer temporal goods, cooperate in parish and diocesan activities, and organize and promote various forms of the lay apostolate. Thus the faithful

106. *Cf. Ibid. 33, 35.*

of the young Churches will be able to take their own part as soon as possible in the life of the Church.[107]

Finally, laymen should willingly offer socio-economic cooperation to peoples undergoing development. This cooperation is all the more praiseworthy to the extent that it concerns itself with founding institutions which touch on the basic structures of social life, or which are oriented to the training of those who bear the responsibility for government.

Worthy of special praise are those laymen who work in universities or in scientific institutes and whose historical and scientific-religious research promotes knowledge of peoples and of religions. Thus they help the heralds of the gospel, and prepare for dialogue with non-Christians.

They should cooperate in a brotherly spirit with other Christians, with non-Christians, and with members of international organizations, having always before their eyes the fact that "the building up of the earthly city should have its foundation in the Lord, and should be directed towards Him."[108]

If they are to shoulder all these tasks, laymen need the necessary technical and spiritual preparation. Such preparation should be given in institutes established for this purpose. Thus their lives will give witness to Christ among non-Christians, according to the words of the Apostle: "Do not be a stumbling-block to Jews and Gentiles and to the Church of God, even as I myself in all things please all men, not seeking what is profitable to myself but to the many, that they may be saved." (1 Cor. 10:32-33).

CONCLUSION

42. The Council Fathers together with the Roman Pontiff, aware of their most solemn duty to spread everywhere the Kingdom of God, lovingly salute all heralds of the gospel. They especially salute those who suffer persecution for the

107. Cf. Pius XII, "Evangelii Praecones" (AAS 1951, 510, 514); John XXIII, "Princeps Pastorum" (AAS 1959, 851-852).
108. Cf. Dogmatic constitution "Lumen Gentium," 46.

name of Christ, and they make themselves companions in their sufferings.[109]

These Fathers and the Roman Pontiff are afire with that same love with which Christ burned toward men. But knowing that it is God who makes His kingdom come on earth, they pour forth their prayers together with all the Christian faithful, that through the intercession of the Virgin Mary, Queen of the Apostles, the nations may be led to the knowledge of the truth as soon as possible (1 Tim. 2:4), and that the splendor of God which brightens the face of Jesus Christ may shine upon all men through the Holy Spirit (2 Cor. 4:6).

Each and every one of the things set forth in this Decree has won the consent of the Fathers of this most sacred Council. We too, by the Apostolic authority conferred on Us by Christ, join with the Venerable Fathers in approving, decreeing, and establishing these things in the Holy Spirit, and We direct that what has thus been enacted in synod be published to God's glory.

Rome, at St. Peter's, December 7, 1965*

I, Paul, Bishop of the Catholic Church

There follow the signatures of the Fathers.

---

109. Cf. Pius XII, "Evangelii Praecones" (AAS 1951, 527); John XXIII, "Princeps Pastorum" (AAS 1959, 864).
*Following the Decree there is an announcement entitled "A Suspension of the Law" (Vacatio legis), declaring June 29, 1966, as the effective date for laws contained in the Decree. The text is the same as that given in note 67, at the end of the Decree on Priestly Formation.—Ed.

A RESPONSE

A proposed statement on missions was presented to Vatican Council II in 1964. A brief document, concentrating largely on juridical and organizational problems, it was rejected by the Council and a new version was asked. This final Decree is a marked improvement, particularly in theological content. A comparison of the texts shows that the theological chapter, however, is primarily an addition. The internal problems of jurisdiction and organization which the Roman Catholic Church faces in its vast and vigorous missionary outreach still dominate much of the Decree.

The theological statement affirms biblically the missionary nature of the Church, affirms that the missionary life of the Church is rooted in the Incarnation and in Pentecost, and sets that life clearly in its eschatological dimension. Thus it provides a dynamic, biblically-based directive for the Church in witness to the nations. This interpretation is a great gain over a once prevalent tendency in Roman Catholic missiology to interpret missions primarily as the extension of that particular Church.

The fundamental agreement at the points listed above to prevailing Protestant understanding of mission enhances the importance of the summons to collaboration "with the missionary activities of other Christian communities" (Art. 29). The total Christian mission stands on a new threshold of hope with the recognition in this Decree that unity and mission are inseparably related, that the scandal of division must be overcome in order to make a fully Christian witness, and that all cooperation must be for the sake of Christ and His gospel.

The missionary call of every Christian—inescapable in his faith and baptism—is rightly stressed. The participation of the laity in mission, however, is to be channeled by the hierarchy. Fulfillment of the missionary obligation which the Christian discovers in Christ demands opportunity for individual, creative initiative and experimentation which the hierarchical controls assumed in this document would seem severely to restrict.

Missions are treated in the Decree primarily as "foreign missions," and missionaries are seen primarily as evangelists sent *abroad*. Even the reality of the missionary task in Latin

America is obscured by the predominant emphasis in this statement upon missions as work in Asia and Africa and Oceania. Related to this limitation is a failure adequately to recognize not only the local missionary task of every congregation, but even of the Churches in Asia, Africa, and Oceania. They are treated fully as Churches, rather than only as missions, and that treatment is a notable advance. However, their own missionary task in their own situation is quite inadequately emphasized. Even in their situation the missionary task seems to be left too much to foreign missionaries, and not made sufficiently the responsibility of local clergy and laity.

The Decree calls for a change in the Sacred Congregation for the Propagation of the Faith. It is to be internationalized. A council of consultants shall be formed, also on an international basis. It is to be composed of persons directly engaged in the missionary task, and its functions are to be determined by the Pope.

Reference is made in the Decree to the need of the individual for conversion and to the process of training that must be provided. There is also reference to the missionary responsibility for the transformation of social and cultural life, for the elimination of poverty and the establishment of peace. In the total context of the document, however, these questions are given surprisingly slight attention. This fact is probably related to the relative absence from the Decree of affirmation of the need of mankind for repentance—both individually and collectively, of the tension between the gospel and the world, and thus of the centrality of the Cross in the Christian mission.

The reader of the Decree is more likely to be impressed by the complexity of the organizational problems within the Roman Catholic missionary enterprise than by the vast complexity of the missionary task today. Questions of massive importance confront the Church in its contemporary mission. Some are touched upon in this Decree; some are not. Obviously, adequate treatment of all is impossible in a statement of this length. A few are listed below:

—Since "the Church on earth is missionary in its very nature" (Art. 2), and "the faithful gathered in the parish church taking part in the Eucharistic liturgy are the Church of God" (Gregory Baum, commenting on the Constitution on the Church), what is the missionary function of the local congregation?

—What is the relationship between missions and the struggle for justice in society?

—What is the relationship between Christian faith and other religions?

—What are the conditions under which cooperation can occur in missionary activity between Roman Catholics and other Christians?

—What is the role of the Holy Spirit today in the Christian mission? Do we understand that role primarily as acting through the institutions of the Church, as seemingly implied in the Decree?

—What future forms of institutional witness should we anticipate in the Christian mission?

The note of desperate urgency of need for the Christian mission is strangely lacking in the Decree. The great vigor of Roman Catholic missionary activity today is evidence that at this point the Decree does not reflect the thinking of many within that Church. As a matter of fact, each of the questions which this Protestant has indicated above about the Decree would have at least some support from individual, and influential, Roman Catholics. The Decree is probably best understood as a beginning rather than an end. This writer joins with a great host of others—Protestant, Orthodox, and Roman Catholic—in gratitude for the increasingly biblical, and therefore ecumenical, nature of Roman Catholic missionary thought.

EUGENE L. SMITH

EDUCATION

ALTHOUGH A SPECIFIC statement on "The Church in the Modern World" is part of the Acta of the Second Council of the Vatican, the whole preoccupation of this historic meeting has been the adjustment of Christian thinking to the modern world.

It would be fair to state that the Church has taken the word "modern" in its proper meaning. A thing is neither good nor bad because it is modern. "Modern" really involves the concept of adjusting to the mode of the present. This is a prime necessity and obligation of the Church, and those who continuously lament the departure of past times are untrue to the Church and to themselves. The very principle of the Incarnation is a principle of living in the present.

It is not, then, surprising that the Church should be preoccupied with her role in formal education. Once again, it would be true to say that the whole concern of the Council is with education in one form or another. In every document, particularly in the most important, such as the Constitution on the Sacred Liturgy, the Constitution on the Church, and the Constitution on Divine Revelation, the prime function of the Church as teacher of mankind has been put into clear focus. Similarly, the Pope, in his historic visit to the United Nations, chose as his motto the text, "Go therefore and teach all nations."

In the present document, the Church comes directly to grips with the problem of formal education, particularly in the schools. We must note that this Declaration is somewhat different from the other Council documents. It states specifically that it deals only with a few fundamental principles and that a more developed point of view is being left to a special postconciliar Commission and to the Conferences of Bishops. This may explain why the Declaration breaks little new ground and limits itself to a strong statement of basic positions.

At a time when the role of the Church in education is again challenged, when even some Catholic laymen seem to feel that the teaching Church, in particular the bishops and the clergy under them, have little or nothing to say about the problems of Christian education, the Church has found it necessary to use the Council in order to redefine the basic rights of all concerned, beginning with the bishops and going right through to the parents, the state, and even the students themselves. This makes for a rather technical document and, in some cases, a somewhat juridical one, but it cannot fail to bring some clarification, if only to establish that the Church has not changed its traditional positions.

What is most distinctive about this document, at least in general terms, is the insistence upon the integration of Christian education into the whole pattern of human life in all its aspects. In this regard, the Declaration on Christian Education is totally in conformity with the spirit of Vatican II. The contrast is with a form of thinking and acting of another age when it was considered best to keep Christians away from the world lest they be contaminated thereby. The stricture of the *Imitation of Christ*—"Son, in many things it behooveth thee to be ignorant"—may have been productive of ascetic monasticism, but it was hardly the proper norm for the 20th-century Christian. This mentality had generated an idea that Catholics were making tremendous sacrifices for a Christian education in order to segregate their children and to protect them.

The present Declaration spells the official and definitive end of any possible false thinking on this score. The Church here states with utmost clarity that it has no desire to remain away *from* the world in a form of isolation but that Christian education is *in* the world and, in a sense, *for* the world, since man must always work out his salvation in the concrete situation in which God has placed him and must achieve this not by protection but by contributing to the whole human community of which he is an integral and inseparable part.

Thus we note the strong emphasis on the intellectual values of all education and an appeal for all to strive to achieve the highest development of the human mind. In making this appeal, the Church remains true to itself by insisting that this must be done in the framework of the moral formation of man and in the fullness of his spiritual, supernatural destiny.

But the formula remains one of integration and total dedication to all of man's legitimate aspirations.

There may be some disappointment that a further development is lacking in terms of what Christian education can mean to the modern world and some suggestions for practical forms of greater collaboration and integration. But the self-imposed limits of the document must be taken into account and it should be used as requested, namely, as a starting point for further dialogue and for a more profound and inspiring presentation of the positive values of Christian education in a world which, while reaching for the stars, is in danger of not seeing their light.

✠ G. Emmett Carter

Declaration on Christian Education

PAUL, BISHOP
SERVANT OF THE SERVANTS OF GOD
TOGETHER WITH THE FATHERS OF THE SACRED COUNCIL
FOR EVERLASTING MEMORY

INTRODUCTION

This sacred Ecumenical Synod has carefully considered the paramount importance of education in the life of man, and its ever-mounting influence on the social progress of this age.[1] In fact, the education of the young and even a measure of continued instruction for adults have grown both easier and more urgent in the circumstances of our times. For as men grow more conscious of their dignity and calling, they prefer to take an increasingly active part in the life of society, espe-

---

1. *Among many documents illustrating the importance of education, see especially:*

Benedict XV, apostolic letter "Communes Litteras," Apr. 10, 1919: AAS 11 (1919), p. 172.

Pius XI, encyclical letter "Divini Illius Magistri," Dec. 31, 1929: AAS 22 (1930), pp. 49-86.

Pius XII, allocution to the youths of Italian Catholic Action, Apr. 20, 1946: "Discorsi e Radiomessaggi," Vol. 8, pp. 53-57.

Pius XII, allocution to fathers of Families of France, Sept. 18, 1951: "Discorsi e Radiomessagi," Vol. 13, pp. 241-245.

John XXIII, message on the 30th anniversary of the publication of the encyclical letter "Divini Illius Magistri," Dec. 30, 1959: AAS 52 (1960), pp. 57-59.

Paul VI, allocution to members of Federated Institutes Dependent on Ecclestiastical Authority, Dec. 30, 1963: "Encicliche e Discorsi di S.S. Paolo VI," Vol. I, Rome 1964, pp. 601-603.

In addition, there may be consulted "Acta et Documenta Concilio Oecumenico Vaticano II apparando," series I, "Antepraeparatoria," Vol. III, pp. 363-364, 370-371, 373, 374.

cially in economic and political matters.[2] Enjoying more
leisure, as they sometimes do, men find that remarkable developments in technology and in scientific investigation, and
new means of social communication offer them readier opportunities for attaining their inheritance of intellectual and
spiritual culture, and for fulfilling themselves and one another
by forging stronger bonds between various groups and even
whole peoples.

As a result, ever-increasing efforts are being everywhere
expended to promote the work of education. The primary
rights of men with respect to education, especially those of
children and of parents, are being emphasized, and are finding expression in public documents.[3] On every side, as the
number of pupils rapidly increases, schools are being multiplied and perfected, and other educational institutions are being established. Techniques of education and training are
being refined on the basis of new experiments. Strenuous efforts are being made so that all men can obtain an education,
though, admittedly, vast numbers of children and young people are still being deprived of even rudimentary training, and
many others lack the suitable kind of education in which
truth and love are simultaneously inculcated.

In fulfilling the mandate she has received from her divine
Founder to proclaim the mystery of salvation to all men, and
to restore all things in Christ, Holy Mother the Church must
be concerned with the whole of man's life,[4] even the earthly
part of it insofar as that has a bearing on his heavenly calling.[5] Therefore she has her role to play in the progress and

2. Cf. John XXIII, encyclical letter "Mater et Magistra," May 15, 1961:
AAS 53 (1961), pp. 413, 415-417, 424.
    Also his encyclical letter "Pacem in Terris," Apr. 1, 1963: AAS 55 (1963),
pp. 278 ff.
3. Cf. the universal profession of the rights of men ("Déclaration des droits
de l'homme") of Dec. 10, 1948, adopted by the General Assembly of the
United Nations; see also "Déclaration des droits de l'enfant" of Nov. 20,
1959; also "Protocole additionnel à la convention de sauvegarde des droits
de l'homme et des libertés fondamentales," Paris, Mar. 20, 1952; regarding
that universal profession of the rights of man mentioned above, cf. John
XXIII, encyclical letter "Pacem in Terris," Apr. 11, 1963: AAS 55 (1963), pp.
295 ff.
4. The Council here states its basic position with regard to the Declaration
on Christian Education. Although the Church is concerned primarily with
the spiritual and supernatural destiny of man, it recognizes the intimate
connection between that destiny and "the whole of man's life." See introductory notes.
5. Cf. John XXIII, encyclical letter "Mater et Magistra," May 15, 1961; AAS
53 (1961), p. 402.
    See also Second Vatican Council's Dogmatic Constitution on the Church,

spread of education. Hence this sacred Synod enunciates certain basic principles of Christian education, especially those applicable to formal schooling. These principles will have to be developed at greater length by a special postconciliar Commission and applied by episcopal conferences to varying local situations.

1. Since every man of whatever race, condition, and age is endowed with the dignity of a person, he has an inalienable right to an education[6] corresponding to his proper destiny[7] and suited to his native talents, his sex, his cultural background, and his ancestral heritage. At the same time, this education should pave the way to brotherly association with other peoples, so that genuine unity and peace on earth may be promoted. For a true education aims at the formation of the human person with respect to his ultimate goal, and simultaneously with respect to the good of those societies of which, as a man, he is a member, and in whose responsibilities, as an adult, he will share.

As a consequence, with the help of advances in psychology and in the art and science of teaching, children and young people should be assisted in the harmonious development of their physical, moral, and intellectual endowments. Surmounting hardships with a gallant and steady heart, they should be helped to acquire gradually a more mature sense of responsibility toward ennobling their own lives through constant effort, and toward pursuing authentic freedom. As they advance in years, they should be given positive and prudent sexual education. Moreover, they should be trained to take their part in social life, so that by proper instruction in necessary and useful skills they can become actively involved in various community organizations, be ready for dialogue with others, and be willing to act energetically on behalf of the common good.

This holy Synod likewise affirms that children and young people have a right to be encouraged to weigh moral values with an upright conscience, and to embrace them by personal

---

Art. 17: AAS 57 (1965), p. 21; also the schema of the Pastoral Constitution on the Church in the Modern World (1965), passim.
6. Pius XII, radio message of Dec. 24, 1942: AAS 35 (1943), pp. 12, 19.
John XXIII, encyclical letter "Pacem in Terris," Apr. 11, 1963: AAS 55 (1963), pp. 259 ff. See also the declarations of the rights of man cited in note (3).
7. Cf. Pius XI, encyclical letter "Divini Illius Magistri," Dec. 31, 1929: AAS 22 (1930), pp. 50 ff.

choice, and to know and love God more adequately.[8] Hence, it earnestly entreats all who exercise government over peoples or preside over the work of education to see that youth is never deprived of this sacred right. It urges sons of the Church to devote themselves generously to the whole enterprise of education, with the special aim of helping to bring more speedily to all men everywhere the worthy benefits of education and training.[9]

2. Since every Christian has become a new creature[10] by rebirth from water and the Holy Spirit, so that he may be called what he truly is, a child of God, he is entitled to a Christian education. Such an education does not merely strive to foster in the human person the maturity already described. Rather, its principal aims are these:[11] that as the baptized person is gradually introduced into a knowledge of the mystery of salvation, he may daily grow more conscious of the gift of faith which he has received; that he may learn to adore God the Father in spirit and in truth (cf. Jn. 4:23), especially through liturgical worship; that he may be trained to conduct his personal life in righteousness and in the sanctity of truth, according to his new standard of manhood (Eph. 4:22-24).

Thus, indeed, he may grow into manhood according to the mature measure of Christ (cf. Eph. 4:13), and devote himself to the upbuilding of the Mystical Body. Moreover, aware of his calling, he should grow accustomed to giving witness to the hope that is in him (1 Pet. 3:15), and to promoting that Christian transformation of the world by which natural values, viewed in the full perspective of humanity as redeemed by Christ, may contribute to the good of society as a whole.[12]

---

8. The theme of personal responsibility which has dominated so many of the deliberations of Vatican II comes out very clearly here. Note the insistence on children and young people and their own development in contradistinction to a previous attitude of education as if it were imposed from above. There is an interesting connection between this paragraph and the Declaration on Religious Freedom.

9. Cf. John XXIII, encyclical letter "Mater et Magistra," May 15, 1961: AAS 53 (1961), pp. 441 ff.

10. Cf. Pius XI, encyclical letter "Divini Illius Magistri," loc cit., p. 83.

11. Here is the most positive statement of the true essence of Christian education. The Christian view of life is simply different and is based on a belief in a supernatural life. The result is that the Christian can never be satisfied with mere material-minded education. It also explains why Christian education is not merely ordinary education with an added dose of religious knowledge.

12. Cf. Second Vatican Council, Dogmatic Constitution on the Church, Art. 36: AAS 57 (1965), pp. 41 ff.

Therefore this holy Synod reminds pastors of souls of their acutely serious duty to make every effort to see that all the faithful enjoy a Christian education of this sort, especially young people, who are the hope of the Church.[13]

3. Since parents have conferred life on their children, they have a most solemn obligation to educate their offspring. Hence, parents must be acknowledged as the first and foremost educators of their children.[14] Their role as educators is so decisive that scarcely anything can compensate for their failure in it. For it devolves on parents to create a family atmosphere so animated with love and reverence for God and men that a well-rounded personal and social development will be fostered among the children.[15] Hence, the family is the first school of those social virtues which every society needs.

It is particularly in the Christian family, enriched by the grace and the office of the sacrament of matrimony, that from their earliest years children should be taught, according to the faith received in baptism, to have a knowledge of God, to worship Him, and to love their neighbor. Here, too, they gain their first experience of wholesome human companionship and of the Church. Finally, it is through the family that they are gradually introduced into civic partnership with their fellow men, and into the People of God. Let parents, then, clearly recognize how vital a truly Christian family is for the life and development of God's own people.[16]

While belonging primarily to the family, the task of imparting education requires the help of society as a whole. In addition, therefore, to the rights of parents and of others to whom parents entrust a share in the work of education, certain rights and duties belong to civil society.[17] For this society

---

13. Cf. Second Vatican Council, schema of the Decree on the Apostolate of the Laity (1965), Art. 12.
14. Cf. Pius XI, encyclical letter "Divini Illius Magistri," loc. cit., pp. 59 ff.: also encyclical letter "Mit brennender Sorge," Mar. 14, 1937: AAS 29 (1937), pp. 164 ff.
Pius XII, allocution to the first national congress of the Italian Association of Catholic Teachers, Sept. 8, 1946: "Discorsi e Radiomessaggi," Vol. 8, p. 218.
15. The rights of parents are set out very much as they were in the encyclical of Pope Pius XI on Catholic education. However, attention should be drawn here to the spiritual and psychological role of parents. It is a development of the concept that the prime educative force in society is the family.
16. Cf. Second Vatican Council, Dogmatic Constitution on the Church, Art. 11 and 35: AAS 57 (1965), pp. 16 and 40 ff.
17. The Declaration limits the powers of the state rather sharply in this paragraph. Note the unusual application of the principle of subsidiarity.

exists to arrange for the temporal necessities of the common good. Part of its duty is to promote the education of the young in several ways: namely, by overseeing the duties and rights of parents and of others who have a role in education, and by providing them with assistance; by implementing the principle of subsidiarity* and completing the task of education, with attention to parental wishes, whenever the efforts of parents and of other groups are insufficient; and, moreover, by building its own schools and institutes, as the common good may demand.[18]

Finally, the office of educating belongs by a unique title to the Church, not merely because she deserves recognition as a human society capable of educating, but most of all because she has the responsibility of announcing the way of salvation to all men, of communicating the life of Christ to those who believe, and of assisting them with ceaseless concern so that they may grow into the fullness of that same life.[19] As a mother, the Church is bound to give these children of hers the kind of education through which their entire lives can be penetrated with the spirit of Christ, while at the same time she offers her services to all peoples by way of promoting the full development of the human person, for the welfare of earthly society and the building of a world fashioned more humanly.[20]

4. In discharging her educative function, the Church is preoccupied with all appropriate means to that end. But she is particularly concerned with the means which are proper to herself,

*For the principle of subsidiarity, cf. footnote on Art. 86c, Pastoral Constitution on the Church in the Modern World.—Ed.

18. Cf. Pius XI, encyclical letter "Divini Illius Magistri," loc. cit., pp. 63 ff.

Pius XII, radio message of June 1, 1941: AAS 33 (1941), p. 200; allocution to the first national congress of the Italian Association of Catholic Teachers, Sept. 8, 1946: "Discorsi e Radiomessaggi," Vol. 8, p. 218.

Regarding the principle of subsidiarity, cf. John XXIII, encyclical letter "Pacem in Terris," Apr. 11, 1963: AAS 44 (1963), p. 294.

19. Cf. Pius XI, encyclical letter "Divini Illius Magistri," loc. cit., pp. 53 ff., 56 ff.

Also his encyclical letter "Non abbiamo bisogno," June 29, 1931: AAS 23 (1931), pp. 311 ff.

Pius XII, letter of the Secretariate of State to the 28th Italian Social Week, Sept. 20, 1955: "L'Osservatore Romano," Sept. 29, 1955.

20. The Church praises those local, national, and international civil authorities who, conscious of the more pressing necessities of these times, expend all their energy so that all people may share a fuller education and human culture. Cf. Paul VI's allocution to the General Assembly of the United Nations, Oct. 4, 1965: "L'Osservatore Romano," Oct. 6, 1965.

of which catechetical training is foremost.[21] Such instruction gives clarity and vigor to faith, nourishes a life lived according to the spirit of Christ, leads to a knowing and active participation in the liturgical mystery,[22] and inspires apostolic action. In her high regard for them, the Church seeks to penetrate and ennoble with her own spirit those other means which belong to the common heritage of mankind, and which contribute mightily to the refinement of spirit and the molding of men. Among these are the media of social communication,[23] many groups devoted to spiritual and physical development, youth associations, and especially schools.

5. Among all the agencies of education the school has a special importance.[24] By virtue of its very purpose, while it cultivates the intellect with unremitting attention, the school ripens the capacity for right judgment, provides an introduction into the cultural heritage won by past generations, promotes a sense of values, and readies for professional life. By creating friendly contacts between students of diverse temperament and background, the school fosters among them a willingness to understand one another. Moreover, the school sets up a kind of center whose operation and progress deserve to engage the joint participation of families, teachers, various kinds of cultural, civic, and religious groups, civil society, and the entire human community.[25]

Beautiful, therefore, and truly solemn is the vocation[26] of all those who assist parents in fulfilling their task, and who represent human society as well, by undertaking the role of school teacher. This calling requires extraordinary qualities

21. Cf. Pius XI, motu proprio "Orbem Catholicum," June 29, 1923: AAS 15 (1923), pp. 327-329; decree "Provide Sane," Jan. 12, 1935: AAS 27 (1935), pp. 145-152; Second Vatican Council, Decree on the Bishops' Pastoral Office in the Church, Art. 13 and 14.
22. Cf. Second Vatican Council, Constitution on the Sacred Liturgy, Art. 14: AAS 56 (1964), p. 104.
23. Cf. Second Vatican Council, Decree on the Instruments of Social Communication, Art. 13 and 14: AAS 56 (1964), pp. 149 ff.
24. Cf. Pius XI, encyclical letter "Divini Illius Magistri," loc. cit., p. 76; also Pius XII, allocution to the Association of Catholic Teachers of Bavaria, Dec. 31, 1956: "Discorsi e Radiomessaggi," Vol. 18, p. 746.
25. Although this paragraph gives priority to the development of intellectual values, there is insistence on the universal value of schools. This is not without interest in view of some of the current discussion concerning the role of the school.
26. The Council is obviously concerned here with restoring the concept of the teaching profession as a vocation as well as an occupation.

of mind and heart, extremely careful preparation, and a constant readiness to begin anew and to adapt.

6. Parents, who have the first and the inalienable duty and right to educate their children, should enjoy true freedom in their choice of schools. Consequently, public authority, which has the obligation to oversee and defend the liberties of citizens, ought to see to it, out of a concern for distributive justice, that public subsidies are allocated[27] in such a way that, when selecting schools for their children, parents are genuinely free to follow their consciences.[28]

For the rest, it is incumbent upon the state to provide all citizens with the opportunity to acquire an appropriate degree of cultural enrichment, and with the proper preparation for exercising their civic duties and rights. Therefore, the state itself ought to protect the right of children to receive an adequate schooling. It should be vigilant about the ability of teachers and the excellence of their training. It should look after the health of students and, in general, promote the whole school enterprise. But it must keep in mind the principle of subsidiarity, so that no kind of school monopoly arises.[29] For such a monopoly would militate against the native rights of the human person, the development and spread of culture itself, the peaceful association of citizens, and the pluralism which exists today in very many societies.[30]

As for the faithful, this sacred Synod exhorts them to offer their services generously to the work of finding suitable methods of education and programs of study, and of forming teachers who can provide young people with an authentic education. Especially through parents' associations, let the

---

27. Note the connection between the allocation of public money and the rights of parents. There is no attempt to enter the practical field, by discussing how the state should subsidize Catholic education, but the principle that parents should not be handicapped in the exercise of their rights in education is clearly established.
28. Cf. Third Provincial Council of Cincinnati (1861): "Collatio Lacensis," Vol. III, col. 1240, c/d; also cf. Pius XI, encyclical letter "Divini Illius Magistri," loc cit., pp. 60 and 63 ff.
29. Once again there is a strong limitation of state control in educational administration.
30. Cf. Pius XI, encyclical letter "Divini Illius Magistri," loc. cit., p. 63; also his encyclical letter "Non abbiamo bisogno," June 29, 1931: AAS 23 (1931), p. 305.
Pius XII, letter of the Secretariate of State to the 28th Italian Social Week, Sept. 20, 1955: "L'Osservatore Romano," Sept. 29, 1965.
Paul VI, allocution to the Christian Association of Italian Workers, Oct. 6, 1963: "Encicliche e Discorsi di Paolo VI," Vol. I, Rome, 1964, p. 230.

faithful make their own contribution to advancing the whole function of the school, above all, its task of providing moral development.[31]

7. The Church is keenly aware of her very grave obligation to give zealous attention to the moral and religious education of all her children. To those large numbers of them who are being trained in schools which are not Catholic, she needs to be present with her special affection and helpfulness.[32] This she does through the living witness of those who teach and direct such students, through the apostolic activity of their schoolmates,[33] but most of all through the services of the priests and laymen who transmit to them the doctrine of salvation in a way suited to their age and circumstances, and who afford them spiritual assistance through programs which are appropriate under the prevailing conditions of time and setting.

The Church reminds parents of the serious duty which is theirs of taking every opportunity—or of making the opportunity—for their children to be able to enjoy these helps and to pace their development as Christians with their growth as citizens of the world. For this reason, the Church gives high praise to those civil authorities and civil societies that show regard for the pluralistic character of modern society, and take into account the right of religious liberty, by helping families in such a way that in all schools the education of their children can be carried out according to the moral and religious convictions of each family.[34]

8. The Church's involvement in the field of education is demonstrated especially by the Catholic school.[35] No less than other schools does the Catholic school pursue cultural goals

31. *Cf. John XXIII, message on the 30th anniversary of the publication of the encyclical letter "Divini Illius Magistri," Dec. 30, 1959: AAS 52 (1960), p. 57.*
32. One of the more original parts of the Declaration, this is an unequivocal statement of the responsibility of the Church to children not in Catholic schools.
33. *The Church highly values the apostolic action which Catholic teachers and associates are able to perform also in these schools. Cf. Second Vatican Council, schema of the Decree on the Apostolate of the Laity (1965), Art. 12 and 16.*
34. *Cf. Second Vatican Council, schema of the Declaration on Religious Freedom (1965), Art. 5.*
35. Catholic schools must: a) have the same cultural aims as all other schools; b) be opened to the contemporary world; c) be illumined by faith.

and the natural development of youth. But it has several distinctive purposes. It aims to create for the school community an atmosphere enlivened by the gospel spirit of freedom and charity. It aims to help the adolescent in such a way that the development of his own personality will be matched by the growth of that new creation which he became by baptism. It strives to relate all human culture eventually to the news of salvation, so that the light of faith will illumine the knowledge which students gradually gain of the world, of life, and of mankind.[36]

So it is that while the Catholic school fittingly adjusts itself to the circumstances of advancing times, it is educating its students to promote effectively the welfare of the earthly city, and preparing them to serve the advancement of the reign of God. The purpose in view is that by living an exemplary and apostolic life, the Catholic graduate can become, as it were, the saving leaven of the human family.

Therefore, since it can contribute so substantially to fulfilling the mission of God's people, and can further the dialogue between the Church and the family of man, to their mutual benefit, the Catholic school retains its immense importance in the circumstances of our times too. Consequently, this sacred Synod proclaims anew a right already made clear in numerous documents of the Church's teaching authority,[37] namely, the Church's right freely to establish and to run schools of every kind and at every level. At the same time, the Council recalls that the exercise of this right makes a supreme contribution to freedom of conscience, the protection of parental rights, and the progress of culture itself.

But let teachers realize that to the greatest possible extent they determine whether the Catholic school can bring its goals and undertakings to fruition.[38] They should, therefore, be

36. Cf. First Provincial Council of Westminster (1852): "Collatio Lacensis," Vol. III, col 1334, a/b; cf. also Pius XI, encyclical letter "Divini Illius Magistri," loc. cit., pp. 77 ff.; Pius XII's allocution to the Association of Catholic Teachers of Bavaria, Dec. 31, 1956: "Discorsi e Radiomessaggi," Vol. 18, p. 746; Paul VI, allocution to the members of Federated Institutes Dependent on Ecclesiastical Authority, Dec. 30, 1963: "Encicliche e Discorsi de Paola VI," Vol. I, Rome, 1964, pp. 602 ff.
37. Cf. especially the documents cited in note (1); in addition, this right of the Church is proclaimed by many provincial councils and in very recent declarations of very many episcopal conferences.
38. Cf. Pius XI, encyclical letter "Divini Illius Magistri," loc. cit., pp. 80 ff.; Pius XII, allocution to the Catholic Association of Italian Teachers in Secondary Schools, Jan. 5, 1954: "Discorsi e Radiomessaggi," Vol. 15, pp. 551-556; John XXIII, allocution to the 6th Congress of the Association of

trained with particular care so that they may be enriched with both secular and religious knowledge, appropriately certified, and may be equipped with an educational skill which reflects modern-day findings. Bound by charity to one another and to their students, and penetrated by an apostolic spirit, let them give witness to Christ, the unique Teacher, by their lives as well as by their teachings.[39]

Above all, let them perform their services as partners of the parents. Together with them, they should pay due regard in every educational activity to sexual differences and to the special role which divine Providence allots to each sex in family life and in society. Let them work strenuously to inspire personal initiative on their students' part. Even after students have graduated, their teachers should continue to assist them with advice and friendship and also by establishing special groups genuinely inspired by the spirit of the Church. This holy Synod asserts that the ministry of such teachers is a true apostolate which our times make extremely serviceable and necessary, and which simultaneously renders an authentic service to society.

As for Catholic parents, the Council calls to mind their duty to entrust their children to Catholic schools, when and where this is possible, to support such schools to the extent of their ability, and to work along with them for the welfare of their children.[40]

9. To this ideal of a Catholic school, all schools which are in any way dependent on the Church should conform as far as possible, though Catholic schools can take on forms which vary according to local circumstances.[41] Thus the Church feels a most cordial esteem for those Catholic schools, found especially where the Church is newly established, which contain large numbers of non-Catholic students.

In the establishment and direction of Catholic schools, attention must be paid to contemporary needs. Therefore, although primary and intermediate schools must still be fostered

Catholic Italian Teachers, Sept. 5, 1959: "Discorsi, Messaggi," Colloqui, Vol. I, Rome, 1960, pp. 427-431.
39. Further illustration of the personalist principle of Vatican II. The importance of the teacher is stressed in terms of personal impact.
40. *Cf. Pius XII, allocution to the Catholic Association of Italian Teachers in Secondary Schools, Jan. 5, 1954, loc. cit., p. 555.*
41. *Cf. Paul VI, allocution to the International Office of Catholic Education, Feb. 25, 1964: "Encicliche e Discorsi di Paolo VI," Vol. II, Rome, 1964, p. 232.*

as the foundations of education, considerable importance is to be attached to those schools which are demanded in a particular way by modern conditions, such as so-called professional[42] and technical schools, institutes for educating adults and promoting social services, as well as for persons requiring special care as a result of some natural deficiency, and also schools for preparing teachers to give religious instruction and other types of education.

This sacred Synod earnestly entreats pastors of the Church and all the faithful to spare no sacrifice in helping Catholic schools to achieve their purpose in an increasingly adequate way, and to show special concern for the needs of those who are poor in the goods of this world or who are deprived of the assistance and affection of a family or who are strangers to the gift of faith.[43]

10. The Church is preoccupied too with schools of higher learning, especially colleges and universities and their faculties. In schools of this sort which are dependent on her, she seeks in a systematic way to have individual branches of knowledge studied according to their own proper principles and methods, and with due freedom of scientific investigation. She intends thereby to promote an ever deeper understanding of these fields, and as a result of extremely precise evaluation of modern problems and inquiries, to have it seen more profoundly how faith and reason give harmonious witness to the unity of all truth.[44] The Church pursues such a goal after the manner of her most illustrious teachers, especially St. Thomas Aquinas.[45] The hoped-for result is that the Christian mind may achieve, as it were, a public, persistent, and universal presence in the whole enterprise of advancing higher culture, and that the students of these institutions may become men truly outstanding in learning, ready to shoulder society's heavier burdens and to witness the faith to the world.[46]

42. Cf. Paul VI, allocution to the Christian Association of Italian Workers, Oct. 6, 1963: "Encicliche e Discorsi di Paolo VI," Vol. I, Rome, 1964, p. 229.
43. Again the emphasis on the interpersonal. The value of the teacher is not only intellectual but, above all, human and spiritual.
44. There is clear refutation here of any anti-intellectualism in the Church. The document evidences preoccupation with a meeting of spiritual and intellectual values.
45. Cf. Paul VI, allocution before the 6th International Thomistic Congress, Sept. 10, 1965: "L'Osservatore Romano," Sept. 13-14, 1965.
46. Cf. Pius XII, allocution to the teachers and students of Catholic Higher Institutes of France, Sept. 21, 1950: "Discorsi e Radiomessaggi," Vol. 12,

In Catholic colleges and universities lacking a faculty of sacred theology, an institute or chair of sacred theology should be set up so that lectures designed for lay students too can be given. Since the sciences progress chiefly through special investigations of advanced scientific significance, Catholic colleges and universities and their faculties should give the maximum support to institutes which primarily serve the progress of scientific research.

This sacred Synod strongly recommends that Catholic colleges and universities and their faculties be conveniently located in diverse parts of the world, and that they be accorded the kind of support which will distinguish them for their academic pursuits rather than for the size of their enrollment. It urges that their doors open readily to students of special promise, even though of slender means, especially those who come from young nations.

Since the future of society and of the Church herself is closely bound up with the development of young people who engage in higher studies,[47] pastors of the Church should not limit their concern to the spiritual life of students attending Catholic colleges and universities. In their care for the religious development of all their sons, bishops should take appropriate counsel together and see to it that at colleges and universities which are not Catholic there are Catholic residences and centers where priests, religious, and laymen who have been judiciously chosen and trained can serve as on-campus sources of spiritual and intellectual assistance to young college people.

Whether they attend a college or university which is Catholic or otherwise, young people of special ability who appear suited for teaching and research should be trained with particular care and urged to undertake a teaching career.

11. The Church looks for rich results from the painstaking work of faculties of the sacred sciences.[48] For to them she

pp. 219-221; Letters to the 22nd Congress of "Pax Romana," Aug. 12, 1952: "Discorsi e Radiomessaggi," Vol. 14, pp. 567-569; John XXIII, allocution to the Federation of Catholic Universities, Apr. 1, 1959: "Discorsi, Messaggi," Colloqui, Vol. I, Rome, 1960, pp. 226-229; Paul VI, allocution to the Academic Senate of the Catholic University of Milan, Apr. 5, 1964: "Encicliche e Discorsi de Paolo VI," Vol. II, Rome, 1964, pp. 438-443.
47. Cf. Pius XII, allocution to the Academic Senate and students of the University of Rome, June 15, 1952: "Discorsi e Radiomessaggi," Vol. 14, p. 208: "The direction of tomorrow's society is principally placed in the mind and heart of the university students of today."
48. Cf. Pius XI, apostolic constitution "Deus Scientiarum Dominus," May 24, 1931: AAS 23 (1931), pp. 245-247.

confides the most serious task of preparing her own students
not only for the priestly ministry, but especially for teaching
in seats of higher Church studies, for advancing branches of
knowledge by their own efforts, and for undertaking the
more arduous challenges of the intellectual apostolate.[49]

It is also the responsibility of these faculties to explore more
profoundly the various areas of the sacred disciplines so that
day by day a deeper understanding of sacred revelation will
be developed, the treasure of Christian wisdom handed down
by our ancestors will be more plainly brought to view, dialogue will be fostered with our separated brothers and with
non-Christians, and solutions will be found for problems raised
by the development of doctrine.[50]

Therefore, these ecclesiastical faculties should zealously promote the sacred and related sciences by an opportune revision
of their own bylaws. Adopting also more recent methods and
teaching aids, let them lead their listeners on to more searching inquiries.

12. At the diocesan, national, and international level, the spirit
of cooperation grows daily more urgent and effective. Since
this same spirit is most necessary in educational work, every
effort should be made to see that suitable coordination is
fostered between various Catholic schools, and that between
these schools and others[51] that kind of collaboration develops
which the well-being of the whole human family demands.[52]

It is particularly in the circle of academic institutions that
increased coordination and joint effort will yield more abundant fruit. Therefore, in every college and university, the
various faculties should be at the service of one another to
the degree that their purposes allow. Let the various colleges

49. Reference should be made here to the Decree on Priestly Formation. In
some ways the same principles apply to those preparing for the priesthood and
for lay persons studying theology. In both cases, a clear adaptation to modern
needs is indicated.
50. *Cf. Pius XII, encyclical letter "Humani Generis," Aug. 12, 1950: AAS
42 (1950), pp. 568 ff. and 578; Paul VI, encyclical letter "Ecclesiam Suam,"
Part III, Aug. 6, 1964; AAS 56 (1964), pp. 637-659; Second Vatican Council,
Decree on Ecumenism: AAS 57 (1965), pp. 90-107.*
51. There is an oblique but important reference here to the growing tendency
to develop collaboration between Catholic universities and secular universities,
or between Catholic schools on the campuses of secular universities. In some
countries this has proven to be of utmost importance and some valuable
formulae have evolved.
52. *Cf. John XXIII, encyclical letter "Pacem in Terris," Apr. 11, 1963: AAS
55 (1963), p. 284 and passim.*

and universities unite in a mutual sharing of effort; together they can promote international conferences, allot fields of scientific research, share discoveries, exchange teachers temporarily, and foster among themselves whatever else contributes to more helpful service.

CONCLUSION

This sacred Synod urgently implores young people themselves to be aware of the excellence of the teaching vocation, and to be ready to undertake it with a generous spirit, especially in those parts of the globe where a shortage of teachers is causing a crisis in the training of the young.

This same Synod acknowledges its profound gratitude toward those priests, religious men and women, and lay people who in their evangelical self-dedication devote themselves to the surpassing work of education, including every kind and grade of schooling. It entreats them to carry on magnanimously in their chosen task and to strive to excel in penetrating their students with the spirit of Christ, in the art of teaching, and in the advancement of knowledge. Thus, they will not only foster the internal renewal of the Church, but will safeguard and intensify her beneficial presence in the world of today, especially the world of the intellect.

Each and every one of the things set forth in this Declaration has won the consent of the Fathers of this most sacred Council. We, too, by the apostolic authority conferred on us by Christ, join with the Venerable Fathers in approving, decreeing, and establishing these things in the Holy Spirit, and we direct that what has thus been enacted in synod be published to God's glory.

Rome, at St. Peter's, October 28, 1965

I, Paul, Bishop of the Catholic Church

There follow the signatures of the Fathers.

A RESPONSE

This Declaration on Christian education does not add to the significance of the Vatican Council. It is something of a holding operation that keeps alive traditional emphases. I do not say this in criticism, because the Council could not say fresh things in all areas and there is a special difficulty in saying much on the broader questions of the relation between Christian education and general education that would be relevant to the changing circumstances in all countries.

The statement of the responsibility of the Church and the outlining of the goals for Christian education are, in general terms, sound. I do not think that Protestants have different goals, at least formally. I am sure that the content of education suggested by such words as "the formation of the human person with respect to the ultimate goal" would involve great differences of emphasis among Christians and not necessarily as between Catholics and Protestants. Also, in general terms, the right things are said about the effect of Christian education on the relation between Catholics and other Christians, and between Christians and non-Christians. The need of relating Christian education to a pluralistic society is recognized. Also, the responsibility of that society to provide education for all children as a matter of justice is given the emphasis that it deserves.

The characteristic Roman Catholic emphasis on the rights and responsibility of parents for the education of their children is present throughout the document, and I welcome this as a check on the tendency of many Protestants to assume that the state or the community acting through agencies of the state is the educator. I think that there is a danger in this country of being too uncritical of the idea of a monopoly of the state in education. The famous Supreme Court decision in the Oregon case (Pierce vs. Society of Sisters) in 1925 was a landmark in the working out of the implications of religious liberty in education.

I do think that in this Declaration the affirmation of the rights and responsibilities of parents is presented in a too unqualified way. Parents presumably should be guided by the Church, but, more than that, the community has the responsibility both to make sure that children have opportunities for education and also to set standards and to determine to some extent the ground that is covered. The relation between parents, community, and the teaching profession is not easily charted. Parents who are narrow and provincial, even though pious, could ruin a school through their pressures on teachers. The principle of subsidiarity does not provide clear guidance here. Chiefly, it gives a basis for stressing the need of balancing various initiatives and authorities in the sphere of education.

I think that American Catholics and Protestants will miss in this document any real recognition of the responsibility of Christians for the public schools. This is not merely a matter of making sure that public education is provided. The interest of Christians in the continuing effort to improve the quality of public education is most important. Here I am led to suggest that probably this will never be given adequate emphasis unless Christians feel that they have a stake in public education in the case of their own children. I believe both in the right of Christians to have their own schools and in the positive contribution which Christian schools make to the education of the nation as a whole. But I think that today any discussion of Christian schools should raise the question as to whether there are limits to what is desirable in terms of separate Christian education.

I see in this document no recognition that many Catholics who believe that there is a place for parochial schools prefer to have their children receive part of their education in public schools. To keep children in separate Christian schools from kindergarten through college is a doubtful procedure educationally. Even though the fact and claims of a pluralistic society are recognized, and even though the Council's splendid statement on religious liberty is seen to have significance for the life of the Christian school, I doubt if a wholly separate Christian education, in most cases under the leadership of the clergy, can really initiate children into the life of a very mixed society or expose them adequately to the subject matter of secular disciplines. I realize that for economic reasons many Catholic authorities are limiting the range of parochial education and project even greater limitations. But there is a strong case for this policy on educational grounds.

Indeed, if one admits any truth in the current emphasis on the need to allow the secular to be itself, I believe that Christians should have the discipline of being exposed to secular disciplines under quite neutral rather than Christian auspices. Any Christian school, high school or college, may often find such encounter with the secular on its own terms the source of fresh understanding of Christian truth. At a time when many American Catholics are thinking through the role of parochial schools with open minds, it is unfortunate that the Council has given them no encouragement. All that I have said applies to the religious schools of any Church or religious Community.

I note that this Declaration calls for subsidies for parochial schools "out of a concern for distributive justice," and in order to enable parents "to be genuinely free to follow their consciences." A few years ago, this would have caused general resentment among non-Catholics in this country. Today I believe that there is a growing willingness to make some adjustment to Catholic claims. The problem of the double educational burden felt by Catholics is a real one. Also, given the fact of the millions of Catholic children in parochial schools, the nation has a stake in the quality of their education, and it should not express its interest here by demanding standards in a way that would drive the parochial schools out of existence. At the same time, Catholics should take account of the objection of many of their fellow citizens to having their taxes used for religious education. Concessions from both sides are necessary.

Non-Catholics should be willing to provide support for nonreligious elements of education in all schools, and they should be willing to make provision for the welfare of children in all schools. The time has passed for great crusades to keep parochial school children off school buses! There should be an ungrudging acceptance of these things. Catholics will need to make some distinctions between religious and nonreligious elements in the subject matter of education. Also, if they should accept the advice of many of their own leaders and welcome the attendance of their children during some of the years of their education at public schools or in other ways make clearer their concern for public education, much of the feeling would go out of the debates on these issues. The idea of "shared time" is another way of giving Catholics a stake in the public schools and of giving their children the experience of being educated with their non-Catholic fellow citizens.

The Council could not go into particular questions of pol-

icy that grow out of the American situation, but it might
have more clearly made room for an open attitude toward
them.

JOHN C. BENNETT

NON-CHRISTIANS

THE HISTORY OF the Declaration on the Relationship of the Church to Non-Christian Religions begins with Pope John XXIII. He wanted the Council to make a statement on the Jews, and he asked Cardinal Bea to see to it. Between that beginning and the outcome there is perhaps the most dramatic story of the Council. It was certainly a story of suspense in the world's newspaper coverage of the Council.

Originally, the material of this Declaration was Chapter 4 in the schema of the Decree on Ecumenism. The early material on religious freedom was contained in Chapter 5. During the second session of the Council, the Moderators called for a vote on the schema's first three chapters; the other two were held over (for lack of time, Cardinal Bea stated).

Just before that decision of the Moderators, Cardinal Bea, on November 19, 1963, in his address to the Council introducing Chapter 4, revealed that Pope John himself had ordered preparation of a text concerning the Jews. Pope John had, in fact, approved the basic lines of the document some months before he died.

A number of bishops, before and after Cardinal Bea's talk, urged that the topic of Catholic-Jewish relations was outside the scope of the ecumenism schema. They advocated that it should be the subject of a separate document. Some, especially patriarchs of the Eastern Churches, did not want the Council to say anything about the Jews, for fear the statement would be considered by Arab governments as a political move favoring recognition of the State of Israel, and the Christian minorities in Arab countries would be made to suffer in reprisal.

During the period between the second and third sessions, the secretariat headed by Cardinal Bea worked out a new draft on the Jews and other non-Christians. The contents became known throughout the world; the text was published in various newspapers. It put an end to the idea held by some Christians through the centuries that the Jews were a "deicide" people.

When the Council Fathers returned to Rome for the third session it was not this text that was presented to them. In the new text, rejection of the charge of deicide had disappeared; the section on non-Christians other than Jews had been extended; special attention was given to Moslems.

Cardinal Liénart began the discussion by insisting that the deleted passages about the Jews be restored—a remarkable development, since he was the senior member of the Coordinating Commission that was said to have made all the changes. He was followed by a long line of cardinals from around the world who, with the exception of Cardinal Tappouni, made the same request—Léger of Canada; Cushing, Meyer, and Ritter of the United States; Frings of Germany; et al.

Cardinal Tappouni, speaking for himself and four other patriarchs of the East, requested that the whole Declaration be dropped, not because they disagreed with what it said but because its adoption would impede the pastoral work of the Church. This final reference to political complications was lost in the tide of three days' speeches by cardinals and bishops who not only called for restoration of the earlier, stronger text but advocated adding to the text a statement that would put an end to some Christians' appealing to Scripture for justification of persecution or hatred of Jews. They called also for condemnation of all persecutions, and for insertion of a request for forgiveness from those who had been wronged by Christian persecution. Cardinal Bea stressed that the document was entirely religious in character and had no political implications, and it was evident that the entire discussion was religious in the very best sense.

In the final text, the statement on the use of Scripture was adopted (Article 4) and reinforced by setting forth so clearly the relationship of the Church with the people of the Old Testament that every pretext for discrimination was excluded. The request for forgiveness was not forthcoming in the document; instead of looking to the past, the document looks forward by fostering and recommending "that mutual understanding and respect which is the fruit above all of biblical and theological studies, and of brotherly dialogues."

The whole story, with its details about the week end when it seemed the statement on the Jews might become only one sentence, and some newspapers carried headlines announcing that the whole Declaration had been shelved, would take many pages in a history of the Council. Suffice it to say here that in the important voting on the sections of the document in October, 1965, there were 2,080 Fathers voting on the proposition that the Jews are not to be regarded as repudiated or cursed by God. There were 1,821 affirmative, 245 negative, and 14 invalid votes. One may perhaps legitimately add to this summary that on the proposition concerning universal brotherhood and exclusion of all discrimination (Article 5) there were 2,128 votes cast: 2,064 affirmative, 58 negative, and 6 invalid.

It has often been said, and rightly so, that if the present document had not been preceded by the earlier one, it would have been universally welcomed as one of the most important advances of the Council. The document certainly ends a sad chapter in Christian history.

Because of the history of its origins, one begins a study of this document with concentration on the part about the Jews. But in the final version that part forms only two-fifths of the text, and it is not what one encounters first.

Bishops from the whole world, meeting together and learning the full scope of the Church's concerns, had their horizons considerably widened. The bishops of Europe had some experience of what Cardinal Bea touched upon when he admitted in an address to the Council that anti-Jewish ideas in Christian history had helped Nazism. Bishops from heavily Jewish parts of the United States were proximately aware of the need to clarify true Christian attitudes toward Jews. The bishops of the most populous parts of the world, however, where Jews are few, presented their preoccupations with other great religions. The result was a world-wide view, with hitherto unheard-of serene outlook.

Some bishops objected: the resulting text would weaken the difference between Catholicism and all other religions, thus leading to indifferentism and the discouraging of missionary vocations. The great majority saw it otherwise, and it was so decreed. Now, in this historic document, the Church affirms that all peoples of the earth with their various religions form one community; the Church respects the spiritual, moral, and cultural values of Hinduism, Buddhism, and Islam. A few, like Dr. W. A. Visser 't Hooft, general secretary of the World Council of Churches, have found this part of the document "very, very weak" because it failed to "come to grips with essential questions raised by these religions" and "confined itself to making polite remarks" about them. Perhaps many readers will find this section of the Declaration rather general and abstruse. However, some historical perspective can be provided by the recollection that it is the first time an Ecumenical Council has expressed such an open approach to the other great faiths of the world.

ROBERT A. GRAHAM, S.J.

Declaration on the Relationship of the Church to Non-Christian Religions

PAUL, BISHOP

SERVANT OF THE SERVANTS OF GOD

TOGETHER WITH THE FATHERS OF THE SACRED COUNCIL

FOR EVERLASTING MEMORY

1. In our times, when every day men are being drawn closer together and the ties between various peoples are being multiplied, the Church is giving deeper study to her relationship with non-Christian religions.[1] In her task of fostering unity and love among men, and even among nations, she gives primary consideration in this document to what human beings have in common[2] and to what promotes fellowship among them.

For all peoples comprise a single community,[3] and have a

1. Originally a chapter in the schema on the Decree on Ecumenism, the material grew into this separate document. Pope Paul prepared for implementation of the Decree by setting up on May 17, 1964, a secretariat for development of relations with non-Christian religions, headed by Paolo Cardinal Marella. The Secretariat for Non-Christian Religions has an episcopal committee of bishops from all parts of the world, consultors in Rome, and consultors throughout the world, including laymen. The secretariat's aims are to create a climate of cordiality between Christians and followers of other religions, to dissipate prejudice and ignorance especially among Catholics, and to establish fruitful contact with members of other religions concerning questions of common interest.

2. The stress on what men have in common was one of Pope John's operative principles. As he often made clear, this approach does not deny or neglect differences; it simply gives *primary* consideration—as this Declaration says— to common goals and interests.

3. The solidarity of mankind was another of Pope John's operative principles,

single origin, since God made the whole race of men dwell
over the entire face of the earth (cf. Acts 17:26). One also
is their final goal: God. His providence, His manifestations
of goodness, and His saving designs extend to all men (cf.
Wis. 8:1; Acts 14:17; Rom. 2:6-7; 1 Tim. 2:4) against the
day when the elect will be united in that Holy City ablaze
with the splendor of God, where the nations will walk in His
light (cf. Apoc. 21:23 f.).[4]

Men look to the various religions for answers to those profound mysteries of the human condition which, today even
as in olden times, deeply stir the human heart: What is a
man?[5] What is the meaning and the purpose of our life?
What is goodness and what is sin? What gives rise to our
sorrows and to what intent? Where lies the path to true happiness? What is the truth about death, judgment, and retribu-
tion beyond the grave? What, finally, is that ultimate and
unutterable mystery which engulfs our being, and whence we
take our rise, and whither our journey leads us?

2. From ancient times down to the present, there has existed
among diverse peoples a certain perception of that hidden
power which hovers over the course of things and over the
events of human life;[6] at times, indeed, recognition can be
found of a Supreme Divinity and of a Supreme Father too.
Such a perception and such a recognition instill the lives of
these peoples with a profound religious sense. Religions
bound up with cultural advancement have struggled to reply
to these same questions with more refined concepts and in
more highly developed language.

Thus in Hinduism men contemplate the divine mystery and
express it through an unspent fruitfulness of myths and
through searching philosophical inquiry.[7] They seek release
from the anguish of our condition through ascetical practices

---

evident from the very beginning of his pontificate and in his first encyclical.
The teaching of this sentence of the Declaration has a detailed history in papal
statements running back for decades.

4. The theme of light connects this document with the great Constitution on
the Church, *Lumen Gentium* (Light of the World).

5. These questions outline a number of the basic, common interests referred
to in the opening paragraph of the Declaration.

6. The Declaration now considers a most basic and fundamental common
interest of men. It speaks in the widest possible terms.

7. The Declaration selects certain key elements of Hinduism without attempting the impossible task of describing in a short space the complex nature of
Hinduism, the distinctions between Vedanta (scriptures) and Puranas (lesser
sacred books), the six philosophical systems, the innumerable sects, etc.
Mention might have been made of the similarities between Hindu and

or deep meditation or a loving, trusting flight toward God.

Buddhism in its multiple forms acknowledges the radical insufficiency of this shifting world.[8] It teaches a path by which men, in a devout and confident spirit, can either reach a state of absolute freedom or attain supreme enlightenment by their own efforts or by higher assistance.

Likewise, other religions to be found everywhere[9] strive variously to answer the restless searchings of the human heart[10] by proposing "ways," which consist of teachings, rules of life, and sacred ceremonies.

The Catholic Church rejects nothing which is true and holy in these religions.[11] She looks with sincere respect upon those ways of conduct and of life, those rules and teachings which, though differing in many particulars from what she holds and sets forth, nevertheless often reflect a ray of that Truth which enlightens all men. Indeed, she proclaims and must ever proclaim Christ, "the way, the truth, and the life" (John 14:6), in whom men find the fullness of religious life, and in whom God has reconciled all things to Himself (cf. 2 Cor. 5:18-19).

The Church therefore has this exhortation for her sons: prudently and lovingly,[12] through dialogue and collaboration

Christian beliefs—e.g., the concept of God's appearance on earth; the concept of grace; sacraments; and similarities between the Christian Trinity and the Hindu ultimate reality—but all this, it was legitimately felt, could be left to the work of dialogue that is endorsed and commended at the end of the Article.

8. As with Hinduism, so with Buddhism—a whole library of knowledge opens up at the mention of the word. Instead of attempting to give detailed summaries of the common areas of interest, the Declaration touches on general themes and leaves the rest to development in competent dialogue.

9. Bishops from Africa, and scholars of religion like Franziskus Cardinal Koenig, Archbishop of Vienna, asked that mention be made of a number of religions in Africa, etc. It was decided, however, to keep to the traditional idea of the great religions in the world (Hinduism, Buddhism, Judaism, Christianity, Islam), giving these explicit mention and referring to all the others in this general summary.

10. The reader of Christian classics will discern here an echo of the famous sentence in St. Augustine's Confessions: "Our hearts are restless and they will not rest until they rest in Thee."

11. This paragraph presents an understanding that is traditional in the Catholic Church. One recalls, for example, Justin Martyr in the early Church attributing all the truths in non-Christian religions to the Word of God who enlightens every man who enters into this world—a concept found at the beginning of the Gospel according to John. Through the centuries, however, missionaries often adopted the attitude that non-Christian religions were simply the work of Satan and the missionaries' task was to convert from error to knowledge of the truth. This Declaration marks an authoritative change in approach. Now, for the first time, there is recognition of other religions as entities with which the Church can and should enter into dialogue.

12. The Declaration gives a good example of prudence in putting aside, for the moment, elements in non-Christian religions that are repugnant to Christians (idolatry, etc.) to focus on the spiritual and moral *goods*. Also, there

with the followers of other religions, and in witness of Christian faith and life, acknowledge, preserve, and promote the spiritual and moral goods found among these men, as well as the values in their society and culture.

3. Upon the Moslems, too, the Church looks with esteem.[13] They adore one God, living and enduring, merciful and all-powerful, Maker of heaven and earth[14] and Speaker to men. They strive to submit wholeheartedly even to His inscrutable decrees, just as did Abraham, with whom the Islamic faith is pleased to associate itself. Though they do not acknowledge Jesus as God, they revere Him as a prophet. They also honor Mary, His virgin mother; at times they call on her, too, with devotion. In addition they await the day of judgment when God will give each man his due after raising him up. Consequently, they prize the moral life, and give worship to God especially through prayer, almsgiving, and fasting.

Although in the course of the centuries many quarrels and hostilities have arisen between Christians and Moslems, this most sacred Synod urges all to forget the past and to strive sincerely for mutual understanding. On behalf of all mankind, let them make common cause of safeguarding and fostering social justice, moral values, peace, and freedom.

4. As this sacred Synod searches into the mystery of the Church, it recalls the spiritual bond linking the people of the New Covenant with Abraham's stock.[15]

is here no undignified breastbeating, no protestation that Catholics were not responsible for unfortunate episodes in history, no exaggerated emotionalism —all of which would not have provided a good basis for persevering in dialogue.

13. Students of the history of relations between Christians and Moslems will find this section a remarkable change in the Church's approach. One thinks inevitably of the Crusades (but note that there were Moslem crusaders as well as Christian). Those were ideological wars. This Council, as it also makes clear in the Pastoral Constitution on the Church in the Modern World, wants to disassociate itself from war.

Many readers will no doubt find it surprising to see how much Christians and Moslems actually have in common in their beliefs. Many Christians have thought of Moslems as fanatical followers of a religion of power and ignorance, sexually excessive (polygamy, ideas about heaven), etc.

14. *Cf. St. Gregory VII, letter XXI to Anzir (Nacir), King of Mauretania.*

15. The Declaration, in taking up the topic of the relationship between Christianity and Judaism, begins on a positive note. It probes to the root of what the two religions have in common: fatherhood in Abraham. In this, and in the acknowledgments of the following paragraphs, the Declaration presents an authentic tradition of the Church rooted in sacred Scripture. Besides this section of the Declaration, the Dogmatic Constitution on Divine Revelation is vital to the dialogue with Jews recommended in the middle of this Article.

For the Church of Christ acknowledges that, according to the mystery of God's saving design, the beginnings of her faith and her election are already found among the patriarchs, Moses, and the prophets. She professes that all who believe in Christ, Abraham's sons according to faith (cf. Gal. 3:7), are included in the same patriarch's call, and likewise that the salvation of the Church was mystically foreshadowed by the chosen people's exodus from the land of bondage.

The Church, therefore, cannot forget that she received the revelation of the Old Testament through the people with whom God in his inexpressible mercy deigned to establish the Ancient Covenant. Nor can she forget that she draws sustenance from the root of that good olive tree onto which have been grafted the wild olive branches of the Gentiles (cf. Rom. 11:17-24). Indeed, the Church believes that by His cross Christ, our Peace, reconciled Jew and Gentile, making them both one in Himself (cf. Eph. 2:14-16).[16]

Also, the Church ever keeps in mind the words of the Apostle about his kinsmen, "who have the adoption as sons, and the glory and the covenant and the legislation and the worship and the promises; who have the fathers, and from whom is Christ according to the flesh" (Rom. 9:4-5), the son of the Virgin Mary. The Church recalls too that from the Jewish people sprang the apostles, her foundation stones and pillars, as well as most of the early disciples who proclaimed Christ to the world.

As holy Scripture testifies, Jerusalem did not recognize the time of her visitation (cf. Lk. 19:44), nor did the Jews in large number accept the gospel; indeed, not a few opposed the spreading of it (cf. Rom. 11:28).[17] Nevertheless, according to the Apostle, the Jews still remain most dear to God because of their fathers, for He does not repent of the gifts He makes nor of the calls He issues (cf. Rom. 11:28-29).[18] In company with the prophets and the same Apostle,

---

16. In practice, at various times in the history of the Church, the facts set forth in this Article have been neglected or obscured by some Christians. Here the Church proclaims her unity with the chosen people of the Old Testament. This, therefore, and not any other, is the authentic and approved tradition.

17. It was felt necessary by some of the Council Fathers to indicate the opposition to Christianity on the part of some Jews, a fact that, among other things, partly explains the subsequent history of tension between Christianity and Judaism. The next two sentences of the Declaration present the Church's official attitude toward this fact.

18. Cf. Dogmatic Constitution "Lumen Gentium," AAS 57, 1965, p. 20.

the Church awaits that day, known to God alone, on which all peoples will address the Lord in a single voice and "serve him with one accord" (Soph. 3:9; cf. Is. 66:23; Ps. 65:4; Rom. 11:11-32).[19]

Since the spiritual patrimony common to Christians and Jews is thus so great, this sacred Synod wishes to foster and recommend that mutual[20] understanding and respect which is the fruit above all of biblical and theological studies, and of brotherly dialogues.[21]

True, authorities of the Jews and those who followed their lead pressed for the death of Christ (cf. Jn. 19:6);[22] still,

19. A reference to "conversion" of the Jews was removed from an earlier version of this Declaration, because many Council Fathers felt it was not appropriate in a document striving to establish common goals and interests first. The sentence as it now stands presents a summary of biblical understandings. ("With one accord" is the RSV and CCD translation of Soph. [Zech.] 3:9. The Latin text, quoting the Vulgate, says literally: "with one shoulder."—Ed.)
20. The word "mutual" indicates that the Council hopes for two-way communication; the Council Fathers here take an initiative (just as the Decree on Ecumenism urges Catholics to take the initiative in proposals for dialogue with other Christians) and hope for a response. The word also tactfully expresses the request of Cardinal Ruffini, Archbishop of Palermo, that Christians should love Jews, and Jews should declare they will not hate Christians (and he asked that certain passages in the Talmud be corrected).
Pope John's deletion of a word from the Good Friday prayer for Jews and Pope Paul's extensive revision of the prayer (now "For the Jews" instead of "For the Conversion of the Jews," etc.) were steps in the direction of mutual understanding and respect. Jules Isaac has related that, after representations made by him in a private audience in 1949, Pope Pius XII made a similar step in this direction in the Good Friday liturgy.
Also, on the day this Declaration was promulgated, the Congregation of Rites issued a decree banning further veneration of Simon of Trent, a small boy allegedly murdered by Jews in 1475 in order that his Christian blood might be used in the synagogue during the Pasch. Investigation had shown that Simon was probably killed by non-Jews who tried to blame Trent's Jewish community for the crime.
21. The Declaration endorses and promotes dialogue between Christians and Jews, just as the Decree on Ecumenism endorses and promotes dialogue between the separated Christian groups. On Oct. 1, 1965, in Rome, it was announced that the Catholic bishops of the United States had established a commission to discover ways to further the dialogue.
22. Some biblical scholars among the Council Fathers pressed for having on the record a reference to the Gospel accounts that relate involvement of Jewish leaders in the arrest and death of Christ. This involvement has, in fact, been a basic element in the thesis that the Jewish people therefore were guilty of the death of Jesus—a thesis held, and pushed to various consequences, by some Christians from early times to the present. In what follows here, the Second Vatican Council repudiates the thesis and its consequences.
The Council has been accused by some (who should have known better) of "playing God" and "absolving," "forgiving," or "exonerating" the Jews of guilt for the crucifixion, and these terms were used in newspaper headlines describing this section of the Declaration. In fact, the Council simply repudiates the notion of a collective Jewish guilt, and instructs Catholics to eliminate false views that in the past have caused Jews to undergo discrimination and suffering. The element of forgiveness was capably handled earlier by Him who said: "Father, forgive them, for they know not what they do."

what happened in His passion cannot be blamed upon all the
Jews then living, without distinction, nor upon the Jews of
today. Although the Church is the new people of God, the
Jews should not be presented as repudiated or cursed by
God,[23] as if such views followed from the holy Scriptures.[24]
All should take pains, then, lest in catechetical instruction
and in the preaching of God's Word they teach anything out
of harmony with the truth of the gospel and the spirit of
Christ.[25]

The Church repudiates[26] all persecutions against any man.
Moreover, mindful of her common patrimony with the Jews,
and motivated by the gospel's spiritual love and by no political considerations, she deplores[27] the hatred, persecutions,

23. The phrase "or guilty of deicide" (deicidii rea) was dropped from this
sentence before the present version of the Declaration came up for discussion
and voting in the final sesson of the Council. Many newspaper accounts attributed the deletion to pressure from Arab governments, etc., but the Secretariat for Promoting Christian Unity, chief architect of the document, explained
that many Council Fathers asked for the deletion because the phrase was
ambiguous and might even suggest to some people that the Church no longer
regarded Jesus as God.

The Secretariat agreed to drop the phrase since the idea is already found
in the preceding sentence: "What happened in His passion cannot be blamed
upon all the Jews. . . ." The Secretariat recommended that the word "deicide"
be eliminated from the Christian vocabulary; it has given rise to false theological interpretations that occasion difficulties in pastoral work and in
ecumenical dialogue.

24. In some sermons of Fathers of the Church, notably the Greek Fathers
(e.g., St. John Chrysostom), and various preachers in the history of the
Church, there has been an attempt to base a pejorative attitude toward Jews
on sacred Scripture. The Second Vatican Council here rejects the attempt.
From now on, no Catholic may quote the Bible to justify calling the Jews
an accursed or rejected people.

As Cardinal Bea and others explained, "His blood be upon us and upon
our children" (Mt. 27:25) is the cry of a Jerusalem crowd that has no right
to speak for the whole Jewish people. The severity of Christ's judgment on
Jerusalem (Mt. 23:37 ff., etc.) does not suppose or prove collective culpability
of the Jewish people for the crucifixion; that judgment caps a long history
of Jerusalem's disobedience to God, crimes against the prophets, etc., and it
is a "type" of the universal, final judgment.

In 1 Th. 2:14-16, St. Paul angrily associates those who are persecuting him
with the spirit of those Jews and their leaders in Jerusalem "who killed both
the Lord Jesus and the prophets." The Council's teaching on the interpretation of sacred Scripture, in the Dogmatic Constitution on Divine Revelation,
is essential reading for all who wish to study this matter.

25. The spirit of Christ is one of love, not hate.

26. Reprobat. Cf. note 33.—Ed.

27. A Latin phrase meaning "and condemns" was dropped at the request
of the Council Fathers who complained that the phrase would put the Council
on record as repudiating discrimination against Jews more strongly than
discrimination against anyone else. Others argued that "condemn" in a Council
document should be reserved for matters of formal heresy, and Pope John
explicitly had requested that this Council not engage in such condemnations.

and displays of anti-Semitism directed against the Jews at any time and from any source.[28]

Besides, as the Church has always held and continues to hold, Christ in His boundless love freely underwent His passion and death because of the sins of all men, so that all might attain salvation.[29] It is, therefore, the duty of the Church's preaching to proclaim the cross of Christ as the sign of God's all-embracing love and as the fountain from which every grace flows.

5. We cannot in truthfulness call upon that God who is the Father of all if we refuse to act in a brotherly way toward certain men,[30] created though they be to God's image. A man's relationship with God the Father and his relationship with his brother men are so linked together that Scripture says: "He who does not love does not know God" (1 Jn. 4:8).

The ground is therefore removed from every theory or practice which leads to a distinction between men or peoples in the matter of human dignity and the rights which flow from it.

28. In four of their seventy canonical enactments, the Fathers of the Fourth Lateran Council (1215 A.D.) dealt with the Jews: Christian princes must watch lest Jews exact too high interest of Christian debtors; baptized Jews may not observe Jewish customs; Jews may not appear in public during Easter week; Jews must give tithes on their houses and other property to the Church and pay a yearly tax at Easter; no Christian prince may give an office to a Jew under pain of excommunication; Jews must wear a distinctive dress from their twelfth year to distinguish them from Christians. If there was anti-Semitism in these laws, it is here repudiated by the Second Vatican Council ("at any time and from any source").

29. This sentence, together with the preceding teaching, puts this declaration on the Jews into a *doctrinal* category. The Fourth Lateran Council's four discriminatory canons on the Jews in the 1215 were *disciplinary* laws. Disciplinary laws are changeable; the content of doctrinal statements is not changeable. The unfortunate laws of 1215 long ago fell into desuetude; the doctrinal statement of 1965, it is to be hoped, removes from the Church the remnants of the thinking that lay behind those laws.

It is curious that the Council makes no reference to the beautiful treatment of the Jews and Christ's death given in the authoritative *Catechism of the Council of Trent for Parish Priests,* published by order of Pope Pius V in 1566, which states that guilt for Christ's death "seems more enormous in us than in the Jews, since according to the testimony of the same Apostle: 'If they had known it, they would never have crucified the Lord of glory' (1 Cor. 2:8); while we, on the contrary, professing to know Him, yet denying Him by our actions, seem in some sort to lay violent hands on Him." Cf. edition by McHugh and Callan (New York: Joseph F. Wagner, Inc., 1923), pp. 50-61, 362-365.

30. The reader will still, no doubt, be thinking of the context of anti-Semitism from the preceding Article. As the next two paragraphs show, however, the Declaration has moved on to a much more sweeping statement: all discrimination against individuals or whole peoples because of race, color, condition of life, or religion, is repudiated by the Church.

As a consequence, the Church rejects,[31] as foreign to the mind of Christ, any discrimination against men or harassment of them because of their race, color, condition of life, or religion.

Accordingly, following in the footsteps of the holy Apostles Peter and Paul, this sacred Synod ardently implores the Christian faithful to "maintain good fellowship among the nations" (1 Pet. 2:12),[32] and, if possible, as far as in them lies, to keep peace with all men (cf. Rom. 12:18), so that they may truly be sons of the Father who is in heaven (cf. Mt. 5:45).

Each and every one of the things set forth in this Declaration has won the consent of the Fathers of this most sacred Council. We too, by the apostolic authority conferred on us by Christ, join with the Venerable Fathers in approving, decreeing, and establishing these things in the Holy Spirit, and we direct that what has thus been enacted in synod be published to God's glory.

Rome, at St. Peter's, October 28, 1965

I, Paul, Bishop of the Catholic Church

There follow the signatures of the Fathers.

31. The word *reprobat* used here is practically as strong as *condemnat*. It means "reprove," "repudiate," etc.—words that are commonly understood to mean "condemn" for all practical purposes. Thus, although obviously trying to follow Pope John's directive not to engage in condemnations, the Council finds racial and religious discrimination too disturbing not to condemn.—Ed.
32. The translator provides a version that catches the spirit of the Council document. Literally, in the Bible, the phrase means "maintain good conduct among the Gentiles" (RSV) or "behave yourselves honorably among the pagans" (CCD, 1941).—Ed.

A RESPONSE

Christian churches are involved in a common guilt for anti-Semitism. They have a common responsibility for making such amends as are possible. Accordingly, the World Council of Churches issued a fairly simple Statement on the subject at New Delhi in 1961, and the Second Vatican Council promulgated a somewhat more complicated Declaration at Rome in 1965.

As to the removal of abuses in the future, both documents are forthright and encouraging. As to the recognition of Christian guilt, both of individuals and of churches, both documents seem to me—as they do to our Jewish friends—inadequate.

Neither document was passed without long and laborious discussion. At one point in the New Delhi meeting of the World Council of Churches, Christians from those parts of the world that do not feel the heritage of guilt for the persecution of the Jews as heavily as do Christians in Western lands were asked to refrain from pressing amendments or theological questions which would have caused the voice of the Assembly to be indecisive on the subject (the New Delhi Report, page 150). While the question of Christian guilt was in the air, in the corridors, in the minds of many participants, and in some of the speeches in the two assemblies, no real confession of guilt found its way into either Declaration. Perhaps a consensus on a complete theological foundation for a Declaration on the relations of Christianity to Judaism would have been as hard to reach in St. Peter's as at New Delhi, where the attempt to reach such a consensus was abandoned. Without an adequate theological framework, perhaps no adequate acknowledgment of the guilt of the Church as such was possible.

One misses in both statements any satisfying expression of the warm human feeling which might in considerable measure have taken the place of the ecclesiastical kinship whose expression was found to be too difficult for formulation.

One is not surprised, therefore, that Jews in general are not enthusiastic over these statements. Rabbi David Polish, for example, finds the Vatican Council Declaration condescending and lacking the spirit of reconciliation. He refers to it as "a unilateral pronouncement by one party which presumes to redress on its own terms a wrong which it does not admit."

Some Jews, however—perhaps most—while not enthusiastic, find substantial grounds for hope for the future. Rabbi Marc Tanenbaum has not only expressed that hope on television programs but has cited examples to indicate that Catholics are already beginning to take the Declaration seriously with regard to the teaching and the practices of the Church.

The Vatican Council Declaration (like the New Delhi one) is not merely a formal statement for the record. It is, on the one hand, an intellectual and emotional culmination; on the other, and more emphatically, it is a new starting point for building brotherly spirit and practices between Christians and Jews. The decisive point was the inclusion of the topic in the Council agenda on the recommendation of Pope John to Cardinal Bea. Once there it could be shifted around, modified, redrafted, bitterly contested by a small minority, but it could not be dislodged. Its necessity was both understood and felt by an overwhelming majority of the bishops.

The goal of the new building is fellowship and partnership between Jews and Christians; it will require good will, mutual esteem, justice, genuine brotherhood. This is not possible unless Jews respond, as they surely will, wherever Christian intentions and efforts are visibly well-meant and honest. The missing warmth is not likely to develop except through personal experience. It would be of help to Christians to know, at least to know of, such Jewish heroes as (in the author's experience) Rabbi Leo Baeck, who resisted the Nazis, and Dr. Roberto Assagioli, who refused to leave his Jewish brethren to the tender mercies of Mussolini's Italy when he might well have re-established himself in England. One needs more examples of genuine participation in lessening Jewish suffering. One thinks of the German Protestant, Dr. Siegmund-Schultze, in Zurich, making certain that Jewish refugees from the Nazis arriving in Zurich could be forwarded to safety within twenty-four hours, though he often did not know where the money for the next ticket was to be found. One thinks also of the American seminary student in Rome sacrificing his own food and clothing and begging and borrowing from friends in order to buy visas at ten dollars per head to bring Jews out of Hitler's Germany. Less dramatic acquaintances and deeds of compassion are possible for every

Christian. In the aggregate, they could change the whole shameful situation.

One difference that these Declarations can make is that in the future no government, no citizenry, can believe, assume, or pretend that it has Christian sanction for any sort of persecution or discrimination against the Jews.

The Vatican Declaration avoided suggestions of conversion, confining itself to the hoped-for reunion of all believers at the end of history. A shift from Christian denunciation of Jews to a Christian strategy of their conversion, advocated and practiced by many Christians, would not improve relations and might greatly exacerbate them. What is needed is that Christians learn and practice truly Christian attitudes and relationships, amounting not to a strategy but to the creation of a new climate.

In a very long run, those sections of the Declaration dealing with Moslems, Buddhists, Hindus, and primitive religions may prove to be even more important than the section on the Jewish religion. One is grateful for their inclusion, and for their respectful and cordial tone. However, if the more immediately practicable call for improvement of Christian conduct with regard to Jews does not produce results, it is hard to see how members of the other non-Christian religions would find any reason to listen to the words addressed to them.

It has seemed proper to refer to the New Delhi statement adopted by Protestants and Eastern Orthodox in the context of the Vatican Council's Declaration. Unless all Christians work together, think together, and pray together, they will not be able greatly to improve Christian-Jewish relationships. It may prove both with regard to the Jewish religion and to other religions that the currency given by the Second Vatican Council to the phrase, the concept, and the spirit embodied in the "People of God" carries a more powerful psychological and spiritual dynamic than the Declaration. Who can set the boundaries of the People of God?

But the Declaration calls forth our commendation and gratitude. It sternly rebukes any effort to make of Christianity an indictment of the Jewish people, and removes the major blocks in the way of cordial and dignified dialogue between Catholics and Jews. It provides the basis, from the Catholic side, for a united and thoroughgoing Christian campaign against anti-Semitism.

Claud Nelson

RELIGIOUS
FREEDOM

ON NOVEMBER 19, 1963, the first schema (draft text) on religious freedom was presented to the conciliar Fathers by the Secretariat for Promoting Christian Unity. In the course of two years, five corrected versions of the text appeared in print, each being the work of many revisions within the secretariat. Three public debates were held in the Aula, during which some one hundred and twenty speeches were made. Some six hundred written interventions were sent to the secretariat, many of them signed by groups of bishops. Moreover, critiques of the successive schemas were made, either orally or in writing, by a considerable number of bishops and theologians who were consulted by the secretariat. Also consulted were a number of the observers at the Council. Before the final vote was taken, more than two thousand *modi* (suggested corrections) were considered (many of them, of course, were identical).

Thus, the greatest argument on religious freedom in all history happily broke forth in the Church. The debate was full and free and vigorous, if at times confused and emotional. Out of it came the sixth and final text, here presented.

The first text had appeared as Chapter V of the Decree on Ecumenism. The second text had appeared as a Declaration, but in an appendix to the Decree on Ecumenism. With the third text the Declaration assumed independent status. From the outset, its intention was pastoral, as was the general intention of the Council in all its utterances. This, however, does not mean that the Declaration contains simply practical advice. Its content is properly doctrinal. In particular, three doctrinal tenets are declared: the ethical doctrine of religious freedom as a human right (personal and collective); a political doctrine with regard to the functions and limits of government in matters religious; and the theological doctrine of the freedom of the Church as the fundamental principle in what concerns the relations between the Church and the socio-political order.

It can hardly be maintained that the Declaration is a milestone in human history—moral, political, or intellectual. The principle of religious freedom has long been recognized in constitutional law, to the point where even Marxist-Leninist political ideology is obliged to pay lip-service to it. In all honesty it must be admitted that the Church is late in acknowledging the validity of the principle.

In any event, the document is a significant event in the history of the Church. It was, of course, the most controversial document of the whole Council, largely because it raised with sharp emphasis the issue that lay continually below the surface of all the conciliar debates—the issue of the development of doctrine. The notion of development, not the notion of religious freedom, was the real sticking-point for many of those who opposed the Declaration even to the end. The course of the development between the *Syllabus of Errors* (1864) and *Dignitatis Humanae Personae** (1965) still remains to be explained by theologians. But the Council formally sanctioned the validity of the development itself; and this was a doctrinal event of high importance for theological thought in many other areas.

Moreover, taken in conjunction with the Pastoral Constitution on the Church in the Modern World, the Declaration opens a new era in the relations between the People of God and the People Temporal. A long-standing ambiguity has finally been cleared up. The Church does not deal with the secular order in terms of a double standard—freedom for the Church when Catholics are a minority, privilege for the Church and intolerance for others when Catholics are a majority. The Declaration has opened the way toward new confidence in ecumenical relationships, and a new straightforwardness in relationships between the Church and the world.

Finally, though the Declaration deals only with the minor issue of religious freedom in the technical secular sense, it

*These are the opening words, in Latin, of the Declaration on Religious Freedom. The opening words of conciliar documents may be cited as titles (usually with each word capitalized, according to the practice for papal encyclicals), but the more common title is the one that heads the document.—Ed.

does affirm a principle of wider import—that the dignity of man consists in his responsible use of freedom. Some of the conciliar Fathers—not least those opposed to the Declaration—perceived that a certain indivisibility attaches to the notion of freedom. The word and the thing have wrought wonders in the modern world; they have also wrought havoc. The conciliar affirmation of the principle of freedom was narrowly limited—in the text. But the text itself was flung into a pool whose shores are wide as the universal Church. The ripples will run far.

Inevitably, a second great argument will be set afoot—now on the theological meaning of Christian freedom. The children of God, who receive this freedom as a gift from their Father through Christ in the Holy Spirit, assert it within the Church as well as within the world, always for the sake of the world and the Church. The issues are many—the dignity of the Christian, the foundations of Christian freedom, its object or content, its limits and their criterion, the measure of its responsible use, its relation to the legitimate reaches of authority and to the saving counsels of prudence, the perils that lurk in it, and the forms of corruption to which it is prone. All these issues must be considered in a spirit of sober and informed reflection.

The issue of religious freedom was in itself minor. But Pope Paul VI was looking deep and far when he called the Declaration on Religious Freedom "one of the major texts of the Council."

JOHN COURTNEY MURRAY, S.J.

Declaration on Religious Freedom

ON THE RIGHT OF THE PERSON AND OF COMMUNITIES TO SOCIAL AND CIVIL FREEDOM IN MATTERS RELIGIOUS

PAUL, BISHOP

SERVANT OF THE SERVANTS OF GOD

TOGETHER WITH THE FATHERS OF THE SACRED COUNCIL

FOR EVERLASTING MEMORY

1. A sense of the dignity of the human person has been impressing itself more and more deeply on the consciousness of contemporary man.[1] And the demand is increasingly made that men should act on their own judgment, enjoying and making use of a responsible freedom, not driven by coercion but motivated by a sense of duty. The demand is also made that constitutional limits should be set to the powers of government, in order that there may be no encroachment on the rightful freedom of the person and of associations.

This demand for freedom in human society chiefly regards the quest for the values proper to the human spirit. It regards, in the first place, the free exercise of religion in society.[2]

1. *Cf. John XXIII, encyclical "Pacem in Terris," Apr. 11, 1963: AAS 55 (1963), p. 279; ibid., p. 265; Pius XII, radio message, Dec. 24, 1944: AAS 37 (1945), p. 14.*
2. Vatican II has been characterized by a sense of history, an awareness of the concrete world of fact, and a disposition to see in historical facts certain

This Vatican Synod takes careful note of these desires in
the minds of men. It proposes to declare them to be greatly
in accord with truth and justice. To this end, it searches into
the sacred tradition and doctrine of the Church—the treasury
out of which the Church continually brings forth new things
that are in harmony with the things that are old.

First,[3] this sacred Synod professes its belief that God him-

"signs of the times." Hence the Declaration begins by noting two facts. The
first is the recent rise of man's personal consciousness, his sense of selfhood. This increasing awareness of the dignity of the human person marks a
progress of civilization. It is the good which has come out of the great evil
of totalitarianism, which brutally refuses to acknowledge the reality of
man's selfhood. The second fact is the related rise of man's political consciousness, his aspiration to live as a free man under a limited government
which puts no obstacles to his pursuit of truth and virtue, and, in particular,
leaves him unhindered in the free exercise of religion in society. (Happily,
the Declaration adopts the classical phrase which the Founding Fathers likewise adopted when framing the First Amendment in 1791.)

In thus acknowledging certain realities of contemporary life, the Declaration
also establishes direct continuity with two basic doctrinal themes of John
XXIII in the encyclical "Pacem in Terris": the dignity of the human person
and the consequent necessity of constitutional limits to the powers of
government. The language of these opening sentences is, in fact, taken from
this great encyclical.

3. The issue of religious freedom arises in the political and social order—in
the order of the relationship between the people and government and between
man and man. This is the order of human rights, and in it the principle of
freedom is paramount. However, man's life is also lived in another order of
reality—in the spiritual order of man's relationship to what is objectively
true and morally good. This is the order of duty and obligation. In it a
man acts freely indeed, but under moral imperatives, which bind in conscience. No man may plead "rights" in the face of the truth or claim
"freedom" from the moral law. The distinction between these two orders
of reality would be admitted by all men of good sense. The underlying intention of these two paragraphs of the Declaration is to make this distinction
clear, lest religious freedom be made a pretext for moral anarchy.

However, the distinction is stated in Catholic terms. For the Catholic, the
"truth" is not a vague abstraction; it subsists in the Church, is taught by
the Church, is believed by the Church. Moreover, this truth about God and
about His will for men is not the private possession of a party or sect; it
is to be taught to all men, and all nations are to be its disciples. It is not
to be thrust by force upon any man; in the order of man's relationship to
truth, coercion has no place whatsoever. Consequently, as the Declaration
will later make clear, religious freedom is an exigence of religious truth as
conceived by the Church.

On the other hand, no man may say of the religious truth which subsists in
the Church: "It is no concern of mine." Once given by Christ to His true
Church, the true religion remains the one way in which all men are bound to
serve God and save themselves. Consequently, religious freedom is not a title
to exemption from the obligation to "observe all things whatsoever I have
enjoined upon you." In fine, a harmony exists between man's duty of free
obedience to the truth and his right to the free exercise of religion in
society. The duty does not diminish the right, nor does the right diminish
the duty.

This frank profession of Catholic faith, at the outset of the Declaration on
Religious Freedom, is in no sense at variance with the ecumenical spirit,
any more than it is at variance with full loyalty to the principle of religious

self has made known to mankind the way in which men are to serve Him, and thus be saved in Christ and come to blessedness. We believe that this one true religion subsists in the catholic and apostolic Church, to which the Lord Jesus committed the duty of spreading it abroad among all men. Thus He spoke to the apostles: "Go, therefore, and make disciples of all nations, baptizing them in the name of the Father, and of the Son, and of the Holy Spirit, teaching them to observe all that I have commanded you" (Mt. 28:19-20). On their part, all men are bound to seek the truth, especially in what concerns God and His Church, and to embrace the truth they come to know, and to hold fast to it.

This sacred Synod likewise professes its belief that it is upon the human conscience that these obligations fall and exert their binding force. The truth cannot impose itself except by virtue of its own truth, as it makes its entrance into the mind at once quietly and with power. Religious freedom, in turn, which men demand as necessary to fulfill their duty to worship God, has to do with immunity from coercion in civil society. Therefore, it leaves untouched traditional Catholic doctrine on the moral duty of men and societies toward the true religion and toward the one Church of Christ.

Over and above all this, in taking up the matter of religious freedom this sacred Synod intends to develop the doctrine of recent Popes on the inviolable rights of the human person and on the constitutional order of society.[4]

freedom. Neither the spirit of ecumenism nor the principle of religious freedom requires that the Church refrain from stating publicly what she believes herself to be. The demands of truth are no more opposed to the demands of freedom than they are opposed to the demands of love.

4. In no other conciliar document is it so explicitly stated that the intention of the Council is to "develop" Catholic doctrine. This is significant, since it is an avowal that the tradition of the Church is a tradition of progress in understanding the truth. The basic truth here is the concept of the "citizen" as stated by Pius XII—the man who "feels within himself a consciousness of his own personality, of his duties, and of his rights, joined with a respect for the freedom of others" (Christmas Discourse, 1945). This conception, as the Declaration will say, is deeply rooted both in the Christian tradition and in the tradition of reason. In recent times, it was Leo XIII (in "Rerum Novarum") who first began to move it, as it were, to the forefront of Catholic social teaching. Pius XII continued this development, drawing out the implications of the dignity of man in terms of his duties and rights. He also brought forward the correlative truth, that the primary function of government is to acknowledge, protect, vindicate, and facilitate the exercise of the rights of man. Both of these truths were taken up by John XXIII, chiefly in "Pacem in Terris," in which they are given an almost systematic form of statement.

However, in regard to the right of man to religious freedom, even "Pacem in Terris" is unclear and even ambiguous. What precisely does religious freedom mean? Does it find place among the inalienable rights of man? These

GENERAL PRINCIPLE
OF RELIGIOUS FREEDOM

2. This Vatican Synod declares that the human person has a right to religious freedom.[5] This freedom means that all men

are the questions to which, for the first time, the Church gives an unmistakably clear and entirely unambiguous answer. The Council brings forth out of the treasury of truth a doctrine that is at once new and also in harmony with traditional teaching.

5. The doctrinal substance of the Declaration is stated in this paragraph, which defines what religious freedom is and affirms its status as a human—and therefore civil—right. A right is a moral claim made on others that they either give me something or do something for me or refrain from doing something. Two questions always arise. First, what is the moral claim I make on others, or in other words, what is the object or content of my right? Second, on what grounds do I make this moral claim, or in other words, what is the foundation of my right?

The Declaration first defines religious freedom in terms of its object or content. The moral claim that every man makes on others—on individuals, groups, political or social powers—is that they refrain from bringing coercion to bear on him in all matters religious. This claim is twofold. First, no man is to be forced to act in a manner contrary to his personal beliefs; second, no man is to be forcibly restrained from acting in accordance with his beliefs. The affirmation of this latter immunity is the new thing, which is in harmony with the older affirmation of the former immunity.

It is to be noted that the word "conscience," found in the Latin text, is used in its generic sense, sanctioned by usage, of "beliefs," "convictions," "persuasions." Hence the unbeliever or atheist makes with equal right this claim to immunity from coercion in religious matters. It is further to be noted that, in assigning a negative content to the right to religious freedom (that is, in making it formally a "freedom from" and not a "freedom for"), the Declaration is in harmony with the sense of the First Amendment to the American Constitution. In guaranteeing the free exercise of religion, the First Amendment guarantees to the American citizen immunity from all coercion in matters religious. Neither the Declaration nor the American Constitution affirms that a man has a right to believe what is false or to do what is wrong. This would be moral nonsense. Neither error nor evil can be the object of a right, only what is true and good. It is, however, true and good that a man should enjoy freedom from coercion in matters religious.

This brings up the second question, concerning the foundation of the right. The reason why every man may claim immunity from coercion in matters religious is precisely his inalienable dignity as a human person. Surely, in matters religious, if anywhere, the free human person is required and entitled to act on his own judgment and to assume personal responsibility for his action or omission. A man's religious decisions, or his decision against religion, are inescapably his own. No one else can make them for are to be immune from coercion on the part of individuals or of social groups and of any human power, in such wise that in matters religious no one is to be forced to act in a manner contrary to his own beliefs. Nor is anyone to be restrained from acting in accordance with his own beliefs, whether privately or publicly, whether alone or in association with others, within due limits.

The Synod further declares that the right to religious freedom has its foundation in the very dignity of the human person, as this dignity is known through the revealed Word of God and by reason itself.[6] This right of the human person to religious freedom is to be recognized in the constitutional law whereby society is governed. Thus it is to become a civil right.

It is in accordance with their dignity as persons—that is, beings endowed with reason and free will and therefore privileged to bear personal responsibility—that all men should be at once impelled by nature and also bound by a moral obligation to seek the truth, especially religious truth. They are also bound to adhere to the truth, once it is known, and to order their whole lives in accord with the demands of truth.

However, men cannot discharge these obligations in a manner in keeping with their own nature unless they enjoy immunity from external coercion as well as psychological freedom. Therefore, the right to religious freedom has its foundation, not in the subjective disposition of the person, but in his very nature. In consequence, the right to this immunity continues to exist even in those who do not live up to their obligation of seeking the truth and adhering to it.

him, or compel him to make this decision or that, or restrain him from putting his decisions into practice, privately or publicly, alone or in company with others. In all these cases, the dignity of man would be diminished because of the denial to him of that inalienable responsibility for his own decisions and actions which is the essential counterpart of his freedom.

It is worth noting that the Declaration does not base the right to the free exercise of religion on "freedom of conscience." Nowhere does this phrase occur. And the Declaration nowhere lends its authority to the theory for which the phrase frequently stands, namely, that I have the right to do what my conscience tells me to do, simply because my conscience tells me to do it. This is a perilous theory. Its particular peril is subjectivism—the notion that, in the end, it is my conscience, and not the objective truth, which determines what is right or wrong, true or false.

6. Cf. John XXIII, encyclical "Pacem in Terris," Apr. 11, 1963: AAS 55 (1963), pp. 260-261; Pius XII, radio message, Dec. 24, 1942: AAS 35 (1943), p. 19; Pius XI, encyclical "Mit Brennender Sorge," Mar. 14, 1937: AAS 29 (1937), p. 160; Leo XIII, encyclical "Libertas Praestantissimum," June 20, 1888: Acts of Leo XIII 8 (1888), pp. 237-238.

Nor is the exercise of this right to be impeded, provided that the just requirements of public order are observed.[7]

3. Further light is shed on the subject if one considers that the highest norm of human life is the divine law—eternal, objective, and universal—whereby God orders, directs, and governs the entire universe and all the ways of the human community, by a plan conceived in wisdom and love. Man has been made by God to participate in this law, with the result that, under the gentle disposition of divine Providence, he can come to perceive ever increasingly the unchanging truth. Hence every man has the duty, and therefore the right, to seek the truth in matters religious, in order that he may with prudence form for himself right and true judgments of conscience, with the use of all suitable means.

Truth, however, is to be sought after in a manner proper to the dignity of the human person and his social nature. The inquiry is to be free, carried on with the aid of teaching

7. It was necessary for the Council to present an argument for the principle of religious freedom, lest anyone should mistakenly think that the Church was accepting religious freedom merely on pragmatic grounds or as a concession to contemporary circumstances. However, it was not the intention of the Council to affirm that the argument, as made in the text, is final and decisive. Complete and systematic study of the arguments for religious freedom is a task left to the scholars of the Church, working in ecumenical spirit with scholars of other religious Communities, and in humanist spirit with scholars of no religious convictions who are concerned with the exigencies of human dignity. The Council merely presents certain lines or elements of argument. It will be sufficient here to indicate the structure.

First, in this paragraph, the objective foundation of the right to religious freedom is presented in terms that should be intelligible and acceptable to all men, including non-believers. The simple essence of the matter is that man, being intelligent and free, is to be a responsible agent. Inherent in his very nature, therefore, is an exigency for freedom from coercion, especially in matters religious. Therefore, in the following three paragraphs, an argument is suggested that will appeal to those who believe in God, in objective order of truth and morality, and in the obligation to seek the truth, form one's conscience, and obey its dictates. To the man who so believes, it will be evident that no one is to be forced or constrained to act against his own conscience (here conscience has its technical meaning).

Two further arguments are advanced to show that a man may not be restrained from acting according to his conscience. First, by reason of man's social nature, inner acts of religion require external expression; hence their external expression enjoys the same immunity from coercion as the inner acts themselves. Second, there is the "further consideration" that no right resides in government to command or inhibit acts of religion, which by their nature lie beyond the reach of government.

American theorists are generally disposed to relate religious freedom to a general theory of constitutional government, limited by the rights of man, and to the concept of civic equality. The Declaration, however, lays less stress on this political argument than it does on the ethical foundations of the right itself. In any event, the elements of the political argument are stated in later Articles (6 and 7). And one is free to construct the argument in the form which may seem more convincing.

or instruction, communication, and dialogue. In the course of these, men explain to one another the truth they have discovered, or think they have discovered, in order thus to assist one another in the quest for truth. Moreover, as the truth is discovered, it is by a personal assent that men are to adhere to it.

On his part, man perceives and acknowledges the imperatives of the divine law through the mediation of conscience. In all his activity a man is bound to follow his conscience faithfully, in order that he may come to God, for whom he was created. It follows that he is not to be forced to act in a manner contrary to his conscience. Nor, on the other hand, is he to be restrained from acting in accordance with his conscience, especially in matters religious.

For, of its very nature, the exercise of religion consists before all else in those internal, voluntary, and free acts whereby man sets the course of his life directly toward God. No merely human power can either command or prohibit acts of this kind.[8]

However, the social nature of man itself requires that he should give external expression to his internal acts of religion; that he should participate with others in matters religious; that he should profess his religion in community. Injury, therefore, is done to the human person and to the very order established by God for human life, if the free exercise of religion is denied in society when the just requirements of public order do not so require.

There is a further consideration. The religious acts whereby men, in private and in public and out of a sense of personal conviction, direct their lives to God transcend by their very nature the order of terrestrial and temporal affairs. Government, therefore, ought indeed to take account of the religious life of the people and show it favor, since the function of government is to make provision for the common welfare. However, it would clearly transgress the limits set to its power were it to presume to direct or inhibit acts that are religious.

4. The freedom or immunity from coercion in matters religious which is the endowment of persons as individuals is also to be recognized as their right when they act in com-

8. *Cf. John XXIII, encyclical "Pacem in Terris," Apr. 11, 1963: AAS 55 (1963), p. 270; Paul VI, radio message, Dec. 22, 1964: AAS 57 (1965), pp. 181-182.*

munity. Religious bodies are a requirement of the social nature both of man and of religion itself.[9]

Provided the just requirements of public order are observed, religious bodies rightfully claim freedom in order that they may govern themselves according to their own norms, honor the Supreme Being in public worship, assist their members in the practice of the religious life, strengthen them by instruction, and promote institutions in which they may join together for the purpose of ordering their own lives in accordance with their religious principles.

Religious bodies also have the right not to be hindered, either by legal measures or by administrative action on the part of government, in the selection, training, appointment, and transferral of their own ministers, in communicating with religious authorities and communities abroad, in erecting buildings for religious purposes, and in the acquisition and use of suitable funds or properties.

Religious bodies also have the right not to be hindered in their public teaching and witness to their faith, whether by the spoken or by the written word. However, in spreading religious faith and in introducing religious practices, everyone ought at all times to refrain from any manner of action which might seem to carry a hint of coercion or of a kind of persuasion that would be dishonorable or unworthy, especially when dealing with poor or uneducated people. Such a manner of action would have to be considered an abuse of one's own right and a violation of the right of others.[10]

9. The freedoms listed here are those which the Catholic Church claims for herself. The Declaration likewise claims them for all Churches and religious Communities. Lest there be misunderstanding, however, it is necessary to recall here the distinction between the content or object of the right and its foundation. The content or object always remains freedom from coercion in what concerns religious belief, worship, practice or observance, and public testimony. Hence the content of the right is the same both for the Catholic Church and for other religious bodies. In this sense, the Church claims nothing for herself which she does not also claim for them. The matter is different, however, with regard to the foundation of the right. The Catholic Church claims freedom from coercive interference in her ministry and life on grounds of the divine mandate laid upon her by Christ Himself (cf. below, note 13). It is Catholic faith that no other Church or Community may claim to possess this mandate in all its fullness. In this sense, the freedom of the Church is unique, proper to herself alone, by reason of its foundation. In the case of other religious Communities, the foundation of the right is the dignity of the human person, which requires that men be kept free from coercion, when they act in community, gathered into Churches, as well as when they act alone.

10. It is customary to distinguish between "Christian witness" and "proselytism" and to condemn the latter. This distinction is made in the text here. Proselytism is a corruption of Christian witness by appeal to hidden forms

In addition, it comes within the meaning of religious freedom that religious bodies should not be prohibited from freely undertaking to show the special value of their doctrine in what concerns the organization of society and the inspiration of the whole of human activity.[11] Finally, the social nature of man and the very nature of religion afford the foundation of the right of men freely to hold meetings and to establish educational, cultural, charitable, and social organizations, under the impulse of their own religious sense.

5. Since the family[12] is a society in its own original right, it has the right freely to live its own domestic religious life under the guidance of parents. Parents, moreover, have the right to determine, in accordance with their own religious beliefs, the kind of religious education that their children are to receive.

Government, in consequence, must acknowledge the right of parents to make a genuinely free choice of schools and of other means of education. The use of this freedom of choice is not to be made a reason for imposing unjust burdens on parents, whether directly or indirectly. Besides, the rights of parents are violated if their children are forced to attend lessons or instruction which are not in agreement with their religious beliefs. The same is true if a single system of education, from which all religious formation is excluded, is imposed upon all.

6. The common welfare of society consists in the entirety of those conditions of social life under which men enjoy the possibility of achieving their own perfection in a certain fullness of measure and also with some relative ease. Hence this welfare consists chiefly in the protection of the rights,[13] and

---

of coercion or by a style of propaganda unworthy of the gospel. It is not the use but the abuse of the right to religious freedom.

11. Implicitly rejected here is the outmoded notion that "religion is a purely private affair" or that "the Church belongs in the sacristy." Religion is relevant to the life and action of society. Therefore religious freedom includes the right to point out this social relevance of religious belief.

12. The internal structure of family relationships and the general style of family life vary widely throughout the world. Still greater variety is exhibited in the organization of school systems, in their relation to the family, to society, and to government, and in the religious and ideological content, or lack thereof, of their teaching. In consequence, the Declaration had to confine itself to a few principles of universal import, which would enforce its doctrinal line—freedom from coercion. To descend to further detail would be to enter the realm of policy, in which contingent circumstances play a determinant role.

13. *Cf. John XXIII, encyclical "Mater et Magistra," May 15, 1961: AAS*

in the performance of the duties, of the human person. Therefore, the care of the right to religious freedom devolves upon the people as a whole, upon social groups, upon government, and upon the Church and other religious Communities, in virtue of the duty of all toward the common welfare, and in the manner proper to each.[14]

The protection and promotion of the inviolable rights of man ranks among the essential duties of government.[15]

53 (1961), p. 417; idem, encyclical "Pacem in Terris," Apr. 11, 1963: AAS 55 (1963), p. 273.

14. The development of Catholic doctrine which the Declaration promised has already shown itself in the clear definition of religious freedom as a human right and in the firm claim that all Churches and religious Communities are entitled to equal freedom from coercion in what concerns religious belief, worship, practice or observance, public testimony, and the internal autonomy of the community itself. Correlative with these developments is the doctrine stated here with regard to the functions and limitations of government in what concerns religion in society. The pivotal notion is the concept of the common welfare which Leo XIII began to put forward in "Rerum Novarum," which Pius XII strongly developed, and which John XXIII defined with greater precision. The common welfare "chiefly consists in the protection of the rights, and in the performance of the duties, of the human person," who is to be the agent of the processes of society and their beneficiary. The care of the common welfare is the common task of all elements within society—individuals, groups, religious bodies, government—each in the way proper to itself.

In a special way, the care of the common good—that is to say, the care of the rights of man—devolves upon government. Consequently, in what concerns religion in society, government has a duty that is twofold. The first duty is to acknowledge the human right to religious freedom, and effectively to protect it and vindicate it against violation. The second duty derives from the general duty of government to assist the people in the performance of their duties; in this case, it is to show a general and undiscriminating favor toward religion in society (cf. above, note 3, at the end) and to assist in the creation of conditions that will help, not hinder, the people in the exercise of their religious rights and in the performance of their religious duties. This latter duty is stated with considerable generality, because the appropriate means for its performance will vary within diverse circumstances.

The concern of the Council was, first, to make entirely clear the duty of government toward religious freedom as a human right, and secondly, to make sufficiently clear the function of government with regard to religion itself as a perfection of the human person and as a social value. This latter function is not easy to define with precision. It is chiefly a matter of avoiding extremes. On the one hand, government is forbidden to assume the care of religious truth as such, or jurisdiction over religious worship or practice, or the task of judging the truth or value of religious propaganda. Otherwise it would exceed its competence, which is confined to affairs of the temporal and terrestrial order. On the other hand, government is likewise forbidden to adopt toward religion an attitude of indifference or skepticism, much less hostility. Otherwise it would betray its duty to the human person, for whom religion is the highest good, and also to the temporal and terrestrial welfare of society, whose content is not merely material but also moral and spiritual. Here then is the principle for finding the golden mean between the extremes.

15. Cf. John XXIII, encyclical "Pacem in Terris," Apr. 11, 1963: AAS 55 (1963), pp. 273-274; Pius XII, radio message, June 1, 1941: AAS 33 (1941), p. 200.

Therefore, government is to assume the safeguard of the religious freedom of all its citizens, in an effective manner, by just laws and by other appropriate means. Government is also to help create conditions favorable to the fostering of religious life, in order that the people may be truly enabled to exercise their religious rights and to fulfill their religious duties, and also in order that society itself may profit by the moral qualities of justice and peace which have their origin in men's faithfulness to God and to His holy will.[16]

If, in view of peculiar circumstances obtaining among certain peoples, special legal recognition is given in the constitutional order of society to one religious body, it is at the same time imperative that the right of all citizens and religious bodies to religious freedom should be recognized and made effective in practice.[17]

Finally, government is to see to it that the equality of citizens before the law, which is itself an element of the common welfare, is never violated for religious reasons[18] whether openly or covertly. Nor is there to be discrimination among citizens.

It follows that a wrong is done when government imposes upon its people, by force or fear or other means, the profession or repudiation of any religion, or when it hinders men from joining or leaving a religious body. All the more is it a violation of the will of God and of the sacred rights of the person and the family of nations, when force is brought to bear in any way in order to destroy or repress religion, either in the whole of mankind or in a particular country or in a specific community.[19]

7. The right to religious freedom is exercised in human so-

16. *Cf. Leo XIII, encyclical "Immortale Dei," Nov. 1, 1885: AAS 18 (1885), p. 161.*

17. This paragraph is carefully phrased. The Council did not wish to condemn the institution of "establishment," the notion of a "religion of the state." A respectable opinion maintains that the institution is compatible with full religious freedom. On the other hand, the Council did not wish to canonize the institution. A respectable opinion holds that establishment is always a threat to religious freedom. Furthermore, the Council wished to insinuate that establishment, at least from the Catholic point of view, is a matter of historical circumstance, not of theological doctrine. For all these reasons the text deals with the issue in conditional terms.

18. This statement about equality before the law as an element of the common welfare has an accent of newness in official Catholic statements. It is important for the construction of the full argument for religious freedom.

19. This condemnation of religious persecution is couched in temperate terms and without naming the guilty. However, the reference to totalitarian regimes of Communist inspiration is unmistakable.

ciety; hence its exercise is subject to certain regulatory norms.[20] In the use of all freedoms, the moral principle of personal and social responsibility is to be observed. In the exercise of their rights, individual men and social groups are bound by the moral law to have respect both for the rights of others and for their own duties toward others and for the common welfare of all. Men are to deal with their fellows in justice and civility.

Furthermore, society has the right to defend itself against possible abuses committed on pretext of freedom of religion. It is the special duty of government to provide this protection. However, government is not to act in arbitrary fashion or in an unfair spirit of partisanship. Its action is to be controlled by juridical norms which are in conformity with the objective moral order.

These norms arise out of the need for effective safeguard of the rights of all citizens and for peaceful settlement of

20. It is a matter of common sense that the exercise of all freedoms in society must be subject to certain regulatory norms. The Declaration states first the moral norm—the principle of personal and social responsibility. Its restraints, of course, are self-imposed. More difficult is the question of the juridical norm which should control the action of government in limiting or inhibiting the exercise of the right to religious freedom. (Note that the right itself is always inalienable, never to be denied; only the exercise of the right is subject to control in particular instances.) The norm cannot be the common welfare, since the common welfare requires that human rights should be protected, not limited, in their exercise. Hence the Declaration adopts the concept of public order. The concept has good warrant in constitutional law. However, it is more frequently used than defined. The Declaration undertakes to define it. In doing so, it makes a contribution to the science of law and jurisprudence.

First, the requirements of public order are not subject to arbitrary definition —at the hands, say, of tyrannical governments, which might abuse the concept for their own ends. The public order of society is a part of the universal moral order; its requirements must be rooted in moral law. Second, public order exhibits a threefold content. First, the order of society is essentially an order of justice, in which the rights of all citizens are effectively safeguarded, and provision is made for peaceful settlement of conflicts of rights. Second, the order of society is a political order, an order of peace ("domestic tranquillity" is the American constitutional phrase). Public peace, however, is not the result of repressive action by the police. It is, in the classic concept, the work of justice; it comes about, of itself, when the demands of justice are met, and when orderly processes exist for airing and settling grievances. Third, the order of society is a moral order, at least in the sense that certain minimal standards of public morality are enforced at all.

Public order therefore is constituted by these three values—juridical, political, moral. They are the basic elements in the common welfare, which is a wider concept than public order. And so necessary are these three values that the coercive force of government may be enlisted to protect and vindicate them. Together they furnish a reasonable juridical criterion for coercive restriction of freedom. The free exercise of religion may not be inhibited unless proof is given that it entails some violation of the rights of others, or of the public peace, or of public morality. In these cases, in other words, a public action ceases to be a religious exercise and becomes a penal offense.

conflicts of rights. They flow from the need for an adequate care of genuine public peace, which comes about when men live together in good order and in true justice. They come, finally, out of the need for a proper guardianship of public morality. These matters constitute the basic component of the common welfare: they are what is meant by public order.

For the rest,[21] the usages of society are to be the usages of freedom in their full range. These require that the freedom of man be respected as far as possible, and curtailed only when and in so far as necessary.

8. Many pressures are brought to bear upon men of our day, to the point where the danger arises lest they lose the possibility of acting on their own judgment. On the other hand, not a few can be found who seem inclined to use the name of freedom as the pretext for refusing to submit to authority and for making light of the duty of obedience.

Therefore, this Vatican Synod urges everyone, especially those who are charged with the task of educating others, to do their utmost to form men who will respect the moral order and be obedient to lawful authority. Let them form men too who will be lovers of true freedom—men, in other words, who will come to decisions on their own judgment and in the light of truth, govern their activities with a sense of responsibility, and strive after what is true and right, willing always to join with others in cooperative effort.[22]

Religious freedom, therefore, ought to have this further purpose and aim, namely, that men may come to act with

21. Secular experts may well consider this to be the most significant sentence in the Declaration. It is a statement of the basic principle of the "free society." The principle has important origins in the medieval tradition of kingship, law, and jurisprudence. But its statement by the Church has an accent of blessed newness—the newness of a renewal of the tradition. The renewal, already hesitantly begun by Pius XII, was strongly furthered by John XXIII. Catholic thought had consistently held that society is to be based upon truth (the truth of the human person), directed toward justice, and animated by charity. In "Pacem in Terris," John XXIII added the missing fourth term, freedom. Freedom is an end or purpose of society, which looks to the liberation of the human person. Freedom is the political method par excellence, whereby the other goals of society are reached. Freedom, finally, is the prevailing social usage, which sets the style of society. This progress in doctrine is sanctioned and made secure by "Dignitatis Humanae Personae."
22. The Council calls attention to the paradox of the moment. Freedom today is threatened; freedom today is itself a threat. Hence the Council calls for education both in the uses of freedom and in the ways of obedience. When freedom is truly responsible, it implies a rightful response to legitimate authority.

greater responsibility in fulfilling their duties in community life.[23]

CHAPTER II

RELIGIOUS FREEDOM IN THE LIGHT OF REVELATION

9. The declaration of this Vatican Synod on the right of man to religious freedom has its foundation in the dignity of the person. The requirements of this dignity have come to be more adequately known to human reason through centuries of experience. What is more, this doctrine of freedom has roots in divine revelation, and for this reason Christians are bound to respect it all the more conscientiously.

Revelation does not indeed affirm in so many words the right of man to immunity from external coercion in matters religious. It does, however, disclose the dignity of the human person in its full dimensions. It gives evidence of the respect which Christ showed toward the freedom with which man is to fulfill his duty of belief in the Word of God. It gives us lessons too in the spirit which disciples of such a Master ought to make their own and to follow in every situation.

Thus, further light is cast on the general principles upon which the doctrine of this Declaration on Religious Freedom is based. In particular, religious freedom in society is entirely consonant with the freedom of the act of Christian faith.[24]

23. Religious freedom is not an end in itself, but a means for the fulfillment of the higher purposes of man. Its religious purpose is clear. But here the Council notes its social purpose. Respect for religious freedom rises out of a consciousness of human dignity; but this consciousness itself confronts man with the responsibilities that his freedom entails. And these responsibilities pervade the whole of community life.

24. The Declaration is the only conciliar document formally addressed to the whole world—Christian and non-Christian, religious and atheist. Therefore it first considers religious freedom in the light of reason. Moreover, in so doing it follows the structure of the problem itself, both theoretical and

10. It is one of the major tenets of Catholic doctrine that man's response to God in faith must be free. Therefore no one is to be forced to embrace the Christian faith[25] against his own will.[26] This doctrine is contained in the Word of God and it was constantly proclaimed by the Fathers of the Church.[27] The act of faith is of its very nature a free act. Man, redeemed by Christ the Savior and through Christ Jesus called to be God's adopted son,[28] cannot give his adherence to God revealing Himself unless the Father draw

historical. Both as a principle and as a legal institution, religious freedom is less than two hundred years old. The First Amendment may claim the honor of having first clearly formulated the principle and established the institution. Only through centuries of experience, as the Declaration says, have the exigencies of the human dignity disclosed themselves to reason. Nevertheless, the question remains, in what sense may religious freedom be called a "Christian" principle? The Council answers by saying that the principle has its "roots in divine revelation." These roots are explored in the second part of the Declaration. This section is of high ecumenical significance. It will furnish a major theme of ecumenical dialogue.

25. *Cf. CIC, c. 1351; Pius XII, allocution to prelate auditors and other officials and administrators of the tribune of the Holy Roman Rota, Oct. 6, 1946: AAS 38 (1946), p. 394; idem, encyclical "Mystici Corporis," June 29, 1943: AAS (1943), p. 243.*

26. The unwavering Christian dogma that the act of Christian faith must be a free response to the Word and grace of God reveals the divine respect for human freedom and for man's inalienable responsibility toward the direction of his own life. The constitutional principle of religious freedom is not a conclusion from this Christian dogma. The connection is rather more historical. That is to say, given the Christian doctrine of the freedom of faith, men would gradually come—as over the centuries they have come—to realize that man's religious life is an affair of responsible freedom, from which all coercion is to be excluded. Given this Christian appreciation of the value of freedom (and given also the growing secular experience of freedom as a social value and a political end), men could not fail to become increasingly conscious that religious freedom is an exigency of the dignity of the person, as this dignity is disclosed by the revelation that man is made in the image of God. Moreover, experience would also make it clear that, where religious freedom prevails, a climate of freedom is created in society which itself favors the free preaching of the gospel and the free living of the Christian life.

27. *Cf. Lactantius "Divinarum Institutionum," Book V, 19: CSEL 19, pp. 463-464, 465: PL 6, 614 and 616 (ch. 20); St. Ambrose, "Epistola ad Valentianum Imp.," Letter 21: PL 16, 1005; St. Augustine, "Contra Litteras Petiliani," Book II, ch. 83: CSEL 52, p. 112: PL 43, 315; cf. C. 23, q. 5, c. 33 (ed. Friedberg, col. 939); idem, Letter 23: PL 33, 98; idem, Letter 34: PL 33, 132; idem, Letter 35: PL 33, 135; St. Gregory the Great, "Epistola ad Virgilium et Theodorum Episcopos Massiliae Galliarum," Register of Letters I, 45: MGH Ep. 1, p. 72; PL 77, 510-511 (Book I, ep. 47); idem, "Epistola ad Johannem Episcopum Constantinopolitanum," Register of Letters, III, 52: MGH Letter 1, p. 210: PL 77, 649 (Book III, Letter 53); cf. D. 45, c. 1 (ed. Friedberg, col. 160); Council of Toledo IV, c. 57: Mansi 10, 633; cf. D. 45, c. 5 (ed. Friedberg, col. 161-162); Clement III: X., V. 6, 9: ed. Friedberg, col. 774; Innocent III, "Epistola ad Arelatensem Archiepiscopum," X., III, 42, 3: ed. Friedberg, col. 646.*

28. *Cf. Eph. 1:5.*

him[29] to offer to God the reasonable and free submission of faith.

It is therefore completely in accord with the nature of faith that in matters religious every manner of coercion on the part of men should be excluded. In consequence, the principle of religious freedom makes no small contribution to the creation of an environment in which men can without hindrance be invited to Christian faith, and embrace it of their own free will, and profess it effectively in their whole manner of life.

11. God calls men to serve Him in spirit and in truth. Hence they are bound in conscience but they stand under no compulsion.[30] God has regard for the dignity of the human person whom He Himself created; man is to be guided by his own judgment and he is to enjoy freedom.

This truth appears at its height in Christ Jesus, in whom God perfectly manifested Himself and His ways with men. Christ is our Master and our Lord.[31] He is also meek and humble of heart.[32] And in attracting and inviting His disciples He acted patiently.[33] He wrought miracles to shed light on His teaching and to establish its truth. But His intention was to rouse faith in His hearers and to confirm them in faith, not to exert coercion upon them.[34]

He did indeed denounce the unbelief of some who listened to Him; but He left vengeance to God in expectation of the day of judgment.[35] When He sent His apostles into the world, He said to them: "He who believes and is baptized shall be saved, but he who does not believe shall be condemned" (Mk. 16:16); but He Himself, noting that cockle had been sown amid the wheat, gave orders that both should

29. Cf. Jn. 6:44.
30. The major purpose here is to show, from the example and teaching of Christ Himself, that coercion in matters religious is alien to the spirit of the gospel. The ways of God with men are not coercive. They are the ways of faithful love. And their supreme illustration is the cross. Rather than impose the truth upon men by force, Christ willingly accepted death at their hands, and He made His death itself the means of redemption, as the revelation of a love than which there is no greater. The way of Christ became the way of His first apostles, whose reliance was on the power of the Word of God, never on earthly forces.
31. Cf. Jn. 13:13.
32. Cf. Mt. 11:29.
33. Cf. Mt. 11:28-30; Jn. 6:67-68.
34. Cf. Mt. 9:28-29; Mk. 9:23-24; 6, 5-6; Paul VI, encyclical "Ecclesiam Suam," Aug. 6, 1964: AAS 56 (1964), pp. 642-643.
35. Cf. Mt. 11:20-24; Rom. 12:19-20; 2 Th. 1:8.

be allowed to grow until the harvest time, which will come at the end of the world.[36]

He refused to be a political Messiah, ruling by force;[37] He preferred to call Himself the Son of Man, who came "to serve and to give his life as a ransom for many" (Mk. 10:45). He showed Himself the perfect Servant of God;[38] "a bruised reed he will not break, and a smoking wick he will not quench" (Mt. 12:20).

He acknowledged the power of government and its rights, when He commanded that tribute be given to Caesar. But He gave clear warning that the higher rights of God are to be kept inviolate: "Render, therefore, to Caesar the things that are Caesar's, and to God the things that are God's" (Mt. 22:21).

In the end, when He completed on the cross the work of redemption whereby He achieved salvation and true freedom for men, He also brought His revelation to completion. He bore witness to the truth,[39] but He refused to impose the truth by force on those who spoke against it. Not by force of blows does His rule assert its claims.[40] Rather, it is established by witnessing to the truth and by hearing the truth, and it extends its dominion by the love whereby Christ, lifted up on the cross, draws all men to Himself.[41]

Taught by the word and example of Christ, the apostles followed the same way. From the very origins of the Church the disciples of Christ strove to convert men to faith in Christ as the Lord—not, however, by the use of coercion or by devices unworthy of the gospel, but by the power, above all, of the Word of God.[42] Steadfastly they proclaimed to all the plan of God our Savior, "who wishes all men to be saved and to come to the knowledge of the truth" (1 Tim. 2:4). At the same time, however, they showed respect for weaker souls even though these persons were in error. Thus they made it plain that "every one of us will render an account of himself to God" (Rom. 14:12),[43] and for this reason is bound to obey his conscience.

Like Christ Himself, the apostles were unceasingly bent

36. *Cf. Mt. 13:30 and 40-42.*
37. *Cf. Mt. 4:8-10; Jn. 6:15.*
38. *Cf. Is. 42:1-4.*
39. *Cf. Jn. 18:37.*
40. *Cf. Mt. 26:51-53; Jn. 18:36.*
41. *Cf. Jn. 12:32.*
42. *Cf. 1 Cor. 2:3-5; 1 Th. 2:3-5.*
43. *Cf. Rom. 14:1-23; 1 Cor. 8:9-13; 10:23-33.*

upon bearing witness to the truth of God. They showed special courage in speaking "the word of God with boldness"
(Acts 4:31)[44] before the people and their rulers. With a firm
faith they held that the gospel is indeed the power of God
unto salvation for all who believe.[45] Therefore they rejected
all "carnal weapons."[46] They followed the example of the
gentleness and respectfulness of Christ. And they preached
the Word of God in the full confidence that there was resi-
dent in this Word itself a divine power able to destroy all
the forces arrayed against God[47] and to bring men to faith in
Christ and to His service.[48] As the Master, so too the apostles
recognized legitimate civil authority. "For there exists no
authority except from God," the Apostle teaches, and therefore commands:* "Let everyone be subject to the higher
authorities . ... : he who resists the authority resists the
ordinance of ·God" (Rom. 13:1-2).[49]

At the same time, however, they did not hesitate to speak
out against governing powers which set themselves in opposition to the holy will of God: "We must obey God rather
than men" (Acts 5:29).[50] This is the way along which
countless martyrs and other believers have walked through
all ages and over all the earth.

12. The Church therefore is being faithful to the truth of the
gospel, and is following the way of Christ and the apostles
when she recognizes, and gives support to, the principle of
religious freedom as befitting the dignity óf man and as being
in accord with divine revelation. Throughout the ages, the
Church has kept safe and handed on the doctrine received
from the Master and from the apostles. In the life of the
People of God as it has made its pilgrim way through the
vicissitudes of human history, there have at times appeared
ways of acting which were less in accord with the spirit of
the gospel and even opposed to it.[51] Nevertheless, the doc-

44. *Cf. Eph. 6:19-20.*
45. *Cf. Rom. 1:16.*
46. *Cf. 2 Cor. 10:4; 1 Th. 5:8-9.*
47. *Cf. Eph. 6:11-17.*
48. *Cf. 2 Cor. 10:3-5.*
*The preceding 14 words are missing from the *L'Osservatore Romano* text of
Dec. 11, 1965.—Ed.
49. *Cf. 1 Pet. 2:13-17.*
50. *Cf. Acts 4:19-20.*
51. The historical consciousness of the Council required that it be loyal to
the truth of history. Hence the Declaration makes the humble avowal that
the People of God have not always walked in the way of Christ and the

trine of the Church that no one is to be coerced into faith has always stood firm.

Thus the leaven of the gospel has long been about its quiet work in the minds of men. To it is due in great measure the fact that in the course of time men have come more widely to recognize their dignity as persons, and the conviction has grown stronger that in religious matters the person in society is to be kept free from all manner of human coercion.

13. Among the things which concern the good of the Church and indeed the welfare of society here on earth—things therefore which are always and everywhere to be kept secure and defended against all injury—this certainly is preeminent, namely, that the Church should enjoy that full measure of freedom which her care for the salvation of men requires.[52] This freedom is sacred, because the only-begotten Son endowed with it the Church which He purchased with His blood. It is so much the property of the Church that to act against it is to act against the will of God. The freedom of the Church is the fundamental principle in what concerns the relations between the Church and governments and the whole civil order.[53]

In human society and in the face of government, the

apostles. At times they have followed ways that were at variance with the spirit of the gospel and even contrary to it. The avowal is made briefly and without details. But the intention was to confess, in a penitent spirit, not only that Christian churchmen and princes have appealed to the coercive instruments of power in the supposed interests of the faith, but also that the Church herself has countenanced institutions which made a similar appeal. Whatever may be the nice historical judgment on these institutions in their own context of history, they are not to be justified, much less are they ever or in any way to be reinstated. The Declaration is a final renouncement and repudiation by the Church of all means and measures of coercion in matters religious.

52. Cf. Leo XIII, letter "Officio Sanctissimo," Dec. 22, 1887: AAS 20 (1887), p. 269; idem, letter "Ex Litteris," Apr. 7, 1887: AAS 19 (1886), p. 465.

53. This statement, together with the declaration of religious freedom as a human right and the enunciation of the principle of the free society, must rank as one of the central doctrinal utterances of the Declaration. Its importance is emphasized by the fact that Paul VI quoted it in his address on Dec. 9 to political rulers: "And what is it that this Church asks of you, after nearly two thousand years of all sorts of vicissitudes in her relations with you, the powers of earth? What does the Church ask of you today? In one of the major texts of the Council she has told you: she asks of you nothing but freedom—the freedom to believe and to preach her faith, the freedom to love God and to serve Him, the freedom to live and to bring to men her message of life." This doctrine is traditional; it is also new. Implicit in it is the renunciation by the Church of a condition of legal privilege in society. The Church does not make, as a matter of right or of divine law, the claim that she should be established as the "religion of the state." Her claim is freedom, nothing more.

Church claims freedom for herself in her character as a
spiritual authority, established by Christ the Lord. Upon this
authority there rests, by divine mandate, the duty of going
out into the whole world and preaching the gospel to every
creature.[54] The Church also claims freedom for herself in her
character as a society of men who have the right to live in society in accordance with the precepts of Christian faith.[55]

In turn, where the principle of religious freedom is not
only proclaimed in words or simply incorporated in law but
also given sincere and practical application, there the Church
succeeds in achieving a stable situation of right as well as of
fact and the independence which is necessary for the fulfillment of her divine mission. This independence is precisely
what the authorities of the Church claim in society.[56]

At the same time, the Christian faithful, in common with
all other men, possess the civil right not to be hindered in
leading their lives in accordance with their conscience. Therefore, a harmony exists between the freedom of the Church
and the religious freedom which is to be recognized as the
right of all men and communities and sanctioned by constitutional law.

14. In order to be faithful to the divine command, "Make
disciples of all nations" (Mt. 28:19), the Catholic Church
must work with all urgency and concern "that the Word of
God* may run and be glorified" (2 Th. 3:1). Hence the
Church earnestly begs of her children that, first of all, "sup-
plications, prayers, intercessions, and thanksgivings be made
for all men. . . . For this is good and agreeable in the sight
of God our Savior, who wishes all men to be saved and to
come to the knowledge of the truth" (1 Tim. 2:1-4).

In the formation of their consciences, the Christian faithful ought carefully to attend to the sacred and certain doctrine of the Church.[57, 58] The Church is, by the will of

54. *Cf. Mk. 16:15; Mt. 28:18-20; Pius XII, encyclical "Summi Pontificatus,"*
Oct. 20, 1939: AAS 31 (1939), pp. 445-446.
55. *Cf. Pius XI, letter "Firmissimam Constantiam," Mar. 28, 1937: AAS 29*
(1937), p. 196.
56. *Cf. Pius XII, allocution "Ci Riesce," Dec. 6, 1953: AAS 45 (1953), p.*
802.
*The CCD translation has "the Lord" instead of "God."—Ed.
57. *Cf. Pius XII, radio message, Mar. 23, 1952: AAS 44 (1952), pp. 270-278.*
58. The Council directs a word of pastoral exhortation to the Christian
faithful. They are urged, in particular, to form their consciences under the
guidance of the authority of the Church. It might be noted here that the
Council intended to make a clear distinction between religious freedom as
a principle in the civil order and the Christian freedom which obtains even

Christ, the teacher of the truth. It is her duty to give utterance to, and authoritatively to teach, that Truth which is Christ Himself, and also to declare and confirm by her authority those principles of the moral order which have their origin in human nature itself. Furthermore, let Christians walk in wisdom in the face of those outside, "in the Holy Spirit, in unaffected love, in the word of truth" (2 Cor. 6:6-7). Let them be about their task of spreading the light of life with all confidence[59] and apostolic courage, even to the shedding of their blood.

The disciple is bound by a grave obligation toward Christ his Master ever more adequately to understand the truth received from Him, faithfully to proclaim it, and vigorously to defend it, never—be it understood—having recourse to means that are incompatible with the spirit of the gospel. At the same time, the charity of Christ urges him to act lovingly, prudently and patiently in his dealings with those who are in error or in ignorance with regard to the faith.[60] All is to be taken into account—the Christian duty to Christ, the life-giving Word which must be proclaimed, the rights of the human person, and the measure of grace granted by God through Christ to men, who are invited freely to accept and profess the faith.

15. The fact is that men of the present day want to be able freely to profess their religion in private and in public. Religious freedom has already been declared to be a civil right in most constitutions, and it is solemnly recognized in international documents.[61] The further fact is that forms of government still exist under which, even though freedom of religious worship receives constitutional recognition, the powers of government are engaged in the effort to deter citizens from the profession of religion and to make life difficult and dangerous for religious Communities.[62]

inside the Church. These two freedoms are distinct in kind; and it would be perilous to confuse them. Nowhere does the Declaration touch the issue of freedom within the Church. Undoubtedly, however, it will be a stimulus for the articulation of a full theology of Christian freedom in its relation to the doctrinal and disciplinary authority of the Church.
59. Cf. Acts 4:29.
60. Cf. John XXIII, encyclical "Pacem in Terris," Apr. 11, 1963: AAS 55 (1963), pp. 299-300.
61. Cf. John XXIII, encyclical "Pacem in Terris," Apr. 11, 1963: AAS 55 (1963), pp. 295-296.
62. At the end, the Council turns once more to the world at large. Two facts claim its attention. First, the principle of religious freedom is widely recognized; this fact takes its place among the signs of the times. Second,

This sacred Synod greets with joy the first of these two facts, as among the signs of the times. With sorrow, however, it denounces the other fact, as only to be deplored. The Synod exhorts Catholics, and it directs a plea to all men, most carefully to consider how greatly necessary religious freedom is, especially in the present condition of the human family.

All nations are coming into even closer unity. Men of different cultures and religions are being brought together in closer relationships. There is a growing consciousness of the personal responsibility that weighs upon every man. All this is evident.

Consequently, in order that relationships of peace and harmony may be established and maintained within the whole of mankind, it is necessary that religious freedom be everywhere provided with an effective constitutional guarantee, and that respect be shown for the high duty and right of man freely to lead his religious life in society.

May the God and Father of all grant that the human family, through careful observance of the principle of religious freedom in society, may be brought by the grace of Christ and the power of the Holy Spirit to the sublime and unending "freedom of the glory of the sons of God" (Rom. 8:21).

Each and every one of the things set forth in this Declaration has won the consent of the Fathers of this most sacred Council. We too, by the apostolic authority conferred on us by Christ, join with the Venerable Fathers in approving, decreeing, and establishing these things in the Holy Spirit, and we direct that what has thus been enacted in synod be published to God's glory.

Rome, at St. Peter's, December 7, 1965

I, Paul, Bishop of the Catholic Church

There follow the signatures of the Fathers.

the principle of religious freedom is also widely violated; this fact can only be deplored. Then the Declaration, which has stated its argument in terms of principle, turns to the pragmatic aspect of the issue—the practical value and necessity of religious freedom in the world today. It is a world of diversity which is striving toward some measure of unity; it is a world of conflict which is yearning for peace; it is, above all, a world in which a new consciousness of human dignity struggles to find expression in social institutions that will guarantee to men the freedom which is due to them in justice. Most necessary of all is freedom of religion. Where it is safe, the way is open for the "glorious freedom of the sons of God" to come to men as God's gift through Christ in the Holy Spirit.

A RESPONSE

The Declaration on Religious Freedom is the single conciliar document addressed to the whole world. Like the encyclical *Pacem in Terris* (April 11, 1963, Pope John XXIII), to which it owes a great deal, it is in effect addressed "to All Men of Good Will." The non-Catholic reader is, therefore, reckoned among those addressed. He is not called upon to express judgment, e.g., as a scholar or a Christian out-grouper, as to whether such a declaration is appropriate to the spiritual government of a community of faith such as the Catholic Church. Rather, he finds himself personally in-volved. The Church, in a legitimate exercise of her freedom to propagate the gospel, speaks bindingly to him.

To the degree that he is capable of meeting the spirit of openness to Truth which informs this and every message fit for dialogue, the non-Catholic reader: (a) acknowledges the right of the Church so to speak to him, and (b) accepts his own duty to listen and to respond in like spirit. If he is a serious student, the obligation to clarity of thought is put upon him. If he is also a fellow Christian, although of an-other communion and discipline, the further obligation of charity and self-examination rests upon him. In either case, only the frivolous will discharge the matter as "merely an-other statement of opinion" or "of interest only to Catholics."

Very appropriately, the Declaration begins its discussion of that attitude and practice which is Christlike and apostolic by reference to the Great Commission (Mt. 28:19-20; Mk. 16:16). This is the precise place where the first Protestant defenders of religious freedom also began.[1] Reading from it, we discern the responsibility of Christians to communicate openly, to avoid coercion, to elicit voluntary commitment, to proclaim the plenary power of Christ (Mt. 28:18, William Penn's favorite text), to announce the coming age. Religious freedom is different in kind from toleration, even from a *pax dissidentium:* it derives, both historically and theologically, from a certain understanding of the nature of true faith. To tolerate dissent is today merely prudent; to respect the con-

---

1. Thus Menno Simons, who wrote strongly against all use of coercion in mat-ters religious, cited the Great Commission repeatedly in "The Foundation of Christian Doctrine" (1539), "Christian Baptism" (1539), etc.

science and the person of another is noble. The cornerstone
of religious freedom is religious, not political. As Claus Fel-
binger, the 16th-century martyr, put it, "God wants no compulsory service. On the contrary, He loves a free, willing
heart that serves Him with a joyful soul and does joyfully
what is right."[2]

Because love ever seeks to communicate, back of religious
freedom there is found a commitment to community. The
notion that "religion is a purely private matter" has no place
in a Christian document. To define religious freedom in purely subjective and individualistic terms is to misconceive its
essential nature and to build on sand. The true end of freedom is the growth of love and service to the neighbor. Here
again Catholics and Protestants are guided along a like path.
"The Reformation did not propose as an end religious liberty
in the political sense. It was not a battle for liberty but for
truth. It did not, and does not, care for liberty except as a
product of the truth and for its sake. Truth is the Church's
aim, liberty only the means thereto."[3]

It has been amply demonstrated in the modern period, of
course, that policies of toleration or freedom which are only
prudential are likely also to be only transitory. Furthermore,
freedoms—and especially religious freedom—which are expounded purely in terms of what is good for the state are
not likely to endure. The case for religious freedom does not
begin with politics but with religion. Both major forms of
totalitarianism have claimed to speak for freedom. Both have
defined freedom in reference to the prior claims of the state.
Both end, under the rubric "absolute separation of church
and state," in policies far more restrictive of the freedom of
religion than the earlier style of coercive Christendom.[4] It is
quite possible to have "separation" without religious freedom.
Indeed, the ideological approach to separation has almost always been accompanied by hostility to and suppression of
the free exercise of religion. The Declaration therefore points

2. Cf. quotation and argument in "The Historical Free Church Tradition Defined," IX *Brethren Life and Thought* (1964), 4:78-90.
3. Forsyth, Peter Taylor, *Faith, Freedom, and the Future* (New York: Hodder
& Stoughton, n.d.), p. 200.
4. Note the almost identical policies for the suppression of religious freedom
in Martin Bormann's program for the Warthegau and Hilde Benjamin's program for the D.D.R.: Gürtler, Paul, *Nationalsozialismus und evangelische
Kirchen im Warthegau* (Göttingen: Vandenhoeck & Ruprecht, 1958), Appendix, Document 8, and "Die Kirchen in der Deutschen Demokratischen Repub-
lik," in Beckmann, Joachim, ed., *Kirchliches Jahrbuch: 1958* (Gütersloh:
Gütersloher Verlagshaus Gerd Mohn, 1958), p. 199.

out repeatedly that no just government may suppress the freedom of religious profession and practice which is the essential style of the Church's life.

In a parallel argument, religious freedom is grounded in "the dignity of the human person," which leads to the demand "that constitutional limits should be set to the powers of government, in order that there may be no encroachment on the rightful freedom of the person and of associations." Religious freedom is thus made secure for all persons of conscience, whether they are professing Christians or not.

A most important advance in the Declaration is the recognition that since there are means improper to serve Christian ends, no true Church and no just government may limit or coerce the religious freedom of non-Christians either. Without weakening whatever the Christian insistence on the ultimate authority of Truth and the final duty of religious obedience, the double standard is thereby eliminated and the pre-condition of open and honest religious dialogue established. As Father Murray puts it, "the Declaration has opened the way toward new confidence in ecumenical relationships, and a new straightforwardness in relationships between the Church and the world."

In one major dimension, the logic of religious freedom remains undeveloped. The theme is thoroughly elaborated in reference to the natural rights of persons and associations. It is soundly grounded in the system of belief of the Church. The implications for the nature of a just government are less thoroughly treated. Governments which persecute are not only defying the rule of reason and the law of the gospel, however: they are also guilty of denying the limits and style of sound government. Governments may "set themselves in opposition to the holy will of God" not only in defying the truth and persecuting the faithful but also by pretending to be something more than limited and—theologically speaking —"creaturely."

The American experience of religious freedom is not only an advance in Church history: it is also an important breakthrough in government. Governments which claim to achieve ultimate aims, which pretend to be more than human instruments to effect limited and specific purposes—whether "sacral" in the old sense, or "ideological" in the sense of contemporary fascism and communism—are theologically disobedient and historically retrogressive. "Secularized" governmental institutions, always to be distinguished from the state committed to secularism as an ideology, have in our situation proved beneficial to both religion and politics.

While appreciating the fact that not all secularist governments respect the integrity of conscience and not all governments with established Churches persecute dissenters today, this writer would note the fundamental difference between toleration and religious freedom and suggest that government which is freed simply to carry on the proper business of government marks a distinct advance in human history.

The assertion of religious freedom, therefore, which begins as a religious understanding and obligation, ends by giving a new institutional formation to the world. As so often has happened in the works of Christ, the work begun among the faithful is completed in the reshaping of the created order. Religious freedom, in sum, makes not only a better Church and a finer obedience among Christians: its constitutional recognition and protection also makes a better government. Thus again, in the end, God's will for the realm of redemption and His purpose for the created order blend in a final harmony.

FRANKLIN H. LITTELL

APPENDIX

ADDRESSES AND DECISIONS OF
POPE JOHN XXIII AND POPE PAUL VI
CONCERNING VATICAN II,
TOGETHER WITH THE CLOSING
MESSAGES OF THE COUNCIL

Unless otherwise noted, the documents in this section are translations from the original Latin provided by the Vatican Press
Office and the Press Office of the Second Vatican Council.

Pope John
Convokes the Council

In this apostolic constitution "Humanae Salutis," dated December 25, 1961, Pope John convoked the Second Vatican Council for sometime in 1962.

JOHN, BISHOP, SERVANT OF THE SERVANTS
OF GOD, FOR PERPETUAL MEMORY:

INTRODUCTION

The Divine Redeemer Jesus Christ, who before ascending into heaven conferred on the apostles the mandate to preach the gospel to all peoples, in support and guarantee of their mission, made the comforting promise: "Behold I am with you all days even unto the consummation of the world" (Mt. 28:20).

This divine presence, which has been alive and active in all times in the Church, is noticeable above all in the most grave periods of humanity. It is then that the spouse of Christ shows itself in all its splendor as the master of truth and minister of salvation. And it is then, also, that it deploys all its power of charity, prayer, sacrifice, and suffering—invincible spiritual means and the same used by the divine Founder, who in the solemn hour of His life declared: "Have faith for I have overcome the world" (Jn. 16:33).

PAINFUL CONSIDERATIONS

Today the Church is witnessing a crisis under way within society. While humanity is on the edge of a new era, tasks of immense gravity and amplitude await the Church, as in the most tragic periods of its history. It is a question in fact of bringing the modern world into contact with the vivifying and perennial energies of the gospel, a world which exalts itself with its conquests in the technical and scientific fields, but which brings also the consequences of a temporal order which some have wished to reorganize excluding God. This is why modern society is earmarked by a great material progress to which there is not a corresponding advance in the moral field.

Hence there is a weakening in the aspiration toward the

values of the spirit. Hence an urge for the almost exclusive search for earthly pleasures, which progressive technology places with such ease within the reach of all. And hence there is a completely new and disconcerting fact: the existence of a militant atheism which is active on a world level.

REASONS FOR CONFIDENCE

These painful considerations are a reminder of the duty to be vigilant and to keep the sense of responsibility awake. Distrustful souls see only darkness burdening the face of the earth. We, instead, like to reaffirm all our confidence in our Savior, who has not left the world which He redeemed.

Indeed, we make ours the recommendation of Jesus that one should know how to distinguish the "signs of the times" (Mt. 16:4), and we seem to see now, in the midst of so much darkness, a few indications which auger well for the fate of the Church and of humanity.

The bloody wars that have followed one on the other in our times, the spiritual ruins caused by many ideologies, and the fruits of so many bitter experiences have not been without useful teachings. Scientific progress itself, which gave man the possibility of creating catastrophic instruments for his destruction, has raised questions. It has obliged human beings to become thoughtful, more conscious of their own limitations, desirous of peace, and attentive to the importance of spiritual values. And it has accelerated that progress of closer collaboration and of mutual integration toward which, even though in the midst of a thousand uncertainties, the human family seems to be moving. And this facilitates, no doubt, the apostolate of the Church, since many people who did not realize the importance of its mission in the past are, taught by experience, today more disposed to welcome its warnings.

PRESENT VITALITY OF THE CHURCH

Then, if we turn our attention to the Church, we see that it has not remained a lifeless spectator in the face of these events, but has followed step by step the evolution of peoples, scientific progress, and social revolution. It has opposed decisively the materialistic ideologies which deny faith. Lastly, it has witnessed the rise and growth of the immense energies of the apostolate of prayer, of action in all fields. It has seen the emergence of a clergy constantly better equipped in learning and virtue for its mission; and of a laity which has become ever more conscious of its responsibilities within the bosom of the Church, and, in a special way, of its duty to collaborate with the Church hierarchy.

To this should be added the immense suffering of entire Christian communities, through which a multitude of admirable bishops, priests, and laymen seal their adherence to the faith, bearing persecutions of all kinds and revealing forms of heroism which certainly equal those of the most glorious periods of the Church.

Thus, though the world may appear profoundly changed, the Christian community is also in great part transformed and renewed. It has therefore strengthened itself socially in unity; it has been reinvigorated intellectually; it has been interiorly purified and is thus ready for trial.

THE SECOND VATICAN ECUMENICAL COUNCIL

In the face of this twofold spectacle—a world which reveals a grave state of spiritual poverty and the Church of Christ, which is still so vibrant with vitality—we, from the time we ascended to the supreme pontificate, despite our unworthiness and by means of an impulse of Divine Providence, have felt immediately the urgency of the duty to call our sons together, to give the Church the possibility to contribute more efficaciously to the solution of the problems of the modern age.

For this reason, welcoming as from above the intimate voice of our spirit, we considered that the times now were right to offer to the Catholic Church and to the world the gift of a new Ecumenical Council, as an addition to, and continuation of, the series of the twenty great councils, which have been through the centuries a truly heavenly providence for the increase of grace and Christian progress.

The joyful echo brought about by its announcement, followed by the prayerful participation of the whole Church and by a truly encouraging fervor in the work of preparation, as well as by the lively interest, or at least respectful attention, on the part of non-Catholics and even of non-Christians, proved in the most eloquent manner that the historical importance of the event has not escaped anyone.

The forthcoming Council will meet therefore and at a moment in which the Church finds very alive the desire to fortify its faith, and to contemplate itself in its own awe-inspiring unity. In the same way, it feels more urgent the duty to give greater efficiency to its sound vitality and to promote the sanctification of its members, the diffusion of revealed truth, the consolidation of its agencies.

This will be a demonstration of the Church, always living and always young, which feels the rhythm of the times and which in every century beautifies herself with new splendor, radiates new light, achieves new conquests, while remaining identical in herself, faithful to the divine image impressed on her countenance by her Spouse, who loves her and protects her, Christ Jesus.

Then, at a time of generous and growing efforts which are made in different parts for the purpose of rebuilding that visible unity of all Christians which corresponds to the wishes of the Divine Redeemer, it is very natural that the forthcoming Council should provide premises of doctrinal clarity and of mutual charity that will make still more alive in our separated brothers the wish for the hoped-for return to unity and will smooth the way.

And, finally, to a world, which is lost, confused, and anxious under the constant threat of new frightful conflicts, the forthcoming Council must offer a possibility for all men of good will to turn their thoughts and their intentions toward peace, a peace which can and must, above all, come from spiritual and supernatural realities, from human intelligence and conscience, enlightened and guided by God the Creator and Redeemer of humanity.

WORKING PROGRAM OF THE COUNCIL

These fruits that we expect so much from the Council, and on which we like so often to dwell, entail a vast program of work which is now being prepared. This concerns the doctrinal and practical problems which correspond more to the requirements of perfect conformity with Christian teaching, for the edification and in the service of the Mystical Body and of its supernatural mission, and, therefore, the sacred books, venerable tradition, the sacraments, prayer, ecclesiastical discipline, charitable and relief activities, the lay apostolate, and mission horizons.

This supernatural order must, however, reflect its efficiency in the other order, the temporal one, which on so many occasions is unfortunately ultimately the only one that occupies and worries man. In this field, the Church also has shown that it wishes to be *Mater et Magistra*—Mother and Teacher—according to the words of our distant and glorious predecessor,

Innocent III, spoken on the occasion of the Fourth Lateran Council.

Though not having direct earthly ends, it cannot, however, in its mission fail to interest itself in the problems and worries of here below. It knows how beneficial to the good of the soul are those means that are apt to make the life of those individual men who must be saved more human. It knows that by vivifying the temporal order with the light of Christ it reveals men to themselves; it leads them, therefore, to discover in themselves their own nature, their own dignity, their own end.

Hence, the living presence of the Church extends, by right and by fact, to the international organizations, and to the working out of its social doctrine regarding the family, education, civil society, and all related problems. This has raised its magisterium to a very high level as the most authoritative voice, interpreter and affirmer of the moral order, and champion of the rights and duties of all human beings and of all political communities.

In this way, the beneficial influence of the Council deliberations must, as we sincerely hope, succeed to the extent of imbuing with Christian light and penetrating with fervent spiritual energy not only the intimacy of the soul but the whole collection of human activities.

CONVOCATION OF THE COUNCIL

The first announcement of the Council made by us on January 25, 1959, was like a little seed that we planted with anxious mind and hand. Supported by heavenly help, we then readied ourselves for the complex and delicate work of preparation.

Three years have passed during which we have seen, day by day, the little seed develop and become, with the blessing of God, a great tree.

Contemplating the long and tiring road covered, there rises from our spirit a hymn of thanksgiving to the Lord for His generous help that everything developed in a suitable manner and in a harmony of spirit.

Before deciding the questions that had to be studied in view of the forthcoming Council, we wished to hear beforehand the wise and enlightened opinions of the College of Cardinals, of the episcopate of the whole world, of the sacred congregations of the Roman Curia, of the general superiors of orders and religious congregations, of Catholic universities, and of ecclesiastical faculties.

This work of consultation was carried out within a year, and there emerged clearly from this the points that had to be submitted to a thorough study.

We then instituted the different preparatory organizations to which we entrusted the arduous task of drawing up the doctrinal and disciplinary projects, which we intend to submit to the Council. We finally have the joy of announcing that this intense work of study, to which the cardinals, bishops, prelates, theologians, canonists, and experts from all over the world have given their valuable contribution, is now nearing its end.

Trusting therefore in the help of the Divine Redeemer, the Beginning and the End of all things, in the help of His most excellent Mother and of St. Joseph—to whom we entrusted from the very beginning such a great event—it seems to us that the time has come to convoke the Second Vatican Ecumenical Council.

After hearing, therefore, the opinion of our brothers the cardinals of the holy Roman Church, with the authority of our Lord Jesus Christ, of the holy Apostles Peter and Paul, and of our own, we institute, announce, and convoke for the forthcoming year 1962 the Ecumenical and Universal Council, which will be held in the Vatican Basilica, on days that will be established according to the opportunty which good Providence may deign to grant us.

We consequently wish and order that to this Ecumenical Council, instituted by us, there should come from all parts our beloved sons the cardinals, the venerable brother patriarchs and primates, archbishops and bishops—both residential and titular—and also all those people who have the right and the duty to attend the Council.

AN INVITATION TO PRAYER

And now we ask each individual member of the faithful and the entire Christian people to continue participating in most lively prayer that it may accompany, vivify, and embellish the preparation of the forthcoming great event.

May this prayer be inspired by ardent and persevering faith. May it be accompanied by that Christian penance which makes it more acceptable to God and more efficacious. May it be strengthened by an effort of Christian life which may be an anticipated token of the decisions taken by each of the individual faithful to apply the teachings and the practical directives that will emerge from the Council itself.

We address our appeal both to the secular and regular clergy, spread throughout the world, to all categories of faithful. But, in a very special way, we entrust its success to the prayers of children, knowing well how powerful is the voice of innocence with God, and to the sick and to the suffering that their pains and life of sacrifice, by virtue of the cross of Christ, may be transformed and rise in prayer, in redemption, in a source of life for the Church.

To this chorus of prayers, we invite also all Christians of Churches separated from Rome, that the Council may be also to their advantage. We know that many of these sons are anxious for a return of unity and of peace, according to the teachings and the prayer of Christ to the Father. And we know also that the announcement of the Council has been accepted by them not only with joy but also that not a few have already promised to offer their prayers for its success, and that they hope to send representatives of their communities to follow its work at close quarters. All this is for us a reason of great comfort and of hope, and precisely for the purpose of facilitating these contacts we instituted some time ago the secretariat for this specific purpose.

May there be repeated thus in the Christian families the spectacle of the apostles gathered together in Jerusalem after the Ascension of Jesus to heaven, when the newborn Church was completely united in communion of thought and of prayer with Peter and around Peter, the shepherd of the lambs and of the sheep. And may the Divine Spirit deign to answer in a most comforting manner the prayer that rises daily to Him from every corner of the earth:

"Renew Your wonders in our time, as though for a new Pentecost, and grant that the holy Church, preserving unanimous and continuous prayer, together with Mary, the mother of Jesus, and also under the guidance of St. Peter, may increase the reign of the Divine Savior, the reign of truth and justice, the reign of love and peace. Amen."

Given at Rome at St. Peter's, December 25, feast of the birth of our Lord Jesus Christ, 1961, fourth year of Our Pontificate. I, John, Bishop of the Catholic Church.

Pope John's Opening Speech to the Council

On October 11, 1962, the first day of the Council, Pope John delivered this address in St. Peter's Basilica.

Mother Church rejoices that, by the singular gift of Divine Providence, the longed-for day has finally dawned when— under the auspices of the virgin Mother of God, whose maternal dignity is commemorated on this feast—the Second Vatican Ecumenical Council is being solemnly opened here beside St. Peter's tomb.

THE ECUMENICAL COUNCILS OF THE CHURCH

The Councils—both the twenty ecumenical ones and the numberless others, also important, of a provincial or regional character which have been held down through the years—all prove clearly the vigor of the Catholic Church and are recorded as shining lights in her annals.

In calling this vast assembly of bishops, the latest and humble successor to the Prince of the Apostles who is addressing you intended to assert once again the magisterium (teaching authority), which is unfailing and perdures until the end of time, in order that this magisterium, taking into account the errors, the requirements, and the opportunities of our time, might be presented in exceptional form to all men throughout the world.

It is but natural that in opening this Universal Council we should like to look to the past and to listen to its voices, whose echo we like to hear in the memories and the merits of the more recent and ancient Pontiffs, our predecessors. These are solemn and venerable voices, throughout the East and the West, from the fourth century to the Middle Ages, and from there to modern times, which have handed down their witness to those Councils. They are voices which proclaim in perennial fervor the triumph of that divine and human institution, the Church of Christ, which from Jesus takes its name, its grace, and its meaning.

Side by side with these motives for spiritual joy, however,

there has also been for more than nineteen centuries a cloud
of sorrows and of trials. Not without reason did the ancient
Simeon announce to Mary the mother of Jesus, that prophecy
which has been and still is true: "Behold this child is set for
the fall and the resurrection of many in Israel, and for a
sign which shall be contradicted" (Lk. 2:34). And Jesus
Himself, when He grew up, clearly outlined the manner in
which the world would treat His person down through the
succeeding centuries with the mysterious words: "He who
hears you, hears me" (Ibid. 10:16), and with those others
that the same Evangelist relates: "He who is not with me is
against me and he who does not gather with me scatters"
(Ibid. 11:23).

The great problem confronting the world after almost two
thousand years remains unchanged. Christ is ever resplendent
as the center of history and of life. Men are either with Him
and His Church, and then they enjoy light, goodness, order,
and peace. Or else they are without Him, or against Him,
and deliberately opposed to His Church, and then they give
rise to confusion, to bitterness in human relations, and to the
constant danger of fratricidal wars.

Ecumenical Councils, whenever they are assembled, are
a solemn celebration of the union of Christ and His Church,
and hence lead to the universal radiation of truth, to the
proper guidance of individuals in domestic and social life,
to the strengthening of spiritual energies for a perennial uplift
toward real and everlasting goodness.

The testimony of this extraordinary magisterium of the
Church in the succeeding epochs of these twenty centuries of
Christian history stands before us collected in numerous and
imposing volumes, which are the sacred patrimony of our
ecclesiastical archives, here in Rome and in the more noted
libraries of the entire world.

THE ORIGIN AND REASON
FOR THE SECOND VATICAN ECUMENICAL COUNCIL

As regards the initiative for the great event which gathers us
here, it will suffice to repeat as historical documentation our
personal account of the first sudden bringing up in our heart
and lips of the simple words, "Ecumenical Council." We
uttered those words in the presence of the Sacred College of
Cardinals on that memorable January 25, 1959, the feast
of the Conversion of St. Paul, in the basilica dedicated to

him. It was completely unexpected, like a flash of heavenly light, shedding sweetness in eyes and hearts. And at the same time it gave rise to a great fervor throughout the world in expectation of the holding of the Council.

There have elapsed three years of laborious preparation, during which a wide and profound examination was made regarding modern conditions of faith and religious practice, and of Christian and especially Catholic vitality. These years have seemed to us a first sign, an initial gift of celestial grace.

Illuminated by the light of this Council, the Church—we confidently trust—will become greater in spiritual riches and, gaining the strength of new energies therefrom, she will look to the future without fear. In fact, by bringing herself up to date where required, and by the wise organization of mutual cooperation, the Church will make men, families, and peoples really turn their minds to heavenly things.

And thus the holding of the Council becomes a motive for wholehearted thanksgiving to the Giver of every good gift, in order to celebrate with joyous canticles the glory of Christ our Lord, the glorious and immortal King of ages and of peoples.

The opportuneness of holding the Council is, moreover, venerable brothers, another subject which it is useful to propose for your consideration. Namely, in order to render our joy more complete, we wish to narrate before this great assembly our assessment of the happy circumstances under which the Ecumenical Council commences.

In the daily exercise of our pastoral office, we sometimes have to listen, much to our regret, to voices of persons who, though burning with zeal, are not endowed with too much sense of discretion or measure. In these modern times they can see nothing but prevarication and ruin. They say that our era, in comparison with past eras, is getting worse, and they behave as though they had learned nothing from history, which is, none the less, the teacher of life. They behave as though at the time of former Councils everything was a full triumph for the Christian idea and life and for proper religious liberty.

We feel we must disagree with those prophets of gloom, who are always forecasting disaster, as though the end of the world were at hand.

In the present order of things, Divine Providence is leading us to a new order of human relations which, by men's own efforts and even beyond their very expectations, are directed toward the fulfillment of God's superior and inscrutable designs. And everything, even human differences, leads to the greater good of the Church.

It is easy to discern this reality if we consider attentively the world of today, which is so busy with politics and controversies in the economic order that it does not find time to attend to the care of spiritual reality, with which the Church's magisterium is concerned. Such a way of acting is certainly not right, and must justly be disapproved. It cannot be denied, however, that these new conditions of modern life have at least the advantage of having eliminated those innumerable obstacles by which, at one time, the sons of this world impeded the free action of the Church. In fact, it suffices to leaf even cursorily through the pages of ecclesiastical history to note clearly how the Ecumenical Councils themselves, while constituting a series of true glories for the Catholic Church, were often held to the accompaniment of most serious difficulties and sufferings because of the undue interference of civil authorities. The princes of this world, indeed, sometimes in all sincerity, intended thus to protect the Church. But more frequently this occurred not without spiritual damage and danger, since their interest therein was guided by the views of a selfish and perilous policy.

In this regard, we confess to you that we feel most poignant sorrow over the fact that very many bishops, so dear to us, are noticeable here today by their absence, because they are imprisoned for their faithfulness to Christ, or impeded by other restraints. The thought of them impels us to raise most fervent prayer to God. Nevertheless, we see today, not without great hopes and to our immense consolation, that the Church, finally freed from so many obstacles of a profane nature such as trammeled her in the past, can from this Vatican Basilica, as if from a second apostolic cenacle, and through your intermediary, raise her voice resonant with majesty and greatness.

PRINCIPLE DUTY OF THE COUNCIL:
THE DEFENSE AND ADVANCEMENT OF TRUTH

The greatest concern of the Ecumenical Council is this: that the sacred deposit of Christian doctrine should be guarded and taught more efficaciously. That doctrine embraces the whole of man, composed as he is of body and soul. And, since he is a pilgrim on this earth, it commands him to tend always toward heaven.

This demonstrates how our mortal life is to be ordered in such a way as to fulfill our duties as citizens of earth and of heaven, and thus to attain the aim of life as established by God. That is, all men, whether taken singly or as united in society, today have the duty of tending ceaselessly during their lifetime toward the attainment of heavenly things and to use, for this purpose only, the earthly goods, the employment of which must not prejudice their eternal happiness.

The Lord has said: "Seek first the kingdom of God and his justice" (Mt. 6:33). The word "first" expresses the direction in which our thoughts and energies must move. We must not, however, neglect the other words of this exhortation of our Lord, namely: "And all these things shall be given you besides" (*Ibid.*). In reality, there always have been in the Church, and there are still today, those who, while seeking the practice of evangelical perfection with all their might, do not fail to make themselves useful to society. Indeed, it is from their constant example of life and their charitable undertakings that all that is highest and noblest in human society takes its strength and growth.

In order, however, that this doctrine may influence the numerous fields of human activity, with reference to individuals, to families, and to social life, it is necessary first of all that the Church should never depart from the sacred patrimony of truth received from the Fathers. But at the same time she must ever look to the present, to the new conditions and new forms of life introduced into the modern world which have opened new avenues to the Catholic apostolate.

For this reason, the Church has not watched inertly the marvelous progress of the discoveries of human genius, and has not been backward in evaluating them rightly. But, while following these developments, she does not neglect to admonish men so that, over and above sense—perceived things —they may raise their eyes to God, the Source of all wisdom and all beauty. And may they never forget the most serious command: "The Lord thy God shalt thou worship, and Him only shalt thou serve" (Mt. 4:10; Lk. 4:8), so that it may not happen that the fleeting fascination of visible things should impede true progress.

The manner in which sacred doctrine is spread, this having been established, it becomes clear how much is expected from the Council in regard to doctrine. That is, the Twenty-first Ecumenical Council, which will draw upon the effective and important wealth of juridical, liturgical, apostolic, and administrative experiences, wishes to transmit the doctrine, pure and integral, without any attenuation or distortion, which throughout twenty centuries, notwithstanding difficulties and contrasts, has become the common patrimony of men. It is a patrimony not well received by all, but always a rich treasure available to men of good will.

Our duty is not only to guard this precious treasure, as if we were concerned only with antiquity, but to dedicate ourselves with an earnest will and without fear to that work which our era demands of us, pursuing thus the path which the Church has followed for twenty centuries.

The salient point of this Council is not, therefore, a discussion of one article or another of the fundamental doctrine of the Church which has repeatedly been taught by the Fathers and by ancient and modern theologians, and which is presumed to be well known and familiar to all.

For this a Council was not necessary. But from the renewed, serene, and tranquil adherence to all the teaching of the Church in its entirety and preciseness, as it still shines forth in the Acts of the Council of Trent and First Vatican Council, the Christian, Catholic, and apostolic spirit of the whole world expects a step forward toward a doctrinal penetration and a formation of consciousness in faithful and perfect conformity to the authentic doctrine, which, however, should be studied and expounded through the methods of research and through the literary forms of modern thought. The substance of the ancient doctrine of the deposit of faith is one thing, and the way in which it is presented is another. And it is the latter that must be taken into great consideration with patience if necessary, everything being measured in the forms and proportions of a magisterium which is predominantly pastoral in character.

HOW TO REPRESS ERRORS

At the outset of the Second Vatican Council, it is evident, as always, that the truth of the Lord will remain forever. We see, in fact, as one age succeeds another, that the opinions of men follow one another and exclude each other. And often errors vanish as quickly as they arise, like fog before the sun.

The Church has always opposed these errors. Frequently she has condemned them with the greatest severity. Nowadays, however, the Spouse of Christ prefers to make use of the medicine of mercy rather than that of severity. She considers that she meets the needs of the present day by demonstrating the validity of her teaching rather than by condemnations. Not, certainly, that there is a lack of fallacious teaching, opinions, and dangerous concepts to be guarded against and dissipated. But these are so obviously in contrast with the right norm of honesty, and have produced such lethal fruits, that by now it would seem that men of themselves are inclined to condemn them, particularly those ways of life which despise God and His law or place excessive confidence in technical progress and a well-being based exclusively on the comforts of life. They are ever more deeply convinced of the paramount dignity of the human person and of his perfections, as well as of the duties which that implies. Even more important, experience has taught men that violence inflicted on others, the might of arms, and political domination, are of no help at all in finding a happy solution to the grave problems which afflict them.

That being so, the Catholic Church, raising the torch of religious truth by means of this Ecumenical Council, desires to show herself to be the loving mother of all, benign, patient, full of mercy and goodness toward the brethren who are separated from her. To mankind, oppressed by so many difficulties, the Church says, as Peter said to the poor who begged alms from him: "I have neither gold nor silver, but what I have I give you; in the name of Jesus Christ of Nazareth, rise and walk" (Acts 3:6). In other words, the Church does not offer to the men of today riches that pass, nor does she promise them a merely earthly happiness. But she distributes to them the goods of divine grace which, raising men to the dignity of sons of God, are the most efficacious safeguards and aids toward a more human life. She opens the fountain of her life-giving doctrine which allows men, enlightened by the light of Christ, to understand well what they really are, what their lofty dignity and their purpose are, and, finally, through her children, she spreads everywhere the fullness of Christian charity, than which nothing is more effective in eradicating the seeds of discord, nothing more efficacious in promoting concord, just peace, and the brotherly unity of all.

THE UNITY OF THE CHRISTIAN AND HUMAN FAMILY MUST BE PROMOTED

The Church's solicitude to promote and defend truth derives from the fact that, according to the plan of God, who wills all men to be saved and to come to the knowledge of the truth (1 Tim. 2:4), men without the assistance of the whole of revealed doctrine cannot reach a complete and firm unity of minds, with which are associated true peace and eternal salvation.

Unfortunately, the entire Christian family has not yet fully attained this visible unity in truth.

The Catholic Church, therefore, considers it her duty to work actively so that there may be fulfilled the great mystery of that unity, which Jesus Christ invoked with fervent prayer from His heavenly Father on the eve of His sacrifice. She rejoices in peace, knowing well that she is intimately associated with that prayer, and then exults greatly at seeing that invocation extend its efficacy with salutary fruit, even among those who are outside her fold.

Indeed, if one considers well this same unity which Christ implored for His Church, it seems to shine, as it were, with a triple ray of beneficent supernal light: namely, the unity of Catholics among themselves, which must always be kept exemplary and most firm; the unity of prayers and ardent desires with which those Christians separated from this Apostolic See aspire to be united with us; and the unity in esteem and respect for the Catholic Church which animates those who follow non-Chistian religions.

In this regard, it is a source of considerable sorrow to see that the greater part of the human race—although all men who are born were redeemed by the blood of Christ—does not yet participate in those sources of divine grace which exist in the Catholic Church. Hence the Church, whose light illumines all, whose strength of supernatural unity redounds to the advantage of all humanity, is rightly described in these beautiful words of St. Cyprian:

"The Church, surrounded by divine light, spreads her rays over the entire earth. This light, however, is one and unique, and shines everywhere without causing any separation in the unity of the body. She extends her branches over the whole world. By her fruitfulness she sends ever farther afield her rivulets. Nevertheless, the head is always one, the origin one, for she is the one mother, abundantly fruitful. We are born of her, are nourished by her milk, we live of her spirit" (De Catholicae Eccles. Unitate, 5).

Venerable brothers, such is the aim of the Second Vatican Ecumenical Council, which, while bringing together the Church's best energies and striving to have men welcome more favorably the good tidings of salvation, prepares, as it were, and consolidates the path toward that unity of mankind which is required as a necessary foundation, in order that the earthly city may be brought to the resemblance of that heavenly city where truth reigns, charity is the law, and whose extent is eternity (Cf. St. Augustine, Epistle 138, 3).

Now, "our voice is directed to you" (2 Cor. 6:11), venerable brothers in the episcopate. Behold, we are gathered together in this Vatican Basilica, upon which hinges the history of the Church where heaven and earth are closely joined, here near the tomb of Peter and near so many of the tombs of our holy predecessors, whose ashes in this solemn hour seem to thrill in mystic exultation.

The Council now beginning rises in the Church like day-break, a forerunner of most splendid light. It is now only dawn. And already at this first announcement of the rising day, how much sweetness fills our heart. Everything here breathes sanctity and arouses great joy. Let us contemplate the stars, which with their brightness augment the majesty of this temple. These stars, according to the testimony of the Apostle John (Apoc. 1:20), are you, and with you we see shining around the tomb of the Prince of the Apostles, the golden candlelabra. That is, the Church is confided to you (Ibid.).

We see here with you important personalities, present in an attitude of great respect and cordial expectation, having come together in Rome from the five continents to represent the nations of the world.

We might say that heaven and earth are united in the holding of the Council—the saints of heaven to protect our work, the faithful of the earth continuing in prayer to the Lord, and you, seconding the inspiration of the Holy Spirit in order that the work of all may correspond to the modern expectations and needs of the various peoples of the world.

This requires of you serenity of mind, brotherly concord, moderation in proposals, dignity in discussion, and wisdom of deliberation.

God grant that your labors and your work, toward which the eyes of all peoples and the hopes of the entire world are turned, may abundantly fulfill the aspirations of all.

Almightly God! In Thee we place all our confidence, not trusting in our own strength. Look down benignly upon these pastors of Thy Church. May the light of Thy supernal grace aid us in taking decisions and in making laws. Graciously hear the prayers which we pour forth to Thee in unanimity of faith, of voice, and of mind.

O Mary, Help of Christians, Help of Bishops, of whose love we have recently had particular proof in thy temple of Loreto, where we venerated the mystery of the Incarnation, dispose all things for a happy and propitious outcome and, with thy spouse, St. Joseph, the holy Apostles Peter and Paul, St. John the Baptist and St. John the Evangelist, intercede for us to God.

To Jesus Christ, our most amiable Redeemer, immortal King of peoples and of times, be love, power, and glory forever and ever.

Synod of Bishops Established

*With this motu proprio, entitled "Apostolica Sollicitudo,"
dated September 15, 1965, Pope Paul took the historic step
of establishing a Synod of Bishops.*

Our apostolic concern whereby, carefully searching the signs
of the times, we endeavor to adapt the principles and the
methods of the sacred apostolate to the growing needs of the
times and the changed conditions of society, impels us to
tighten the bonds of our union with the bishops "whom the
Holy Spirit has placed . . . to rule the Church of God"
(Acts 20:28).

To this we are inspired not only by the reverence, esteem,
and gratitude which we rightly nurture for all our venerable
brothers in the episcopate, but also by the very heavy charge
of universal shepherd which has been laid upon us and
whereby we have the duty to lead the People of God to everlasting pasture. In this day and age, disturbed and filled as it
is with dangers and yet so open to the salutary inspirations
of heavenly grace, we have learned from daily experience
how helpful for our apostolic office is this union with the
shepherds of the Church, a union which it is our intention
to promote and encourage in every way lest, as we declared
on another occasion, we be deprived of the consolation of
their presence, the help of their prudence and their experience,
the safeguard of their counsel and the assistance of their
authority" (AAS, 1964, p. 1011).

Wherefore it was most fitting, especially during the sessions
of the Second Vatican Ecumenical Council, that we should
be profoundly convinced of the importance and the necessity
of a broader use of the assistance of the bishops for the welfare of the universal Church. Still more, the Ecumenical
Council provided us with the occasion for the project of
setting up permanently a special body of bishops to the end
that, also after the end of the Council, there would continue
to flow out upon the Christian people that vast abundance
of benefits which happily resulted from our close collaboration with the bishops during the Council.

But now, with the Second Vatican Ecumenical Council

drawing to a close, we feel that the opportune moment has come to finally implement a plan which has long been in mind, and we do this all the more willingly because we know that the bishops of the Catholic world are favorable to this plan, as is clear from the desire expressed by many bishops during the Council.

Therefore, after careful consideration, as an expression of our esteem and respect for all Catholic bishops, and in order to provide them with a clearer and more effective means of sharing in our solicitude for the universal Church, on our own initiative and by our apostolic authority, we erect and constitute in this city of Rome a body for the universal Church, directly and immediately subject to our authority, to which we give the special name of Synod of Bishops.

I. This Synod, which like all human institutions can be still more perfected with the passage of time, will be governed by the following general norms:

1. The Synod of Bishops, whereby bishops chosen from various parts of the world lend their valuable assistance to the Supreme Pastor of the Church, is so constituted as to be:

a) A central ecclesiastical institution,

b) Representing the complete Catholic episcopate,

c) By its nature perpetual,

d) As for its structure, performing its duties for a time and when called upon.

II. By its very nature it is the task of the Synod of Bishops to inform and give advice. It may also have deliberate power, when such power is conferred on it by the Sovereign Pontiff, who will in such cases confirm the decisions of the Synod.

1. The general aims of the Synod of Bishops are:

a) To encourage close union and valued assistance between the Sovereign Pontiff and the bishops of the entire world;

b) To insure that direct and real information is provided on questions and situations touching upon the internal action of the Church and its necessary activity in the world of today;

c) To facilitate agreement on essential points of doctrine and on methods of procedure in the life of the Church.

2. The special and proximate ends of the Synod of Bishops are:

a) To communicate useful information;

b) To proffer advice on the topics proposed for discussion in the individual meetings of the Synod.

III. The Synod of Bishops is directly and immediately subject to the authority of the Roman Pontiff, to whom it consequently pertains:

1. To convoke the Synod as often as he may deem it advisable, designating also the place of meeting;

2. To confirm the election of the members mentioned in articles VII and VIII;

3. To determine topics for discussion at least six months, if possible, before the date for the convening of the Synod;

4. To decide on the dispatching of material to those who are to take part in the discussion;

5. To determine the agenda;

6. To preside over the Synod either personally or through a representative.

IV. The Synod of Bishops can be convoked in general, extraordinary, or special meeting.

V. The Synod of Bishops convoked in general meeting consists first and per se of the following:

1. a) Patriarchs, major archbishops, and metropolitans outside the patriarchates of the Catholic Churches of the Eastern Rites;

b) Bishops elected by the individual national episcopal conferences, according to the provisions of article VIII;

c) Bishops elected by the national episcopal conferences of several nations, for those nations which do not have their own national conference, according to the provisions of article VIII;

d) Ten religious to represent clerical religious institutes, elected by the Roman Union of Superiors General.

2. The cardinals in charge of the dicasteries of the Roman Curia take part in the general meetings of the Synod of Bishops.

VI. The Synod of Bishops convoked in extraordinary session is composed of the following:

1. a) Patriarchs, major archbishops, and metropolitans

outside the patriarchates of the Catholic Churches of the Eastern Rites;

b) The presidents of the national episcopal conferences;

c) The presidents of the episcopal conferences of several nations which do not have their own individual conferences;

d) Three religious representing clerical religious institutes, elected by the Roman Union of Superiors General.

2. The cardinals in charge of the dicasteries of the Roman Curia take part in the extraordinary meetings of the Synod of Bishops.

VII. The Synod of Bishops assembled in special meeting includes patriarchs, major archbishops, and metropolitans outside the patriarchates of the Catholic Churches of the Eastern Rites, as also the representatives both of the episcopal conferences of individual nations or of several nations, as well as the representatives of religious institutes, as stated in articles V and VIII. All these members, however, must belong to the regions for which the special meeting of the Synod was convoked.

VIII. The bishops representing the national episcopal conferences are elected on the following basis: (a) one for each national conference having no more than 25 members; (b) two for each national episcopal conference having no more than 50 members; (c) three for each national episcopal conference having no more than 100 members, (d) four for each national episcopal conference having more than 100 members.

The episcopal conferences of several nations elect their representatives conformably to these same norms.

IX. In the election of those who will represent the episcopal conference of one or several nations and clerical religious institutes in the Synod of Bishops, special attention shall be paid not only to their learning and prudence in general, but also to their theoretical and especially their practical knowledge of the matters to be discussed in the Synod.

X. If he so wishes, the Sovereign Pontiff may add to the members of the Synod of Bishops, adding either bishops or religious, to represent religious institutes, or, finally, ecclesiastical experts, up to 15% of the total membership mentioned in Articles V and VIII.

XI. The conclusion of the session for which the Synod of Bishops was convoked entails the automatic cessation of both the personal membership of the Synod and of the offices and functions filled by the individual members as such.

XII. The Synod of Bishops has a permanent or general secretary, who will be provided with an appropriate number of assistants. Besides, each individual synod of bishops has its own special secretary, who remains in office until the end of the said session.

Both the general secretary and the special secretaries are appointed by the Sovereign Pontiff.

Given at Rome, in St. Peter's, on the 15th day of September, in the year 1965, the third of Our Pontificate.

POPE PAUL VI

Catholic-Orthodox Declaration

On December 7, 1965, Pope Paul in Rome and Patriarch Athenagoras in Istanbul issued this text concerning the events of 1054 that led to a breach between the Roman Catholic Church and the Orthodox Church of Constantinople.

1. Grateful to God who mercifully favored them with a fraternal meeting at those holy places where the mystery of salvation was accomplished through the death and resurrection of the Lord Jesus, and where the Church was born through the outpouring of the Holy Spirit, Pope Paul VI and Patriarch Athenagoras I have not lost sight of the determination each then felt to omit nothing thereafter which charity might inspire and which could facilitate the development of the fraternal relations thus taken up between the Roman Catholic Church and the Orthodox Church of Constantinople. They are persuaded that in acting this way, they are responding to the call of that divine grace which today is leading the Roman Catholic Church and the Orthodox Church, as well as all Christians, to overcome their differences in order to be again "one" as the Lord Jesus asked of his Father for them.

2. Among the obstacles along the road of the development of these fraternal relations of confidence and esteem, there is the memory of the decisions, actions, and painful incidents which in 1054 resulted in the sentence of excommunication leveled against the Patriarch Michael Cerularius and two other persons by the legate of the Roman See under the leadership of Cardinal Humbertus, legates who then became the object of a similar sentence pronounced by the Patriarch and the Synod of Constantinople.

3. One cannot pretend that these events were not what they were during this very troubled period of history. Today, however, they have been judged more fairly and serenely. Thus it is important to recognize the excesses which accompanied them and later led to consequences which, in so far as we can judge, went much further than their authors had intended and foreseen. They had directed their censures against the persons concerned and not the Churches; these

censures were not intended to break ecclesiastical communion between the Sees of Rome and Constantinople.

4. Since they are certain that they express the common desire for justice and the unanimous sentiment of charity which moves the faithful, and since they recall the command of the Lord: "If you are offering your gift at the altar, and there remember that your brother has something against you, leave your gift before the altar and go, first be reconciled to your brother" (Mt. 5:23–24), Pope Paul VI and Patriarch Athenagoras I with his Synod, in common agreement, declare that:

a) They regret the offensive words, the reproaches without foundation, and the reprehensible gestures which, on both sides, have marked or accompanied the sad events of this period.

b) They likewise regret and remove both from memory and from the midst of the Church the sentences of excommunication which followed these events, the memory of which has influenced actions up to our day and has hindered closer relations in charity; and they commit these excommunications to oblivion.

c) Finally, they deplore the preceding and later vexing events which, under the influence of various factors—among which, lack of understanding and mutual trust—eventually led to the effective rupture of ecclesiastical communion.

5. Pope Paul VI and Patriarch Athenagoras I with his Synod realize that this gesture of justice and mutual pardon is not sufficient to end both old and more recent differences between the Roman Catholic Church and the Orthodox Church. Through the action of the Holy Spirit, those differences will be overcome through cleansing of hearts, through regret for historical wrongs, and through an efficacious determination to arrive at a common understanding and expression of the faith of the apostles and its demands.

They hope, nevertheless, that this act will be pleasing to God, who is prompt to pardon us when we pardon each other. They hope that the whole Christian world, especially the entire Roman Catholic Church and the Orthodox Church, will appreciate this gesture as an expression of a sincere desire, shared in common, for reconciliation, and as an invitation to follow out, in a spirit of trust, esteem, and mutual charity, the dialogue which, with God's help, will lead to living together again, for the greater good of souls and the coming of the kingdom of God, in that full communion of faith, fraternal accord, and sacramental life which existed among them during the first thousand years of the life of the Church.

Closing Messages
of the Council

*On December 8, at the close of the solemn ceremonies mark-
ing the end of the Second Vatican Council, Pope Paul spoke
to the Council Fathers, and cardinals read messages, in the
name of the Council Fathers, to various groups of people:
rulers, intellectuals and scientists, artists, women, the poor,
sick, and suffering, workers, and youth.*

Pope Paul to the Council Fathers

The hour for departure and separation has sounded. In a
few moments you are about to leave the Council assembly
to go out to meet mankind and to bring the good news of the
gospel of Christ and of the renovation of His Church at
which we have been working together for four years.

This is a unique moment, a moment of incomparable significance and riches. In this universal assembly, in this
privileged point of time and space, there converge together
the past, the present, and the future—the past: for here,
gathered in this spot, we have the Church of Christ with
her tradition, her history, her Councils, her doctors, her
saints; the present: for we are taking leave of one another
to go out toward the world of today with its miseries, its
sufferings, its sins, but also with its prodigious accomplishments, its values, its virtues; and lastly the future is here in
the urgent appeal of the peoples of the world for more justice,
in their will for peace, in their conscious or unconscious
thirst for a higher life, that life precisely which the Church
of Christ can and wishes to give them.

We seem to hear from every corner of the world an immense and confused voice, the questions of all those who look
toward the Council and ask us anxiously: "Have you not a
word for us?" For us rulers? For us intellectuals, workers,
artists? And for us women? For us of the younger generation,
for us the sick and the poor?

These pleading voices will not remain unheeded. It is for all
these categories of men that the Council has been working for
four years. It is for them that there has been prepared this

Constitution on the Church in the Modern World, which we promulgated yesterday amidst the enthusiastic applause of your assembly.

From our long meditation on Christ and His Church, there should spring forth at this moment a first announcement of peace and salvation for the waiting multitudes. Before breaking up, the Council wishes to fulfill this prophetic function and to translate into brief messages and in a language accessible to all men, the "good news" which it has for the world and which some of its most respected spokesmen are now about to pronounce in your name for the whole of humanity.

To Rulers

(Read by Achille Cardinal Lienart of Lille, assisted by Bernard Cardinal Alfrink of Utrecht and Giovanni Cardinal Colombo of Milan.)

At this solemn moment, we, the Fathers of the twenty-first Ecumenical Council of the Catholic Church, on the point of disbanding after four years of prayer and work, with the full consciousness of our mission toward mankind, address ourselves respectively and confidently to those who hold in their hands the destiny of men on this earth, to all those who hold temporal power.

We proclaim publicly: We do honor to your authority and your sovereignty, we respect your office, we recognize your just laws, we esteem those who make them and those who apply them. But we have a sacrosanct word to speak to you and it is this: Only God is great. God alone is the beginning and the end. God alone is the Source of your authority and the Foundation of your laws.

Your task is to be in the world the promoters of order and peace among men. But never forget this: It is God, the living and true God, who is the Father of men. And it is Christ, His eternal Son, who came to make this known to us and to teach us that we are all brothers. He it is who is the great artisan of order and peace on earth, for He it is who guides human history and who alone can incline hearts to renounce those evil passions which beget war and misfortune. It is He who blesses the bread of the human race, who sanctifies its work and its suffering, who gives it those joys which you can never give it, and strengthens it in those sufferings which you cannot console.

In your earthly and temporal city, God constructs mysteriously His spiritual and eternal city, His Church. And what does this Church ask of you after close to two thousand years of experiences of all kinds in her relations with you, the powers of the earth? What does the Church ask of you today? She tells you in one of the major documents of this Council. She asks of you only liberty, the liberty to believe and to preach her faith, the freedom to love her God and serve Him, the freedom to live and to bring to men her message of life. Do not fear her. She is made after the image of her Master, whose mysterious action does not interfere with your prerogatives but heals everything human of its fatal weakness, transfigures it, and fills it with hope, truth, and beauty.

Allow Christ to exercise His purifying action on society. Do not crucify Him anew. This would be a sacrilege for He is the Son of God. This would be suicide for He is the Son of man. And we, His humble ministers, allow us to spread everywhere without hindrance the gospel of peace on which we have meditated during this Council. Of it, your peoples will be the first beneficiaries, since the Church forms for you loyal citizens, friends of social peace and progress.

On this solemn day when she closes the deliberations of her twenty-first Ecumenical Council, the Church offers you through our voice her friendship, her services, her spiritual and moral forces. She addresses to you all her message of salvation and blessing. Accept it, as she offers it to you, with a joyous and sincere heart and pass it on to your peoples.

To Men of Thought and Science

(Read by Paul-Emile Cardinal Leger of Montreal, assisted by Antonio Cardinal Caggiano of Buenos Aires and Norman Cardinal Gilroy of Sydney.)

A very special greeting to you, seekers after truth, to you, men of thought and science, the explorers of man, of the universe, and of history, to all of you who are pilgrims en route to the light, and to those also who have stopped along the road, tired and disappointed by their vain search.

Why a special greeting for you? Because all of us here, bishops and Fathers of the Council, are on the lookout for truth. What have our efforts amounted to during these four years except a more attentive search for and deepening of the message of truth entrusted to the Church and an effort at more perfect docility to the spirit of truth?

Hence our paths could not fail to cross. Your road is ours. Your paths are never foreign to ours. We are the friends of your vocation as searchers, companions in your fatigues, admirers of your successes, and, if necessary, consolers in your discouragement and your failures.

Hence for you also we have a message, and it is this: Continue your search without tiring and without ever despairing of the truth. Recall the words of one of your great friends, St. Augustine: "Let us seek with the desire to find, and find with the desire to seek still more." Happy are those who, while possessing the truth, search more earnestly for it in order to renew it, deepen it, and transmit it to others. Happy also are those who, not having found it, are working toward it with a sincere heart. May they seek the light of tomorrow with the light of today until they reach the fullness of light.

But do not forget that if thinking is something great, it is first a duty. Woe to him who voluntarily closes his eyes to the light. Thinking is also a responsibility, so woe to those who darken the spirit by the thousand tricks which degrade it, make it proud, deceive and deform it. What other basic principle is there for men of science except to think rightly?

For this purpose, without troubling your efforts, without dazzling brilliance, we come to offer you the light of our mysterious lamp which is faith. He who entrusted this lamp to us is the sovereign Master of all thought, He whose humble disciples we are, the only one who said and could have said: "I am the light of the world, I am the way, the truth, and the life."

These words have meaning for you. Never perhaps, thank God, has there been so clear a possibility as today of a deep understanding between real science and real faith, mutual servants of one another in the one truth. Do not stand in the way of this important meeting. Have confidence in faith, this great friend of intelligence. Enlighten yourselves with its light in order to take hold of truth, the whole truth. This is the wish, the encouragement, and the hope, which, before disbanding, is expressed to you by the Fathers of the entire world assembled at Rome in Council.

To Artists

(Read by Leo Cardinal Suenens of Malines-Brussels [Belgium], assisted by Lawrence Cardinal Shehan of Baltimore and Jaime Cardinal de Barros Camara of Rio de Janeiro.)

We now address you, artists, who are taken up with beauty and work for it: poets and literary men, painters, sculptors, architects, musicians, men devoted to the theater and the cinema. To all of you, the Church of the Council declares to you through our voice: if you are friends of genuine art, you are our friends.

The Church has long since joined in alliance with you. You have built and adorned her temples, celebrated her dogmas, enriched her liturgy. You have aided her in translating her divine message in the language of forms and figures, making the invisible world palpable. Today, as yesterday, the Church needs you and turns to you. She tells you through our voice: Do not allow an alliance as fruitful as this to be broken. Do not refuse to put your talents at the service of divine truth. Do not close your mind to the breath of the Holy Spirit.

This world in which we live needs beauty in order not to sink into despair. It is beauty, like truth, which brings joy to the heart of man and is that precious fruit which resists the wear and tear of time, which unites generations and makes them share things in admiration. And all of this is through your hands. May these hands be pure and disinterested. Remember that you are the guardians of beauty in the world. May that suffice to free you from tastes which are passing and have no genuine value, to free you from the search after strange or unbecoming expressions. Be always and everywhere worthy of your ideals and you will be worthy of the Church which, by our voice, addresses to you today her message of friendship, salvation, grace, and benediction.

To Women

(Read by Leon Cardinal Duval of Algiers, assisted by Julius Cardinal Doepfner of Munich and Raul Cardinal Silva of Santiago [Chile].)

And now it is to you that we address ourselves, women of all states—girls, wives, mothers, and widows, to you also, consecrated virgins and women living alone—you constitute half of the immense human family. As you know, the Church is proud to have glorified and liberated woman, and in the course of the centuries, in diversity of characters, to have brought into relief her basic equality with man. But the hour is coming, in fact has come, when the vocation of woman is being achieved in its fullness, the hour in which woman acquires in the world an influence, an effect, and a power never hitherto achieved. That is why, at this moment when the human race is undergoing so deep a transformation, women impregnated with the spirit of the gospel can do much to aid mankind in not falling.

You women have always had as your lot the protection of the home, the love of beginnings, and an understanding of cradles. You are present in the mystery of a life beginning. You offer consolation in the departure of death. Our technology runs the risk of becoming inhuman. Reconcile men with life and above all, we beseech you, watch carefully over the future of our race. Hold back the hand of man who, in a moment of folly, might attempt to destroy human civilization.

Wives, mothers of families, the first educators of the human race in the intimacy of the family circle, pass on to your sons and your daughters the traditions of your fathers at the same time that you prepare them for an unsearchable future. Always remember that by her children a mother belongs to that future which perhaps she will not see.

And you, women living alone, realize what you can accomplish through your dedicated vocation. Society is appealing to you on all sides. Not even families can live without the help of those who have no families. Especially you, consecrated virgins, in a world where egoism and the search for pleasure would become law, be the guardians of purity, unselfishness, and piety. Jesus, who has given to conjugal love all its plenitudes, has also exalted the renouncement of human love when this is for the sake of divine love and for the service of all.

Lastly, women in trial, who stand upright at the foot of the cross like Mary, you who so often in history have given to men the strength to battle unto the very end and to give witness to the point of martyrdom, aid them now still once more to retain courage in their great undertakings, while at the same time maintaining patience and an esteem for humble beginnings.

Women, you who know how to make truth sweet, tender, and accessible, make it your task to bring the spirit of this Council into institutions, schools, homes, and daily life. Women of the entire universe, whether Christian or non-believing, you to whom life is entrusted at this grave moment in history, it is for you to save the peace of the world.

To the Poor, the Sick, and the Suffering

(Read by Paul Cardinal Meouchi, Maronite-rite Patriarch of Antioch; assisted by Stefan Cardinal Wyszynski of Warsaw and Peter Cardinal Doi of Tokyo.)

To all of you, brothers in trial, who are visited by suffering under a thousand forms, the Council has a very special message. It feels fixed on itself your pleading eyes, burning with fever or hollow with fatigue, questioning eyes which search in vain for the why of human suffering and which ask anxiously when and whence will come relief.

Very dear brothers, we feel echoing deeply within our hearts as fathers and pastors your laments and your complaints. Our suffering is increased at the thought that it is not within our power to bring you bodily help nor the lessening of your physical sufferings, which physicians, nurses, and all those dedicated to the service of the sick are endeavoring to relieve as best they can.

But we have something deeper and more valuable to give you, the only truth capable of answering the mystery of suffering and of bringing you relief without illusion, and that is faith and union with the Man of Sorrows, with Christ the Son of God, nailed to the cross for our sins and for our salvation. Christ did not do away with suffering. He did not even wish to unveil to us entirely the mystery of suffering. He took suffering upon Himself and this is enough to make you understand all its value. All of you who feel heavily the weight of the cross, you who are poor and abandoned, you who weep, you who are persecuted for justice, you who are ignored, you the unknown victims of suffering, take courage. You are the preferred children of the kingdom of God, the kingdom of hope, happiness, and life. You are the brothers of the suffering Christ, and with Him, if you wish, you are saving the world.

This is the Christian science of suffering, the only one which gives peace. Know that you are not alone, separated, abandoned, or useless. You have been called by Christ and are His living and transparent image. In His name, the Council salutes you lovingly, thanks you, assures you of the friendship and assistance of the Church, and blesses you.

To Workers

(Read by Paul Cardinal Zoungrana of Ouagadougou [Upper Volta], assisted by Jose Cardinal Quintero of Caracas and Jose Cardinal Bueno y Monreale of Seville.)

In the course of this Council, we, the Catholic bishops of the five continents, have, among many other subjects, reflected together on the grave questions posed for human conscience by the economic and social conditions of the contemporary world, the coexistence of nations, the problem of armaments, of war and peace. We are fully aware of the repercussions which the solution provided for these problems can have on the concrete life of the working men and women of the entire world. Thus, at the end of our deliberations, we wish to address to all of them a message of confidence, peace, and friendship.

Very loved sons, rest assured first of all that the Church is aware of your sufferings, your struggles, and your hopes, and that she appreciates highly the virtues which ennoble your souls—namely, courage, dedication, professional conscience, love of justice—and that she recognizes fully the immense services which, each in his own place and in positions often the most obscure and the most ignored, you render to the whole of society. The Church is grateful to you for this and thanks you through our voice.

In these recent years, she has never ceased to keep before her eyes the increasingly complex problems of the working world; and the echo which recent pontifical encyclicals have found in your ranks has proved to what degree the soul of the workingman of our time was attuned to that of his highest spiritual leaders. Pope John XXIII, who enriched the patrimony of the Church with his incomparable messages, knew how to find the road to your heart. He, in his own person, gave a shining example of the Church's love for the workingman as well as for truth, justice, liberty, and charity, on which is founded the peace of the world. We wish also to be before you witnesses of this love of the Church for you workingmen, and we declare to you with all the conviction of our souls: The Church is your friend. Have confidence in her. In the past, regrettable misunderstandings have, over too long a period, maintained a spirit of mistrust and lack of understanding between us, and both the Church and the working-class have suffered from this. Today the hour for reconciliation has sounded and the Church of the Council invites you to celebrate this hour without suspicion.

The Church is ever seeking to understand you better. But on your part you must endeavor to understand what the Church means for you, workingmen, who are the chief artisans of the prodigious changes which the world is undergoing today. For you know full well that unless a mighty spiritual inspiration animates these changes, they will cause disaster for humanity instead of bringing it happiness. It is not hatred which serves the world. It is not only the bread of this earth which can satisfy man's hunger. Thus, accept the message of the Church. Accept the faith which she offers you to light your path. It is the faith of the successor of Peter and of the two thousand bishops assembled in Council. It is the faith of the Christian people. May it be your light. May it be your guide. May it bring you to the knowledge of Jesus Christ, your Companion in work, Master and Savior of the whole human race.

To Youth

(Read by Gregorio Cardinal Agagianian of the Roman Curia, assisted by Joseph Cardinal Ritter of St. Louis and Valerian Cardinal Gracias of Bombay.)

Lastly, it is to you, young men and women of the world, that the Council wishes to address its final message. For it is you who are to receive the torch from the hands of your elders and to live in the world at the period of the most gigantic transformations ever realized in its history. It is you who, receiving the best of the example of the teaching of your parents and your teachers, are to form the society of tomorrow. You will either save yourselves or you will perish with it.

For four years the Church has been working to rejuvenate her image in order to respond the better to the design of her Founder, the great Living One, the Christ who is eternally young. At the term of this imposing re-examination of life, she now turns to you. It is for you, youth, especially for you that the Church now comes through her Council to enkindle your light, the light which illuminates the future, your future. The Church is anxious that this society that you are going to build up should respect the dignity, the liberty, and the rights of individuals. These individuals are you. The Church is particularly anxious that this society should allow free expansion to her treasure ever ancient and ever new, namely faith, and that your souls may be able to bask freely in its helpful light. She has confidence that you will find such strength and such joy that you will not be tempted, as were some of your elders, to yield to the seductions of egoistic or hedonistic philosophies or to those of despair and annihilation, and that in the face of atheism, a phenomenon of lassitude and old age, you will know how to affirm your faith in life and in what gives meaning to life, that is to say, the certitude of the existence of a just and good God.

It is in the name of this God and of His Son, Jesus, that we exhort you to open your hearts to the dimensions of the world, to heed the appeal of your brothers, to place your youthful energies at their service. Fight against all egoism. Refuse to give free course to the instincts of violence and hatred which beget wars and all their train of miseries. Be generous, pure, respectful, and sincere, and build in enthusiasm a better world than your elders had.

The Church looks to you with confidence and with love. Rich with a long past ever living in her, and marching on toward human perfection in time and the ultimate destinies of history and of life, the Church is the real youth of the world. She possesses what constitutes the strength and the charm of youth, that is to say, the ability to rejoice with what is beginning, to give oneself unreservedly, to renew oneself and to set out again for new conquests. Look upon the Church and you will find in her the face of Christ, the genuine, humble, and wise Hero, the Prophet of truth and love, the Companion and Friend of youth. It is in the name of Christ that we salute you, that we exhort and bless you.

Papal Brief Declaring the Council Completed

At the closing ceremonies, on December 8, 1965, Archbishop Pericle Felici, General Secretary of the Council, read the papal brief declaring the Second Vatican Council closed and stating that all of its decrees should be "religiously observed by all the faithful."

Pope Paul VI: for perpetual memory of the event:

The Second Vatican Ecumenical Council, assembled in the Holy Spirit and under protection of the Blessed Virgin Mary, whom we have declared Mother of the Church, and of St. Joseph, her glorious spouse, and of the Apostles Sts. Peter and Paul, must be numbered without doubt among the greatest events of the Church. In fact it was the largest in the number of Fathers who came to the seat of Peter from every part of the world, even from those places where the hierarchy has been very recently established. It was the richest because of the questions which for four sessions have been discussed carefully and profoundly. And last of all it was the most opportune, because, bearing in mind the necessities of the present day, above all it sought to meet the pastoral needs and, nourishing the flame of charity, it has made a great effort to reach not only the Christians still separated from communion with the Holy See, but also the whole human family.

At last all which regards the holy Ecumenical Council has, with the help of God, been accomplished and all the constitutions, decrees, declarations, and votes have been approved by the deliberation of the Synod and promulgated by us. Therefore, we decided to close for all intents and purposes, with our apostolic authority, this same Ecumenical Council called by our predecessor, Pope John XXIII, which opened October 11, 1962, and which was continued by us after his death.

We decide moreover that all that has been established synodally is to be religiously observed by all the faithful, for the glory of God and the dignity of the Church and for the tranquility and peace of all men. We have approved and established these things, decreeing that the present letters are and remain stable and valid, and are to have legal effectiveness, so that they be disseminated and obtain full and complete effect, and so that they may be fully convalidated by those whom they concern or may concern now and in the future; and so that, as it be judged and described, all efforts contrary to these things by whoever or whatever authority, knowingly or in ignorance, be invalid and worthless from now on.

Given in Rome, at St. Peter's, under the [seal of the] ring of the fisherman, December 8, on the feast of the Immaculate Conception of the Blessed Virgin Mary, the year 1965, the third year of our Pontificate.

THE ECUMENICAL COUNCILS

1.	Nicaea I	Sylvester I	May to June, 325
2.	Constantinople I	St. Damascus I	May to July, 381
3.	Ephesus	Celestine I	June to July, 431
4.	Chalcedon	St. Leo the Great	Oct. to Nov., 451
5.	Constantinople II	Vigilius	May to June, 553
6.	Constantinople III	St. Agatho; Leo II	Nov., 680 to Sept., 681
7.	Nicaea II	Hadrian I	Sept. to Oct., 787
8.	Constantinople IV	Nicholas I; Hadrian II	Oct., 869 to Feb., 870
9.	Lateran I	Callistus II	Mar. to Apr., 1123
10.	Lateran II	Innocent II	Apr., 1139
11.	Lateran III	Alexander III	Mar., 1179
12.	Lateran IV	Innocent III	Nov., 1215
13.	Lyons I	Innocent IV	June to July, 1245
14.	Lyons II	Gregory X	May to July, 1274
15.	Vienne	Clement V	Oct., 1311 to May, 1312
16.	Constance	Martin V	Nov., 1414 to Apr., 1418
17.	Florence	Eugene IV	Dec., 1431 to Aug., 1445[?]
18.	Lateran V	Julius II; Leo X	May, 1512 to Mar., 1517
19.	Trent	Paul III; Pius IV	Dec., 1545 to Dec., 1563
20.	Vatican I	Pius IX	Dec., 1869 to July, 1870
21.	Vatican II	John XXIII; Paul VI	Oct., 1962 to Dec., 1965

IMPORTANT DATES OF VATICAN II

Jan. 25, 1959: Pope John, at St. Paul's Outside the Walls, first announces his intention to summon a Council.

June 5, 1960: Pope John, by the motu proprio "Superno Dei Nutu," establishes the preparatory commissions and secretariats.

Dec. 25, 1961: Pope John, in the apostolic constitution "Humanae Salutis," convokes the Council.

July 20, 1962: Invitations are sent to separated Christian Churches and Communities to send delegate-observers to the Council.

Sept. 5, 1962: Norms of the Council are established in the motu proprio "Appropinquante Concilio."

Oct. 11, 1962: The Council solemnly opens.

Oct. 12, 1962: The Council adjourns at its first meeting, to prepare to elect its own commission members rather than those suggested by prepared list.

Oct. 20, 1962: The Council issues "A Message to Humanity."

Dec. 8, 1962: The Council's first session is concluded without any completed results.

June 3, 1963: Pope John XXIII dies.

June 21, 1963: Pope Paul VI is elected and announces his intention to continue the Council.

Sept. 29, 1963: The second session of the Council opens.

Oct. 30, 1963: Orientation vote is taken, favoring sacramentality and collegiality of bishops, the divine right of the episcopal college, restoration of the diaconate as a distinct and permanent order.

Dec. 4, 1963: The second session of the Council closes, with promulgation of the Constitution on the Sacred Liturgy and the Decree on the Instruments of Social Communication.

Jan. 4–6, 1964: Pope Paul makes an ecumenical journey to the Holy Land and meets with Patriarch Athenagoras.

May 17, 1964: The Secretariat for Non-Christian Religions is created.

Sept. 14, 1964: The third session of the Council opens.

Nov. 21, 1964: The third session closes with promulgation of the Dogmatic Constitution on the Church, the Decree on Ecumenism, and the Decree on Eastern Catholic Churches.

Pope Paul proclaims the title of Mary as Mother of the Church.

Sept. 14, 1965: The fourth and final session of the Council opens.

Sept. 15, 1965: Pope Paul, in the apostolic constitution "Apostolica Sollicitudo," sets forth the norms governing the new Episcopal Synod established to help him in governing the Church.

Oct. 4–5, 1965: Pope Paul goes to New York to address the United Nations General Assembly, and reports to the Council on his visit.

Oct. 28, 1965: The following documents are promulgated: the Decree on the Bishops' Pastoral Office in the Church, the Decree on the Appropriate Renewal of the Religious Life, the Decree on Priestly Formation, the Declaration on Christian Education, the Declaration on the Relationship of the Church to Non-Christian Religions.

Nov. 18, 1965: The Dogmatic Constitution on Divine Revelation and the Decree on the Apostolate of the Laity are promulgated. Pope Paul also announces the beginning of the reform of the Roman Curia, the introduction of the process for the beatification of Pope Pius XII and Pope John XXIII, a Jubilee period, and convocation of the Episcopal Synod not later than 1967.

Dec. 4, 1965: At St. Paul's Outside the Walls, where Pope John first announced the Council, there takes place a function entitled "A Prayer Service *(Sacra Celebratio)* for Promoting Christian Unity at which the Holy Father, Paul VI, will assist along with the Fathers of the Ecumenical Council as well as the observers and guests delegated to attend the Council."

Dec. 7, 1965: The Declaration on Religious Freedom, the Decree on the Ministry and Life of Priests, the Decree on the Church's Missionary Activity, and the Pastoral Constitution on the Church in the Modern World are promulgated.

Dec. 8, 1965: The Council solemnly closes.

CONTRIBUTORS

The Rev. Walter M. Abbott, S.J., associate editor of *America,* national Catholic weekly review, and General Editor of this volume, has furnished the Introduction and Notes for the key Decree on Ecumenism. Father Abbott, an American ecumenist, is Director of the John LaFarge Institute, an interfaith and interracial center in New York. He is also the author of the book *Twelve Council Fathers,* and was present at the Vatican Council.

The Rev. Calvert Alexander, S.J., who was for twenty-five years the editor-in-chief of the publication *Jesuit Missions,* provided the Introduction and Notes for the Decree on the Church's Missionary Activity. Father Alexander followed the entire work of the Council in Rome for four years.

President John C. Bennett, Union Theological Seminary, New York City, writes the essay-response to the Declaration on Christian Education. Dr. Bennett is a leader in the ecumenical movement and co-chairman of the editorial board of *Christianity and Crisis.* He is the editor of *Christian Social Ethics in a Changing World,* the first in a series of four volumes issued by the World Council of Churches early in 1966. He is also author of *Social Salvation, Christian Ethics and Social Policy,* and *Christianity and Communism Today.* He has lectured at many colleges and theological seminaries.

Dr. Robert McAfee Brown is professor of religion at Stanford University. He is author of such books as *Observer in Rome* (giving his day-by-day experiences at the second session of Vatican II), *The Spirit of Protestantism,* and *An American Dialogue* (with the late Gustave Weigel, S.J.). Before going to Stanford, he was Auburn Professor of Systematic Theology at Union Theological Seminary, New York City. He contributes the essay on the Pastoral Constitution on the Church in the Modern World.

The Rev. Thomas J. M. Burke, S.J., who is presently Director of the Center for the Advancement of Human Communication, Fairfield University, Connecticut, and who holds a doctorate in his subject from New York University, has prepared the Introduction and Notes for the Decree on the Instruments of Social Communication.

The Rev. Donald R. Campion, S.J., former associate editor of *America* and a leading Catholic sociologist, is the author of the Introduction and Commentary on the Church in the Modern World.

The Most Rev. Alexander Carter, Bishop of Sault St. Marie (Ont.), and brother of Bishop G. Emmett Carter, has done the commentary on the Council Decree on Priestly Formation. Bishop Alexander Carter is vice-chairman of the Conference of Canadian Bishops.

The Most Rev. G. Emmett Carter, Bishop of London (Ont.), has done the commentary on the Council Declaration on Christian Education. Bishop Carter, the leading authority on education in the Canadian hierarchy, was the Newman chaplain at McGill University, Montreal, for fifteen years; he was also a member of the school board of the Archdiocese of Montreal and founder of St. Joseph's College in Montreal.

Dr. Samuel McCrea Cavert, former general secretary of the National Council of Churches and author of *On the Road to Christian Unity* and other books, writes the response to the Decree on Ecumenism. Dr. Cavert had a leading part in both the formation of the National Council of Churches and the World Council of Churches. He is now chairman of the advisory board of the Religious Book Club.

Bishop Fred Pierce Corson of the Methodist Church (Philadelphia area), president of the World Methodist Council, served as an observer at the Second Vatican Council. He has been pastor of churches in New York State and president of Dickinson College. He is a trustee of several schools and colleges, and holds many honorary degrees. He is author of such books as *Education and the Arsenal of Democracy, The Minister and Christian Higher Education,* and *How Good Is Communism?* He provides the essay in response to the Decree on the Bishops' Pastoral Office in the Church.

The Rev. Avery Dulles, S.J., son of the late John Foster Dulles, Secretary of State, comments on the most important document of the Council, the Dogmatic Constitution on the Church. Father Dulles, a convert to the Catholic Church during his student years at Harvard University, is now a professor of theology at Woodstock College, Woodstock, Maryland.

The Very Rev. Msgr. Joseph Gallagher has been archivist of the Archdiocese of Baltimore since 1957, and editor of the archdiocesan newspaper, *The Catholic Review,* since 1957. He has contributed articles to the *New Catholic Encyclopedia,* the *Catholic Youth Encyclopedia,* the *Catholic Historical Review,* and many other periodicals.

The Rev. Robert A. Graham, S.J., authority on Vatican diplomacy, has written the Introduction and Notes for the Declaration on the Relationship of the Church to Non-Christian Religions. Father Graham's book on Vatican diplomacy won the John Gilmary Shea Prize and was published by Princeton University Press.

Prof. Frederick C. Grant, official observer at the Second Vatican Council, is professor emeritus of biblical theology, Union Theological Seminary, New York City, and author of *Rome and Reunion.* He writes the response to the Dogmatic Constitution on Divine Revelation. He has been president of Seabury-Western Theological Seminary and senior Fulbright scholar at Oxford.

The Most Rev. Paul J. Hallinan, Archbishop of Atlanta, who comments on the Decree on the Bishops' Pastoral Office in the Church, was Bishop of Charleston, South Carolina, when Pope John established the Archbishopric of Atlanta and promoted Archbishop Hallinan to this key post. The Archbishop is noted for his progressive views and his courageous handling of the race question in the United States.

Dr. Franklin H. Littell, professor of church history at the Chicago Theological Seminary, is a leader in the ecumenical movement and is author of such books as *The Anabaptist View of the Church, From State Church to Pluralism,* and *Introduction to Sectarian Protestantism.* He is a member of the American Society of Church History. He writes the response to the Declaration on Religious Freedom.

The Very Rev. R. A. F. MacKenzie, S.J., rector of the Pontifical Biblical Institute in Rome, and one of the highest ranking biblical scholars in the world, has provided the notes for the Dogmatic Constitution on Divine Revelation. Father MacKenzie, a Canadian scholar, is president of the International Society for Old Testament Studies and a former president of the Catholic Biblical Association of America. Among his predecessors as rector of the Pontifical Biblical

Institute was the eminent biblical scholar Augustin Cardinal Bea.

The Rev. Paul Mailleux, S.J., head of the John XXIII Center for Eastern Christian Studies at Fordham University, has written the Introduction and Notes for the Decree on Eastern Catholic Churches.

The Most Rev. John J. McEleney, S.J., Bishop of Kingston, Jamaica, has provided the notes on the Decree on the Appropriate Renewal of the Religious Life. Bishop McEleney was Provincial of the Jesuit Order in New England before being consecrated Bishop of Kingston.

The Rev. C. J. McNaspy, S.J., member of the board of the Liturgical Conference, vice-president of the Catholic Fine Arts Association, associate editor of *America,* and one of the top liturgical scholars of the United States, explains the Constitution on the Sacred Liturgy.

Bishop Reuben H. Mueller, president of the National Council of Churches and a bishop of the Evangelical United Brethren Church, with headquarters at Indianapolis, writes an introductory note. Bishop Mueller has long been a leader in the ecumenical movement. He holds honorary degrees from colleges in this country and abroad. He is author of *Lay Leadership in the Church, Being a Christian,* and *What is Christian Teaching?*

The Rev. John Courtney Murray, S.J., provided the Introduction and Notes for the much-discussed Declaration on Religious Freedom, which is largely his own work. Father Murray is generally thought to be one of the leading theologians of the world today, and the chief exponent of the Council's teachings on Church and State.

Dr. Claud D. Nelson, official Religious News Service correspondent at Vatican II for the National Conference of Christians and Jews, and author of *The Vatican Council and All Christians,* authors the response to the Declaration on the Relationship of the Church to Non-Christians. Dr. Nelson served for several years as a YMCA secretary in Rome, Italy. He was a Rhodes scholar.

Dr. John Oliver Nelson is the director of Kirkridge, a retreat and study center in Bangor, Pennsylvania. Until recently he was on the faculty at Yale Divinity School as professor of

Christian vocation and previous to that was chairman of the Commission on the Ministry at the National Council of Churches. At present he is chairman of Association Press (publishing wing of the YMCA) and of the United Presbyterian Peace Fellowship. Dr. Nelson is author of *Look at the Ministry, Protestant Religious Vocations,* and *Vocation and Church Occupations.* He contributes the essay-response to the Decree on the Ministry and Life of Priests.

The Rev. William A. Norgren, a priest of the Protestant Episcopal Church, is head of the Department of Faith and Order of the National Council of Churches. He was a guest of the Secretariat for Promoting Christian Unity at Vatican II. He edits the ecumenical booklet *Trends* and is co-author of *Living Room Dialogues.* He writes the essay in response to the Decree on the Appropriate Renewal of the Religious Life.

Dr. Albert C. Outler is professor at the Perkins School of Theology, Southern Methodist University, Dallas. He was an official observer at Vatican II, and on several occasions was selected as the representative and spokesman for the observers at special functions in Rome. He is author of *The Christian Tradition, The Unity We Seek,* and other books and articles. He provides the response to the Dogmatic Constitution on the Church.

Prof. Jaroslav J. Pelikan of Yale University provides the essay in response to the Constitution on the Sacred Liturgy. Professor Pelikan is author of *The Riddle of Roman Catholicism, Obedient Rebel,* and *Luther the Expositor,* and is the editor and translator of Luther's works. He is a member of the Department of Faith and Order of the World Council of Churches.

Prof. Warren A. Quanbeck, professor of systematic theology at the Lutheran Theological Seminary, St. Paul, Minnesota, and a contributor to *Dialogue on the Way,* a book dealing in depth with Vatican II, writes the response to the Decree on Priestly Formation. He was an observer at the Council.

The Very Rev. Alexander Schmemann is dean at St. Vladimir's Orthodox Seminary, Yonkers, New York. He was an official guest-observer at the second session of Vatican II. He has served as a member of the Faith and Order Department of the National Council of Churches and is lecturer in Eastern Orthodoxy at Union Theological Seminary. He is author of

Historical Roots of Eastern Orthodoxy, Sacraments and Orthodoxy, and *Introduction to Liturgical Theology.* He contributes the essay-response to the Decree on Eastern Catholic Churches.

Dr. Eugene L. Smith is general secretary of the U.S.A. office of the World Council of Churches. Before taking this major responsibility, he was general secretary of the Board of Missions of the Methodist Church. He contributes the response to the Decree on the Church's Missionary Activity. He has been lecturer at several colleges and is the author of *The Power Within Us, They Gird the Earth,* and *God's Mission and Ours.*

Dr. Stanley I. Stuber, director of Association Press, New York City, and an official guest-observer at Vatican II, provides the essay-response to the Decree on the Instruments of Social Communication. Dr. Stuber is author of *Primer on Roman Catholicism for Protestants, Public Relations Manual for Churches,* and several other books. For fourteen years he was chairman of the Commission on Religious Freedom of the Baptist World Alliance.

Dr. Cynthia Wedel (Mrs. Theodore O. Wedel) writes the response to the Decree on the Apostolate of the Laity. She is associate general secretary for Christian unity, National Council of Churches. She has also served as president of United Church Women. She is author of *Women in the Church, The Glorious Liberty,* and *Employed Women and the Church.*

Mr. Martin Work, who is recognized in the United States as the Catholic laity's most official spokesman, has prepared the Introduction and Notes for the Decree on the Apostolate of the Laity. Mr. Work is Executive Director of the National Council of Catholic Men, with headquarters in Washington, D.C. He was also the official observer at the Vatican Council for the American laity.

The Most Rev. Guilford C. Young, Archbishop of Hobart, Tasmania, provides the Introduction and Commentary for the Decree on the Ministry and Life of Priests. Archbishop Young is vice-chairman of the International Liturgical Commission, which is at work on a new liturgy for the English-speaking world; this project is scheduled for completion in about three years. Archbishop Hallinan is the United States representative on this commission.

INDEX

Prepared by Joseph W. Sprug

Abbot: blessing of, 157
Abraham: Islam and, 663
  plan of salvation, 113
Academic freedom: acknowledgment
  of, 265
Activity: bond with religion, 233
  Church and the world, 238
  norm: good of mankind, 233
  purification of, 235
  significance of, 233
Actors: moral responsibility, 324
Adam: figure of Christ, 220
Adaptation of religious life: *see* Religious orders: Adaptation
Adaptations: approval of Apostolic
  See required, 152
  cultures in mission lands, 612-613
  liturgical commission, 153
  liturgical laws for mission lands,
  152
  liturgical reform, 151
  liturgical year, 169
  preliminary experiments, 152
  rites and ceremonies, 151
  Roman rite, 151
  sacraments, 151
  sacred art and furnishings, 176
Administration: gift of, 472
Adolescents: *see* Youth
Adult education, 637, 648
Adultery: profanation, 253
Advent: bible services, 150
Aesthetics: ethics and art, 322
Agape: early church, 498
Aged: apostolate to help the, 503
Agnosticism: science and technology,
  263
Agriculture: antiquated methods, 301
  economic justice, 274
Altars: construction, 176
Anointing of the sick: *see* Extreme
  Unction
Anxiety: death, 215
  modern problem, 210
Anti-Semitism: rejection by the
  Church, 666-667

Apologetics: polemical theology, 253
Apostles: coercion and conversion,
  691
  commissioned to hand on revelation, 115
  foundation of the Church, 344, 589
  Gospels and, 123
  intentions in writing Gospels, 124
  Jews, 664
  mission, 35, 396, 584
  mission; Pentecost, 38
  passion of Christ and, 590
  powers passed on, 41
  prayer, 164
  preaching to be preserved, 115
  select men to teach others, 556
  selection, 38
  sent by Christ, 140
  successors of, 534
  veneration of, 81-82
  witnesses to truth, 691-692
  work of salvation, 588
Apostolate: aids in formation, 520
  aim of organizations, 510
  all lay persons called to, 506-507
  areas where the Church is in difficulty, 503
  areas widened today, 490
  as individuals or in groups, 506
  associations, 509
  associations, appreciation of, 511
  associations; characteristics, 510
  associations or institutes, 494-495
  associations recommended, 511
  associations recommended and promoted, 510
  basis of formation, 516
  bishops and, 409
  bishops' support of, 400
  catechetical instruction, 501
  centers; higher institutes, 520
  charisms, use of, 492-493
  chastity (vow) and, 474
  children, 504
  Christian social action, 498
  Church authority for, 513

Apostolate *(cont'd)*
clergy's esteem and concern for, 612
communications media, 326, 329
and bishops, 329
national offices, 329
community nature of, 508
conferences of major superiors, 480
contemplative life, 471
conversations with others, 519
cooperation necessary, 512
cooperation of Catholics with other Christians, 515
cooperation of clergy, religious, and laity, 513
coordination and direction by bishops, 409
coordination of associations, diocesan, 515
councils, types of, 515
culture, 517
dialogue: clergy and laity, 514
diocesan councils, 515
diocesan harmony and unity, 421
direction of organizations, 510
divine law in the earthly city, 244
doctrinal instruction, 517
duty for all to spread the Faith, 613
duty of the faithful, 409
early Church, 489
educational institutions, 518
effectiveness related to formation, 516
evangelization, 492
exhortation, 521
explicit recognition by the hierarchy, 513
ex-seminarians, 444
extending beyond local areas, 501
family activities, 503
family as school of, 61
family groups, 503
formation always needs improvement, 517
formation for, 516
formation: groups and associations, 519
formation of lay people, 512
formation: secular and lay aspects, 516-517
forms, 506
forms adapted to current needs, 410
forms; relationships with the hierarchy, 513
gifts of the Spirit, 492, 494
hierarchy and, 513
hierarchy over, 511
holiness in the Church, 69
human relations, 517
in non-Catholic schools, 645

incorporated into work of the whole Church, 512
individual work as basis, 506
individuals gathering in groups, 508
inspiring the laity, 455
intellectual, 650
international organizations, 509
laity as commissioned, 59
laity in mission lands, 628
laity in society, 504
life of the lay person, 517
manifestation of Christ's message, 496
married persons and families, 502
Mary as model, 93
mission of the Church, 491
missionary activity, 502
missions, 602
modern conditions, 490
motive: love, 498
mutual esteem, 512-513
national and international, 505
natural abilities and formation, 517
necessity of, 500
new associations; justification, 510
objectives, 495
of teachers, 647
opportunities for, 496
organic action, 511
organized form must be strengthened, 509
parish activities, 501
particular selection and promotion by hierarchy, 513
pastoral ministry and the laity, 496
pastoral promotion of, 419
persecutions and, 507-508
preservation of distinctiveness of each, 513
priests and promotion of, 514
priests engaged in works of, 417
professional workers, 511
promotion by religious, 514-515
purpose, 603
reach out to all, 505
religious and diocesan coordination, 423
religious communities assist in, 421
religious orders, 421
religious rules adjusted to demands of, 472
right and duty, 492
right and duty common to all the faithful, 514
salvation of the world, 507
secretariat at the Holy See proposed, 515
secular institutes, 474
seeking opportunities for, 496

Apostolate *(cont'd)*
significance of group apostolate, 508
social milieu, 504
solidarity and brotherhood, 506
spirit of religion in, 472
spiritual and temporal orders, 495
study and, 571
supplying a lack, 500-501
support of lay workers and their families, 512
teachers and educators, 518
technical and spiritual preparation, 629
temporal order, 288, 518
theological virtues, 492
training of children and young people, 518
transferring from one nation to another, 510
union with Christ, 493
union with the hierarchy, 512
united effort, 508
unity and charity, 512
universal obligation, 36
value of religious life, 467
variety of associations, 509
various fields, 500
vocation of the laity, 489
women, 500
works of charity and mercy, 520
youth and, 504
see also Catholic Action; Laity
Apostolic Succession: bishops in place of the apostles, 39
continues without a break, 399
Eastern churches, 359
mission of the apostles, 39
teaching in place of apostles, 115
tradition; St. Irenaeus, 40
willed by Christ, 37
Archbishops: metropolitan jurisdiction, 427
patriarchs and, 378
Armaments: arms race, 295
Art: evil, portrayal of, 322-323
moral norms, 322
new forms of, 269
Art, Sacred: appreciation, 176
approved by the Church, 171
bishops and, 175
Church and, 174
diocesan commission, 153, 175
history; principles, 176
judging, 175
purpose, 174
schools or academies, 176
study by clerics, 176
styles, freedom, 175
works of value, 175
Artists: bishops and, 176
clergy and, 176

imitation of God the Creator, 176
Arts: advancement of, 355
Church use of, 269
value recognized by the Church, 269
Assent: accept teachings of bishops, 48
adherence to truth, 681
Assistant pastors: contribution to pastoral ministry, 419
relations with pastors, 419
Associations: apostolic dynamism, 509
appreciation of apostolic, 511
bishops' promotion of, 409-410
communications media, 324
development of man, 224
family, 258
international, appreciation of, 511
lay apostolate, 511-512
Atheism: applications of the word, 216
causes, 217
Christianity and social problems, 219-220
economic and social emancipation, 218
freedom claimed by, 217
governmental promotion of, 218
modern expression of, 217
modern problem, 216
remedy in the Church's teaching, 219
repudiation by the Church, 218
study of questions raised by, 218
Attitudes: war and peace, 296-297
Audiences: cultural and moral betterment, 328
moral obligations, 323
Augustine, Saint: love of the Church, 446
on brotherhood, 59
Authority: civil, 410
civil defense against abuses, 285
civilization and the state, 266
communications media and public authority, 324-325
compatible with freedom, 286
division of functions and bodies, 285
essential in the political community, 284
family rights and, 257
founded on human nature, 284
obedience in matters of faith and morals, 30
obedience to civil, 284
obedience to lawful, 687
papal, 397
political life, 283
politics and the moral order, 284
refusal to submit to, 687

Authority (cont'd)
  religious superiors, 476-477
  seminarians' attitude, 448
  war, elimination of, 295
Autonomy: apostolate and, 490
  creature and God, 240-241
  increasing sense of, 261
  of culture, 262, 265
  of earthly affairs, 233-234
  private ownership, 280
Auxiliary bishops: see Bishops,
  Auxiliary

Baptism: bond of unity, 363-364
  Christ present in, 141
  Christian education, 640, 641
  communion under both kinds, 156
  consecrated religious life and, 470
  consecrated to God, 74
  Easter mystery, 601
  incorporation into Mystical
    Body, 363-364
  lay apostolate, 492
  Lent and, 169-170
  licit and valid administrations;
    Eastern Churches, 379
  life as witness to, 597
  liturgical participation, 144
  Mass, special, 160
  members of the Church, 345
  mystery of Christ, 140
  Mystical Body of Christ, 20
  necessary for salvation, 32
  necessity, 593
  priesthood of the faithful, 27, 28
  seeking for perfection, 557-558
Baptismal promises: at confirmation, 160
Baptismal rites: for adults, 159-160
  for converts, 160
  for infants, 160
  Order of Supplying What Was
    Omitted in the Baptism of an
    Infant, 160
  shorter rite, 160
  variants, 160
Baptismal water: blessing, 160
Baptistery: construction, 176
Beatitudes: Christian social
  action, 282
  lay apostolate, 494
Beauty: fine arts, 174
Belief and doubt: see Faith; Unbelief
Benefices: bishops' freedom in
  bestowing, 416
  reform of, 573
Bible: bishops and instruction on
  use of, 128
  both Testaments canonical because of inspiration, 118

  canon known through tradition,
    116
  Church as judge of interpreta-
    tion, 121
  Church teaching authority, 363
  Common Bible idea approved, 126
  condescension of eternal wis-
    dom, 121
  deposit of the word of God, 117
  divine office; readings, 165
  editions for non-Christians, 128
  error in, 119
  Holy Spirit as author, 119
  honored by non-Catholics, 34
  inspiration of the Spirit, 118
  interpretation by men; careful
    investigation, 120
  interpretation in same spirit as
    written, 120
  interpretation; teaching office of
    the Church, 117-118
  languages, 449
  life of the Church, 125
  life of the Spirit, 128
  literary forms and interpreta-
    tion, 120
  love and reverence for, 362-363
  meaning related to literary
    form, 120
  men chosen to compose, 119
  ministry of the word, 127
  moral theology and, 452
  more representative portions to
    be read, 155
  prayer and reading of, 127
  preaching, 125
  priestly learning, 571
  reading by all, 127
  reading; easy access, 125
  reading in religious communi-
    ties, 471
  reading scriptures in church, 141
  readings; reform, 149
  reform in the liturgy, 147
  reverence for, 117
  rule of faith, 125
  seminary professors and
    liturgy, 145
  seminary studies, 451
  services encouraged, 150
  study: the soul of theology, 127
  study by clergy, 127
  study encouraged, 126
  tradition closely connected
    with, 117
  translations; accessibility, 126
  translations made with non-
    Catholics, 126
  unity of the whole, 120
  word of God in human dis-
    course, 121
  written word of God, 117

Biology: advances in, 203
Birth control: conscience; divine law; family size, 254-255
dishonorable solutions, 255
family increase temporarily halted, 255
family size; right of parents, 302
illicit practices, 249
methods; objective moral standards, 256
scientific efforts toward regulation, 258
Bishops: administering church property, 400
aid to other dioceses, 45
apostolate and, 409
apostolate of communications media, 329
apostolate, support of, 400
art and, 175
artists and, 176
as Ordinary of different rites, 413
authority, 146
authority and reserved cases, 401
authority over religious in some matters, 422-423
bestowing offices and benefices, 417
biblical instructions, 128
brotherly interest in persecuted bishops, 401
canonical mission, 47
care for those strayed from truth, 404
Christ present through, 40
civil authorities and selection of, 411
communications media: day of instruction, 329
communion under both kinds, 156
concern for all the churches, 400
concern for non-Christian areas, 400
consecration of, 41, 161
consultations with coadjutor, 415
continue the work of Christ, 397
cooperating for common good of many churches, 424
dialogue with men, 405
diocesan, 403-412
dispensations and reserved cases, 401
duties related to diocesan boundaries, 412
earthly concerns of the faithful, 244
Ecumenical Councils, 399
ecumenical participation, 349-350
ecumenism, 409
erection or suppression of parishes, 420
evangelization, support of, 400

extension of the Body of Christ, 625
example of the Good Shepherd, 52
father and pastor, 407-408
fraternal association between offices, diocese, and conferences, 427
fullness of sacrament of orders, 406
good example, 51
good shepherds, 407
heralds of the faith, 609
higher education of seminarians, 453
holiness, example of, 407
individual exercise of office, 398
infallibility, 48
interdiocesan office, 427-428
jurisdiction, 44
jurisdiction over worship, 50
liturgical life of diocese, 152
liturgy and, 406
lives arranged to fit needs of the times, 408
love and solicitude, 408
mandate to preach, 624
members of episcopal conferences, 425
members of the episcopal body, 398-399
members of the Roman Curia, 402
military chaplains and, 428
missionary vocations and, 625
missions and, 45-46
missions; communion with the whole Church, 608
mission to teach all nations, 47
nomination and appointment, 411
office of teaching, sanctifying, governing, 403
office related to the Supreme Pontiff, 397
one priesthood with their priests, 53
parishes and, 152
participation in ministry of, 54
pastoral office, 51
pastors as cooperators of, 417-418
popular devotions, 143
power exercised with agreement of Pope, 399
power to govern, 51
preaching, 47
"prelates," 52
priestly communion with, 546
priestly vocations, 439
priests and, 446
priests, special love for, 408
priests' study and knowledge, 571

Bishops *(cont'd)*
  principal dispensers of mysteries
    of God, 406
  promotion of missionary
    activity, 621
  recognition of rights of other
    hierarchical authorities, 403
  relations with coadjutors and
    auxiliaries, 414-415
  relations with diocesan
    priests, 417
  relations with religious; meet-
    ings, 423
  religious as helpers of, 421
  religious in the active aposto-
    late, 421
  religious orders and, 76
  remuneration for priests, 572-573
  reserved blessings, 162
  resignations because of age,
    health, etc., 412
  responsible for the Church, 400
  role in the universal Church, 398
  roles of Christ, 40-41
  sacraments and, 50
  salvation of souls; State rela-
    tions, 410
  sanctification of, 68
  sanctifying, office of, 406
  seminarians, 445
  seminary relations, 443
  share in Christ's mission, 534
  social and material care of the
    faithful, 410
  social circumstances of the faith-
    ful, 408-409
  solicitous for the whole
    Church, 45
  Synod of, 399-400
  teachers, 47
  teachers, pontiffs, and pastors, 397
  teaching duty, 404-405
  testing candidates for the priest-
    hood, 448-449
  united in a college, 397-398
  unity of the Church, 44
  vacation projects for seminari-
    ans, 455
  vernacular question, 150
  witness of Christ before men, 404
  work for the whole world, 624
  worship with non-Catholics, 352-
    353
  see also Apostolic Succession;
    Archbishops; Collegiality;
    Episcopacy; Episcopal Con-
    ferences; Hierarchy
Bishops and priests: body or
    senate of priests, 548-549
  friends and brothers, 547
  respect for bishops, 549

  responsibility for sanctity of
    priests, 548
Bishops, Auxiliary: faculties, 414-415
  powers when See becomes
    vacant, 415
  reasons for, 414
  requests for, 415
  vicar generals or episcopal
    vicars, 415
Bishops, Coadjutor: faculties, 414-
    415
  vicar general, 415
Blessings: reserved, 162
Body, Human: dignity; value, 240
  goodness of, 212
Books: increased circulation
    of, 267-268
Brotherhood: salvation in, 59
Brotherhood of man: Church as
    sign of, 306
  Church's fostering of, 201
  establishment not hopeless, 236
  one family, 223
  peace and, 290-291
  universal, 305
  vocation, 307
Brotherly love: *see* Love
Brothers: lay apostolate and,
    514-515
  ordination of, 473
Buddhism: religion, 662
Buildings: *see* Church
    architecture
Burial rite: of infants, 163
  revision, 162

Calendar: revision, 177-178
Canon law: mystery of the
    Church in, 452
Care of souls: collaboration of
    pastors and other clergy, 418
  community life for priests, 418
  diocesan priests, 416
  general directories, 428
  missionary spirit, 418
  qualifications of pastors, 419
  religious priests, 420-421
Catechetics: basis, 406
  Bible and, 127
  bishops and, 406
  directory for instruction, 428-429
  duty of pastors, 418
  lay apostolate, 501
  method suited to students, 406
  priestly vocations, 440
  results, 643
  seminary studies, 454
Catechists: association for, 606
  auxiliary, 606
  biblical study, 127
  canonical mission, 606

Catechists (cont'd)
  conventions or courses, 606
  importance, 605
  missionary work, 605
  training, 406, 606
  training of Brothers and
    Sisters, 616-617
  wages, 606
Catechumenate: entire community
  involved in, 601
  rite of admission to, 600
  training period, 600
Catechumenate for adults:
  restoration, 159
Catechumens: gradual education
  of, 545
  instruction of adults, 406
  instruction, rites, sacraments
    of initiation, 600-601
  intention to join the Church, 33
  juridic status, 601
  witness of lives, 601
Cathedral church: choirs, 171
  diocesan liturgical life, 152
Catholic Action: associations recommended and promoted, 510
  promotion of, 409
Catholic Church: Church of Christ,
  22
  communications media, 320
  esteem for other religions, 239
  government, 23
  hierarchy, Churches, Rites in, 374
  necessity for salvation, 32
  one true religion subsists in, 677
  renewal a prime duty, 348
  see also Church; Mystical Body;
    etc.
Catholicity: destiny of the Church,
  26
  divisions an obstacle to, 349
  Pentecost, 588
  People of God in all ages, 30
  temporal values of each people, 32
  variety of local rites, 46
Catholic press: purpose, 327
Catholics: failure; imperfection, 348
Catholic schools: see Schools, Catholic.
Celibacy: ascetical norms, 567
  beneficial, 475
  gift of the Spirit, 447
  honor for, 71-72
  mastery and maturity, 447
  not demanded by nature of priest-
    hood, 565
  seminary training, 446
  sign of the world to come, 566
  suitability for the priesthood, 565-
    567
  supernatural and natural aids, 567

  value, 446-447, 565
Ceremonies: see Rites and ceremonies.
Certitude: human knowledge of God,
  114
  sin and reality, 213
Chalcedon, Council of: Eastern
  schism, 355-356
Chant, Gregorian: pride of place,
  172
  simpler melodies, 172
  typical editions, 172
Chaplains: military, 427
Chapters, cathedral or collegiate:
  choral office, 166
  reorganization, 416
Character: of missionaries, 615
  seminarians, 448
Charisms: apostolate, 492
  lay apostolate, 519
  missionary vocation, 613-614
  special gifts for needs of the
    Church, 30
Charities: collection and distribution
  of aids, 303
  duty and right of the Church, 499
  freedom and dignity of person
    helped, 499
  more urgent and universal, 499
  recipients freed from dependence,
    499
  relief of the poor; obligation, 278
Charity: sacraments and, 158
  see also Love
Chastity: dangers in celibacy, 447
  in marriage, 256
  preparation for marriage, 253
  virtue of religious, 470
Chastity (vow): brotherly love an
  aid to, 475
  gift of grace, 474
  observance of, 474
  symbolism, 474
  test of candidates for, 475
Children: apostolate, 504
  apostolic formation, 518
  apostolic formation in the
    home, 502
  education in the family, 267
  gift of marriage, 253-254
  making parents holy, 252
  vocational education, 257
  see also Family; Parents; Youth
Choice: freedom and dignity, 214
Choir: piety and decorum, 148
  promotion, 171
Choral office: obligation, 166
Chosen People: community aspect,
  230
  see also Jews
Christian education: see Education,
  Christian; Religious education

Christianity: all called to, 30
 Church helped by other religions,
  239
 freedom to embrace, 690
 life and culture renewed by, 264
 messianic people, 25
 modern culture as preparation for,
  264
 new and definitive covenant, 113
 People of God, the, 25-36
 related to non-Christians, 34
 voices of our age and, 246
 see also Church
Christian life: adaptation in mission
  lands, 612
 autonomy and, 490
 building a more human world,
  262
 change of heart, 351
 charity for others, 544
 Christian family, 61
 Christians as witnesses, 695
 constantly vigilant, 80
 duty: fuller understanding of
  truth, 695
 education, 640
 Eucharistic basis, 545
 example and witness, 597
 family manifestation, 252
 formation of the world, 640
 forming the Christian community,
  601
 grace rather than merits, 33
 inspiring lives of the faithful, 82
 laity and the Spirit, 60
 laity as witnesses to, 244
 maturity in mission lands, 608
 ministries needed for growth, 603
 modern world problems, 199-200
 more fruitful witness to, 597-598
 neglect of temporal duties, 243
 non-Catholics, 364
 pastors and, 418-419
 penetrated by faith, 219
 personal gifts and duties, 68
 priesthood of the baptized, 27
 priestly vocations, 439
 proper nationalism and patriotism,
  603
 prudence and patience in dealing
  with others, 695
 religious persons, 77
 renewed by the Spirit, 221
 sacraments, 158
 seminary studies, 454
 service in this world, 307
 sign of God's presence, 602
 social virtues, 495
 spread of the faith, 623
 temporal order, renewal of, 498
 Vatican Council (2nd), 137
 vocation to apostolate, 491

 witness in mission lands, 609
 witness of the laity, 496
 witness of the lay apostolate, 507
 witness to Christ, 624
 witnesses to Christ, 307
 works, 142
 works of charity and mercy, 520
 see also Evangelization
Christian literature: Divine Office
  readings, 165
Christians: collaboration in socio-
  economic problems, 598-599
 earthly duties, 242-243
 political vocation, 286
Christian social action: see Social
  action
Christian unity: Church linked with
  non-Catholics, 33-34
 Church's work for, 15
 citizens of a heavenly kingdom, 31
 common dignity of the People of
  God, 58
 common sharing of gifts, 31
 concern for attainment of, 350
 concern for restoration, 341-342
 cooperation among Christians,
  354-355
 culture and, 262
 desire aroused by the Spirit, 34
 desire for, 306
 division contradicts will of Christ,
  341
 Eastern Churches and promotion
  of, 383
 Eucharistic Sacrifice, the, 16
 faith, hope, and charity, 343
 holier lives, 351
 hope, 365-366
 laity in mission lands, 612
 liturgical life, 138
 missionary activity, 592-593
 missionary activity; God's plan,
  594
 prayer of Christ, 343, 352
 restoration; no unnecessary burden,
  360-361
 seminary study of separated
  churches, 453
 sins against, 351
 testimony of a good life, 623
 Vatican Council (2nd), 137
 way to, 348
 see also Ecumenical Movement;
  Unity of the Church
Church: appearance in time, 79
 arts and, 174
 as society, 239
 biblical interpretation, 121
 bride, 141
 bride of Christ, 22
 brotherly community, 231
 building of God, 19

Church *(cont'd)*
children and family life, 641
Christ present in, 140-141
Christ's work the goal of, 201
Christ works through, 562
communication of divine life, 239
communion with various civiliza-
  tions, 264
continual reform, 350
dialogue with the world, 646
diocese and, 403
dissensions in and separations
  from, 345
diversity among its members, 31
diversity of ministry in, 491
earthly glory, 23
education a duty of, 642
elements outside boundaries of
  Catholic Church, 345-346
eschatological nature of, 78-85
established by Christ, 37
foreshadowed in the Old Covenant,
  15
foundation and mission, 17, 589
founded on the apostles, 344
function: to make God present,
  219
guided by the Spirit, 17
hands herself to all generations,
  116
hierarchical structure, 37-56
historical reality, 245-246
Holy Spirit in, 153
holy temple, 19
human culture advanced by, 264-
  265
human failings, 245
human interests, 210
images, 18
inauguration and growth, 16
indefectibly holy, 65-66
independence from particular cultures, 242
independence from race, nation, or
  culture, 264
in exile on earth, 20
influence related to education, 651
inner nature and universal mission,
  15
intention to join, 33
kingdom of God, 18
laity working with hierarchy, 610
leaven in society, 239
life of the, 128
liturgical year, 167-170
living body, 491
living in union with, 471
local congregations or churches, 50
love of, 446
mandate to evangelize the world,
  35
manifesting nature of, 137

marriage and Christ, 251
Mary as type of, 92
maternal solicitude for all men,
  405
membership through baptism, 345
members in likeness of Christ, 20
members liable to sin, 346
members: role in this world, 238
mission, 65, 305-306, 491
missionary by nature, 585
mission, differences in exercising,
  590
mission, fulfillment of, 589
mission: kingdom of God and salvation of men, 247
mission: means suited to situation,
  591
mission of salvation, 23
mission related to temporal order,
  289
mission to mankind, 599
mother and virgin, 92-93
motherhood toward souls, 546
movement toward fullness of truth,
  116
mutual service of members, 231
mysteries of salvation in, 452
mystery of Christ, 450
mystery of the, 15
necessary for salvation, 32
new Israel, 26
new People of God, 666
one complex reality, 22
one with men of every condition,
  598
organic union of members, 491
path of Christ, 590
perfection in heaven, 78
place of particular Churches in,
  32
prayers for success of mission of,
  694
presence and activity in world of
  today, 200
profit from antagonism, 247
purification of members of, 245
recognition of lawful diversity, 305
redemptive act of Christ, 139
religious life, 467
religious mission; temporal aspects, 241
religious orders in, 73
religious responsibility, 642
renewal in various spheres, 351
reveals the mystery of the Lord, 22
role in the modern world, 238
sacrament of unity, 147
salvation and renewal of all men,
  585
salvation of the world, 163
saving and eschatological purpose,
  238

Church (cont'd)
Scripture and, 363
seminarians' spiritual formation, 446
seminary curricula, 452
service in religious life, 470
sheepfold, 18
spouse, 19
teacher of truth, 694-695
teaching office and interpretation of Scripture, 117-118
temporal and eternal life of man, 638
temporal order, mission in, 495
tillage of God, 18
transcendence of, 594
values in non-Catholic Churches, 349
visible incorporation of members, 33
visible social structure, 22, 246
world's need of, 244-245
united with souls in heaven, 81
universality, 242
use of different cultures, 264
willed by Christ, 344
see also Catholic Church; Christianity; Evangelization; Kingdom of God; Missions; Mystical Body; Unity of the Church; etc.
Church and social problems: controversial solutions, 244
understanding our world, 202
see also Social problems
Church and state: atheism, 218
autonomy and independence of each, 288
bishops' independence, 410-411
Church as minister to man, 599
Church not identified with any political community, 287
civil recognition of one community, 685
conditions favorable for religious life, 685
contributions of the Church, 288
cooperation, 288
desires of the Church, 242
freedom for the Church, 288-289
freedom in care for salvation of men, 693
freedom of the Church as spiritual authority, 693-694
freedom of the Church, the fundamental principle,
freedom to exercise duty of preaching, 694
imposition or repudiation of any religion, 685
independence of the Church, 694
political action by Christians, 287

religious liberty and the common welfare, 681
right and fact of liberty, 694
tribute to Caesar, 691
see also Religious liberty
Church architecture: liturgy and, 175
Church history: mystery of the Church in, 452
Church of England: partial Catholic traditions, 356
Church property: administration, 568
bishops' administration of, 400
purpose, 568
religious liberty, 682
Church Unity: see Christian Unity; Unity of the Church
Churches: houses of prayer, 543
Citizenship: duties binding on all citizens, 285-286
extensive participation in public affairs, 229-230
freedom, responsibility and the Church, 288
progress a duty of, 274
City life: growth of, 204
Civil authorities: honors, 148
prayer for, 156
Civil authority: see Authority
Civil community: see Community life
Civil rights: defense against abuses, 285
Civil service: praise for, 285
Civilization: Christ the center of, 247
Christian, 77
Church history; profit, 246
public authority and, 266
treasures of, 260
Civilization, Modern: better world; basis, 261
features of, 202
hopes and anxieties, 199-200
imbalance in intellectual life, 206
meaning and value, 231
oppositions in, 207
spiritual agitation, 203
stranger to things divine, 598
thirst for full and free life, 207
Clergy: biblical study, 127
bishops and diocesan priests, 417
bishops and lack of, 400
common fund for, 573
contribute to material needs of diocese, 417
diocesan priests, 416-420
distribution of, 554
higher education; priests from mission lands, 605
inter-ritual education, 375
lay apostolate and, 612
liturgical instruction, 144-145

Clergy *(con't)*
  number and qualifications for each
    diocese, 413
  outward activity, 562
  priests charged with supra-
    parochial duties, 417
  promotion of lay apostolate, 514
  religious liberty, 682
  remuneration for, 572
  seeking ecclesiastical office and
    benefits, 568
  social assistance, 573
  unworthy ministers, 559
  variety of ministries in the
    Church, 37
  works of apostolate, 417
  see also Bishops; Deacons; Hier-
    archy; Pastors; Pope; Priests;
    Religious persons; *etc.*
Clergy and laity: obligations of the
    faithful, 554
  promote dignity of the laity, 552
  spiritual life, 553
  unity of charity, 553
Clergy: Education: importance of
    priestly training, 437
  priestly training after the semi-
    nary, 456
  see also Seminaries: Curricula
Clerics: liturgical formation, 145
  sanctification of, 69
Cloister: adjustment to conditions
    of time and place, 478
Coadjutor bishops: *see* Bishops,
    Coadjutor
Code of canon law: revision of, 427
Coercion: excluded from matters
    religious, 689-690, 693
  in conversion work, 691
  Jesus Christ and, 690
  religious practices, 682
Collectivism: economic growth, 273-
    274
Colleges and universities: Catholic,
    648
  cooperative endeavors, 650
  exchange of professors, 650-651
  matriculation, 649
  numbers or quality, 649
  spiritual and intellectual assistance,
    649
  theology in, 649
Collegiality: action when bishops
    are dispersed, 399
  early Church, 42
  Ecumenical Councils, 42-43
  expresses unity of the faithful, 44
  papal primacy and, 43
  power exercised with the Pope, 43
Commentators: function, 148
Commerce: developing nations, 299
Common Bible idea, 126

Common good: Catholic apostolate,
    505
  Christians and politics, 286
  civil society, 641-642
  communications media, 324
  contributions by all, 228
  cooperation of bishops, 424
  cultural autonomy, 265
  culture and, 266
  education and, 639
  education and state, 642
  government recognition of, 242
  idea of, 284
  international organization, 298
  laboring classes, 277
  lay apostolate, 519-520
  moral force toward, 284
  news and information, 322
  papal concern, 397
  peace, 290
  political community, 284
  political duties, 286
  political life; basis, 283
  political parties, 287
  political systems reproved, 283
  politics and moral order, 284
  private property, 281
  progress in underdeveloped areas,
    274
  public authority and communica-
    tions media, 324-325
  seeking solutions to problems, 244
  social change and politics, 282-283
  temporary restriction of rights, 286
  universal complexion, 225
  voting and, 285
  see also Temporal goods
Common life: among priests, 551
  religious communities, 477
Common prayer: restored, 155
Common welfare: *see* Common good;
    Public welfare
Communal celebration: preferred
    form, 148
Communicatio in Sacris: Catholics
    and Eastern separated brethren,
    384
  conciliatory policy; Eastern
    Churches, 384-385
  Eastern Churches, 359, 383-384
  practice of common worship, 352
  times when forbidden, 383
Communications media: advances in,
    260
  aid in Christian education, 643
  apostolate: persons with proper
    skills, 328
  apostolic uses, 326
  Christian spirit in, 321
  Church's right to use, 320
  commission of bishops in each
    country, 330

Communications media *(cont'd)*
conscience and moral code, 323
critics, 328
cultural aspects, 638
day of instruction in every diocese, 329
duty of readers, viewers, or listeners, 323
duty to maintain and support, 328-
329
evil, portrayal of, 322-323
harm by evil use, 320
instruction of consciences, 329
instructions on proper use, 328
international associations, 330
manner of achieving effect, 321
mass and individual influence, 319
mission lands, 608, 624
mission use, 624
moderation and self-control, 323-
324
moral norms, 321
moral outlook of those concerned
with, 321
national offices; apostolate, 329
new and more efficient, 204
pastoral instruction to be issued,
330
patronization of evil presentations,
323
persons morally responsible for,
324
priestly vocations, 440
professional associations, 324
religious education, 405
religious presentations, 324
Secretariat for the Supervision of
Publications and Entertainment,
329
service to mankind, 320
use for good of society, 330
use impeded by technical delays
or expense, 328
Communion: Christian life, 140
Eastern Churches, 380
participation in entire Mass, 157
reception at Mass, 156
under both kinds, 156
unity of the People of God, 28
Communion of Saints: worship
enriched by, 84
Community: parish, 153
pastoral concern for, 545
Community life: divine plan, 230
education and, 639
religious freedom and, 687-688
united efforts, 284
welfare of the Church, 246-247
Community of nations: *see* International organization
Compline: revision, 164
Composers: liturgical training, 172

Concelebration: communion of
priests and bishops, 546
Eastern Churches, 358
meetings of priests, 157
new rite to be drawn up, 157
permission extended, 157
permission of the Ordinary, 157
right of each priest to celebrate
individually, 157
Conduct of life: modern imbalance,
206
order in accord with truth, 679
Confession: faculties; Eastern territories, 380
pastors' availability, 418-419
religious superiors, 477
Confessors: languages, 419
Confirmation: given at Mass, 160
lay apostolate, 492
life as witness to, 597
minister; Eastern Churches, 379
revision of rite, 160
witness bearing, 28
Confraternity of Christian Doctrine:
establishment by pastors, 418
Conjugal love: *see* Love; Marriage;
Sex
Consecration: of bishops, 41
Consecration of virgins: rite, 162
Conscience: divine law, 681
fidelity to, 214
formation: attend doctrine of the
Church, 694
formation of true judgments, 680
habitual sin, 214
imbalance in concern for, 206
invincible ignorance, 214
law recognized, 213
man bound to serve God, 690
moral values, 639-640
obligations re true religion, 677
reverence for, 240
war and, 292
see also Liberty of conscience
Conscientious objection: legal provision for, 292
Constitutional law: religious freedom in, 679
Contemplation: apostolic love joined
to, 470
preservation of faculty of, 261
Contemplative life: apostolate, 471
conversion of souls and, 627
example, 471
foundations in mission areas, 628
honorable place in the Church,
471
manner of living to be revised, 471
mission lands, 607
Continence: false doctrines concerning, 474
motivation, 71-72

Contracts: institutes in mission
  lands, 621
Controversy: on solutions to problems, 244
Conventual Mass: concelebration,
  157
Conversion: call to, 142
  Christ and, 600
  force; improper methods, 600
  progressive change of outlook, 600
  spiritual journey, 600
Conversion work: coercion and the
  apostles, 691
  contemplative life and, 627
Converts: motivation, 600
Cooperation: apostolate of Catholics
  and other Christians, 515
  in education, 650
  scientific studies, 263
  social, technical, and Christian,
  354-355
Councils and Synods, Provincial:
  purpose, 424
Councils, Ecumenical: conditions
  for, 44
  Eastern Churches, 357
  power of bishops exercised in, 399
Councils, Plenary: see Plenary
  councils
Counsels, Evangelical: authority of
  the Church, 73
  divine call, 470
  example of Christ, 73
  following Christ, 466
  holiness of the Church, 71
  love quickens and directs, 470-471
  practice of, 66
  purpose of the religious life, 469
  renewal of life of, 466
  Secular Institutes, 473
  vows, 74
  see also Religious life
Courage: students and, 639
Covenant: Eucharist, 142
  marriage and, 251
  old and new, 25
  old, as preparation, 122
  Old Testament, 664
  plan of salvation, 121
Created goods: see Temporal goods
Creation: autonomy of earthly affairs, 233-234
  creature unintelligible without the
  Creator, 234
  fashioned anew, 200
  man the center of, 210
  subjection of all things to man,
  232
  value of the, 62
  see also Nature
Creatures: proper use of, 235
Critics: training of, 328

Culture: as political or economic
  instrument, 266
  authors and artisans of, 260-261
  autonomy, 262
  benefits extended to all, 207
  Catholic higher education, 648
  Catholic schools, 645
  Christianity and, 264
  Christian spirit, 268
  Christian unity, 262
  Church's missionary use of, 264
  Church's promotion of, 264-265
  classical; and modern technology,
  261
  communications media, support
  of, 329
  conditions impeding, 267
  conscious of right to, 267
  development of the whole person,
  262
  duties of Christians, 266
  dynamism and expansion of, 261
  education and, 638
  education and state, 644
  education to higher degree of, 229
  elevation of mankind; learning
  and arts, 263
  harmony with Christian teaching,
  268
  help for those poor in, 264
  heritage of tradition, 261
  home education of children, 267
  keep pace with science and technology, 269
  lay apostolate, 63, 517
  legitimate autonomy, 265
  liberty necessary for, 265
  living exchange, 246
  meaning for the person, 268
  minorities, 266
  mission growth in, 612
  missions, 602
  mission seminaries, 604
  modern characteristics, 260
  new ways for extension of, 260
  perfecting, 611
  plurality of cultures, 259
  possibility for full development,
  266-267
  profit for the Church, 245-246
  proper development of, 259
  public authority and, 325
  renewal of religious life, 469
  renewal through Christianity, 264
  respect and inviolability, 265
  responsibility for progress of, 261
  right of all men to, 266
  safeguarding cultures, 261
  sociological sense, 259
  subordination to person and
  community, 265
  true and full humanity, 259

Culture *(cont'd)*
  union with men of the time, 269
  universal, 268
  universal form of, 260
  values in, 263
  vocation of man, 262
  word, the, 259
Curia, Diocesan: organization, 416
  value, 416
Curia, Roman: act in name of the
    Pope, 401-402
  bishops as members of, 402
  coordination of work, 402
  laity and, 402-403
  members taken from various
    regions, 402
  reorganization, 402
Current events: renewal of religious
    life, 468

Deacons: apostolic institution, 164
  biblical study, 127
  dependent upon the bishop, 406
  duties of, 55
  restoration of the diaconate, 56
  sanctification of, 69
  time before promotion to priest-
    hood, 449
Dead, The: faith and, 215
  fellowship with, 83-84
  piety toward, 81
  union of church militant with, 81
Death: anxiety over, 215
  Christ's victory over, 215
  danger of, 161
  example of Christ, 221
  meaningful in Christ, 222
  riddle, 661
Democracy: choice of systems and
    rulers, 284
Deposit of faith: tradition and
    Scripture, 117
Desire: human longings, 236
  imbalance in heart of man, 207
  satisfaction of, 240
Despair: modern problem, 210
  riddles of life and death, 218
Developing nations: *see* Underde-
    veloped areas
Devil: mission work, 596
  struggle against powers of dark-
    ness, 235
Devotions: bishop's mandate, 143
  clerics, 145
  harmonized with liturgical seasons,
    143
  popular, 143
Diaconate: permanent, in Eastern
    Churches, 380
  permanent state; restoration, 605

Dialogue: lay apostolate, 517, 519
  see also Religious relations
Dialogue, Ecumenical: *see* Ecumen-
    ical dialogue
Dictatorship: violation of rights, 286
Dignity: basis of, 215-216
  charities and, 499
  Church and, 239
  Church and the world, 238
  concern for neighbor, 226
  conjugal love, 256
  conscience and, 213
  culture and, 266
  discrimination and, 667-668
  education, 637
  equality of persons, 228
  false autonomy and, 241
  ferment of the gospel, 226
  foundation of religious freedom,
    679, 688
  free choice, 214
  free will, responsibility, truth, 679
  God and human autonomy, 240-241
  God and religion, 690
  growing awareness of, 225
  human body, 212, 240
  husband and wife, 253
  increasing sense of, 675
  in economic and social life, 271
  insults to human, 226
  living conditions and, 229
  love in marriage, 252-253
  married state, the, 250
  modern man, 210
  mutual respect for, 222
  peace and, 290-291
  politico-juridical order, 283
  public and private institutions, 228
  religion and, 218
  religious liberty, 692
  revelation, 688
  sick and the aged, the, 275
  social betterment and the Church's
    message, 220
  social order, 206
  temporal order, 497
  truth and, 680-681
  vow of obedience, 476
  wider recognition of, 693
  work for, 305
Diocesan curia: *see* Curia, Diocesan
Dioceses: bishop-centered liturgical
    life, 152
  clergy, number of, 413
  commissions for music and art,
    153, 175
  councils on the lay apostolate, 515
  definition, 403
  ecclesiastical provinces and, 426-
    427
  harmony in the apostolate, 421

Dioceses *(cont'd)*
  language groups in, 414
  lay appreciation of, 501
  liturgical commission, 153
  local clergy, 604
  mission spirit, 625
  offices, institutions, and organizations, 413
  pastoral commission, 416
  provision for different rites, 413
  purpose related to boundaries, 412
  religious priests in, 420-421
  resources for support of activities, 413
  senate, or council, 416
  unity in the apostolate, 409
Dioceses: Boundaries: characteristics of regions and peoples, 412-413
  civil boundaries and, 413
  continuous territory, 413
  criteria for revision, 412-414
  distribution of clergy and resources, 412
  episcopal conferences on revision, 414
  geographic size and population, 413
  organic unity, 412
  population factor, 412
  purpose of diocese, 412
  revision; methods, 412
  revision proposals to Apostolic See, 414
Directories: use in care of souls, 428
Disarmament: beginning of, 296
Disasters: bishops and relief of, 400
Discipline: Councils and Synods, 424
  seminaries, 448
Discrimination: all forms rejected, 227-228
  economic inequalities, 274
  laboring classes; wages, 274-275
  not to exist, 685
  rejection of, 667-668
  right to culture, 266
Discussion: solutions to problems, 244
Dispensations: faculty of bishops, 401
Disposition: efficacy of the liturgy, 143
Divine law: *see* Law, Divine
Divine Office: as perfect as possible, 166-167
  canonical time for hours, 165-166
  chief hours celebrated in common, 167
  choral, 166
  Christ and the Church, 163
  clerics in major orders, 166
  day-night made holy, 163

dispensation from, 166
Eastern Churches, 380, 382
hymns, 165
in common, 166
institutes dedicated to acquiring perfection, 166
liturgical service as substitute, 166
minor hours, 165
music; language, 171
norms for revision, 164
pastoral ministry, 164
pastoral work, 542-543
piety, source of, 165
praise of God, 164
prayer of Christ, 163
priestly work, 561
psalms, distribution of, 165
readings, 165
restoration, 164
seminarians, 445
short office for certain institutes, 166
sung when possible, 167
those in major orders or solemnly professed, 166
traditional sequence of hours, 164
vernacular for nuns and certain institutes, 167
vernacular provisions, 167
Divorce: plague of, 249
  profanation, 253
Dogma: definitions of Pope or bishops, 49
  development; methods, 116
  explanation; terminology, 354
  hierarchy of truths, 354
  study of history of, 452
Dogmatic theology: arrangement for seminary studies, 452
Drama: communications media, 328

Earth: development of, 262
  divine plan for, 278
Earthly goods: *see* Temporal goods
Easter: calendar revision, 177
  fixed date for celebration of, 382
  resurrection celebrated, 168
Easter season: liturgical restoration, 601
Eastern Churches: Catholic tradition, 373
  causes of schism, 358
  celibacy, 565
  conciliatory policy regarding communicatio in sacris, 384-385
  education of Latin Rite persons dealing with, 376-377
  equal in dignity, 374-375
  esteem for institutions, rites, traditions, 373

Eastern Churches *(cont'd)*
feast days, transferring or sup-
pressing, 381
full communion, 360
inter-ritual meetings, 426
joining unity of the Catholic
Church, 383
law and custom, 359
liturgical languages, 382
liturgical obligations, 380
liturgy, 358
liturgy, preservation of, 376
merit owed to, 376
missionary activity, 619
origin and growth, 357
particular or local churches, 357
Pope and, 374-375
preservation of spiritual heritage, 376
priesthood, valid, 383
relations with separated churches,
383-385
religious of the Latin Rite and,
377
reunion efforts, 361
reunion prayed for, 385-386
right to self-rule, 376
sacraments, 359, 379-381
separated; communicatio in sacris,
384
separated in good faith; valid
sacraments, 384
special consideration for, 357
theological differences, 360
treasury of, 357
Ecclesiastical goods: *see* Church
property
Ecclesiastical property: *see* Church
property
Ecclesiastical provinces: all dioceses
are to belong to one, 427
boundaries to be revised, 426-427
grouped into regions, 427
Ecclesiastical studies: revision of, 449
Economic assistance: duty of advanced nations, 300
world commerce and developing
nations, 299
Economic conditions: balance lacking, 272
dignity of man, 271
extravagance and wretchedness together, 271-272
inequalities; discrimination, 274
international aspects, 272
reform needed, 272
Economic development: determination by largest possible number
of people, 273
false liberty, 273
growth, 273
international agencies, 300-301

international organization, 300
laity in mission lands, 629
material and spiritual aspects, 301
mitigation of social inequalities,
271
mobility of workers, 274
progress depends on utilization of
resources, 300
service of the whole man, 273
world commerce and developing
nations, 299
Economic goods: national wisdom
and, 213
Economic problems: aggressive demand for benefits, 206
collaboration of Christians, 598-599
untimely solutions, 301
Economics: domination by, 271
international order, 299
modern characteristics, 271
person superior in, the, 275
Ecumenical Councils: *see* Councils,
Ecumenical
Ecumenical dialogue: Bible in, 363
encouragement in spite of differences, 362
moral problems as topic, 365
presentation of dogma, 354
theological problems, 353
value, 347
Ecumenical Movement: Catholic participation, 347
Catholic principles, 345
Catholics join in prayers for
unity, 352
cooperation; norms, 602
false irenicism, 354
fostered by the Spirit, 342
full Catholic communion, 348
growth hoped for, 362
guidance for Catholic efforts, 365
increasing Catholic participation,
349
initiatives and activities, 347
mission seminaries, 605
missions, 353-354
personal renewal and, 351
priests and, 554
renewal in the Church and, 351
soul of the, 352
spiritual aspects, 352
see also Christian unity
Education: associations of parents,
644-645
authors of, 641
collaboration and cooperation, 650
community role in, 641-642
experiments, 638
family life, 251-252
for all, 638-639
for everyone in all parts of the
world, 640

Education (cont'd)
 functions of schools, 643
 importance, 637
 influence, 637
 influence of the Church, 645-646
 liberty of choice by parents, 644
 love and truth in, 638
 missions, 602
 motivation for, 637-638
 of religious persons, 478
 opportunities for, 267-268
 pastoral methods and theological
   science, 571-572
 poor and the deprived, the, 648
 progress and the Church, 638-639
 provision for higher studies, 266
 purpose, 639
 rights of men, 638
 social aspects, 229, 639
 universal right, 639
 see also Adult education; Clergy:
   Education; Culture; Moral education; Parents; Religious education; Schools; Seminaries:
   Curricula; Students; Teachers
Education and state: atheism, 218
 civil rights and duties, 641-642
 functions of the state, 644
 monopoly and subsidiarity, 644
 public subsidies and liberty of
   choice, 644
 religious principles of families,
   645
 right to free choice of schools,
   683
 subsidiarity; parents' rights, 642
Education, Christian: aids to, 642-643
 goal, 640
 pastors' obligation, 641
Education, Higher: formation; lay
   apostolate, 520
 priests from mission lands, 605
 seminarians, 453
 spiritual life of students, 649
 see also Colleges and universities
Education, Liturgical: see Liturgical education
Education, Special: Catholic schools,
   648
Educators: dedication, 651
 vocation, 643
 see also Teachers
Elections: civil right and duty, 285
Embellishments: proper ordering,
   176
Employment: creation of opportunities for, 275
End of the world: completion of the
   Church, 15
 time unknown, 237
Enemies: love of, 227
Eparchies: right of establishing, 378

Ephesus, Council of: Eastern schism,
   355-356
 Mariology, 358
Episcopacy: institution; purpose, 411
Episcopal conferences: bishops of
   many nations, 426
 communications, 426
 conferences of major superiors
   and, 480
 coordination of mission efforts, 613
 counsel on mission problems, 621
 decisions; binding force, 425-426
 description, 425-426
 immigrants from mission lands,
   626
 members, 425
 missionary cooperation, 626
 mission lands, 609-610
 national or regional associations,
   425
 personnel in mission lands, 617
 problems of those deprived of
   parish life, 410
 Propagation of the Faith, 620
 question of boundaries, 427
 statutes, 425
Epistles: content of apostolic writings, 124
Equality: diversity of ministries in
   the Church, 58
 no inequality in the Church, 58
 of all men, 227
 of rites, 138
 religious liberty, 685
Error: see Truth
Esthetics: see Aesthetics
Eternal life: divine testimony, 113
 way to, 404
Ethics: art and morality, 322
Eucharist: center of Christian life,
   545
 covenant; grace, 142
 foretaste of the heavenly banquet,
   236-237
 growth in love, 70
 in Catholic life, 407
 lay apostolate, 492, 508
 Mystical Body of Christ, 20
 other sacraments directed to, 541
 perfects the Church, 626
 religious life, 477
 seminarians, 445
 source and apex of Church's
   work, 542
 strength for life's journey, 236
 unity of the Church, 343
 see also Communion; Mass
Eucharistic Sacrifice: see Mass
Evangelical Counsels: see Counsels,
   Evangelical
Evangelization: accommodated
   preaching, 246

Evangelization *(cont'd)*
  bishops' support of, 400
  communion of Churches, 624-625
  division among Christians as obstacle, 592
  duty of pastors, 45
  duty of the Church, 589, 593
  gospel message not yet heard, 597
  laity, 61, 628
  lay apostolate, 491-492
  mandate of the Church, 35
  prayer and penance for, 625
  preaching as chief means, 591
  purpose of missionary activity, 591
  responsibility for, 623
  responsibility of the apostolate, 492
  seminary and university professors, 627
  study and, 571
  universal mission, 47
  will of God as source, 593
  work of all the faithful, 623
  zeal for, 627
Evil: *see* Good and evil
Excardination: revision of norms, 555
Exemption (religious orders): jurisdiction of bishops, 422
  meaning of, 422
Ex-seminarians: lay apostolate, 444
Extreme Unction: anointings, number of, 161
  fitting time for, 161
  prayers for the suffering, 28

Faith: act of, 114
  act of, a free act, 689-690
  act of, and religious freedom, 688
  and salvation, 538-539
  as knowledge, 265
  Christian education, 640
  coercion opposed to, 693
  discernment in matters of, 29
  free human response to God, 689-690
  future life and, 215
  life penetrated by, 219
  liturgical life, 142
  modern conditions, 205
  necessary for salvation, 32
  necessity, 593
  new light on life, 209
  non-Catholics, 364
  nourished, 149
  nourished by the word, 540
  preparing to receive and profess, 36
  priests, 575
  revelation and obedience of, 113
  rule of, 125
  sacraments and, 158

seminarians, 450
submission to, 601
Synods and Councils and, 424
teaching as duty of bishops, 404
word of God, 125
Faithful, The: *see* Laity
Fall of man: promise of redemption, 112
  revelation and experience, 211
Family: apostolic activities, 502-503
  apprenticeship for the apostolate, 518
  associations, 258
  basis of society, 502-503
  causes of discord, 206
  Christ and, 230
  Christian and apostolic life, 502
  Christian education, 641
  communion of minds in, 257
  community of love, 249
  dignity and autonomy, 502
  domestic Church, 29
  educational role, 267
  foundation of society, 257
  government and needs of, 502
  judgment of parents on number of children, 302
  large, 255
  manifestation of Christ's presence, 252
  material and spiritual conditions, 254
  missions, 602
  nobility of, 249
  priestly vocations, 439
  promotion of values of, 257-258
  religious liberty in, 683
  social changes and, 249
  transformed by Christianity, 61
  values, 404-405
Farmers: culture and, 267
  income, 274
  modern conditions, 207
Fastings: Lent, 170
Fathers: family life, 257
Fathers of the Church: Eastern, 359
  study encouraged, 126
Feast days: Eastern Churches, 381
Feasts: liturgical year; preference, 169
  local celebration, 170
  of saints, 168
Fidelity: in marriage, 251
Films: *see* Moving pictures
Finance: international, 280
  international cooperation, 299
Fine arts: nobility, 174
  public authority and, 325
Foreign countries: human relations, 506
Fortitude: virtue of religious, 470

Freedom: abuse of, 687
  and education, 639
  atheism and, 217
  crippled by poverty, 229
  honored by priests, 553
  human activity joined with re-
    ligion, 233
  license and, 214
  of inquiry, thought, and expression,
    270
  private ownership, 280
  responsible; sense of duty, 675
  strength; social aspects, 229
  unity and, 349
  usages of society, 687
  see also Liberty
Freedom of religion: *see* Religious
  liberty
Freedom of speech: opinions of the
  laity, 64
Free will: dignity, 679
Friendship: in marriage, 252
  lay apostolate, 494
Funeral rites: revision of, 162-163
Furnishings, Sacred: liturgical use,
  174, 175, 176
Future: dominion over, 203
Future life: earthly values perfected
  in, 237
  faith in, 215
  human longings, 237
  pledge of glory, 154

Gentiles: grafted wild shoots, 664
Glory of God: liturgy, 142, 171
God: ancient recognition of Supreme Being, 661
  autonomy of man and, 240-241
  Church as witness to, 219
  glorified; mission activity, 593
  glory; purpose of priesthood, 536
  human longings for, 240
  human reason and certain knowl-
    edge of, 114
  knowledge and love of, 639-640
  man called to share life of, 585
  manifestation in created realities,
    112
  man's common, final goal, 661
  ways with men; the Old Testa-
    ment, 122
Godparents: *see* Sponsors
Good and evil: communications
  media, 322-323
  duty to fight evil, 221
  experience of the Fall of man, 211
  freedom necessary for goodness,
    214
  indifference to goodness, 227
  mission activity, 596

questions remain, despite progress,
  208
riddle, 661
social circumstances as factor in,
  224
struggle against powers of darkness, 235
Good example: of bishops, 51
Good Shepherd: example for priests,
  561
Gospels: apostolic origin, 123
  historical character, 124
  intention in writing, 124
  preeminence in the New Testa-
    ment, 123
Government: *see* State
Grace: acknowledgment of the
  Word, 263
  administering to others, 544
  apostolate, 492
  Christian life, 695
  cooperation with, 143
  liturgical year, 168
  liturgy as source, 142, 149
  Mass, 154
  passion of Christ, 667
  priestly vocations, 440
  sacraments, 158
  saints, 168
  works unseen, 221
  worship in common, 352
Greed: priests, 568
Gregorian chant: *see* Chant
Guilt: judgments about internal, 227

Habit, Religious: norms for, 478
Happiness: moral order, 322
  progress and, 235
  riddle, 661
Health: habit of religious, 478
  mind and body; vow of chastity,
    474-475
  students and the state, 644
Heaven: Church on earth united
  with, 81
  Church perfect in, 78
  liturgy, 83, 141
  saints, feasts of, 168
Hermits: religious life, 467
Hierarchy: diocesan provision for
  different rites, 413
  for special rites, 375
  lay apostolate and, 60, 512
  patriarchates, 377
  promotion of the apostolate, 513
  structure of the Church, 37-56
  temporal order, 514
  see also Bishops; Clergy; *etc.*
Higher education: *see* Education,
  Higher
Hinduism: religious search, 661-662

History: advances in, 260
  becoming all of a piece, 203-204
  Christ and, 236
  Christ the center of, 247
  Christ the key to, 208
  Church has profited by, 246
  Church's role in, 239
  consummation of, 247
  ecumenical study of, 353
  private, disappearing, 203-204
  religious sense in, 661
Holiness: followers of Christ, 67
  fostered by bishops, 407
  fruitful ministry of priests, 559
  imitation of Christ, 72
  lay apostolate, 493
  love as way to, 70
  motivation, 78
  oneness of, 67
  universal call to, 66-72
  see also Perfection; Sanctification
Holy orders: *see* Orders, Holy
Holy Scripture: *see* Bible
Holy Spirit: apostles, 396
  apostles' mission, 115
  biblical inspiration, 118
  bishops, 397
  Christ in the heart of man, 236
  Christian life, 517
  Christians led by, 200
  Christian unity, 342
  Church and, 219
  diocese and, 403
  diverse gifts of, 236
  faith and, 601
  faith and revelation, 114
  fidelity of the Church, 245
  fullness of truth, 125
  gift: knowledge of the divine
    plan, 213
  gifts for welfare of the Church,
    21
  gifts; lay apostolate, 494
  impulses of, 306
  indwelling, 17
  infallible definitions and, 49
  laity and, 490
  life of the Church, 21-22
  liturgical movement in the
    Church, 153
  love in religious life, 477
  love of the Church, 446
  man renewed by, 221
  ministry of Christ, 588
  ministry of priests, 575
  missionary activity, 619
  missionary spirit, 576
  mission in the Church, 31
  non-Catholics and, 34
  religious life, 467
  religious obedience, 476
  renewal of religious life, 468

  resurrection of man, 222
  rule of faith, 125
  saving work of, 587-588
  seminarians and celibacy, 447
  social order and, 226
  special gifts for the apostolate, 492
  strength for suffering Christians,
    385
  teaching office of the Church, 118
  tradition and, 116
  tradition and Scripture, 118
  truth led to by, 116-117
  unity of the Church, 242, 343
  work in the Church, 588
  see also Charisms; Pentecost
Holy Thursday: concelebration, 157
Homily: at Mass, 155
  liturgical, 127
Honors: civil authorities, 148
Hope: lay apostolate, 494
  Mary as sign of, 95
  resurrection, 221
  temporal and eternal, 218
Hospitality: family, 503
Human activity: *see* Activity
Human body: *see* Body, Human
Humanism: autonomy of culture
    and, 262
  denial of God or religion, 205
  emancipation and rule by human
    efforts, 208
  new; extension of responsibility,
    261
Human race: *see* Man
Human relations: lay apostolate, 517
  respect and love for those of dif-
    fering views, 227
  sports and, 268
  union of the faithful with men of
    the times, 269
Humility: Christ and priests, 565
  lay apostolate, 494
  priests, 563
  virtue of religious, 470
Hunger: sharing earthly goods, 279
  social problem, 207
  wealth and, 202
Husband and wife: *see* Marriage
Hymns: Divine Office, 165

Ideology: social problem, 206
Ignorance: free humanity from, 266
Illiteracy: common good and, 266
  modern problem, 202
Image of God: brotherly treatment
    of man, 667
  in neighbor, 499
  man's final goal, 223
Images: number in churches, 175
  of saints, 170
  proper ordering, 176

Immigrants: from mission lands, 626
Imposition of hands: episcopal consecration, 41
Incardination: revision of norms, 555
Incarnation: mystery of man
 and, 220
 plan of salvation, 586
 purpose, 396
Independence: of temporal
 affairs, 234
Individual, The: social participation, 229
Individualism: rejected, 228
Industrialization: social change, 204
Infallibility: bishops as a body, 48
 extent of, 48
 Holy Spirit and, 49
 individual bishops, 48
 papal, 48-49
 universal agreement in matters of
 faith and morals, 29
Information: common good, 322
 freedom of, 265-266
 necessity of freedom of, 325
 right to, 322
Inheritances: renouncing by
 religious, 475
Initiation rites: in mission lands, 159
Institutes, Missionary: *see* Religious
 orders, Missionary
Institutes, Religious: *see* Religious
 orders
Institutions: for bettering conditions
 of human life, 228
 good and just elements in, 242
 serve human purpose, 228
Intellect: dominion over time, 203
 material universe surpassed by,
 212
Intellectual life: apostolate, 650
 development of human
 faculties, 265
 modern imbalance in theory and
 practice, 205-206
 progress in, 212-213
 sciences and technology, 203
 synthesis difficult today, 267
International agencies: apostolate, 509
 business affairs, 300-301
 Catholic associations, 304
 cooperation with, 629
 for peace, 298
 provision for human needs, 298
 world community, 298-299
International associations: communications media, 330
International cooperation: Christian
 activities, 304
 Church and, 304
 economic matters, 299
 population increase, 301

Internationalism: efforts toward universal community, 207
International organization: Christian
 cooperation, 302, 304
 common good, 298
 cooperation with non-Catholics, 304
 coordination and promotion of
 economic growth, 300
 interdependence growing, 222
 nations more conscious of
 unity, 289-290
 see also International agencies
International relations: causes of
 discord, 297
 differences and conflicts, 206
 economic aspects, 271
 economic development, 273
 mutual distrust, 206
 see also War
Inventions: communications
 media, 319
Investments: objectives, 279-280
 underdeveloped areas, 280
Irenaeus, St.: apostolic succession, 40
Israel: *see* Jews

Jerusalem: heavenly liturgy, 141
Jesus Christ: acknowledgment of, 263
 active in the world, 79
 apostles commissioned to hand on
 revelation, 115
 apostles; mission, 140
 apostolate and, 493
 bearing witness to, 534
 center of Christian unity, 362
 center of history and civilization, 247
 coercion not used by, 690
 cornerstone, 596
 death on the cross, 16
 divine praise, 163
 exemplar for religious, 481
 following the evangelical counsels, 466-467
 foundation of the Church, 17
 freedom of religion and, 688
 fullness of religious life in, 662
 Good Shepherd, 18
 government's rights recognized
 by, 691
 head of the Church, 21
 holiness, 66
 humanity of, 220-221
 human nature, 586
 human nature; solidarity, 498
 humility and obedience, 564-565
 imitation of, 72, 494
 impelled by the Spirit, 588
 in hearts of men, 236
 key to mystery of man, 208
 kingship, 62

Jesus Christ (cont'd)
knowing through Holy Scripture, 471
light of nations, 14
love, 258
love of neighbor, 498
man's need of, 595
Mary and, 89-90
Master; meekness, 690
Mediator, 586
Mediator and fullness of revelation, 112
Messiah, 18
mission, 30-31
mission; mediation, 139
mission: redemption, 16
Moslems and, 663
mystery affects all history, 450
mystery manifested in the New Testament, 123
obedience, 476
on temporal duties, 243
passion and death freely undertaken, 667
passion and death, the Jews, 665-666
passion; the apostles, 590
peace and, 291
perfection in following, 240
perfect man, 220, 236
poverty, 475
poverty and oppression, 24
prayer for unity, 343
presence in the Church, 140-141
present in the bishops of the Church, 40
priestly office, 141
priestly work in the Church, 163
prophetic office, 29
prophetic office and the laity, 61
purpose in the world, 201
redemptive work, 139
religious following Him as the one thing necessary, 470
resurrection; Sunday, 168, 169
revelation perfected by, 113
salvation completed by, 113
seminarians conformed to, 445
seminary model, 442
social life, 230
social thought, 230
suffering and death, 221
teaching the mystery of, 404
transcendence of, 594
true vine, 19
unity of Christians, 341
victory over death, 215
world emancipated by, 200
see also Christianity; Church; Kingdom of God; Mystical body; Sacraments; Salvation; etc.

Jews: Christian beginnings, 664
Christ's passion and death, 665-666
covenant with Israel, 24, 121
exodus as foreshadowing the Church, 664
Israel as church of God, 24
mutual understanding and respect, 665
non-acceptance of the gospel, 664
plan of salvation; chosen people, 113
salvation, 34
spiritual patrimony common to Christians and, 665
Joy: Lord's Day, 169
Judgment: internal guilt of others, 227
Judgment Day: Moslems, 663
render account for each life, 214-215
render to each according to his works, 247-248
Justice: action against any injustice, 287
Christian cooperation, 307
Christian social action, 282
common good, 228
family apostolate, 503
in human relations, 686
peace and, 290
political life, 283
principles worked out by the Church, 272
religion and society, 685
social order, 225

Kingdom of God: all creation subjected to God, 62
earthly progress and, 237
Good News, the, 17
mission of the Church, 247, 584
People of God, 25
present on earth in mystery, 237-238
redemption in the Church, 16
religious orders, 75
seen in words, works, and presence of Christ, 18
spread of, 603
temporal welfare and, 31
see also Christianity; Church
Knowledge: Catholic higher education, 649
certitude about reality, 213
faith and reason: two orders, 265
limits of human, 450-451
perfecting, 571
priests and, 571
Knowledge, Pursuit of: see Education

Labor and laboring classes:
  apostolate, 69
  culture and, 267
  disgraceful conditions, 226
  disputes and negotiations, 277
  leisure, 276
  mobility, 274
  modern conditions, 207
  organization adapted to persons,
    276
  pastoral concern for, 419
  persons, not tools of pro-
    duction, 275
  provision for technical and pro-
    fessional formation, 275
  religious persons, 475
  superiority of the person, 275
  workers as slaves, 276
  workers share in determining
    conditions, 277
Labor unions: responsibility in
    economic development, 277
  right to form, 277
Laity: apostolic and pastoral work,
    62
  assistance in pastoral work, 418
  as witnesses, 65
  belong both to Church and
    society, 611
  benefits of dialogue with
    pastors, 64-65
  brothers of the, 59
  charitable and social work, 499
  charities, 507
  collaboration with clergy, 501
  communications media; apos-
    tolate, 326-327
  cooperation with the hierarchy, 60
  dignity and responsibility, 65
  diocese, appreciation of, 501
  Divine Office, 167
  evangelization work, 61, 628
  formation in sacred sciences, 270
  freedom of inquiry, thought, and
    expression, 270
  gifts of God found in, 553
  holiness, 493
  Holy Spirit, 490
  instruction concerning rites, 375
  leaven of the temporal order, 603
  life an evangelization, 61
  life conformed to faith, 505
  mission areas, 608
  obedience, 64
  pastoral duties entrusted to, 513
  pastoral services, 518
  perfection of the Church, 610
  proclaiming and communicating
    Christian teachings, 612
  proper share in Church affairs,
    409
  prophetic office of Christ, 61

  relations with pastors, 64
  renewal of the temporal order, 498
  right to found and control as-
    sociations, 510
  role in building up the Church,
    514
  role in the Church, 489
  Roman Curia, voice in, 402-403
  sacramentals, 162
  sanctification, 70
  secular competence, 63
  secular duties and activities, 243
  share in offices of Christ, 491
  share in priestly function of
    Christ, 60
  sharers in functions of Christ, 57
  shortage of priests; apostolate, 490
  social apostolate, 504
  spiritual life, 493
  spiritual life related to state, 494
  spread the Kingdom of God, 62
  teaching authority of the
    Church, 244
  technical, doctrinal, and moral
    training, 328
  temporal activity, 491-492
  temporal apostolate, 491-492
  temporal order and the Church,
    495
  temporal vocation, 58
  term, the, 57
  unity and solidarity, 612
  vocation to the apostolate, 491
  welfare of the Church, 57
  witness and instrument, 60
  witness and service of Christ, 60
  witness as main duty, 611
  witnesses to Christ, 244
  witness of daily life, 61
  witness of life of, 507
  work for growth of the Church,
    59, 61
  world consecrated to God by, 60
  see also Priesthood, Universal
Land: distribution of owner-
    ship, 301
  reforms of ownership for the
    common good, 281
Language of the liturgy: ad-
    ministration of sacraments, 159
  Divine Office in vernacular, 167
  Latin to be preserved, 150
  marriage rite, 162
  ordination rite, 161
  translations from Latin, 151
  vernacular: competent territorial
    authority, 150
  vernacular in the Mass, 156
  vernacular; neighboring re-
    gions, 150
  vernacular use may be ex-
    tended, 150

Languages: confessors, 419
diocesan provision for different
groups, 414
missionaries, 617
Lapsed Catholics: pastoral work
with, 553
Last Supper: institution of the
Eucharist, 154
Latin language: preservation in the
liturgy, 150
seminary study, 449
see also Language
Lauds: importance, 164
Law: civil obedience to just
laws, 411
observance of just laws, 228-229
Law, Constitutional: see Constitutional law
Law, Divine: conscience and, 681
highest norm of life, 680
human rights and, 241
laity and establishment of, 244
man's participation in, 680
Lay apostolate: see Apostolate
Lay Brothers: drawn into life of
the community, 477
Lazarus: concern for, 226
Learning and scholarship: blend new
sciences with Christian
teaching, 269
Christian faith and, 268
elevation of mankind, 263
method; religious aspects, 234
pastoral care and secular
sciences, 269
synthesis, 261
synthesis difficult to form, 267
Lectors: function, 148
Legates, Papal: office to be more
precisely determined, 402
Leisure: education and, 638
increase of, 268
laboring classes, 276
modern culture, 260
Lent: baptismal features, 170
Bible services, 150
fasting, 170
liturgical restoration, 601
penance, practice of, 170
penitential elements, 170
Liberty: authority compatible
with, 286
constitutional limits on powers
of government, 675
culture, development of, 265
personal and social responsibility
in, 686
temporary restriction of rights, 286
see also Coercion; Freedom
Liberty of conscience: civil
right, a, 694
freedom to follow, 681

Liberty of religion: see Religious
liberty
Libraries: pastoral studies, 571
Life: eternal destiny of man, 256-
257
safeguarding, 256
things opposed to, 226
Life, Conduct of: see Conduct
of life
Literature: in life of the Church,
269
Liturgical books: chant, 172
revision, 147
revision; people's parts, 148
Liturgical celebrations: see
Liturgy; Rites and ceremonies
Liturgical commission: diocesan, 153
to be established, 153
Liturgical education: art, 176
Bible, 144-145
clergy, 144-145
instruction during rites, 150
music, 172
professors, training, 144-145
seminaries, 144-145
Liturgical laws: authority, 146
clerical formation, 145
territorial bodies of bishops, 146
Liturgical life: clergy, 145
diocese and bishop, 152
manifesting Christ and Church, 137
parish, 153
sacrifice and sacraments, 140
Liturgical movement: Holy
Spirit, 153
Liturgical reform: see Reform
of the liturgy
Liturgical services: see Liturgy;
Rites and ceremonies; see also
particular rites; e.g. Marriage
rite
Liturgical year: adaptations for
local conditions, 169
martyrs and saints, 168
Mary in, 168
mystery of Christ, 168
pious practices, seasonal, 168-169
Proper of the Time, 169
revision, 169
saving work of Christ, 167
Liturgy: art and, 269
bishops as guardians of, 406
culture and, 264-265
devotions, popular, 143
Eastern, 358
foretaste of heavenly liturgy, 141
fount of Church's power, 142
honors for private persons, 148
importance in Church's life, 139
instruction in participation, 542
instruction of the faithful, 149
languages; Eastern rites, 382

Liturgy *(cont'd)*
  languages, study of, 449
  local culture and traditions, 151
  more than laws of celebra-
    tion, 143
  nature of, 139
  non-Catholic Churches, 346
  participation in parishes, 418
  participation; lay apostolate, 493
  participation through education,
    643
  pastoral work, 541
  prayers said in name of all, 149
  priestly office of Christ, 141
  primary source of true Christian
    spirit, 144, 148
  public functions, 147
  restoration and promotion; general
    principles, 139
  sacred action surpassing all others,
    141
  sanctification, 137, 142
  seminary studies, 452-454
  source of spirituality, 471
  spirit of the, 144, 148
  training of seminarians, 604
  translations from Latin, 151
  understanding, 165
  union with the Church in heaven,
    83
  whole body of the Church, 147
  see also Rites and ceremonies
Lord's day: *see* Sunday
Lord's Supper: non-Catholic
    Churches, 364
Love: agape, 498
  apostolate motivated by, 498
  chastity and brotherly love, 475
  Church manifests God's love
    for men, 247
  common good, 228
  conscience and, 213-214
  contemplation and, 470
  cult of the saints, 84
  draws men to Christ, 494
  family life, 641
  first and greatest command-
    ment, 223
  for those who think or act
    differently, 227
  fraternal charity, 505
  God's presence revealed by, 219
  greatest commandment, 498
  growth in, 70
  human: affection of the will,
    252-253
  human recognition of divine, 216
  impelled to promote God's
    glory, 492
  in education, 638
  in marriage, 258

  in ordinary circumstances of
    life, 236
  lay apostolate, 492
  man and his brothers, 667
  married couples, 69
  missionary activity, 593
  of created things, 235
  of enemies, 227
  of God and of neighbor, 470-471
  passion of Christ, 667
  peace and, 291
  religious life, 477
  salvation and, 33
  social order, 225
  testimony of the saints, 83
  truth and, 306
  truth and error; indifference, 227
  union with Christ in apostolic
    activity, 472
  union with God, 351
  unity and, 351
  universal, 598
  war vanquished by, 291
  way to holiness, 70
  world problems and, 305
  world's transformation, 236
  see also Marriage; Sex
Luxury: religious poverty, 476

Major seminaries: *see* Seminaries
Man: activity, 233
  as sufficient to himself, 263
  basic questions of modern
    man, 208
  biblical teaching, 210
  bodily composition, 212
  called to share God's life, 585
  center of all things on earth, 210
  Christ the key to mystery of, 208
  community and fellowship, 660
  condition and calling, 594
  creature as rival of Creator, 232
  desire for a higher life, 215
  desires and limitations, 207
  destiny, 212
  development of human faculties,
    265
  development; social aspects, 224
  develop the earth, 262
  dynamic, evolutionary concept of
    reality, 204
  emancipated by Christ, 200
  exaltation and despair, 210
  find self through gift of self, 223
  grandeur and misery, 212
  guiding forces unleashed by, 207
  humanity an offering accepted by
    God, 236
  image of universal man, 267
  imbalance in heart of, 207
  interior qualities, 212

Man *(cont'd)*
isolation, 230
literature and arts, 269
male and female, 211
mandate over nature, 232
material and spiritual needs, 273
meaning of his existence, 240
modern anxiety, 200
modern new stage of history, 202
mutual service in answering
questions of, 210
mystery of, and the Incarnation,
220
new creation, 20
new creature in the Holy Spirit,
235
participation in divine life, 15
political formation, 285
preserved by God's love, 216
puzzle to himself, 218
reality in heart of, 212
restoration of divine likeness, 220
reverence for, 226
riddle, 661
sanctified by Christ, 240
service of men, 262
social nature of, 211
struggle with good and evil, 211
superior to bodily concerns, 212
unity of, 212
value in what he is, 233
whole man, the, 201
wisdom, 213
see also Dignity; Humanism; Person; Society; *etc.*
Marriage: apostolate of married
persons, 502, 503
basis of society, 502
childless, 255
Christ and the Church, 474
Christ and the Church as model,
251
Christian education of children,
641
conjugal love; divine law, 255
cooperation with love of the
Creator, 254
danger when intimacy broken off,
255
dignity and value, 250
disfigurements of, 249
faithfulness and harmony in, 253
fidelity in, 251
form and validity; Eastern
Churches, 381
friendship, 252
God the author of, 250
husband and wife: true love, 252
indissolubility, 502
irrevocable covenant, 250
love in, 251
mutual help and service, 250

mutual love, growth of, 255
nobility of, 249
pastoral counseling, 258
perfection in, 250
power and strength of the institution, 249
preparation for, 257
procreation and education of
children, 250, 253-254
profaned by self-love, 249
promotion of values of, 257-258
pure love; undivided affection, 252
renewal in, 253
responsible parenthood, 254
sacramental sign: Christ and the
Church, 447
sacrament; consecration, 251
sacrament; the Church, 28
sex in, 253
virtue demanded in, 253
vocation; witness to Christ, 258
Marriage rite: apart from Mass, 162
blessing, 162
customs and ceremonies, 161
prayer for the bride, 162
revision, 161
time at Mass, 162
usage of place and people, 161-
162
Martyrdom: non-Catholics, 34
proof of love, 71
readings, 165
Martyrs: as witnesses, 692
feasts, 168
veneration of, 81-82
witness to faith, 219
Mary, Blessed Virgin: assumption
into heaven, 90
cult in the Church, 94
docility, 570
Eastern tribute, 358
Eve and, 88
faith, 89-90
free from all sin, 88
honored by non-Catholics, 95-96
honored in the liturgy, 168
intercession by religious, 481-482
intercession of, 96, 630
model of virtues, 93
Moslems and, 663
mother in the order of grace, 91
Mother of God, 86
place in the mystery of Christ, 85
pre-eminent member of the Church,
86
prophetically foreshadowed (O.T.),
87
public life of Jesus, 89
redemption and, 88
reunion and, 385
reverence for, 85-86

Mary, Blessed Virgin *(cont'd)*
  role in the economy of salvation,
    87
  salvific influence on men, 90
  seminarians' veneration of, 445
  sign of hope, 95
  spiritual and apostolic life, 495
  subordinate role, 91-92
  titles, 91
  type of the Church, 92
  union with her Son, 89
  warning against false exaggera-
    tions, 95
Mass: at baptism, 160
  center of Christian community life
    418
  Christian community, 602
  Christian life, 143
  Christ offered sacramentally in,
    535
  Christ present in, 141
  "common prayer" restored, 155
  communal celebration, 148
  communion from the same sacri-
    fice, 156
  daily celebration, 560
  death of Christ made present, 140
  diocesan liturgical life, 152
  entire Mass: word and Eucharist,
    156-157
  greatest work of priests, 560
  homily, 155
  institution; Last Supper, 154
  instruction in participation, 541
  Latin parts, 156
  life of the Church strengthened
    by, 128
  Liturgy of the Word, 540
  music; language, 171
  participation, 28, 143
  pastoral charity; life of a priest,
    563
  priestly function, 53
  radio or television, 145
  regulated by bishops, 50
  revision of rites; nature and con-
    nection of parts, 155
  rites; pastorally efficacious, 155
  rites to be simplified, 155
  source of spirituality, 471
  Sunday, 153
  two parts, 156-157
  understanding; union, 154
  united with the Church in heaven,
    83
  vernacular in, 156
  work of redemption, 16
  see also Eucharist
Material goods: *see* Temporal
  goods
Materialism: culture and, 263
  lay apostolate, 519

Material things: sanctification, 158
  used in worship, 176
  problem for modern man, 208
Matins: revision of, 164
Maturity: chastity, vow of, 475
  discipline in seminaries, 448
  obedience, vow of, 476
  self-knowledge, 519
  seminarians, 447
Media of communication: *see* Com-
  munications media
Meditation: seminarians, 445
Messiah: preparation for, 113
Metropolitans: rights and privileges;
  new norms, 426
Migrants: family rights, 502
  international agencies, 298
Migration: social changes, 204
Military service: proper role of,
  293
Military vicariates: establishment;
  bishops' cooperation, 427
Ministers: *see* Clergy; Priests; *etc.*
Minorities: culture; liberty, 266
  political rights, 283
Minor orders: Eastern Churches,
  380-381
Minor seminaries: *see* Seminaries,
  Minor
Miracles: kingdom of God, 17
Missionaries: character, 615
  doctrinal training, 616
  esteem for local language and
    customs, 616
  formation completed in mission
    lands, 617
  goals; unity, 620-621
  habits of mind, 615
  knowledge of language and social
    milieu, 555
  language studies, 617
  life; qualities, 614
  lifetime vocation, 614
  local priests united with, 609
  missiological studies, 616
  musical training, 173
  qualified, 610
  renewal of spirit, 615
  salute to, 629
  scientific preparation for work,
    622
  special vocation, 614
  spiritual and moral training, 615
  subject to the bishop, 621
  vocation; charismata, 613-614
  vocations and bishops, 407
Missionary activity: *see* Missions
Missionary institutes: *see* Religious
  orders, Missionary
Mission lands: baptismal rite, 160
  initiation rites, use of, 159

Mission Lands *(cont'd)*
  liturgical variations and adaptations, 151, 152
  musical traditions, 172-173
Mission of the Church: *see* Church
Missions: activities of the Congregation for the Propagation of the Faith, 619
  activity extends to second coming of Christ, 595
  adaptation as obstacle to conversions, 610
  adaptation; syncretism, 612
  as epiphany, 595
  bishops and, 45-46
  bishops' concern for, 619
  bishops provide priests for, 400
  changes and circumstances affect activity, 592
  Church's inner nature as source, 592
  clergy volunteering for, 609
  collaboration of missiological institutes, 622
  collection of funds for, 625
  communion between communities, 624
  contemplative houses, 628
  contracts between Ordinaries and institutes, 621
  coordination of efforts, 621
  ecumenical approach, 353-354
  eschatological aspects, 596
  for glory of God, 593
  forming the Christian community, 601
  growth in local cultures, 612
  human nature and aspirations, 594
  immigrants from mission lands, 626
  institutes of the active life, 628
  lack of priests and material support, 608
  lay apostolate, 502
  love as motive for, 593
  maturity of Christian life in, 608
  missionary spirit, 576
  necessities of the Christian community, 602
  papal mission works, 625
  particular traditions; Catholic unity, 613
  pastoral activity and, 592
  pastoral council, 621
  personnel, 617
  planting the Church with stability, 607
  pooling of resources, 621
  power and necessity, 593
  prayer and penance for, 624
  priests sent two or three together, 555
  purpose, 35

  range of charity, 624
  research assisting, 629
  rooted in the people, 602
  seminary training, 604
  stages, 592
  term, the, 591
  truth and grace found in non-Christians, 595-596
  use of talents for, 618-619
  work not done by lone individuals, 617
  zeal, 610
Modern world: *see* Civilization, Modern
Mohammedans: *see* Moslems
Monasticism: adaptation of traditions to needs of today, 473
  apostolic life joined to choir duty, 473
  Eastern Churches, 359
  mission lands, 607
  preservation of, 472-473
  principal duty of monks, 472
Moral education: communications media, 328
  parents and schools, 644-645
  parents' responsibility, 302
Morality: individualistic, 228
  keep pace with science and technology, 269
  objective norms of, 214
Moral order: Church as teacher, 694-695
  economic aspects, 273
  errors undermining, 496
  lay apostolate, 63
  man affected in his entire being, 322
  political authority, 284
  public authority and, 326
  respect for, 687
Moral problems: ecumenical dialogue, 365
Moral theology: perfecting of, 452
Mortification: chastity and, 474
  priests, 558
Moses: priests and, 547
Moslems: Christian hostility; history, 663
  Church's regard for, 663
  religion, 35
Mothers: domestic role, 257
Moving pictures: communications media, 327
Musical instruments: liturgical use, 173
Music, Sacred: composers, 172
  compositions; sources, 173
  diocesan commission, 153
  higher institutes, 172
  holiness, 171
  language, 171

Music, Sacred *(cont'd)*
 local traditions, 172-173
 nobility of liturgical worship, 171
 pre-eminence, 171
 purpose, 171
 teaching in seminaries and other
  institutions, 172
Mystical Body of Christ: apostolate
  in, 491
 bishops and welfare of, 45
 bringing to fullness, 623
 building up by members, 20
 Christ as head, 21
 Christian education, 640
 creation of, 20
 growth through missionary activity, 593
 growth through mission work, 596
 membership, 374
 public worship, 141
 royal priesthood, a, 533
 work for growth of, 546
 see also Church

Nationalism: Christians and, 603
Nations, Developing: *see* Underdeveloped areas
Native clergy: gift of vocations,
  603-604
 united with foreign missionaries,
  609
Natural law: permanent binding
  force, 292
Nature: control over, 206
 culture and, 259
 mastery over, 231
Necessities: available to all men, 225
Neighbor: as another self, 226
 every man, 226
 image of God in, 499
Neophytes: ecumenical spirit, 602
New churches: *see* Missions
News: moral aspects of reporting,
  322
 reporting; common good, 322
New Testament: hidden in the Old,
  122
 new covenant, 25
 power of the word of God, 123
 witness to mystery of Christ, 123
Non-Catholic churches: acknowledge
  values in, 349
 active faith, 364
 differences among themselves, 361-
  362
 liturgical actions, 346
 study and understanding by Catholics, 353
 unity lacking, 346
Non-Catholics: bishops and the
  separated brethren, 409

Church linked with other Christians, 33-34
 cooperation with, in the apostolate,
  515
 graces from the Holy Spirit, 34
Non-Christians: bishops' concern
  for, 409
 charity in dealings with, 695
 religions and the Church, 660
 truth and grace in, 595-596
Nuns: apostolic work, 478
 papal cloister, 478
 suggestions regarding adaptation
  and renewal, 470

Obedience: assent to teachings of
  bishops, 48
 Christ and priests, 564-565
 civil obligation, 284
 laity, 64
 making light of duty of, 687
 mature freedom, 564
 missionaries, 614-615
 of faith, 113
 of priests, 549, 564
 seminarians, 446
 teaching authority of the Church,
  30
Obedience (virtue): religious life,
  470
Obedience (vow): dignity; maturity,
  476
 humility, 476
 surrender of will, 476
Old age: dignity; livelihood, 275
 extreme unction, 161
 parents and children, 252
Old Testament: Church foreshadowed
  in, 15
 contents, 122
 knowledge of God in, 122
 meaning in the New, 122
 plan of salvation, 122
 received through the Jews, 664
 value permanent, 122
Order: peace, 290
 see also Moral order; Social order
Orders, Holy: nourishing the
  Church, 28
 providence and vocations, 440
 special sacrament, 535
Ordination: bond of union among
  priests, 550
 ceremonies and texts to be revised,
  161
 communion under both kinds, 156
 extending time before promotion
  to priesthood, 449
 of brothers, 473
Organ (musical instrument): liturgical use, 173

Organizations: religious liberty in
	establishment of, 683
Oriental Churches: see Eastern
	Churches
Ornaments: noble beauty, 175

Pagans: salvation, 35
Papacy: willed by Christ, 38
Parents: apostolic formation of
	children, 518
	children and the apostolate, 502
	communications media and, 324
	community of love, 249
	educational associations, 644-645
	educational role, 641
	education and welfare of children,
		302
	education, state, and rights of,
		642
	encourage vocations, 29
	judgment of family size, 254-255
	liberty of choice in education, 644
	mission: transmission of life, 254
	old age; children, 252
	partners with teachers, 647
	religious example of, 251
	religious vocations, 481
	rights; Catholic schools, 646
	rights in religious education of
		children, 683
	see also Children; Family
Parishes: erection or suppression,
		420
	for special rites, 375
	lay apostolate, 501
	liturgical life, 153
	priestly vocations, 439
	purpose: good of souls, 419
	religious called to serve in, 421-
		422
	vacant pastorates, 419
Participation: acclamations, etc., 148
	bodily attitudes, 148
	church architecture, 175
	clerics, 145
	communion celebration to be
		preferred, 148
	diocesan liturgical life, 152
	pastoral efforts, 145
	promotion, 144
	proper disposition, 143
	purpose of apostolic works, 142
	right and duty of Christian people,
		144
	sacred music, 171, 173
	spiritual life, 143
Particular Churches: see Missions
Passion: dignity and, 214
Past: dominion over, 203
Pastoral commission: duties, 416

Pastoral institutes: priestly training
	after the seminary, 456
Pastoral Liturgy: Institute for, 153
Pastoral work: building up the
	Church, 544
	care for those deprived of parish
		life, 410
	directory for special groups, 428-
		429
	evangelization and, 627
	formation of the laity, 518
	functions of priests, 53
	gather the People of God together,
		543
	holiness and, 559
	importance of formation of priests,
		353
	laity entrusted with, 513
	lay apostolate and, 490, 496
	lay assistance, 418
	new approaches and methods, 564
	promotion of participation, 144
	religious communities called on
		for, 421-422
	secular sciences and, 269
	seminarians' initiation into, 455
	seminary preparation, 442
	seminary studies, 454
	spiritual life, 446
	unified in the diocese, 418
	unity of the human race, 54
	vocation of married people, 258
	see also Care of souls
Pastors: bishop's representative, 152
	charisms and the lay apostolate,
		493
	Christian education of the faithful,
		641
	communications media, 326
	community spirit, 545
	cooperators of the bishop, 417-418
	daily conduct and concern, 244
	evangelization a duty of, 45
	imbued with liturgical spirit, 144
	judging suitability for administra-
		tion, 419
	laity and, 64, 244
	law of concursus suppressed, 419
	liturgical instruction of the faith-
		ful, 145
	ministers to the faithful, 58-59
	removable and irremovable, 419-
		420
	resignations because of age, etc.,
		420
	right of religious, 419
	rights of nomination, etc., sup-
		pressed, 419
	sanctification of their people, 418
	shepherds, 419
	stability of office, 419-420

Pastors *(cont'd)*
support for those who have resigned, 420
teaching office, 418
transferring and removing procedure, 419-420
visitations, 419
work with special groups, 419
see also Assistant pastors
Patriarch: meaning of the term, 377
Patriarchate: antiquity of, 377
Patriarchates: equal in dignity, 377
establishment of new, 378
Patriarchs: authority; Synods, 378
rights and privileges, 378
rights as of time of union, 378
special honor, 377-378
Patriotism: Christians and, 603
cultivation of, 286
Paul, Saint, Apostle: all things to
all men, 536
Peace: and education, 639
arms as deterrents to war, 294
Catholic unity, 32
causes of, 290
ceaseless efforts for, 290
Christian unity and, 306
community of nations, 289-290
contribution of the Church to,
303-304
cooperation in achieving, 290
economic inequality and, 272
enterprise of justice, 290
eternal life, 237
false hope, 297
instruction in sentiments of, 297
international bodies working for,
298
join with all true peacemakers, 291
love of neighbor, 291
military service and, 293
mutual trust essential, 296
personal aspects, 290
religion and society, 685
result of order and justice, 687
studies of the problem, 296
working together for, 307
Penance: conversion, 142
Lent, 169-170
missions and, 624
priestly vocations, 440
Penance (sacrament): Christian life,
418-419
contrite heart, 542
members of the Church, 28
readiness to administer, 561
reception by priests, 570
rite and formulas to be revised,
161
Pentecost: apostles as witnesses, 47
Church and, 588
Mary, 90

mission of the apostles, 38-39
mission of the Holy Spirit, 16
People of God: *see* Christian life;
Church
Perfection: all called to holiness, 29
bishops as leaders, 407
common welfare, 683
culture and, 265
following Christ, 67
goal of Catholic life, 348-349
in marriage, 250, 251
love and, 236
moral order, 322
obligation to strive for, 72
priests' life, 557
promotion of temporal good, 642
saints, 168
Periodicals: lay apostolate, 520
Persecution: bishops, 401
government attempts to destroy
religion, 685
lay apostolate, 507-508
life made difficult for religious
communities, 695
missionaries, 629
profit from, 247
rejection by the Church, 666
united with Christ, 70
Person: culture and perfection of,
265
distinctions made by the liturgy,
148
education, 639
laboring classes, 275
preservation of, 201
socialization, 286
social order to benefit the, 225
transcendent character; Church
as sign, 287-288
understanding the whole, 267
values, 404-405
violations of integrity of, 226
Personality: modern development,
240
private property and, 280
temporal goods and, 567
Peter, Saint, Apostle: foundation of
the Church, 344
office permanent, 40
primacy, 38, 43
Philosophy: Church's use of, 246
revision of ecclesiastical studies,
449-450
seminary studies, 450
teaching the history of, 450
theology and, 451
training in mission lands, 604
true problems of life, 451
Piety: Divine Office, 165
liturgical offices, 148
seminarians, 445-446
Pipe organ: liturgical use, 173

Pius X, Saint, Pope: liturgical
   books, 172
   sacred music, 171
Plenary councils: purpose, 424
Pluralism: education and state, 644
Political action: Church relationship,
   287
   dedication to justice and service,
      287
   protection of rights, 283
Political ethics: relations between
   rulers and citizens, 286
Political parties: work for common
   good, 287
Politics: basis of establishment, 283
   Christians and, 286
   culture and, 266
   formation of man under, 285
   formation of the population, 287
   free will of the citizens, 284
   juridical foundations, liberty in
      establishing, 285
   leaders, 284
   order, 284
   participation by all citizens pos-
      sible, 229-230
   participation increasing, 283
   preparation for career in, 287
   purpose of the political com-
      munity, 284
   social change and, 282-283
   systems reproved, 283
   variety of solutions to problems
      possible, 285
Polygamy: disfigurement, 249
Polyphony: in the liturgy, 172
Pontificals: use reserved, 177
Poor, The: bishops and, 405
   Catholic education, 648
   Church's love for, 24
   contempt for, 271
   missionary zeal, 609
   pastoral obligation to, 544-545
   pastoral work, 419
   relief an obligation, 278
   religious orders and, 475-476
   united with Christ, 70
Pope, Primacy of: collegiality of
   bishops and, 43
   particular Churches in the
      Church, 32
   reaffirmation of, 38
Popes: exempt religious orders and,
   422
   over individual Churches and
      rites, 374-375
   primacy of ordinary power, 397
   principle and foundation of unity,
      44
   religious orders; jurisdiction, 76
   supreme authority, 397
   see also Infallibility

Popular devotions: see Devotions
Population, Increase of: forecasting
   and regulating, 203
   international cooperation, 301
   rights and duties of government,
      301
   solutions contrary to moral law,
      302
Poverty: freedom crippled by, 229
   spirit of, 282
   voluntary, 568
   worldwide, 303
Poverty (virtue): lay apostolate, 494
   social security for the clergy, 574
Poverty (vow): diligent practice
   of, 475
   poor in fact and in spirit, 475
   right to possess necessities, 476
   sharing of temporal goods, 476
Power: problem for modern man,
   202
   responsibility and, 232-233
Practicality: imbalance in concern
   for, 206
Prayer: family life, 251
   Lent, 170
   mental and vocal; priests, 570
   missions and, 624
   pastoral ministry, 164
   presence of Christ, 141
   priestly vocations, 440
   private, 143
   proficient in, 542
   sacred music, 171
   seminarians, 446
   spirit and practice in religious
      communities, 471
Prayer of the faithful: restored, 155
Preaching: accommodation in, 246
   bishops' duty, 47
   chief means of evangelization, 591
   development of tradition, 116
   duty of pastors, 418
   effective, 539-540
   gift of, 472
   ministry of, 149
   nourished by Scripture, 125
   priestly vocations, 440
   relevant to actual conditions, 269
   religious education, 405
   religious liberty, 694
   religious vocation, 481
   sacred duty, 535
   seminary studies, 454
   word of Scripture, 127
Presbyters: see Priests
Press: freedom of the, 325
   good press fostered, 327
Pride: social disturbance, 224
Priesthood: excellence of the order
   of, 532
   power and force from Christ, 535

Priesthood *(cont'd)*
  purpose: glory of God, 536
Priesthood, Universal: interrelated
    with hierarchical priesthood, 27
  sacraments and virtues, 27
Priestly training: *see* Clergy; Semi-
    narians; Seminaries
Priests: asceticism, 561-562
  as disciples, 552
  associations, 551
  biblical study, 127
  bishops' concern for, 408
  bound to acquire perfection, 558
  brotherhood of, 54
  building up the Church, 550, 557
  common life, 551
  community life, 418
  concern for the newly ordained,
    456
  cooperators of the episcopal order,
    416-417
  coordination of lives of, 562
  dependent upon the bishop, 406
  dialogue with the world, 245
  difficulties; failing, 552
  diocesan priests volunteering for
    mission work, 625-626
  docility, 570
  ecumenism, 554
  education related to contemporary
    problems, 270
  educators in the faith, 544
  episcopal co-workers, 534
  Eucharistic Sacrifice, 36, 53
  examination of works and projects,
    563
  exhortation to, 574
  failings; bishops and, 408
  faith, 575
  fidelity and faithfulness, 563
  freedom and docility, 567
  functions, 538, 626
  gift of self, 562
  Good Shepherd as example, 561
  good shepherds, 537
  greatest task: the Eucharistic Sac-
    rifice, 560
  greed, 568
  growth in holiness, 559
  hierarchical communion with
    bishops, 546
  hierarchically bound with the
    bishop, 541
  holiness; bishops' responsibility,
    548
  holiness through duty, 559
  hospitality and sharing among,
    551
  humility, 563
  humility and obedience; Christ's
    example, 564-565
  institutes and meetings for, 408

  joining forces with other priests,
    549
  joining self with Christ, 562
  knowledge; study, 571
  lead in seeking Christ, 552
  liturgical life, 145
  loneliness, 575
  loyalty to their bishops, 68
  manual labor, 550
  ministry of the word, 540
  mortification, 558
  mutual assistance, 551
  never alone, 575
  obligation to the poor and weak,
    544-545
  obstacles in life of, 575
  one priesthood with their bishop,
    53
  paternity in Christ, 566
  pattern to the flock, 55
  possessions of, 569
  power from God, 560
  prayer life, 570
  primary duty: proclaiming the gos-
    pel, 538-539
  receive the word themselves, 559-
    560
  recreation, 551
  relations between older and
    younger, 550-551
  relationship to the world, 567
  relations with others, 546
  research or teaching, 549-550
  sacramental brotherhood, 549
  sacred duties, 535
  sanctification of, 68, 569-570
  seminary relations, 443
  service of the missions, 626
  service to men, 537
  share in care of the whole
    Church, 556
  share in Christ's ministry, 533
  special grace, 558
  spending themselves, 564
  spiritual, intellectual, and material
    welfare, 408
  spiritual life; aids, 569
  spiritual requirements, 563
  sufficient number of, 556
  supra-diocesan works, 417
  to the end of time, 556
  union; obedience, 564
  united, 550
  united with the bishop, 53
  unity, 438, 446
  unity among diocesan, 417
  universal mission, 554
  vacation, 573
  virtues required, 538, 563
  vocation to life of perfection, 557
  voluntary poverty, 568

Priests *(cont'd)*
　volunteer for work outside dio-
　　cese, 554-555
　work for growth of the Church,
　　546
　working alone, 563
　see also Clergy; Pastors; Religious
　　priests; Seminarians
Priests: vocations: belated vocations,
　441
　means of fostering, 440
　organizations; aids, 440
　priests' zeal in fostering, 439
　shortage of, 439
　transcend local boundaries, 440-441
　urgent fostering of, 439
Prime: suppressed, 164
Production: increase of, 272-273
Professional education, 648
Professional workers: capacities as
　property, 280
Professors of liturgy: training, 144-
　145
Profit: developing nations, 300
Profit sharing: promotion of, 277
Progress: advances in, 233
　citizens' duty, 274
　culture, 259
　in developing nations, 204
　kingdom of God and, 237
　purpose of, 300
　temptation, 234-235
　true happiness, 235
Propagation of the Faith, Congre-
　gation for the: administra-
　tion; methodology, 620
　episcopal conferences; consultors,
　　620
　planning missionary activity, 619
Property: autonomy; freedom, 280
　common destination of earthly
　　goods, 281
　large estates; expropriation, 281
　ownership fostered, 280
　proper use of, 278
　public and private, 280-281
　security in, 280
Prophets (O.T.): on earthly duties,
　243
Prosperity: bishops' regard for, 411
Protestant Churches: *see* Non-Cath-
　olic Churches
Providence: knowledge of the divine
　plan, 213
　priestly vocations, 439-440
　signs of God's presence and pur-
　pose, 209
Provincial councils: *see* Councils
　and Synods, Provincial
Psalter: revision of divine office, 165
Psychology: advances in, 203, 260
　in education, 639

pastoral use, 269
Public opinion: moral aspects, 323
　war and peace, 296-297
Public welfare: basic component
　of, 687
　Catholics and the common good,
　　505
　collaboration with civil authorities,
　　411
　social conditions for, 683-684
Public worship: Mystical Body, 141
　see also Liturgy
Pupils: *see* Students

Race prejudice: discrimination re-
　jected, 668
Race problems: modern conditions,
　206
Radio: apostolate, 327-328
　liturgical use, 145
Readings, Scriptural: *see* Bible
Reality: dynamic, evolutionary con-
　cept of, 204
　heart of man, 212
　science and religion, 234
Reason: faith and, 265
Recreation: clergy, 551
Redemption: liturgical year, 168
　Mary and, 88
　Mary in the liturgy, 168
　mission of Christ, 16, 139
　purpose of Christ's coming, 396
　renewal of the temporal order, 495
　unity and, 343
Reformation: divisions stemming
　from, 356
Reform in the Church: continual
　need, 350
Reform of the liturgy: adapting to
　culture and traditions, 151
　authority, 146
　Bible; importance, 147
　clarity of texts and rites, 146
　general norms, 146
　innovations, 147
　intimate connection between
　　words and rites, 149
　investigations, 146
　local variations and adaptations,
　　151
　needs of modern times, 138
　norms based on didactic and pas-
　　toral aspects, 149-151
　norms to be established, 138
　restoration related to change, 146
　rites in adjacent regions, 147
　Roman and other rites, 138
　scriptural readings, 149
　simplicity, 149
　tradition, 146
　Vatican Council (2nd), 137

Reform of the liturgy *(cont'd)*
 zeal, 153
 see also Adaptation
Refugees: international agencies, 298
Relics: veneration, 170
Relief work: Catholic organism proposed, 304-305
 duty of, 278
 international volunteers, 303
 national and personal duty, 499
Religion: acts transcend temporal
  affairs, 681
 ancient times, 661
 binding in conscience, 690
 coercion excluded from, 690
 earthly affairs and, 243
 errors undermining, 496
 external expression of internal acts,
  681
 indifference to problems of, 240
 modern conditions affecting, 205
 obligation to seek the true, 677
 social value, 685
 way to serve God revealed, 677
Religion and state: *see* Church and
  state; Religious liberty
Religions: answers to unsolved riddles, 661
 Catholic Church's esteem for, 239
 free selection, etc., of ministers,
  682
 in advanced cultures, 661
 non-Christian, and the Church,
  660
 recognition of diversity, 306
 respect for, 283
 rights of communities, 682
 seminary studies, 453
 truth and goodness in, 453
 truth and holiness in, 662
Religious conditions: modern man,
  598
Religious education: Bible and, 127
 family life, 251-252
 lay apostolate, 517
 media, 405
 non-Catholic schools, 645
 presentation adapted to needs of
  the time, 405
 right and duty of parents, 502
 rights of parents, 683
 teaching as duty of bishops, 404-
  405
 see also Catechetics
Religious liberty: buildings and
  properties, 682
 care of right to, 684
 communicating abroad, 682
 communities free to show their
  values, 683
 constitutional law, 679, 694

denial of, an injury to the human
  person, 681
 dignity as foundation of, 679
 dignity of man the foundation of,
  688
 education and state, 645
 effective constitutional guarantee
  necessary, 696
 equality of citizens, 685
 establishment of organizations,
  683
 exercise subject to norms, 685-686
 faithfulness to the gospel, 692
 family rights, 683
 free act of faith, 688
 free acts according to conscience,
  681
 free exercise of religion, 675
 free profession in public and private, 695
 government duty to protect, 684-
  685
 immunity from civil coercion, 677
 immunity in state of indifference,
  679
 international documents; recognition, 695
 Jesus Christ, 688
 meaning; application, 678-679
 meetings, 683
 necessity, 696
 personal right to, 678-679
 practice of religion in society, 694
 public teaching by communities,
  682
 purpose; community aspect, 687-688
 religious communities, 681-682
 right of society to defend against
  abuses, 686
 sincere and practical application
  of, 694
 see also Church and state
Religious life: apostolic spirit, 472
 Christ the ultimate norm of, 468
 common life; brotherhood; love,
  477
 following Christ, 467
 harmony; superiors, 477
 hidden with Christ, 470-471
 live for God alone, 470
 mission lands, 606
 purpose, 75, 469
 seek and love God above all, 470
 service of the Church, 470
 special consecration; baptism, 470
 state complete in itself, 473
 state of life, 74
 trust in provident care, 475
 union with Christ, 472
 unity of the brethren, 477
 use to pastoral mission of the
  Church, 473

Religious life *(cont'd)*
  value to the Church, 467
  virtues; share in Christ's emptying
    of Himself, 470
  see also Chastity (vow); Cloister;
    Contemplative life; Evangelical
    counsels; Habit, Religious; Mo-
    nasticism; Obedience (vow);
    Poverty (vow)
Religious orders: active life; mis-
    sion work, 628
  apostolic and charitable activity,
    472
  apostolic works; coordination with
    the diocese, 423
  authority of local Ordinary in
    some matters, 422-423
  bishops and, 76
  chapters and deliberative bodies,
    477
  communications media; apostolate,
    329
  conferences of major superiors, 480
  cooperation with diocesan clergy,
    423
  cultivation in young Churches, 607
  development related to local life
    and customs, 479
  duty to extend kingdom of God,
    75
  external works of apostolate, 420
  federation, union, association, 480
  foundations; new communities, 479
  inheritances, 475
  jurisdiction over, 76
  Latin foundations of the Eastern
    rite, 377
  meetings with bishops, 423
  men: clerics and lay on equal
    footing, 478
  ministries proper to each, 479-480
  multiple and miraculous growth,
    73
  pastoral ministries, 421-422
  regulation by the hierarchy, 76
  role in evangelization of the
    world, 627
  rules, 76
  schools; authority of local Ordi-
    naries, 423
  sharing of temporal goods, 476
  spiritual life, 471
  suppression of communities with-
    out hope of development, 480
  training of directors, spiritual
    father, teachers, 478-479
  variety of, 467
  see also Exemption; Secular In-
    stitutes
Religious orders: adaptation and
    renewal: abandon less rele-
    vant works, 479-480

adjustment to modern needs, 472
approbation of competent author-
    ities, 469-470
constitutions, directories, etc., to
    be re-edited, 469
cooperation of all members, 469
faithful observance the hope of,
    470
fit demands of their apostolate, 472
founders' spirit; sound traditions,
    468
governing, manner of, 469
missionary spirit, 480
modern physical and psychologi-
    cal circumstances, 469
principles and norms, 467-468
renewal of spirit, 469
requirements of time and place,
    479
return to sources; original spirit,
    468
share in life of the Church, 468
social conditions; current events,
    468-469
Religious orders, Missionary: coop-
    eration with institutes in home
    lands, 622
  coordination of work, 622
  local traditions and, 606-607
  multiplication of congregations,
    607
  necessity, 618
  purpose of the mission, 621-622
Religious orders of women: Propa-
    gation of the Faith, 620
Religious persons: active apostolate;
    observance of their rule, 422
  bishops' helpers, 421
  Christian example, 77
  cooperation for the good of
    churches, 420
  diocesan family, 421
  education, 478
  exhortation to make vocation ef-
    fective, 481
  first duty: building up the Church,
    420
  holiness as goal of, 78
  human development, 77
  instruction in arts and science,
    478-479
  love and dedication, 471
  pastoral care for, 545
  perfection of culture, talents, edu-
    cation, 479
  strengthening kingdom of God,
    603
  talents and gifts, 471-472
  work, 475
  zeal, 609
  see also Brothers; Lay Brothers;
    Nuns; Sisters

Religious practice: coercion in, 682
  modern abandonment of, 205
Religious priests: diocesan respon-
    sibilities, 421
Religious profession: at Mass, 162
  communion under both kinds, 156
  liturgical setting, 76
  renewal of vows, 162
Religious relations: bishops'
    dialogue with men, 405
  cooperation with others, 629
  dialogue and collaboration, 662-
    663
Religious superiors: see Superiors,
    Religious
Religious truth: see Religion; Truth
Religious vocation: see Vocation,
    Religious
Renewal of religious life: see Re-
    ligious orders: adaptation and
    renewal
Reporting: moral aspects, 322
Research: encouraging careers in,
    649
  missions and, 629
  religious and social, 410
Reserved cases: bishops and Pope,
    401
Responsibility: dignity, 679
  education and, 639
  family size, 302
  growing consciousness of, 696
  increasing sense of, 261
  in exercise of rights, 686
  new humanism, 261
  relative to power, 232-233
  sense of, 229
  universal, 304
Restoration: see Reform
Resurrection of the body: Christian
    hope, 222
  future blessedness, 237
  glory and happiness, 84
Reunion movement: see Christian
    Unity; Ecumenical Movement
Revelation: application to human
    problems, 452
  Christ the fulfillment of, 113
  culture and, 264
  definitions of the Church, 48
  God communicates Himself and
    His will, 114
  God speaks to man, 112
  handing on, 114
  inner unity of deeds and words,
    112
  kingdom of God, 17
  man in the purpose of God, 112
  message of salvation, 111
  no new public revelation awaited,
    113
  obedience of faith, 113

religious freedom in, 688
Revision: see Reform
Rights: cooperation to guarantee for
    all people, 283
  cultural autonomy and, 265
  discrimination rejected, 227-228
  divine law and, 241
  dynamic movements of modern
    world, 241
  false autonomy, 241
  government recognition of, 242
  growing discovery of, 240
  juridical norms of government ac-
    tion, 686
  parents and education, 638
  preservation; apostolate of the
    married, 502
  protection and promotion by gov-
    ernment, 684-685
  protection of, 283
  respect for rights of others, 686
  restricted for the common good,
    286
  system for protection of, 285-286
  universal and inviolable, 225
  universal right to education, 639
Rites: adaptation to time and place,
    374
  diocesan provision for different,
    413
  education of clerics, 375
  evidence of catholicity, 46
  inter-ritual meetings; exchange of
    views, 426
  love among Catholics, 602
  membership in the Church, 374
  Pope as guide of, 374
  retention and observation, 375-376
  those living outside area of their
    own rite; calendar, 382
  traditions retained by, 374
Rites and ceremonies: communal
    celebration, 148
  decorum in, 148
  educational aspects, 544
  instruction during rites, 150
  local adaptations, 151
  parts pertaining to each person,
    148
  piety and decorum, 148
  words and rites; intimate connec-
    tion, 149
  see also Liturgy
Rites, Eastern: see Eastern Churches
Rites (liturgies): equality, 138
  reform, 138
  revision to fit modern needs, 138
  see also Roman rite
Rituale Romanum: local rituals and,
    159
Rituals: revision for local needs, 159
Roman Curia: see Curia, Roman

Roman rite: local adaptations, 151
  reform, 138
Roman Ritual: local rituals and, 159
Rulers, Civil: protection of rights,
  286

Sabbath: made for man, 225
Sacramentals: administered by laity,
  162
  institution; purpose, 158
  language, 159
  new, 162
  revision; participation, 162
  rites; revision, 159
Sacraments: ancient discipline; Eastern Churches, 379
  bishops and, 50
  Christ present in, 141
  Christ the source, 158
  communal celebration, 148
  Eastern Churches, 379
  Eastern Churches separated in
    good faith, 384
  ecumenical dialogue, 364
  Eucharist as object of, 541
  frequent reception; parishes,
    418
  from non-Catholic ministers of
    Churches with valid sacraments,
    384
  growth in love, 70
  in Catholic life, 407
  language; administration, 159
  lay apostolate, 59, 492
  local adaptations, 151
  ministers of, 541
  music; language, 171
  of initiation, 601
  priesthood of the faithful, 27
  purpose, 158
  rites; revision, 159
  salvation, 140
  signs, 149, 158
  valid administration; Eastern and
    Western rites, 379
Sacred art: see Art
Sacred music: see Music
Sacred sciences: faculties of, 649-650
  reappraisal of programs, 650
  refresher courses; episcopal con-
    ferences, 609-610
  research in, 650
  study by the laity, 270
Sacred Scripture: see Bible
Sacrifice: ministry of priests, 535
  work of salvation, 140
Saints: companionship with, 82
  Eastern Churches, 358-359
  feasts, 168, 170
  fellowship with, 141
  images, 170

love as cult, 84
  readings; Divine Office, 165
  relics, 170
  veneration of, 82
Salvation: achievement of, 496
  all-embracing means of, 346
  Church and the world, 163
  Church necessary for, 32
  conversion; penance, 142
  ecclesiastical studies, 450
  faith and, 538-539
  faith and baptism, 593
  God's universal design, 586
  helps for fallen man, 15
  humanity of Christ, 139
  lay apostolate, 507
  Mary's role in; 87
  mission of the Church, 247
  news of, 200
  non-Catholic Churches, 346
  non-Christians, 35
  Old Testament revelation, 122
  passion of Christ, 667
  perseverance in search for, 112
  persevere in charity, 33
  plan; the chosen people, 121
  purpose of the Incarnation, 586
  temporal duties and, 243
  training of seminarians, 604
  universal, 586-587
  work of the Church, 599
Sanctification: assisting one another,
  62-63
  bishops' office, 406
  clergy, the, 68
  efficacy of the liturgy, 137, 142
  furthering Christian unity, 351
  in marriage, 251
  lay apostolate, 491-492
  Mary as model, 93
  pastoral work, 541
  purpose of Christ's coming, 396
  sacraments and sacramentals, 158
  seminary preparation, 442
  signs, 141
  see also Holiness
Schism: Eastern and Western, 355-
  356
Scholarship: see Learning and scholarship
Schools: conducted by religious;
    authority of local Ordinary, 423
  expansion of, 638
  importance, 643
Schools, Catholic: areas of new
    churches, 647
  duty of parents to support, 647
  function, 646
  primary and secondary, 647-648
  rights of the Church, 646
  sacrifice for, 648
  special education, 648

Schools, Catholic *(cont'd)*
  temporal goods, 646
  types, 647
Science: agnosticism and, 263
  autonomy of, 265
  Catholic higher education, 649
  denial of God or religion, 205
  keeping pace with, 269
  meaning for the person, 268
  modern culture, 260
  modern intellectual formation, 203
  seminary studies, 450
  values in, 263
Science and religion: Catholic higher
    education, 648
  method; no conflict, 234
  new findings and faith, 268
Scientific method: limitations of, 263
Scripture: *see* Bible
Second coming of Christ: missionary
    activity, 595
Secretariat for Promoting Christian
    Unity: planning missionary ac-
    tivity, 620
Secular Institutes: apostolate, 474
  conferences, 480
  full profession of evangelical
    counsels, 473-474
  missions and evangelization, 628
  principles of renewal, 467-468
  spiritual training, 474
  total dedication, 473-474
Secularism: rejection of, 63-64
See, Episcopal: location of, 412
Self: gift of self, 223
Self-denial: change of heart, 351
  seminarians, 446
Selfishness: social disturbance, 224
Self-knowledge: advances in, 203
Seminarians: attitude to authority,
    448
  Catholic spirit, 455
  consideration of the candidates,
    443
  dedication and joy, 450
  deliberate choice of vocation, 448
  formation for service, 446
  higher education, 453
  hope of the Church in, 457
  humanistic and scientific training,
    449
  joy, 443
  knowledge of burdens and dangers, ·
    446
  maturity, 447
  ministry of the word, 442
  mystery of the Church, 446
  obedience and self-denial, 446
  pastoral end in formation, 442
  personal formation, 444
  pious practices, 445-446

  practical initiation into pastoral
    work, 455
  selection and testing, 444
  spiritual training, 444-445
  testing fitness of, 49
  training; mission areas, 604
  vacations, 455
  virtues, 448
Seminaries: administrative training,
    605
  community spirit, 443
  discipline, 448
  example of teachers, 443
  faculties of sacred sciences, 649-
    650
  international, 555
  life patterned on future priestly
    life, 448
  liturgical studies and formation,
    144-145
  necessity, 442
  obedience to the bishop, 442
  pastoral needs of the region, 604
  piety and silence in life of, 448
  regional or national, 444
  selection of teachers and admin-
    istrators, 442-443
Seminaries: Curricula: adapted to
    times and localities, 438
  aids; methodology, 455
  Biblical studies, 451
  development of maturity, 448
  dialogue with men, 450, 455
  multiplication of courses, 453
  pastoral concern throughout, 454
  pastoral end, 450
  program of priestly training, 438
  teaching methods to be revised,
    453
  understanding the contemporary
    mind, 450
  understanding the separated
    Churches, 453
Seminaries, Minor: daily routines,
    441
  formation of students, 441
  social and cultural contacts, 441
  studies provide for change of vo-
    cation, 441
Separated Churches: *see* Non-Catho-
    lic Churches
Sermons: content, 149
Servers: function, 148
Sex: dignity in conjugal love, 256
  in marriage, 253
  true practice of conjugal love, 254
Sex differences: in education, 647
Sex education: prudent, 639
Sick, The: pastoral care for, 545
  pastoral work, 419
  united with Christ, 70
Sickness: extreme unction, 161

Signs: chosen by Christ or the
  Church, 149
  sacraments, 158
  sanctification, 141
Silence: proper times, 148
Simplicity: revision of rites, 149
Sin: allurements of, 264
  bondage, 240
  certitude obscured by, 213
  Christ needed to free from, 595
  conquest of, 62
  conscience and habitual sin, 214
  earthly and heavenly city, 239
  fulfillment of man blocked by, 211
  inducements to, 224
  rebellious stirrings in the body, 212
  riddle, 661
  sinners and the Church, 24
  social consequences, 170
Sin, Original: errors resulting from,
  497
Singers: liturgical training, 172
Singing: fostered, 172
  see also Music
Single people: holiness in the
  Church, 69
Sisters: lay apostolate and, 514-515
  one class of sister in communities
  of women, 478
Slavery: fight against, 228
  social and psychological, 202
Social action: activities of family
  apostolate, 503
  Christians fighting for justice, 282
  cooperation with all men, 505-506
  laity in mission lands, 629
  lay apostolate, 498
  rights to culture, 266
  technically competent laity, a, 63
Social change: in institutions, 282-
  283
  intellectual and technological
  aspects, 203
  in traditional local communities,
  204
  modern cultural and social transformation, 202
  political aspects, 282-283
  questioning accepted values, 205
Social communication media: see
  Communications media
Social conditions: culture impeded
  by, 267
  dignity of man, 271
  excessive economic and social differences, 228
  more unified world, a, 229
  work for betterment of, 219
Social education: family life, 641
Social ethics: cultural and educational obligations, 229
  observance of obligations, 228-229

observe social necessities, 229
Social groups: interrelationship, 225
Social institutions: dealing with destination of earthly goods, 279
  progress; apostolate, 509
  subject and goal of, 224
Socialization: advantages to the person, 224
  effects, 204
  human autonomy and, 286
  worthy elements in, 241-242
Social justice: Catholic organism
  proposed, 305
Social order: Church's activities in
  behalf of, 241
  constant improvement, 225
  destruction of the human race, 235
  disturbances, 224
  founded on truth, justice, love, 225
  meaning of, 687
  service and dignity of man, 206
  work for benefit of the person, 225
Social problems: assistance for every
  man, 305
  bishops' knowledge of, 408-409
  collaboration of Christians, 598-599
  conditions poisoning society, 226-
  227
  cooperative action, 354
  government and family needs, 502
  marriage and family problems, 249
  renewal of religious life, 468-469
  special urgency, 248
Social reform: necessity of, 272
Social relations: participation in, 229
Social research: bishops' use of,
  408-409
Social sciences: advances in, 203
Social security: clergy and, 574
Social teachings: lay apostolate, 520
Social welfare: Catholic schools, 648
Social work: laity and, 499
Society: basic truths about, 223
  Church as leaven of, 239
  closed in on itself, 501
  culture and, 265
  errors undermining, 496
  moral and spiritual nature of
  man, 222
  permeate and transform, 611
  renewal, 201
  temporal values, 404-405
  uncertainty of direction, 202
  usages related to freedom, 687
Sociology: pastoral, 410
  pastoral use, 269
Solidarity: authority and freedom,
  286-287
  Christ and human nature, 498
  Church and the world, 201
  Eucharist and, 236-237
  increasing sense of, 506

Solidarity *(cont'd)*
  international cooperation, 299
  laity in mission lands, 612
  mutual dependence, 202-203
  perfection; future life, 231
  scientific studies and, 263
  social unity, 230
  universal, 304
Soul: recognition of, 212
Special education: *see* Education,
    Special
Spirit: human culture, 263
Spiritual direction: minor seminaries,
    441
  priestly vocation, 556
  seminary studies, 454
  see also Care of souls
Spiritual directors: seminaries, 445
Spirituality: national traditions, 301
Spiritual life: care for those de-
    prived of parish life, 410
  in ecumenism, 352
  laity, 493
  lay apostolate, 514, 516-517
  liturgical formation of clerics, 145
  of priests, 408
  participation in the liturgy, 143
  pastoral work, 446
  religious persons, 470
  seminarians and theology, 451
  theological virtues, 493
  word of God, 125
Spiritual reading: by priests, 570
Sponsors: rite of baptism, 160
Sports: value of, 268
State, The: economic policy, 271
  intervention in social, economic,
    and cultural matters, 286
  protection of human rights, 684-
    685
  see also Education and state;
    Church and state; Politics
State and Church: *see* Church and
    state
State and education: *see* Education
    and state
Strikes: recourse to, 277
Students: health, 644
  spiritual life of students in non-
    Catholic colleges, 649
Students, Seminary: *see* Seminarians
Study: leisure and, 268
  priests and, 571
  see also Liturgical education
Subdiaconate: Eastern Churches,
    380-381
Subsidiarity: education and state, 642
  international community, 300
  school monopoly, 644
Suffering: associated with Christ, 28
  Church's love for, 24
  example of Christ, 221

riddle, 661
Sunday: calendar revision, 177-178
  Eastern rite obligation, 380
  importance, 169
  Mass, 153
  resurrection of Christ, 168, 169
Superiors, Religious: conferences of
    major superiors, 480
  counsel with members regarding
    renewal, 470
  education of religious, 479
  exercise of authority, 476-477
  obedience, vow of, 476
Superstition: modern view of re-
    ligion, 205
Syncretism: mission lands, 612
Synod of Bishops: deliberative body,
    399-400
  missionary concern, 619
Synods: purpose, 424

Tabernacle: construction, 176
Talents: Christian use of, 618-619
  service of God and man, 240
Taxes: avoiding, 228
Teachers: ability; duty of the state,
    644
  apostolate, 647
  Catholic schools, 646-647
  encouragement of careers as, 651
  lay apostolate, 518-519
  qualifications; skill, 647
  relations with students after grad-
    uation, 647
  seminaries, 442-443
  witness to Christ, 647
Teaching: encouraging careers in,
    649
  gift of, 472
  see also Liturgical education
Technology: agnosticism and, 263
  discoveries, 319
  education, 638
Technology and civilization: classi-
    cal culture and, 261
  keeping pace with science, 269
  mounting importance of, 203
  transforming the earth, 203
Television: apostolate, 327-328
Television broadcasting: liturgical
    use, 145
Temporal goods: Catholic educa-
    tion, 646
  common use of, 569
  competence of the laity, 63
  customs related to modern needs,
    279
  disposed for man's salvation, 404
  duty of the Church, 642
  duty to be concerned with this
    world, 237

Temporal goods *(cont'd)*
  earthly vocation, 236
  education and the Church, 638
  idolatry of, 497
  kingdom of God on earth, 31
  lay vocation, 57
  necessity for personal develop-
    ment, 567
  neglect of, 243
  political and economic progress,
    206-207
  priests and, 567
  purpose in use of, 567-568
  right to sufficient share, 278
  science, learning, and religion, 234
  share in, 278
  sharing by religious orders, 476
  true meaning and value, 519
  use in Church's mission, 288
  use of; moral aspects, 497
  values, 404-405, 493
  see also Common good
Temporal order: apostolate, 288
  Christian service to, 307
  components of, 497
  cooperation in apostolic work, 516
  goodness, 497
  laity as leaven of, 603
  lay apostolate, 491-492, 494, 518
  man's eternal vocation, 288
  mission of the Church, 289
  motives for action, 507
  natural and supernatural united,
    497
  redemption and, 495
  renewal in Christ, 497-498
  renewing and perfecting, 497
  role of the hierarchy, 514
  values, 497
Theologians: priests and study, 571
Theology: Bible and tradition, 127
  communicating to men of the
    times, 268
  deeper study of, 572
  East and West, 360
  ecumenical study of, 353
  in Catholic universities, 649
  mission seminaries, 604
  philosophy and, 451
  revision of ecclesiastical studies,
    449-450
  seminary education, 451
  seminary professors and liturgy,
    144
  studies in contact with the times,
    270
  teachers collaborate with men of
    science, 270
Thomas Aquinas, Saint: Catholic
  higher education, 648
  dogmatic theology in seminaries,
    452

  papal texts on study of, 452
Time: dominion over, 203
Totalitarianism: violation of rights,
  286
Tourism: value of, 268
Trade unions: *see* Labor unions
Tradition: apostolic succession and,
  115
  as word of God, 117
  Bible closely connected with, 117
  biblical canon known through,
    116
  content of, 116
  deposit of the word of God, 117
  development in understanding, 116
  languages, 449
  reverence for, 117
  rule of faith, 125
  Scripture and the magisterium, 118
Travelers: apostolate, 506
Trent, Council of: on revelation, 111
  Vatican II and, 456-457
Trinity: unity, 223
Truth: assent to, 681
  assisting others in quest of, 681
  Christ and use of force, 691
  Christian education, 640
  conscience and search for, 214
  dramatic portrayal of evil, 322-323
  duty to seek, 680
  establishment; force, 691
  free search for, 265
  fullness of, 125
  Holy Spirit leads to, 116-117
  imposing itself on the mind, 677
  in education, 638
  life ordered in accord with, 679
  love and, 306
  love and indifference to error, 227
  movement toward fullness of, 116
  non-Catholic religions, 662
  non-Christians, 595-596
  obligation to seek, 679
  rigorous search for, 450
  scientific method and, 263
  seeking related to dignity, 680-681
  social order, 225
  unchanging, 680

Unbelief: judgment of, 595
Underdeveloped areas: dependence
  increasing, 206-207
  development requires changes in
    world commerce, 299
  industrialization and urbanization,
    204
  investments in, 280
  landowners and tenants, 281
  progress a duty in, 274
  volunteer services in, 303
  see also Economic development

Union with Christ: lay apostolate, 493
Union with God: brotherly love, 351
    participation at Mass, 154
Unity: and education, 639
    Christian unity and, 306
    civic, economic, and social, 55
    community of all peoples, 660-661
    human family founded on Christ, 241
    international, 696
    mankind and the Trinity, 223
    mission of the Church, 305-306
    preservation of civilizations, 260
    promotion of, 242
    see also Solidarity
Unity of the Church: baptism as bond of, 364
    Christ as source and center, 362
    Christ founded one Church, 341
    diversity of customs, 359
    equality in diversity of ministries, 58
    Eucharist and, 343
    freedom in, 349
    love among believers, 21
    mystery, 344
    Pope and bishops as principle of, 44
    rites and Churches in, 374
    sharing riches, workers, resources, 32
    social unity and, 242
    Trinity and, 17
    worship in common and, 352
    see also Christian unity
Universal community: see Internationalism
Universality: see Catholicity
Universe: intellect and, 212
Universities: see Colleges and universities

Vacation: for priests, 573
Values: change in attitudes, 205
    cooperation in apostolic efforts, 516
    cultural, 261-262
    development of culture, 259-260
    disordered, 234-235
    freedom in quest for, 675
    hierarchy and temporal order, 514
    human person, the, 267
    human relations and the apostolate, 517
    man, 233
    modern civilization, 203
    modern culture, 263
    motivation, 639-640
    non-Catholic religions, 663
    priests and temporal, 567

    public authority and, 325
    purification of, 209
    science and civilization, 263
    temporal and eternal, 237
    temporal goods; doctrine of the Church, 404-405
    temporal order, 497
    universal, 263
Vatican Council, (1st): foundation of the Church, 37
    on revelation, 111
Vatican Council, (2nd): aims, 137
    on calendar revision, 177-178
Vernacular: see Language
    see also under Divine Office; Mass
Vespers: importance, 164, 167
Vestments: liturgical use, 175, 176
Viaticum: rite, 161
Vicar general: importance of office, 415
Vicars: auxiliary bishops, 415
    episcopal; authority, 415-416
Vigils: Bible services, 150
Violence: renunciation of use of, 291
    vanquishing of, 291
Virginity: excellence of, 447
    particular honor for, 71-72
Virgins, Consecration of: see Consecration of virgins
Virtue: lay apostolate, 63
Virtues: for priests, 538
    moral and social, 229
    priesthood of the faithful, 27
    religious life, 470
    seminarians, 448
    social, 495
Virtues, Theological: lay apostolate, 492
    spiritual life, 493
Visitations: by pastors, 419
Vocation: children and the apostolate, 502
    clerical and lay, 57
    earthly duties of Christians, 242-243
    earthly service, 236
    educational work, 643
    human activity, 233
    to the priesthood, 556
    voice of the Lord calling, 556
    works favoring, 557
    see also Priests: Vocations
Vocation, Religious: candidates carefully chosen, 481
    example and recruiting, 481
    fostered by priests and educators, 481
    generous living of, 481
    right of communities to recruit, 481

Vocations: bishops and, 407
  encouraged by parents, 29
  missionary institutes, 625
  mission lands, 604, 609
  response to the Spirit, 614
Voting: civil right, 285
Vows: consecration to divine service,
    74
  religious life, 74
  renewal of, 162

Wages: discrimination in, 275
  of catechists, 606
  sufficiency, 276
War: arms race as cause, 295
  attitudes toward, 296-297
  avoidance of, 291
  causes, 297-298
  criminal actions, 292
  danger increasing, 295
  destruction of entire cities, 294
  freedom from slavery of, 295
  guerrilla warfare, 292
  hazard of modern weapons, 294
  international agreements, 292
  leaders working to eliminate, 296
  massive and indiscriminate de-
    struction, 293
  outlawed by international consent,
    295
  right to legitimate defense, 293
  seeking conquest of other nations,
    293
  terrorism, 292
  threat of, 289
  threat vanquished by love, 291
  total slaughter, 293
  weapons as deterrents, 294
  weapons of modern science, 291
Wealth: enslavement to, 494
  modern conditions, 202
  passionate desires for, 281
  religious poverty, 476
  squandering, 271
Wealth, Distribution of: dependence
    of developing nations, 206-207
  unequal, 303
Weapons: see War
Widowhood: continuation of the
    marriage vocation, 252
Widows: holiness in the Church, 69
Wisdom: attraction of, 213
  eternal, 263
  nations rich in, 213
  observation and, 261
Witness-bearing: baptized, the, 27
  Catholic dialogue with other re-
    ligions, 662-663

Catholic higher education, 648
Christian education, 640-641
Women: apostolic work, 500
  cultural life, 267
  domestic role, 257
  equality in law and in fact, 207
  rights not universally honored, 228
Word of God: see Bible; Revelation
Work: development of self, 233
  duty and right, 276
  results of, 275
  subjection of all things; divine
    plan, 232
Working classes: see Labor and la-
    boring classes
Works: Christian life, 142
Works of mercy: apostolic forma-
    tion, 520
World: biblical usage of the word,
    235
  presence and activity of the
    Church in, 200
  see also Temporal order
World community: growing recogni-
    tion of, 231
  see also International organization
Worship: Christian education, 640
  monastic life, 472
  Moslem, 663
  non-Catholics, 364
  sacraments, 158
  seminary preparation, 442
  spirit drawn to, 263
Worship in common: see Com-
    municatio in Sacris

Young churches: see Missions
Youth: adults and, 504
  apostolate, 504
  apostolic formation, 518
  communications media and, 323-
    324
  culture, 267
  exhortation to the apostolate, 521
  inadequate in responsibilities, 503
  influence in society, 503
  international community and, 304
  pastoral work, 419
  political formation, 287
  preparation for marriage, 253
  printed matter and performances,
    326
  questioning of accepted values, 205
  social and political importance, 503
  zeal, 504

Zeal: promotion of the liturgy, 153

Prayer of Pope John XXIII to the Holy Spirit for the Success of the Ecumenical Council

O Holy Spirit, sent by the Father in the name of Jesus, who art present in the Church and dost infallibly guide it, pour forth, we pray, the fullness of Thy gifts upon the Ecumenical Council.

Enlighten, O most gracious Teacher and Comforter, the minds of our prelates who, in prompt response to the Supreme Roman Pontiff, will carry on the sessions of the Sacred Council.

Grant that from this Council abundant fruit may ripen; that the light and strength of the gospel may be extended more and more in human society; that the Catholic religion and its active missionary works may flourish with ever greater vigor, with the happy result that knowledge of the Church's teaching may spread and Christian morality have a salutary increase.

O sweet Guest of the soul, strengthen our minds in the truth and dispose our hearts to pay reverential heed, that we may accept with sincere submission those things which shall be decided in the Council and fulfill them with ready will.

We pray also for those sheep who are not now of the one fold of Jesus Christ, that even as they glory in the name of Christian, they may come at last to unity under the governance of the one Shepherd.

Renew Thy wonders in this our day, as by a new Pentecost. Grant to Thy Church that, being of one mind and steadfast in prayer with Mary, the Mother of Jesus, and following the lead of blessed Peter, it may advance the reign of our Divine Savior, the reign of truth and justice, the reign of love and peace. Amen